D1587050

Yeomanry Wars

Frontispiece   Norwich Businessmen's Club

The 1st Marquess Townshend as Colonel, The Norfolk Rangers. The
regiment formed in 1782 served as the germ of an idea in the formation of
the later Yeomanry.

Yeomanry Wars

The History of the Yeomanry, Volunteer and Volunteer Association Cavalry

---

A Civilian Tradition from 1794

by

Peter D Athawes

SCOTTISH CULTURAL PRESS
Aberdeen

To Billy and Bridger

Published by:
Scottish Cultural Press
PO Box 106, Aberdeen AB9 8ZE, Scotland
Tel/Fax: 0224 583777

© **Peter D Athawes 1994**

The right of Peter D Athawes to be identified as Author of this work has been asserted by Peter D Athawes in accordance with the Copyright, Designs and Patents Act 1988

All rights reserved.

British Library Cataloguing in Publication Data
A catalogue record for this book is available from the British Library

ISBN   1 898218 02 1

Designed and Word Processed in Times New Roman and Arial by the author

Printed by BPC Wheatons Ltd, Exeter, England

Contents

List of Illustrations
Colour

PREFACE

Although the Yeomanry were originally raised in 1794 as a volunteer cavalry force to defend this country from French invasion during the Napoleonic Wars - throughout the Boer and two World Wars they demonstrated their ability to serve in whatever role was demanded of them - and so today the successor units of those Regiments can be found throughout all arms of the British Army's order of battle.

This book provides the reader with a picture of the Yeomanry at work over the past two hundred years - it is a fascinating story.

A story of officers and men from the same counties or cities recruited in peacetime, who trained and fought together in whatever role was required of them.

Their good humour, resourcefulness and determination to serve their comrades and their regiments was their prime consideration - their equipment and sometimes lack of it their second.

Ralph Carr. Ellison

Colonel Sir Ralph Carr-Ellison, TD
The Colonel Commandant of the Yeomanry
March 1994

Foreword

by

The Seventh Marquess Townshend

I am delighted to be able to write a foreword to this book on the Yeomanry.

The 4th Viscount, later the 1st Marquess Townshend (1724-1807), was a champion for the rôle of the Non-Standing Army although he had had a very successful career in the regular army, including serving as a Brigadier-General under Major-General James Wolfe in the expedition to capture Quebec in 1759. His earlier experiences of serving in the army under the Duke of Cumberland and his dislike of foreign mercenaries, led him, as Colonel the Hon. George Townshend, into piloting Pitt's Militia Bill through the House of Commons in 1757. Under this Act men balloted for service, however the Government allowed the principals elected to appoint substitutes and the scheme fell into disrepute, indeed the Militia became very unpopular. There followed a long period of agitation in which he sought various reforms whereby an economic way could be found for producing a more broadly based reserve army. One glaring deficiency was the absence of a Cavalry Arm, because the Government was unwilling to fund its creation adequately.

Frustrated by the arrangements and this lack of willingness to reform, he believed that private enterprise in military matters was a more potent force. Hence his involvement in setting up a truly volunteer cavalry Corps in the Norfolk Rangers at Raynham Hall, in his county home of Norfolk, during September 1782. To this Horace Walpole is claimed to have rather doubted if Knights of the shires accustomed to shooting woodcock would survive in real combat! Just twelve years later the Volunteer Act for raising infantry and cavalry was passed on 17th April 1794 and further Volunteer Corps were added to counter the threat of a French invasion. This Act broke new ground by introducing the principle of large, economical and high quality volunteer forces. The new mounted men completed that vital missing cavalry element for the Reserve Army and remains with us today.

Agitation by public-spirited individuals is a distinctly British trait. This has continued for two hundred years with regard to the volunteer part-time forces from which developed the Territorial Army that we now know. The Yeomanry Cavalry has always been particularly strong in driving reluctant governments to take the defence of the United Kingdom seriously. In uniform they have performed their tasks with flair and enthusiasm and in the Wars of the 20th Century have played a significant part in defeating the enemies of our nation.

Peter Athawes has painstakingly researched the origins and intricate succession of the Corps and regiments of Yeomanry Cavalry from its inception to the present time. In many respects he has carried on the work of Commander Benson Freeman and produced a very valuable source document. The light touch and dry humour with which he comments on the facts makes his book very readable. I commend it to those who are interested in Military matters and the history of local society in many parts of the country and for an insight into how matters worked in Britain over times past.

Raynham Hall, Norfolk. April 1994

Author's Introduction

My arrival at the Yeomanry stable door came about by chance: I was parachute trained. So many years ago, or so it seems, National Service came in two parts. Following the completion of the full-time obligation one was posted to the Territorial Army for a few days training. It didn't seem to matter what your speciality, I in fact was infantry trained, the fact of airborne training meant you were posted to their nearest Drill Hall and this for me was just across the River Avon from Park Lane, Bath. The Independent Airborne Squadron, North Somerset Yeomanry were the anti-tank gunners of the then 16th Airborne Division.

It was that period which shaped my curiosity about the Yeomanry, yet getting into the history took longer. As the quirks of regimental custom forge important traditions, so it is the inconsistencies in history which draw the enquirer to take a closer look. The initial study, first taken up in 1986 started to list the independent Troops and when these passed the 300 mark there was a problem of multiple dimensions. Firstly, consolidating all the separate histories was out of the question, besides which the information available was a patchwork quilt with many lost beyond recall. Secondly, very early on it became apparent that there was much else beside the Yeomanry competing for attention and the one story was impossible to tell without the other. Lastly, name dropping introduced confusion in the way related topics do and these needed clarification. A free rein has been given to the inclusion of any material having a bearing on the Yeomanry ethos. Thus, there are appendices detailing the Irish Yeomanry and the First Aid Nursing Yeomanry. This advances the work of Dr Frederick in his *Lineage Book of British Land Forces* in this area: similarly it adds material to Arthur S White's *Bibliography of British Regimental Histories.*

Most readers will be surprised to see the very large number of Corps formed as the result of the French Revolutionary and Napoleonic Wars. It is regrettable that many of their histories are inaccessible or even unwritten.. It seems clear from the strictures of the Honourable John Fortescue that Britain's administrative abilities were not always up to scratch. Later, these volunteers were badly mismanaged by officialdom as the latter grappled to contain the expense of a huge reserve army, and this only succeeded in souring relations and squandering the money anyway.

The chapter dealing with Support of the Civil Power and the associated rioting of the period makes unedifying reading and catalogues the actions of the Yeomanry in more detail, than any account so far published and establishes the Yeomanry as a power for good, so that within the narrow confines of the law it strove to uphold, it exercised a kindly discretion and humanity over those less fortunate than themselves. The author presents a contemporary military account for the *1819 Peterloo Massacre* and illustrates how difficult it was to police the country before the days of the County and Borough Constabularies.

The reforms introduced during the Victorian and Edwardian eras are well covered elsewhere and therefore only lightly touched upon. However, many misconceptions surrounding the Boer War are carefully delineated, because the facts do not appear to be very generally available, nor do they accord with the public ballyhoo of the times.

The vast scale of The Great War led to many changes in the Yeomanry, where the poor horse found life virtually intolerable. The writer has worked very hard to codify the formations employed in the various theatres and a similar account covers The Second World War. It will be apparent how those brought in from civilian life fought more than half the armoured battles of the latter period.

Useful additions have been made for the intervening periods and are not without interest to the Yeomanry because they included two important stages of Army reform and its mechanisation. Besides this there are appendices covering, legislation, precedence, thumbnail histories and Battle Honours.

The post-war reforming of the Territorial Army is well known, also the numerous amalgamations which have followed 1947, leading up to its disbandment in 1967. These moves are detailed, including those Yeomanry transferred to other Arms and Services or making a welcome return to the armoured fold. The early days of The Territorial and Army Volunteer Reserve, the natural successor to the Territorial Army and its eventual renaming is all traced and tabulated, to the present day.

Inevitably such a large remit leads to errors and omissions, though hopefully these will act as a spur to future investigation. Whether this is satisfactory to the reader must be left to them. The Orkadians have a saying "it is better to be ill-treated than ignored"

Acknowledgements

Writing a notice of thanks to all those responsible for making this book a worthwhile reality is both a pleasant duty and privilege. Money, interest, persistence and fellow feeling have each contributed to the score and although many were paid professionals, they so often went that extra mile. I see from my letter book that I wrote to the War Office, Whitehall Library as early as March 1988 and there started a useful correspondence with Judithe Blacklaw. Let us therefore start by thanking the staff of the various libraries of the country, out of which was initiated most of the research.

At Aberdeen I have to thank Mr J Pratt and the Reference Section for identifying and accession of a large list of books, through the Inter-Library Lending Service and The British Library. The mere sight of the bibliography, at Appendix C1 and the chapter ends, illustrates the daunting extent of that task and there was much other material besides. At Aberdeen University there was a similar willing team at the Queen Mother Library and outlying collections able to coach one through the vagaries of legislation, reports or simply able to reveal that such and such a book even existed. Next, though not in order of importance came the legislative aspects using the vast resources of the Scottish National Library, where Margaret Deas and Pauline Thomson were so helpful.

The County Local History sections at some thirty locations have been able to pinpoint the locale of long defunct Yeomanry Corps and newspaper articles dealing with their history. Getting to grips with this special type of history called for the advice of the more experienced users of this class of material. Some people have a natural instinct for getting at the core with effortless ease. This writer has not been blessed with such an insight let alone 'second sight' and there are a number of advisers who must share the kudos, though none of the blame in arriving at my point of view. Thus, I am happy to acknowledge a fruitful correspondence with Major Patrick Mileham, late of the RTR, in helping to firm-up the methods for listing the numerous Yeomanry Corps. However, that gentleman is not only trained in matters military, but is also as a historian and has been able to put much helpful comment and advice my way.

The practical guidance of Kenneth Goodson of Lincoln, introduced by Doctor, the Reverend JBM Frederick, has been invaluable whilst logging and charting the virtually impenetrable jungle of British Army Orders and its related organisation. There are few people able to interpret this specialised area with confidence or accuracy. Much of it starts life as 'Restricted' or even 'Secret' and later when declassified, there is nobody able to remember how it all started. A considerable liaison has resulted, leading to the inclusion of all units with a Yeomanry appellation of whatever Arm or Service, leading to a similar treatment of the T&AVR till the present day. Even as I write the pot is once more on the boil. Of course, Dr Frederick made a signal contribution in publishing his *Lineage Book of British Land Forces*: this power-house of information has been a driving force for writing this history and no doubt many others.

Lastly, I showed the manuscript to Roy Bridges, Professor of History at Aberdeen University, who was able to correct errors of fact, though unable to support many of my more judgmental conclusions over the period of the Industrial Revolution. As the consequence that important chapter, Support of the Civil Power has been factually strengthened, with the rôle of the Yeomanry more clearly defined. That era presented me with a long historical dilemma. I make no boasts that all is secure. I have striven to make best use of the advice so well given to shape and explain events surrounding the Yeomanry, in a way which may appeal to a decerning readership.

Major John Tamplin of Army Museums Ogilby Trust, now retired, provided me the first sight of the 1803 Parliamentary Return listing the re-acceptance of the Volunteers following signature of The Peace Treaty of Amiens, which possibly constitutes the single most valuable benchmark for work in this field. The Benson Freeman archive remains at that location, to be combed for missing Yeomanry details. It followed from this that I fell under the guiding hand of Ruth Wilson of The Scottish United Services Museum at Edinburgh Castle, who provided most of the Yeomanry and Volunteer Lists and where I first discovered a discrete mention on the Association Troops.

Much later, during 1991, Peter Longworth as a book collector and uniform specialist joined in a most fruitful correspondence, helping to fill out numerous missing facts not easily available because many libraries were unwilling to loan scarce historical tracts.

In seeking to balance and lighten the text I was indebted to Harry Hay, Dave Potter and Douglas Rawson as 'average readers'. Each being an engineer in the practical mould, was not given to flights of fancy in the use of words. The reasoning was that if the story was to be got across to a civilian readership, it had to pass their muster. The comments they made have been acted upon and were much appreciated.

Illustrations are a further avenue where a variety of museums and trusts have been helpful with details, most often granting a free use of copyright: David Fletcher and The Tank Museum at Bovington serves as an example, though numerous others are cited in the text.

To all these people and many others I offer my sincere thanks. I hope that I shall be able to provide some service in return or to others starting out on a new project, who may feel entitled to receive from me the same courtesy and support I have had in working up my own thesis.

Glossary and Abbreviations

Abbreviations, acronyms, and abridgements are a necessary evil. Good ones avoid ambiguity whilst relieving text from a space consuming repetition. Also, their use is necessary in overcoming the constraints on space and there are a lot of tables: most regrettable are the truncated regimental titles, for the same reason.. The following basis has been adopted in deciding their use.

Regimental titles have in general been condensed to less than a five number-letter group, though mentions in the text are given in full. The list of whole regimental titles quoted below are those applying at the time of The Great War or later. When the need arises to check out a particular title recourse should be made to Succession Listings in Appendices D and E. There follows a compilation of the numerous regiments associated with the Yeomanry as the result of the latter being converted, formed and absorbed into other arms. The final list relates to words used in explaining how formations were affected by change. A need arose to treat these more severely than the conventional abbreviations, purely to have information fit in as entries. These are shown as an additional option in the listing below and the context makes their meaning clear.

Regiments

1, 2, 3, etc.	See MxY, WD, SS, KEH and others
A(Ayr)Y	The Ayrshire Yeomanry (Earl of Carrick's Own) (Hussars)
BY	Bedfordshire Yeomanry (Lancers)
B&WD	The Berkshire and Westminster Dragoons
BYH	Berks Yeomanry (Hungerford) (Dragoons)
CY	The Cheshire Yeomanry (Earl of Chester's) (Hussars)
DenY	Denbighshire Yeomanry (Hussars)
DerY	The Derbyshire Yeomanry (Dragoons)
DLOY	The Duke of Lancaster's Own Yeomanry (Dragoons)
ERY	East Riding of Yorkshire Yeomanry (Lancers)
EY	Essex Yeomanry (Dragoons)
FFY	Fife and Forfar Yeomanry
FFY/SH	The Fife and Forfar Yeomanry/Scottish Horse
GY	Glamorgan Yeomanry (Dragoons)
HBY	Hertford and Bedfordshire Yeomanry
HCY	Hampshire (Carabiniers) (Dragoons)
HdY	Highland Yeomanry this was a Cadre under RCT (!969 till 1st april 1975)
HY	Herts Yeomanry (Dragoons)
IoCY	Inns of Court Regiment
ICY	Inns of Court Yeomanry
IC&CY	Inns of Court and City Yeomanry
KEH	King Edward's Horse (The King's Oversea Dominions Regiment) also 4 CoLY
2KEH	2nd King Edward's Horse
KCLY	Kent and County of London Yeomanry
KSY	Kent and Sharpshooters Yeomanry
KY	Kent Yeomanry
LkY	The Lanarkshire Yeomanry (Lancers)
LncY	Lincolnshire Yeomanry (Lancers)
L&BH	Lothians and Border Horse (Dragoons)
LDY	The Leicestershire and Derbyshire Yeomanry (Prince Albert's Own) RAC (TA)
L&RGY	Lanarkshire and Royal Glasgow Yeomanry
LH	The Lancashire Hussars Yeomanry
LS	The Lovat Scouts
LY	The Leicestershire Yeomanry ('Prince Albert's Own') (Hussars)
MxH	1st County of London Yeomanry (Middlesex, Duke of Cambridge's Hussars)
MY	Montgomeryshire Yeomanry (Dragoons)
NH	The Northumberland Hussars (Yeomanry)
NorY	Norfolk Yeomanry (The King's Own Royal Regiment) (Dragoons)
NIH	North Irish Horse
NS&BY	North Somerset and Bristol Yeomanry
NSY	The North Somerset Yeomanry (Dragoons)
44/50RTR	44th/ 50th Royal Tank Regiment RAC (TA)
NSY/44RTR	The North Somerset Yeomanry/ 44th Royal Tank Regiment RAC (TA)
NY	Northamptonshire Yeomanry (Dragoons)
PembY	Pembroke Yeomanry (Castlemartin) (Hussars)

QODY	Dorset Yeomanry (Queen's Own)
QOLY	Queen's Own Lowland Yeomanry RAC (TA)
QOMY	Queen's Own Mercian Yeomanry
QOOH	Oxfordshire Yeomanry (Queen's Own Oxfordshire Hussars)
QOY	The Queen's Own Yeomanry
QORGY	Queen's Own Royal Glasgow Yeomanry (Dragoons)
QOWH	Worcestershire Yeomanry (The Queen's Own Worcestershire Hussars)
QOWWY	The Queen's Own Warwickshire and Worcestershire Yeomanry RAC (TA)
RDY	Royal Devon Yeomanry
R1DY	Royal 1st Devon Yeomanry (Hussars)
RBH	Buckinghamshire Yeomanry (Royal Bucks. Hussars)
REKY	R East Kent Yeomanry (The Duke of Connaught's Own) (MR) (Hussars)
RGH	Gloucestershire Yeomanry (Royal Gloucestershire Hussars)
RM&LY	Royal Mercian and Lancastrian Yeomanry
RNDY	Royal North Devon Yeomanry (Hussars)
RR	City of London Yeomanry (Rough Riders) (Lancers)
RTC etc	Royal Tank Corps for 19th-26th Armoured Car Companies.
RWY	The Royal Wiltshire Yeomanry (Prince of Wale's Own) (Hussars)
(R)WxY	(Royal) Wessex Yeomanry
RY(R)	The Royal Yeomanry (Regiment)
SH	The Scottish Horse
ScotY	The Scottish Yeomanry
SIH	South Irish Horse
SNH	Nottinghamshire Yeomanry (South Nottinghamshire Hussars)
SNY	Suffolk and Norfolk Yeomanry
SRY	The Nottinghamshire Yeomanry (Sherwood Rangers) (Hussars)
SS	3rd County of London Yeomanry (Sharpshooters) (Hussars)
3/4SS	3rd/4th County of London Yeomanry (Sharpshooters) RAC (TA)
4SS	4th County of London Yeomanry (Sharpshooters), RAC
S(Shrop)Y	Shropshire Yeomanry (Dragoons)
StfY	The Staffordshire Yeomanry (Queen's Own Royal Regiment) (Hussars)
SfY	Suffolk Yeomanry (The Duke of York's Own Loyal Suffolk Hussars)
SyY	Surrey Yeomanry (Queen Mary's Regiment) (Lancers)
SxY	Sussex Yeomanry (Dragoons)
WCY	Westmorland and Cumberland Yeomanry (Hussars)
WDGN	2nd County of London Yeomanry (Westminster Dragoons)
WHY	Welsh Horse (Lancers)
WkY	The Warwickshire Yeomanry (Hussars)
WKY	West Kent Yeomanry (Queen's Own) (Hussars)
WSY	West Somerset Yeomanry (Hussars)
YD	Yorkshire Dragoons (Queen's Own)
YH	The Yorkshire Hussars Yeomanry (Alexandra, Princess of Wale's Own)
Y(Yorks)Y	Yorkshire Yeomanry

Dismounted Yeomanry

Formed	From Yeomanry Regiments into 74th (Broken Spur) Division
10Buffs	10th (Royal East Kent and West Kent Yeomanry) Bn The Buffs (East Kent Regiment)
14BW	14th (Fife and Forfar Yeomanry) Bn The Black Watch (Royal Highlanders)
16Dev	16th (Royal 1st Devon and Royal North Devon Yeomanry) Bn The Devonshire Regt
12Norf	12th (Norfolk Yeomanry) Bn The Norfolk Regiment
10KSLI	10th (Shropshire and Cheshire Yeomanry) Bn King's Shropshire Light Infantry
12RSF	12th (Ayr and Lanark) Bn Royal Scots Fusiliers
16RSx	16th (Sussex Yeomanry) Bn The Royal Sussex Regiment
24RWF	24th (Denbighshire Yeomanry) Bn Royal Welsh Fusiliers
25RWF	25th (Montgomeryshire and Welshh Horse Yeomanry) Bn The Royal Welsh Fusiliers
12SLI	12th (West Somerset Yeomanry) Bn The Prince Albert's (Somerset Light Infantry)
15Suff	15th (Suffolk Yeomanry) Bn The Suffolk Regiment
24Welsh	24th (Pembrokeand Glamorgan Yeomanry) Bn The Welsh Regiment

Formed	Into Infantry Regiments
7Bdr	7th (Westmorland and Cumberland Yeomanry) Bn Border Regiment
15Hamp	15th (Hampshire Yeomanry) Bn The Hampshire Regiment
18HLI	18th (Royal Glasgow Yeomanry) Bn The Highland Light Infantry
18King's	18th (Lancashire Hussars Yeomanry) Bn The King's Regiment
12Manch	12th(Duke of Lancaster's Own Yeomanry) Bn The Manchester Regiment
9NF	9th (Northumberland Hussars Yeomanry) Bn Northumberland Fusiliers
10Q's	10th Bn The Queen's (Royal West Surrey Regiment) Abs Surrey Yeo less C Sqn

10QOCH	10th (Lovat's Scouts) Bn The Queen's Own Cameron Highlanders
7RIrish	7th (Royal Irish Horse) Bn The Royal Irish Regiment
9RIF	9th (North Irish Horse) The Royal Irish Fusiliers
17RS	17th Bn Royal Scots took in HQ & B Sqns Lothians and Border Horse
13(SH)BW	13th (Scottish Horse) Bn The Black Watch (Royal Highlanders)
6Wilts	6th (Wiltshire Yeomanry) Bn Wiltshire Regiment
9WYks	9th (Yorkshire Hussars Yeomanry) Bn West Yorkshire Regiment

Bn/Sqn   Machine Gun Corps

100MG	B Bn Machine Gun Corps (later 100th) fr WksY and SNH
101MG	C Bn Machine Gun Corps (later 101st) fr RBH and BYH
102MG	D Bn Machine Gun Corps (later 102nd) fr ERY and LncY
103MG	E Bn Machine Gun Corps (later 103rd) fr RR and SS
104MG	F Bn Machine Gun Corps (later 104th) fr WD
17MG	17th (Bucks & Berks Y) Sqn MGC
18MG	18th (ERY & Lincs Y) Sqn MGC
19MG	19th (Warwick Yeo?)
20MG	20th (SRY & SNH) Sqn MGC see above B Bn
21MG	21st (RR & SS) Sqn MGC
26MG	26th (Scottish Horse) Sqn MGC (from 1/3rd Scottish Horse less a Coy)

Abbrev.   Other Terms

abs	absorbed
amal	amalgamated
Anzac	Australian and New Zealand Army Corps
arty	artillery
A tk	Anti-Tank
attd	attached
Bde	Brigade
Bn	Battalion
BTE	British Troops Egypt
Bty	Battery
b/u	broken up
C	Corps or Cadre
cav	cavalry
CCR	Corps Cavalry Regiment
Cdn	Canadian
CMF	Central Meditteranian Force
Co	County
comp	composite
consol	consolidated
conv	converted
Coy	company
Cy	City
D	Dragoons
desig	designated / designation
DC(Sqn)	Divisonal Cavalry (Squadron)
disb	disbanded / disbandment
disemb	disembodied
dismtd	dismounted
div	division
DMC	Desert Mounted Corps
dup	duplicate unit (TA)
EEF	Egyptian Expeditionary Force
emb	embodied
f	formed
fr	from
GHQ	General Headquarters
H	Hussars
HQ	Headquarter(s)
Hse	Horse
ICC(B)	Imperial Camel Corps (Brigade)
IMD	Imperial Mounted Division
indep	independent
IY	Imperial Yeomanry
j	joined
L	Lancers
LH	Light Horse

lt	light
ME(L)F	Middle East (Land) Forces
MG(C)	Machine Gun (Corps)
mob	mobilized
MR(V)	Mounted Rifle(s)(Volunteers)
mtd	mounted
orbat	order of battle
pdr	pounder
pers	personnel
RAC	R.A.C./ Royal Armoured Corps
reconst	reconstituted
redes	redesignated
red/c	reduced to cadre
Regt(l)	regiment(al)
regtd	regimented
reorg	reorganise(d)
ret(d)	return(ed)
RHQ	Regimental Headquarters
RTC / RTR	Royal Tank Corps / Royal Tank Regiment
sec	section
S/A	suspended animation
SP	Self-propelled
s/u	split up
Sqn	squadron
(T)	Territorial
TA	Territorial Army
TAVR	Territorial and Army Volunteer Reserve
temp	temporary
TC	Tank Corps
TF	Territorial Force
Tp	Troop
tp(s)	troop(s)
trg	training
(V)	Volunteer(s)
VC	Volunteer Cavalry
VLH	Volunteer Light Horse
WF	War Formed (unit)
WFF	Western Frontier Force
WO	War Office
Y, Yeo	Yeomanry
YC	Yeomanry Cavalry

Yeomanry Directory

1. Royal Armoured Corps

a. The Royal Yeomanry

RHQ	071 414 5240
HQ (WDgn) Sqn	071 414 5259
IC & CY Band	071 414 5261
Duke of York's Headquarters	
King's Road, SW3 4SC	

A (RWY) Sqn 0793 523865
Yeomanry House
Church Place
Swindon
Wilts SN1 5EH

B (LDY) Sqn 0533 778566
TA Centre, Tigers Road
Glen Parva
Leicester LE8 2UD

C (KSY) Sqn 081 688 2138
The Barracks, Mitcham Rd
Croydon
Surrey CR0 3RU

b. The Royal Wessex Yeomanry

RHQ	0285 648351
HQ Sqn	0285 648380
RGH Band	0285 648385
Highfield Ho, Somerford Rd	
Cirencester, Glos GL7 1TT	

A (RGH) Sqn 0452 302636

TA Centre
Eastern Avenue
Gloucester GL4 7PF

B (RWY) Sqn 0722 327325
TA Centre, Old Sarum Ho
Portway, Old Sarum
Salibury, Wilts SP4 6BY

D (RDY) Sqn 0271 45471
TA Centre, Fortescue Lines
Oakleigh Rd, Barnstable
Devon EX32 8JT

c. The Royal Mercian & Lancastrian Yeomanry

RHQ	0952 672926
HQ (Shropshire Y) Sqn	0952 506644
Bridgeman Ho, Cavan Drive	
Dawley Bank	
Telford, Salop TF4 2BQ	

A (QOWWY) Sqn 0384 394543

TA Centre, Swinford Road
Stourbridge
West Minlands DY8 2LQ

B (Staffordshire Y) Sqn 0384 230166
TA Centre, 5 Vickers St
Dudley
West Midlands DY2 8JT

D (DLOY) Sqn 0942 48882
TA Centre,
Kearsley Ho, Canal St
Wigan WN6 7NQ

d. The Queen's Own Yeomanry

RHQ	091 261 1046 x3125
HQ (NH) Sqn	091 261 1046 x3127
Fenham Barracks,	
Barracks Rd	
Newcastle-upon-Tyne	
NE2 4NP	

Y (Yorkshire) Sqn 0904 620320
Yeomanry Barracks
Fulford Road
York YO1 4ES

C (Cheshire Y) Sqn 0244 381050 x2736
Fox Barracks, The Dale
Liverpool Road
Chester CH2 4BU

B (SRY) Sqn 0602 618722 x2673
TA Centre, Cavendish Dr
Carlton
Nottingham NG4 3DX

D (NH) Sqn 0670 733974
Fox Barracks, High Pit Rd
East Cramlington
N'berland NE23 6RA

e. The Scottish Yeomanry

RHQ	031 336 1761 x5564	A (Ayr Yeo) Sqn	0292 264649 x5860
HQ (Lothians) Sqn	031 310 5564		
Inchdrewer House	QM 031 3105565	Yeomanry House	
Colinton Road		Chalmers Road	
Edinburgh EH13 0LA		Ayr 2JQ KA7	

B (LGY) Sqn	03552 25499	C (FFY/SH) Sqn	0334 56155
TA Centre, Whitemoss		Yeomanry House	
East Kilbride		Castlebank Road	
Glasgow G74 2HP		Cupar, Fife KY15 4BL	

f. North Irish Horse (Independent Squadron)

North Irish Horse	Dunmore Park Camp		0232 429545/6
	Antrim Road	Belfast BFPO 806	

2. Royal Artillery

a. 100 (Yeomanry) Field Regiment RA

RHQ	081 857 2151	201 (HBY) Field Bty RA	0582 572032
Napier House, Baring Road		TA Centre, Marsh Road	
Grove Park		Leagrave, Luton	
London SE12 0BH		Beds LU3 2RX	

202 (SNY) Field Bty RA	0284 753407	307 (SNHY) (RHA) Field Bty RA	0602 272251
Blenheim Barracks		South Notts Hussars Band	As above
Newmarket Road		TA Centre, Huchnall Lane	
Bury St Edmonds		Bulwell	
Suffolk IP33 3SQ		Notts NG6 8AQ	

b. 104 AD Regiment RA

211 (Glamorgan	Raglan Barracks	Newport	0633 214707
Yeomanry) AD Bty RA	Barrack Hill	Gwent	

3. Royal Engineers

a. 78 (Fortress) Engineer Regiment (V)

127 (Surrey & Sussex	0273 556041	227 (Hampshire	0252 340131
Yeomanry) Field Engineer		Yeomanry) Amphibious	
Sqn (V)		Engineer Sqn (V)	
TA Centre, 198 Dyke Rd		Seeley Ho, Shoe Lane	
Brighton		Aldershot	
East Sussex BN1 5AS		Hants GU11 2EZ	

4. Royal Signals

a. Squadrons serving with non-Yeomanry Regiments

47 (MY) Sig Sqn Royal	081 427 6890	Middlesex Yeomanry	071 272 2404
Signals,	081 863 1778	Band, c/o Lt Col SJ	
31 Signal Regiment (V)		Williams MBE TD	
TA Centre, Elmgrove Rd		88 Hornsey Lane	
Harrow		Highgate	
Middx HA1 1QA		London	

69 (North Irish Horse) Sqn Royal Signals, 32 (Scottish) Sigs Regt (V) BFPO 807 Clooney Military	0504 43211 x Clooney 228	**80 (CY) Sig Sqn, 33 Signal Regt (V)** Gilwern, Abbotts Park Liverpool Road Chester CH1 4AX	0244 390958 / 347203
95 (Shropshire Yeomanry) Signal Sqn, 35 Signal Regt (SM) (V) Territorial House Sundorne Road Shrewsbury SY1 4RL	0743 353365	**67 (QOWWY) Signal Sqn, 37 Signal Regt (V)** 77TA Centre, New Broad St Stratford-on-Avon CV37 6HW	0789 292266
70 (EY) Signal Sqn, 38 Signal Regt TA Centre, Victoria Rd S Chelmsford EssexCM1 1LN	0245 251152 or 284815	**Essex Yeomanry Band, c/o Major J Clarke** 175 Station Road Leigh on Sea Essex SS9 3BN	0702 76330
5 (QOOH) Sqn Royal Signals, 39 (City of London) Signal Regt	0295 262178	TA Centre, Oxford Road Banbury Oxon OX16 9AN	

b. 71 (Yeomanry) Signal Regiment

RHQ HQ (K&CoLY)Sqn 265 (K&CoLY) Signal Sqn Phoenix House, TA Centre Watling Street Bexleyheath Kent DA6 7QQ	0322 529225 0322 525522	**68 (IC & CY) Signal Sqn** 10 Stone Buildings Lincoln's Inn London WC2A 3TG	071 405 0702
		94 (BY) Signal Sqn TA Centre, Bolton Road Windsor, Berks SL4 3JG	0753 860600

5. Infantry - Correspondence via RHQ

a. Lovat Scouts (A & D Coys) **2 Bn 51 Highland Volunteers** TA Centre, Edgar Road Elgin IV30 3YQ	0343 543821 x3850	**6/7 Bn Princess of Wale's Royal Regt** Norfolk TA Centre Denne Rd, Horsham	**b. A (Surrey Yeomanry) Coy** 0403 266111	W Sussex RH12 1JF

6. Royal Logistic Corps

224 (Pembrokeshire (Castlemartin) Yeomanry) Sqn RLC,	**157 (Wales & Midland) Transport Regt (V)**	Picton Barracks Carmarthen SA31 3ZZ	0267 237114

7. Women's Transport Service (First Aid Nursing Yeomanry)

F.A.N.Y.	E Block King's Road	Duke of York's Headquarters London SW3 4RX	071 730 2058

8. Regimental and Old Comrades Associations, Museums,

Besides those museums noted below there are a number of national and local ones with information and collections of Yeomanry memorabilia. Where nothing is shown against a particular Yeomanry an existing formation may be able to assist with information. Local History Sections of the County Library network are also a prolific source of information. Old Comrades Associations are more ephemeral and where nothing can be elicited from these sources an enquiry should be lodged with;

The Yeomanry Association, Hon. Sec: Colonel JEB Hills DL
The Priory Cottage, Long Newnton, Tetbury.
Glos. GL8 8RN ☎ 0666 502681

Army Museums Ogilby Trust, 2 St Thomas Centre, Southgate St, Winchester, Hants SO23 9EF ☎ 0962 841416

Ayrshire Yeomanry - Hon Sec OCA
Maj GA Hay, Messrs D&J Dunlop, 2 Barns St, Ayr KA7 1XA

Ayrshire Yeomanry Museum
Rozelle House, Alloway by Ayr

Berkshire Yeomanry - Hon Sec OCA
55 South Hill, Godalming, Surrey

Royal Berkshire Yeomanry Museum
TA Centre, Bolton Road, Windsor, Berks SL4 3JG

Buckinghamshire Yeomanry - Hon Sec OCA

Cambridgeshire Yeomanry - Hon Sec OCA

Cheshire Yeomanry - Hon Sec OCA
3 Larchfields, Sanghall, Chester

The Cheshire (Earl of Chester's) Y Museum
Manley Lane, Manley, Cheshire WA6 9JF

Derbyshire - See Leicestershire Hon Sec OCA
Taylor Simpson & Mosley, 35 St Mary's Gate, Derby

Derby Museum & Art Gallery
The Strand, Derby

Royal Devon Yeomanry - Hon Sec OCA
33 Sunset Heights, Barnstable, Devon

The Devon Yeomanry Museum
Barnstable, Devon

Dorsetshire Yeomanry - Hon Sec OCA

Essex Yeomanry - Hon Sec OCA
The Old Rectory, Burgate, Diss, Norfolk

Fife & Forfar Yeo/ Scottish Horse - Hon Sec OCA
Capt J Dolan, Yeomanry House, Castlebank Rd
Cupar, Fife

Flint & Denbigh Yeomanry

Glamorganshire Yeomanry - Hon Sec OCA

Royal Gloucestershire Hussars - Hon Sec OCA
A(RGH) Sqn, TA Centre, Eastern Ave,Gloucester

Regiments of Gloucestershire Museum
Gloucester Docks, Gloucester

Hampshire Yeomanry - Hon Sec OCA
2 Copse Mead, Woolnaugh, Reading

Herts & Beds Yeo - Hon Sec OCA
Mr Currill, 28 St Margarets Rd, Old Fletton,
Peterborough PE2 9EA

Herts Yeomanry - Hon Sec Assn
Maj Tony Olford, 21 Beech Avenue, Eastcote,
Middx HA4 8UG

Inns of Court & City Yeomanry - Hon Sec OCA
22 Bron Court, Brondsbury Rd, NW6 6AH

North Irish Horse - Hon Sec OCA
CR McDonald Esq, 19 Dalboyne Park, Lisburn
Co Antrim BT28 3BY

Lothian & Border Horse Regtl Assn, c/o RHQ
RTR, Bovington, Wareham, Dorset BH20 6JA

Lovat Scouts Regimental Assn - Hon. Sec.
Flat 4, 20 Culduthel Rd, Inverness IV2 4AJ

Royal Mercian and Lancastrian Yeomanry

Middlesex Yeomanry - Hon Sec OCA
17 Queensbury Pl, Blackwater, Camberley, S urrey

Norfolk - See Suffolk

Northamptonshire Yeomanry - Hon Sec OCA
Upper End, 12 Seaton Rd, Uppingham, Rutland

Northumberland Hussars - Hon Sec OCA
31 Winchester Walk, Wideopen, NE13 6JF

Nottinghamshire - Hon Secs OCA
SRY - Eastthorpe House, Southwell, Nottingham
SNH - 35 Metro Avenue, Newton DE55 5UF
SNHB Fund TA Centre, Hucknall La, Bulwell, Notts

Q's O Oxfordshire Hussars - Hon Sec OCA
2 Juniper close, , Banbury, Oxon

Pembrokeshire Yeomanry - Hon Sec OCA
Hean Castle, Saundersfoot, Dyfed SA69 9AL
Perthshire - See Fife

Q's Own Yeomanry - Hon Sec OCA
Town Farm, Langton, Malton, N Yorks

Royal Yeomanry - Hon Sec OCA

Shropshire Yeomanry - Hon Sec OCA
Bridgeman House, Cavan Drive, Telford

Herts Yeomanry and Artillery Historical Trust
8 Mornington, Digswell, Welwyn, Herts AL6 0AJ
Also Hertford Yeomanry Museum, Hitchin , Herts

Inns of Court and City Yeomanry Museum
10 Stone Bldgs, Lincoln's Inn, London WC2A 3TG

Scottish United Services Museum
The Castle, Edinburgh EH1 2NG

Fort George Museum
Ardesier, Inverness

Norfolk Yeomanry Museum
Shirehall, Market Ave, Norwich Norfolk

The Northamptonshire Yeomanry Museum and
Abington Museum, Abington Park, Northampton

SNH Non Sec Assn - Col AJ Haines, 54 Rivergreen
Crescent, Bramcote, Notts WG9 3ET

The Castle Museum of Arts & Crafts
The Castle, Haverfordwest, Dyfed

The Scottish Horse Regimental Museum
The Cross, Dunkeld, Perthshire

Somerset, Hon Secs, OCA
NSY, The Lord Wraxall, Tyntesfield, Wraxall
Bristol BS19 1NT
WSY, W Richards Esq, 6 Luxhay, Taunton TA2
8ET

The Somerset Military Museum Trust
14 Mount St, Taunton, Somerset

Staffordshire Yeomanry - Hon Sec OCA

Surrey Yeomanry - Hon Sec OCA
21 Devon Road, Cheam, Surrey

Suffolk & Norfolk Yeomanry - Hon Sec OCA,
Mr RP Kidd, 18 Coral Drive, Ipswich, Suffolk IP1
5HS

The Suffolk Yeomanry Museum
T&AVR Centre, Bury St Edmunds, Suffolk

Sussex Yeomanry - Hon Sec OCA
31 West Park Crescent, Burgess Hill, Sussex

Warwickshire Hon Secs OCA
QOWWY CTrust TA Centre Swinford Rd
Stourbridge, W Midlands
WY- 10 Ashlawn Cresecent, Solihull, Warks

Worcestershire Y, City Museum & Art Gallery
Foregate St, Worcester WR1 1D
Warwickshire Yeomanry Museum
Court House Vaults, Jury St, Warwick

Westminster Dragoons - Hon Sec OCA
21a Blackberry Lane, Four Marks, Alton

Westminster Dragoons Museum, London

Westmorland & Cumberland

Dalmain House Museum, Penrith, Cumbria

R Wiltshire Yeomanry - Hon Sec RWY Assn
19 Smitan Brook, Covingham Park
Swindon Wilts

The Royal Wiltshire Yeomanry (PWO) Museum
Town Museum, Swindon, Wilts

Worcestershire - Sec **QOWWY** Charitable Trust
TA Centre, Swinford Rd, Stourbridge, W Midlands

Yorkshire - Hon Secs OCA

Yorks Hussars & Yorks Yeomanry -
Hoover House, Main Street, Harome, York

Q'sOYD - 14 Church Bank, Thorne, Doncaster
ERY - 35 Parkstone Road, Hull

Prologue

A Tale of Revolutions

During the middle of 18th Century there was a totally unexplained population explosion across the whole of Europe. In a disconnected way the agricultural methods were vastly improved which averted mass starvation. Famine and pestilence were no strangers to this part of the world. Had there not been an improvement in food productivity then many would have starved but this would have been unremarkable for the time. The survival of so many additional people meant economic growth gathered momentum and it was a question of national policy how different countries should manage this opportunity. The French it seems closed their eyes, because this would have required the Aristocracy sharing power with the Middle Class and loosening their hold over the serfs.

In almost the converse way, the British started to industrialise the various productive processes without much in the way of official guidance. Various dates are given for the onset of industrialisation. What is certain is that it predated the American War of Independence and the revolution in France. The profits of empire were used to fund a vast canal building programme necessary to improve communications for the transport of raw materials. This had to be done, quickly, cheaply and reliably if industry was to prosper. Only by this method were the cities to be adequately supplied or more to the point the factories they contained. Equally the products of manufacture needed to be hauled away for national consumption and export. Latterly steam eclipsed water power and the railways took over from the canals to transport not only goods but people. In terms of the urban masses feudalism was dead, also redundant were the large number of craftsmen put out of work by the machine methods of the new factories.

The Industrial Revolution over the period 1760-1830 was created out of the Country's own resources using every form of commercial and technical innovation. It was the process whereby a rich, ingenious and ruthlessly single minded society contrived to transform the threat of a social catastrophe into an opportunity and to create wealth on a scale previously unknown.

The catastrophe was the population explosion across Europe which followed no conceived logic from about 1750. In the normal way plague, famine and pestilence would have carried away large numbers, but the year 1665 marked the last plague. Notwithstanding, crowded towns continued to be large killers well into the industrial age with a combination of cholera, typhus, tuberculosis, scarlet fever, diphtheria and smallpox, but their actions were slow compared to the devastating rates experienced during a plague. The average age of town dwellers may have been no more than 16 years but this was henceforth calculated on a vastly increased population.

In the terms of the age, trading meant the capture of markets by the expansion of empire. Britain maintained a strong navy for the defence of her trade routes and to place her armies in overseas possessions. The North American Colonies were one such interest. They were the suppliers of the once famous potato, which became the staple diet of the masses and latterly tobacco and cotton. In return they imported our manufactures, including 'tea'.

The American War of Independence started in 1775 and had an inevitability about it. 'No taxation without representation' taken with the 'self evident truth' were powerful slogans, albeit the slave remaining not so equal! At home in the United Kingdom an increasing percentage of people were governed without representation according to the precepts of a broken down feudalism. By the time of the Reform Act of 1832 many of its protections were in process of being eroded, encouraged by a laissez-faire Government. Under the feudal right, a forty shilling tenancy gave the occupant a vote as he was ranked a Yeoman; below this there were no votes. However the process of urbanisation meant that even those with a qualification often had no place to exercise it by virtue of the system of 'rotten boroughs' and that places such as Birmingham and Manchester had no representation in the democratic process. The 1832 Act increased the property qualification to one of £10, but this was meaningless since the yeoman's rate had not changed since the middle of the 16th Century.

Apart from the colonies, North America embraced French interests in Louisiana and Canada, a Spanish one in California and Mexico. The Dutch maintained strong commercial links with the New England states. The French most notably sided with the colonialists, also the Dutch, because of the commercial potential. The British navy was badly stretched and when she wished to concentrate forces in 1780 at the Chesapeake Bay landings the Royalist French made a decisive intervention. It was no more than a spoiling tactic and totally devoid of altruism. This exposure of their 'Lower Deck' to the free thinking and actions of the colonials, redounded on France: their fleet, homeward bound, carried with it the fatal virus of Liberté-Egalité-Fraternité!

The French revolution was about the abolition of privilege. In a country with a highly centralised government and the aristocrats more or less bound to the nearby Court of Versailles, the established order of things fell like a house of cards. The much talked about storming of the Bastille was in fact a negotiated surrender by the Swiss garrison, to avoid bloodshed. Agreement notwithstanding, the Revolutionaries butchered them before emptying the cells of just two inmates! There followed a three year experiment to devise a constitutional monarchy: it didn't work. Revolutions are at best chancy affairs and only rarely do their inventors profit. As was the case in the later Russian Revolution, the situation arose where a well organised minority seized power. They proceeded to guillotine the Royal Family and concocted the 'Reign of Terror' lasting a year in which some 2600 souls perished. Many of these were able people and genuine democrats and in any case few aristocrats had stayed to witness the excesses of Jacobinism. This concluded the third of the revolutions, except to say the French were most enthusiastic to export their radical ideas. Whatever the justice of their cause, the deafening rantings of the French had their frontiers in flames. All the surrounding countries were feudal and led by aristocratic elites as France had been: they viewed the situation with dismay.

Fortress United Kingdom
The main strength of Britain against chance revolution, bearing in mind our own experience at cutting off Royal heads, was a 'weak' central government. Ironically, it was supported by a well developed county system with a strong Middle Class imbued with a love of freedom and good mercantile talents. When France declared war during the last days of January 1793 it suited neither aristocrat nor merchant to divert attention from the affairs of commerce and trade; not immediately anyway. Equally, they were not about to enfranchise all in sight. In any case, the fact of war was to close ranks bottom to top against an ancient foe. Politically, the Opposition took virtually no initiatives against the Government and this situation continued until the end of the Industrial Revolution, long after the war with France had been concluded. Considering the seduction of these radical politics, it called for steady nerves on the part of Government. Much was done to slow, mute and confuse the aspirations of the non-voting masses, also of those who had it but exercised it in public, under the eyes of their masters. Firstly, the Jacobin influence was played up as grounds for preventing the formation of Trades Unions or the circulation of tracts. The Combination Acts effectively outlawed the unions whilst the Corresponding Societies were taxed for their publications, with the printers liable for adjudged sedition and the authors guilty of 'High Treason'! At the time the penalty for this latter offence was 'hanging, drawing and quartering'! When in the case of Hardy, a jury refused to convict, the Government suspended Habeas Corpus. For the lesser offences there was transportation to Australia, with multiple prosecutions to tame the spirit of unruly printers. To assist in the task, a host of spies and agents provocateur were employed to ensure nobody got carried away with any stupid, new fangled and untried democratic notions. Trade was the thing.

Parliamentary reform excepted, the two vexing problems of the day were the displacement of skilled craftsmen by factory machines and curiously the lack of cheap food in country districts. Both were the cause of some of the worst riots seen in village, town or city. They occurred periodically throughout the Napoleonic war and thereafter until the mid-century and so far as can be ascertained Jacobinism played little or no part. With some reason the period following 1793 could be christened the 'English Reign of Terror'. It put a stain on the Establishment impossible to erase, except by playing heavily on patriotic sentiment. It divided the country into 'them' and 'us', where the former consisted of nearly 95% of the population!

Under the Feudal system everyone had a place. There were 'rights' and ways of righting wrongs. People had privilege, but with it went responsibility and duty. Magistrates were empowered to ensure the poor obtained food at prices related to their pay. Dramatic improvements were made in farming methods, making the land more productive. Such was the urban appetite for food that, more not less people were required on the land. However the intensive methods of cultivation increased costs without raising wages. As a consequence, food moving to the towns left behind a population of starving labourers and their wretched families. When pressed to apply feudal law, the Government turned the situation on its head by abolishing its main provisions, including the repeal of the Corn Laws. Even so, rural magistrates often persisted in the old ways. They turned a Nelsonian eye on a complaining farmer who had his corn ambushed on the way to market, for sale locally at popular prices, provided the money was paid over: People were not all bad.

The first really powerful surge of the Industrial Revolution came at about the same time as feudalism ended 'officially'. The Great Reform Act of 1832 did this, but feudalism had already died a death many years earlier at the hands of a callous Government. The £10 tenancy was easy enough to pay if you had one of the modern type jobs, however it disenfranchised a large number of the population, put out of work by the new machines. It is against this backcloth and a war with France that the initial work of the Yeomanry has to be judged. It called for local knowledge, a sense of fair play and a resolute spirit.

French Designs

Even before her internal differences were settled or external ones of method with her neighbours, France was at war notably with Austria and Prussia. An invading Prussian army was brought to battle. The Cannonade of Valmy on 20th September, 1792 lasted a mere seven hours and cost no more than 500 lives, yet it is credited with changing battlefield conduct, as previously known, into Total War! This was no mean feat for a near bankrupt nation with its officer ranks sorely depleted. Efforts to 'free' Belgium and separate Holland from Austrian domination were next embarked upon. The execution of the French King on 21st January, 1793 caused England to sever diplomatic relations and the French retaliated by declaring war on 1st February, 1793. In this, the external intentions of the Revolution were crystallised and as Fuller says 'The French wars ploughed up the feudalism of Europe' and they lasted for 22 years.

Although most of Europe became involved it was England who had to be brought to terms. For this there were two strategies: either to gain command over the Channel or to strangle Continental and Colonial trade.

Command of the Channel required not so much the defeat as the *annihilation* of the British Royal Navy. There has been much theorising over when this might have been and even an open shoreline still presented the intending aggressor with a list of imponderables. Not the least of these was the possibility of ambush and certain discovery, followed by a struggle in which the Royal Navy had to do no better than lose slowly. Yet by custom and practice it could expect to do a lot better, even with a scratch fleet and a late arrival. A trade blockade called for closing a circle of ports around Europe from the Baltic to the Adriatic and a strong and well supported navy, if it was intended to interfere with the Colonies. None of these requirements could be met initially. Time and events had to wait on the man. Meantime, a series of pinpricks were inflicted around the shores of Britain. These were mere distractions from the far more hurtful growing pains of the Industrial Revolution. England was as disinterested in the hysterical rantings of her erstwhile neighbour as she had been over the legion of émigrés who fled to her shores. Trade was the thing.

Now Napoleon was that 'man'. Trained in artillery, by a country boasting the best artillery of the day, he gained promotion to Brigadier by master-minding the ejection of the Royalists and English from Toulon during August 1793. Later he was promoted to General for stabilising a faltering government in Paris by ordering the famous 'whiff of grapeshot' over an unruly mob during 1794. Appointed to the command of the Italian campaign, he concluded by taking Austria and separating Holland from it. Appointed C-in-C of the invasion force for England in October 1797, he appeared opposite our shores on the 11th of February 1798. Previous attempts by the French navy to land a sizeable military force at Bantry Bay, Ireland failed in December 1796, due to bad weather. A successful but ridiculous landing followed in February 1797 at Fishguard, south Wales, but the so-called troops quickly surrendered to amongst others the Castle Martin Yeomanry. This later unit secured a unique place in the annuls of British military history by the award of the sole Battle Honour granted within the United Kingdom!

Presumably, the French did not get to hear of in time, or were unable to organise events to benefit from, the naval mutinies at Spithead on the 15th April, or The Nore on 2nd May, 1797. Whatever, with a mere two ships the British bluffed and blockaded the Texel preventing a prospective Dutch landing in England. Dutch and French invasion fleets then returned their attentions to Ireland. The Dutch were engaged at Camperdown on 11th October, 1797, which action aborted a diversionary landing of troops in the Clyde, with eight out of sixteen ships captured along with 6,000 troops. This brought to a close any early or cheap victories for the French, hence the appointment of Napoleon. His detailed appreciation was to halt precipitate attacks until a sizeable invasion fleet could be built up including invasion barges. Never at a loss for fruitful projects, he proposed to attack Egypt sitting astride a main trade route, whilst initiating as effectively as possible a Continental blockade against British trade. When the time was right, command of the Channel was to be secured for at least 24 hours. Between his arrival and the battle off Cape Trafalgar, near Gibraltar, this right time kept eluding him and after Nelson's victory there was no more than the glimmer of hope.

Prologue

Unwillingly to War

There was never a question of the French blockading British ports! Even at the middle of 1803 their fleet numbered no more than 23 Ships of the Line, 25 frigates, 107 corvettes with 167 small craft belonging to the invasion flotilla of 1800 barges. Many more were building but only their periodic allies, the Dutch and the Spanish could bolster these numbers. For the British it was 'business as usual' following the declaration of war except for the obvious consideration of avoiding French controlled ports. Naturally our merchantmen needed to apply prudence in planning voyages. Progressively Europe became a closed shop to our trade and threw people out of work. It was this that succeeded in focusing the national mind. A threat to our shores gave birth to the Volunteers Act of 1794 and a gradual overhaul of our Army and Navy. Very little else was done to deflect attention from the business of 'business', by which was meant an ever developing industry. It was with extreme bitterness that Napoleon referred to the English as 'a nation of shopkeepers', because he was unable to distract them from their productive aims, despite every ploy. Politically, Britain took initiatives to limit economic damage by forming coalitions with friendly states. This involved the payment of subsidies for standing armies and the employment of mercenaries which included the large French émigré Corps of soldiery opposed to the revolution. A Treaty obligation by Britain toward Belgium however, made an expedition imperative. This was so badly equipped and serviced that the remnants had to be extracted through Holland, the following year under the protection of Austrian guns; how humiliating! Even so, attempts were made at securing a peace during 1797 as there was a strong Peace movement at home, but these foundered against the dogged ambitions of the French philosophy.

The parties to a coalition, living as they did on the Continent, were subject to the political and military pressures of the French. Over the war period as many as eight were formed and foundered on the rock of this reality. During the period 1801-1803 Britain was alone except for the dubious Peace of Amiens calling a brief halt to the fighting, for 14 months. Although no more than a truce it enabled both sides to follow their separate interests and to break its provisions as it best suited them. During this period Napoleon cemented his grasp on power, when a grateful people elected him consul for life. Britain for her part was able to take a more strategic view, whilst making the best attempt so far at securing her shores. By January 1803 the English fleet comprised: Thirty-four Ships of the Line, those with three gun decks; eighty-six 50-gun ships and frigates, with 77 Ships of the Line and forty-nine 50-gun ships and frigates in reserve.

With the failure of the 'Peace' the British were at last roused to the threat of invasion. The Royal Navy imposed a blockade on French ports. Also, by the end of that year the Army with volunteers reached 463,000 and the figure was increased to 600,000 a year later. The blockade provided a stand-off arrangement as regards an invasion which was now taken seriously. It was also subtle, for it had the debilitating effect of depriving the crews of ships permanently in port of proper sea service and gunnery practice. Napoleon and those under him had worked hard to create a fleet capable of invading England. By the end of 1804 this comprised, including those of his Dutch and Spanish allies some 67 Ships of the Line. The English had 61 on blockade duty, 5 in port and 12 in the East and West Indies. This was a fragile control made good only by an Admiralty strategy of holding the Western Approaches of the Channel against invasion, with the sea off Brest as the rallying point. That is to say, if the French wished to assemble a battle fleet, it was necessary for them first to break out from a number of blockaded ports. If any of the blockading Squadrons were unable to prevent this their duty was to make for Ushant. Accordingly Napoleon's aim was to decoy a significant English fleet long enough to effect the landing of an army in England, whilst the Admiralty had a plan *almost* bound to make this impossible.

The battle 10 miles off Cape Trafalgar in the Atlantic between Cadiz and Gibraltar is well known; but what it achieved less so: a combined French and Spanish fleet of 33 ships fought 27 British; no British ships were lost; eighteen of the opposing force surrendered and four more were taken off Corunna; superior tactics and superb gunnery inflicted 14,000 casualties in return for 1,500 killed or wounded. Britain was become mistress of the seas for a 100 years.

Of course invasion became a near impossibility and Napoleon had only the Continental System or economic blockade to fall back on. This caused the English economy distress periodically. Militarily it made a 'Second Front' necessary if the French were to be brought to terms! Soon the Peninsular War opened through Portugal and with Spanish irregulars passed into Spain and South-Western France. This campaign became the effective training ground for a revitalised British Army, with the rise to eminence of the Duke of Wellington.

1. Volunteers

Early Days

The fact of the Volunteers Act of 1794 obscures a long civilian tradition of service whenever the Country was threatened. In this, National duty to defend the Homeland was an accepted tenet of citizenship. Governments of varying complexion have abused this facility when finding themselves unprepared to field a properly equipped and trained army. Never was this more true than at the time of the French Revolution. Even up to 1804 there seemed an extreme reluctance either to recruit a proper army or to train the population in the use of arms. The Government of that day swithered between compulsion and volunteering and contrived to miss the obvious feature of national duty. As a consequence they ended up with the worst of all Worlds: a depleted Regular Army, a mass of conscripted Militia and a huge force of Volunteers they were unable either to arm or train.

Theoretically the Regular Army was 'all volunteer', but the main thrust of legislation enacted for the period, was to squeeze the Militia, which was not. Some small part of the Volunteers were just that, whilst others volunteered to obtain the best from a number of unwelcome choices. If persons failed to volunteer they were liable to the Militia ballot. This was a conscript force. Volunteers were granted a variable set of reliefs from the Militia Ballot, also the widespread use of Substitutes enabled those determined to avoid such service to purchase an exemption and it seems the Government never expected the Principals to serve anyway.

In the Public mind there was a distaste for the Military. This dated from Cromwell, his Model Army and the 'Interim Administration' which had sat uneasily in the social strata of the times. Thereafter, matters were organised to divide command and control of the military both at the Governmental level and of the reserves on a county by county basis.

Presented with an impending disaster, it was decided to form a broader based military reserve. Normally the Militia would have been expanded, but this conscripted a mixed bag of people into a force universally detested and service in it was avoided where possible; besides which the Cavalry element had withered away, nor was there Artillery. Unspoken went the fear that although it might fight an external enemy, it was unlikely to be reliable when used at home on riot duty. The destabilising effects of the Industrial Revolution were beginning to work through and became an added factor to the social infrastructure of the times, though riots as such were no new phenomena. The final damnation in the eyes of the Treasury was the Militia represented a large standing charge; they had to be fed, clothed, accommodated and equipped until disbanded. A cheaper way had to be found to raise a willing number of high potential recruits, preferably mobile, as an uncertain future unravelled.

Armed Associations of horse borne soldiery were active in a guerrilla capacity during 1745 against the uprising led by Bonnie Prince Charlie and earlier during the reign of William III for use in Scotland and Ireland overcoming Catholic opposition. A Regiment of Light Cavalry was raised, during the Jacobite Rebellion, by the Yorkshire landowners and received the King's permission to be styled, the Royal Regiment of Hunters. It was disbanded directly following the end of the rebellion. Also identified with this period was The Northampton Defence Association. A more permanent unit in The London and Westminster Light Horse Volunteers dates from 1779. Thereafter, with one exception here and another in North America, all had been disbanded by 1785. This famous and unique corps, the London and Westminster Light Horse Volunteers sprang into being at the time of the Gordon Riots and demonstrated the possibility of citizen cavalry. There was some doubt in the Military mind of the time whether mere civilians could absorb the necessary lessons and discipline to make Cavalry work. This regiment discontinued in

Chapter 1

1783, lodging its standards in The Tower, for later use in 1794 [1] as part of the Yeomanry.

Only one other corps of cavalry of this period has a direct connection with the Yeomanry, the Norfolk Rangers, organised by the Marquess Townshend, who was convinced by what he had seen in the American War of Independence of the utility of Volunteer Light Cavalry. This Corps was never officially disbanded and was therefore in being, even if officially forgotten, and finally reorganised in 1794 [1] as Corps of Yeomanry.

Under the new, close at hand and pressing dangers, an interim solution of the Government was to have the Army resort to the wholesale creation of Fencibles. Presumably, no one was willing to wait on the results of recruiting Volunteer Cavalry or cynical of its likely abilities. There were 36 Regiments of Fencible Infantry and 41 of Cavalry pencilled in, though only 33 of the latter were actually embodied, each with varying numbers of Troops. A (de)Fencible is best described as a full-time Army Volunteer enlisted for an indeterminate period of crisis, for 'Home Service' only. Their object was to release their Regular counterparts to more distant projects, or simply close-up holes in the Establishment. Fencibles are first noted in the records from 1759 with the formation from Clan Campbell of the Fencible Men of Argyllshire with disbandment following in 1763. This was before two further crises, this time giving rise to the formation of Regiments. In these, Infantry, Cavalry and Sea Fencibles (An Admiralty Port defence responsibility) are variously noted. Prior to the French Revolutionary Wars, thirteen formations were ranked as Infantry and one as Cavalry (The Yorkshire Light Dragoons 1779-83). Those formed from 1794 are shown in Table 1.

The next gambit of Officialdom was the re-incarnation of the horse-borne Militia in 1796 as Provisional Cavalry. The force itself was unpopular and it is unclear who was the architect of this grand design, but it seemed intended to make up for the shortfall in the Yeomanry. An early clamour for its repeal led to the substitution of Yeomanry, if they came forward in three-quarters of the prospective numbers set for the Provisional scheme. Even so, some units were formed, placing further strain on the overworked Lieutenancies. Those areas failing the test had Provisional units formed as follows: Berkshire, Cinque Ports, Kent, Northumberland, Princess Royal's Own, Somerset, Suffolk, Suffolk Cavalry and Worcester. According to

Beckett only six regiments were actually embodied of which Worcestershire was alone in serving in Ireland. The timing was around the series of French pinpricks (Castlebar in Ireland, where serving Yeomen died and Fishguard in Wales resulting in a bloodless surrender) and although these never amounted to much, they succeeded in galvanising the Country into action because of the risks that one or another might succeed. The Parliamentary Return, made in 1798 [2] shows the extent of augmentation and new additions made to the Volunteer Movement. Those of the Provisional Cavalry not embodied were allowed to dwindle away until 1800-01 when the remnants were absorbed into the Yeomanry. Some were subsequently ostracised, according to Beckett, [3] providing an interesting though unpleasant forerunner to the 1956 amalgamations between Yeomanry and the RTR.

Table 1 Fencible Cavalry

Ayrshire	McDonnell's
Berwickshire	Midlothian
British Ancient	New Romney
Cambridgeshire	Norfolk
Cavalry 1st Regt	Oxford
Cornish	Pembroke
Dumfries	Perthshire
Durham	Princess Royal's
Essex	Roxburgh & Selkirk
Fifeshire	Rutland
Hampshire	Somersetshire
Ireland,Lt,1st&2nd	Suffolk
Lanark & Dumbarton	Surrey
Lancashire	Sussex
Linlithgow	Warwick
Lothian East & West	Windsor Forester's

Over this war period the Yeomanry were employed periodically on coast watches. Here Yeomanry mobility combined with the dispersed nature of their numerous 'headquarters' made them eminently suitable for defensive duty. Naturally it was the coastal counties that required to have the most effective forces. On the few occasions an alarm was raised, it followed on the lighting of beacons around the coast. It now seems unlikely that large cohesive forces could have been assembled at a danger spot in time. Cynics of the day observed that, "if the Royal Navy failed to save us, so would the Army; making the latter superfluous and if the Navy did not fail, there was no need for the Army; so it was unnecessary". No doubt these self appointed critics would have had some other equally vociferous complaint to make if the French had landed to set their thatch alight! To the pragmatist, a large, organised but scattered force, operating in friendly country would have given a good account of itself, particularly after being blooded. A major enemy lodgement, itself a considerable military achievement, would have been almost impossible to sustain and small ones of little consequence.

As Coast Watches became established the Regular Army Cavalry were withdrawn, for more offensive service elsewhere and were on occasion replaced by Volunteer Cavalry.

The only remaining forces not included here are those formed around 1860, variously titled Mounted Rifle Volunteer Corps or Light Horse Volunteer Corps and the Metropolitan Mounted Rifles a little later.

Administration

Many will claim that the English have a peculiar way of going about their business, the organisation of the military being no exception. In the case of the Royal Navy there was an unambiguous purpose and not the vaguest likelihood of its taking over the country. Insofar as the military was concerned, there remained the lurking suspicion that it or its masters could usurp the function of constitutional government, because it had done so once: rather a case of giving a dog a bad name. Charles M Clode in a monumental tome, [4] makes a number of apposite remarks:

"Parliament ensured the Army was kept small, in small formations and that allied foreign troops were not permitted to land on our shores. (They had done so at some earlier time, with unpleasant consequences for the Government stupid enough to proffer the invitation.) At the central level, control was exercised by as many as six people, whilst all the reserve forces came under the charge of individual Lords Lieutenant of the numerous counties, with the exception of the Pension Force. He was responsible for the efficiency and discipline of all the county reserves, holding both by Constitutional usage and Statutory authority, the place of Chief Command. The appointment and displacement of officers devolved upon him: The Ministers of the Crown had only the power of vetoing an improper person should such be named by a Lord Lieutenant. And it had been agreed between statesmen that Political motive should never interfere with such function nor should the appointments of Lords-Lieutenant be negatived upon the ground of political disagreement alone. (But see later the aftermath of Peterloo.)

Clode goes on to observe that; "two Non-Political offices of totally distinct import are often found united in the same person. As Custos Rotulorum, the appointee is the Civil functionary responsible in a sense for the Preservation of Order and the due Administration of Justice in his County and in that capacity properly communicates with the Home Office. As Lord Lieutenant he is essentially a Military officer and communications as such are to be made, not to the Home Office, but the War Office; for obviously the interference of a Military officer, either the Commander-in-Chief of the Militia in each county, or the General of the Army in each district, with the Administration of Justice or Civil police, would be unconstitutional. The Lord Lieutenant as a Military officer is liable to dismissal by the Crown, although a rarely considered necessity. His position is that of a General of a district, reporting through the Secretary of Sate for the War Department. Such communications are of a confidential nature and not for usual disclosure".

These features are important, as they underpin both the administration of Second Line defence and social order. Running the Army required team-work of a high order, just to make it work at all, whilst going to war needed concerted Parliamentary activity. The British Army of the time was not conscripted, that is to say men joined because they wanted to or because relative to the society of the day, it was the best deal they could get. To bring the Army up to size to meet the periodic emergencies relied upon a form of conscription to the Militia, which enabled the Regulars to be released for more pressing duties. Aside from this, a flow of part-trained militiamen were attracted, by the payment of bounties, into the Regular Forces. The generation and operation of the numerous Militia laws lays outwith the scope considered here. Those dealing with Volunteers are next considered.

The Volunteer Act of 1794 broke new ground and was clear on a number of points. It identified the authority of the Lord Lieutenant of each County, it specified both the external threat and the likelihood of civil unrest and most importantly it made clear that discipline was to remain in the hands of its appointed officers and no others. This latter feature was important having regard to the savagery with which punishment was meted out in the Regular Army of the day. *It was also specified that with a peace there was an automatic disbandment of any force raised under its provisions.* It was not specific about what form the units would take, contenting itself with saying Corps or Companies. It seems from this that the legislation was a broad brush affair, providing officialdom with a large canvas upon which to trace out their designs. Previously Home defence had been given the secondary support of an enlarged Militia. The new Act was careful to release the Volunteers from any liability to serve with the Militia and made it largely self-governing. Only later was this seen as unwise.

The extreme emergencies during 1797 produced some practical measures of a sort. With the mutiny at the Nore, a bridge of boats was strung out across the Thames from Essex to Kent, which effectively blockaded London for a period. In response to this the Government resorted to closing access to the land, with every road and lane patrolled as far as Tilbury, so that by these means many sailors were taken into custody and the remainder forced to live offshore. The Kent Troops of Yeomanry were active in containing 'sailors on the loose' and the Provender Troop was ordered to the Isle of Sheppey to arrest mutineers. Others Troops were brought in to patrol the coasts between Sheerness, Faversham, Whitstable and the Isle of Thanet. In one comical episode the frigate Beaulieu threatened to bombard Margate unless five arrested sailors were released.

There followed the Peace Treaty of Amiens, commencing on the 25 March 1802. By definition of the 1794 Act, the Volunteers were released from their service by legislative self-destruct. The Government of the day wished to retain the Force and had conducted a canvas, though the Continuation Act of 22 June 1802 (See Appendix A) was necessary to make it constitutional to accept offers and these had to be accepted by the Sovereign, to make them legal. However, by the stratagem of the canvas and some mumbo-jumbo, the Yeomanry was kept alive and only a few units were formally disbanded. Britain was without coalition partners at this time, yet placed little faith in the 'Peace'; accordingly the bulk of the Yeomanry were re-accepted over the ensuing 14 months. Hostilities were re-opened during May 1803, after which it was business as usual with Napoleon.

From this point the British had completed the equation between the Regular Forces necessary to pursue the war with France and a Reserve Army needed to defend the shores and keep peace in town and village. The war with France ended in 1815 at Waterloo, now a suburb of Brussels.

Legislation

It may at first appear perverse to put Administration ahead of Legislation, however the tradition and sense of history behind the shires has always provided them with an unquestioned ascendancy. Effectally, the rule of law was and remains by consent. Until the Peace of Amiens very little in the way of legislation had been enacted for the Volunteer Cavalry. There was the founding Act of 1794, the let-out granted under the Provisional Cavalry Act of 1796 and the 1802 Act enabling Volunteers to continue their services. This latter provision, although first mooted before the signing of the Peace Treaty, actually followed it to avoid upsetting delicate negotiations and as a consequence the Volunteers lapsed.

The chief defect over this eight year period, was the absence of any military consolidation for Home defence and the wasted effort in raising two sets of units not required in the longer term. The main, and as it turned out, misguided effort became focused upon the raising of formations and drilling these according to the precepts of the Prussians, as opposed to training individuals in military skills. If this was lamentable, the rush of confused legislation which followed, cemented the unsatisfactory arrangements together for years to follow. By way of example, Fortescue [4], talks of the confusion in that quarter and how it redounded on Home defence. In this he dismisses the many demonstrations of activity by saying 'its true significance was poverty of thought and of power of organisation'. To help his reader he summarised the effect of the Government Acts and Circulars of the period, affecting the Yeomanry and Volunteers:

"In 1802 they called them into existence upon their own terms of service, and granted them exemption from the Militia ballot in return for *five days'* exercise annually, together with certain allowances. On the 31st of March 1803 they called for more Volunteers, and proposed to give them what were afterwards known as the June Allowances. Having called for them, they became nervous lest the exemption of a number of Volunteers would interfere with the various ballots, and left many of their offers of service unanswered. On the 11th of June they passed the First Defence Act for general training of the people, and exempted the Volunteers from its operation. A few days later they issued the June Allowances, which offered pay to the men for *85 days'* exercise in the year, and required of them an agreement to serve within the Military District, in return for which pay was granted to a limited number of officers and to a permanent staff. (Clearly the listing of the Districts embraces groups of counties greatly extending the previous areas of service.) While circulating these allowances the Secretary of State announced that Corps accepted after the 16th of June would not be exempt from the ballot for the Army of Reserve. Ministers then again became nervous as to the expense of raising Volunteers upon the June Allowances, and delayed the acceptance of (these) offers of service. They then passed the Levy en Masse Act on the 27th of July for the compulsory training of all able-bodied men, with a clause to suspend the operation of the measure if a sufficient proportion of Volunteers should be produced by each county, which Volunteers should be bound to serve in any part of Great Britain. A circular of the 30th of July directed that immediate training should be given to a number of men equal at least to six times the quota of the Ordinary Militia. Then on the 11th of August they passed two Acts, the one to cancel the rigid rule as to the proportion of Volunteers to be raised under the Levy en Masse; the other to grant Volunteers exemption from the Army of Reserve, on condition that the Infantry underwent 24 days' and the Cavalry *12 days'* training within the year. Finally, on the 31st of August Ministers accepted the offers of all Volunteer corps, only stipulating that any men over and above the quota of six times the old Militia should be supernumeraries and not entitled to exemption of any kind."

He remarks that it was hardly surprising the Lords Lieutenant should have been puzzled by the successive measures and goes on to say that added to the difficulty of ascertaining the law of the land, was that of divining the wishes of the Government: did Ministers really want Volunteers or not? This was a question which the Lieutenancies found hard to answer, and they found it none the easier when direction of the Volunteers reverted to the Home Office in the course of 1803 (Circular of 31st August). Earlier he had put his finger on the fatal flaw of dissociating the Volunteers from the Militia and identified it as a lost opportunity in team building at the strategic point in time. He also noted how the War Office had taken over the Volunteers for no explained reason (An alarming presumption having regard to what Clode [3] says later) but nevertheless giving it a free hand to rationalise an unsatisfactory state of affairs and how it transpired

that Lord Hobart, the Minister responsible, was incapable of making much of the opportunity. The Home Office then finding itself saddled with a mountain of unanswered offers, prompted the new Minister to accept them all, 'providing' they did not militate against the Defence or Levy en Masse Acts, or general rules adopted or to be adopted: even then it was still the case of a definite possible maybe!

Today's reader may be forgiven in not following the theoretical implications of the Acts and Circulars at this stratospheric level. In practice the combination of inactivity and the inter-action of the various bits of legislation was to paralyse administration. However, even then the newspapers of the day were key informants! Most of the Lords Lieutenant of the day were exasperated to find their new instructions in them, along with verbatim tracts of the new laws and circulars, so slack were the clerks at the Home Office in providing copies of direct communications. In simple terms the impact of legislation worked out as follows:

Between 1794 and the 1802 Peace, the position of the Volunteers was simple: The terms of the 1794 Act applied. (See Appendix A1) After Corps Acceptance and the officers Gazetted, arms were issued by the Board of Ordnance (when held in stock) and the former were free to develop their soldiering skills. The important fact was an absence of allowances and that no one was paid.

They were reconstituted under the 1802 Act, which gave each mounted volunteer £2 to cover clothing and appointments, whilst each Troop of no fewer than 40 persons was given £60. The members were exempt from the Militia Ballot in return for five days' exercise per year.

From the 31st March 1803, it was proposed to attract more Volunteers by offering two days' (presumably paid) exercise in every week between Lady Day and Michelmas (54 days), with exemption from the Ballot during the term of service. These arrangements remained tentative and not actual, for two months until the Government fixed on a definite plan. But also on this date the 1st Defence Act (what amounted to preparations for general mobilisation) gave impetus to the affairs of June.

Then the Government circulated the 'June Allowances'. They amounted to a new code, in which every man had to take the oath of allegiance, every corps that claimed pay had to engage to serve in any part of its Military District (greater than the county as heretofore) and that Companies (or Troops) were not to be fewer than 50 men. The Volunteers were also tempted to undergo 85 days training per year, however only 20 were for pay!

There followed on the 3rd of August, the 'August Allowances', which effectively re-wrote the previous enactment, to which few enough persons had managed to engage successfully. These amounted to: £120 per Troop and exemption from the Army of Reserve in return for 12 days exercise, pay for up to 20 days service (to which was later added a further six), in return for an undertaking to serve in any part of Great Britain!

Now a difficulty arose in attempting to combine the requirements of the June and August Allowances. The absence of permanent staff hindered training and lengthened the time it took to bring both the man and Corps up to effectiveness. If this failed to worry the Yeoman, the play on training days did. The man on the August terms was required to put in 85 days for which he would be paid for 20 and failure to put in the remainder meant that the permanent staff were not supplied, even according to the adverse numbers game, meaning a Corps of at least 300. The theory picked up by Fortescue was that 52 of the 85 Drills were to be held on Sundays (An early form of Nationalisation; in this case the Sabbath) on which day no man received wages, which when added to the 20 paid days made 72 and that Corps should make shift to eke out the remaining 13, or, in other words, must be indemnified by the officers. This presumption was bitterly resented, since the officers rarely received pay and already made good the shortfall on clothing allowances and any others associated in retaining essential staff.

On the 10th of February 1804 a day's pay was added to the 20 for each inspection by a General or Inspecting Field Officer, provided they were not held more than once in every two months. However the Billeting Act of 11th August contained more, as it subjected the Yeomanry to the Mutiny Act when called to repel invasion and placed the Force under the command of Generals of Districts. Yet, on the credit side the officers were given custody of all funds and items purchased by such funds, which at last provided the beginnings of a legal remedy for recovering misappropriated property.

As can be imagined the import of the above measures, far from providing a firm and easily understood lead, left the Volunteers confused and some with soured relations. Then there followed on 5th June 1804 the Volunteer Consolidation Act which did away with the Billeting Act, continued the exemption of Effective Yeomen and freed them from the Mutiny Act whilst on Permanent Duty. Resignation was codified by making it conditional upon giving 14 days notice, the giving up of arms and the settlement of outstanding fines. No further rules were to be binding unless approved by the Secretary of State and the King was free to annul any rules made in the past or should be made in the future. These latter considerations were a good if belated move, but Governments change.

During 1806 a further onslaught was launched against the conditions under which Volunteers qualified for allowances, in the form of the Training Act of 16th July. Already by Circular of 9th June, the contingent expense of £120 per Troop was replaced by one of £2 per Yeoman. The June Allowances were swept away and replaced by £3 per man allowed for clothing, with £2 for all other expenses. An Adjutant was added to Corps comprising three Troops of 40 men. Somewhat divisively those under the August Allowances were henceforth to receive £2 for all expenses and an Adjutant for a Corps over 300 strong or a Sergeant-Major for one between 120 to 300 men. Lastly, to Corps raised after 24th July 1806 no allowances whatever were to be given. For the three classes mentioned the number of paid exercise days were now made 26.

From the records of the period leading up to the Peace of Amiens, the best attempt at preparing the Volunteers for 'Active Service' was agreeing places of rendezvous, plus plans for general mobilisation during 1797 and 1802. As later discussed the idea of driving the counties free of live and dead stock, in the event of an invasion, was strongly condemned, as a task of such enormity, by an august Duke of Richmond, in his capacity as Lord Lieutenant of Sussex and the former Master-General of Ordnance. Any criticism the Regular Army of the time had in regard to these auxiliaries was muted by the fact of their own unpreparedness. In any case it was the Militia which supplied them their steady stream of partially trained volunteers.

Of course it was left to the Lieutenancies to put their finger on the men for the Militia, whilst the Home

Secretary and War Secretary had to agree between themselves, if agree they could, to channel any flow of volunteer recruits to the Regular Army. Conflicting arrangements served both men badly. The large market for substitutes bid up their price, which was further aggravated by a depletion to the Volunteers and in turn the twin effects raised bounties for the Regular Army to astronomical levels. As the pool of willing men dried up, any shortages were thenceforth requisitioned from the Parishes where failure to supply them attracted fines. It may be thought this latter charge fell uniformly upon the people, but in reality it was the landed proprietors who had to pay, notwithstanding their likely efforts to form Volunteer Corps. Many that could not afford these arbitrary and periodic charges, shut up their country homes and repaired to urban parts.

During 1798 Guides were formed in Kent and Sussex, followed in 1801 by Surrey and in 1803 by Cornwall. These were allied to the Yeomanry or Volunteer Cavalry although serving in an intelligence gathering rôle, by virtue of their specialised local knowledge. These are mentioned in a footnote by Benson Freeman. [5]

"Corps of Guides had been formed in foreign armies, notably the French and were at first detachments of picked men, to act as their name signifies as guides and as scouts to the army. Later, as they were attached to the staff, such duties as escorts to their respective generals, the carrying of dispatches, special reconnaissance work, espionage and control of routes and minor police duties were performed by the Corps. The high standard of intelligence required naturally soon resulted in a very superior quality of man being recruited for them and caused whole regiments of guides to be subsequently organised, who were equipped as Hussars and regarded as superior form of light cavalry. They were favourite troops with Napoleon, who frequently appeared in their uniform. Disbanded after Waterloo, they were revived under the Second Empire. In the Belgium Army the Guide Regiments still exist and are regarded as crack light cavalry units. One regiment (the 19th Light Cavalry) still bears the names of Guides in the Italian Army and in the Indian Army, The Queen's Own Corps of Guides have the highest reputation. None of these Corps now differ in training or essentials, from the armies of which they are a part, though they would all claim to be a little better than their fellows."

French Pressure

The French had identified England as the country to be brought to terms, if their expansive schemes were to bear fruit and but for bad weather and a lack of experience in combined operations their early pinpricks might have been successful. As it was, they only succeeded in awaking Britain to her perils, giving time to organise adequate but always economical defences.

The Peace Treaty of Amiens was a watershed militarily speaking. In retrospect, before it neither Britain nor France was in a position to do the other mortal harm. By the time it failed it was clearly possible for France to damage Britain, provided she could immobilise our Royal Navy, so it became from the British viewpoint a naval war. Whilst the French knew there was no chance of a victory before securing our maritime defeat, the British began to realise how something more than a successful navy was required to secure the Continental trading interests. What this says is that both a strong army and navy were a prerequisite for the side intending to win and it took until after 1812 with the abortive Russian Campaign before England could qualify and even this required a generous contribution from others. As the consequence of this realisation, the War Office commenced a complete overhaul of the Army system, ready to prosecute a Continental strategy. The Government no longer placed more than a secondary faith in the use of subsidies and coalitions, indeed the market for takers had virtually dried up. On the Home front this manifested itself in stricter training and service requirements, to facilitate a maximum release of Regular Army personnel.

Mobilisation

A practical difficulty arose at the Corps level because of the varying terms under which units were accepted. As the 1803 Parliamentary Return shows, Troops within a Regiment were sometimes split between the June and August Allowances, leading to defections to obtain better terms. Independent Troops adjoining each other and serving on different terms had already intense rivalries made worse. If this wasn't complication enough, likely commanding Generals could foresee Corps serving under them with conflicting terms of service, varying from the Military District or City and Great Britain in case of Invasion, the Military District only, the County, the County and ten miles, within the Hundred only, according to the original 1802 Act continuing the Yeomanry, the coast of North Wales, England and Wales, with supernumeraries serving at no pay or allowance and claiming no exemption and lastly those generally serving under the Defence Acts: This constituted both a legislative nightmare and a military morass. If the War Office wanted the consolidation of Volunteer Cavalry to progress, they utterly failed in getting their message across to the Legislature. In the event Officialdom tinkered about to provide a niggardly fit. There was an eventual consolidation of the Acts previously mentioned.

It may be thought that having at last 'solved' the problem under which men now served, the training of units could proceed effortlessly: no chance! Initially the August Allowances carried no grant for Permanent Staff such as Adjutants and Sergeant Majors and 65 days were at no pay. These stupid conditions were partially abated in time, but served to sour relations. Added to this the Government paid no more than a third of the *actual* cost of uniforms. Most generally these additional charges fell upon the officers, but more unfortunately these most often manifested themselves only months later when bills were returned unpaid by the Exchequer.

Cavalry Corps under 300 men (the majority) received no professional instructors unless, by chance, they numbered such within their own ranks. Only volunteers could have been expected to serve and prosper under such demoralising conditions, but this wasn't the end of difficulties, there remained the question of arms. Colonel Vyse, an officer of extensive experience, had been consulted earlier by the Government on the underlying philosophy when forming a large auxiliary army. He had cautioned against creating Corps they could not arm, nevertheless they boldly enrolled hundreds of thousands of men on the understanding that 25 muskets for every 100 men would be sufficient for purposes of instruction and that pikes would be cheerfully accepted by the remaining 75. Never were the authorities more pitifully deceived. The proposed pike was eight feet long whilst the contemporary French model was thirteen, hardly a matter designed to embolden a fledgling soldiery; very few would requisition or use them.

However, arms of whatever sort could not be issued until the officers were Gazetted and the clerks at Downing Street were extremely casual, so that some issues took over three months to effect. More serious was the failure to procure the quantity of arms needed

for the new army. It was the partial issue of arms within a county which caused the most trouble as this fanned the flames of local resentment and jealousy. The volunteers had been allowed by the patchwork quilt of regulations to degenerate into a series of private fiefdoms and these engendered the most parochial of outlooks, so that far from coming together many Corps set their faces against it to the point of disbandment. The final act in this tragi-comedy came when the Government ordained by Act of Parliament, that to gain their exemption from the Militia, Volunteers must appear at exercise 'properly armed and equipped'. The period of direct interest closes with Nelson's victory at Trafalgar.

All the above may cast the War Office in a poor light, which is unfair, since the area was bedevilled by politics, into which area they were forbidden to stray. Where a military plan could be made against the reality of an invasion, the most masterly preparations for mobilisation were drafted. The following notes derive from the State Papers of the time [6], articulating the stratagems to be adopted for local defence. These had been assiduously developed over the years from as early as 1796:

"A Corps of Guides on horseback, consisting of those who are best acquainted with the Roads, Lanes, Footpaths, Bridges, Creeks, Rivers, Fording Places, and other Communications in the several Parts of Country, should be selected in the Maritime Counties, in Number from *Three to Six* from each Parish, according to its size. The rendezvous of this Corps to be the Head Quarters of the Army within the District, to which they should be bound to repair the moment it is known the Enemy has landed. To be Officered and paid as Yeomanry: Arms to be provided by Government". In this context the Corps of Guides had the function of providing local intelligence and for guiding bodies through what would otherwise be strange country. Units of such size were never formed, but more nearly approximated to a Squadron of two Troops. In many ways this initiative was a forerunner to the NW Frontier Guides and today's SAS. The point to note is that proper thinking was given to the question of Home defence.

Also included in this plan were further measures designed to make the best use of resources, human and otherwise and to ensure any invader was hemmed in and denied all sustenance. Under these conditions the Home Army was to bring the enemy to battle on the least favourable of terms or have him surrender.

The Mobilisation Plan included Pioneers, with the express purpose of making the going easy for the Home Army and as tough as possible for the invader. The country was to be 'driven', clearing it of all forms of livestock and deadstock. (i.e. grain, forage etc.) Roads were to be blocked, bridges dropped, wagons removed or their axle-trees smashed. To do their work, axes, saws and hammers were to be made available, on an agreed scale.

Besides this there was room for bands of fighting volunteers under their own elected leaders, mounted or dismounted, to be paid on the daily basis applicable to Privates and Lieutenants of the Volunteers, mounted or otherwise. This was an entirely separate provision from the Volunteers of the time.

Other initiatives included forming registers of bakers, millers, wagon train drivers and barge owners, so that they were available to provide essential services if the need arose. Next the problem of communications and leadership was addressed. Each county was divided into divisions and further subdivided into Hundreds, Rapes, Lathes or Wapentakes (according to local custom), with a gentleman in charge to ensure all necessary measures were implemented.

The protection of the coasts and their ports saw the recommendation to create Sea Fencibles, which was taken up as an Admiralty responsibility. Also included was the arming of flat bottomed vessels to act as inshore and river gunboats. Boats abandoned were to be sunk. These latter measures were backed by a Government undertaking to provide the necessary guns and stores and also to pay for the fitting with ring bolts to run-out cannon. It appears from this that the Admiralty could make their writ run.

To motivate the local inhabitants to perform this orgy of self-destruction willingly a scheme of indemnification was framed. These measures were backed by a Royal Warrant and Orders in Council. Thus, the English got down to the business of defending the Homeland in a way never witnessed before, nor equalled till the Second World War. These propositions had first emanated from Whitehall during 1776 and again in 1799 and 1801. The Lord Lieutenant of Sussex, The Duke of Richmond, a former Master-General of Ordnance and commander of a Yeomanry Artillery then examined their implications

and pronounced them unworkable by virtue of the sheer enormity of the task facing county authorities. Thus by November 1803 the scheme was scrapped, although it was still intended to drive horses and draught animals from the path of any French landing.[3][6] But of course the invasion never came!

Wartime Conclusions

Centering on the French Revolutionary war and concerning the use of Auxiliary Forces, come the conclusions reached by Fortescue, a hundred years later. As a preface to his County Lieutenancies and the Army, 1803-1814 [7], he describes the work as an *overflow* from his 13 volumes dealing with the History of the British Army. He remarks that possibly the subject could have been covered in 20-30 pages, and that if the reader finds the volume impossible to digest, he had found it maddening to write. As it was the text ran to 312 pages. Luckily we are concerned with nothing more than the mounted portion of the Volunteers, but the interaction between the War Office, the Home Office, the Lieutenancies and the Militia make it difficult to separate them at times. It was for this reason and with the formation of the Territorial Force in mind that it may be presumed Haldane prevailed upon Fortescue, with a small subsidy, to articulate at greater length than he was minded to.

The records for this period are extensive, confused and incomplete. The most instructive preserved at the Public Records Office are entitled *Home Office, Internal Defence* of which 250 volumes embrace the period, arranged by counties in date order: A further 76 were and possibly remain in a state of chaos. As the result of studying some 100,000 documents it was possible to reach some conclusions for the period:

- Compulsion cannot be applied for service outside the British Isles.
- The admission of the principle of substitution in any scheme of compulsory service leads to ruinous expense, demoralisation and inefficiency.
- Compulsory personal service for home-defence has been tried and not found wanting.
- The ultimate end for which all our military organisation must exist is the maintenance of the Regular army, our only offensive force
- The true basis of such an organisation is National training
- Learning the use of arms should be imposed as a positive duty upon all individuals within certain ages, to be enforced by fine

Chapter 1

- A Volunteer who asks more from the State than his arms, except on active service, is no Volunteer. False volunteers are alike troublesome, expensive and useless.

Prior to 1803 Fortescue shows that Pitt's whole organisation and system of the Part-time Volunteers had been vicious and false and later became impossible to change. This statement he necessarily qualified, under a number of headings, but basically it was the failure of the Administration to give a clear lead, and make a proper financial contribution, which led to their loss of control. Granted the Duke of York saw to the appointment of Inspecting Officers and in 1806 their returns were consolidated by the War Office, however there was no initiative taken to angle the training or it seems any means of communicating such a need. *Thus the Volunteers, left to themselves, adopted a false system of training, spending days on valueless classical manoeuvres, when a few hours could have inculcated worthwhile military skills.* Overall it made no economic sense, because the money was still spent, whether from the State purse or the private pocket and at the end no proper army was created. The best return came from the mounted Corps, who were better disciplined and served a practical need in the form of police, although this facet is no more than lightly touched upon. When called to this duty they received Regular Army rates of pay and continued to do so for the bulk of their service.

Hopefully the reader can flavour the perplexing and random situation facing the volunteers of the period. As said elsewhere, from Nelson's victory at Trafalgar, the need for a Home Defence Army against invasion was less than pressing, but this remark is now made with the benefit of hindsight and the assumption that our Regular Army was not otherwise engaged.

In talking legislation, the importance attached to the implications of the Law can be assumed by the later publication of Precedents of Proceedings on the Yeomanry Cavalry Act [8]. This is concerned with the civil actions of a Yeoman, in regard to membership, property and the right to resign. It seems from this that convictions were difficult to obtain until a specific law was passed as late as 15th May 1822 (3 GIV c.23, s,1). The work is dedicated by an un-named author, to Edmund Pollexfen Bastard Esq. a member of Parliament for the County of Devon and Lieutenant-Colonel Commandant of the South Hams Yeomanry Cavalry.

References
1 Freeman FM Benson & Fellows G. His. Records of the S Nottinghamshire Hussars. (Gale & Polden, Aldershot 1928)
2 Parliamentary Session Papers. 1797 Vol XLV 910, folio pages1-9
3 Beckett IFW. The Amateur Military Tradition, 1558-1945. (Manchester University Press, 1991(2))
4 Clode CM. Military Forces of the Crown: Their Administration & Government. (Murray 1869)
5 Benson Freeman FM. The Yeomanry of Devon, 1794-1927. (St Catherine Press, London 1927)
6 Parliamentary Sessional Papers, 1803-04 Vol XI Folio pages from 117
7 Fortescue Hon JW. The County Lieutenancies and the Army. (Macmillan, London 1909)
8 A County Magistrate. Precedents of Proceedings on the Yeomanry Cavalry Act. (J Butterworth, London 1822)

2. Part-Timers

The Invention of Part-time Volunteers

The war with France caused the formation of the mounted volunteers, or at least it provided the strongest pretext. In a tentative manner this had happened earlier. On this occasion politicians turned events to their advantage. The primary need was for a military defence against French aggression, but clearly the pressure generated by the import of radical ideas unsettled matters at home, whilst the other radicalism of the Industrial Revolution added a sense of urgency. On balance therefore, a need arose for Parliamentary action.

Out of the flawed genius of the 1794 Volunteers Act came the initial few formations of mounted troops. It produced part-time cavalry, but not in great quantity or uniformity. Although no responsibility of the Army, it was a matter for its concern, since in the event of an invasion ALL land forces would need to team-up. Given the legislation, the counties were left to get on with its execution. Fortescue[1] summarises the position succinctly. 'Where no individual's station marked him out among his fellows as a natural leader and most notably in the towns, the proceedings were uniformly as follows:

A meeting of the citizens or parishioners was summoned, an individual was called to the chair and after a solemn preamble setting forth the ambitions and vices of the hated Bonaparte, a series of resolutions was passed that an Association for the defence of the locality should be formed, that subscriptions should be invited and that a committee should be organised for the general direction of affairs. Then followed the rules of the Association, which included the conditions of service and the regulations for internal economy and discipline. *The committee did not contain none but officers of the corps. On the contrary, it consisted commonly of the largest subscribers who, with sound commercial instinct, claimed an influence proportioned to their contribution.* It was the great ambition of every Association to be, if possible, self-supporting, to the end it might be self-controlled. In fact the Associations were, or aspired to be, simply clubs formed for the purposes of defence, on the principles of equality that govern social clubs; that is to say, the Committee was elected; that the officers also were either elected or chosen by the committee; and that the general proceedings of the Committee, together with any matters of extraordinary importance, were subjected to the criticism of General Meetings, ordinary and extraordinary'.

One is inclined to remark, 'how reasonable', but there were professional soldiers, at the time, of great experience who demurred. However, it is to be remarked how recurrent a theme it is in British history for officialdom to make recourse to the Mutiny Act, flogging and other measures of compulsion upon erstwhile free and volunteer citizens. (Even Navvies constructing a railway during the Crimean War were not free of this danger and heaven only knows what sort of a railway would have resulted from official intervention.)

Such a meeting when held in Kent was a most undignified affair. The Lord Lieutenant was roundly abused as a 'place-man' and only by virtue of the numerous competing interests was he able to take the chair and then with great difficulty, because the meeting threatened to break up. This county it will be noted was nearest France, was most populace and on the high road to London. Over the period of threat it formed more independent Troops than the total comprised within its combined East and West Regiments, which numbered 16.

Dorset however furnishes a particular example of how well things could be done. A Government circular was issued to the Grand Jury sitting at the Dorchester Lent Assizes on March 13th 1794, entitled PLAN of AUGMENTATION of the FORCES for INTERNAL DEFENCE. Basically this outlined the idea of forming

Chapter 2

Volunteer companies, Fencibles and 'other Bodies of Cavalry'... to consist of Gentlemen and Yeomanry or such persons...etc. "It was immediately, and unanimously, Resolved.

- To give at this crisis the utmost Support to Government.
- That the experience of giving such support be defrayed by a Voluntary Subscription throughout the county.
- That a Committee be formed etc. etc.
- That the Committee do meet etc.
- That the Subscription be immediately be opened. (noting Banks in London and locally.)
- That the Subscriptions be paid by Instalments, at the Call and under the Directions of the Committee.
- That the Proceedings of the committee be from Time to Time inserted in the Salisbury and Sherbourne papers.
- That a Copy be delivered by the foreman of the Grand Jury to each of the Judges of Assize.

A sum of £1,425 10s. subscribed by 19 persons was raised. The resolution to form a Volunteer Cavalry was carried unanimously, so they moved directly to the Articles of their Enrolment:

- That we are to receive no Levy money.
- That we are to have no pay unless called out and embodied.
- That we are to find our own Horses and Clothing, Government to provide Arms and Accoutrements and pay for one Serjeant per Troop
- That we are liable to be embodied or called out of the county by special direction from His Majesty in Case of appearance of actual Invasion, or in aid of any Corps which may be formed for the defence and security of any adjoining County, (viz. Hampshire, Wiltshire, Somersetshire, and Devonshire), when riots and tumults do exist in that County and during the continuance of the same: And to be liable to be called upon by order from His Majesty, or by the Lord Lieutenant, or by the Sheriff of the County, for the suppression of riots and tumults within the County: In either case when actually on service to receive pay as Cavalry and to be liable to the provisions of the Mutiny Bill.
- That we will attend at such times and places as shall be appointed by the Commanding Officer with the approbation of the Lord Lieutenant, in order to be trained and exercised, not oftener than two days in the week, and not during the time of Harvest or Sheep Shearing.
- That we shall forfeit the sum of five pounds in case of non-attendance without sufficient Cause upon the days appointed for training and exercising.
- That we will forfeit the sum of two Pounds in case of non-attendance without sufficient Cause upon being called out to suppress riots and tumults, in this, or in Adjoining Counties.
- That we will forfeit the sum of fifty pounds in case of non-attendance without sufficient Cause upon being called out on the appearance of actual Invasion.
- That the Cause of non-attendance in the above three Cases shall be decided to be sufficient or insufficient by a Majority of the Volunteers serving in person.
- That the sums forfeited shall be paid into the hands of the Paymaster of the Corps for the use and benefit of the Corps as shall afterwards be determined by the Majority.

It was understood, though not stated that no servants were to be admitted and that the Corps was to consist *solely of Gentlemen, Yeomen, and respectable Tradesmen*. At this time the Gentlemen of the County balloted amongst themselves for rank as officers. Perhaps this should help to settle the unreal situation into which the Yeomanry subsequently argued itself. Writers today have gone to great lengths to correct a false impression which has had absolutely nothing to do with the reality of this period. The Yeomen were always recruited from amongst those with a community of interests in property and the established order of things, else how could they have remained so steadfast in the face of frequent brickbats?

There is no implied criticism of other Corps when one says Dorset was the epitome of all that was good in the Volunteer Movement: They were quick off the mark to form a complete mounted regiment, were precise and clear on all service objectives and determined to be highly disciplined over their conduct of affairs. At the same time they asked for nothing more than arms from the Government. Any weak features were endemic to the Volunteers as a whole, by virtue of the manner in which the Government had constituted them. And directly the need was over this Corps was as equally keen to disband.

This said, the Grand Jury meeting in Oxford threw out the measure as 'inexpedient'. Also this proceeding on the part of Government excited some opposition in

Chapter 2

Parliament, led in the Upper House by Lord Wycombe and in the Commons by Sheridan. On the 24th March the latter moved that a copy of the circular be laid before Parliament and denounced its issue without the consent of the both Houses as unconstitutional and an attempt by the Crown to increase the land forces without the consent of Parliament. This explains a rather shrewd move by Mr Pitt in bringing in the curious 'Bill to Encourage and Discipline Volunteers' (Appendix A1).

Dealing first with the formations of the mounted Corps from the country districts: Where a landed proprietor or magnate formed them, it was generally the tenants who filled the ranks and his friends and acquaintances the officer appointments. The system varied very little from the ongoing rural economy, in which landlords exerted a compelling ascendancy, and the people accepted the status quo on the basis of accepted custom and practice. It must be remarked that this writ of bucolic rectitude did not always run and people did fall out and officers resigned, but not often. Many regard these as the true Yeomanry, but this begs a large question, as instanced by Dorset, besides which their numbers were indeed very small in proportion to the movement as a whole.

Most of the mounted Association Corps sprang to life with a view to protecting private property in the towns, with local and restrictive terms of service. Committees deliberated over their conditions of service and were supported by private subscriptions. The committee members were not necessarily holders of commissions. During the formative days meetings tended to be rowdy, in which local notables, such as a Lord Lieutenant was paid scant respect, as was the case in Kent. These local bodies frequently addressed the Secretary of State directly and it was open to question whether they or the officers were the true commanders of the Corps. The founding Act was used as a bargaining point and members rarely intended fulfilling its full terms. As is shown elsewhere the word Yeomanry was used with great economy until after 1804, so most Corps were titled Volunteer Cavalry and as a consequence it is difficult to separate them unless specifically described as 'Association'.

Many Association Cavalry later accepted the full terms of service and signified it by the inclusion of the words Yeomanry and Volunteer in their titles, however by then many other Corps did the same, making it difficult to trace the actual dates of transition. The Letter Books of the War Office for the period running up to 1802 also showed other conversions from Volunteer Cavalry to Yeomanry. The social distance was less here in the towns, between officers and men, making discipline more difficult to enforce, although major infractions were rare within the mounted element. Disbandment was the final arbiter on those occasions when a complete breakdown in discipline occurred.

A further grouping of Corps was formed in the cities, without a feudal influence but prepared to serve under the full rigours of the Act. They were frequently called Volunteer Light Horse (not to be confused with the later formations circa 1860). The standards of a self-imposed discipline were of a drastically higher order, providing the commanding officer an unambiguous right to command.

Corps had a list of rules or objectives, most commonly supported by a system of fines for the non-performance of specified duties. Unfortunately, it was impossible to enforce a fine on a person without property and expulsion became the only viable option, in the event of non-payment. Earlier, some mounted Corps had identified this weakness and for other reasons, a property qualification was imposed when seeking membership. A problem arose from the acceptance of a volunteer unable to provide for himself in all respects: For a mounted trooper, the charges were considerable, taking into account, a horse, horse furniture, sometimes arms, accoutrements and uniform. More insidious came the creeping-up in the number of service days needed, from 1803, to secure exemption from the Militia ballot, for which no pay was granted, whilst pay from an employer might be deducted for absence.

Initially the Government had given undertakings to provide arms and at other times the provision of uniforms, so when these failed to materialise, it was either the officers or the men who had to take up the shortfall. Patriotic subscriptions and the private funding of the Associations, held this problem in check over the early years, but when these funds became exhausted it was only a matter of time before the Volunteer Corps started to dwindle.

In all this Fortescue remarks on the paucity of documents over the period 1793-1801 and that it was impossible to speak of them except in general terms. There is no mention of anything to do with money and only the 1798 Parliamentary Return to underpin the fact of many unit's acceptance, apart from the War Office Letter Books and these seem notoriously incomplete. This explains the vagueness evinced by many writers covering the period, though rarely admitted. Later, Parliament fixed on obtaining better documentation and an explanation of how money was spent, but all of this follows 1803.

During that year a Parliamentary wrangle broke out over a Volunteers right to resign and the Government attempted three stratagems until agreeing. Fortescue[1] reports the single sentence by Fox, summing up Minister's action: "First it was intended that Volunteers *might* resign, then the Attorney-General said that they *could not* resign; then the Court of the King's Bench said they *could* resign; and now Minister's bring in a Bill to say that they can resign, and insert a provision which renders it *impossible* for many to resign": But on this latter point the Ministry was eventually obliged to withdraw.

Next the question of Commanding Officers disciplining men was decided by giving them the right to discharge them, thereby making them liable to the Ballot. By 1804 it was also apparent that the only remedy for disagreement between the Government and Corps was the latter's disbandment. Whatever the efficiency, or lack of it, by January 1804 the Cavalry Volunteers numbered 28,943. However, the whole system of training was wrong in the opinion of the Soldier Robert Crauford, but it was a fatal defect when unable to enforce discipline. Notwithstanding, the Government persevered by encouraging Permanent Service periods[8]. The Maritime Counties turned out their Cavalry and Infantry Corps between 1st November 1803 and 5th March 1804 and by ten days continuous exercise worked a salutary good effect over the efficiency of the movement. At this time the first steps were taken to 'Brigade' the Corps in the Military Districts, as shown in Table 2.

Table 2 Volunteer Brigading

District	Cavalry	Infantry
Eastern	2	4
Southern	1	3
South Western	1	4
South Inland	1	4
London	1	7
Home Counties	0	6

This was part of plans to group small isolated Corps into regiments, but very rarely with success owing to the bitterness of local jealousies. Norfolk and Suffolk gave particular trouble. In the latter county their were 13 Troops and not one regiment. Accordingly, the creation of brigades was problematical. This lack of military cohesion, in the case of Norfolk lead to an Inspector reporting, in May 1804, only three out of 33 Corps fit for service and the Lord Lieutenant, himself a General felt obliged to agree. This aura of parochialism showed badly when the officers were required to undertake instruction together. The Corps would clamour for Regular sergeants and corporals (their inferiors) and felt hard done by when Colonels of the Line refused their requests (for lack of this scarce resource) but revolted against the provision of Officers who were unaware of their local importance and treated them purely according to a fitness for duty. At this stage the Volunteers were under the protection rather than the control of the Home Office. Only on Permanent Duty (which was not compulsory) and when called out to repel invasion were they under military law and most of the time they snapped their fingers at all in authority. Well might Crauford exclaim that so delicate a machine was unfit for war, though the real test of foreign steel never materialised and it was this temper needed to make forces battleworthy.

As it transpired Napoleon's preparations for invasion were faulty. In trying to design an invasion barge suitable both as a transport and a fighting ship he obtained a craft unsuitable for both. Added to this was the problem of assembling the Channel Fleet in view of British cruisers. The ports were such that no more than 90,000 men could be put to sea over a period of two tides. Apart from the reality of Trafalgar, Napoleon perceived the uselessness of the project and broke it up.

The demands for enhanced efficiency in the Volunteers reached their maximum point during 1806. At this time the June Allowances were effectively swept away for individual ones of £3 for clothing and £2 for other expenses, with an Adjutant for any Corps comprising three Troops of 40 rank and file and upwards. For those on August Allowances it was £2 per individual to cover all expenses, with an Adjutant to cover Corps over 300 men or a Sergeant-Major for between 120 and 300 men. These facts are repeated here again for it was these revisions which went to explain the number of disbandments occurring at this time. The Yeomanry Force numbered 32,728 on 1st January 1805, 30,927 a year later and continued to fall until 1812 when the

Rank and file were down to 19,207.

From this point, the recruitment of Volunteers most often reflected the imposition of Militia ballots, which they wished to avoid and for this reason such men were not at all well received. Added to this was a new type of man attracted by regular pay at a time when work was scarce. Indiscipline continued leading the Isle of Wight Yeomanry declining to serve under an officer, in defiance of an Act of Parliament and when the Commanding Officer resigned, the Troop even attempted to appoint their own. The Yeomanry was not called out for Permanent Duty during 1811 and during 1812 the consolidation of the Militia proceeded, with the run-down of the Volunteers encouraged. This appears to have included the Yeomanry. The process was to have men volunteer to serve in the Militia, without filling their places by ballot, until six months had been given for volunteers to fill such vacancies.

The conclusion of hostilities would have normally brought to a close the need for Volunteers, indeed the Infantry was disbanded in 1812-3, to loan their arms to the Prussians for more martial service elsewhere. However the Yeomanry with all their faults had demonstrated an ability at Crowd Control out of all proportion to their size or expense and so were retained. This story is taken up in the succeeding chapter.

Formation Anomalies

General Considerations As a generality the Lords Lieutenant were responsible for all military matters in their respective counties. Initially they gave acceptance to those offering to establish a Corps of Yeomanry and granted the necessary commissions, which enabled those in charge to draw arms from the Board of Ordnance. This was both a good and a bad thing, but in any case from the middle of 1798, such authority passed upwards to the Secretary of State, Home Department, who thereafter informed the Lords Lieutenant when the Sovereign had accepted their offers of service. Why a good thing? Basically arrangements were enabled to proceed rapidly in an age of slow communications and provided strong local supervision. The accepted mode of individual travel at that time was horseback, so that each Lord-Lieutenant often spent an arduous day in the saddle sorting out his County's arrangements. Why a bad thing? Obviously the display of local initiatives engendered a degree of organisational drift and in this the Volunteer Corps

was already about as variable as any organisation could be, making central planning uncertain. However quaint, anomalies were extremely unwelcome at a time when the administrative machine was under strain. Possibly this explains the transfer of arrangements.

The Confederation of the Cinque Ports At the time of the 1794 Volunteers Act the Cinque Ports enjoyed specific privileges turning on the military situation. Firstly, they were free from the impressment of their citizens into the Royal Navy and secondly the Militia Ballot did not apply. Under the circumstances they felt morally bound to do something and volunteering was one.

The Cinque Ports numbered '14' members strung out along the Sussex and Kent coasts, so frequently threatened by an intending invader. Originally, as their name implied they were five in number: Hastings, New Romney, Hythe, Dover and Sandwich. They provided ships, men and materials, prior to the Norman Conquest, as an Anglo-Saxon response to further Saxon encroachment. Following the conquest, Winchelsea and Rye were added to their number with equal privileges. Later, seven more 'Limbes' were added, by name Lydd, Faversham, Folkstone, Deal, Tenterden, Margate and Ramsgate. The Lord Warden of the Cinque Ports was also Warden of Dover Castle with an official residence at Walmer Castle. It is obvious that in times of peril the inhabitants of these 14 towns could hardly evade taking some responsibility, which was the reason for the initial grant of privileges. In the event they formed a large Corps of Volunteers, with amongst other things a number of Troops of Yeomanry. Presumably, as they were not beholden to the Lords Lieutenant, the acceptance of their services was taken by the Lord Warden and over the period 1794-1806 this luminary was none other than the Prime Minister Pitt, the progenitor of the Volunteers Act! Whilst those in Kent formed some Corps identified with the Cinque Ports, it appears nothing was done in Sussex, though some of the Ports did form mounted Corps.

County Parts Durham County is a true example of the Church Militant, where the Bishop, doubled as the Lord Lieutenant. In early history it was the King's writ which did not run: Rather the case of a privilege taken, not one granted. At the time of the Yeomanry formation the County came in three parts. The second consisted of a sizeable triangle tapering inland to West of Coldstream, facing the Border with Scotland.

Obviously the Bishop of Durham was able to brush aside any objections voiced by Northumberland. The third portion was situated by Blyth.

Hales Owen is a further example of a marooned portion of a County (Salop, surrounded by Worcestershire). As the consequence of these arrangements, the reader will come upon a number of apparently displaced units.

London, Environs and Other Parts A cursory glance at the Troop names for the counties of Essex, Kent, Middlesex and Surrey, make it patently obvious how London has grown since the latter years of the Eighteenth century. Besides this The City of London was never London and the latter was most frequently referred to as Westminster, unless it was some other place falling within the counties just named. Even then it is pertinent to look at some of the early Militia and Yeomanry Returns and to consider into which category did, for example, Tower Hamlets fall.

Similarly the Isle of Wight was a separate county entity, whilst a number of the smaller Scottish Counties have since coalesced into more Regional units.

The Isle of Man, then as now, was a separate constitutional part of Great Britain, despite attempts of Inspecting Officers to ignore the fact. During the war with France it formed Militia, Fencibles and Yeomanry Corps. One reason for not forming a Yeomanry earlier than it did was the existence of a volunteer mounted Militia or Constitutional Dragoons between 1793-6, something which had ceased to exist elsewhere.

Lost and Changing Troop Titles Elsewhere the pull of demographic events can be remarked upon. It was always a moot point with the War Office, the variability and frailty of some Volunteer formations. However, Troops were where the people were. As the strains of the Industrial Revolution worked through the system, so the population distribution changed and some villages shrank and so did the make-up of Troops and so titles changed.

An unfortunate feature of the Militia and Yeomanry Lists were the purely alphabetical order of things with very little geographical guidance. When Ireland joined the Union in 1801, the problem was compounded by the addition of about the same number of Irish place names, applying to an *undivided* Yeomanry; that is one

in which a Corps could be either Infantry or Cavalry. As the consequence of this and any differences in Parliamentary or Military Returns, one is often left with a handful of names which cannot be allocated. To ensure identification it is often necessary to have its place name, that of its commander and the county. Within the Official listings appeared a number of confusing titles. Rangers were either Cavalry or Infantry. Light Horse and Guides were classified as Cavalry, whilst a solitary Forester unit was Infantry. There were a number of surprising and sometimes quaint titles in use at this time such as; the Gilcomston Pikemen, the Ramsgate Marksmen, the Tavistock Miners (Artillery), The Muncaster Mountaineers, Loyal Flint Fusiliers, Hertford Horse Artillery, the Glasgow Sharpshooters, the Grocer's Armed Association, Artillery Company (1120 Infantry!), Pioneers and the Sherwood Rangers (as Infantry).

Terminology It has already been remarked how few units carried the appellation Yeomanry during the earlier days. Whilst most Volunteer Cavalry was so called, a number carried what are now confusing titles. Added to this were those embodied within larger formations such as the legion.

In the military sense the term Yeomanry was not specific to Cavalry, although it became so. It could and did contain on occasion both Infantry (Renfrew) and Artillery elements (Sussex). A truly Irish situation arose with their local armed associations, which later became termed Yeomanry. These formations were both Cavalry, Infantry or mixed and they seemed perfectly free to change the constitution, though the general direction was toward Infantry. This feature explains the specific use of the word Cavalry, whilst the word Volunteer distinguished them from the Fencible and Provisional Cavalry of the times.

The most perplexing Corps were those formed by local associations, entirely independent of Government support. Under no debt or obligation to others they frequently failed to provide returns or information to those outside, indeed they seemed oblivious that such existed. *What the dividing line really was between the Yeomanry and Volunteer Cavalry cannot be divined for nowhere has it been stated what conditions **had to** be fulfilled.* The best guess seems to be a ready acceptance of the ever changing conditions of service, but this far from infallible, as the most cursory examination of the records shows and the 1803 Return is as good an example as any. Many obliged to earn a living found these impossible to satisfy, hence Fortescue's strictures, however he must have had his tongue in his cheek, for even he had to earn his fee!

A number of Yeomanry Corps adopted Infantry companies, or formed part of associations or legions which contained both arms. The Honourable Artillery Company at some later date integrated the three arms, creating a true forerunner of the Panzer Armee principle mooted by Fuller, post The Great War. A Legion was generally a mix of Cavalry and Infantry and sometimes Artillery or Pioneers, but it could mean a simple group of either Cavalry or Infantry. Individually there are Corps noted as Pioneers; Rangers who were either cavalry or infantry, Light Horse and Guides who were mounted, a sole Forester Corps as infantry, and an Artillery Company with 1120 infantry. The point considered here is the advisability of actually confirming the Arm of the service to which any Corps belonged.

Cavalry Formations till 1838

The 1794 Act slowly attracted the Yeomen. Taking the Parliamentary Return of 1798[2] as a starting point the record of acceptances is shown in Table 3.

Table 3 Cavalry Numbers

Year	Corps	Troop	Numbers
1794	46	152	7,472
1795	60	168	8,222
1796	64	176	8,572
1797	114	251	12,826
1798	225	374	19,190

The combination of French pin-pricks and the operation of the Provisional Act had the obvious effect of jolting the 1797-8 figures upwards. Already the highly dissociated nature of the movement was apparent, despite half a dozen large regimental formations, the ratios between Corps and Troops drop from 3.3 to 1.6 over the period, whilst the numbers in a Troop remain fairly constant around 50. Of course failure to achieve the latter figure would have led to non-acceptance.

Fortescue has already remarked over this rugged independence. The numerous small Corps were not the way the Military saw it and no doubt, through the medium of attached permanent staff, their thinking became known. In tandem with independence came a fierce pride and sense of duty. One unfortunate at Weymouth, who failed to put in an appearance though not incapacitated when the defences were tested during 1798, was dragged from out of his house by indignant townsfolk. The street was lined on both sides as he was led down it with a halter round his neck, accompanied by jeers of the spectators. After this his uniform was stripped off and he was chased out of town.

We are indebted to Fellows and Freeman[3], for an alternative listing of formations over The 1794-6 period. This appears as Appendix B. As they remark, had no disbandments taken place, this listing would have given the precedence of the various regiments, based upon the acceptance dates of each senior troop. One pitfall avoided, was of accepted units not actually materialising, as happened in the cases of Bedford, Glamorgan and Roxburgh during 1794. Also, the Marquess of Townshend's Norfolk Rangers existed as a Yeomanry body at this time, having been first created in September 1782 and thus rank 'right of the line'! Their are additions for 1797, with most of the Lowland counties of Scotland joining. A good proportion of these names represent groupings which eventually gave rise to County Regiments.

Gentlemen & Yeomanry Lists appeared for 1799-1801. That for 1801 indicates no less than 205 Corps, but that figure is insecure and possibly unimportant in the run-up to the prospective Peace of Amiens. The Government of the time was most anxious to retain the services of any Yeomanry, whatever their numbers, because of their effectiveness in quelling public disorder.

By virtue of the Act raising the Volunteers, it was necessary to have them volunteer and be re-accepted, if they were to continue their services. However Dorset, Leicester and the Southern Regiment of the West Riding were not prepared to give such an undertaking and were formally disbanded. The dating of the enabling legislation and the need for it, confirms the 'constitutional gap' between the onset of peace and the re-acceptances. In simple terms all the Volunteer Cavalry Corps lapsed as from 28th March 1802, the operative date for the Treaty of Amiens. To this extent Officialdom took the opportunity to reshape the Volunteer Cavalry, by ensuring only those wanted were re-accepted, if they volunteered which most did.[5] The actual sequence of events in the case of the Wiltshire is illustrative of how the Official mind operated over this period. As early as 12th November 1801 Lord Bruce[4] informed Lord Hobart at the War Office (for during this period and into the Peace they had charge) of their willingness to serve beyond it.

Note, the Association were not the only bodies to go over the head of their Lord Lieutenant. On the 14th November Hobart responded saying the offer had been laid before the King *who would consider continuance*. On the 28th of March 1802 the Peace Treaty was signed and the reduction of forces to a peace establishment was at once commenced. On 24th April, the Earl of Pembroke, then Lord Lieutenant of Wiltshire wrote to Lord Bruce enclosing a further letter from Hobart. In essence the latter wished to be informed what proportion would serve *should circumstances ever render it necessary to call for them and that His Majesty did not wish to avail himself of these offers until those making them had had an opportunity to reconsider them.* As the consequence of this, the letters were laid before the Troops, who re-affirmed their willingness to serve. Hobart was informed accordingly and acceptance was made by the King on 31st August 1802. It is significant that in only a single instance (Pimhill, Salop, 11th June 1798) does an Acceptance over this period predate the enabling legislation of 22nd June 1802 and that is possibly an oversight. It is upon this re-affirmation that a new line of Acceptance Dates were granted as recorded in the 1803 Parliamentary Return. In the light of this and the last clause in the 1794 Volunteers Act, it is difficult to support the fiction of unbroken service across such a divide.

The fact of civilian unrest was a feature from 1795, when riots took place all over Devon, which must have been most worrying to the authorities, seeing as to its strategic setting. This unrest continued, on and off until 1803. As has been remarked, French threats to our shores added further impetus to the formation of more units, also the Blockade Napoleon exacerbated an already unsatisfactory employment situation with further civil unrest. Support of the Civil Power became a cardinal feature of Yeomanry work and this forms the subject of the ensuing chapter.

Ostensibly the failure of the Peace of Amiens stemmed from a quarrel over the ownership of Malta, but it was a failure waiting to happen and nobody believed it to be other than a pretext. During the interim period the British Government, bereft of coalition partners, addressed the question of military preparedness. On the renewal of war, the disbanded Yeomanry were re-raised and that force as a whole augmented. A basic worry for the War Office remained the large number of independent troops, likely now to become their direct responsibility. Some counties achieved regimentation but most Troops evaded such orders, because *no one would provide the necessary funds needed to change uniforms!*

The Yeomanry and Volunteer Corps Parliamentary Return for 9th December 1803[5] and that for Military Districts in 1806[6] provide the most complete picture we have of these reserves at any time in their history. Also during 1806 there appeared the Willson Chart[7], although his figures are of uncertain origin.

The 1803 Return formed the basis for calling the Force to Permanent Duty, which had such a salutary effect on its erstwhile poor discipline. There are figures for both Establishment and Effectives respectively, the Terms of Service under which they were accepted, with a new line of Acceptance dates and is noteworthy as it clarifies the constitution of Legions and other Corps with unusual mounted and dismounted combinations. The limitation in forming larger units was more a problem of finding commanders of ability and appropriate experience, than getting small units to come together, willy nilly. The shape of these particular forces was extremely variable. Sometimes the component Cavalry Troops were reported separately and on other occasions as part of the Legion etc., which is the reason for tabulating them below. The components making up the Legions etc. are shown in Table 4 below.

Chapter 2

Table 4 Legionary Formations

Name & Composition of Force	Cav Tp	Inf Coy	Artil Coy	Period	Men
East Cornwall Volunteers	1	12	-	1803-1810	1058
Cheshire Legion	6	6	-	1806-1813	710
Cumberland Rgrs & Inf.	1	7	-	1803-1813	556
Denbigh Legion	1	8	-	1803-1808	530
East Devon Legion	6	7	5	1803-1808	1341
Southern Regt (Devon)	2	36	-	1803-1806	2646
Usworth Legion	4	5	-	1803-1806	496
Darlington Legion	2	5	-	1803-1806	400
Hatfield Peverel Vols	1	2	-	1803-1813	198
Essex 2nd Trp & Dism'ted	1	2	-	1803-1813	187
Essex 5th Trp & Infantry	4	3	-	1803-1804	
Essex Union Legion	4	2d	-	1803-1806	344
W Essex Legion	1	2d	-	1803-1806	214
1st Essex Legion + Pikemen	1	15 +1P	-	1803-1806	1240
Maylor Legion	4	5	-	1803-1806	680
Swansea Legion	2	3	-	1803-1806	436
Hertford Volunteers	1	1	1	1803-1806	255
Lovedon Volunteers	1	7	-	1803-1806	904
London & W'minster Vols	6	3	-	1802-1806	815
Royal Spelthorne Legion	1	10	-	1803-1810	842
Montgomery Legion	3	20	-	1803-1810	1680
Lynn & Freebridge + M'ted Rifles & Artillery.	2	1/2Rif	1/2	1803-1813	128
Royal Cheviot Legion	4	10	-	1803-1813	810
Percy Tenantry	6	17	-	1803-1813	1311
Glendale Volunteers	1	1	-	1803-1813	130
Nottingham Sqn + Rifles	2	1/2	-	1803-1808	130
Selwood Forest Legion	2	4	-	1803-1804	520
Mendip Legion East	1	10	-	1803-1807	800
Mendip Corps	4	1	-	1803-1806	290
W Stirling Legion	2	6	-	1803-1806	607
Clapham Volunteers	1	3	-	1803-1813	299
Richmond Legion	1	2	-	1803-1806	205
Croydon Volunteers	1	4	-	1803-1813	317
North Pevensey Legion	2	14	-	1803-1813	1220
Craven Legion	5	12	-	1803-1806	1280
Rutland	4	4	-	1803-1806	495
Warwick	5	1	-	1803-1813	386
Richmond Foresters	1	3	-	1803-1806	270

Some care is necessary in naming the parts comprised in a legionary formation to avoid double counting. Also later, when the Volunteer Infantry and Artillery components were dissolved, it was not uncommon for the Cavalry to soldier on under the old legionary title, giving a thoroughly confusing idea of who they were or their numbers. Beside this, although not listed above, there were purely Infantry formations titled as legions. Perhaps the most interesting Legion was the East Devon with its sequence of acceptances as follows:

The Hemiock & Culmstoke Corps of Cavalry of two Troops was accepted on the 29th October 1802, followed by the Royal East Devon Corps, also of two Troops, on the 5th November. Three separate Companies of Infantry followed on the 21st May 1803 and one of Artillery on the 12th August. On the 20th August two further but separate Infantry Companies were accepted, similarly two more of Artillery.

Two further separate Infantry Companies joined on the 3rd September, plus another of Artillery. Lastly, on the 15th October 1803 a further Company of Artillery arrived to be joined by the Upottery and Churchstanton Corps of Cavalry, each of single separate Troops. The first five pledged to serve within the Military District and obtained the June Allowances. The remainder came under the Defence Acts and got the August Allowances. In modern terms such a force would constitute a Quartermaster's nightmare, but then there was without doubt a high degree of autonomy, nevertheless it is interesting to speculate over the degree of arm-twisting necessary to create and hold together such a miracle command!

The listing of a completely new set of Acceptance Dates poses a problem for the practitioners of 'precedence'. Table 7 shows the effective numbers serving for 1803 and 1806, when known. Later, the concept of 'service without pay' was noted by the Home Office, during the 1828 and 1838 economies, but at this time it was conveniently forgotten, possibly in view of that last clause in the 1794 Volunteers Act.

The varying conditions of service have been traced already in the legislation. Using this return a number of useful data can be derived. Firstly, the ratio of Troops to Corps is now 2:1, with 302 Corps and 604 Troops. The Establishment total has risen to 33,992, providing an average Troop manning of 56, whilst the total All Arms Effective Force is 380,183, a mere 10,387 below Establishment. Isolating the Cavalry element, there is a shortfall on the Establishment of 2,160 men, which figure ignores the Legions. Accordingly, the Cavalry appears to be well up to establishment.

Next there is the question of varying terms of service. Of the 302 Corps, 115 elected to serve under the Defence Acts, 169 within their Military Districts and anywhere in Great Britain in case of invasion, with 111 of them in receipt of the June Allowances. The remaining 18 Corps restricted their service to the County or Hundred, yet even so seven of these qualified for the June Allowances. Particularly hard hit were 30 Corps suffering split allowances, where either so many men or specified Troops obtained June Allowances and the remainder those for August or like 37 other Corps, none at all. Aspects of this situation have been discussed already, so the lack of cohesion generated by these treatments can be imagined. Bedford serves to illustrate the divisive nature of such administration; the Force numbered 177 men, divided into four Troops, of which 100 were to be 'clothed' by the Government and two Troops were to receive £120 each, so who got what? Well might Fortescue inveigh against any other than the true volunteer, but in fairness, *'the goal posts had been moved'.*

There is a considerable variation in the numbers and names of formations over this, the most important war period. In the case of 1803 the figures are taken from the Effective Rank and File. In the case of missing numbers, those for Establishment are shown. This overcomes the difficulty of separating the Cavalry element from the Legions. For 1806, a similar approach is taken, excepting the Willson figures[7] are first used, when those of Effectives are not available. In the absence of this figure the Establishment value is then cited.

The 1806 Return[6] is interesting because it is based upon Inspecting Officers' from the Regular Army, qualified to comment upon fitness for duty. These range from 'Fit to act with Troops of the Line', 'Advancing in discipline', 'Deficient in discipline, for want of practice', 'the Officer's very attentive', 'scattered state and bad attendance' and 'in want of permanent duty'. Specific comments include ' --- 2 Sergeants and 44 Rank and File, included in the absent, are not allowed to parade on account of bad conduct' and in the case of the South Hampshire Cavalry, 'Not fit to act in line - majority of the horses much under size for service'. A number of units are not reported in this Return, but appear in the Willson Chart. He makes the single specific mention of the word Yeomanry. By this date all the War Office inspired Provisional and Fencible cavalries had been disbanded. Most of the titles line up exactly with the Yeomanry, so it may be taken those mentioned, were the ones in common usage at the time, as opposed to those in Official documents. In passing, Table 5 provides a matrix into which the cavalry numbers have been slotted for 1806, but no equivalent figures are yet found for 1803.

Table 5 Military Districts & Volunteer Cavalry

1803	District	1806	District	R & F
1	N Eastern	1	Northern	698
2	Yorkshire	2	Yorkshire	2,618
3	Eastern	3	Eastern	2,472
4	Southern	4	Kent	853
-	---	5	Sussex	489
5	S Western	6	S-Western	852
6	Western	7	Western	2,666
7	Severn	8	Severn	2,262
8	N Western	9	N Western	2,128
12	Home	10	Home	2,675
10	N Inland	11	N Inland	2,307
9	S Inland	12	S Inland	2,348
11	London	13	I of Wight	74
13	N Britain	14	N Britain	2,266
--	Total	–	Total	24,999

This total excludes the three Buckinghamshire Corps not making a return, quoted by Willson as having a complement of 1126, giving a total for the Yeomanry Force of 30,103, which is more in line with the 30,903 quoted elsewhere. A further aspect of the Military Return is the relationship between counties and District areas. For example, the Home District centred on London takes in large portions of the surrounding counties, whilst Dorset, Somerset and the Principality of Wales are split between Districts, presumably upon Military advice. Also to be noted is a slight variation of these Districts from those used in the earlier 1803

Mobilisation Plans. A detailed comparison between the 1803 and 1806 figures is made and appears at the end of the chapter in Table 7.

From 1805 the military purpose of the Volunteers was relaxed and they were allowed to dwindle away, until in 1813 the Infantry portion, with a few exceptions were dissolved by a circular dated 17th March. (Their arms were required for the Prussians to fight Napoleon.) The Yeomanry was left untouched, indeed steps were taken to raise its efficiency by encouraging it to come out for 12 days permanent duty at Regular Army rates of pay. By this time the Government was, in the words of Fortescue, awakening to the fact that it was the most valuable element in the Volunteers, notwithstanding the first attempts at Yeomanry economy or put more precisely, military efficiency occurred during 1813. These were aimed solely at regimenting the independent Troops, but these refused to die. Regimentation, it must be admitted, involved a dreadful upheaval of bruised sentiments on the part of independent commanders, plus being hit in the pocket by uniform changes. Since the Government offered no incentive, once again such requests fell on deaf ears and so long as the war lasted, nothing much could be achieved by Officialdom. The Dorset Yeomanry disbanded yet again in 1814, with the overthrow of Napoleon.

A Parliamentary Return is available to make safe the figures and units cited for 1817[8]. The main value of this latter document resides in the figures for the Cavalry Establishment being set against Effectives: These are 20,839 and 17,818 Rank and File respectively.

On the 3rd April 1822 the War Office issued a Return dealing with 1821. This lists unit titles, with the names of commandants and the various sums of money paid out. The total sum came to £118,614, with £33,085 paid for Permanent Duty in the suppression of riots. Fifteen Corps failed to make any claims for allowances and at that late date it seems unlikely that such would be forthcoming, so possibly they were then in the process of disbanding?

A very confusing Yeomanry Cavalry and Volunteer Infantry List appeared during 1825[9]. It is difficult to decode, both because of a Cavalry and Infantry admix and for the fact that Ireland is included in its alphabetical ordering. (With their Yeomanry shown undivided.)

On 5th September 1827 the Government set about the significant disbandments mentioned earlier. During 1828, twenty-four Yeomanry regiments each with about 33 years of service were disbanded. Fellows and Freeman remark "A force which had reached an establishment of 33000, was already reduced to 31000 had then to come down to 7725 officers and men in the following 22 corps consisting of 144 troops. The remainder of the Yeomanry corps, many of whom were compact regiments, some 102 in number, containing 354 troops were selected for disbandment. To their credit sixteen corps containing 66 troops and a total strength of 3152 men, offered to continue their services *and were accepted* without either pay or allowances. The total number of corps thus serving being raised to 38, containing 210 troops and an establishment of 10,877 privates." The Corps identified with this period are listed in Table 6. These economies were made as a result of those paying taxes remonstrating over the high level thereof. These were hardly the toiling masses, but they had the political muscle and so favoured attention. The Government was in a dilemma, for it was positively aware that insurrection, even rebellion could break out at any time. The obvious strategy was to identify the Yeomanry who were vitally needed and to disband the rest. This of course called for the exercise of sound logic.

Table 6 Yeomanry Corps Economies of 1828

Selected to Serve	Serving Gratuitously
Ayrshire	2nd Buckingham
Cheshire	1st Cornwall
Glamorgan (Gower)	2nd Cornwall
Glamorgan (E)	Denbigh
Glamorgan (Cen)	Derby
Lanark	1st R Devon
Lancashire (D of)	N Devon
Leicester	S Devon
Midlothian	Glasgow
Northumberland	E Lothian
S Nottingham	Oxford
Sherwood Rangers	Bloxham & Banbury
Renfrew	Pembroke
N Shropshire	W Somerset
S Shropshire	E Somerset
N Somerset	Westmoreland
Stirling	
Stafford	
Warwick	
Wiltshire	
Yorkshire Hussars	
SW Yorks.(Y Dgns)	

However this judgement was clouded, for where efficient Corps operated, there was little or no record of unruly mobs, hence these were most frequently chosen for disbandment. Accordingly the selection was botched, setting a time bomb ticking under the

Southern counties and the economy very soon redounded on the head of political expediency, in the form of the (Captain) Swing Riots. The Return for 1827[10] places the cost of maintaining the Yeomanry at £127,419 and it goes on to select those units, as listed in the above table, destined to remain after the bulk of the Corps were disbanded.

At this juncture the story has been completed from the onset of a war with France, to its conclusion during 1814-5, through the aftermath into a recession, concluding with the 1827-8 economies. There were further economies made in a similar manner in 1838 and with similar results. However, from that point things began to come right. The Industrial Revolution started to pay-off and increasingly the various Police Forces took up the maintenance of public order. To illustrate the creation, development and curtailment of the numerous Corps over the periods 1794-1802 and 1802-1828, two spreadsheets have been developed as shown in Appendices C2 and C3.

TABLE 7 1803 & 1806 Rank & File Effectives

County	Accept.	1803	Corps	1806	County	Accept.	1803	Corps	1806
Ayr	22 10 02	144	Ayrshire	144		12 10 03	38	Barnstable	----
Beds	16 09 02	177	Bedford	----		----	L Biddeford	70	
	26 10 02	----	Woburn	69		----	Ermington	51	
	20 08 03	----	Warden	48		----	Kingsbridge	42	
Berks	31 08 02	50	Abingdon	----		----	Exeter	54	
	30 09 02	35	Windsor	24		----	Swinbridge	108	
	08 10 02	90	Woodley	65		12 10 03	96	Teignbridge	88
	22 03 03	61	Wargrave	41		12 10 03	40	Teignmouth	40
	13 07 03	80	Maidenhead	40	Dorset	27 05 03	442	Dorset	369
	13 08 03	60	Aldermaston	40		----	Sadborough	47	
	22 08 03	60	Donnington	----	Dunbn	09 05 03	88	Dumbarton	80
	22 08 03	50	Thatcham	38	Dumf	22 02 03	84	Dumfriesshire	118
	05 10 03	82	White Horse	----	Durham	16 09 02	114	Durham	120
	30 10 03	42	Hungerford	----		13 10 02	50	N Durham	50
		----	Berkshire C	158		13 08 02	176	L Usworth Lgn	137
Berwick	03 12 02	160	Berwickshire	154		24 11 02	100	Darlington Lgn	79
Bucks	16 07 03	390	1st Regiment)	----		16 09 02	52	Staindrop	45
	16 07 03	322	2nd)	1126		----	Gibside	40	
	16 07 03	253	3rd)	----		05 11 02	42	L Axwell	38
Cams	17 10 03	44	Arrington	51	Essex	26 10 02	59	Epping Forest	49
	04 08 03	56	Doddington	39		26 10 02	68	Hatfield P	----
	30 08 03	46	Whittlesey	39		26 10 02	54	Uttlesford & C	33
Carm	13 10 02	80	Dynevor	74		01 09 03	63	Chafford/Barst	----
	13 10 02	40	Howell	41		06 09 03	65	E Essex (Cock)	44
Ches	13 08 03	251	W Cheshire	202		----	2nd E Essex	38	
	22 08 03	60	Norton	58		26 10 02	79	1st Essex	60
	16 09 02	291	E of C Lgn	293		26 10 02	67	Chelmesford	183
	08 09 03	35	Stockport	40		26 10 02	65	3rd Essex	59
Clackmn	05 09 03	40	Clackmannan	40		26 10 02	80	4th Essex	----
Cornwall	23 05 03	104	Penwith	77		01 10 03	160	Harlaw (EUL)	----
	23 05 03	43	Cornwall	50		26 10 02	50	Threshwell	48
	30 09 03	50	E Cornwall	37		----	1st Essex Lgn	23	
		----	St Germain's	35		----	W Essex Lgn	57	
	20 08 03	55	Bodrean	49		----	Essex U Lgn	113	
		----	Mounts Bay	40		26 10 02	48	Halstead	47
	13 04 03	123	L Meneage	116		26 10 02	56	Haverill	45
Cumbld	18 05 03	56	Cum Rangers	47		09 05 03	40	Wakering	41
Denb	01 03 03	140	Wrexham	129		26 12 02	120	Havering	119
	17 03 03	50	Denbigh Lgn	601		10 08 03	80	Colchester	----
Derby	15 04 03	330	Derbyshire	285	Fife	03 03 03	309	R Fifeshire	289
Devon	05 11 02	418	R 1st Devon	370	Flint	12 06 03	180	Maylor Lgn	146
	20 03 03	487	N Devon	522		03 03 02	96	Mold	80
	05 11 02	38	S Devon	41	Forfar	18 11 02	40	Angus	47
		----	E Devon Lgn	157		----	W Troop	38	
	29 10 02	100	Hemiock & C	----	Glam	31 08 02	49	Fairwood	48
	05 11 02	102	R E Devon	73		31 08 02	38	Cardiff	39
	12 10 03	38	Churchstanton	----		31 08 02	106	Swansea Lgn	96
	20 03 03	44	Plymouth D	37	Glous	13 08 02	58	Cheltenham	56
	20 08 03	100	S Regt	100		13 08 02	116	Bristol	76
	00 00 00	120	C of Guides	120		22 08 02	54	Doddington	53
	12 10 03	30	Torbay	25		13 09 03	40	Dursley	39

County	Accept.	1803	Corps	1806	County	Accept.	1803	Corps	1806
	22 08 03	50	Grumbolds A	49			----	N Wold 1st	40
	12 07 03	62	Stow	79			----	N Wold 2nd	43
	08 11 03	42	Tewkesbury	39	Linlith	31 08 02	77	Linlithgow	70
	12 08 03	48	Cirencester	48	Middx	31 01 03	287	Midlothian	192
	22 09 03	70	Gloucester	59		15 04 03	310	R Midlothian	256
	01 09 03	50	Longtree B	62	London	04 08 03	180	L London	156
	01 09 03	52	Tortworth	49		01 07 02	360	Lon & W LHV	643
		----	Winterbourne	33		01 07 02	170	L & W Supers	----
Hadd	13 08 02	205	E Lothian	189	IoM		---	Manx Y C	40
Hants	09 05 03	50	Bere Forest	39	Middx	12 10 03	40	Edmonton	26
	01 09 03	50	Fordingbridge	34		05 09 03	(42)	R S'thorne Lgn	----
	01 09 03	150	Ringwood	54		27 09 02	260	Westminster	155
	06 09 02	152	NE or A & P	96	Mon	06 11 02	58	Chepstow	70
	06 09 02	160	N or B'stoke	122		22 08 03	53	Monmouth	46
	08 08 03	50	Dogmersfield	54	Mont	02 11 03	120	Mont Legion	107
	06 09 02	50	Fawley	53	Norfolk	22 10 02	56	Blofield & S W	56
	06 09 02	380	S Hampshire	301		02 09 03	47	Clackclose	70
	09 05 03	152	SE Hants	109		22 10 02	44	E Dereham 1st	40
	12 11 03	20	Sir H Mildmay	----		22 10 02	60	E D'ham 2nd	30
	08 08 03	40	Whitchurch	46		22 10 02	42	S Erpingham	30
Here	27 09 02	175	Herefordshire	159		09 07 03	40	S Greenhoe	22
Herts	13 08 02	85	Southern*	66		22 10 02	64	Hingham	33
	13 09 03	42	Ashridge	40		22 10 02	53	Loddon etc	44
	13 08 02	114	Midland	90		23 09 03	30	Marshland	----
	31 08 02	58	Northern	47		22 10 02	92	Norwich	76
	31 08 02	59	Eastern	52		22 10 02	80	Norfolk Rgrs	80
	07 05 03	80	Western	47		13 08 03	26	Smithdon & B	28
	22 12 02	58	Sawbr'worth	44		22 10 02	34	Swaffham	40
	16 09 02	66	Hertfordshire	49		22 10 02	67	Tunstead & H	39
Hunts	05 11 02	165	Huntingdon	103		05 09 03	55	Wymondham	38
Kent	13 08 02	50	Chislehurst	42		22 10 02	55	Yarmouth	44
	13 08 02	50	Nonington	----		22 10 02	104	Lynn & F	60
	13 08 02	57	Barham D	51		16 09 03	43	Holkham	----
	13 08 02	78	Elham	61	N'thnts	17 09 02	649	Northampton	606
	13 08 02	68	Blackheath	58		12 07 03	129	Peterborough	129
	13 08 02	38	Denton	27		16 09 02	51	Wellinboro	43
	14 06 03	74	Deptford	56		13 08 02	70	Northampton	71
	13 08 02	411	W Kent Regt	468	N'thum	13 08 02	50	Bywell	59
	22 08 03	53	Hunton	56		13 08 02	160	R Cheviot Lgn*	160
	30 07 03	60	C of Guides	63		30 07 03	240	Percy T'try*	240
	14 06 03	45	Isle of Sheppy	35		18 08 03	54	Glendale	44
	13 08 02	53	Isle of Thanet	54			----	Coquet D Rgrs	50
	13 08 02	45	Lydd (CP)	49	Notts	22 03 03	60	Bunny	64
	14 06 02	50	Bridgehill	45		06 12 03	77	H'pierrepoint	77
	13 08 02	141	Provendor	116		08 08 03	60	Mansfield	41
	06 09 03	40	Squerries	40			----	Newark	79
	13 08 02	49	Walmer (CP)	44		08 08 03	100	Notts (Chaplin)	130
	06 09 03	54	Penshurst	36		08 08 03	65	Notts (Wright)	113
	06 09 03	60	Ifield Court	42		08 08 03	60	Retford	41
Kirkcud	05 07 03	200	Kirkcudbright	179		05 09 03	50	Rufford	49
Lanark	23 07 03	65	R Glasgow LH	48	Oxon	10 11 02	88	Bloxham & B	90
Lancs	03 08 02	160	Liverpool LH	106		13 07 03	80	L Oxford	72
	03 08 02	48	L Ashton	47		20 08 03	53	Oxford	49
	03 08 02	100	Bolton Le Moor	56		03 09 03	60	Ploughley 100	39
	09 08 03	34	Preston	----		13 08 02	70	Bullington	70
	17 08 03	180	Manchester LH	96		13 08 02	71	Watlington	73
Leics	05 09 03	450	Leicestershire	398		22 09 03	70	Wootton North	72
	05 09 03	42	Lutterworth	37	P'bles	23 05 03	52	Peebleshire	40
	05 09 03	50	A-d-l-Zouch	50	Pemb	28 07 03	72	Castle Martin	79
Lincs	15 08 03	60	Boston	57		02 05 03	54	Dungheddy	17
	12 08 03	65	Grantham	40		07 10 03	300	Owen	169
	12 08 03	64	Loveden	47	Perth	01 08 03	160	Perth	150
	22 02 03	64	Market Raisin	51	Rox	19 08 02	100	Roxburg	98
	22 02 03	68	Spalding	39	Rutland	03 08 02	160	Rutland Lgn*	167
	28 07 03	140	Falkinghham	126	Shrops	05 11 02	88	Oswestry Rgrs	79
	03 09 03	60	Ness	54		11 06 98	54	Pimhill LH	46
	03 09 03	45	Lincoln City	33		xx 03 03	108	1st Shrews'	108
	12 08 03	87	Louth	63		26 10 02	160	Shrewsbury	124

County	Accept.	1803	Corps	1806	County	Accept.	1803	Corps	1806
	13 08 02	232	N Shrops Regt	246		30 07 03	100	N P'ensey Lgn	39
	09 06 03	46	Hales Owen	35		13 08 02	54	Ch'ter R H Artil	37
	19 08 02	153	Ludlow etc	138		02 09 03	37	Ringmer	26
	07 09 03	40	Acton Reynold	40		01 10 03	30	Rye	23
Selkirk	31 08 02	48	Selkirkshire	37		26 05 03	61	C of Guides	60
Som	20 08 03	112	Bath	41		23 11 02	47	W Coast	30
	15 09 03	43	East Coker	43		23 11 02	55	Midhurst	37
	05 09 03	200	Mendip	223		23 11 02	64	Lewes	61
	20 08 03	50	E Mendip Lgn	----		23 11 02	48	E Grinstead	35
	13 08 03	132	Selwood F Lgn	----		13 06 03	44	Ashburnham	46
	13 08 03	46	Wells	41		06 12 03	40	Henfield	29
	06 08 02	452	E Somerset	422		20 10 03	180	Mr Curteis	----
	12 02 03	477	W Somerset	432	Warks	09 09 03	56	Atherstone	50
Staffs	16 09 02	75	Bilston	64			----	Coleshill	45
	07 10 03	50	L Handsworth	33		13 10 02	49	Nuneaton	41
	16 09 02	541	Staffordshire	374		13 10 02	318	Warwickshire	301
	07 10 03	64	Stone & E	51		13 10 02	62	Warwick	74
	07 10 03	47	Tamworth	41	IoW		----	Isle of Wight	74
	12 08 03	47	Uttoxeter	48		13 08 02	60	East Medene	----
	21 10 03	80	Walsall	80		13 08 02	60	West Medene	----
Stirling	13 08 02	----	(St Ninian's & S	----	Wigtwn		----	Galloway Rgrs	41
	27 09 02	160	(Strath Enrick	----		13 08 02	63	Wigtownshire	61
		----	(Stirling E	----		15 09 03	42	Stranraer	----
	30 09 02	129	Stirling S	----	Wilts	31 08 02	800	Wiltshire	542
		----	Stirlingshire	145		01 12 03	50	Draycott	38
		----	W Stirling Lgn	105	Worcs	31 08 02	157	Worcester Y	147
Suffolk	08 10 02	68	1st Suffolk	59		12 02 03	50	Bromsgrove LH	42
	08 10 02	123	2nd Suffolk	169		27 09 03	47	Kings Norton	41
	08 10 02	54	3rd Suffolk	46		06 11 02	57	1st Stourbridge	47
	08 10 02	120	4th Suffolk	80		12 09 03	40	2nd Stourbridge	31
	08 10 02	80	5th Suffolk	47		11 10 03	60	Dudley	42
		----	6th Suffolk	66		15 11 02	50	Kidderminster	50
		----	7th Suffolk	68		27 09 03	40	Wolverley	40
		----	8th Suffolk	57	WRiding	20 08 03	42	Knaresboro	49
		----	9th Suffolk	64			----	Stockeld Park	41
	28 07 03	80	Hadleigh	57		06 09 02	343	WR N Regt	354
	28 07 03	80	Baberg	80		06 09 02	40	Attd to N Reg,	120
	22 08 03	60	Heveningham	48		15 08 03	616	WR S Regt	552
	05 09 03	55	Southelmham	52		15 08 03	120	W York	120
Surrey	22 09 03	48	Croydon*	32		22 08 03	42	West Riding	----
	21 08 03	94	Guildford & B	54		07 09 03	200	Craven Lgn	202
	21 08 03	50	Richmond Lgn	28		20 08 03	72	Harewood	67
		----	Wimbledon LH	44		13 08 02	78	Leeds	47
	21 08 03	42	Woking	31	NRiding		----	Barton Le St	42
	22 08 03	43	Clapham Lgn	37		15 00 03	41	Kiplin & L	40
	21 08 03	42	Godley/Egham	41		05 09 03	70	Helmsley	72
	22 09 03	63	Lambeth	73		30 09 02	60	Scarborough	51
	31 10 02	360	Lord Leslie	292		05 09 03	50	N'burgh Rgrs	44
	21 08 03	100	Southwark	100		20 09 03	40	B Hambleton	----
	22 08 03	80	Wandsworth	30	ERiding	19 08 03	40	Everingham	38
Sussex	23 11 0?	67	Parham	60		05 09 03	81	Grimston	78
	31 12 02	87	Petworth	66		31 08 02	247	Yorks Wolds	228

References

1   Fortescue, Hon JW. The County Lieutenancies and the Army. (Macmillan, London 1909)
2   Parliamentary Sessional Papers. 1797 Vol XLV 910, pp1-9
3   Freeman FM Benson & Fellows G. Hisl Records of the S Notts Hussars. (Gale & Polden, Aldershot 1928)
4   Graham H. Annals of the Yeomanry Cavalry of Wiltshire, 1794-1884. (Marples, Liverpool 1886)
5   Parliamentary Sessional Papers. Vol. and Yeo. Corps accepted by His Majesty. 1803-04 Vol XI pp117-178.
6   Parliamentary Sessional Papers, 1806 Vol X Folio pages 2-101
7   Cambridge, Marquess The Vol. Army of GB, The Willson Chart, 1806. (JAHR Vol XII pp113-126,163-174)
8   Parliamentary Sessional Papers. 1817 Vol XIII p225
9   List of Yeomanry Cavalry and Volunteer Infantry 1825.
10   Parliamentary Sessional Papers. 1828 Vol XVII p251.

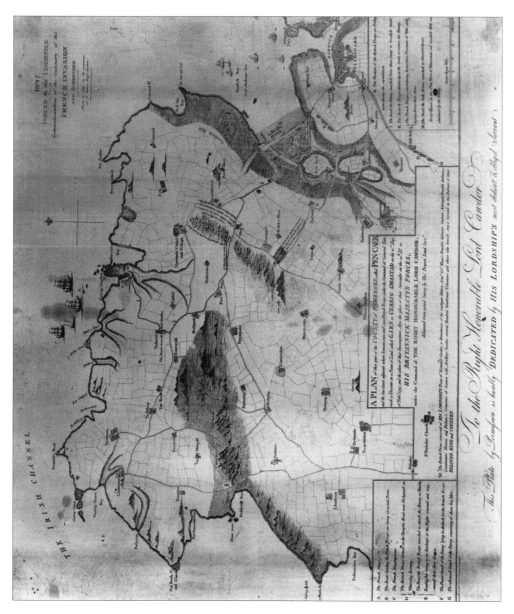

Carmarthen Museum and Antiquarian Society

Plate 2/1

Map of the French Invasion and Surrender at Fishguard, Carmarthen, Wales.

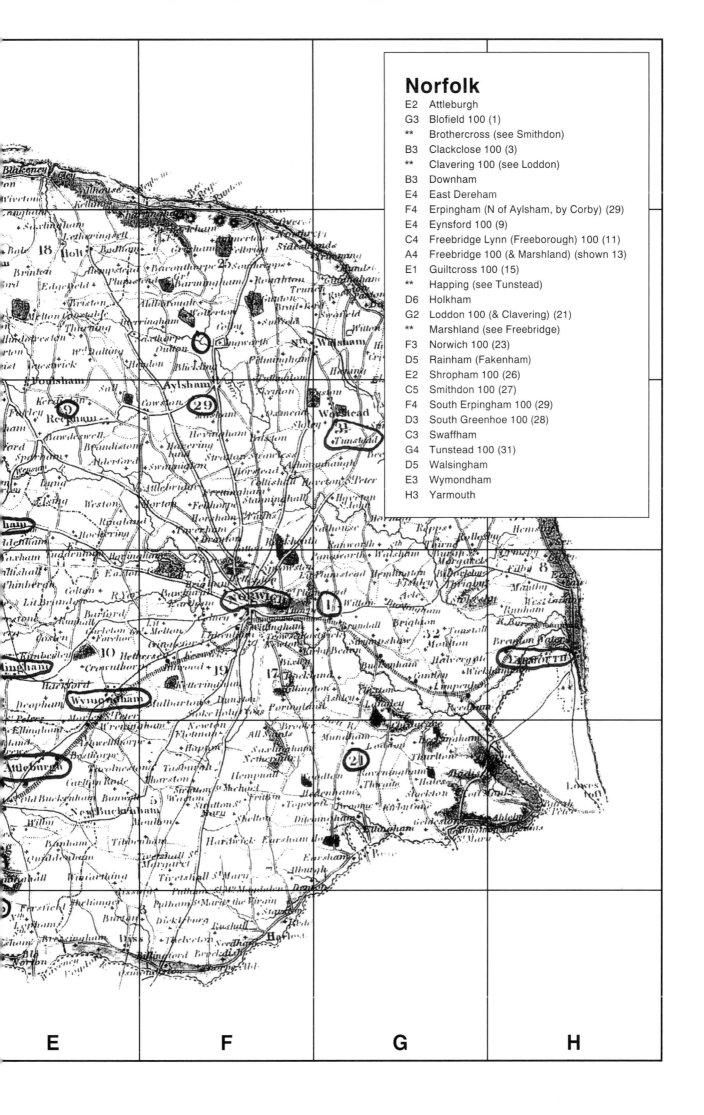

Norfolk

E   F   G   H

Suffolk

**	4th Troop (part of 1st L Suffolk)
C2	Baberg 100
G4	Blything 100
D4	Botesdale
C3	Bury St Edmunds
E4	Eye
G3	Fornham
D1	Hadleigh
C4	Ickworth
E2	Ipswich
C2	Long Melford
H5	Lowestoft
G3	Saxmunden
F5	Southelmham
D3	Stowmarket
**	1st L Suffolk (See Bury)
F2	Woodbridge

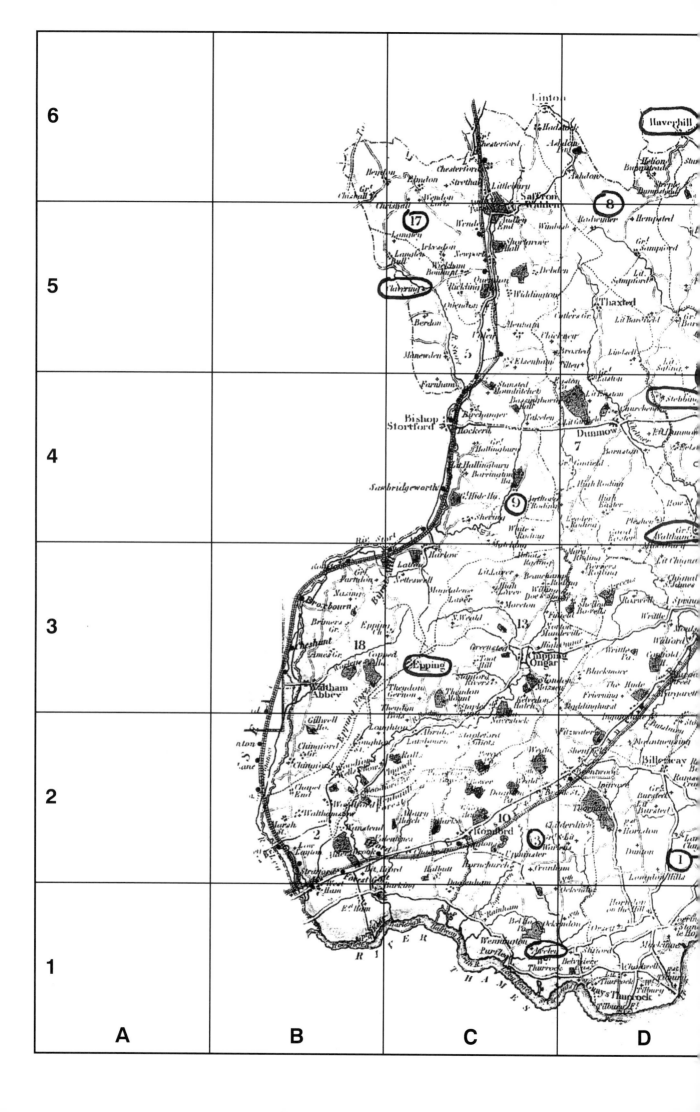

Essex

C1	Aveley
D2	Barstable 100 (Basildon)
E5	Castle Headingham
C2	Chafford 100 (3) (Churford supra)
D3	Chelmsford
B5	Clavering 100 (5)
F4	Colchester
B3	Epping Forest
D6	Freshwell 100 (8)
D5	Halstead
B4	Harlow 100 (9)
E3	Hatfield Peverill
D6	Haverhill
B2	Havering (R Liberty of)
E5	Hinckford 100 (11)
E4	Kelvedon
D5	Saling
D5	Stebbing
G4	Tendring 100 (15)
**	Threshwell (see Freshwell)
B5	Uttlesford 100 (17)
F2	Wakering (Great & Little)
D4	Waltham (Great)

E   **F**   **G**   **H**

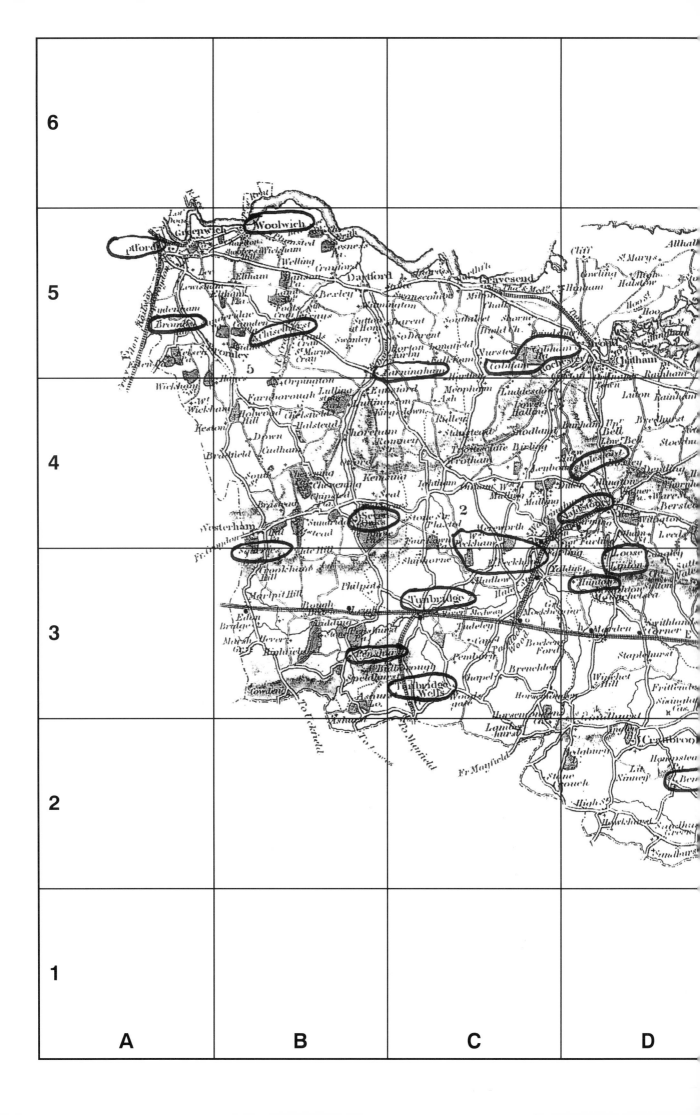

Kent

D4	Aylesford	A5	Deptford	C4	Peckham
G3	Barham Downs	G3	Elham	B3	Penshurst
A5	Blackheath (Bromley)	F3/H4	E(l)vington (by Ashford or Sandwich?)	E4	Provender (Ho in Norton)
	Blenhooth (?W Kent)	B5	Farningham	D2	Rolvendon
F4	Bridge Hill (?by Canterbury)	D3	Hunton	B4	Sevenoaks
B5	Chislehurst	C5	Ilfield Court (Ho in Ilfield)	B3	Squirries
H3	Cinique Ports (Dover)	E5	Isle of Sheppey	C3	Tonbridge
C5	Cobham West	H5	Isle of Thanet	C3	Tunbridge Wells
D3	Cox Heath (see Linton/Loose)	F1	Lydd	H4	Walmer
H4	Deal	D4	Maidstone	G4	Wingham
F4	Denton (by Canterbury)	G4	Nonnington	B5	Woolwich

E F G H

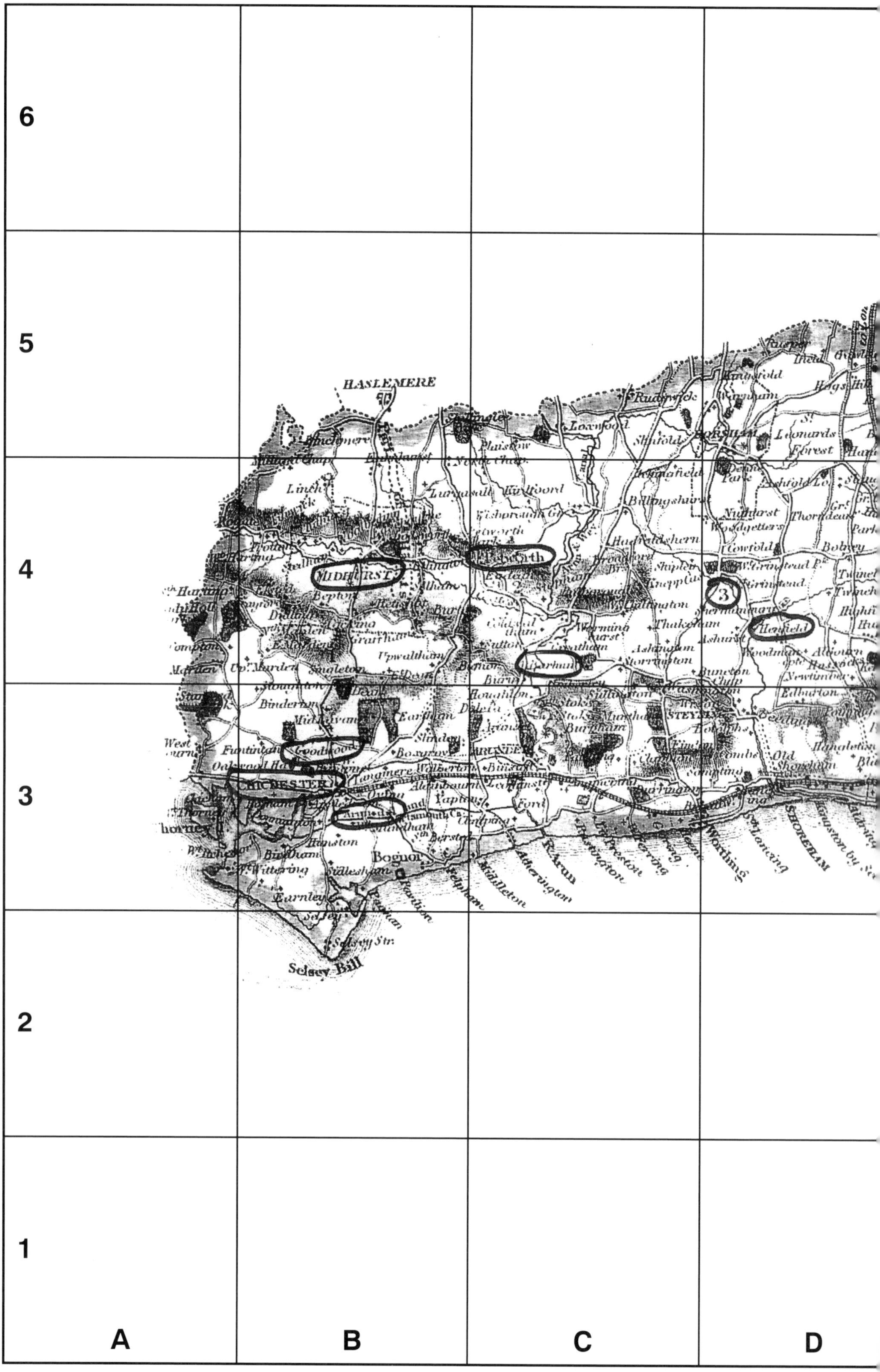
6
5
4
3
2
1
A
B
C
D
HASLEMERE
MIDHURST
CHICHESTER
Goodwood
Petworth
Henfield
Horsham
Rudgwick
Loxwood
Billingshurst
Cowfold
Shipley
Ashurst
Thakeham
Storrington
Ashington
Upwaltham
Singleton
Binderton
Funtington
Bognor
Selsey Bill
Earnley
Worthing
SHOREHAM
Old Shoreham
Edburton
Newtimber
Lancing
Steyning
Bolney
Twineham
Woodmancote
St. Leonards Forest

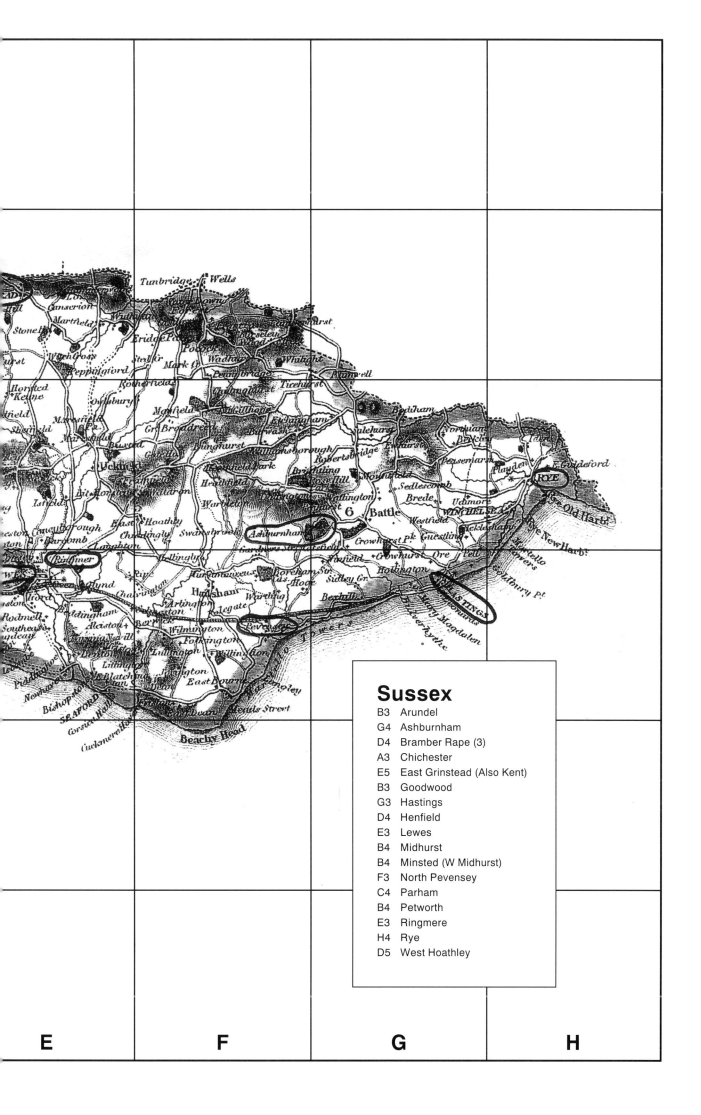

Sussex

E F G H

6
5
4
3
2
1
A
B
C
D
SALISBURY
Downton
Romsey
Stockbridge
Cranbourne
Fordingbridge
Ringwood
Lyndhurst
Lymington
Christ Church
Poole
The Needles
Salt Works
Christ Church Bay

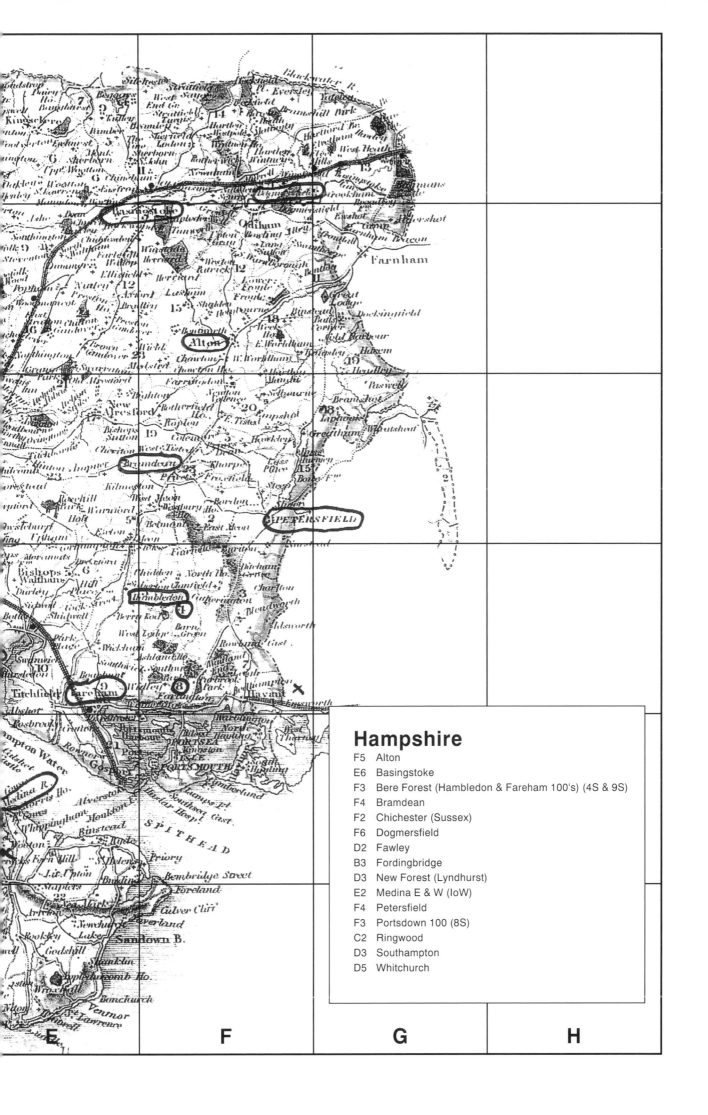

Hampshire

F5 Alton
E6 Basingstoke
F3 Bere Forest (Hambledon & Fareham 100's) (4S & 9S)
F4 Bramdean
F2 Chichester (Sussex)
F6 Dogmersfield
D2 Fawley
B3 Fordingbridge
D3 New Forest (Lyndhurst)
E2 Medina E & W (IoW)
F4 Petersfield
F3 Portsdown 100 (8S)
C2 Ringwood
D3 Southampton
D5 Whitchurch

E   F   G   H

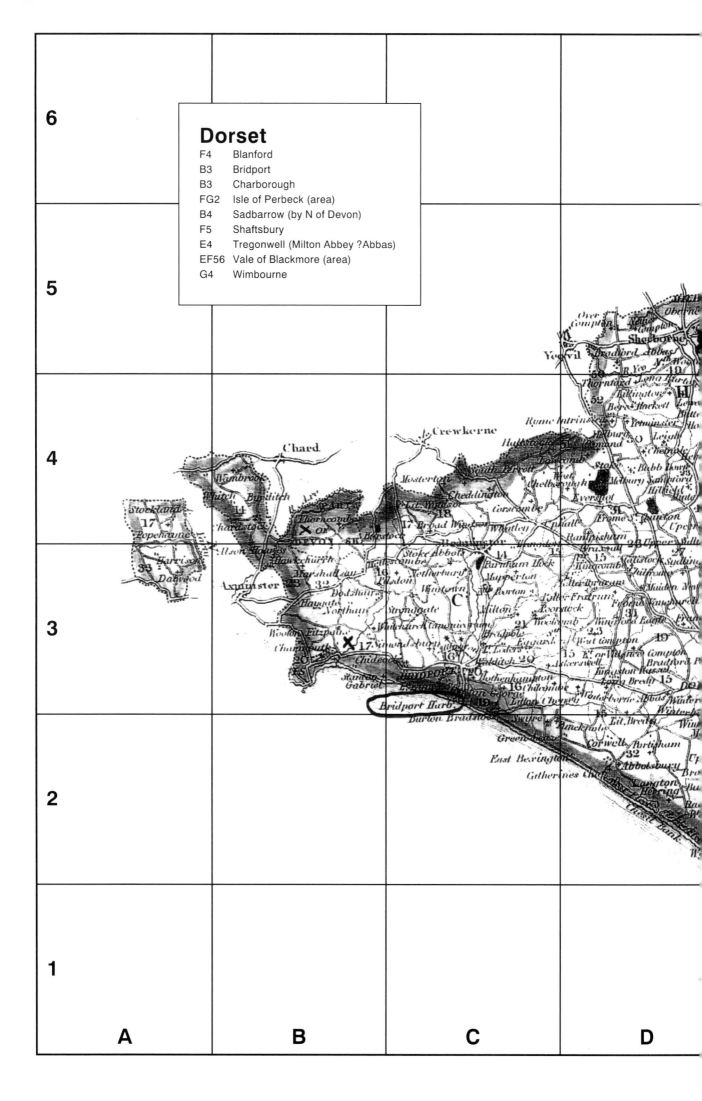

Dorset

F4	Blanford
B3	Bridport
B3	Charborough
FG2	Isle of Perbeck (area)
B4	Sadbarrow (by N of Devon)
F5	Shaftsbury
E4	Tregonwell (Milton Abbey ?Abbas)
EF56	Vale of Blackmore (area)
G4	Wimbourne

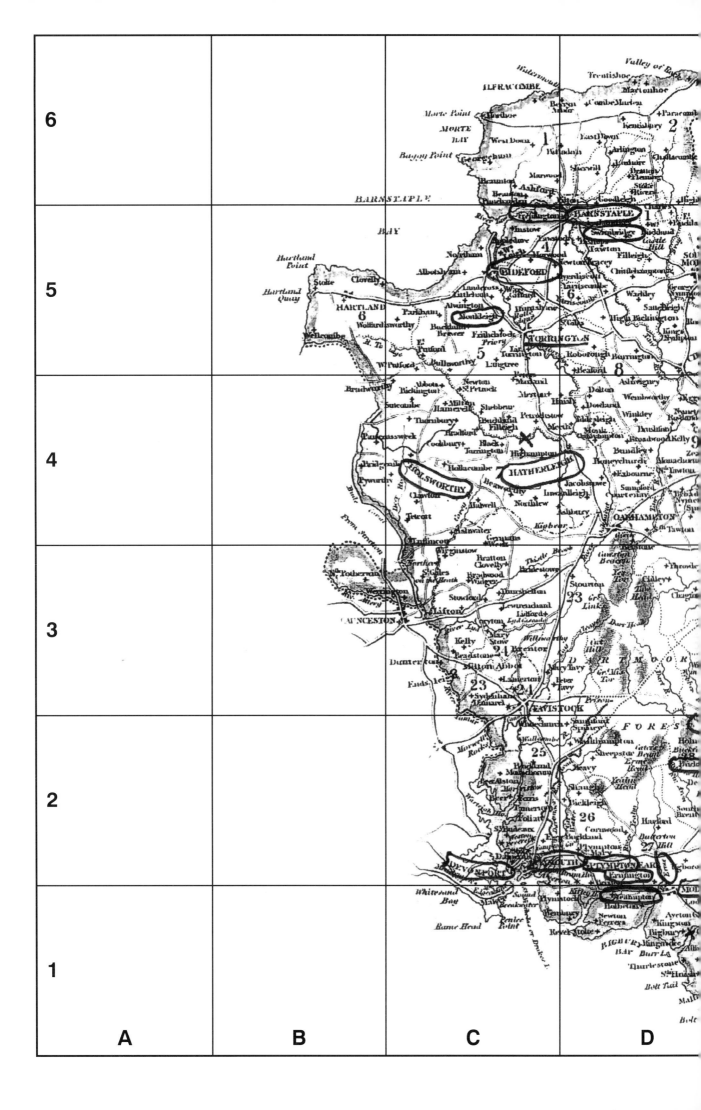

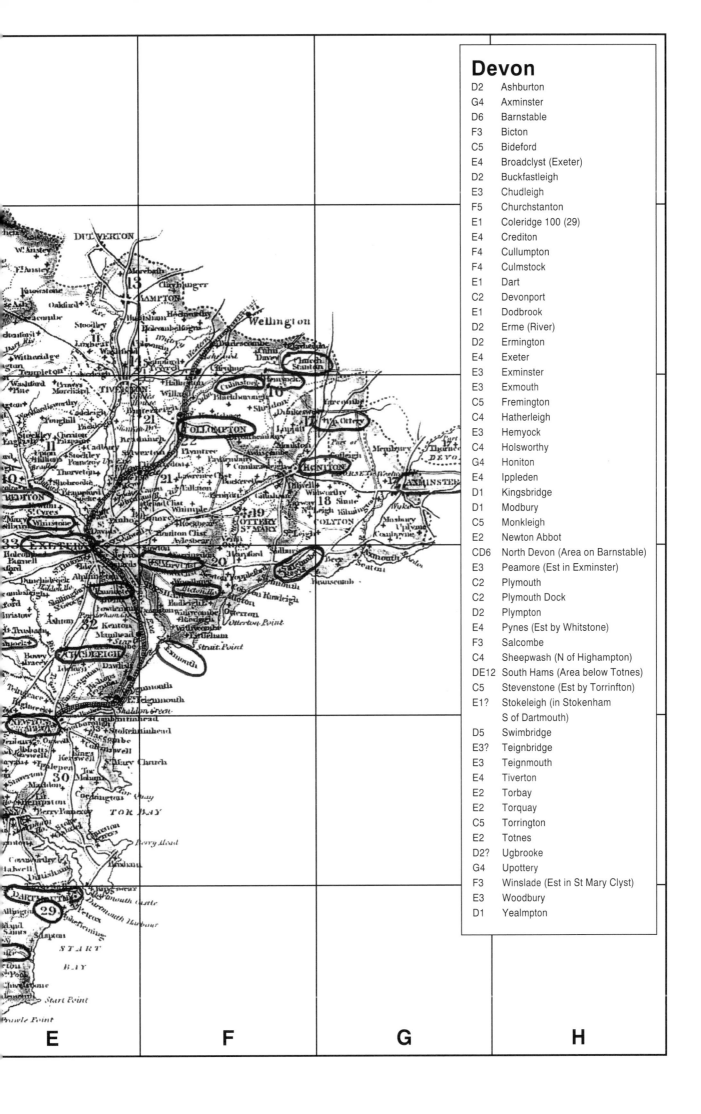

Devon

D2	Ashburton
G4	Axminster
D6	Barnstable
F3	Bicton
C5	Bideford
E4	Broadclyst (Exeter)
D2	Buckfastleigh
E3	Chudleigh
F5	Churchstanton
E1	Coleridge 100 (29)
E4	Crediton
F4	Cullumpton
F4	Culmstock
E1	Dart
C2	Devonport
E1	Dodbrook
D2	Erme (River)
D2	Ermington
E4	Exeter
E3	Exminster
E3	Exmouth
C5	Fremington
C4	Hatherleigh
E3	Hemyock
C4	Holsworthy
G4	Honiton
E4	Ippleden
D1	Kingsbridge
D1	Modbury
C5	Monkleigh
E2	Newton Abbot
CD6	North Devon (Area on Barnstable)
E3	Peamore (Est in Exminster)
C2	Plymouth
C2	Plymouth Dock
D2	Plympton
E4	Pynes (Est by Whitstone)
F3	Salcombe
C4	Sheepwash (N of Highampton)
DE12	South Hams (Area below Totnes)
C5	Stevenstone (Est by Torrinfton)
E1?	Stokeleigh (in Stokenham S of Dartmouth)
D5	Swimbridge
E3?	Teignbridge
E3	Teignmouth
E4	Tiverton
E2	Torbay
E2	Torquay
C5	Torrington
E2	Totnes
D2?	Ugbrooke
G4	Upottery
F3	Winslade (Est in St Mary Clyst)
E3	Woodbury
D1	Yealmpton

E   F   G   H

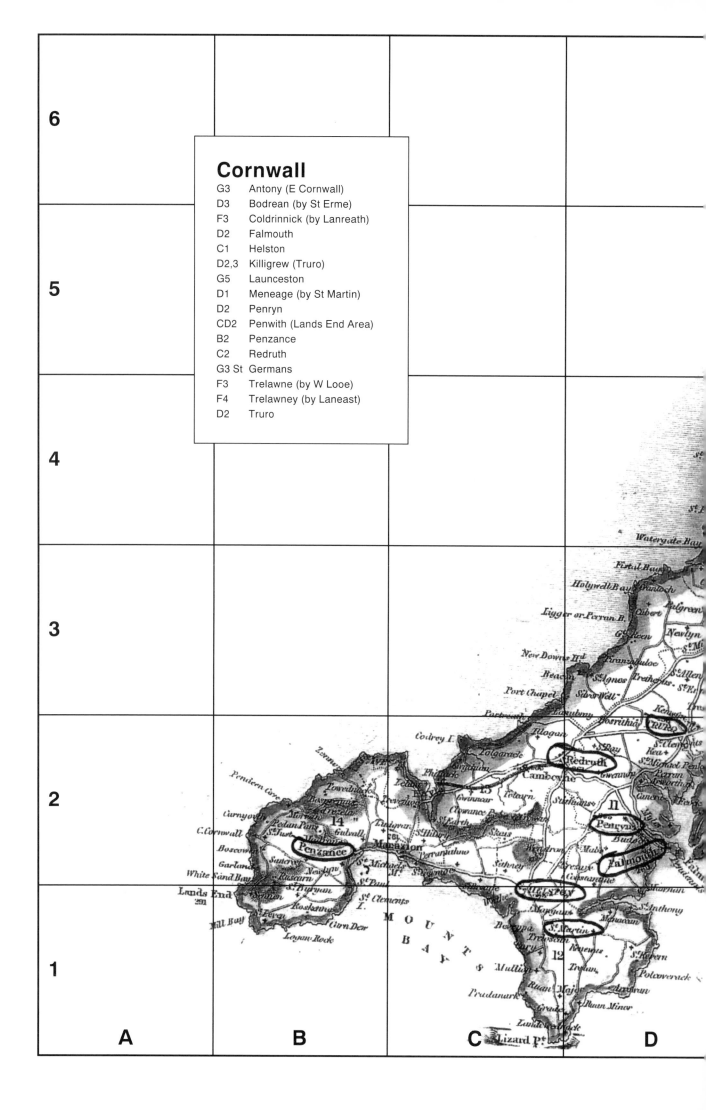

Cornwall

G3	Antony (E Cornwall)
D3	Bodrean (by St Erme)
F3	Coldrinnick (by Lanreath)
D2	Falmouth
C1	Helston
D2,3	Killigrew (Truro)
G5	Launceston
D1	Meneage (by St Martin)
D2	Penryn
CD2	Penwith (Lands End Area)
B2	Penzance
C2	Redruth
G3 St	Germans
F3	Trelawne (by W Looe)
F4	Trelawney (by Laneast)
D2	Truro

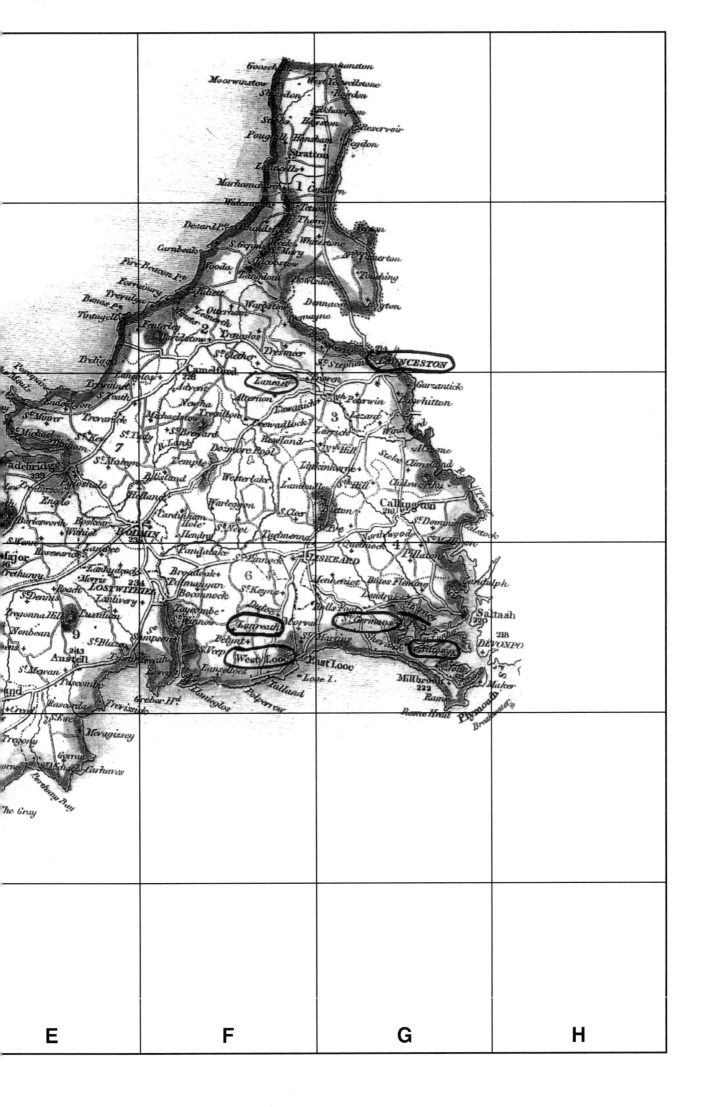

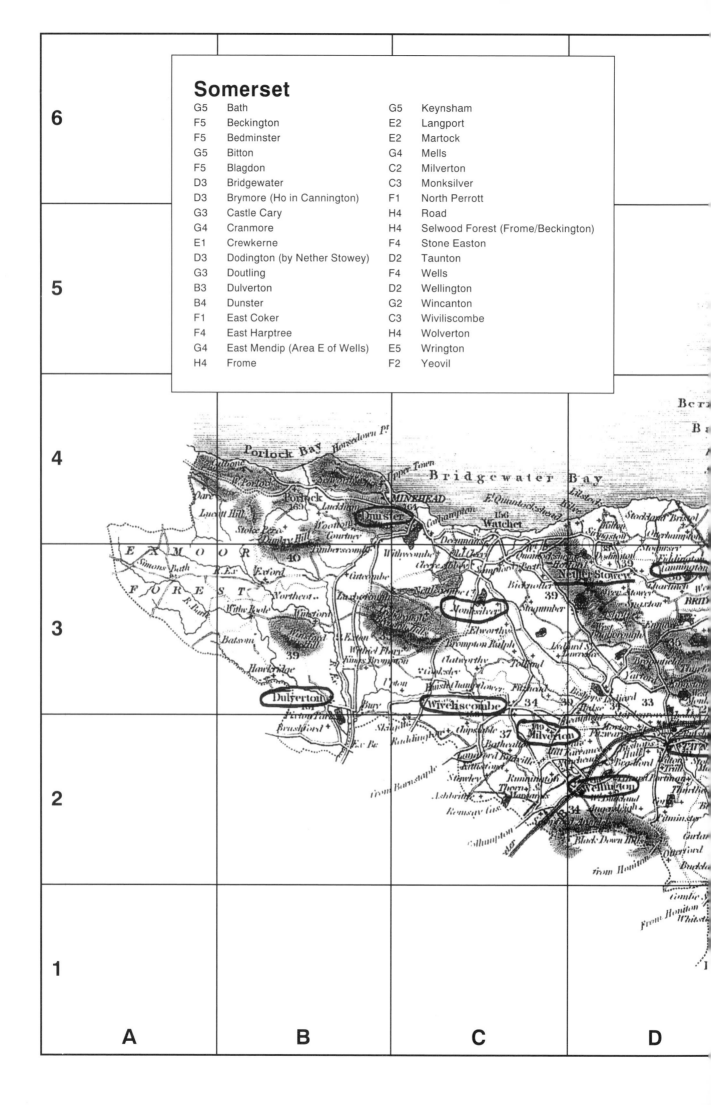

Somerset

G5	Bath	G5	Keynsham
F5	Beckington	E2	Langport
F5	Bedminster	E2	Martock
G5	Bitton	G4	Mells
F5	Blagdon	C2	Milverton
D3	Bridgewater	C3	Monksilver
D3	Brymore (Ho in Cannington)	F1	North Perrott
G3	Castle Cary	H4	Road
G4	Cranmore	H4	Selwood Forest (Frome/Beckington)
E1	Crewkerne	F4	Stone Easton
D3	Dodington (by Nether Stowey)	D2	Taunton
G3	Doutling	F4	Wells
B3	Dulverton	D2	Wellington
B4	Dunster	G2	Wincanton
F1	East Coker	C3	Wiviliscombe
F4	East Harptree	H4	Wolverton
G4	East Mendip (Area E of Wells)	E5	Wrington
H4	Frome	F2	Yeovil

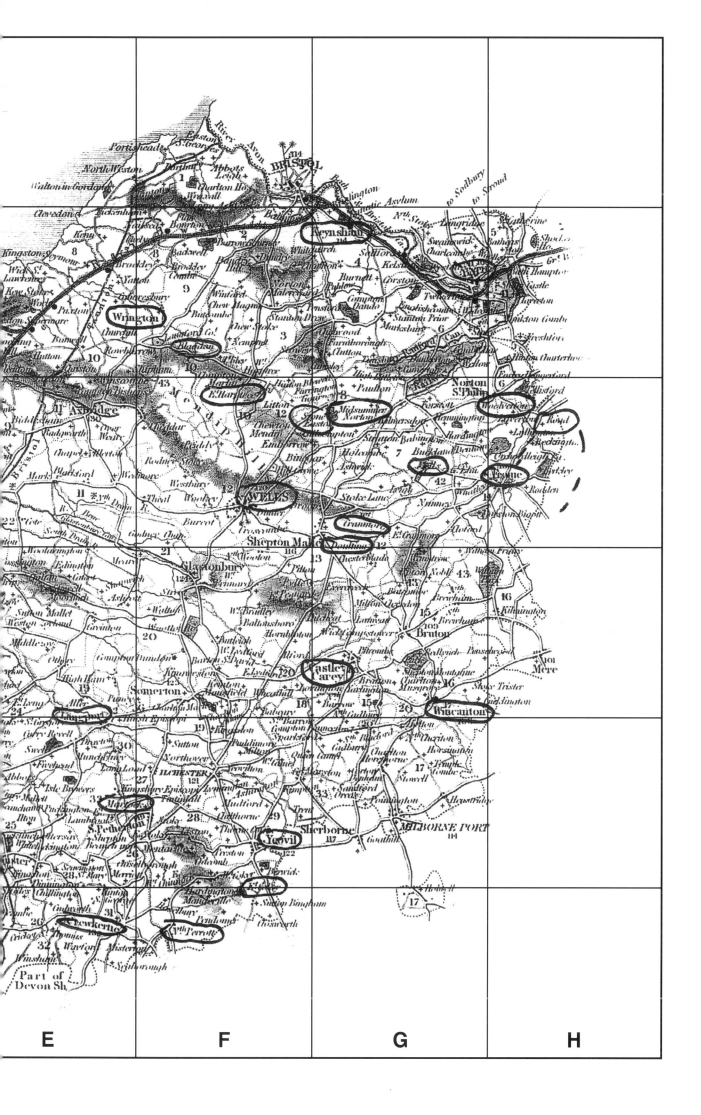

E   F   G   H

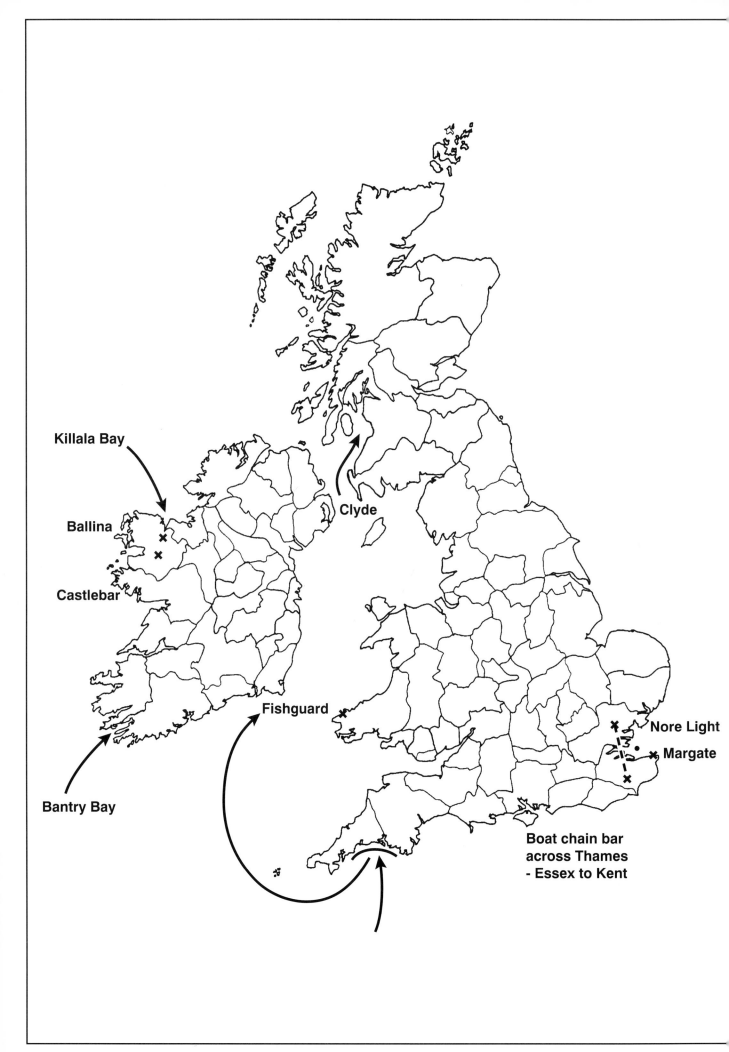

Killala Bay

Ballina

Castlebar

Clyde

Fishguard

Nore Light

Margate

Bantry Bay

Boat chain bar
across Thames
- Essex to Kent

Plate 2/12 Historical Events

3. Aid to the Civil Power

"After two major continental wars and a number of limited wars overseas it is not surprising that servicemen and the civilian community nowadays consider war against foreign enemies - or its prevention - to be the 'proper' task of the British Army. It may come therefore as something of a surprise when it is discovered that the Army raised, or retained, by King Charles II in 1661 was intended to maintain law and order within the realm and troops have been used far more often on this civil duty, both at home and in the colonies, than they have on purely military duties. In the days before Sir Robert Peel reorganised the police the few Bow Street Runners, and the Revenue Officers who waged an incessant struggle against smuggling, depended heavily upon the support of the Army. The Scots Greys, for example, who have been criticised for charging too far at Waterloo, had not been on campaign since 1794! Small wonder if they were a bit too keen! While their contemporaries had been winning laurels in the Peninsular the Royal North British Dragoons, broken up into small bodies seldom more than a troop strong, had been doing the work of a non-existent police force. Aid to the civil power was but an indifferent preparation for the battlefields of Belgium."

From the foreword by Brigadier Peter Young to Kenneth O Fox's *Making Life Possible*. 1982

The more things change, the more they are the same. Alphonse Karr   1808-1890

The People, the Authorities and the Military [1]
Between the abolition of the Star Chamber in 1641 and the passing of the Riot Act in 1715 there were no measures to define rioting or the specific punishment of rioters. As a consequence, the legal recourse fell between a remonstrance for creating a disturbance and the charge of treason, for threatening the safety of the Realm. In between it was possible to suspend the Habeas Corpus Act, which meant persons rotted in gaol until they had effectively served a sentence, which was obviously unlawful and therefore rarely adopted. First introduced in 1679, the Act was designed to ensure prisoners were either charged with an offence or released. More importantly, treason being a capital offence led to the extreme punishment, amounting to the indescribable torture and suffering of hanging, drawing and quartering. As a consequence juries, even when bullied, were unwilling to convict a rioter for treason. Beyond this, there were over 200 offences carrying the death penalty and when charges exceeded even the rough equity of those times, the defendant often got off scot free. The law over this period was unsatisfactory.

The Riot Act provided a well understood civil remedy, so long as it focused on Catholic insurrection, for which it had been designed in 1714, added to which the magistrates could confidently expect support from the military. This then developed to embrace religious tolerance, to the extent the 'Gordon' riots were correctly policed against the determined efforts of a Protestant rabble rouser. In other riots the Regular Army were often faced by ambiguous situations. However, given a clear-cut order they were obliged to react when a magistrate issued a requisition, though obviously this had to pass through channels longer than those to the Yeomanry. Both forces became spectators of the magistrates making up their minds and taking action. Where circumstances centred on hunger, support for the law was not always forthcoming from either side, being often constrained by the natural justice of the rioter's case.

The burgeoning townships and urban conurbations produced a huge demand for food. Strangely the country labourer hardly benefited from this, in fact in some parts it went against him when 'enclosure' deprived him of his patch of private ground and share of the common. The effect was for him to become wage dependent and when followed by a failed harvest spelt hunger as the price of corn and potatoes doubled and trebled. This pool of unemployed was a useful bargaining counter to the employers, against wage demands and for periodic employment, such as at harvest times. Officialdom was in a quandary. The land magnates were more distant and less accountable to the natural regulation of country affairs. The periodic social explosions were random and uncoordinated, though the justice of the case was with the worker. Added to this the Yeomanry were only beginning their apprenticeship in riot control, besides which they had a distinct distaste over interfering in this matter. In the instance of a food shortage it was common for farmers carts to be ambushed and stores broken into, so that the contents could be sold off at 'popular prices', though generally a scrupulous reckoning was handed to the erstwhile owner.

The next stage was one of a progressive escalation, at which juncture the Yeomanry and other military were obliged to apply a restraining hand. In the larger townships and cities the riots were more ugly and often became very dangerous affairs as the following account underlines.

The second major cause of unrest was a result of the industrial revolution. Contention frequently centred on machine produced products, both of good and bad quality. It was this that struck society's Achilles heel, for local merchants felt unwilling to band together, to defend their property. If they dealt roughly with their workforce, it frequently proved counterproductive. Short of anarchy the magistrates increasingly turned to the doubtful military and the Volunteers.

The Corn Law of 1815, introduced price-fixing on imported grain successively at 50, 63 and even 80 shillings a quarter (28lb.). These were measures chiefly designed to satisfy the land magnates who had discovered how to operate agriculture in England at a profit. This insulated them against European imports.

Income Tax first introduced in 1797, to help fund the war, at 7d in the Pound on incomes over £60 per annum in 1797, was next abolished in 1816. To replace the lost revenue the Government of the day re-introduced an early form of value added tax first tried in 1730, this time on tea, sugar, beer, paper, soap and candles. These measures taxed those least able to pay and distorted the economy, because so few had money to spend. Then the Game Law of 1816 further restricted the country folk in their efforts at self-help.

With the end of the war, public pressure mounted against Government. There were 200,000 demobilised soldiers and seamen, bringing unemployment to 500,000 in 1816. The general trend of improved methods of productivity was, in any case, to squeeze industrial wages. The industrial slump saw exports plummet 30% by 1818 and half of the blast furnaces shut down with a consequent reduction in the demand for coke. These difficulties could not be overcome until secure markets had been developed world-wide and that time was still distant.

Aspirations for political power led the new urban populace over the years to seek representation in Parliament. From this time it was usual for petitions to be signed in huge numbers and for these to be presented to Parliament with great show and for the latter to reject them, because they were not made through the channels of the elected representation. It thereby set in train the political rally. The Government was not slow to perceive the danger held by these rowdy concentrations of people, with their potential for riot, insurrection and even open rebellion. However, it did not wish to be seen competing with the leadership of those who felt unrepresented. The government's response was to attempt the removal of the latter by the use of informers and political ambush. In this they were singularly inept and unsuccessful, so the speakers and the rallies they addressed flourished. It culminated in the sort of political meeting called at Saint Peter's Fields, Manchester during 1819. There was nothing illegal about the meeting, so it was very much a matter of judgement when or if the Riot Act should have been read.

The Government had then an urgent choice to make; either to address the jumbled grievances of the time or to suppress such outbreaks resolutely. It seemed safer to choose the latter course. The 'Gagging Acts' were passed into law that year. These six Acts provided for: the powers of search without warrant for arms; the powers of search without warrant for seditious literature; the forbidding of military drilling by private individuals; the restriction of meetings to present petitions; the raising of Stamp Duty on pamphlets and periodicals to 6d; and trial by magistrates of political offences immediately to avoid jury trials. In *droll fashion* historians have noted how the subsequent period was one of apparent tranquillity!

Periodic pressure on the economy or a failed harvest, brought about the sabotage of both agricultural and industrial machines as they were seen as the cause of the attendant wage cuts or price increases. A workforce would strike and threaten others brought in as replacements, hoping to bring the manufacturers to make an improved offer. One encouraging sign was the passing of a Factory Act in 1819 regulating the hours of work for children, though with characteristic oversight or by cunning, no provision for inspection was considered and hence it was largely unenforceable.

In 1820 Import Duties were reduced and in 1823 there was a Reciprocity of Duties Act with an increasing number of countries entering into agreements, which helped the growth of international trade. This was the beginning of Free Trade, though it took time for the measures to bear fruit.

Meantime the cauldron of discontent bubbled away. The military without the means to repress popular uprisings counselled restraint, which enabled them to eke out their slender resources. The Regular Army was thin on the ground, the Volunteers could not be mustered indefinitely, whilst the Militia were only available by misusing their annual camp training period. The Generals of District were obliged to make it clear to the magistrates that those unable to demonstrate practical measures taken against riot would not receive military support. They in turn explained the situation to the reluctant millowners. Unfortunately the debates in Parliament were conducted largely by persons distanced from the problems far from London. A disproportionate amount of Parliamentary time was spent, from 1825 onward, passing a plenitude of Acts helping the new railways and it is pertinent to add how these were better designed than the townships they serviced, mainly because they had been planned!

Short-sightedly, the Government felt impelled in 1824 to an economic drive related to war debt. The Great War as it was then called had lasted 22 years and cost £800,000,000, so protests soon erupted against 'high taxation'. The rates by modern day standards were paltry. The search for economies, combined with the reduction in overseas trading had the Government delude themselves that the Yeomanry could with safety be greatly reduced and this took place during 1827-8.

A more positive measure was the move to stabilise the price of bread, when the Corn Law was modified in 1828 to allow for a sliding scale according to the home price of wheat, but this was not enough to ameliorate the plight of the worker.

The now 'undefended' counties in the South of England soon erupted into an orgy of agricultural machine breaking, brought about by the change to commercialism on the farms. Land purchased on borrowed money to make a profit also required interest to be paid. Machines enabled a previously better off worker to be squeezed out. The large land owners were able to capitalise such agricultural ventures, though many of the smaller farmers, like the earlier Yeomen at the time of the Enclosures were forced out of business and effectively joined an already large pool of wage labour. Farmers pleading poverty when approached by the breakers, were advised by them and recognised the need to secure better lease rates from the land magnates. The latter proposed the re-forming of the Yeomanry to the self same farmers, in an effort to protect threatened interests and the quid pro quo was a reduction in rents and tithes. A further development was for the generous rates paid to those in public office to be challenged.

There is a question mark over the 1832 Reform Act, though the rumpus in its passing was for all to see. Politically the centre of gravity of representation moved northwards across a line drawn between the Wash and the Bristol Channel, though it remained very much in the hands of the propertied classes. When it came to the matter of reform, it was a *three* cornered fight, though it was the interests of the industrial middle class which prevailed. The Bill generated much heat in debate and was the cause of many riots around the country. To some extent it saw the landed interests in retreat, though it did little for the northern cities.

Chartism erupted during 1838. There had been stirrings from 1834 as it became apparent how little had been achieved for the working class by the Reform Act. When the first petition was thrown out by Parliament, methods became brutally physical and middle-class support melted away. The latter wished to pursue similar objectives by different methods namely, the abolition of the Corn Law. Whilst one interest attempted a jumble of measures, the Anti-Corn Law League set out to achieve *one* by Parliamentary means. By a combination of superb organisation, extensive propaganda, talented speakers and adequate funding, allied to the single objective, the campaign largely succeeded where the others failed. Perhaps that is not entirely true, for although the Chartists spent a lot of time disrupting the anti-Corn Law League meetings and failed to succeed directly, the combined pressure induced a line of Government action by passing Acts of Parliament governing, public health, mining and factories. The end of these two movements brought to a close the period in which the Yeomanry played a major part in protecting property and the public from violence. Free trade, improved living and working conditions, with cheap bread combined gradually to make for a peaceful society. Thus rioting in the general sense became less and less frequent.

The Ramifications of the Riot Act

It is necessary now to discover how military deterrence or an actual use of force was implemented during the period from 1715 onwards. The Yeomanry shared this mantle from 1794 until it was released in 1908, with the formation of the Territorial Force. The maintenance of internal security, put euphemistically, 'Support of the Civil Power', rested on the use of military force. There were no police and the town constables were overwhelmed by the scale of events their office was not designed to take. They were mainly concerned with the protection of individual property. The Metropolitan Police Act of 1829, was possibly the reason for disbanding so much of the Yeomanry. This was followed in 1838 by the initial steps to found the County Constabularies, a process hardly completed before 1856. Until these measures were implemented any fracas in town or village was most generally handled by a local constable, often acting as an individual. Larger events called for military intervention.

The Riot Act (Appendix A3) was placed on the Statute Book in 1715, as the result of the First Jacobite Rebellion. It was never intended as an antidote for these troubles, though its workings became central to the whole being of the Yeomanry, in which its main provisions were as follows:

"That if twelve or more persons unlawfully and riotously assemble together to the disturbance of the public peace, and after being required by any Justice, by proclamation to be made in the King's name, to disperse, and peaceably to depart to their habitations shall remain or continue together for one hour after the proclamation, then such continuing together shall be adjudged felony, and the offenders felons.

After the hour, every Justice and such other persons as he shall command to assist him (such Justice being thereby authorised to command all (His/Her) Majesty's subjects), then every such Justice, and all and singular persons aiding and assisting, shall be free discharged,

and indemnified of, for or concerning the killing, maiming, or hurting of any such person as shall happen to be so killed, maimed, or hurt as aforesaid".

Clode[2] makes a number of points in explanation, such as the Act serving notice on a mob to disperse or take the consequences. Nor was it necessary for the Act to be read before 'force could be met by force' or for an hour to elapse after its reading before force could be used. Particular care was necessary on the part of the military not to interpose in any of these matters except at such times as they should be desired by the Civil Magistrate. This of course amounted to the need for a formal requisition.

From the passing of the Riot Act until 1794 and beyond, a lack of understanding developed between the Civil and Military authorities. The commanding generals of the Military Districts had often to stress to the local authorities how their small forces were insufficient to produce order in a situation of general rebellion. This scenario was acted out time and again in the respective Military Districts. Here generals struggled with every force of their considerable personalities to coach magistrates and local notables on getting their act together. They were able to co-ordinate a response to virtually anything, so that they often appeared to have far larger forces than was the case. Some were extremely clever and diplomatic and were soon dealing successfully with the most complex situations. The best example was Lieutenant-General Byng, who nevertheless found it necessary to complain both up and down the chain of command, over his problems of commitments and resources. Others lacked the touch for this obscure form of guerrilla warfare, chiefly because they failed to develop proper sources of 'Intelligence'. However, when they did so, their information was frequently more up-to-date, accurate and reliable than that of magistrates, leading the Government to draw the conclusion that these sometimes self-important officials were inept, lazy and sometimes even downright misleading.

The affairs of the Yeomanry were inextricably bound up with the magistrates, the military forces including other Volunteers, initially the Fencibles and later the Provisional Cavalry, the Militia and the Regular Army. When death resulted from troop action in the course of a riot, the Attorney General sometimes refused to prosecute and on others entered a sufficient defence.

The Regular Army indeed was not disposed to have its

troops ordered about by others nor to get involved without orders from 'a high level', meaning the Lord Lieutenant of the county in question or the general of a Military District. There was a clearer need for the Yeomanry to turn out, reading the Volunteers Act. According to Benson Freeman,[3] this latter Act came to the Statute Book "without much being said on this delicate subject, although it is almost certain that East Coast MPs had mentioned in the Lobbies of Parliament, if not in debate, the utility of the Norfolk Rangers and that the three counties of Berkshire, Dorset and Rutland had each independently suggested the Volunteer Cavalry, presumably not with disinterest nor specifically as a counter to French aggression."

Devon demonstrated the pressing need for such a force by the application for Regular Troops, at Tiverton on May 27th 1794. It was anticipated there was to be a tumult by the woolcombers of that town and the Yeomanry thereabouts had not yet formed and mustered. This brings out a further aspect of Yeomanry duty, that of being 'turned out'. It now appears obvious that the Authorities could hardly wait until a full-scale riot was in progress before calling for help. In times of peace the Regular Cavalry forces were disposed about the country in 'penny packets' and thus available to show the flag when deemed necessary. The new war changed all that as they were drawn off to the coasts and further afield. It left behind the locals with no more than a tenuous hold over a patchwork quilt of the newly formed townships and swollen conurbations.

The practical need was for the magistrates to exercise a more finely calculated approach to solving military problems than heretofore. As we shall see later, there were occasions when plans miscarried, either because they allowed other considerations to blur their judgement or instructions to the Military allowed for a varied interpretation. This still left the Military with the problem of execution and the Yeomanry had now to be woven into the fabric of events and even stand alone. However, if these part-timer's were to be brought in from the fields and marched a number of miles to the latest seat of trouble, proper warning times had to be calculated. Also this call to duty gave rise to expenses, over and above those agreed in the budgets of the period. There were to be many occasions when they were 'called to' or given a warning order, when no riots ensued. However, the fact of a Troop jingling through the lanes and byways or standing at ease in a town or village square, held trouble-makers in check and steadied the less ruly elements. Thus the true measure of their service was the number of times they interrupted their daily round to ensure certain things *did not happen*. As Mileham[4] makes out, the riots the Yeomen attended were often bruising affairs, but as local men it was often the intimidation suffered whilst at home which cut deeper. There was always the probability that a few hardened characters would descend upon an isolated dwelling to take away a member's arms.

The period between 1794 and 1856 marks the longest period that any volunteer force has had to be ready to take the field in Britain. The total Yeomanry service in three subsequent wars pales into insignificance when compared with this period. It did so remarkably effectively. More often than not it achieved its aims without the use of force and at worst employed only that minimum to achieve legitimate ends. There were to be few military honours, not because these were not deserved, but for the reason officialdom could not be brought to admit a responsibility for the inadequacy of government.

Wartime Employment

Whatever the practical difficulties, the Yeomanry provided the bulk of the manpower for the policing service. It constituted a major source of employment during the early part of the 19th century and they had had to act frequently before that. The Government was well informed and for that reason took positive steps later to retain the Yeomanry Corps, if only for riot suppression. Major Teichman quotes the requirements laid on the Yeoman[5], as contained in his conditions of engagement and articles of enrolment:

" The Corps to be subject to be embodied within the County by Special Direction of His Majesty on Appearance of Invasion, and to be marched out of the County to any part of the Kingdom of Great Britain by the like Authority of His Majesty in case of actual Invasion. To be liable to be called on by Special Direction of His Majesty, in the suppression of Riots and Tumults existing in any adjoining County in which a Corps shall have been raised for its Internal Defence, to assist such Corps during the continuance of such Riots and Tumults. To be liable to be called on by Order of His Majesty, or by the Lord Lieutenant, or by the Deputy Lieutenant commissioned to act in his absence, or by a Sheriff of the County for the suppression of Riots or Tumults within the County."

"As all Yeomen were volunteers, it was considered a point of honour to attend drills, obey orders and be ready to turn out at a moments notice in order to assist in repelling invasion or aiding the Civil Power; and discipline could only be enforced by means of fines and threats of dismissal."

The practicalities called for and often showed compromise between people who had to live close together.

Emerging from the War

When the end of the war came, it was far from being a time for rejoicing, because it brought economic recession. Not only were the existing Yeomanry retained, but even augmented and new units raised to face widespread insurrection, arising from unemployment and the dislocation following the end of the war. The immediate question of independent Troops was forgotten. Matters quietened for a few years. Then once again the independent Troops became the focus of attention. By dint of 'searching inspections', many of these were worried out of existence and disbanded on their own volition. Also, there was a scheme introduced from 1827 to disband as many of the Yeomanry regiments who were unable to show active service by way of being called out by the magistrates during recent years. When the Metropolitan Police were established in 1829 it caused the Government to seek a further offset in costs. Some of the Yeomanry caused their own demise by being seen to be effective in the policing rôle. The undoubted but grudging respect shown them by an otherwise rebellious population, signed their death warrant.

The authorities had already got to hear of Captain Swing as early as 1826 as an active though unidentified organiser of agricultural machine breaking in East Anglia. Nevertheless, they went ahead with their economies at precisely the time he moved into Kent, which had been rendered virtually defenceless by the economies. The 'Swing' riots spread Westwards from Orpington and Canterbury leaving a trail of broken threshing machines and burnt corn ricks. So widespread were disturbances that all the disbanded units were re-raised and others added. A further effort at Yeomanry economy came in 1838, allied to a start in the formation of the Police in the major cities and the County Constabularies. Gradually these measures got results. A number of Yeomanry departed the scene

during that year, though a few were recalled in the early 1840s.

The formation of the County Constabularies was more or less completed by 1854. This opened the way for Horse Guards to take over command and the management of the Yeomanry for its own purely military tasks in 1856. In all this, it was the eventual prosperity of industry that brought public disorder down. But as a precautionary measure, the liability of the Yeomanry for call-out during civil insurrection was not finally removed until 1908, the year it came under the Territorial Force Act.

The Story of Riots

It is against the backcloth of these preliminaries that actual rioting can now be reviewed in sequence year by year. The account by Major Teichman is the most far ranging but additional material has been taken from a variety of additional sources [1][9-16] and others, indeed it is hardly possible to open a Yeomanry history without coming across some bruising and life threatening instance of civil strife. The newspapers of the period carried fulsome accounts of these disturbances. Further information is gleaned from the Parliamentary Returns [6][7][8] for the periods of Permanent Duty paid for and associated with riot suppression over the years 1816-29 and 1843-49. Beginning in 1793 riots were fuelled by a very real sense of injustice, as made out in pamphlets such as Thomas Paine's *The Rights of Man* that had sold 200,000 copies in that year. In the following years so many meetings, legally defined as seditious, under the law of the times, were held up and down the country that Habeas Corpus was suspended (1817 Spa Fields, London, at which Mr Hunt made a noted appearance). Frequent demands for the improvement of conditions and the lowering of the basic food prices were made both in the countryside and the towns. Later, demands for Constitutional and Parliamentary reform created situations of tension and widespread violence.[4] The calendar of events given below is a generous though still incomplete sampling for the period under review.

Riots During the Revolutionary War

Corn, Bread and Food Riots

The features of hunger-inspired rioting have been set out in some detail above. The specific instances below were caused by numerous local circumstances at a moment in time, about which generalisation is not particularly helpful.

Plate 1

The Carmarthen Museum

The Surrender. The French landed an ill equiped force of 1400 persons at Goodwick Sands, Fishguard on 22nd February 1797. They were without food and intended living off the country. After a few skirmishes they surrendered to amongst others The Castlemartin Yeomanry who were later awarded the uniqye Battle Honour 'Fishguard', the only one granted within the United Kingdom.

The Kent and Sharpshooters Yeomanry

Plate 2

The Review of the Royal East Mounted Rifles and the Queen's Own West Kent Yeomanry by HRH The Prince of Wales in 1888.

1794 The first on record involving the Yeomanry appears to be in October, when the Rutland Yeomanry were called to Oakham to quell a riot: "but in vain" says the historian.

1795 There were riots all over the country. One of the many instances took place in Devon when Sir Stafford Northcote's Volunteer Troop of Cavalry was despatched to Crediton to assist the 25th Light Dragoons to restore order and make arrests. This was the beginning of the so-called *Bread Riots*. On 18th April a Troop of the South Nottingham Yeomanry were utilised at Nottingham to quell a bread riot. But disturbances were also widespread and as a reward for their services all members of Yeomanry Cavalry were in future exempted from the hair powder tax. The first occasion the Warwickshire Yeomanry were asked to aid the Civil Power came on 29th June, when a riot broke out in Birmingham. Mr Legge's Troop marched to offer assistance, the Riot Act was read and a striker was shot by one of the Dragoons present.

At the Devon July Assize, a man was sentenced to death for 'notoriously assisting in destroying' a mill at Kingsteignton. "The execution was fixed for August 6th and as the sentence had aroused considerable feeling and sympathy for the criminal, an outbreak was feared. Prisoners in those days were frequently executed near the scene of their crimes, as a deterrent to others; and to convey the condemned man from Exeter, not only was the 1st Devon Troop called, but the 25th Light Dragoons, the East Devon Troop, two Troops from Exeter, with the Honiton and Cullumpton Volunteer Infantry. Under this imposing escort the prisoner was conducted in a Mourning coach to Bovey Heath".

The Staffordshire Yeomanry were called out to Radford Bridge on the 6th August, where a mob were attempting to detain corn. On this occasion the magistrate was able to convince the unruly elements to disperse voluntarily. The first call on the Wiltshire Yeomanry came on 17th August, in connection with a *bread riot* anticipated at Devizes. Five Troops were called out by the magistrates and no rioting took place. The Rotherham and Barnsley Troops of Yeomanry in the West Riding of Yorkshire also assisted the Civil Power at Wath.

1796 Further *bread riots* occurred in Nottingham and the Yeomanry were compelled to fire on the rioters by order of the chief magistrate.

1797 On August 22nd the Roxburgh Yeomanry were called out to aid the Civil Power at Jedburgh. The rioters were present in an attempt to avoid the Militia Act coming into operation, however this business had been carried the previous day. The appearance of the Yeomanry therefore gave them an object to vent their frustration upon and they were accordingly pelted with stones. The Major in command was knocked from his horse and then further struck whilst on the ground.

1798 The Portsdown Troop of the Hampshire Yeomanry were called to look after French prisoners at Porchester castle on 15th September and relieved on the 17th.

1800 On 21st April the Cullumpton Troop provided assistance in escorting as far as Taunton, a party of 450 French prisoners, who were being marched from Plymouth to Bristol. Also during April, disturbances took place in Edinburgh, due to the high price of meal. Two Troops of the Midlothian Yeomanry attended duty for a week. Two more *bread riots* took place in Nottingham; the first in April was quickly subdued but the second in August lasted for three days, with looting of granaries and shops. It took three troops of the Blues, three of the South Nottinghamshire Yeomanry and a violent thunderstorm before the mobs were finally dispersed. The Southampton Cavalry were called out to a serious riot at the local market on 18th September, when order was speedily restored. Later, on the 25th a further riot erupted to which the Fawley Light Dragoons attended. To disperse the rioters, the magistrates eventually ordered them to charge, which solved the problem and by not using more than the flat of their swords few persons were harmed. Later in the day the Bramsdean Volunteer Association Cavalry arrived to assist. Next, the Stafford Troop were twice called during September to quell local disturbances. On one occasion firearms were used and some persons wounded. In the Potteries trouble continued for a week, where the Colliers and Journeymen Potters 'controlled the prices' at provision merchants. The Newcastle, Lichfield and Walsall Troops were each busy preventing outrageous acts, over the period 11th till 15th of September. The Berkshire Yeomanry were called out during the year for riot duty.

1801 Benson Freeman writing on Devon stated, "local troops were called out in connection with a serious riot in Plymouth, where, on March 30th, a mob assembled and began to interfere with the proceedings of the market. Two carts, laden with potatoes, going out of the town at Old Town Gate, were stopped and the potatoes retailed at popular prices. The Plymouth Troop and the Volunteers were called out. On March 31st - it being market day at Plymouth Dock - another and much more serious, riot occurred. The mob, after completely upsetting the market, proceeded to break into shops of the bakers and provision dealers. The Riot act was read and the Queen's Bays 'were obliged to charge down Fore Street'. The Plymouth Dock Troop was called out and with the Volunteers and other troops, paraded and cleared the streets. Several rioters were arrested and though several persons were injured before order was at length restored, no lives were lost. The following from the *Exeter Flying Post* gives an account of the subsequent proceedings:"

"It is believed the business would have ended here, but at about four o'clock, on the dockyard men coming out of the yard, the tumult again commenced. Joined by the yardsmen, they proceeded towards the Main Guard, with the avowed purpose of liberating the prisoners. The cavalry and picquets were, however, thrown across the streets and prevented them approaching nearer than within 100 yards of the Guard House. But no entreaties could prevail on the mob to either retreat or disperse. With the utmost insolence they passed the military and dictated to the Magistrates, who at length complied with the demand and liberated the whole of the prisoners, a compliance which, whatever might be the motive, may eventually produce more real evil than firmer measures would have done.

The infuriated people concerned in this disgraceful riot little appreciated the danger they were in. . . . Several field pieces, loaded with grape and canister shot, were brought, unknown to them, to bear upon them and a few moments would have been sufficient to have sent hundreds of them in an instant before that God, whose religion proscribes tumult and enjoins obedience to the laws.

It is but justice to add the troops of the garrison, together with the Dock Associated Cavalry, behaved with a steadiness and patience not to be surpassed."

This was the year a large number of persons made an unlawful assembly at the Southernhay in Exeter. Two Troops went into barracks on 31st March at 6 am and later scoured the neighbouring villages, whilst the Exeter Troop with other Volunteers, paraded the streets of the town. By this show of force any tendency to riot was checked. On 6th April another riot being

feared in the Plymouth area, a certain General England ordered the whole of the garrison to parade at nine the next morning, consequently both Plymouth and Plymouth Dock Troops turned out at Eight. This show of force overawed the malcontents at the Dock, so that no riot took place.

Once more the Midlothian Yeomanry were suddenly requisitioned during June, by the Edinburgh Sheriff for a further period of duty. As the consequence of a grain riot at Errol during November, there were prisoners to be escorted to Perth by the local Volunteers and Yeomanry. The latter behaved well but the Volunteers became terrorised by rioters and 21 of the Company resigned the next day.

Riots During the Napoleonic War

1803 On 28th December an affray occurred in Chester between a Press Gang and some Volunteers on duty. One of the latter was thought to have seagoing experience and despite his dress was seized and lodged in Northgate gaol. A large crowd collected to assist the Volunteers and to release their man and the Western Cheshire Yeomanry were got under arms to police affairs, but all was quiet by the time they appeared on the scene.

1805 On 11th September, the Manx Yeomanry detailed a corporal and three privates to assist a Lieutenant Clarke, in apprehending a secreted seaman and escorting him to gaol, a distance of 16 miles. Later, during November three detachments were out on night duty as information had been received of men who had deserted from the Royal Navy and they were helping to round them up. Another sergeant's patrol was out on the 27-28th November to arrest 'some smugglers and proper persons to serve in the Navy' and on the 29th escorted those arrested to Douglas.

1806 May was a busy month for the Manx Yeomanry with no less than three parties engaged with officers of the Royal Navy in the pursuit of deserters, mainly at night time.

1808 The Castlemartin Yeomanry stood guard over the Frigate Leda of 38 guns on 31st January when it was wrecked at the entrance to Milford Haven.

1809 The enclosure of Duddleston Heath, Shropshire, enraged the natives who defied all law and order. The Oswestry Rangers were called to keep the ground whilst the Surveyors went about their work.

1810 The Wiltshire Yeomanry were called to deal with a mutiny of the 2nd Wiltshire Local Militia at Devizes. A further Militia riot took place on 16th May when the West Mendip Regiment of Local Militia assembled for training at Bath. The Lancashire Militia took in the ringleaders but the prison was stormed overnight and the North Somerset Yeomanry were called to help restore order, which they did. Three Troops of Staffordshire Yeomanry were next involved at the Wolverhampton Market, on 30-31st May, where a mob were throwing the provisions into the street. The ringleaders were taken into custody and committed to the local gaol.

Shoddy, 1811-12 and Luddism till 1817
Shoddy was the name applied to a product of substandard materials and weaving techniques adopted by some manufacturers to make quick profits in the South American market. Another term used at the time was 'cut-ups' as stockings were made up from pieces of cloth woven on the larger pantaloon frames, then going into disuse. They had turned here for trade as the result of the Blockade Napoleon and the 1811 Non-Intercourse Act with North America. Whilst this date is given as the commencement of Luddism, the Shoddy Riots did not involve the breaking of weaving frames. Their action was to remove the vital 'Jackwires'. These lifted selected warp threads as the shuttle shot back and forth and a programme provided a means for varying the pattern in the cloth. At first sight this seems analogous to the removal of the rotor arm to immobilise a car, but in reality it was nearer to upsetting the timing mechanism as their replacement called for re-tuning the loom. The actions were carried out at night by commando style teams of skilled craftsmen, with a hammer-man in the lead, who would burst into offending premises. Often this sabotage was carried out with the connivance of the quality goods manufacturers, who were left in peace. These earlier riots have to be distinguished from the machine breaking named after Ned Ludd, a Leicestershire 'Hot Head', who had in a passion destroyed some stocking frames thirty years previously. Even so there was some legality under statute law for frame breaking when products failed an acknowledged quality standard. This was immediately reviewed and frame breaking made a capital offence.

As applied to the power looms of the Lancashire cotton trade and the Yorkshire Woollen industry,

Luddism had little to do with the maintenance of quality products. Some owners here fought resolutely in the defence of their property, such as at Middleton by Manchester in April 1812. The mill was attacked by several thousands, but they were driven back by musket fire, killing 10 of their number. They next retaliated by burning down the mill owner's house. Troops were used to break up gatherings and at York 17 adjudged Luddites were hanged in January 1813. This strong line by government closed the main affair of Luddism though sporadic outbreaks continued until 1817.[11]

1811 On March 26th the Manx Troop were on duty quelling riots resulting from corn being sent for export following a bad harvest. During this year it was on duty at Ramsay for 61 days before being relieved. The Luddite Riots commenced in March and lasted intermittently for about seven years. The results had been a reduction in wages and an increased cost of living, an early example of 'stag-flation'. They marched on Arnold, destroyed 63 frames and dispersed before the Yeomanry could be called. However the areas were kept under arms until the 21st, when the Holme and Clumber Troops were dismissed. On 10th November more trouble broke out at Bulwell and an owner was killed by the rioters. The Lord Lieutenant of Nottinghamshire called out six troops of the South Nottinghamshire Yeomanry who remained spread out amongst the local villages for two weeks. Fresh outrages occurred in Nottinghamshire and on 1st December the Bunny Troop was called to Nottingham and to Sutton-in-Ashfield, to be followed by two further Troops on the 2nd. Thereupon the mobs resorted to night raids. The Bunny Troop was dismissed after eight days duty, with the Holme Troop released on the 12th and the Mansfield on the 19th.

1812 Rioting recurred in Nottingham and the surrounding counties, on an increased scale from January and became so serious that the Bays, the South Devon Militia and the Royal Buckingham Militia were out. In addition the South Nottingham, Derbyshire, Leicestershire, the West Riding and the Craven Yeomanry Regiments were under arms. Upwards of 900 frames were broken in a month as the rioters became crafty at quickly assembling and dispersing. At Nottingham, from 13th January, when all the frames were broken, the rioters resorted to personal violence and placarded the streets with notices offering a reward for the Mayor, dead or alive, because he had put up one of £500 for information leading to the arrest of the Luddite responsible for the death of a Mr Trentham. Quiet was restored by the end of April, with a trail of damage stretching through New Radford, Lenton, Ruddington across the Trent and Clifton. Later, although the Military managed a scheme of general control, the rioters became even more subtle. At Basford three soldiers protecting a house were confined by a party of strikers. Whilst one stood at the door as a dummy sentry, the remainder completed their work of destruction. On departing they discharged the weapons and bade the soldiers goodnight. On 13th April it was the turn of the whole 1st Cheshire Yeomanry to start duty for three weeks. The Penwith and Killigrew Troops in Cornwall were also called out during the year in connection with food riots in their district. The Manx Yeomanry repeated their duties of the previous year, but this time at Douglas.

1813 The Midlothian Yeomanry, during July escorted two criminals for execution at Coltbridge, where they had robbed and murdered an old man. Also during the year there was a riot at King's Lynn, Norfolk, attended by the local Yeomanry Troop.

1814 On May 12th the Western Troop of the Roxburgh Yeomanry escorted a convicted murderer from Jedburgh gaol to the gibbet at the Common Haugh at Hawick, without incident. One of the earliest colliery riots occurred at Radstock, Somerset towards the end of the year and the Bath Troop of the North Somerset Yeomanry secured order, but not before a miner was shot. A Captain Wiltshire was charged with manslaughter and acquitted, 'his defence being that his pistol went off by accident'. During the year a riot erupted at Norwich and was attended by the local Yeomanry.

The Seamen's Strike 1814
This strike followed hard on the heels of the war's end. Large numbers of seamen were discharged from service by the Transport Office, where they had received relatively high rates of pay. Amongst those remaining in work were a number of foreigners who were to be 'largely excluded' from the peacetime labour force under the 1794 Act (34 Geo.III, cap.68). The principal action took place on Tyneside. The original demand was for the removal of the foreigners but this was soon extended to one for a fair wage, proper vessel manning and safe practices. They gave edge to their demands by blockading the river at Newcastle.

The Government did not wish to become embroiled in something between employer and employee, besides which they had learned to mistrust the employers as more interested in profit than patriotism. Also the Admiralty was preoccupied with a large decommissioning programme and knew from experience how profitless any action on their part might be. As anticipated the employers settled and the only concern at any level had been the maintenance of public order.

1815 During November three Troops of the Staffordshire Yeomanry were sent to Wolverhampton; disturbances here were expected after reduction in wages and unemployment in the collieries and iron-works. At Bilston, a running fight developed with a hostile mob. As the disturbances spread, the whole of the Staffordshire Yeomanry was called out. Order was restored after three days, assisted by 9th Light Dragoons. The Manx Yeomanry were again on duty from 13-17th June, 'the town of Ramsay being riotous'.

1816 General discontent spread to West Country. The Frome food riots were suppressed by the North Somerset Yeomanry. Two Troops of North Devon Yeomanry, at Bideford, dispersed an angry mob, trying to prevent the export of potatoes. Later, the same mob besieged the local jail attempting the release of the ringleaders. The Yeomanry apprehended four rioters and sent them to Exeter under escort of the North Devon Yeomanry. Further information came in of a great number of disorderly people collecting at Appledore and Clewhouses, but these ran off directly the Yeomanry appeared. This was an example of a mob being quelled in its infancy. This year experienced a scanty harvest and brought on serious rioting at Ayr on 12th June. The Miller's house and mills were destroyed, so the Yeomanry was warned. A detachment assembled at 1am on the 14th, consisting of seven officers and 41 other ranks, who remained on duty for eight days. The Monmouthshire Yeomanry were called twice, on 22nd June and 19th October, to Abergavenney, whilst in neighbouring Glamorgan the Yeomanry was busy keeping order in the colliery districts. October 9th saw the Staffordshhire Yeomanry asked to assist in the quelling of a riot at Walsall, in which they succeeded with a detachment of Regulars. The Southern Regiment of the West Riding were called out to support the Civil Power. As an indication of charges on the Public Purse, the following Corps were paid sums of money this year, in aiding the

Civil Power: Arrington and Royston £12, Doddington £23, Derbyshire £88, Cardiff £22, Swansea and Fairwood £203, Huntingdon £21, Leicestershire £ see 1817, 2nd Norfolk £22, 3rd Norfolk £41, and Warwickshire £138.

This year witnessed the three Spa Fields Meetings in London over November and December. The second ended in a riot. The main speaker was Orator Hunt. It was an early form of a political rally and its business was to have a reform of Parliament, universal suffrage, voting in secret and annual elections. It was to all extents a forerunner of Chartism.

1817 The March of the Blanketeers
The Blanketeers were essentially an extension of protests by poor weavers who wanted amongst others things to present a petition to the Prince Regent asking for help for their industry. About 600 men, with blankets on their backs, walked in groups of 10, the maximum allowed by law when presenting a petition. About 200 were arrested at Stockport and most of the remainder were chased away by cavalry at Macclesfield. One man was allowed through to present his petition though nothing came of this pathetic incident except that 13 of the leaders were sent to prison. [11]

1817 The Derbyshire Rising
The Brandreth riots started around March in the Midlands. Many violent speeches were followed by open rebellion. Encouraged by a government spy known as Oliver, about 300 poor stocking-makers led by Jerimiah Brandreth, set off from Pentridge and Ripley in Derbyshire to seize Nottingham Castle, 14 miles away. Brandreth had assured his followers that the whole country was about to rise with them and that a provisional government was to be set up to provide relief. Oliver had alerted cavalry at Nottingham, so the men ran off. Brandreth and two others were hunted down.

Elsewhere in the Ayrshire mining districts the Ayrshire Yeomanry, as two regiments were in almost constant use against miners. The 1st Cheshire Yeomanry had the Stockport Troop called out on 13-15th January. A large military force was collected, including three Troops of Staffordshire Yeomanry, at Newcastle-under-Lyme on 27th January to attend a meeting, but it went off peacefully. Over March 9-15th the whole of the 1st Cheshire Yeomanry was called out for duty in the Manchester, Stockport and Macclesfield areas.

And again on the 29-30th March the whole of the 1st Cheshire Yeomanry were out in Stockport, Macclesfield, Ashton-under-Lyme and the neighbourhood of Manchester. The first riot in Nottingham took two days to quell, by the South Nottingham Yeomanry. Later that month, 'Blanketeers' were stopped at Leek by Troops of the Stafford and Derby Yeomanry, en route for London to petition the Prime Minister. The ringleaders were arrested but Brandreth escaped. He was later to be captured by the Derbyshire Yeomanry and subsequently executed for High Treason. In June the followers of Brandreth were still active in Derby and liable to join those in Nottingham. The latter township was 'defended' by the South Nottingham Yeomanry, with the Leicestershire Yeomanry on standby to support Nottingham. Also in June the state of country was so serious that an order was issued to all Yeomanry "to ensure their immediate attention for assistance to the Civil Authorities in England." There was a further riot amongst the Somerset miners and serious riots at Ely, so that the generally disturbed state of affairs had the Government suspend Habeas Corpus. Monies paid out in support of the Civil Power amounted to: 1st Cheshire £548, Clackmannan £76, Northamptonshire £43, Stirling £26, Warwickshire £12, Wigtownshire £12, Worcestershire £133, Kidderminster £49, and Huddersfield £162.

1818 Once again the Manx Yeomanry, both on the 6th and 24th March were detailed to assist the authorities in taking into custody persons dealing in 'base' coins and to convey them to Castle Rushem, which they did. On April 13th they were on riot duty at Jurby and on the 18th the Revenue Officer was requesting help in arresting the Captain and crew of the vessel Earl St Vincent for the illegal export of spirits! Then the South Wold Corps in Lincolnshire were called out. Further disorders broke out in Nottinghamshire with the Woollaton Troop called on the 22nd June and the Watnall Troop the following day. The former was dismissed on the 25th and the other on the 27th and the Wiltshire Corps was called out on that latter day. The Stockport, Mere, Knutsford and Tabley Troops of the Prince Regent's Cheshire Yeomanry were called out over the 14-19th July and 24th August, each for duties at Stockport. The Manchester and Salford Yeomanry Cavalry were called on the 17th September on account of shots being fired on the authorities and persons being wounded. This was connected with the eviction of work people from a cotton manufactory at Ancoats, Manchester. The Worcestershire Yeomanry were summoned by the magistrates, on 29th September, to the **Freeman's Riots** at a place known as the Little Pitchcroft. The Mayor swore-in Special Constables and read the Riot Act, but nobody took notice. Here some locals were demolishing structures which occupied Common Land. The Yeomanry when they appeared were greeted by a shower of stones and they retired to the local hostelry. The mob also retired having completed their work. The Carmarthen Yeomanry were called out on the 30th September.

1819 Peterloo

This was the year of the much publicised 'massacre' which occurred on the 31st July, in St Peter's Fields on the then environs of Manchester. So much has been written about this event that it has passed into folklore, with every attendant imperfection. Most of the accounts make uncertain history because authors take an off-centre socio-political stance. Without doubt the events leading up to the rally shaped the event itself: a disaster waiting to happen. There were infinitely more bloody events at Bristol, Nottingham and lastly South Wales where far more were killed by the Argyll and Sutherland Highlanders. This latter event obviously coloured the later thinking of the Duke of Wellington over the use of infantry in riot control. Britannica carries an account that follows the conventional wisdom, but leaves out crucial military aspects which need to be addressed: for instance, the fact that the Yeomanry would not have been present unless requisitioned and the specific rôle of the Manchester Yeomanry being misrepresented. It seems that the only reporting to provide a balanced military perspective comes from Leary's History of the Earl of Chester's Yeomanry, present at the rally and given by Benson Freeman[13] in succinct detail, whilst penning the history of the much maligned and unfortunate Corps. This runs as follows:

"As to the man 'Orator' Hunt, there seems little doubt that he was a vainglorious and mischievous agitator, who while foremost in inciting disorder managed to take very good care to avoid personal danger. He began life as a Yeoman farmer in Wiltshire. Having joined the Yeomanry of that county, then commanded by Lord Bruce, he lost no opportunity of displaying his patriotic sentiments, giving on every parade animated orations to his Troop on loyalty, discipline and similar subjects. But finally this unnecessary loquacity disgusted Lord Bruce, who was a somewhat peremptory personage and he was dismissed from the Regiment. Hunt then sent a challenge to Lord Bruce,

who at once brought him before the King's Bench on a criminal information. The judges after some severe comments, sentenced Hunt to six weeks' imprisonment and a fine of £100, and this had the result of transforming a loyal and worthy person into one of the most mischievous demagogues of the times."

Other useful background is that this meeting formed the third attempt to arrange a venue that had been thwarted by the magistrates, though for no legal cause: The first was for the same place on the 2nd August and the second for a Town's meeting on the 9th. Also that one of its main purposes was to have Hunt elected as an *Legislative Attorney,* whence he could attempt a dialogue with the Westminster Parliament, for at this time the whole of Manchester and its environs was without Members of Parliament. And lastly, that Hunt had reputedly, the previous evening made it known to the magistrates that he would facilitate his own arrest, though presumably it had to be seen done publicly.

"The Authorities had foreseen trouble and called in a considerable military force including, the 1st Dragoon Guards, three squadrons of the 15th Hussars, the Cheshire Yeomanry, two battalions of infantry and two batteries of artillery and two troops of the local Yeomanry! These were each in nearby holding areas, as the day's events unfolded. The point being made was the absence of surprise or the need for anything to be done at more than a leisurely pace or without mature consideration. The magistrates were alert and had it on oath that the demonstrators meant to attack Manchester and that formidable preparations were being made, with large bodies of pikemen assembling near Middletown and at Oldham. The military forces mentioned earlier assembled at 11 am and at about this time the magistrates took up their viewing stance in a house in Mount Street, overlooking the ground. Soon the numerous bodies of special constables assembled on the ground and the military moved to various positions assigned to them, each some distance from the ground. The so-called reformers started to arrive from different routes in regular military array. Each 'Battalion' had its leader and banners bearing such inscriptions as "Let us die like men and not be sold as slaves", "Liberty or Death", "Equal representation or death". As the local business people saw this build-up they became alarmed and shut up shop for the day. The crowd numbered possibly 60,000, whilst the ground measured 100 by 160 yards.

A short consultation took place between the

magistrates who decided to arrest the leaders and Mr Nadin, as Deputy Constable, was appointed to execute it. At the commencement of the proceedings a lane had been formed by two lines of special constables, from the house in which the magistrates stood and the cart upon which the speakers stood. the latter seeing the meaning of the lanes moved back the cart, closing it off. Mr Nadin refused to proceed without the aid of the military. The magistrates now thoroughly alarmed, sent for the troops and the first to arrive by accident of station was a Troop of Manchester and Salford Yeomanry, consisting of about 60 men under a Captain Birlay, who was immediately ordered to assist the Deputy Constable to arrest the speakers. Before the Yeomanry advanced Mr Nadin fearing mischief withdrew as many special constables as he was able with the result the lane was completely destroyed.

At the time the Yeomanry advanced, Hunt was addressing the meeting and had just used the words, "I hope gentlemen, that if your enemies attempt to interrupt the proceedings or cause a riot or disturbance, that there are some amongst you who possess courage enough to put these down, quieten them and keep them down". The influence which such advice was calculated to have upon the mob was shown by one of them shouting "why that's like killing them."

The Yeomanry were now seen advancing and were met with a shout of defiance, with stones, brickbats and sticks freely used. As the Yeomanry reached the cart on which the orators had taken up their position, orders were given for the mob to stand firm and those that surrounded the hustings linked themselves together arm in arm. The Yeomanry persevered in their onward course until they reached and surrounded the cart, when the Civil Authorities seized the leaders of the meeting. Up to this time not a blow had been struck by the Yeomanry, but now the confusion became so great that the little band was hemmed in by the dense crowd, overpowered, overwhelmed and broken up into small knots of twos and threes, they were entirely at the mercy of the mob and it was clear that without assistance they would be annihilated.

Till then there had been no question of dispersing the meeting, but only of arresting the leaders. The question of dispersing the meeting came in when the danger to the Yeomanry from the mob's resistance to the execution of the warrant under which they acted, was perceived. At this point the Cheshire Yeomanry and the 15th Hussars moved up presumably on advice

and the chief magistrate ordered them to disperse the meeting. The order was obeyed and the mob seeing the two regiments scampered away in every direction, in their terror and confusion pressing one another down and the ground was cleared as by magic.

The utmost exertion was required by the authorities for the rest of the day and the whole of the evening till midnight in many parts of the town, but more especially at New Cross. Between 7 and 8 pm the Riot Act was read, and three or four persons were wounded by shots fired by the Infantry, who the mob defied. One had his legs amputated at the Infirmary and another was so severely wounded that he afterwards died. Strong bodies of the Yeomanry and Regular Cavalry patrolled the streets of the town and it was not before the early hours of Tuesday morning that quiet was restored.

There was a bad Press, but most of it derived from poor or exaggerated second-hand information, besides which there was the political dimension in which the Whigs wished to score over the Tories. Of the six killed, one was shot by the Infantry at New Cross, another was a constable in the execution of his duty, a woman and child were killed by the pressure of the crowd, one died in the Infirmary from a sabre cut and another was a man found dead on St Peter's Fields from no known cause. If there were more deaths they were not related to this event at the time. There were very few sabre wounds, although possibly a large number of the wounded crept away and hid them for fear that they might be identified with events of that day. It is necessary to ask this question, was there stronger proof of moderation that such a large meeting was dispersed by the military with so few casualties arising from the use of arms?

There is another side to this use of military force, which has been generally overlooked. It has been the fashion to represent this meeting as being composed of quiet law abiding citizens and yet the 15th Hussars had two officers, two non-commissioned officers and privates and seven horses forcibly struck with stones or brickbats and also four horses cut with sharp instruments. One of these horses was seen to be cut with a crooked instrument attached to a long pole and one of the others received a deep stab wound. One of the privates received a severe blow to the head and had his arm broken. The commander of the troops received a tremendous blow on the forehead temporarily depriving him of his senses. Of the 116 members of the Manchester and Salford Corps who were on duty, two officers, 41 others and nine horses were cut with sharp instruments. The Cheshire Corps had three men hurt and one horse killed. One of the men was cut desperately by a brick thrown at him at Deansgate, where he was knocked from his horse and his helmet kicked through the streets.

Whence came the stones thrown at the military? At a subsequent trial the Assistant Surveyor of Manchester swore that acting under orders he had had the area cleaned prior to the meeting of all stones, brickbats and sticks, yet afterwards he had collected some scores of sticks and a cartload of stones and brickbats. Then again the pressure of the crowd would have prevented the gathering of stones from off the ground. The gross estimate of crowd density works out at a quarter square metre per person, whilst other contemporary accounts speak of hat brims touching, people dressed in their Sunday best, with pretty girls at the front.

Wheelers Manchester Chronicle, an impartial source, remarked "it was scarcely to be expected that great numbers of the Reformers would come to a meeting prepared with offensive weapons but such was the case. A class of them were dressed as brewery servants usually are, with long coats with deep pockets and these it appears were filled with stones. Leastwise the presence of the stones has never satisfactorily been accounted for."

At the trial later, which lasted five days the behaviour of the Yeomanry was completely vindicated, a result which was fully sustained by the Lord Chief Justice. After ten days in prison those arrested were released on bail. Charges of murder brought against certain members of the Yeomanry were thrown out, by the Grand Jury, and at length it was decreed the ringleaders should take their trial at the York Assizes. After a long and patient investigation five were found guilty of attending an illegal meeting, for which Hunt as the principal was sentenced to two and a half years in prison at Ilchester gaol and the others for lesser periods. As to the situation following the riot, matters were so unsettled that the Manchester and Salford Yeomanry were not dismissed until 19th August, receiving the thanks of the magistrates of Lancashire and that of the Prince Regent, through the Home Secretary. From the foregoing it pertinent to observe as academic how well the Yeomanry were seated.

The authorities were resolute and when the Lord Lieutenant of the West Riding protested for a Public enquiry he was removed from office. The General Officer of the District, Major-General Byng made a report to the Home Secretary of the time, but such cannot be found in the records for the period, so that rightly or wrongly it might be concluded it failed to support the official line. Certainly the illegality of the meeting is hard to make out, yet that was the basis for charging Hunt.

Of course there was the need for an improved political articulation. The stupidity of the Rotten Boroughs returning many MP's, whilst Manchester, Birmingham and other large urban centres were allowed none needed to be addressed. It does well to note that *all* persons domiciled thereabouts, whether with property or not had no franchise. Business suffered as the result of unruly elements, something known and best designed to bring down the wrath of the authorities. The meeting was an early form of Chartism and those calling the meeting were well in tune with the status quo and could have been better advised, whatever the frustration, for it was their world. From this it might be assumed that Hunt had already recognised the illusory nature of his quest for legislative attorney: it was a pipe-dream. As with so many events of this kind, an unfortunate mix of circumstances set the scene for a disaster. Whatever the moralities of the case, it had the perverse effect of attracting a veritable flood of Yeomanry volunteers and triggered the passing of the 'Gagging Acts'.

Aside from Peterloo the calendar of events for the year commenced with the Liverpool Light Horse being called out on 13th February and the Stockport Troop on the 15th, whilst the Manx Yeomanry were called on April 13th. The Fife Yeomanry were next called on the 8th July, the Montgomeryshire Yeomanry on the 12th and the Bath Troop of the North Somerset Yeomanry on the 21st. In August the Oldham Troop was called on the 9th and 16th, also the whole of the 1st Cheshire Yeomanry until the 18th for duty in Manchester, followed by the Huddersfield Troop being mustered on the 20th. Later, the South Tyne Corps were called to duty on 15th October, the Bywell Troop of Northumberland on the 16th, the Durham Corps on the 30th and the Staffordshire Corps on the 31st. During November the Leicestershire Corps were called on the 3rd, the Ashton in Makerfield Corps on the 8th and the Manx once again on the 14th when the further quelling of riots commenced over a three month period. The 2nd Ayrshire Yeomanry were called to duty on the 15th November. A party of five privates was told off to proceed to Dumbarton to collect ammunition. The issue was double the normal amount, being 60 rounds and three flints per man on their establishment. The noteworthy features was the absence of anyone holding rank, and the fact that the party were passing through strongly radical territory (of which more later), taking two days out and two days back. And once again the Manchester and Salford Corps were called on 29th. For the second time both the South Tyne Corps were called on 3rd December and Durham on the 4th. This was followed by the Huddersfield Corps on the 6th, also the Mold Corps of Flint, the Coquetdale Rangers and the Corps from Wigtownshire. At this time the Radical Riots commenced in Scotland. On 10th December the Midlothian Yeomanry received orders to proceed to Hamilton and then on to Glasgow, where it remained on duty till the 16th. The Midlothian Corps was called on the 11th and the Berwickshire Corps on the 12th, whilst the East Lothian Corps assembled on the 13th at Haddington and moved up to Musselburgh and Dalkeith two days later. Also called to this day were the Linlithgow and Stirling Corps and in more southerly climes the Ashton, Oldham, Staffordshire, Manchester, the 1st Cheshire Yeomanry (until the 16th), the Holmpierrepoint, Wollaton and the South West York Corps. Then the 3rd and 4th Troops of the 1st Ayrshire Yeomanry were stationed at Ayr from the 13th because of disturbances there and only dismissed on Christmas Day. False intelligence caused three Troops of South Nottinghamshire Yeomanry to be mustered between 13-14th, whilst the Kinross Corps was called out on the latter day. The Berwickshire Yeomanry were both mustered and ordered to Dalkeith on the 14th as a back-up to the forces moving across to Glasgow; they moved on to Dunbar and finally Haddington before returning home on the 18th. The Lanarkshire also mustered at this time in an successful effort to overawe the mobs in the county. Further south the Swansea and Fairwood Corps were called on the 20th. There were riots during the year which the Berkshire Yeomanry attended.

1820 The Scottish Radical War[14]
This year heralded the Radical War in Scotland which engaged the largest portion of their Yeomanry. It followed the Brandreth Riots of 1817 and Peterloo of 1819, so officialdom was well informed over the probable pattern events would follow. It seems that

April 1st was targeted for a general strike and uprising in and around Glasgow, in notices signed by a 'Committee for forming a Provisional Government', using the motto 'Liberty or Death'. The Radicals had been preparing for the day, with secret drillings and military instruction taking place at convenient spots. In preparing arms, blacksmith's shops were taken over, often forcibly. The area affected embraced Glasgow, a number of towns and villages in the counties of Dunbarton, Stirling, Renfrew, Lanark and Ayr. Once this proclamation was brought to the attention of the authorities the order went out for all military forces to muster on 2nd April. The Clyde-Forth valley was heavily garrisoned by Regular Cavalry and Infantry, to which could be added 3000 Volunteer Infantry and 2000 Yeomanry Cavalry. Ayrshire contributed ten Troops divided into two regiments, the Glasgow Yeomanry comprised two Squadrons, Lanark a further five Troops, Renfrew four, Dumbarton three and Stirling a further five. Added to this were those in outlying areas, able to nudge across, fire brigade style, as those above moved into the Glasgow frame. As a precautionary measure the largest portion of the Yeomanry were drawn into various parts of Glasgow, so that the very size of the opposition should be seen by the intending rebels. A great number of these skulked away reasoning over the stupidity of the project. The plan was to strike and move across Scotland to Edinburgh picking up people on the way. Indeed 60,000 persons struck, but no more than two to three hundred could be induced to bear arms and much less took part in the actual marching.

Possibly it was a separate event, but the Airdrie Cavalry were called on the 28th February, though the first real inkling of trouble connected with the Radicals came the following day. The Commander of the Western District asked the Lords Lieutenant to put their various Corps on Standby. As the consequence both the Ayrshire Corps were on permanent duty from the 29th February till 4th March. This appears to have been premature or that rioting was put off by the prompt action taken by officialdom. The Upper Ward, Lanark Yeomanry were also called on this date with the Hamilton and Stirling Corps, to be followed on 1st March by Dumbarton and Cambuslang. The only action occurred at the "Battle of Bonnymuir" which was joined by a Troop of 10th Hussars and the Kilsyth Troop of the Stirlingshire Yeomanry, in heading off rebels on their way to Edinburgh. The fact that the rebels fired on the troops caused surprise, but in the subsequent mêlée they were scattered, hunted down and 19 taken into custody. A few persons were wounded on both sides and a single horse was killed. The Falkirk Troop was 'pelted a little upon' in passing through Camelon during the morning, yet all was quiet later that afternoon. By 6th April the Fintry Troop was reporting the absence of acting magistrates in their area and would steps be taken to have two Troops of Clackmannan Yeomanry placed in readiness. Obviously there was still a sense of unease, yet the insurrection as such was at an end. However there were numerous minor scuffles. Two Troops of Ayrshire Yeomanry were attacked with weighted darts, called clegs and brickends. One of the Yeomen who had told off his officer during the morning how he had scruples over attacking an unarmed mob, announced at the end of the day; "I'm no' that man noo, for I've had a brick on the side of my head and anither on my shoulder, and I'm ready to gie them two for't." Glasgow was a similar proposition. The overall result was that 41 persons were charged with treason. If this was the end of insurrection, it didn't satisfy the miners. On the 2nd April the 2nd Ayrshire, the Hamilton, the Paisley and Airdrie Corps were each called. The 1st Ayrshire were hard pressed on the 2nd, 9th, 10th, 12th, and 22nd. Yet on the 3rd April it was the turn of Dumbarton, Cambuslang, Glasgow, Kilbride, the Upper War of Lanark and the Stirling Corps. The newly raised Edinburgh Troop was ordered out on 4th April and sent to Glasgow on the 8th, whilst the other Troops of the Midlothian Yeomanry assembled in Midlothian and West Lothian. They patrolled the streets of Glasgow for several days, were sent to Kilmarnock on the 13th, where they effected several arrests and escorted prisoners to Ayr. They were next on a similar errand to Strathhaven and Lanark before returning home on the 16th. Also on the 4th the Midlothian Corps was called, followed by Clackmannan and Linlithgow on the 5th and the Johnstone Corps on the 10th. Elsewhere the 2nd Troop, Berwickshire Yeomanry were called to suppress a riot on 6th January at Berwick.

Elsewhere the Manx Yeomanry took the field on the 16th February. Then the Bloxham and Banbury Corps of Oxford were called out a second time, followed by South West York on the 11th and Wigtown on the 27th. During the remainder of this month, the Bloxham and Banbury Corps was called on the 10th, Perthshire on the 12th, possibly independently of the Radicals and Huddersfield on the 31st.

During May the Johnstone Corps were called again on

the 12th and 17th and the Dungleddy and Pembroke Corps on the 15th. June was relatively quiet, except for South Salop on the 15th, Shrewsbury on the 15th and Stirling for a third occasion on the 25th. The Johnstone Corps went out for the fourth time on the 13th July. The Surrey Corps was called on the 18th August and later in November to keep order during riots which took place in connection with the acquittal of Queen Caroline. Later on 8th September riots were anticipated at Girvan and these occupied, for three hours some 70 men from the 1st and 5th Troops of the Ayrshire Yeomanry and again in December the Carrick Troop were on duty in Ayr. November brought a call for the Staffordshire Yeomanry on the 15th and Perthshire for the second time on the 20th. There is a single record for a Bitton Troop in Somerset warned for duty by the Civil Power during November, whilst in conclusion there was a riot by miners and ironworkers at Wellington which was subdued by the South Shropshire Yeomanry.

1820 The Cato Street Conspiracy [11]
Although no part of the Yeomanry piece, it was related to the radicalism of the period. The leaders included Arthur Thistlewood and James Ings, who moved the most extreme act of protest with a half-baked plan to murder the entire cabinet at dinner, parade the heads of the ministers on pikes, capture the Tower, Bank and Mansion House (The Lord Mayor's residence) and proclaim a republic. Once again the government had spies in place, so the plot came to nothing. Five leaders including Thistlewood were executed and a further five transported. Unfortunately their actions, unimportant in themselves, seemed to vindicate the government passing the 'Gagging Acts' and thus put back the cause of reform.

1821 Over the period 2nd, 3rd and 10th February there was further trouble around Wellington, owing to reduced wages, leading to the 'Battle of Cinderloo' and considerable machine damage. Two Troops of South Shropshire Yeomanry dispersed 3000 rioters and arrested ringleaders. The Yeomanry was pelted with stones and cinders and opened fire, killing two rioters. They were reinforced the next day by two Shrewsbury Troops and a Troop of 6th Dragoons before order was restored. The new King was not popular and the Divorce Bill against the Queen aroused the lower classes against him. As the consequence there were a number of troop movements to make the Capital safe. In these the Surrey, London and Westminster Light Horse, the Mid and South Buckingham Yeomanry were selected for duty, whilst the East Berkshire went to Windsor Castle to relieve the Life Guards for the City. The 3rd Troop of the Berwick Yeomanry were called to suppress a riot at Lauder, between Irish sheep shearers and the townspeople on 30th September. Two of the offenders leading the mob, set on abusing the residents were taken into custody, but were subsequently released. Then constables and the Yeomanry made arrests and the peace of the neighbourhood was restored with a detachment of 4th Dragoon Guards. Once again on the Isle of Man there were riots on 1st October. One of the ringleaders was locked up by a Deemster the following day and the Manx Yeomanry were called to quell more riots at Peel and Douglas. The mob overpowered the whole Troop and rescued the prisoner, however he was re-taken and subsequently lodged in Rushem Castle. Then on October 4th a further riot took place at Douglas, headed by a man in woman's clothing and another who was taken into custody. The riots continued until the Corn Law embargoes were removed, but these were then reimposed leading to a further spate of rioting through the winter.

1822 The Wiltshire Yeomanry were called to riots on the 21st and 26th January, with the North Somerset Yeomanry on the 22nd. The 3rd Norfolk Regiment was called on 4th of March, followed by the 2nd Regiment on the 5th, along with the 1st Regiment of Suffolk. Once again the Monmouth Yeomanry were called on 31st March, keeping rebellious colliers in check until 5th April. The 1st Suffolk Regiment were again called on the 13th and 15th, the South Salop on the 16th and 29th, the Staffordshire Corps on the 17th and once again Monmouth on 20th April. The Staffordshire stand-to was against striking miners, who were intimidating those prepared to work. The Bilston Troop was first sent to protect those not on strike and they were able to handle the numbers, but subsequently these so increased that large reinforcements became necessary. A detachment of Greys, the Dudley Troop and four companies of Regular Infantry went into action for two weeks. Later the Tiddesley Troop co-operated in rounding-up the escaped ringleaders and order was restored. These actions had occupied seven Troops of Yeomanry, a detachment of Scots Greys, the Handsworth Cavalry, four companies of Infantry, with staff of the Militia, covering the areas of Bilston, Dudley and Tipton. The Himley Troop remained on duty for 23 days, the Walsall and Bilston Troops were called out twice and later the Himley Troop was called out to Dudley for a further four days. Unrest next

spread to the West Country, resulting in the Weavers' Riots of Wiltshire and Somerset. At Warminster 1200 weavers surrounded and wrecked houses of those prepared to work. Other trouble spots were, Bradford-on-Avon, Frome, Trowbridge and Warminster, each connected with improved machines and reduced wages for piece output. The Wiltshire and North Somerset Yeomanries were each called out for a number of days. The Chepstow Troop were called out to duty on 1st May when more trouble erupted and remained on duty till the 7th. Later a Troop was requisitioned for duty at the Rock Colliery on the 23rd and it was between these dates that the colliers took action to prevent the movement of coal to Tredegar. A ringleader was seized and almost immediately released by his comrades. The Riot Act was read without effect, whereupon the Yeomanry went in to disperse the mob using the flat of their swords. With the task of escorting the wagons handed over to the Regulars, the Yeomanry was dismissed. A few days later the escort of wagons was once more entrusted to the Yeomanry. A furious attack across a culverted position made progress impossible until the Regulars worked along the heights. On the 6th May once again the Handsworth Troop was called on, whilst the Monmouth Corps was mustered for the third time on the 22nd. The 1st Regiment of Suffolk was called for the fourth time on 28th June and lastly the Ravensworth Troop on 9th October.

1823 The Wiltshire Yeomanry were mustered on 16th June, whilst the North Somerset Yeomanry were called on the 1st and 8th July. Then an Election Riot at Newcastle-under-Lyne on the 24th saw the Staffordshire Corps quelling disturbances. The Berwickshire Corps were called to a riot on 15th September, due to trouble at the market at Duns in hiring sheepshearers. They were requisitioned by the sheriff to take up duty on the morning of the 20th at 5 am and a detachment 18 strong remained on duty through the day. Again the Berwickshire Corps was called out on 22nd. During October the Wigtown Corps was called on the 2nd, the Berwick on the 28th and the Roxburgh and Ayr Corps on the 29th. The action of the 28th involved a detachment of three officers and 106 men ordered to attend the execution of one Robert Scott. The criminal was escorted from the Jedburgh Gaol to the border of the County at Earlston Bridge, by a large body of Roxburgh Yeomanry and handed over to the Berwickshire Corps. They protected the man from an enraged mob, until his execution at Fans. The condemned man had killed and mutilated two persons for no known motive. The Troops were dismissed on the 30th. Finally for the year, the Ayrshire Corps was called on no less than the 16th and 23rd November and the 11th and 12th December.

1824 There were considerable disturbances in Cheshire leading to the call-out of the King's Cheshire Yeomanry on 5th April to Sutton. The Midlothian Corps were next called during November to preserve order during a great fire which raged for several days in Edinburgh and during which, large blocks of houses and tenements between Parliament Square and the Tron Church were completely destroyed. The year concluded with the Glamorgan and Llantrissent Corps called out on the 21st December.

This was the year the Combination Laws were repealed. Thus Trade Unionism became legal for the first time since 1799-1800. So obviously a good measure, the initial reaction was for a rash of Unions to be formed with a confusing array of objectives, strikes and mayhem, which horrified Radicals and Industrialists alike. Only as the result of some quick thinking by the main proponents of the Act was a reintroduction averted by an Amending Act of 1825 which outlawed molestation and obstruction.

1825 The Midlothian Yeomanry were assembled with special constables on New Year's Day, in anticipation of riots which often took place on that day. Their services were not required. The Staffordshire Corps were called on the 11th of January, followed by the Glamorgan and Llantrissent Corps on the 14th May and the Tyne Hussars on 4th August.

1826 The 3rd Norfolk Corps was called out on the 2nd February. The Maylor Legion was out on 6th March, followed by the Mold Corps on the following day. The Craven Legion was next called on 22nd April, the Bolton Corps on 26th, followed by the 1st and 2nd Cheshire, Oldham, Wigan and the Yorkshire Hussars Corps on the 28th. During April there was rioting throughout the manufacturing areas of the Midlands, leading to the large scale destruction of machines. Great damage and several lives were lost. Disturbances then reached the scene of Peterloo and a further meeting. Speakers there urged machine destruction and the opposing of the Military. The King's Cheshire Yeomanry were called to Manchester on the 27th, but trouble erupted before they arrived.

At 6 pm on the 28th orders for the 1st Squadron of the Prince Regent's 2nd Regiment of Yeomanry to march on Warrington without delay. Luckily the Bays and a company of the 60th Rifles were stationed in town and able to stop rioters entering it and they proceeded to restore order by midnight. Rioting recommenced the next morning however and the Yeomanry then on duty was heavily stoned by the mobs. The rioting became daily more violent, so that the two Cheshire Regiments were employed in Manchester, Stockport and Hyde, under the direct orders of Lt-General Sir John Byng. The 1st were dismissed on the 30th, whilst the 2nd provided eight days continuous service. It seems there was considerable sympathy for the plight of the working people at the time as subscriptions were collected from amongst the Yeomanry to be distributed by a Distress Fund. At this time the Yorkshire Hussars were called on the 26th April to Addingham to prevent loom breaking. The action spread to Otley on the 28th and back to Addingham on May 1st and from there to Bingley, Baildon, Bradford and Halifax, finally subsiding on the 3rd. There were two killed and 14 wounded amongst the loom breakers. The North High Peak Corps were also called on the 1st, whilst the 1st Cheshire and Staffordshire Corps were called on the 3rd. The *Weavers' Riots* recurred in Wiltshire on the 7th May. A mob released the riot leaders at Bradford-on-Avon by tearing the roof from the jail and much damage was done in Trowbridge. Eventually order was restored by four troops of the Wiltshire Yeomanry and two of the 6th Dragoon Guards, brought up from Dorchester and Weymouth by train. On May 3rd the Himley Troop of Staffordshire was called to duty for five days, without active employment resulting. Fresh disturbances next broke out in West Bromwich on 27th July, caused by miners from Dudley and Tipton not accepting a wage cut. Three troops of the Staffordshire Yeomanry managed to disperse a considerable mob. Later on 14th December two Troops of Staffordshire Yeomanry were mustered for a contested Election.

One is entitled to ask why the use of Yeomanry was so popular with the authorities. The Duke of Wellington giving evidence before the Parliamentary Finance Committee said: "It is much more desirable to employ cavalry for the purpose of police than infantry; For this reason, cavalry inspires more terror at the same time that it does much less mischief. A body of twenty or thirty horse will disperse a mob with the utmost facility, whereas 400 or 500 infantry will not effect the same object without the use of their firearms and a great deal of mischief may be done."

1827 The Castlemartin Yeomanry were called on 14th January, the 3rd Norfolk Corps on the 12th February and again on 21st March. Wigtown were next called on 31st March and the 3rd Norfolk Corps for the third time on 12th June. There is the rare example of a magistrate complaining over the non-attendance to a request for help on the 7th and 9th of May, against the Monmouth Yeomanry. At that time they were away on annual training. The outcome is not on record, though it indicates a poor liaison, though the record shows £10-19-7d paid during the year in respect of their Aiding the Civil Power.

1828 The Lanark Yeomanry once more took the field in the cause of Catholic rights and riots at Carluke. A small detachment of Ayrshire Yeomanry were called out during the year.

1829 The Metropolitan Police Act

It will be obvious that the instant creation of a Police Force across the United Kingdom, as a whole was an administrative impossibility, but gradually the Yeomanry were eased from their onerous duties. The Act provided for 1000 paid constables, soon to be increased to 3000. They were unarmed except for a truncheon, to avoid the charge they were military. The result was a spectacular reduction in the crime rate as the criminal fraternity flocked out of London. Soon the surrounding towns copied London, mostly due perhaps to their recent unwelcome arrivals.

1829-30 Captain Swing

A variety of dates and places are given for the first outrage, though all are located in Kent. The word 'swing' refers to the swinging stick or flail used in hand threshing. It was to be the last agricultural labourer's revolt. First heard of in East Anglia in 1826, Swing reappeared in Orpington and Canterbury, although never formally identified. Two out of four army officers sent into the field as government agents, were arrested in a comical error by the local authorities because of being military and foreigners to those parts. By the third week in November rioting had become general in Kent, Surrey, Sussex, Hampshire, Berkshire, Buckinghamshire, Wiltshire and the Southern parts of Oxfordshire and Hertfordshire. Here it will be remembered that only the Wiltshire and North Somerset Corps were on pay and allowances, with but three Devon and one Buckingham Corps available,

serving for no pay. The identity of Swing has remained a mystery. Groups of farm workers turning up at a farm were most careful to state their aims, basically the need for a living wage and the requirement to smash the new threshing machines, each able to put 75 persons on poor relief, whilst making a 10% better grain return than hand methods. When the farmers gave high rents and tithes as a difficulty it was suggested they ask the landed proprietors and the clergy for a reduction and some undertakings were given. Those going back on their word, which some did later, had their ricks fired[11]. Although officialdom cobbled together a response and effectively broke the riots, it was without the sympathy of the community at large. The problem was that by this time the unemployed were dealt with under the Poor Law, which was a tax on the locals. In this, farmers felt disinclined to pay proper wages or to engage labourers for a whole week as the Poor House would make up any shortfall.

1829 More trouble erupted in Devon and was avoided by letting the likely rioters know that the Yeomanry was assembled, in particular the Swimbridge, Fremington and Torrington Troops, nevertheless a number of threshing machines were broken. The Hindon Troop of Wiltshire Yeomanry faced 500 rioters at Tisbury. One rioter was killed, possibly by a farmer before the Yeomanry arrived. There were many other actions by Troops in the south of Wiltshire. The Salisbury Assize tried 330 prisoners; Two were sentenced to death and the remainder to terms of imprisonment or transportation. The riots had started in Kent and stopped directly there was a response over the wages question.

Other actions included a Troop of the Lancashire Yeomanry called out on 6th May, whilst the Biddeford Troop in North Devon was called to *'Wreck Duty'* on 11th September with the cargo ship Daniel on the Northam Burrow, to prevent looting.

1830 On September 5th the Oxford Corps was called, followed by five Troops of Mid-Buckinghamshire with two of the latter's artillery pieces on the 6th. This had to do with the draining of the Otmoor, by diversion of the river Ray, which effectively transferred flooding elsewhere. When the users of this land returned the routing of the stream to its old course, they found themselves in breach of the law, but refused to acknowledge its equity. Some 57 taken were taken into custody by 21 Yeomen for escort to Oxford at the time of the St Giles Fair. On passing through the town the escort was set upon by a throng of over 1000 with sticks, stones and brickbats and those under arrest, untied and released, which illustrates graphically the parlous situation in which the Yeomanry was placed: they were in no position to arbitrate on the law of the land, yet the shift in events opened a credibility gap. In a final fling, during December the Stockport and Dunham Massey Troops of the 1st Cheshire were called out to Hyde.

1831 The Reform Bill

There were disturbances around the country during 1831 with the passage of the Bill through the House of Commons and again in the House of Lords. Basically the scheme of representation had not changed for over a 100 years, therefore it took no account of the demographic changes brought in by the industrial revolution. As the consequence constituencies were not organised to give fair and equal representation. [11] Counties were represented by two MPs irrespective of size, but not Scotland or Wales who had only one. Boroughs of some five different varieties were most generally represented by two MPs, but not Scotland, Wales or Ireland, who had one. However the right to vote for a borough was restrictive, with some 56 having less than 40 voters. Cities such as Birmingham, Manchester, Leeds and Sheffield had no MPs, because they did not qualify as Boroughs! In 1831, Lancashire with a population of 1.3 million had only 14 MPs, while Cornwall with 300,000 people had 42 MPs. Also, it will be remembered that women at this time did not have votes of any sort. A further issue was that the new class of prosperous businessman objected to domination of Parliament by landowners. The appearance of revolution once again in France, the death of the King (the enemy of reform) and the estrangement of a Tory lobby because of the grant of Catholic emancipation laid open the way to the passing of the Bill. Nevertheless tempers rose around the country which made it a testing time for the Yeomanry.

Wiltshire The Salisbury Troop, of the Wiltshire Yeomanry was in a near state of mutiny. The Troop Sergeant-Major and 30 privates signed a 'remonstrance' when Lord Arundell, their commander voted against the Great Reform Bill. Eight privates resigned, to be followed by his Lordship and a Cornet who had been overly supportive of him.

Edinburgh The Midlothian Corps was eventually called out on 3rd May, to control an Election riot in connection with the Reform Bill. The mob attempted to throw Edinburgh's Lord Provost over the parapet of the North Bridge. With 1000 constables, order was restored after some hours, during which more than a third of the Yeomanry were wounded.

Nottingham Between October 7th to 20th the Reform Bill was rejected by the House of Lords. Immediately riots broke out in many large towns, of a violence seldom equalled in the history of England. The Riot Act was read in numerous places. Further trouble erupted at nightfall at Nottingham. The Mayor was wounded and trampled by the crowd, but refused to summon the Yeomanry. Order was restored by the 15th Hussars. Rioting re-commenced during the afternoon of the 11th, when the whole of the South Nottingham Yeomanry were called out on the insistence of the 15th Hussars' Colonel. Before they could be mustered the 15th Hussars were over-run and the mob burned the castle to the ground. By dawn of the 12th, both forces commenced clearing the town and surrounding areas of unruly elements. Two Troops of the Sherwood Rangers were called out at this point for duty in Mansfield. Further trouble was sparked on October 13th, with disturbances put down at Plumtree and Mansfield by two Troops of the Sherwood Rangers. These concluded actions which lasted 6 days.

On the 4th January riotous Denbigh miners marched on Shrewsbury to release comrades from jail. The South Shropshire Yeomanry assembled the next day to repel the 'Welsh invasion' and the miners dispersed. Early in the year a panic-stricken Government recalled the disbanded Yeomanry and augmented the force, so that within a few months this was brought up to 20,000 men. The Himley Troop of Staffordshire was called out on 15th January for seven days service. The Enclosure Acts next brought the Oxfordshire Hussars into the frame at Otmoor during May and again in July and September. In May the miners of the Pottery district were on strike. A Squadron of 10th Hussars and the Newcastle Troop of Staffordshire Yeomanry, with a company of the 43rd Regiment were called out to aid the Civil Power: Order was restored after four days. From the 1st June the Burton Troop of the Staffordshire Yeomanry was called to quell a riot caused by the find of a silver hoard, discovered during alterations to the course of the river Dove. They restored order and remained on duty for three days until relieved by Infantry.

During June there was a serious rash of riots around Swansea and Merthyr Tydfil, connected with coal mining. In one incident a major and 34 men of the Swansea and Fairwood Troop of the Glamorgan Yeomanry, gave up their arms to 400 miners who had sprung a friendly ambush and had in any case first taken the major hostage. According to Beckett[12] a Regular officer reported this as an agreed surrender of arms and the make-up of the force was low on farmers. Later that year some 25 people were killed and about 100 seriously wounded. Three Corps of Yeomanry were disbanded on 11th July 1831, following the orders of the Home Secretary, for adjudged mis-behaviour.

On October 8th, Derby was defended by firearms, with the jail saved on the 9th, only by a detachment of 15th Hussars, who were in action on the 10th. The Yeomanry arrived that day from Derby, Leicester and Stafford, just in time to prevent the position being over-run. On the 19th October disturbances occurred at Sherborne. The rioters refused to disperse on the evening of the 20th. A Troop of Dorset Yeomanry were employed, with the threat of using firearms. On the 21st October threshing machines were destroyed at Stower Provest and order was restored by the Sturminster Troop of the Dorset Yeomanry. On the 24th October, owing to a reduction of wages in the lace industry, men at Tiverton struck. That night the mob attacked the house of an unpopular foreman and although he managed to escape, they proceeded to smash up his furniture. The Tiverton and Exeter Troops assembled and remained on duty till the 28th to maintain order. Obviously there was much sympathy here for the strikers, as there were resignations from Lord Rolle's Yeomanry, whilst the *London Alfred* , a London Paper, remarked on how slow the Tiverton Troop were in making themselves useful on the 24-25th October.

The Queen's Square Riot, Bristol

Over the period 29th to 31st October a most severe riot played itself out at Bristol, on the appearance of the Recorder. The Mansion House was sacked, with the jail and Bishop's Palace burnt to the ground. Due to inept handling these three days of riots go down as the worst in the history of England. Officially, twelve people were killed and 67 wounded taken to hospital, although in the latter case there were obviously more. Other accounts talk of 500 dead, through drunkenness,

wounds and then being burnt to death in the blazing buildings. Regular Cavalry and the Bedminster Troop of North Somerset Yeomanry were called, dismissed and re-called again, but poorly used. Trouble spread into surrounding parts. The Doddington Troop of Gloucestershire Hussars and the whole of the North Somerset Yeomanry next converged on Bristol.

The 5th November saw the Exeter Reform riots promptly subdued by 1st Devon Yeomanry. Also during November the whole of Worcestershire Yeomanry was put at short notice. During the ensuing riot the ringleaders were extracted from within the disorderly crowds and later confined. Also on the 30th November the Staffordshire Yeomanry mobilised to subdue a large body of miners who were marching on Wolverhampton, releasing prisoners at Oldbury Court House and looting shops. The 1st December saw the whole of Worcester Yeomanry called out to occupy Dudley, Oldbury, Halesowen and Kidderminster. They assisted a troop of Dragoons to retain prisoners under escort and during the evening escorted 120 prisoners to Stafford, Worcester and Shrewsbury jails. The following day there was a serious riot at Dudley. Three Troops of the Worcester Yeomanry endured much stone throwing, before the mob was dispersed. The following day the ringleaders were rounded-up. There were sporadic outbursts about the county, the most serious being at Castle Bromwich. This was dispersed by four Troops of the Worcester Yeomanry, against mobs with sickles and poles. The period from 6th to 20th December marked the last riots due to Reform Bill. The South Shropshire Yeomanry was called out to aid the Civil Power at Shrewsbury, Wellington, Shifnal and Ironbridge. Again the Berkshire Yeomanry were called out during the year to control riots.

1832 On January 11th the North Devon Yeomanry were requisitioned by two magistrates to supply 60-70 men at Great Torrington for 9 am the following day, because of a tumultuous assemblage threatening to obstruct the taking of prisoners to the County gaol. In response the Sheepwash and Torrington Troops mustered and remained on duty till 1 pm. A Troop of 83 men turned out from the Ayrshire Yeomanry to protect the execution of a criminal and Fairlie's Troop performed the same unpleasant duty the following June, when the culprit was a man called Ramsay, who had shot a constable at an Orange Procession in Girvan. The Islip action of the previous year was next repeated in April and May, the Oxford Corps remaining on duty for 18 days on one occasion. Objections now arose over Land Enclosure and provided the next eruption with the Oxford Hussars once again called to Otmoor. The Worcester Yeomanry put a stop to tow rope cutting on the Severn between Worcester and Gloucester, during June. Below Tewkesbury a similar duty was performed by the Gloucestershire Yeomanry. After 20 offenders had been arrested the practice died out for want of leaders. There was a serious election riot in December at Frome lasting two days with the North Somerset Yeomanry in attendance. Lastly, the 1st Duke of Cornwall's Yeomanry were called to guard a wreck during the year.

1833 A meeting at Oldbury during October was followed by a strike by colliers for shorter working hours. Although it finished peacefully, there had been alarm, so that the magistrates had assembled a detachment of 3rd Dragoon Guards, the Himley Troop from Staffordshire and the local Dudley Troop. Two Troops of North Devon Yeomanry were called in December for nine days for 'wreck protection duty'. Here there were 2000 prospective looters of the cargo vessel *Elizabeth* with a £40,000 cargo stranded on the bar at Bideford.

1834 A Parliamentary Election took place this year and the 5th Ayrshire Troop was requisitioned to march into Ayr, where the police had been overpowered and the mob were in control. On arrival they had to clear the barricades and withstand a barrage of stones and blue lights thrown to frighten the horses. Things played out by 11 pm and the Troop stood-down leaving a sergeant and 12 men on guard and the Troop remained on duty for four days.

1835 Kent was a very disturbed county and in May the 'E' Troop of the East Kent Regiment was stoned all the way up Canterbury High Street, whilst escorting 20 prisoners from Sittingbourne, held as the result of a riot at Rodmersham. They were obliged to retreat into Fountain Yard and barricade themselves.

1836 The North Devon Yeomanry were called to subdue a riot at Sheepwash, arising from the introduction of the new Poor Laws. Some hayricks were fired. The Fremington Troop beat off an attack from a menacing crowd on 2nd February and delivered prisoners to the Torrington jail. Later on the 10th a riotous mob assembled at Sheepwash when the Relieving Officer of the Torrington Union arrived to disburse money and doles of bread. Previously the crowd had broken the windows of his house and wrecked the local bread depot. The ensuing trial of five ringleaders on the 12th was threatened by gangs wanting to rescue them, but they were successfully transferred to the Exeter gaol. On February 17th the Fremington and Sheepwash Troops marched to Combemartin following disturbances and their presence restored order. Once again the Berkshire Yeomanry were called during the year to perform riot duty.

1837 Riots in the Potteries arose because of the defeat of the Liberal candidate at Stoke-on-Trent in the General Election. The Newcastle Troop of the Staffordshire Yeomanry were called out following the sacking of a Police Office. Two days later three Troops stood by whilst Police made house to house searches and arrested 40 persons. On 26-7th July the Morley Troop of the 1st Cheshire Corps was called to Stockport. And again the Berkshire Yeomanry were called out for riot duty during the year.

1834-6-8, 1838, 1842, 1848 Chartism [11]

The movement arose from unfinished business taken up from the Reform Act, which had its origins in the industrial revolution. The period was broken into four phases of which the first was evolutionary and had little in the way of a public face. The working population were disenchanted with their lot to the point of rebellion. In briefest of terms: they had poor conditions in the factories, workshops and mines; poor living conditions; they were disillusioned with the practical effects of the Reform act; they had witnessed the collapse of Trade Unionism under government hostility; they were angered by the 1834 Poor Law first introduced into the North during 1837. Perhaps the most cogent reason for action was the trade depression, with consequent unemployment and hunger. The Charter had six main objectives: universal male suffrage; vote by secret ballot; equal electoral districts; annual Parliaments; payment of Members of Parliament; removal of the property qualification; and much else besides.

The second phase sprang into life for a two year period. As the result of threatening meetings, a rejected petition and the ensuing riots most of the leadership went to gaol. As these emerged in 1842 a further spate of ugly meetings followed. Characteristically the House refused a second petition and riots immediately broke out in many large towns

Plate 3

'Battle of Pythouse' 1830. Part of the picture covering the last agriculture worker's revolt.

The Royal Wiltshire Yeomanry

Plate 4   The Abbot of Downside

Yeomanry Gallop, South Africa. A Lady Butler portrait. So often the Boers got away because our horses were overburdened with equipment. Our mounted troops were also poorly armed against the hunting rifles carried by the other side. The British employed 518,000 horses, of which 347,000 died from overwork, malnutrition and disease, with less than 2% lost in battle. Wars are not won decisively by the wanton misuse of scarce resources.

including, Birmingham, Bolton, Chester, Derby, Leeds, London, Manchester, Nottingham and Stoke-on-Trent. These abated and the membership fell away as the trade cycle revived. In 1847 a further trade depression set in with a huge increase in the unemployed. There were grandiose plans made by the leadership but badly organised and the movement began to fade away after 1848. The movement was destined to fail, through lack of Middle Class support, which meant not much representation in Parliament. The campaign was widespread, long fought and riven by factions and of course, deeply penetrated by spies. If it offered any lesson it was the need for teamwork.

1838-46 The Anti-Corn Law League [11]
This movement more or less paralleled Chartism but aimed to achieve a similar objective using opposite methods. It was a further bitter fight against landed interests, though using entirely constitutional means. In a long running public debate it fielded superb orators and informed the whole electorate of its single objective, using the newly invented penny post. The country was administered as 12 districts and the whole operation properly financed. It introduced a corps of 12 MPs into Parliament and hammered the issue relentlessly there and around the country with regular well run public meetings. It forced the Tories to adopt a measure it avowedly despised and split the party in the process. The Chartists often attempted to disrupt these meetings but were thwarted by Irish working class support, brought in as ushers.

1838 A Troop of the Ayrshire Yeomanry were called to Kilwinning by the Sheriff during the election due to quarrels between electors and considerable rioting, to the point that one of the candidates had his clothes torn from his body. Order was restored. This matter when raised adversely in the House of Commons was quickly withdrawn when the true facts became known.

1839-1843 The Rebecca or Turnpike Riots [15]
These began for two main causes. Poor Relief in Wales was considered unfair, for although relief was granted, it had to be repaid when work was resumed. Also, parishes were too poor to maintain the roads, which were built by contractors who reimbursed themselves by establishing toll gates, often illegally close together. Bands of men roamed the country, burning down these offending gates. They are said to have been clad in long white shirts, with faces blackened, and to have accompanied their moonlight wanderings with the blowing of horns and the firing of

guns. Their motto was taken from the Bible, Genesis XXIV v60. 'And they blessed Rebekah, and said unto her, Thou art our sister, be thou the mother of thousands of millions, and let thy seed possess the gate of those that hate them.' These disturbances found the Government at a disadvantage. Due to the disbandment of Glamorgan and Carmarthen Yeomanry some 15 years previously and the absence of any Yeomanry in Cardiganshire or Brecknockshire, there existed no more than three Troops of the Castlemartin Yeomanry to cover the whole of West Wales. It appears the legislation allowing the erection of turnpikes was poorly thought out by the Government and under the pressure of public opinion they gave ground. The first incident occurred at Efailwen, on the Cardigan to Narberth road, when a newly erected turnpike was hacked down by an angry crowd. More serious riots took place by St Clear's in Carmarthenshire during 1842.

1839 Over April the South Shropshire Yeomanry was called to put down riots in Wales. They marched to Newtown, Montgomery and Llanidloes and dispersed rioters, who had held the town for five days and took prisoners. Monmouth was next attacked by miners! As with the agricultural riots in 1829-31 it had the effect of bringing back many of the Yeomanry disbanded or slimmed by the 1838 economies.

In May more riots erupted at Westbury and Trowbridge and were put down by the 10th Hussars, working with the Warminster, Melksham and Devizes Troops of Wiltshire Yeomanry. At Trowbridge the mob consisted of 5000 persons armed with cutlasses, pistols and staves. Also during May the Sherwood Rangers were ordered to march to Mansfield, the stronghold of the local Chartists. Four days later the South Nottinghamshire Yeomanry relieved them and remained on duty for 12 days. The use of two complete regiments avoided such riots as occurred in Wales. Again in May riots broke out in the Potteries. The new Police were unpopular and at Lane End a disturbance developed into a riot when they arrested some ringleaders. The Staffordshire Yeomanry Troop appearing the following day were pelted with stones whilst escorting prisoners to Newcastle. Order was then restored with a further two Troops, but they were not dismissed for three days, when they were relieved by detachments of the 79th Regiment and the Rifle Brigade. On the 14th July at Birmingham, there were many seditious meetings and riots following police 'interference'. The following day the whole of the

Worcestershire and Staffordshire Yeomanries were called out. The Dudley, Birmingham, Hagley, Moseley, Stourbridge, Lye, Himley, and Handsworth areas were each occupied by the Yeomanry. It was not until the 25th August that the Regiments were dismissed. Notwithstanding such events, the Government pressed on with economies, linked to the establishment of police. The Tabley and Tatton Troops of Cheshire were called out to Macclesfield on July 22-23rd. Later in August, over the 12-18th the whole of the Regiment was called to Chester, Hyde and Macclesfield. Several arrests were made in connection with the Rebecca riots and two Troops of the Castlemartin Yeomanry rode to Tavernspite to maintain order during the ensuing trial.

1840 There was a nil expense this year under Public Order and no record of riots.

1841 The 1st Cheshire Yeomanry turned out 10 Troops for a day and the Congleton Troop served locally during July. The Sherwood Rangers turned out three Troops for a day and the Staffordshire Corps turned out two Troops for four days.

1842 This year was notable for the long overdue reintroduction of Income Tax. For an initial period of three years it was set at 7d. per Pound on incomes over £150 per annum. Income Tax has been with us ever since! The Southern Regiment of the West Riding had six Troops on duty for six days suppressing the Chartist Riots. On April 24th, after nearly three years of comparative quiet, riots recommenced in the Midlands. A mob of some 2000 nail makers assembled at Dudley and took the local magistrates prisoner. The next day the Himley troop of the Staffordshire Yeomanry restored order. The day following, the Worcestershire Yeomanry was called and the Regiment was quartered in Stourbridge, Dudley, Oldbury, Bromsgrove, Kidderminster and Cradley. For about a month the whole area was patrolled until peace was restored. In total the Staffordshire Corps had 11 Troops deployed for 25 days and the Worcestershire Yeomanry for the phenomenal 10 Troops for 71 days! The Yorkshire Hussars were placed on standby on 3rd June and warned over disturbances due on the 13th August. Various dispositions were taken up over the ensuing days. The Riot Act was read at Leeds and the Mill of Messrs Maclea and March attacked, when 25 prisoners were taken on the 17th. More mill attacks took place over the following days with some prisoners taken and general actions took place at various points

within the West Riding until the 22nd, when the Yeomanry was dismissed to their homes. The service totalled 10 Troops serving 14 days. During July serious Chartist disturbances broke out in Lancashire, spilling over into other counties. There the services of three Troops was necessary for 20 days. It spread into Cheshire, requiring the services of 10 Troops for 28 days. In particular the Congleton Troop served at Ashton-under-Lyne over July 15-18th and from 22-23rd, in company with the Tatton Troop. They were followed by the whole Regiment on 26th August until 8th September, working Stockport, Congleton, and Macclefield. The troubles moved into Staffordshire where 11 Troops were employed over 25 days, whilst Warwickshire needed six Troops for three days and Yorkshire, where the Hussars mobilised 10 Troops for 14 days and the South West Yorkshire Yeomanry called out six Troops for six days. From here the disturbances spread into the manufacturing towns of Scotland and to the Welsh collieries. In the Potteries and collieries of Staffordshire the riots were particularly serious, lasting from early July until the middle of September. During these critical times the troops were forced to use firearms and charge with the sword. Detachments of the 1st and 2nd Dragoon Guards, the Staffordshire and the Cheshire Yeomanry were employed. Many requisitions were made for the escort of prisoners and for the patrolling of the roads surrounding the areas in ferment. Each Troop was on duty for an average of 22 days, but the Himley troop was not relieved for 50 days at a time they were required for harvesting. Meanwhile fresh disturbances were dealt with by the Worcestershire Yeomanry at Dudley, Stourbridge and Oldbury. From early July their Squadrons took it in turns to patrol the districts affected. The Lanarkshire Yeomanry were called out on 12th August, with four Troops employed for 34 days, in connection with a colliers strike. The effect of this was to close down a large number of surrounding furnaces, thus throwing some 30,000 people out of work. Without any means of support or sustenance these people were starving and took to the fields, robbing farmers of their potato and turnip crops. The Yeomanry in patrolling a wide area had some hard bouts with the locals and many broken heads, but none was killed. They remained on duty till 15th September. Troops of the Ayrshire Corps were also called in connection with collier's strikes, using six Troops for 71 days. Some were on duty for a fortnight occupied mainly in night patrols. Others spent 33 days on duty because the locked-out miners had attacked new hands and even shot one of them. The Chartist

Riots now seemed over and a Horse Guards order for 8th October 1842 was published stating the Yeomanry was relieved from permanent duty. The emergency had been such that all forces had been placed under the orders of the Commander-in-Chief, the Duke of Wellington. In the winter the more serious *Rebecca Riots* took place by St Clear's in Carmarthenshire and the Castlemartin Yeomanry took duty, turn and turn about for 25 days. Whilst they were guarding the Pwlltrays Gate, the gate and tollhouse on the other side of town were burnt down. Unconnected with the above the following Corps were turned out: The Derby and Chaddeston Troop for 11 days, the Radbourne Troop for five days, the Gloucester Hussars with the portion of a Troop for a day, the Leicester Corps with three Troops for 10 days, the North Salopian Regiment with two Troops for two days, the Ilminster Troop for two days and the Westmorland Yeomanry with three Troops for nine days.

1843 The previous riots grew more serious in January, spreading into the counties of Glamorgan, Brecon and Cardigan. So on the 7th February three Troops of The Pembroke Corps were called out for 26 days of active duty. They were out again on 28th June and set to guard Narberth, St Clears and Lampeter, but without positive results. The end came in November 21st with a trial at which the perpetrators were dealt with lightly because the Government perceived they had a genuine grievance. Thus ended a trying and persistent duty for three Troops over a period of 115 days. Once again those Yeomanry serving for no pay, were placed on pay and allowances, when fresh disorder again called for their services: Also the 2nd West Yorkshire and Midlothian Yeomanry were revived.

1845 On December 23rd the North Devon Yeomanry were again recalled to wreck-protection duty. Two wrecks - the *Ness* and the *Albion* - had to be protected from the public, who were anxious to loot, the Ness, with a cargo of sugar and rum especially. During the year the following additional detachments were provided: The Oxford Hussars, a detachment for two days; The Westmorland Corps, a single Troop for 10 days and detachments from three Troops for seven days. The Berkshire Corps were again out during the year on riot duty.

1846 A serious riot in Exeter arose over the middlemen cornering the market in potatoes. Cornmills and shops were looted. The Kenn, Exeter, 2nd Bicton and Powderham Troops were stoned on arrival. Order was restored on the fourth day with the arrest of the ringleaders. Less dramatic perhaps was, the prevention of a 'war' between English and Irish navvies building the Carlisle to Lancaster railway, by the Westmoreland and Cumberland Yeomanry. Lastly, the East Lothians were re-raised as the consequence of the Chartist movement.

1847 On May 21st the Fremington Troop of the North Devon Yeomanry, was called to quell a bread riot. Altogether the Devon action comprised, the 1st Devons with one Troop out for six days and five Troops out for three and the North Devon Corps with two Troops for a day. Somerset was another unsettled county. The North Somerset Corps were called on for, five Troops for a day, two Troops for two days, and one Troop for three days. Then the West Somerset Yeomanry were even more extended, with two Troops called for 11 days, one Troop for 10 days, two Troops for nine days, two Troops for six days and a single Troop for five. The Ayrshire Corps was also active with single Troops out for two and eight days and two Troops out for four, six and seven days respectively.

1848 The whole of the Ayrshire Yeomanry was called out on 8th March and kept on duty for a week due to the most serious rioting in Glasgow. Later in July news was received of the *Smith-O'Brian* outbreak, so the whole regiment was once again assembled and the question put, whether in the case of an emergency they would be prepared to serve in any part of the Kingdom, to which they responded with three rousing cheers. Next, on March 9th the Lanark Corps received orders to march to Hamilton, which it did the following day, where it remained until the 16th. The process was repeated between the 2-9th August at Holytown because of more striking colliers. The Midlothian Corps had been warned to be ready during March, in connection with the *Chartists Movement*. In the event they were not ordered out until 31st July, when they worked with Regular Cavalry to disperse rioters. Again, but less seriously, the Ayrshire peace was broken at the *Battle of Ballock Broe*. On the famous 12th of July a band of Orangemen met an almost equal number of Catholics halfway between Maybole and Crosshill, obviously by arrangement and an awful set-to began. A Troop of Yeomanry was called, whereupon the two bands joined together and sent the Yeomen fleeing: an intelligent thing to do under the circumstances! Whatever the truth of this supposed incident, an Orangeman was sent to prison in Ayr at this time. On the 5th April the South Nottingham

Yeomanry were called, for the last time, as the government became alarmed at the renewed activity of the Chartists, who aimed at establishing an *English Republic*. The various meetings were broken up or managed. The Newark Troop spent several weeks maintaining order in Mansfield. Elsewhere as the result of unsettled conditions the following Corps were active. The 2nd Buckinghamshire with eight Troops for eight days; The 1st Cheshire with the Tatton and Congleton Troops on the 10th April; The Derby and Chaddesden with two single call-outs for two and four days respectively; The Radbourne Troop for three days and the Repton and Gresley Troop for two; The West Essex with a detachment for a day; The Upper Ward of Lanark, with two Troops for eight days; The Duke of Lancaster's Own with a single Troop for a day. The Leicester Corps were active during the year with five Troops for six days, one Troop out for two and two Troops out for four. The Royal Midlothian Corps had five Troops out for a day and the Uxbridge Troop for a day also. The South Nottinghamshire Corps had five Troops on duty for three days, the Staffordshire a single Troop for one and two days respectively. The Warwickshire Corps was involved with six Troops for three days, two Troops for two days, three Troops for three and a single Troop for three days. Lastly, the 2nd West Yorkshire had four Troops out for six days, a single Troop for three and a further four Troops for two days.

1855 March was a further troubled month with the miners and Pottery workers of Staffordshire, owing to a reduction in wages. There were riots in Bilston, Walsall and other places with order restored when the Wolverhampton and Walsall troops of the Staffordshire Yeomanry were assisted by a detachment of the Essex Rifles over a period of five days. November saw a food riot at Teignmouth, where a mob of 2000 attacked bakers' and butchers' shops. Two days later this was followed by a riot in Exeter, where nearly every provision shop was looted. On the following day, detachments of the Exeter, Powderham, Exmouth and Bicton Troops of the 1st Devon Yeomanry were called to assist two companies of the Devonshire Regiment, which had arrived from Plymouth.

1856 Industrial troubles next caused the Forfar Yeomanry to be revived, only to be disbanded again in 1862. This was the last regiment to be raised under the old order as Yeomanry Cavalry. The Glasgow Yeomanry was called out as a precaution during the

great strike of miners in the coal districts of the Lothians, Lanarkshire and Ayrshire. Once again the Lanarkshire Corps were out for several weeks, when 40,000 colliers struck for more wages and would allow no others to work. On the 15th of May 70 men of the Upper Ward were stationed at Holytown and the same number at Coatbridge. During the rioting the Yeomanry frequently drew swords and charged into the rioters. The women, as is so often the case, were fiercer than the men, seizing the Yeomen by the legs and trying to unhorse them. The Corps remained on duty till 10th June when the strike collapsed.

Conclusions
There was a Call-out to the food riots in Devon in 1867 and possibly this was the last riot attended by Yeomanry. In fact, Devon County was literally, the first and the last, when it came to riots! Owing to an efficient police force being established, they were gradually relieved of their civil duties, whilst events on the Continent caused them to be gradually brought back to their original status as the Cavalry of the Home Defence Army. In 1860 the corps numbered 49, but by 1871 these were reduced to 45. Even then, three were single troops and these were now disbanded. The Force was then organised as 42 regiments. The South and North Shropshire Corps were next amalgamated in 1872, the Midlothian disbanded in 1873, also the West Essex in 1877, so the Force numbered 39 regiments until the 2nd West York Yeomanry was broken up for want of officers in 1890, bringing the number to 38.

Professional historians have counselled restraint in arriving at judgmental conclusions, over this complex era. Social disorder was no stranger to the United Kingdom though the causes changed. Initially failed harvests and a slump in international trade provided the impetus, since there was not enough money to buy food. Added to this came a period of regressive taxation, meaning the poor had virtually no disposable income and were thus unable to stimulate the economy. Only slowly did the Government perceive the nature of the problem and set out to rectify it. Thus, the Yeomanry were drawn deeply into the resulting troubles directly the Napoleonic War ended. The Government was faced by three competing interests; the landed magnates, the industrial middle class and the industrial and agricultural labour force. The first used all the advantages of an entrenched position, whilst the latter two had different perceptions over how best to advance their causes: one used political guile, but not before the latter had adopted rebellion threatening rallies and mounting attacks on the peaceful meetings of the former. The Yeomanry involvement was that of maintaining public order and the protection of property: that is to say they played no rôle as social arbiters.

Were the Yeomanry loyal and were they effective? Such a question is apt to make military moustaches twitch since it has always been a matter of honour to serve constitutionally. Against this, they were hardly uncaring, though if they had been unsuccessful at their work they would have been promptly disbanded. Two attempts at economy, in 1828 and 1838, redounded on the head of ministers with increased costs and the reforming of disbanded units. If English society of the period had its faults, it was the inability of central government to orchestrate a scheme representing the interests of society *as a whole*. In today's parlance this amounts to strategic planning, something which flies in the face of *laissez faire*. It seems the British are inherently bad at the former and successive Governments feel the ultimate costs of the latter are worth paying.

As noted in an earlier chapter, the Government was one thing and the law another. If the former could not or would not make it clear, it had to settle for what it got and even during those early days a strong pull existed against central government. Let us examine the protocol. Power to govern locally was diffused through lords-lieutenant to magistrates, the courts of law and all the imperfections of the jury system. There was no universal power and this remains the case today. Now whilst the Army could go away, the Yeomanry were always to remain to attract the plaudits or opprobrium of the latest fracas. Being so much closer to the affairs of disorder meant the limits were skimmed repeatedly, revealing the inadequacies of the law and more importantly the lack of redress it offered those they faced. Also the 'other ranks' comprising a Troop had more than a small stake in local enterprise and they were never a mindless appendage awaiting the bidding of their officers. Between the determined response to do their duty and mutiny lay various shades of compliance. Since there is no specific record of mutiny as such, it is the intensity of these shades that needs examination.

So did the Yeomanry wait upon such requisitions as they got? They would have exceeded their powers without, though adjudged laggardly when failing to turn out promptly when such were issued. The instances below serve to illustrate when their arrival at some scene was estimated to have been 'slow'. Then, did the rank and file offer blind obedience to their officers interests as opposed to orders? Certainly not in matters of social policy, particularly at the time of the Reform Bill. Lastly, how well was Government served by swithering in national policy toward the Yeomanry with its large scale disbandments during 1828 and 1838? Well, it very quickly produced the undignified spectacle of the monied interests, who had so vociferously lobbied for economy, pleading for a return of the former yeomen. Many of these had been undertaken at a personal cost, besides which any recall was open to negotiation, hardly orders, which is what happened.

The way is now open to catalogue a number of events bearing on the question of loyalty. In the following Ian Beckett[12] cites some occasions when a response to a call was less than prompt, or there were undercurrents dissuading those in command from issuing certain orders. It was always crucial for dispositions of the Yeomanry to be made in advance, so the two questions need to be taken together, also the matter of impartiality. The reported instances are few and whilst none makes a convincing case, many others may well have been 'swept under the carpet' of the times.

In August 1820, for example members of the Hertfordshire Troop were reported as unlikely to act against rioters sympathetic to the cause of Queen Caroline. The treatment of a Royal wife had been the cause of national disaffection, taken up by the working-class and it was something best avoided by the Yeomanry. As instanced earlier , the Swing riots found it impossible to re-raise the Yeomanry directly amongst the tenant farmers of East Sussex and Kent, but it was as a matter distinct from those actually serving. Other suspicions then focused upon the Reform crisis and extended to Birmingham (1830), Carmarthen (May 1831) and Cheltenham (1832). On these occasions those in command picked up the mutterings of disaffection and tailored their dealings with the rank and file, so as to avoid gratuitous provocation. In March 1831, there was much talk amongst men of the Andover Troop over an unwillingness to act against Reform riots and the threat of resignations if such orders were issued and as a consequence none were issued. Many resignations came at this time from the Hertfordshhire Yeomanry, that in Wolverhampton and in Salisbury. In the latter instance officers seen to have allowed their prejudices to become too public also found it necessary to resign. A similar round robin occurred in the Doncaster Troop with the resignation of 22 men, whilst elements of the Dorset Yeomanry were similarly considered unreliable. This freedom to resign was not something open to common soldiery, yet since it formed a legitimate avenue to all yeomen it seems beyond complaint for them to use it. Thus they were free to exercise conscience without dishonour; a novel military situation!

Less admirable, however, was the overt political motivation of the Hindon Troop, dubbed the 'Wiltshire Cossacks' in supporting a Tory candidate at the hustings during 1818-19. Granted this was done in mufti and in a county not famous for tolerating unruly elements. Then there was the ruse for disarming the 34 man Swansea and Fairwood Troop, at Merthyr Tydfil on 4th June 1831. Here it was alleged that arms were given over voluntarily though by that time their major was a hostage of 400 miners, who held his life in jeopardy. This resulted in the later disbandment of the unfortunate Corps and two others adjoining.

It was from there one hears how the Corps were low on farmers, though how a predominantly industrial area was to be policed by farmers has not been satisfactorily explained. However, over and above the availability of the *right types*, the farming community had to face the unwelcome fact that civil disturbance when it came almost always coincided with a major agricultural activity, such as harvesting, which couldn't wait ; so it was catch-22 all over. This former argument has persisted into the present days with the so-called 'right types' unable to service their industrial equipment properly. At the time of Chartism, which erupted after two swingeing Yeomanry economies, the imbalance between the rural and urban Corps was so upset, as to deny cover to large areas of the industrial North and the Midlands. A better case of disloyalty can be laid at the door of those in government, who created a raft of unworkable situations.

As to the question of effectiveness, we have the earlier opinion of the Duke of Wellington, in regard to use of cavalry at riots and likely dangers of employing infantry. From the context it can be assumed it was light cavalry he had in mind and all Yeomanry was light cavalry. In a letter by Major Mileham, in 'History Today', [16] he very precisely delineates elements of the problem facing the Yeomanry commanders of the time. He writes "As the author of a book on the Yeomanry regiments, I was much interested in Phillip Lawson's article 'Reassessing Peterloo' (March 1988). I remain, however, very sceptical about one aspect, conventionally held by historians; that is the supposition that regular troops, the Yeomanry Cavalry, Volunteers or Militia, were efficient and well trained in 'crowd control' during the eighteenth and nineteenth centuries. The efficacy of minimum force was certainly implicit in the understanding of military aid to the civil power and deliberate and heavy-handed provocation of the rebellious factions was almost always avoided - discretion being the better part of valour. Mounted troops could indeed be sensibly used to deter crowds from turning violent and destructive and this worked in the great majority of instances when regular or part-time troops were called out. Deterrence always involves bluff. Occasionally, when matters appeared to be turning really ugly, deliberate military intimidation also worked. The use of cavalry, however, for shock action (a heavy cavalry role over true cavalry country, i.e. the wide open spaces of Continental Europe) was enormously risky in the context of crowd control, even if the 'flat of the sword' was ordered and crowd dispersal routes were considered. Furthermore, 'snatch squad' and arrest tactics were not in the drill books of the period and anyway could not have been carried out by men mounted on horseback. They could and did assist in running incidents where mobility and speed was essential, but Peterloo could not have been so described.

Military efficiency was not of the highest order amongst the Yeomanry Corps at the time and any training that they did was of little relevance to the difficult task of keeping the peace; appropriate techniques were worked out much later. Thus Captain Nicolson, commanding the Falkirk troop embodied at the height of the troubles in central Scotland eight month after Peterloo, wrote to his commanding officer at Stirling stating: 'I am just going to take the troop to the moors and practice themselves [sic] and myself a bit...' And then 'My troop have not turned out well and I should have been ashamed to show ourselves in Glasgow,'[where the trouble was expected]. 'I must have a reform of the troop. I hope there will be no occasion for our going to Glasgow, or Kilsyth or anywhere, as there must be an overwhelming force in the neighbourhood...'. So much for troops who might be expected to keep their nerve in a crisis.

Perhaps the incident which best highlights another 'danger' of attempts at crowd control took place in 1830. A troop of the Swansea Yeomanry Cavalry was met by a crowd, which appearing to be peaceful, first good naturedly engulfed the yeomen and then quickly disarmed them. It was a deliberate ruse; happily no physical harm came to either side, but the embarrassment can be imagined.

Effective military assistance to the civil power always demands well disciplined troops, trained in sensible tactics and set reasonable tasks. In my view, too much was asked of the Yeomanry and regular cavalry at Peterloo: their bluff was called and in a very frightening situation they lost their 'cool' - as did the crowd."

This letter admirably sums up core military philosophy; which is to manipulate, if one must, a situation short of a blood bath. The latter is not only counter-productive, it has also to be explained! Bluff and fright are far more likely to attain desired objectives, besides which there were no resources to meet an ongoing rebellion.

Turning to the subject of historical conclusions leads onto more contentious ground. Perhaps it is simplistic and more theoretical than real, but the single and most over-riding conclusion for the period was the need for universal suffrage, because that would have placed the responsibility for the election of government in the hands of the governed. All of this is so easy to say now with the benefit of hindsight, however, the social problems of the time required the full machinery of government and this at least should have been perceived. The *three cornered nature of the struggle for representation* meant that many of the social ills of the period were not addressed for 20-30 years, by which time they had assumed epidemic proportions. The first inroads came by way of the 1848 Public Health Act, chiefly due to the work of Edwin Chadwick, though cholera entered England by Sunderland in 1832 and was no respecter of persons.

The Riot Act solved few problems, though it provided a decorum against which each side was able to gauge their actions. It was much later repealed in 1967 and no thought given to its re-introduction during later riots associated with the introduction of new technology. As an attempt to criminalise political dissent it was a failure. Many, yet only a small percentage, were unjustly imprisoned and transported to Australia it is true, though as a rule, juries refused to convict in capital cases, so executions were few.

An important lesson for large concentrations of people meeting up in contention was the need for discipline. Whilst this might be expected on the part of law officers and the military it was also characteristic of those they met to oppose, particularly skilled artisans, despite the numerous confusions set up by the former. The Yeomanry can derive much satisfaction from emerging with credit after a long period of a wretched employment in solving other men's problems. What for us is a mere fragment of history was to them a living reality. They had to think and act rationally under a brutal pressure and ride home with the hope that none of their number had besmirched the reputation of the Corps of which they were proud members. They rarely got the rate for the job, collected a fair share of bruises, their horses were frequently abused and terrified and for long periods they enjoyed no such thing as a private life. So often they were pitched into the conflict, as the sticky mortar holding together the brittle building blocks of a fragmented society.

The celebrated instances when matters went awry stemmed from blurred judgements or the lack of resolution, such as at Manchester, Bristol, Nottingham and possibly South Wales. There never was any room for playing clever games. Many apologists have attempted to incriminate the Yeomanry, as at Peterloo with the charge of partiality, though in the full review none of these have stood up. The clear message was either to manage events or be managed by them. Many affrays were made worse by a refusal of the prime movers to meet and discuss issues or having done so, to go back on their word. In this can be traced the early confrontational patterns of unionism, which had in any case been stunted by the Combination Acts introduced as early as 1799-1800, though later repealed in 1824.

The periodic suspension of Habeas Corpus was little more than a holding measure until officialdom could get its act together. The Industrial Revolution succeeded more clearly in separating society than feudalism with all its Lords and Squires. The 'dog eat dog' class of boss which emerged was, in the main, a talented brute and one detached from duties and obligations. From this, one concludes a better bridge needed to have been built, but at who's cost? The aristocratic elites must surely bear some responsibility for only they were in a commanding position to enquire, legislate and control the obvious developments of the period. This, however, meant they had to volunteer the giving away of a vast fortune to a far from clearly defined cause. Unfortunately, their experience in the main taught them to work down a chain of command. In earlier feudal times the process was well understood and contained a scheme of checks and balances, designed to guarantee fair play. With the new industrial mercantile class it was a bad assumption to make, besides which vital preparatory ground work was never laid. Whatever the cause, only they had the inestimable advantages of travel and education to shape the necessary thinking and in its absence loomed a social chasm.

The early days of industrialisation carried few benefits for the toiling masses. The pressure of public opinion eventually saw the necessary legislation passed into law, but it got off the ground too late, with catastrophic results. Three streams of Acts were passed during the civil lifetime of the Yeomanry and much more thereafter, including: Public Health in 1848; Mines in 1842, 1850, 1860, 1862; Factories in 1819, 1831, 1833, 1844, 1847 and 1850. The problem was establishing root causes of the various ills. There was no universal cure-all and the various remedies took time to develop. Those governing health and education were less visible and only later, at the time of The Great War, did these damages become strikingly apparent in those called to the Colours. High quality manpower is and was a national resource and a military imperative and therefore not something to be frittered away. The extent of social ills during the 1830s and 1840s is best summarised by the following statistics: the annual death rate in the population climbed to 25%, whilst the average life expectancy of a labourer in a Manchester slum was only 17 and as low as 15 in Liverpool. The periodic riots must not be seen as a mindless rejection of law and order, quiet the reverse. The problem of visibility was hampered by the unlikelihood of any person without specific business in a slum being likely to enter one, which of course included the Yeomanry.

It is fashionable today, when schemes fail to work out, to talk of fault lines. The 1832 Reform Act was a small beginning and hardly an ambitious undertaking. Social reform during the 19th century Britain had to take giant strides, to keep pace with the scale of the enterprise. A major crime was hobbling a political leadership at a time of an occupational and health catastrophe in England's conurbations. There was an unbelievable obstinacy against accepting reality, all of which had to be bought and paid for later. Progress was also hampered by regressive taxation because people did not understand economic and fiscal policy then, as we do now claim.

Perhaps we can take heart by recognising the instinctive genius of the British in knowing how far to take civil violence, while avoiding bloody revolution.

A considerable body of information has originated from the individual Corps histories listed under Appendix C, Spreadsheet Bibliography, to which frequent reference should be made. This is based on and arranged similarly to AS White's "A Bibliography of Regimental Histories of the British Army" (SAHR and the Army Museums, Ogilby Trust, London 1965) with a number of additions made since that date.

Table 8 overleaf consolidates various quantitive and financial elements of the Yeomanry of the period, so far as data can be found.

Chapter 3

Table 8 Yeomanry General Particulars and Aid to Civil Power

Year	Corps	Troops	Expenses £	All Ranks	Troops to Riot	Riot Days	Riot £'s
1816	134		76,237		15*		2,052
1817	143		110,820	17,818	20*		6,110
1818			95,858		9*		580
1819			104,179		41*		8,759
1820	182		154,800	30,791	47*		8,837
1821	179		118,564		5*	587	+33,035
1822			117,245		19*		4,108
1823			124,591		13*		549
1824			126,357		2*		63
1825			111,247		3*		100
1826			144,593		16*		4,474
1827	127		133,242		6*		302
1829	36		45,337	8,351	1	1	?
1831	93		167,332	20,213			
1832	93		81,769	20,339			
1833	103	346	88,661	19,672			
1834	98	346	77,329	19,618			
1835	94	338	104,212	19,287			
1836	93	335	101,842	19,365			
1837	93	325	103,072				
1838	55	244	79,684	14,040			
1839	55	247	90,786	14,119			
1840	55	247	93,227	14,285	nil	nil	nil
1841	55	238	82,383	14,274	15	90	
1842	54	239	101,458	14,203	90	30,420	
1843	54	251	95,471	13,911	4	116	
1844	54	255	87,622	14,207	nil	nil	nil
1845	54	224	82,182	12,494	1+3d	27	
1846	54	254	87,989	13,908	nil	nil	nil
1847	54	235	87,948	12,798	30	83	
1848	53	232		12,867	64+1d	79	

References

1 Fox Kenneth O. Making Life Possible. (privately by Roundwood Press, Kineton, Warwick, 1982)
2 Clode CM. Military Forces of the Crown; Their Administration and Government.(John Murray, London 1869)
3 Benson Freeman, Edited Earl Fortescue. The Yeo. of Devon, 1794-1927. (St Catherine Press, London 1927)
4 Mileham, Maj PJR. The Yeomanry Regiments; A pictorial History. (Spelmount, Tunbridge Wells 1985)
5 Teichman, Maj O. Yeomanry in Support of the Civil Power, 1795-1867. (JSAHR Vol XIX. 1940)
6 Parliamentary Sessional Papers. 1828 Vol XVII pp 283-287
7 Ditto .... 1829 Vol XVI pp 178-183
8 Ditto .... 1850 Vol XXXV pp 128-139
9 by QL. The Yeomanry Cavalry of Worcestershire: 1794-1913 (G Simpson, Devizes. 1914)
10 Marquess of Angelsey. A History of the British Cavalry. Vol 1 (1816-1860) (Lee Cooper, London 1973.)
11 Lowe N. Modern British History (MacMillan Press Ltd Basingstoke and London 1989)
12 Beckett IAF. The Amateur Military Tradition. (Manchester University Press, Manchester. 1991(3)
13 Hargreaves P & Benson Freeman. Old Time Yeomanry: The Manchester Corps. Chester Courant. Fr 23 03 10
14 Mileham, Maj PJR. The Stirlingshire Yeo Cavalry and the Scottish Insurrection of 1820. (JSAHR Vol LXIII 1985)
15 Howell, Lt-Col RL. The Pembroke Yeomanry. The Pembrokeshire Museum's Military Collection, Dyfed CC
16 Mileham, Maj PJR. Controlling Peterloo. History Today , Letter to the Editor Vol 38, June 1988

Plate 4/1   The Royal Wiltshire Yeomanry

'Lorried Infantry'. This picture dating from 1860 shows a dismounted section of the Royal Wiltshire Yeomanry. A number of Yeomanry units formed these sections to assist in the military purpose of holding positions directly the cavalry had taken them.

4. Victoriana

National Alarms

The first fright came in 1846 when France had a second revolution bringing Louis Napoleon to power and again in 1851 when it was proposed he become Emperor, which he did the following year. The Orsini affair in 1858-9 brought Britain and France back again into the traditional confrontational frame. With accomplices in London this man organised a plot to assassinate Napoleon III. He was caught and duly executed for the failed attempt. However, the French protested so strongly to London that the Government felt it necessary to introduce a Bill into Parliament making amends for harbouring an assassin. This was more than the Country or the Opposition would stand, so the Government was forced to resign.

Overseas skirmishes were no concern of a Reserve Army constitutionally bound to the Home shores.

Thus the Crimea and the First Boer War passed the Yeomanry by. As already mentioned the Yeomanry left the jurisdiction of the Home for the War Office in 1854-5. At the County level, this made little difference, since the chief official remained the same.

In retrospect, from consolidation following the end of the war with Napoleon, the Yeomanry increased in size far more as the result of social unrest at home than any external military threat. These, when they came, failed to extract a military response and this situation pertained until the end of the century. Of course the raising of political temperatures, saw the Volunteers seeking ways and means of serving. It was around this time that the rifle began to make a strong impact on military thinking.

Table 9 Mounted Rifle Volunteers & Light Horse Volunteers

Formed	Disb.	Formation Title	Formed	Disb.	Formation Title
10 08 60	1865	1st Cambridgeshire MRV C	15 02 61	1864-5	Redes 2nd Hampshire LHVC Disb as 2nd Hampshire MRVC
12 05 60	1863	2nd ditto	19 11 62	1880	1st Hertford LHV C
22 06 60	1871	1st Derbyshire MRVC	14 04 60	1861	1st Huntingdonshire MRVC
23 02 60	1878 .	1st Devonshire MRVC	01 61	1882	Redes 1st Huntingdonshire LHVC
05 03 60	1861	2nd ditto	22 03 60	1861	1st Lancashire MRVC
10 04 60	1865	3rd ditto (Amal with 1st)	02 61	1872	Redes 1st Lancashire LHV C
30 04 60	1865	4th ditto (Renumbered 3rd)	05 60	1861	1st Lincoln MRVC
65	1874-5	4th ditto (became new 3rd)	03 61	1861	Redes 1st Lincoln LHVC
24 05 60	1861 .	5th ditto	10 07 67	1887	2nd Lincoln LHVC
04 61	1875-6	Redes 1st Devonshire LHV C	18 01 61	1866	1st Middlesex LHVC
13 07 60	1875	6th Devonshire MRVC	25 03 61	1861	2nd Middx LHVC(Amal. with 1st)
14 06 60	1865	7th ditto	25 03 61	1862	1st Norfolk MRVC
65	1874-5	Redes 2nd Devonshire LHV	62	1867	Redes 1st Norfolk LHV C
25 11 74	1880	1st Dumfriessshire MRVC	03 03 60	1869	1st Northamptonshire MRVC
03 07 68	1871	1st Elgin MRVC.	12 01 64	1870	1st Oxfordshire LHV C
61	—	1st Essex MRVC (Authd not formed)	13 02 72	1880	1st Roxburgh MRVC
15 02 61	1861	1st Glamorgan MRVC	22 01 80	1891	Redes. 1st Rox (Border MR) MRV
Late 61	1873	Redes 1st Glamorgan LHV C	12 91	1892	Redes. 1st Rox (Border MR) VMR
19 05 64	1867	1st Gloucester LHV C	02 04 60	1861	1st Surrey MRVC
25 04 60	1861	1st Hampshire MRVC	02 61	1868	Redes 1st Surrey LHV C
15 02 61	1863	Redes 1st Hampshire LHV C	01 08 71	1875-6	1st Sussex LHV C
04 01 61	1861	2nd Hampshire MRVC			

This combined with the general needs for mobility prompted the formation of the Volunteer Mounted Rifles. Even when the first Corps of Yeomanry were forming up there had been a move to have the rifle adopted, but it was in its infancy and besides which it wasn't a Cavalry weapon, so the proposition was dropped. To avoid any confusion with the Yeomanry as such, over the period 1860-87 these are listed in Table 9. [1]

Military Developments

Apart from Colonial skirmishes Britain was only involved in one war between the Battle of Waterloo and the end of the century; the Crimea. In this she did so badly in all departments, save crass bravery, that it set in train important military reforms. These were long overdue, but in these matters the Yeomanry had to wait on events.

As the Cavalry of the volunteer Reserve Army it adopted uniforms of the Light Cavalry, dressing as Hussars, Lancers or Dragoons. These can never have been the most comfortable of garbs given the main role as 'Maintenance of Public Order'. Considerable latitude appears to have been allowed, as the result of which, some intriguing variations in turnout have been noted, but as a generality the dress followed many Regular Army styles then passing into disuse.

The basic Yeomanry unit remained the Troop, formed within the confines of the county. Those most in 'action' often had many Troops. Each, or any agreed group were termed Yeomanry Corps, indicating a unity of command and of course the formation of Regiments was in the ascendancy. Sparsely populated areas did form cross-county links and this was especially true for Scotland. The idea of Squadron formations was essentially a Regular Army idea which paid scant regard to the demographic strains placed upon a local community, although funnily enough these same Regulars very rarely met up as regiments.

As a benchmark, where precisely were the Yeomanry meant to fit into the scheme of things? Basically they were a form of Light Cavalry. During the war they provided a portion of the coast-watch which released scarce Regular troops for foreign service. Its main strength resided in local knowledge and friendly locals. In a series of six letters[2], dated 13 February 1797, F P Elliot illustrates and details to the Colonel of the Staffordshire Volunteer Cavalry the training of Yeomanry as follows:

1 Discipline and nature of service.
2 Utility and Expediency of Establishment.
3 Method of giving the Word of Command.
   Troop exercises as a Squadron.
4 National advantages arising from Establishment of Yeomanry Corps and plans to make permanent.
5 Cavalry Evolutions for Squadron, Regiment or Line.
   Sword Exercise.
6 General principles of Movement.
   Selected Manoeuvres founded on new Instructions and Regulations.
   Brief Directions for obtaining changes in formation.

This publication, which it must be assumed obtained Royal approval, is beautifully printed and includes detailed illustrations showing the changes from one formation to another. Subsequently, nothing much is heard of its application. It seems unlikely that the formations of the time were large enough and time too short to enable the drills to be practised. Far better any time was spent teaching men to shoot straight and to use a sabre to good effect. Presumably this was the sort of thing that Fortescue spoke against in preparing a Reserve Army against invasion.

As regards the training of mounted troops, the best authority for the period leading up to the Crimea was Nolan [3]. It seems unlikely that much of this detail, published in 1852, would have percolated down to the Yeomanry, much more likely were the practicalities and peculiarities of hunting, shooting and fishing, as practised regionally. Nolan goes into considerable detail over the use of Cavalry, covering training, qualities of officers, men, materials and availability of mounts. His general submission was: "that Continental armies of Napoleonic times were oversized, not properly mounted, nor very well trained. Some of these faults were due to a shortage of the right types of horse but the remainder stemmed from poor systems of command which hampered proper leadership. Accordingly and only on rare occasions did the Cavalry in question give their best service to the Commander-in-Chief. He goes on to make the not unheard of plea that, "England should not imitate foreign armies as she was rich in men, money and above all in horses and that she ought to make her own Cavalry so superior as to defy comparison and all competition". After dividing Cavalry into Heavy, Middle and Light, he enumerates their duties. He also makes the point that no one type is fit to perform *all* the duties required of horse soldiers in the field. This sort of argument has clattered on into the present mechanised days. The integral nature of fighting forces was not lost on him then and it should not be lost now, by those pundits of the solo Arm victory.

"Heavy Cavalry was composed of large men in defensive armour, mounted on heavy, powerful horses, held in hand for decisive charges on the day of battle, and their horses were so deficient in speed and endurance (being so overweight) that they required Light Horse to follow up the enemy they had beaten. The greatest possible care was taken of this sort of cavalry in the field. They did no outpost duty, no foraging, no reconnoitring: they could not be made use of even to escort a convoy, because if kept out long on the road their horses tired quickly and become incapable of carrying their riders. They were calculated only to show an imposing front in the line of battle, and their history proves them to be more formidable in appearance than in reality." Pretty hard words from an acknowledged expert. In no case was the Yeomanry ever invited to join the ranks of the Heavy Cavalry and the latter, for the reasons given, had no place at an industrial riot.

Next came the Dragoons, "These were originally intended to be mounted Infantry, in order that they might arrive quickly at a position in which they were to fight. In a battle they dismounted, formed line and acted with the infantry. At first they served as Light Cavalry but gradually took heavier horses to enable them to charge with advantage but at the same time lightly equipped to be skirmishers, foragers etc." In summary Nolan says, "dismounted cavalry have done good service in covering a retreat, in defending defiles and passes against cavalry and in pushing forward to seize bridges and dismounting to maintain them; but they would be quite out of place if used in storming positions, or if expected to take their post in line of battle with the infantry." It seems their position was somewhat analogous to the modern day medium tank, they had the disadvantages of the light without the advantages of the heavy, but someone, somewhere had felt the compromise worthwhile.

Light Cavalry, Nolan identified as the most important in the field, "They were called upon to watch over the safety of the army, and they are constantly hovering in advance, on the flanks and in the rear of the columns, to prevent all possibility of surprise on the part of the enemy. In enclosed country they are supported by Light Infantry: In the open country they pushed on and

kept the enemy at a proper distance from the army; they were constantly employed in cutting off the enemy's supplies and communications and in reconnoitring. This varied and often impromptu work required a combination of numerous qualities in officers and men. And in addition to all these duties, peculiarly their own, they often had to perform those expected of the heavy cavalry."

Both Wellington and Napoleon were skilled users of the heavy cavalry, when they could get their commanders to pick the right moment or simply follow orders. Frequently this was not the case. Many opportunities were lost, because they were dispersed and not available at the time of military necessity. Without a force of heavy cavalry an army lost the ability to make decisive interventions, whilst its ability to defend itself at a critical stage in a battle was lost. Taking Waterloo as an example, both sides gambled away opportunities with bad handling of Heavy Cavalry accounting for serious losses. Not until Blucher joined the fray was a critical flank of the French Army rolled-up. At precisely that moment Napoleon saw his battle as lost and Wellington, his won, for both had expended their own resources.

Lancers by virtue of their weaponry could reach those parts that other weapons could not reach; no pun intended. They were light and fast. In support of operations they could be expected to act as a pursuit force to prevent a routed enemy regrouping, forces of 'spent' Heavy Cavalry forming a natural prey. Their purpose was to seize points of interest to the commander and to bring in stragglers for interrogation. In defence the services were doubtful. Basically they would make things positively unpleasant for the enemy in a peripheral sense and by so doing prevent the enemy effecting these self same essential duties. Hussars were also light and fast but without the lance.

Peter Young in Cavalry [4] states: "that the manuals of the time have nothing to say about security or reconnaissance but from his writings Napoleon had a very clear idea of what he expected from his outpost commanders. In an advance for instance, he wanted defiles and fords reconnoitred, guides secured, notables such as schoolmasters and postmasters questioned, good relations established with the locals, any letters seized and translated if felt useful, spies sent out, measures taken to form magazines and food stocks provided for the refreshment of his troops. At the halt, the same forces would attempt to bring in spies, stragglers or couriers and provide escorts." It can be presumed that in a retreat anything which would make it more difficult for the enemy to advance or to secure these self same services would be denied by Hussars. No wonder there was no manual, but the common sense of it all was plain to see.

Nolan comes down strongly in favour of speed as opposed to weight in action. In this he cites the exploits of the Swedes and the German Hussars, to which may be added the legendary Cossacks in action against the Napoleonic French in the German provinces. In the course of the Peninsular War Wellington was most careful to create a strong Cavalry force and it secured notable victories against many redoubtable and experienced foes. In the case of Yeomanry, there was no experience of battle. The riots they attended in a civil capacity must have equated very nearly to a battlefield; wearing, frustrating and bruising affairs, as they were. However, their local knowledge would have been most un-nerving to an invader and attractive to a Home General. They would have enjoyed an almost inexhaustible re-supply position. Beyond this, they would have had the ability to merge into a background, not unlike the earlier Hussars and Cossacks, until called forward.

The prosperity, brought on by Industry, meant there was little social unrest. Therefore the Government was required to enact little reform, so long as their foreign policy held. Apart for a short period of occupation in France, the British Regular Army returned to the United Kingdom and over a short period of years was quickly run down to a shadow of its former glory.

At the time of the Crimea, the main occupation of higher command were taken up with organising transportation of supplies to the field of engagement. The chief problem was achieving this, as we shall see, with not much in the way of a General Staff. Generalship was conspicuous by its absence; on the British side at least. In an epic of maladministration, a cargo of left boots was delivered to the battle site (the latter day National Serviceman must have wondered why it was his boots came to him either stapled or strung together). The poor performance of the military, particularly the Officer Corps, provoked a Public outcry and at least two subsequent Secretary's of State for War tinkered with the War Office machinery following the numerous recommendations submitted by Official enquiries. Nothing of any note was achieved.

Something has been said already about the good development and performance of French field artillery up to the time of Waterloo. The next system to take a leap forward was the rifle. Firstly, smokeless powder was introduced and rifling of the gun barrel. This cleared the pall of smoke which hung over a battlefield, to blind everyone including the respective commanders. Breech loading rifles supplanted muzzle loading, which meant that this could now be effected lying down, although considered very sneaky up to the time of the Boer War. Sinusoidal shaped bullets were substituted for ball ammunition and these were fitted with a soft self sealing driving band working against the spiralled grooves in the barrel. This ensured to all practical intents that the driving gasses were all used to propel the bullet forward and that it was spun so that it would not tumble through the air wasting momentum. The range, accuracy and rate of fire were each improved. At this stage initial steps were also taken to mechanise the firing process, so that a belt of cartridges could be fed into the weapon automatically!

The rifle was the weapon of the Century. It was to transform military tactics. Only the American Civil War with large river and rail movements and the Prussians building a rail system for military use made equal contribution to the art of war, but these were strategic considerations. The proper use of the rifle altered the military tactical doctrine, because Cavalry formations were made ineffectual and the Artillery was obliged to step behind the Infantry.

Army Reformer: Edward T Cardwell

Arvil B. Erickson[5] in his study published in 1959 states, "that Cardwell was one of the best administrators in an age of eminently great public servants; also a highly esteemed financial adviser to two of the greatest Statesmen of his age - Peel and Gladstone". Born in 1813, the son of a prosperous Liverpool merchant, he was schooled at Winchester and Balliol where he obtained a double First Degree. Entering Parliament in 1842, he became Secretary to the Treasury at the young age of 34. Thereafter he held a string of Ministerial appointments including the Colonial Office. In 1867 he was appointed Secretary of State for War until he was elevated to the Lords in 1874. It is the extraordinary events over this six year period that concern us.

The Army machine of the period was divided between

the War Office at Pall Mall, under the Secretary of State for War and the General-Commanding-in-Chief across the road at Horse Guards. But this was only the half of it, for at the time, thirteen offices conducted their business independently and communicated with each other by formal letter:

The Secretary of State for War and the Colonies was responsible for determining the size of the forces required and for allotting garrisons to the colonies. During war, he was charged with the responsibility for selecting commanders and for approving military operations.

The Commander-in-Chief was responsible for efficiency and discipline of the Infantry and Cavalry, the enlistment of troops, and the promotion of officers. All officers were recommended for their posts to the Crown by the Commander-in-Chief. If the command was at a Home station, the prior approval of the Home Office was required; if at a foreign station, the appointment had to be approved by the Secretary of State for War and the Colonies. And, while the Commander-in-Chief commanded the forces in England, he did not have charge of the supplies of arms, ammunition, and equipment. He could not increase nor diminish any garrison; nor could he move a single man without the previous sanction of the Secretary of State of War, by whom the route order was signed upon a requisition made by the Quartermaster-General on the War Office. Furthermore, he had no command of troops outside the United Kingdom.

For such things as quartering of troops, billeting, rates of pay, food and clothing for the Army (exclusive of the Royal Artillery and Engineers), military schools, military prisons, and pensions, the Secretary of War was responsible. If the Commander-in-Chief objected to any of his arrangements, the Secretary of War had to consult with him, with the First Lord of the Treasury, with the Chancellor of the Exchequer, or with all of them.

The Treasury had full responsibility for Army finances and directly managed the Commissariat Department which, in turn negotiated all contracts.

The Master-General of Ordnance had responsibility for the discipline, pay and allowances of the Royal Artillery and Royal Engineers, and for all construction, maintenance, and armament of all fortifications and barracks. He it was who provided and regulated the issue of artillery, arms, ammunition, accoutrements and other stores both for the Army and the Navy, camp equipage, barrack furniture, great-coats for the Army, and clothing for the Artillery and Sappers, in fact everything for the Army except the regimental clothing of the Infantry and Cavalry, which was supplied by the Colonels of Regiments. In this work the Master-General was under the authority of the Treasury. Always an officer of high rank, he was also a member of the Government and often had a seat on the Cabinet. In the performance of his civil duties, he was assisted by the Board of Ordnance consisting of The Storekeeper, Clerk of Ordnance and the Surveyor General of Ordnance.

The Deputy Adjutant-General of Artillery and the Director-General of Artillery advised the Master-General on artillery problems, while the Inspector-General of Fortifications advised him on matters relating to the Royal Engineers.

The Home Secretary had control over the Militia, Volunteers and Yeomanry as well as the regular troops when used in aid of the civil authorities at home.

The Board of General Officers had responsibility for the clothing of the Cavalry and Infantry. In addition to these officials, there were the Judge-Advocate General, who advised on disciplinary problems and courts martial, the Controllers of Accounts, the Army Medical Board, the Commissary General of Musters, two Paymasters General, the Commissioners of the Chelsea Hospital and the Commissaries of Barracks.

"This bewildering array of uncoordinated offices led to hopeless confusion and incredible inefficiency." As Erickson comments, "Cardwell knew, through his tenure as Colonial Secretary, that the War Office, in the collective sense, if collected it could be, was about as inefficient as an institution could be and still survive." It seemed all the more farcical that the War Office was able to complain, periodically, over inefficiency of the Yeomanry when chaos reigned in its own domain, but such was the case.

A great problem called for a great man. Cardwell was intelligent, experienced, hardworking and above all tactful, a rare even unique combination of skills. In a series of studies the various problems were reduced to basics. The first was to unify the War Office and Horse Guards under the civil authority of the

Secretary of State for War, with the Commander-in-Chief performing the duty of military adviser. This was achieved by 1871. Historically the command of the Army was under the Sovereign or a person appointed by him or her and this accounted for the separation of offices, but increasingly there was a need to at least co-ordinate the function through the Civil Office of the Secretary of State. The second problem was to abolish the purchase of commissions. The system, as then in existence, could be made to work within the Regular Army, if pursued with vigour and taken in isolation. The problem arose when mixing it with the Reserve Army which formed the linchpin of the proposed economies. It was impossible to mix the same arm of two services when working according to different precepts. Besides this, a positive push had to be given to raising the competence of the long serving Regular officer. After much wrangling the device of a Royal Warrant was used to end Purchase, also in 1871. It is fair to observe that Purchase had been first created by this means. The third problem arose from the proposed integration of the reserve forces with the Regular Army, thus to allow the latter to be reduced in size, particularly the overseas portion. To make the scheme work it was necessary to have a quick response in sending forces to a trouble spot and for the gap so created at Home to be immediately replenished from the reserves. Basically, the most outward sign of reform or economy came from a reduction in the standing army. Parliament was more interested in the latter, whatever the state of the Army! However a vital component was for the reserves to become standardised, so that all and sundry down the long line of the planning process knew what to expect when reserves joined the Colours. Not only were the units to be trained alongside the Regular Army, but the personnel, particularly the officers had to match their Regular counterparts. This measure was passed into law during 1872.

There was much to do in making this latter measure work because the Reserve Forces had to attend annual manoeuvres. The fact that subsequent Secretaries of State failed to keep this Force up to scratch is no reflection on Cardwell or the needs so identified, as subsequent events were to prove. The main arm of the reserves was the Militia. This was grouped with the Regular Army and trained by and with them at the various Regimental depots throughout the Country. Cardwell did not ignore the Volunteers which included the Yeomanry. Since passing various reforms the periodic need for the latter to deploy in aid of the Civil

Power declined and with it its numbers. Periodic economies had further depleted its numbers and there was little that could be done to regularise formations: They had always been raised on demographic lines. Under the circumstances it was decided that any Corps below four troops of fifty men each, would not be trained, by the Regulars. The desired aim was for units of eight troops, trained as *mounted riflemen*. However, those not under training were left in being where it was considered they could perform a useful function on escort or ceremonial duty.

It would do less than justice to Cardwell to leave this account without listing the improvements made to the soldier's lot by way of pay, conditions and equipment. Through bad health care and poor barracks, the death-rate of soldiers was five times that of civilian life in the United Kingdom and much worse at Foreign Stations. This statistic excludes the business of accidents in training for war or actual war! The barracks were improved and reading rooms provided. Proper health care was introduced. Enhanced long service pay was substituted for bounties paid on enlistment and re-enlistment. Corporal punishment was abolished in 1869 and branding (tattooing) for desertion in 1871. The education of officers was reorganised in 1870. Serving officers were henceforth debarred from patenting inventions for private gain. Work continued in an open minded manner to perfect the breech loading rifle, for which there were many contenders.

Cardwell left behind him a first-class military machine, it was more efficient and far less costly than anything that went before and as Erickson goes on to say, "it was no fault of his that immediate successors at the War Office allowed it to run down, failed to remove the obstructionist Commander-in-Chief or neglected to form a much needed General Staff". So much can a man do. From 1879 Cardwell was increasingly ill, eventually dying at Torquay in 1886.

Yeomanry Establishment
We can now review the creation, expansion and contraction of the Yeomanry from the small, locally independent Troops to fully fledged regiments, in appendices C and D. It is hoped to consolidate revisions, as these come to hand (from whatever source) and to reprint them periodically. In order to pace historical developments these are divided between the periods: Appendix C1. The French Revolutionary War 1794-1802; Appendix C2. The Napoleonic War 1802-1828; and Appendix D. 1829-onwards. From

1829 there is certainty in the history, so the last appendix provides a short and complete outline history, up to the time of the Territorial Army disbandment. During the earlier period we are considering some 400 independent Corps and a proliferation of titles.

1794-1802 The main points illustrated are, the initial creation of the Yeomanry in 1794, the panic to bolster our forces in 1797-8 and the Peace Treaty of Amiens bringing about a wide scale disbandment of our forces in general.

1802-1828 The realisation was the so-called Peace Treaty was not going to hold and that England had to get her act together. This meant taking decisions over how to win the war, as opposed to not losing. As the Blockade Napoleon took effect, so did our social problems of unemployment and starvation. Since the end of the war brought a recession, there was no let-up for the Yeomanry and their chief duty was riot and strike breaking. Nevertheless the Government were badly placed financially and disbanded two thirds of the Yeomanry force in 1827-8.

1829-1967 The third period takes up the story from 1829 till the War Office assumed responsibility for managing Yeomanry affairs in 1856. At the start there was the question of political reform. As so often happens, it was a case of too little too late. The over reaction of the Government in disbanding so large a part of the Yeomanry redounded on its head, leaving the Southern Counties unprotected against incessant rebellion. Granted there were not to be a repetition of the disgraceful conflagrations of the previous period, nevertheless industrial action and rough demands for reform of representation figured up and down the Country till beyond 1850.

The Battle for Precedence
Right of the Line is pride of place in the Army and apocryphal tales abound where military disaster has followed fast on the heels of the usurper. It doesn't make much sense today, at least on the battlefield. Pride of place drives one to try a little harder or outdo another, if the competition is meaningful, but that is a different story. On Parade it is a useful device for bringing order to a noisy and confusing place. In other respects it plays no useful part, for as we shall see, one small break in an otherwise continuous service (or the necessary supporting record) can lose a Corps years of 'seniority'. There is no military virtue in being 'right of the line' unless the order is open to change as the

result of *on-going* performance.

When the knife cuts deep, in the name of economy, the more senior regiments demand to survive, on no other pretext: Perhaps it stopped, and even now stops, a lot of bickering! However, this may have been unjust to the Yeomanry in particular and for the following reasons, illogical. Demographic and sometimes geographic considerations decided what and where units could be best raised and in turn what size was prudent. Regular units may achieve a compromise through the use of mergers and amalgamations. Clearly the Yeomanry had to achieve the best military solution possible, within the confines of the enabling legislation of the times, but it has been largely county driven. Practical duties varied from coast watches to riot duty in a variety of places, subject always to population developments and movements. During peacetime Regular Cavalry was rarely together on a regimental basis, but Yeomanry could hardly conduct their peacetime routine on this basis.

Correct placement within the scheme of precedence depended upon the accuracy of records and those called upon to arbitrate taking the trouble to consult such records as existed. Clearly the War Office was about the last place to disregard precedence or associate with slapdash rulings (So it was felt). However, the Yeomanry were a peculiar kettle of fish, not conforming to so many military nostrums. Also, during the first sixty years of its existence, it served under the Home Office. Had it been a Regular Army matter it might have exercised better brains, now it is no longer clear who actually did the Staff work or whether they cared!

The prospect of a Royal Review in 1887, to celebrate the Golden Jubilee of Queen Victoria set the Yeomanry colonels wondering in which order they were to parade. By 1885 the problems were so intractable that the War Office was called in, as honest broker, to make the necessary rulings; recriminations flew. It is difficult to imagine what records the War Office actually consulted, to counter the claims. Certainly the Letter Books, showing the daily transaction of business by the Home Office, were not. It was accepted that broken service meant a loss of seniority and only the most recent period of unbroken service was to count. Memories were distinctly hazy, but service without pay was certainly meant to count and this was a matter of record, however it seems it was rarely, if at all, taken into account. Each colonel was asked to provide details and if necessary support claims of service. At the beginning some of the details amounted to the bizarre. When the lists closed, an order of precedence was issued with, in many cases, entirely fictitious dates of raising. Messrs Fellows and Benson Freeman in writing the Historical Records of the South Nottinghamshire Hussars Yeomanry, 1794 to 1924 make a thorough research of the matter showing the development and consequence of the numerous errors. The present reader may not agree with all they said, but at least the case has been committed to writing for the benefit of posterity. It is reproduced here as Appendix B.

In closing, it is as well to admit that the story of Yeomanry precedence, so far told, is incomplete. Properly it began with the Middlesex Hussars taking exception to the Infantry Section of the Honourable Artillery Company marching ahead of them in any proposed parade. The matter was referred to the War Office who ruled in favour of the latter. Their argument was always a loser since even the Yeomanry embodied a number of mixed Cavalry and Infantry formations. Besides which the Honourable Artillery Company could boast an unbroken service dating from 1537. In many respects it equated to a Staff College for the Reserve Forces: Something the Regular Army had still to recruit.

Also in 1885 the War Office were able to publish the Establishment to take effect from 1st April for the various Yeomanry Cavalry, in Army Regulations, volume X [6]. This shows very clearly the high state of integration achieved with the Regular Army since the days of Cardwell. The various Yeomanry now served in Districts: Northern, Eastern, Western, Southern, South-Eastern, Home and North British (Scotland). There were 39 units, as cited earlier, each with a Lieutenant-Colonel, a Major, an Adjutant, a Surgeon, a Veterinary Surgeon (for 25 of the units with maximum establishments of 375 or more) and a Sergeant Major. Units came in three approximate sizes: 538-434, 405-375 and 291-251. The largest units had eight Troop Sergeant Majors or Quartermasters, eight Permanent Staff Sergeants, eight Trumpeters, 24 Sergeants and 24 Corporals. The next in size had three-quarters this establishment and the smallest half the number.

The most interesting figures are the maximum-minimum figures for Privates in the total Force; 11,412-10,122 and an All Ranks maximum total of 14,405. It appears that from 1877 the minimum establishment for a Yeomanry Cavalry regiment had been laid down at 200 non-commissioned officers and privates and for 42 to be the minimum for a Troop.

References

1 Frederick. JBM. Lineage Book of British Land Forces, 1660-1978. Vol I (Microform Academic Publishers, Wakefield, 1984)
2 Elliot FP. Six letters on the Subject of the Armed Yeomanry. (T Egerton, Military Library, Whitehall. London 1797)
3 Capt. Nolan. Cavalry; Its History and Tactics. (London 1853)
4 Edited by J Lawford. The Cavalry. (Purnell Book Services Ltd. Abingdon, Oxon, 1976)
5 Erickson. Arvil B. Reformer: Edward T Cardwell. (Trans Amer. Phil Soc Vol 49 Pt2, Philadelphia. 1959)
6 Army Regulations, Volume X. 1885

5. The Boer Wars

Background to the Dutch Cape [1]

During the course of their early mercantile voyages to the East Indies, the Dutch naturally stopped off at the Cape of Good Hope. At this time the area was unpopulated but the land was plainly suitable for farming. It was decided to colonise the Cape Province and farmers were sent out from the mother country from about 1650; Huguenots and Germans followed from 1688.

Britain paid the Dutch East India Company £6 million for the Colony in 1815. This Company had been bankrupted as the result of the Napoleonic wars. It would appear that the then colonists were not consulted! The British interest, at the time, lay in securing her route to India.

Mainly as a result of the 1834 Act freeing slaves, but also to be free of British interference, a large proportion of the Boers left the Province to establish the Orange Free State and the Transvaal. Full independence was not then acknowledged by the British which rankled in the Boer mind. To secure full independence they fought and won what became known as the First Boer War in 1880-1. In this they defeated an army at Majuba, under Colley who was killed along with half his force and Premier Gladstone acknowledged their cause in a somewhat vague treaty.

The discovery of gold at Witwatersrand in Transvaal, during 1886 provoked a gold-rush, attracting a veritable host of outsiders, promptly named Uitlanders, by the Boer inhabitants. They were taxed heavily and denied political rights. In protesting they were supported by the British authorities in the Cape. In 1895 Jameson and party led an unsuccessful raid on the Boers. Attempts to settle the problem peacefully failed. The Boer Republics joined to make increasing demands upon the British and to stockpile arms. On 9th October 1899 Kruger presented an ultimatum which meant war by 5 pm 11th October unless accepted and it wasn't!

There is little doubt, in retrospect, that a combination of self interests in Cape Province had manipulated the London authorities. The former was unable to fight a war without resources they did not possess, whilst the latter were misinformed over crucial political factors. The Government of the time was weak and easily pushed by a bellicose public flushed by successes against natives. When war became inevitable they failed to take account of the form it would take. This was lamentable, as the following account shows.

Michael L. Melville in his Story of the Lovat Scouts picks out a number of statistics concerning the Boer War and the Republics we came to fight:

"The Boer War lasted three years, cost £222 million and involved roughly 450,000 Imperial troops, of whom 22,000 died, nearly three-quarters of them from disease. The Boer armies amounted at most to 88,000 irregular soldiers, men and boys, who fought in their working clothes often providing their own horses and weapons and above all were acclimatised to the country. They were organised in locally raised 'Commandos', sub-divided into 'Precincts' and 'Corporalships'."

Also quoted is a masterly description of the Boer, by Conan Doyle [2], who was a military surgeon there at the time:

"Take a community of Dutchmen of the type who defended themselves for 50 years against all the power of Spain when Spain was the greatest power in the world. Intermix with them a strain of those inflexible French Huguenots who gave up home and fortune and left their country for ever... The product must be one of the most rugged, virile, unconquerable races ever seen upon earth. Take this formidable people and train them for seven generations in constant warfare against savage men and ferocious beasts, in circumstances in which no weakling could survive, give them a country which is eminently suited to the tactics of the huntsman, the marksman and the rider. Then finally put a fine temper upon their military qualities by a dour, fatalistic, Old Testament religion and an ardent and consuming patriotism. Combine all these qualities and all these impulses in one individual, and you have the modern Boer - the most formidable antagonist who ever crossed the path of Imperial Britain. Our military history has largely consisted in our conflicts with France, but Napoleon and all his veterans have never treated us so roughly as *these hard-bitten farmers with their ancient theology and their inconveniently modern rifles.*"

"The Boers were delighted with our generalship, for one captured Boer even reported it was a capital offence for any one of them to shoot a British General! Changes in outlook, method and tactics were necessary...the British Army was no match for an elusive enemy with his superior use of speed and surprise and his far greater ability in fieldcraft, reconnaissance and marksmanship."

Oh dear! It should not be forgotten that a large British Boer population remained in the Cape, after the time of the Great Trek. Reading Conon Doyle, it seems not unlikely that the top Boer political leadership could have launched a reverse take-over, indeed this almost came about.

The Invention of Khaki [3]
The Boer War was the first in which the Yeomanry was to serve overseas and they donned khaki. The word comes to us from India where it is the Urdu for *dusty colour*. Later as we know it was applied to the light drab cloth used in uniforms. The invention arose from an obvious need for camouflage when taking the field against rifles of ever increasing accuracy and range. As adopted by the British Army of the day it came in a light and dark shade, the latter for use in the African colonies.

During the times of close quarter engagements, the dust, smoke and confusion made a commander's control of events an uncertain affair. Once battle was joined a soldier's chief fear was being shot by his own side. To overcome this, distinctive and often brilliant coloured uniforms were worn. The advent of the rifle and smokeless powder changed all that.

When Henry Lawrence was appointed Resident of the independent Sikh Kingdom he found it necessary to create his own military force. He approached Harry Lumsden, then serving in the 59th Bengal Native Infantry to form the first unit of his Punjab Irregular Force. By irregular was meant, not part of the Regular Empire forces. Both were agreed that for a soldier to do his work best, a comfortable and inconspicuous dress was necessary. At the time uniforms were generally the reverse; colourful yet uncomfortable. A composite or double regiment of cavalry and infantry was formed in line with the best military traditions, of the period. The dress comprised a long smock, baggy trousers and a turban. All was made of homespun cotton, which was coloured drab grey, using the dwarf mazari palm for dye.

In many respects the new formation, which became known as Queen Victoria's Own Corps of Guides, was a forerunner of the present day S.A.S. Although trained in the more conventional military techniques they were above all required to be highly resourceful and able to take initiatives. In this, they trained to work in small groups, gathering intelligence, conducting road watches and giving advance warning of enemy intentions. To do the latter, they mounted long range intruder patrols or sent agents into the local hills forming the North-West frontier. The cold climate called for what has become known as the Afghan sheepskin coat. When the first deliveries were made the Contractor had found it impossible to dye them grey from the materials to hand. Accordingly mulberry juice was applied to the bleached skins and from this emerged the drab yellow colour we have come to call Khaki.

Initially this escaped the notice of their Regular counterparts, because they were miles away from the seat of government. However with the Indian mutiny, the Guides were brought in as a relief force and force-marched at a heroic pace to Delhi ridge. They covered 540 miles at an average of 27 miles per day, infantry and cavalry alike, with 30 miles on the last morning, to be in action within half an hour. The colour was adopted by a number of units after the Mutiny, because of its camouflage properties, but then discarded. Later at the time of the Second Afghan war in 1879 it reappeared as standard issue except for British units joining an expedition. In their case they were obliged to use river mud to dull down their white uniforms! However, by 1881 all troops in India wore Khaki and a darker shade variant was made available to Africa.

Further uniform trials followed in England, using grey

tweed, until in 1902 when 'drab mixture' was adopted for World-wide service. It was a close run thing that, but for the difficulty in dyeing an Afghan jacket grey and the success of mulberry juice, the British Army might have gone to war in 1914 wearing *'Field Grey'*.

Mounted Rifles [4]

Such a term calls for a double definition: What constitutes mounted and what a rifle? The rifle had hung over the Yeomanry, since its inception. Herein reside a set of implications jostling for attention. Arguments, often heated and rarely rational, arose throughout the 19th Century and later, quite stupidly, clouded more important issues in the run-up to The Great War. At the time of their initial formation there was talk of making Mounted Rifles of what became the Yeomanry. Obviously this was a very different matter to that arising in the Boer War, for the following reason: The British Light Cavalry of the Napoleonic period had to be taught their work by German Hussars. The duties of the various types of Cavalry have already been described, but for some reason the British found Outpost Duty and reconnoitring distasteful and therefore something they rarely performed. On the Continent the absence of prior knowledge of enemy intentions severely handicapped operations. Possibly the close nature of the English countryside engendered a lack of appetite for this category of work. The attendant risks of sniping were real enough, even before the time of the 'enclosures'. By comparison the Continent was a wide open plain, of which we had little knowledge.

Whatever the arguments over rifles and these were in their infancy, the Yeomanry opted for the role of Light Cavalry, with all its acknowledged faults. Possibly a recruitment problem could have arisen, without the exclusive attractions of Dragoon and Hussar dress. It has to be acknowledged that recruitment over the period 1794-96 was a slow affair and needed the *Provisional* legislation to provide a positive impetus.

Rifle developments took giant strides during the 19th Century, albeit the weapon remained *muzzle* loaded for the earlier years. The rifling technique was adopted to spin the projectile, which enhanced accuracy. It consisted of a number of shallow grooves winding along the length of the barrel. Unfortunately the propellant powders of the day quickly fouled the bore making reloading progressively more difficult, added to which, reloading after the first shot necessitated the conventional muzzle loading routine of standing up!

Under the circumstances it is hard to imagine what advantages the mounted rifleman enjoyed, unless he was to dismount! Bore fouling was overcome by finding ways of reducing groove depth, to a few thousandths of an inch and ultimately by the adoption of *smokeless* powder. However, the basic requirement was for breech loading. This enabled the rifleman to reload in a variety of positions. All that remained was for the range and accuracy of the rifle to be further extended to thoroughly upset the battlefield scheme. For example, it was possible to pick off artillerymen, so they were obliged to fall back behind their infantry. The range and freedom of action for the Cavalry was also circumscribed, since the horse offered a target four to five times as large as an infantryman. Effectively what the Squares achieved with great difficulty and stubborn bravery, against cavalry at Waterloo, was now reduced to a routine... *can you stand?* Without alternative initiatives, the way was presaged to siege warfare and the calamitous events of 1914-18.

Between the adoption of the breech-loading rifle and the trenches came the Boer War: Superficially a cavalryman's dream, with wide open spaces outstripping the imagination. In this the British were caught between two stools. The potential of the rifle was not fully understood nor developed in the tactical sense, whilst the wide open spaces gobbled up the small number of mounted troops available. Both problems were the proper concern of a non-existent General Staff. That of solving the fault of our immobility was seen as the most pressing. In modern parlance, the cavalryman and his horse could be regarded as a *weapon system,* that is to say they were indivisible. Unfortunately the straightened finances of the Army made it double as a *transport system* as well. When more infantry were wanted up front in a hurry, they doubled behind the Cavalry mounts. Whether a mounted rifleman or infantryman on a horse would suffice was questionable, because he was not so well wedded to his horse. The reality was the horse could no longer venture onto the battlefield, anymore than Infantry could continue launching frontal assaults. However, in the absence of anything else, the horse was at least required to provide mobility.

An Infantryman requires a lot of additional training to suit him for the saddle and the truth was some could never ride. It is vital for him to arrive in time for battle, fit enough to fight and not crippled by bad riding habits. Also he has to be knowledgeable enough to maintain his animal for future use. All in all, training a soldier in a combination of infantry and cavalry disciplines takes a long time and costs a lot of money. Dependent upon the view taken over the employment of this hybrid soldier, follows the choice of equipment to be borne by horse and man. The Light Cavalry horse was not big, nor strong enough to carry the rider and the accoutrements of two fighting Arms, in fact it was over-encumbered by the requirements of one. Some selection of equipment was necessary to keep such a force in the field, like a commissariat of high speed light weight wagons designed to keep pace. During The Second World War recourse was to the Platoon 15 Cwt Bedford. The problem was as much that of shedding past notions and traditions, before making a critical re-examination of a task: The enhancement of mobility.

The arrival of the first efficient breech loaded rifles spelt doom for the Cavalry, directly a meaningful tactical doctrine had been evolved for their use and this should have been foreseen. Already the rifle had forced the Artillery to give ground, so why did the Cavalry take so long to grasp military imperatives: Possibly a lack of Continental wars; but then the Boer War was essentially a Whiteman's affair. The sheer audacity of the Boer succeeded in paralysing rational military thought at the time. Afterwards, very little thinking followed through to solve the dilemma. Matters were delayed long enough, until a long and tragic Continental war drove home its lessons. In the meantime Cavalry sabres, never much of a weapon, were handed in, a breech-loader rifle handed out and the Light Cavalry became *Mounted Rifles*. Attempts to mount Infantry on the horse were doomed to failure, because it was poorly thought out and eventually tackled in a *cheap and nasty* manner. Without doubt the redundant Cavalry could have provided better help than they did, but they were more intent on proving their worth, not enhancing the prospects of another Arm. Nolan had much earlier argued for a small highly trained Cavalry force, but he died disappointed. When the Boer War opened there was no time to create a properly trained force of mounted infantry and most of the lead time was spent in fruitless bickering.

Had the Boers inherited a martial tradition there seems little doubt the Cape would have become theirs, by right of conquest. As it was the British were obliged to throw numbers at the problem and to pay dearly for an equally messy peace. Mobility has always been a chief tactical factor in war and until a substitute was found for the horse, it remained a vital component in the military arsenal, not Light Cavalry. To this extent Lancelot Rolleston [4] and references to Major-General Hallam Parr on the Training of Cavalry or Mounted Rifles ignore the unpalatable fact that a small force of properly trained mobile infantry, had the means to annihilate any Cavalry force not brought up to the same standards of musketry.

Boer War Yeomanry Formations
A war of mobility required large numbers of horse mounted and rifle trained soldiers, preferably those experienced in the saddle. By analogy it was hoped that these people would also bring countryside skills to the business of war making. In a word, the Yeoman was ideal. However, let no one be deluded into thinking the Yeomanry were the only form of horse soldier. Large numbers came from other parts of the Empire, whilst locally many units were formed comprising colonials well used to the country, the saddle and the ways of the Boer.

Fieldcraft was still emerging as a necessary yet distasteful tool of war. Those that stood up to face the enemy *like a man* had their heads shot through, often at ranges exceeding 600 metres, by *sporting* rifles of the Mauser and Mannlicher types. Marksmanship posed a problem. The best Army rifles were with the infantry who were not mobile, whilst the cavalry who had the mobility were armed with carbines which were entirely useless, under the new circumstances. Militarily, the first efficient rifle rendered obsolete the infantry frontal assault. Flanks were difficult to turn, because so few could extend so much front, so far. Although these features were perceived by some there was *too little time* for the new doctrine to filter through to higher echelons before the grisly events of 1914 unfolded. This can be identified as the first casualty of a non-existent General Staff.

Generalship or properly speaking the lack of young, up to date and well trained generals posed a double problem for the Home government. Lack of success in any part of the military sphere redounded on the head of the leader up front; a sort of bricks without straw situation. Administration was hopelessly entwined with the tactics and strategy of bitty campaigns. The question of officer training was something else that hadn't properly worked itself through the system since the Cardwell reforms. The prospective General learnt his trade by watching the *Muffin* ahead! The Government had only a small handful of talented

Generals to call upon, mostly elderly. When these few failed to obtain success the few remaining options were; Scorched earth, barbed wire, concentration camps and shooting those captured not wearing uniforms.

A new and improved rifle had been developed by 1895 and a carbine version some 4 inches shorter was hurriedly issued to the Cavalry. Eventually with further improvements a combined shorter rifle was developed in 1902 and became standard issue in 1907. The Cavalry handed in their carbines gratefully, but their sabres with bad grace, why one will never know; Perhaps the comparison with Mounted Infantry had become too transparent. Notwithstanding, this brings us to the finest hour of the Yeomanry, so far. For Constitutional reasons their way out of the United Kingdom was blocked. Considering the patriotic fervour of the times, it was a lame excuse and soon rectified. Perhaps it was a ruse by the War Office to force structural changes upon them and to ensure they and not the Counties should have an unquestioned right to their management. During their deliberations it became apparent that the Treasury was not prepared to provide funds for the transport of horses nor equipment to South Africa. There may have been some sense in this since crossing the Equator confused the horse as to when it should grow its winter coat. Nevertheless these *own goals* tended to indicate how skin deep was our military preparedness and was perceived by unfriendly onlookers for use at a later time. The various considerations pressing on the Government changed during the early months and enabling legislation was passed in December 1899, leading to the appeal of the 18th for volunteers to serve in the Imperial Yeomanry. The fight promised to be rough and tough and unfortunately much of the lead-time was eaten up in fruitless planning by inexperienced and untrained staff.

The first contingent of Imperial Yeomanry were at first sponsored by the Regiments at Home, with any deficiencies in personnel and material made good by the Regular Army. Sometimes and not amusingly, this amounted to the provision of unbroken Argentine mules. The basic organisation was four Sabre companies to a battalion. Very few of the Home Regiments could man-up a whole battalion, so the appeal for volunteers meant that people outside the existing Yeomanry were taken, provided they could ride. The Battalion was an administrative device, since companies were used as the building blocks for the

Field formations. From this point a mythology has grown up thoroughly obscuring who did what and how. Many of the then existing Yeomanry regiments bathe in the glow of supposed South African service, yet with half a dozen exceptions it is a misnomer. The generalised description above does much to veneer and varnish the situation covering the creation, maintenance and reinforcement of these hybrid formations. The following note has been abstracted from a Doctoral Thesis submitted by Colonel Dunlop to London University. [5]

"The backdrop to the employment of the Yeomanry came in February 1900 when it was known that all the Regular Army was committed and all those of the reserves, including the Militia would be used up by September. Granted there were 100,000 Regulars left in the United Kingdom, but these were mainly immature boys, besides which some few forces had to be retained for essential duties. Clearly the military appreciation of requirements varied from that of the Yeomanry. General Buller on the morrow of Colenso wired asking, 'would it be possible to raise 8,000 *irregulars* in England, organised not in regiments but in companies of 100 each. They should be equipped as *mounted infantry*, be able to shoot as well as possible and ride decently, I would amalgamate them with the colonials.' These proposals bore no resemblance to a home force priding themselves as cavalry."

"On 24th December, 1899, War Office instructions were communicated to the press nominating an Imperial Yeomanry Committee authorised to take all the steps for raising of the first contingent Imperial Yeomanry. The Government provided arms, a capitation grant and also a sum for horses. The responsibility for spending the money fell on the committee and was supplemented by additional funds raised by the various County Associations. The first contingent was, thanks to the large sums subscribed by the public, sent out to South Africa equipped in a far superior manner to the Regular Army. Many regiments had machine guns and light carts supplied from private funds while the jackets, hats and breeches were of superior material. On the other hand, Yeomanry stores of clothing were not replenished from England, and after some months of campaigning most of the Yeomanry were wearing ordinary government issue. This duplicate system of clothing supply led to difficulties, but a much more serious defect was a separate remount department organised by the Imperial Yeomanry. This latter system worked so badly, in fact, so very badly that it was abolished early in the campaign."

"A very small proportion of the total Imperial Yeomanry were recruits from the existing Yeomanry Regiments. A larger proportion came from volunteers and much the greater percentage came from the civilian population. Compared with the volunteer service companies, the conditions of enlistment were not strict as no fixed standards were laid down. Three contingents of Imperial Yeomanry were sent out to South Africa and owing to different methods employed in the raising of these contingents it is important to differentiate between them."

"The first contingent was raised in the early Spring of 1900. It was composed, for the most part, of men of good character who came in as volunteers at a critical period of the war. Quite a number of them could ride, though their knowledge of horsemanship and the grooming and care of horses was not good. Quite a number of them, once again, could shoot in the sense understood by the English countryside, that is to say, they could shoot with ordinary 12-bore shot-guns or a rook rifle, but their knowledge of a service rifle and service ranges was not good. The officers and NCO's were, to a certain extent recruited from Yeomanry Regiments and were not always very good. In few cases were squadrons entirely officered by Yeomanry and in some cases they were under 50%. Recruiting was carried out through local committees. Setting aside, however, all the defects necessarily inherent in an improvised force, the first contingent consisted for the most part of a good type of man who only required training to make him a first-class soldier. The faults as they showed themselves were, first, that insufficient training had been given before the force left England. The result was a good many companies went into the field in an unprepared state and suffered sickness or casualties which might have been avoided. Again, owing to the careless nature of enlistment some obviously unsuitable men were taken all the way to South Africa and up country. A few bad cases had an unnecessarily severe reflection on the force as a whole. Although battalions were raised, it was very seldom they were used in larger units than a company and these had to develop an esprit de corps of their own."

"While recruitment was proceeding extremely satisfactorily and men coming forward readily, the War Office was urged to continue enrolment of men even though the required numbers for the first contingent had been attained. Unfortunately this was refused and recruiting shut down. Men for this contingent had been engaged for twelve months and any longer period would have meant financial hardship. After the capture of Pretoria it could no longer be claimed that the existence of the country was at stake. During the period 27th January till 14th April the organising committee dispatched 550 officers and 10,571 other ranks. It was then dissolved on 25th May 1900."

"The slow but triumphal progress through the Orange Free State and the Transvaal was a reasonable excuse for failure of the War Office to maintain an adequate supply of drafts to the first contingent. However, subsequent events were to prove how unfortunate it was not to maintain a steady flow of new men to the existing units of the first contingent. A Major Wyndham Knight made a careful Précis of Evidence before the Elgin Commission enquiring into aspects of the Boer War and said, 'There should never have been any second or third contingents'. And reading between the lines it is obvious that the method eventually adopted as an emergency measure in January 1901 was expensive and unsatisfactory. It was not clear why men of the first contingent came home when they did as their engagement was for one year or the duration of the war, should the war last longer than a year. There is no doubt that the Yeomanry were influenced by the terms of service of the Colonials and particularly the South African Corps. Many were enrolled for periods as short as six months and the suchlike were continually terminating their service with one Corps, going home to settle private business and then joining another. The upshot of all this was that in the spring of 1901 the formation of a second contingent was looked upon as providing a relief force for the first. A number of Imperial Yeomen who went out in the 1900 remained on. Even so, the fact they were in a minority in the reconstituted force proved a disadvantage and there were certain difficulties because some of this first contingent who were seasoned men with junior rank found it difficult to fit in with newcomers who had been promoted in England. A steady stream of drafts would have avoided this difficulty."

"The total casualties of the first contingent were 3,093 out of 10,000. Of these 1,397 were invalided home, 216 killed in action, 330 died of disease and 606 were taken prisoner."

"In the early days of January 1901, Kitchener took

over as C-in-C South Africa and decided to raise a field force of 35,000 mounted men. A three man committee was set up at home to raise the second contingent and to provide each man with two or three months training before they went overseas. This was promptly countermanded by Kitchener who asked for them immediately following enrolment, apparently without realising many men could hardly maintain their seat upon a horse. Thereafter the committee considered themselves as a recruiting organisation pure and simple, indeed their resources and influence were slim."

"One important alteration was made to the rate of pay. The first contingent encountered Colonial contingents, who they considered their equals, paid at the rate of 5s (25p) a day, whilst they drew normal Cavalry rates of half this figure. After the capture of Pretoria had changed the general aspect of the war, such a differentiation caused some grumbling and it was represented that it would not be possible to raise a new contingent or induce men of the first to stay on unless the rate of pay was equalled."

"The second contingent was to include four special corps raised as battalions, the Sharpshooters, Paget's Horse, the Roughriders and the Duke of Cambridge's Own. For the rest a Yeomanry centre was established at Aldershot with another at the Curragh and all recruits were attested at local recruiting offices whether through the Yeomanry regiments or special agencies and sent direct to Aldershot. The result was for small parties of men to arrive without officers or often without NCO's, enrolled for various county Imperial Yeomanry corps. A large number of small details thus collected at Aldershot. There the men were equipped and thence sent forward, as transport to South Africa became available. Men went forward knowing little or nothing of the officers under whom they were to serve, small parties of various corps were mixed up in the same troopship and commanding officers in South Africa had little idea of what drafts they would receive. A large depot was opened at Elandsfontein where theoretically the confusion was to be sorted out."

"The order authorising the second contingent laid down the physical standard required and that the recruit was to be 'a good rider and a marksman according to Yeomanry standard'. These tests were only carried out perfunctorily, besides which there was no organisation in place to maintain standards. As the consequence, a great number of the officers and the men proved inefficient in South Africa and had to be weeded out. From some 17,245 men and 395 officers it appears that between 700 to 1,000 men and 42 to 100 officers were rejected. It seems the physique and intelligence of the men was on a higher level than for the Regular Army, though the glamour and patriotism was not burning as brightly as in 1900. However 5s. a day and some excitement were quite a good attraction for a reasonably high standard of artisan and competed for the first time with the labour market. It was the lack of organisation and a percentage of bad characters which gave an unfortunate start to the second contingent."

"The treatment of Sharpshooters, one of the specially selected Corps designed to be a crack unit is illustrative of the difficulties encountered as a whole. Each applicant was subjected to severe testing and then sent to Aldershot. As soon as 110 men were kitted, they were shipped overseas and it is quite obvious that only the privileged position of Colonel Jarvis, the commanding officer was able to intercept all his own drafts at Elandsfontein and reconstruct his regiment in the field at Standerton. Probably the officers were the weakest point in the second contingent, though the poor selection could not be blamed upon the committee, bearing in mind their straightened circumstances. The whole lesson underlines the impossibility of the improvisation of officers."

"After the great second wave of the second contingent had been sent, the War Office decided that no drafts would follow, though once again this decision had to be rescinded."

"A third contingent was authorised from 1st January 1902. The War Office learning from its mistakes decided on special training camps at Aldershot and Edinburgh where at least two and possibly three months training would be given. As the result undesirable men were quickly eliminated. Although the recruits were for the most part indifferent shots and riders when they came into the depots, they were of good physique and intelligence. A total force of 7,221 men were thus raised but the war was over before it could take the field and it is not possible to give any comparative comment upon their fighting capabilities."

"In all, a total of 34,124 men of all ranks in the Imperial Yeomanry were dispatched to South Africa between the outbreak of the war and 31st May 1902."

Special measures were adopted to attract likely recruits from Ireland: There was no Yeomanry there, nor existing legislation under which men could be taken. Directly the field force found its feet it developed a very useful organisation. The Establishment of each Company comprised a Captain, four subalterns, six sergeants including a Quartermaster, a farrier sergeant, two shoeing Smiths, a saddler, a bugler, 115 rank and file, including six corporals, two cooks and officers' servants. Organisationally each company was designed to divide into four sections of 28 and of real importance to the men a further division into seven four-man subsections. These four would in future stand, march, mess, sleep and fight together and membership was for their own choosing.

The listing forming Table Ten is made up from from Frederick, Till and Kipling & King [6, 7, 8] and illustrates the extent of the Imperial Yeomanry contribution to the

Boer War. Some of the inter-battalion moves and other variations are indicated in the text of the table. These relate to 1902, with the single exception of The Queen's Own West Kent Yeomanry in 1901. Throughout the period of hostilities, or nearly so, the 113th and 114th Companies, the Lovat Scouts were operating independently. Also out of the Caledonian Society of Johannesburg was formed The Scottish Horse. This latter unit was subsequently reinforced from Home, though it is not noted as such, unless the Highland Horse figures. There were a number of city units, not part of the Yeomanry proper, such as Belfast, Dublin, Manchester, Irish Horse and the Metropolitan Mounted Rifles, latterly formed into the Westminster Dragoons. Other contingents were also formed under the names of their commanders, such Paget, Fincastle and Lord Donoughmore. Also to be noted are the companies involved in the Colt's Gun. The listing of Imperial Yeomanry is shown in Table Ten.

Table 10 South African I Y Companies[6, 7, 8]

County, City etc	Coy	Bn	County, City etc	Coy	Bn
Ayrshire	17 (Colt's Gun)	6	Middlesex	34, 35, 62(11Bn 1902), 112	11,14(11)
Bedfordshire	28	4	Westminster Dgns	127-130	28
Belfast	46, 54	12, 13	(Sharp Shooters)	67, 70, 71, 75, 80 -83, 90-93, 115-118	18, 21, 23, 25
Berkshire	39, 58	10, 15	Metro' Mtd Rifles	94-97	24
Buckinghamshire	37, 38, 56, 57	10,15,19	Lothian	19(2nd & Colt's Gun)	6
Cheshire	21, 22	2	Lothian & Berwick	19 (1st & Colt's Gun)	6
Denbighshire	29	9	Lovat's Scouts	113, 114	Indept
Derbyshire	8, 104	4	Manchester	77, 105 (8 Bn 1902)	8
Devonshire	27	7	Montgomeryshire	31, 49, 89	9
Donoughmore's	47	13	Northumberland	14, 15, 55, 100, 101, 105 (M'chester), 110	5, 11, 14, 2
Dorsetshire	26	7	Notts Sherwood R	10	3
Dublin	45, 74	13, 16(8)	Notts, South	12	3
Fife & Forfar Lt H	20	6	Oxfordshire	40, 59	10, 15
Fincastle's Horse	139-142, 177	31	Paget's Horse	51&73 (12Bn 1902), 52, 68	(12), 19
Glamorganshire	4	1	Pembrokeshire	30	9
Glasgow	18 (Colt's Gun), 108	6	Scottish Horse	Not numbered	1st & 2nd
Gloucestershire	3	1	Shropshire	13	5
Hampshire	41(4th Bn 1902), 50	12 (4),17	Somerset, North	48	7
Hertfordshire	42	12	Somerset, West	25	7
Highland Horse	163-166	37	Staffordshire	6, 106	4
Irish	99	8	Suffolk	43, 44	12
Belfast	46 (12th Bn 1902), 54	13 (12)	Sussex	69 (7 Bn 1902)	7, (14)
Dublin	45, 74 (8 Bn 1902)	13,16	Warwickshire	5, 103	2
Irish Horse	131-134, 175, 176	29	Welsh Yeomanry	88	9
Irish, North	60	17	W'morland&C'land	24	8
Irish, South	61	17	Wiltshire	1, 2 ,63(1 Bn 1902)	1, (16)
Kent, East	33, 53 (11Bn 1902)	11,14(11)	Worcestershire	16, 102	5
Kent, West	36 (also 30 in 1901)	11	Yorkshire	11, 66 (3 Bn 1902)	3, (16)
Lanarkshire	107	6	Yorks (Doncaster)	9	3
Lancashire	23, 32	8, 2	Yorkshire Dgns	111	3
Leicestershire	7, 65	4, 17	Yorkshire Hussars	109	3
London, City of (Rough Riders)	72, 76 & 78 (22 Bn 1902), 79, 84-87	20, 20 (22), 22	North Riding Vols	98	3
			Younghusband's	119 -122	26

Chapter 5

The Doctor's Dilemma

As a conclusion to his book, The Great Boer War, Conon Doyle includes a chapter, Some Military Lessons of the War and it is worthwhile to review these:

"That war is far too important to be left to the military alone": An old saw. "With modern weapons every brave man with a rifle is a formidable soldier. It is the fresh eye undimmed by prejudice and tradition which is most likely to see clearly": Again, how true, for why did "the War Office declare for an Infantry war or the General on the spot select 10,000 men to march on Pretoria?"

"One of the most certain lessons of the war, as regards ourselves, was once and for all to reduce the bugbear of an invasion of Great Britain to an absurdity; because of the use of rifle and hedgerows, combined with the advantages of defence over attack, even without a fleet."

"The lesson of the war was to have a small, well trained army of high calibre soldiers who were well paid. It costs as much to feed, clothe and transport a worthless man as a good one. Persons incapable of becoming marksmen, the unfit and the unintelligent should not be recruited. The attractions of the service should be such as to make dismissal a real punishment."

So much for the generalities:

"Infantry - Their use as pikemen was mediaeval and dangerous. There is only one thing which wins modern battles and that is straight shooting. The standards of musketry were disgracefully poor. The taking of cover and its use were ignored and peace time training bore little resemblance to that of war. Entrenching was a weak point, amounting to rabbit scratchings compared to those of the opposing amateurs. The officer should carry a rifle like his men, dress alike and take his profession seriously. *If junior officers are unable to think for themselves or keep themselves informed as they might expect lawyers or doctors to be, they will be incapable of thinking for themselves when they reach senior rank.*"

He goes on to say; "Passing on to the cavalry, we come to the branch of the service which appears to me to be the most in need of reform. In fact, the simplest and most effective reform would be one which would abolish it altogether, retaining the Household Regiments for public functions." (Cardwell had more or less adopted this philosophy for the Yeomanry, rather than become enmeshed in a bed of nettles.)

And, "We have not realised what first-class mounted infantry can do, for we have never trained any first-class mounted infantry. Let a man be a fine rider, a trained horsemaster, a good skirmisher and a dead-shot and he becomes more valuable than any mere cavalryman can be. Cavalry it seems would be equally unable to attack it as resist it. If they were attacked, the magazine fire would shoot them out of the saddles. If they attacked, the best shots and best skirmishers must win." Then, "When we compare the doings of cavalry and of mounted infantry in this war we must remember that it is not a fair comparison, as the one force was highly trained, while the other was rapidly improvised."

Further on he says that only in one instance was there an essentially cavalry exploit: The charge at Diamond Hill. But on the other hand the mounted infantry did things which the cavalry as presently constituted could never have done - such as the ascent of Elandslaagte, or the surprise at Gun Hill. "Let them have only the rifle and let them be trained to fight on foot."

Lastly he enters a plea --- "for a vital change which *must* be effected. That is to relieve the poor horse of seven stone of extra weight which is carried by each and which brings the creature on to the field of battle too weary for his work. With the military saddle, the rug, the oat bag, the saddlebags and all the other hangings, the poor beast is weighed down. It is not an exaggeration to say that the Boer war was prolonged for months by this one circumstance, for we should certainly have cut off the Boer retreat and captured their guns had our horses not been handicapped so severely. Whether spare horses should carry the things or galloping carriages (Galloper Guns had been in service a century earlier), or whether this gear should be dispensed with, must be left with the leaders. But that seven stone must in some way be removed if we are ever to get full value out of our mounted force."

In further paragraphs the remaining departments of the military are dissected. The Artillery obtains the best

Chapter 5

plaudits, although deficient in equipment. It was unable to take the high ground, through no fault of its own and this severely limited results.

It reveals the blinkered thinking of the times, that no public reply was thought necessary and it seems unlikely that the Military of the time would have engaged in a private dialogue, that they were sure to lose. The book was published late, during 1900 and received widespread critical acclaim written as it was in an open and direct style. Such adverse comments, of course stood in danger of being dismissed as the demented rantings of a meddler, but this was untrue. Doctor Conon Doyle was Knighted for his work, at that time, in counter-espionage, refuting spurious Boer propaganda, when Britain was being pilloried by the World. And to do his work he had access to the facts and opinions of those best qualified to advise.

There is a vast literature dealing with the Boer War and a number of general works covering the British Army. None of these succeeds clearly in bringing out the situation in which the Yeomanry found itself. Lest this be considered special pleading the reader may like to consult JW Fortescue's History of the British Army or P Young & J Lawson under the same title. The Yeomanry played, as the numbers already quoted show, no more than a small part in a large and celebrated disaster. The resultant tragedy was actually made worse by winning, because it fooled us into adopting a practised indifference to its future implications.

The Yeomanry was poorly prepared and badly misused in the field. There were of course notable exceptions, where proprietorial rights allowed the Kitchener grasp of imperatives to be loosened. United Kingdom examples were some of the London Regiments, The Scottish Horse and of course The Lovat Scouts. However the local Colonial and most of the Dominion Light Horse were less hampered by traditional Cavalry thinking of the period, in which they rode into battle and the Infantry walked!

References

1 Melville.ML. The Story of the Lovat Scouts. (The Saint Andrew Press, Edinburgh 1981)
2 Conan Doyle, Sir A The Great Boer War. (Smith Elder, London 1900)
3 Indian Army Soldiers and Uniforms.
4 Rollaston. L Yeomanry Cavalry or Mounted Infantry. (Smith Elder, London 1901)
5 Dunlop Col JK. The Development of the British Army - 1899-1914. (Methuen, London 1938)
6 Frederick. JBM. Lineage Book of British Land Forces, 1660-1978. (Microform Academic, Wakefield, 1984)
7 Till. Paul H. Imperial Yeomanry Companies of the Boer War. The Orders & Medals Research S, London. Autumn 1992 pp 167-174
8 Kipling, AL & King, HL. Head Dress Badges of the British Army. (F Muller. London 1972)

Plate 5/1   The Imperial War Museum

A Yeoman in the Saddle. The seeds of trouble are sewn here as the weight of equipment increased with the range of operations. At the end the Boers would outrun pursuing troops to get away from many a well established ambush. When cornered they were liable to ride through the British lines so sure were they that their use of firearms was superior to those they opposed.

Plate 5/2   The Imperial War Museum

Mounted Infantry! Only with reluctance would the cavalry accept infantry training.
Perversely, the infantry were not offered proper training when mounted. Whilst the Boer
War called for a high degree of mobility, neither the cavalry nor the infantry was ever
properly trained as 'mounted riflemen', hence the Boer got away so often from a numerically
superior force.

Plate 5/3   The Imperial War Museum

Mounted Riflemen? It is entirely uncertain what this martial scene illustrates. Whether
Infantry or Cavalry they seem ill prepared for the saddle.

Plate 5/4   The Imperial War Museum

The Enemy. It was 14-15 year olds who competed for a place to assault Majuba Hill in the 1st Boer War.

Plate 5/5   The Cheshire Yeomanry

Kit Inspection. These are not always the bugbear supposed as at least the individual was encouraged to review the order of his stuff!

6. The Edwardians

Additions to Establishment

As the consequence of the Boer War many new units were formed, though this did not of itself ensure their acceptance onto the Home Establishment. Accordingly, disbandments and re-raisings altered the precedence accorded them. In the precedence listing issued in 1885 the 2nd West Yorkshire were shown as 36, but they were disbanded in 1894, meaning that four lesser units gained one point each in precedence. The new units added to Table 11 commence their order from 39:

The creation of the Special Reserve, in 1908, took out those holding precedence numbers 50, 51 and 52, whilst the Lovat Scouts were next split into two regiments, leading to a revision of the tables.

Further changes were made during 1914, which are listed here for the sake of completeness. On mobilisation the Scottish Horse divided into three regiments: 54 - 55 - 56. Also early in the war the Welch Yeomanry Horse was raised on 15th August 1914 making it 57 in the corrected order of precedence,

though it was interposed incorrectly at 44. However in the 1903 table, there were further Official errors: Lincoln was numbered 44 when it should have been 42 (hence Sussex was really 43 and Glamorgan 44), thus when the Welsh Horse were interposed it became 45 (officially) and all the following numbers were in the words of Fellows and Freeman, were 'fleeted up one'.

Swinton's Cautionary Tale

Major Ernest Swinton published an amusing yet instructive booklet on Subaltern tactics in 1904, entitled The Defence of Duffer's Drift [1]. The plot concerned the defence, by a platoon of riflemen, of a road and ford across a dried out river, overlooked by a small hill. The hero, the redoubtable Lieutenant Backsight Forethought, after a tiring day's march and a heavy meal, settles into a nightmarish sleep. In this the Boers succeed in devastating his defences and making use of the road to re-supply their forces. As a result, the next morning certain changes were made to improve dispositions. However, the succeeding four nights were accompanied by equally disturbing dreams,

Table 11 Additions to Yeomanry Establishment following the Boer War

No	WO Date	Title	No	Actual Date	Title
39	12-04-01	Surrey		07-06-60	Fife & Forfar
40		Fife & Forfar		12-04-01	Surrey
41	14-05-01	Norfolk		14-05-01	Norfolk
42	04-06-01	Sussex		18-05-01	Lincoln
43	14-06-01	Glamorgan		04-06-01	Sussex
44	26-06-01	Lincoln		14-06-01	Glamorgan
45	18-07-01	County of London (RR)			Westminster Dgns
46	18-07-01				
47	18-07-01	3 County of London (SS)			
48	10-08-01	Bedford			
49	28-10-01	Essex			
50	29-11-01	King's Colonials	50	07-02-02	Northampton
51	07-01-02	N of Ireland	51	02-04-02	E Riding
52	07-01-02	S of Ireland	52	11-02-03	1 Lovat Scouts
53	07-02-02	Northampton	53	11-02-03	2 Lovat Scouts
54	02-04-02	E Riding	54	16-02-03	Scottish Horse (two regts)
55	11-02-03	Lovat Scouts (two regts)	55	Mobn	Scottish Horse
56	16-02-03	Scottish Horse (two regts)	56	Mobn	Scottish Horse

leading to successive changes. On the sixth night, the defences hold as the result of careful positioning of men on the hill and along the river bank. The object lessons above were an early perception of the changes brought about by the best tactical use of the rifle. Swinton went on to write the Official analysis of the war between Russia and Japan, fought around Port Arthur. This revealed a continuation of the trench and barbed wire principle, in which the carnage was dramatically increased by the use of the machine gun, a sort of belt fed rifle! This 'developed' to the point where military operations became static. It was indeed a return to siege warfare, because it relied upon the reduction of defences, by bombardment, before the infantry could rise up to do their job. Essentially this presaged a transfer of initiative from the infantry to the artillery, just as the rifle had earlier grounded the cavalry in offensive operations. Granted the horse, or something like it, was required to provide mobility, but it no longer fought with a man on its back, so henceforth it was destined to become a mere beast of burden: well almost!

As with so many lessons, they needed time to sink in. Britain was at its Imperial cross-roads. The Army was designed and equipped for Colonial operations but increasingly the power vacuum in Europe drew it into a Continental Strategy. The Admiralty had the situation in hand by about 1905, at the time of the Dreadnought crisis. True to form, the public were blissfully unaware of a looming disaster, still bathing in the glory of defeating - farmers! Parliament were chiefly concerned in our having any sort of Army, so long as it was cheap. Thus there were two dimensions to the problem. As we have seen the tactical one waited on a horse substitute; one impervious to bullets! The failure to solve this conundrum timeously led to indescribable carnage later. The other side of the coin concerned Army administration and this was about to be taken up, more or less where Cardwell had left it in 1872.

More Military Reform: Edward Burdon Haldane
Governments rarely volunteer reform, but the bad press during and directly following the recent war focused hard on the shortcomings of the War Office, in all its departments, save that of military intelligence. A succession of enquiries and two ministerial appointments collected the facts and tinkered away for three and a half years but failed to provide a remedy. This was more or less a re-run of the post Crimea situation. Also, despite the horrendous results in South Africa, Parliament still contained a strong lobby against raising and equipping the military; basically the Government could do virtually anything it wished, so long as it didn't cost money. On the other hand, directly the defence was seen as compromised an equally vociferous lobby would take up the task of harrying the Minister responsible.

The situation inherited was a unified though thoroughly demoralised War Office. Happily, the authority of the War Minister at least was absolute. Its effectiveness had been blunted by what can be termed *organisational drift*. In this, individual developments were incorporated into departments piecemeal, but without due regard to the organism as a whole: It was not a team. Cardwell had much earlier left the formation of a General Staff for later consideration, although absolutely clear in his own mind that it was a vital requirement. This was linked to the vexed question of dispensing with the services of a redundant Commander-in-Chief. These two aspects were not finalised until after the Boer War, in the period leading up to Haldane taking office. In the event the period from 1872 till 1905 was frittered away. The once new organisation gelled without the leadership of a trained General Staff and subsequently lost its edge. As the mind directs the body, this minus made it impossible for the various departments to operate efficiently or economically. And worst of all, there had been no one in Government prepared to grasp the nettle. This was to change!

The essence of Cardwell was the provision of *rapid* Home Country response to Empire crisis. This unfortunate phraseology is resurrected periodically, where speed of movement is substituted for cash input. Against this, forces elsewhere had been disbanded to achieve a balancing economy. The foreseen need for a General Staff was, amongst other things, to ensure a strategic balance was struck in military affairs and these might be quite disconnected from ongoing events. The provision of lead-times in weapon and training development had to be such that the manuals of the day were up to date and troops suitably practised, also staff procedures needed testing before being immersed in the cauldron of war. The fact of the Boers being able to butcher whole troop columns by a rudimentary combination of fieldcraft, rifle fire and movement rocked the military establishment and the public at home when first it became news. If these were the headlines, there were other even less palatable facts, such as the large number of troops taken prisoner and that the largest killer remained bad health, not bullets!

Chapter 6

These features pointed to faulty administration which was hopelessly enmeshed with command and almost out of touch with reality. It was impossible in the most celebrated instance for three Field Forces to co-ordinate their activities to obtain mere average results; instead of which, each was routed!

All this was history to Richard Burdon Haldane when he became Secretary of State for War on 11th December 1905. [2] By that time the scenario had changed: There was an *entente cordial* with France, whilst Germany was perceived as a potential threat. Whatever the difficulties, he intended to reshape the army machine with those about him most able to help. This meant three things; the reorganisation of the Army as a whole, to provide better value for money; the introduction of a General Staff to oversee ongoing activity and to prepare for the future; and the writing, testing and implementation of procedures for application throughout its sphere of governance, of which more later. It was the first item that loomed above all other considerations, indeed the house stood or fell on that foundation. He had less than three months in which to prepare and submit the Army Estimates. There was a complex array of interlocking considerations, some of which relied upon agreement with other departments. In the absence of time, the figure of £28m was chosen upon which to build the new Army machine. The genius of this was it provided a much needed planning target for *In-house* use, but it was felt anyway to be the maximum figure Parliament itself would tolerate.

Agreement was made with the Admiralty, according to the *Blue Water Policy*, for them to be responsible for the first line of Home Defence. This released a large number of troops from coastal defences and that of London. Similarly a reduction in overseas garrisons was negotiated with the Colonial and Foreign Offices, taking into account improved response times possible with enhanced communications and methods of transportation. These arrangements allowed the shape and disposition of the Regular Army to be revised. Not until the Overseas element of this was set could the question of Home forces be tackled. Thus by 1908 the overseas army was established at 74 battalions. The remaining army at Home, which included all the reserves, served the peacetime function of finding drafts and providing a readiness for war on mobilisation. And from this was fashioned the *British Expeditionary Force!*

No one, it appears, ever questioned to what use a force of such size could be put. It comprised six large divisions of 66 line and six Guards Battalions, four Cavalry brigades, 63 six gun batteries of Artillery and 'the advance provision of the ancillary services in the manning of the ammunition columns, transport, supply, clerical, medical and veterinary services; and the maintenance of a draft level in peacetime able to offset the first six months of war wastage, estimated at 40% of all ranks and arms.' Although this was the beginning of a Continental strategy, it was never advertised as such. Continuation of the Cardwell principle of unit reinforcement combined with the reduced periods of overseas Imperial Service, for individuals, must have deflected attention from a number of significant pointers, such as the new relationship with France and the German Battlefleet construction programme: Nevertheless Britain was engaged upon something distinctly *Continental*.

Having established the size of the Army stationed around the Empire and its vital organ of replenishment, with its hidden vehicle for supporting the French, by obligation of treaty, it was now time to address the case for a Reserve Army. Of all the problems to be surmounted, this was to prove the least tractable. Excluding the element of reservists from the Regular Army, these comprised; the Militia, the Volunteers and the Yeomanry.

Since the end-play was for one united Territorial Force it is worthwhile to consider the status quo. The Militia cost £2m per annum, was without Artillery or Cavalry, besides which it was under strength to the extent of 1,000 officers and 46,000 men, based upon the establishment of 131,000. It was not liable for service overseas besides which many were too young for this service, it lost 10% through desertion and a further 25% through premature discharge. Its main blessing was the 12,000 'troops' it furnished to the Regular line, but in all other respects it had little military value. A saving grace during the recent war was all save four battalions volunteered to serve overseas, but they lost a high proportion of their best officers and men to Regular units to replace casualties, leaving the remainder to be relegated to garrison and lines of communication duty. The Volunteers dated from the 1859-61 period when it seemed likely the French would invade us and previous formations under that category had been disbanded during the Napoleonic war. At the outset, this force was largely independent, but through the ravages of time, came to Haldane at an annual cost of £1.75m. Analysis showed it to be lacking in organisation; Basically the requirement for a service age range of 20-34 and preferably unmarried could not be met, so at the time of the recent war, out of 230,000 men, only 22,000 actually served. The troops remaining at home were equally disorganised; They had neither a command structure, nor administrative and supply services, no transport, and not even the arms to ward off an invader! The condition of the Yeomanry was more satisfactory, though one might add the rider, *by comparison.* It comprised some 25,500 all ranks and trained annually for 14 to 18 days. Three contingents of Imperial Yeomanry were raised during the war, of which two served in South Africa. The true nature of these has been examined already in the previous chapter. The main defect, as then constituted, was the absence of Staff, Brigade organisation or administrative services. It also lacked a specific wartime role. In essence it remained very tied to the counties but formed a nucleus from which the Cavalry of a second line might be fashioned.

These reserves presented an unhappy picture. The common thread running through the volunteer forces was a rugged independence, an absence of any higher formation staff and minimal administrative machinery. These latter features, were of course the principal shortcomings across the Army as a whole. Haldane felt that reorganisation was vital and quantity, not quality, was to be the watchword in the Territorial Force. Thereafter a process of long term education would, to his mind, provide a reserve army able to attract a large reservoir of manhood needed during a national emergency. During the interim something had to be done at the local level to provide for the education and the infrastructure of a modern force. He proposed County Associations to handle this business need, whether out of originality is not important. However, a number of unwelcome difficulties reared their heads from this stage and became perennial up to the time of The Great War. The Territorial Force as proposed would bring together all the existing auxiliary Army forces into 16 divisions Each would have Infantry, Cavalry and Artillery components, plus the necessary staff and services making them mobile. The whole organisation was planned to number 300,000 men.

The enabling Bill was first tabled on 4th March 1907, received its Second Reading on the 9th, 10th and 23rd of April and entered the Committee stage on 6th May. The Third Reading was on the 19th June, when it was passed by 286 to 63 votes. Surprisingly, the debates throughout were poorly attended. The significant ground given was to change the purpose of the Force from support of the Second Line to one of Home defence. In passing to the Lords, the Militia was removed from its provisions. On this basis the Bill received the Royal Assent on 2nd August.

The Act was blighted by the exclusion of the Militia from the scheme, at the behest of its colonels. They would neither agree to joining the Territorials, whatever the blandishments, nor would they accept that of engagement for overseas service as drafts for the Regular Army. Those that wished were able to transfer to a Special Reserve, whilst the remainder served out their term of service, so the Militia as such was allowed to whither on the vine. It can be seen that the withdrawal of such a large infantry reserve meant that new numbers had to be raised to balance the scheme before the time of an emergent crisis. On the credit side the reform rounded off the requirements for Brigade and Divisional staffs, produced Line services, provided artillery of a sort and rationalised an inefficient system into separating command from administration! If this was the maximum the country was prepared to pay for, it was certainly the most it could expect for its penny.

Haldane strove for many years after the passing of the Territorial and Reserve Forces Act to have it accepted as a popular measure, though recruiting never reached the target figure. A succession of notables subjected the Territorial Force to minor and seemingly unnecessary slights. Field Marshal Lord Roberts, a former Artillery man, arose in the House of Lords to say how ineffectual the newly created gunnery arm was, even a positive danger to those around, by comparison to its quick firing Continental counterpart. But then it was early days and the guns were perforce conversions of outdated equipment and part-time training took longer than in regular units. These pricks sowed doubts in the mind of the public and it was always on a basis of popular enthusiasm that the scheme was destined to succeed or fail. Also, the War Office was slow off the ground to prompt the new or hardly created County Associations to establish Drill Halls and rifle ranges and thus the educational element was hampered. The Regulars had also to forge a range of new relationships to keep on terms with something they regarded as an extension of *their* army.

Next there came the creation of a Staff Corps, but not upon the French or German model. From inception there was to be no division between those performing staff duties and those in charge of troops, so that officers on the ladder of promotion alternated between one type of appointment and the other. Whether the arrangements included Staff 'tabs' down to the rank of captain and something like 60 differing armbands as employed in the Great War on the Western Front is uncertain. In essence this training would acquaint officers from all arms and services with the modus operandi and capabilities of their counterparts and entry was to be by open competitive examination.

Turning again to Colonel Dunlop [3] and closely linked with the reforms was the requirement for a central doctrine to the new Army organisation and a provision of the means for its direction and command in war. Little seen at the time were the efforts of the Directorate of Military Training, working under a man called Haig. Douglas Haig became Director of Staff Duties on November 9, 1906 and he assembled a group to produce the necessary works. Admittedly something had already been done in the issue of Combined Training, but the essence of the new scheme was codified for all arms by the issue of 'Field Service Regulations, Part I - Operations - 1909'. This provided a much needed statement of generally agreed Strategic and Tactical principles, resulting from the recent war. The concept of a military staff work was poorly understood, yet an essential part of military education. The idea that tactics and strategy should relate was not in question, nor the positive steps taken to integrate the Territorial Army. At the end it was desired that any operation became transparent to the people charged with its execution, thus everything had to be thought through and an agreed procedure adopted. This was revolutionary; Written orders were one thing but for everybody to follow a standard procedure, to which they were accountable was another. It was at this stage, the one dealing with administration and the responsibilities of the services that the Treasury raised objections, most possibly on historical grounds. Now Haig was thoroughly convinced over the need for a companion volume covering the whole organisation of the Army and for the duties and functions of officers, units and commands in the Lines of Communications and at the base to be as clearly defined as for an army in the field.

'Field Service Regulations - Part II - Organisation and Administration, 1909' was next published with the powerful backing of Haldane. The consequences flowing from these measures were immense, as all arms and services henceforth sung from the same hymn sheet. [3]

It may be thought that having laid the foundations for a revitalised Yeomanry the remaining elements over the Haldane tenure of office were of no real concern. This was untrue since for the first time in its long history the United Kingdom had an integrated reserve army. Despite strenuous effort to explain the remarkable features of the new scheme, the idea did not get across by 1914 when Lord Kitchener took over as Secretary of State for War. His decision was to create his own reserve army and to pay little attention to the Territorial Force much to the latter's chagrin. Thus for the second time the same man stood in the way of having reserve forces used to their best advantage. Haldane's achievements were later vindicated, during the 1920's and all the machinery so painstakingly assembled before the Great War was put to good use, even the artillery with its decrepit field pieces.

The creation of an Imperial General Staff created a meeting point at the head of the military through which the various departments of the War Office were to be encouraged to filter their considerable but otherwise uncoordinated services to distant forces: They hated it, but it began to work. Various *rides* or supervised exercises were organised to throw up a range of administrative shortcomings, which could be studied and corrected before the next. Haldane was able to insist upon this, mainly because he had attended German exercises and also knew that country possessed a modern railway system geared to placing their armies in position within three days. This, to the public mind, goes under the heading of *mobilisation*, but it is no more than half the story. More often it was the mobilised troops which froze, starved and lost sleep, simply because no steps had been taken to follow through and organise affairs, at the end of an otherwise uneventful rail journey. In this way good troops lost their fighting edge, before starting to do what they had been trained for. Each plan was to be properly thought through and tested. That was the essence of the good administration Haldane was determined to instil. *Mobilisation* was to be the acid test of the Government's intention to put into operation a well thought out plan and not some vague twelve letter word.

To achieve it required supervision, *at the workface*. The problem with the British Army of 1908 was a missing element of 4,419 Subalterns for the Expeditionary Force, the most junior grade of officer in the Army. Cardwell had got rid of the Cornets and Ensigns, but the pay of a Subaltern had not been raised since 1806! Competent men in the ranks were unlikely to volunteer for promotion leading to a pay cut, besides which they were the least likely to have the private income necessary to make life liveable. Without this element made good it was unlikely the Expeditionary Force would work, at that date. This of course was another story.

It hardly bears thinking about, what the state of our Army might have been, without a man of Haldane's stature. That he was helped by others of great ability and influence is agreed. Yet even in the decadent Edwardian era, many of his critics should have exercised more sense. Basically, for all that was said, he cut his cloth according to his measure. Though no gambler, he obviously felt things would come right, but in the meantime admitted no weaknesses. Perhaps this annoyed some and provoked others who felt he should be more forthcoming in his dealings. Through his dogged perseverance, it did work out to have an Expeditionary Force in place to deny the Germans a success for their flawed Schlieffen offensive in 1914. Like Cardwell he worked to and beyond the limits of his considerable abilities with consequent permanent damage to his health. Taken with Cardwell, this duo were the most influential Secretaries of State for War the United Kingdom has had and the accident of history makes it difficult to choose between them.

First Aid Nursing Yeomanry
Popular accounts dealing with the First Aid Nursing Yeomanry vary from the picturesque to the bizarre. Thus, Hugh Popham [4] quotes from a 1946 Tokyo newspaper, and as he remarks, "at least they got the name and the date of founding right".

"Four beautiful English ladies wearing khaki uniform over their harmonious bodies talk about their impression of the water paradise, Matsue . . . FANY, the First Aid Nursing Yeomanry, is an army organised by female patriots of Britain who are proud of an old brilliant tradition and is so famous that it is distinguished among all the British forces . . . They were as brave as 'Joan of Arc' in the Crimean War,

who is world famous as a brave and gentle nightingale.

FANY is one of such women's troops and its history is old. It is the very origin that in 1907 they served in the riding on horseback . . . They usually stayed in British Colonies, but during the Second World War they showed their active endeavour in the European Front, France and Belgium and the Far Eastern Front . . . As truck drivers and aeroplane pilots their service did not fall behind men's and some of them are told, pitifully to say, to have died in the battle."

The real truth is slightly more prosaic. The first grains of truth: A wounded man had much time to contemplate his situation, even misfortune, over the journey betwixt battlefield and base hospital. The gap between the field dressing stations and the hospital was a veritable killing ground for the seriously wounded. Many perished en route, whilst postponing the journey had an equally deadly effect. Cavalry Serjeant-Major EC Baker, recounted how the idea of the Corps occurred to him at such a time:

"During my period of service with Lord Kitchener in the Sudan Campaign, where I had the misfortune to be wounded, it occurred to me that there was a missing link somewhere in the Ambulance Department, which, in spite of the changes in warfare, had not altered very materially since the days of the Crimea when Florence Nightingale and her courageous band of helpers went out TO SUCCOUR AND SAVE the wounded. On my return from active service I thought out a plan which I anticipated would meet the want, but it was not until September of the year 1907 that I was able to found a troop of young women to see how my ideas would work . . . but I refused to take the public into my confidence until I was certain that I was progressing ON THE RIGHT LINES."

The Edwardian era was a veritable spawning ground for all manner of voluntary bodies, such as The Boy Scouts, The Girl Guides, the Voluntary Aid Detachments of the Red Cross and latterly an offshoot from the Corps itself, the Women's Sick and Wounded Convoy Corps, to mention a few. Captain Baker hardly rates a mention in the national records, although his idea was both original and ingenious and led to the formation of unique and useful organisation. However, for an organisation of this type to prosper called for determination ranged behind sound principles, whilst at the time of the suffragettes, any strident female activity stood in danger of attracting public odium and official indifference. Notwithstanding the bleak prospects, the stated objective of the Corps was to provide services to the Government in the event of hostilities. For membership, each had to qualify in First Aid and Home Nursing, Horsemanship, Veterinary Work, Signalling and Camp Cookery. But the mere passing of tests satisfied nobody and the members had to demonstrate resourcefulness, the ability to exercise initiative and the determination to bring each task to a successful conclusion. Finally to dissuade the faint hearted, there was a joining fee, prospective members had to provide their own uniforms and immediate wants, added to which they received no pay. To these qualities, summed in a man as 'having what it takes', they added the requirement for a gentlewomen.

A carefully cultivated liaison took place with officials during the pre-war period. On the one hand the organisation wished to gain acceptance and to attract recruits, whilst on the other it had to train along parallel lines of the services it sought to assist. Colonel FC Ricardo of the Grenadier Guards was able to inspect them at their riding school, when the initial preliminaries had been completed and as a result invited them to appear at the Royal Naval and Military Tournament and subsequently he became Honorary Colonel. Riding instruction took place at the Surrey Yeomanry Riding School and latterly with the 19th Hussars at Hounslow. A Captain LCV Hardwicke, MD, RAMCT, acted as adviser on First Aid and Ambulance matters, at this time. The Guards Depot at Pirbright was able to provide tentage for the camps and when their drill reached a satisfactory standard they were invited to join their Church Parade: a signal honour. At a later stage when motor vehicles came on the scene, the routine procedures of the Army Service Corps were incorporated.

Growing pains around 1910 led to a schism between those wanting to take on more immediate activities. The larger part left to form The Women's Sick and Wounded Convoy Corps. Also, there had been a muddle over the finances, although its exact nature was neither discovered nor disclosed. Those that remained took stock of the unhappy situation and initiated a reorganisation. The uniform was changed to a divided skirt with the abandonment of riding side-saddle. Captain Baker stepped back, remaining as titular head until January 6th 1912 when Colonel Ricardo formally took over command of the Corps. Effectively this was now led by two very determined and capable women, Lillian Franklin (FANY No 1) and Grace Ashley-Smith (FANY No 2) and by 1912 the ravages of these earlier troubles had been repaired. Under the latter it was arranged for RAMC Sergeants to give stretcher drill and teach bandaging, whilst a signalling officer gave semaphore and morse instruction.

When the principles set down in founding this voluntary and unpaid Corps are studied it can be seen how it so successfully thwarted the later take-over ambitions of others and how its rugged independence should have never been confused with arrogance or pride.

Two further events occupy this account until the onset of The Great War. The first of these were the troubles in Ireland and although the Corps was given a provisional acceptance as "The Ulster Ambulance", this came to nothing. The second came after the 1914 Summer Camp, where under the good offices of a Major Smallman RAMC, Surgeon-General Woodhouse was induced to inspect them and somewhat grumpily agreed thinking them to be VADs. In collusion with their RAMC instructor, a Sergeant Pepper, they put up such an impressive show of medical expertise that he recommended Ashley-Smith to Sir Arthur Sloggett, then Chief Commissioner of the Red Cross at the War Office and the latter gave her a sympathetic hearing. At that stage they had every right to think they had made it, but with the commencement of hostilities in 1914 events were to prove otherwise.

The further account dealing with the evolution of the Corps appears under Appendix H, for as with the Yeomanry its scope developed far beyond the initial ideals, across two World Wars and remains with us today, as one of the oddest of registered charities, but with a cogent peace-time purpose and a latent war making capability.

References
1 Swinton.E. The Defence of Duffer's Drift. (G Ronald Oxford 1904, (United Service Magazine)
2 Spiers.EM. Haldane - An Army Reformer. (Edinburgh University Press, Edinburgh 1980)
3 Dunlop Col John K. The Development of the British Army 1899-1914. (Methuen, London 1938)
4 Popham Hugh. F.A.N.Y The Story of The Women's Transport Service 1907-1984. (Leo Cooper/Secker Warburg. London 1984)
5 Ward Irene. F.A.N.Y. Invicta. (Hutchinson. London 1955)

7. The Great War

Schlieffen

The essence of German strategy was for a quick war on one front, followed by a conclusion on the other. To out-distance the ability of the Allies to respond, they proposed using their rail network for a rapid mobilisation. Germany knew it took its potential enemies three weeks longer to mobilise than themselves and their plan took three weeks to put into effect. However useful this lead-time, there was a conundrum. If they chose to mobilise one way, until it was fully effected, they were unable to mobilise in the other, because railway movements became wrong-ended. Also, practical considerations favoured an attack on France, with whom Germany had no conceivable quarrel! To achieve their aims, the Germans dusted off a plan dating from 1905. Count Alfred von Schlieffen, as Chief of the General Staff revised an earlier one by von Moltke, to take account of recent developments (the war between Russia and Japan). The strategy was to place relatively weak forces on the left flank, facing the French across easily defended ground and strong forces on the right flank, in good fighting country. In disregard of Belgian neutrality these latter forces were to move obliquely pinning down the French, enabling a crushing flank attack to open the way round Paris, severing Allied communications and to hammer the remaining forces against the anvil of their left flank. So much for the plan.

Between plan and execution came Moltke, now as Commander-in-Chief, who proceeded to meddle with the balance of the forces. This more than anything saved the Allies from defeat, seeing as the French, Russians and the British, had each contrived defective military arrangements. In the case of the British, they delayed mobilisation for purely political reasons. Nevertheless there was just time to have the British Expeditionary Force in place: Well almost.

There is not much to be said about the Western Front for all its casualties. By dint of improvisation, the enemy thrust was deflected. The Admiralty, always perceptive and of course responsible for the transport and supply of any British expedition, were wide awake to the threat posed and had gratuitously interposed a screening force to enable the essential Channel ports of re-supply to be secured. Thereafter it was siege warfare. Trench warfare when it developed, gelled around two facts. Firstly, although the Germans had no thought of failure, a natural Staff prudence ensured that it was the 'high' ground that was occupied when movements ground to a halt. Thus it was the Allies came to occupy a *well irrigated* front-line, whilst the Germans sat in a high proportion of well engineered trench constructions, very often impervious to shellfire. Secondly, the British had Staff, hardly by an oversight, at the tender stage in their development, without any experience of campaigning in formations above the Light Division. Added to this was the dead-hand of the Treasury ensuring trench building and other supplies for the front, when they came, were generally of inferior quality, even to those of the French, when the latter sourced them from the United Kingdom!

Some British Army Statistics[1][2]

It does well to review the status of the British Army from the point where the impetus of the German onslaught stalled. There was a stalemate with a static front running from the Channel to the Swiss Frontier. At the start of the war the British had just 447 Staff College graduates and an Army of three-quarters of a million. Virtually the only portion of it that was equipped and trained for Continental war was the BEF and this was severely mauled by its head-on collision with the forces of Schlieffen. At the end there were 5,514 Staff officers connected with this front and possibly 10,000 overall. The Army total manpower soared to 3,563,466, which figure excluded losses. Casualties amounted to about two million wounded and 900,000 killed, with 190,000 prisoners. Such a loss represents about a third of the whole and one assumes predominantly on the Western Front, sadly depleting the proportion of the troops present. A percentage of the combatants returned to the field, indeed people were wounded more than once. Again, such figures are not quoted to jerk sympathy from the reader, but to indicate the compound nature of the management problem. Much has been written about the poor standards of generalship, with the troops advertised by the *Lions Led by Donkeys* fable. There seems to be neither basis for the former nor the latter and as General Mangin at Verdun remarked 'whatever you do (attack or defend), you lose a lot of men' and this applied to both sides equally. In a short series of paragraphs John Terraine paints an objective and more plausible picture of the Western Front and the huge armies developing there.

The first problem has already been alluded to, that of scale. The British Staff had little experience of campaigning in large formations and none at all on the Continent when the war opened. There was the relaxed Victorian attitude and practised amateurism toward the profession of arms, unlike the Royal Navy. In a space of under two years many of the better products of the Military Schools had to shoulder four advances in rank. The Staff usually worked from before nine in the morning till ten at night with the promise of leave after three months a dream, but six months the reality. This went on, seven days a week for months on end, whilst during an offensive it was most likely 8.30 am till midnight and half hour meal breaks. A more macabre aspect, as the war progressed was for the staff to be made up from the fit and unfit in the ratio 2:5. All of them faced a torrent of new technology, in which their reverie was shocked by:

"...the first war of aviation, with all the implications of that new medium the first real undersea war, entirely altering the nature of naval power; the first war of the internal combustion engine, therefore also the first war of the mechanics, a new breed of men in uniform; the first war of wireless telegraphy (but not unfortunately the walkie-talkie); the first of two great artillery wars, with all *their* destructive implications; the first chemical war, using (among other things) poison gas, and napalm (flame throwers, petroleum based); the first war of modern mass production, mass logistics and mass administration (by 1916 British GHQ in France was administering a population bigger than any single unit of control in England, except Greater London). And much else besides."

In terms of education, the Staff rode a near vertical learning curve. They were expected to survive the ride and come on performing just about every form of managerial technique then known whilst continuing a rôle as leaders and in all their dealings still appear rational human beings. At the firing line the absence of voice control came at precisely the moment battle was joined! The Western Front was the largest theatre of the war and the first. As the war progressed other theatres opened, notably when Turkey sided with Germany. In due course to enlarge the size of the Army, Second and Third Line Regiments were formed. Whilst the Army had their problems so did the Royal Navy, who also had a foot on the land, with responsibilities on both sides of the English Channel.

The Admiralty Landships Committee
Some words of explanation are necessary before immersing ourselves in one of the most far reaching military developments of the 20th Century. It may be thought by some readers that the Admiralty were tinkering in an area none of their business. In fact they were in the hapless situation of securing any land installations necessary for the security of the fleet or those operations undertaken by the military, either at home or abroad. That constituted a broad canvas! As already discussed the Boer war was for the mobile rifleman. Bereft of mobility the Great War degenerated into a gigantic siege, making it an artillery war. The thousands of dead and wounded infantry paid the price of our inability at cutting barbed wire, bridging trenches or a means of moving up with something bullet proof to silence enemy machine gunners.

The Haldane preparations for Continental war included the defence of the Homeland, provided by the Royal Navy under the *Blue Water* strategy. Also agreed with the Admiralty was the requirement to transport any expeditionary force to France and to maintain a re-supply capability. This meant securing ports against enemy infiltration and occupation. In this they faced the dilemma of deciding, before the event, *what form modern war would take*. In response to the various invitations proffered it set out to take some practical initiatives.

Firstly, it set up a forward airbase at Dunkirk, to observe enemy intentions. In defence of this, it equipped itself with armoured cars, manned by the RNAS. Later, it threw an RM brigade into the breach at Ostend to deter enemy feelers and a little later, a scratch division of its own making into Antwerp. Acting in the Hussar role came the armoured cars, now manned by the RNVR and RM Artillery personnel and also the Oxfordshire Hussars, providing a vital screening function, to this very Light Division. This apparent side-show caught the last steam of Schlieffen, causing just enough delay to allow the front to be stiffened by the Army. In all this the Admiralty was motivated solely by strategic considerations and in matters for which it had agreed *to carry the can*.

Thus it was the Admiralty continued to take an interest in military developments. This of course included something along the lines of a 'bullet proof horse'; one able to leap wide ditches, crush barbed wire entanglements and carry weaponry into the plague of our enemies. It formed the Admiralty Landships Committee to work out proposals.

Continuing his earlier thoughts came Swinton, who by this time had visited the various sectors of the Western Front. The upshot of his proposals and those of the Admiralty came together in London and the action was made joint between the Army and the Navy. A secret weapon, code named *TANK,* was developed and offered as the means of breaking the military impasse. Thus the end of The Great War saw the Cavalry arm presented with a new weapons system able to recapture the initiative and to secure for itself a premier position in the military hierarchy. What did it make of this opportunity? Well, not very much, yet the problems were more than technical or material deficiencies; they were in the minds of those able yet unwilling to evolve a tactical doctrine. But it is too trite to leave the problem there: the Cavalryman had had too long and a lasting relationship with the horse.

Cavalry Upheaval

The fact of an almost immediate stalemate meant there was an upheaval within the Cavalry Arm, if only through their being virtually unemployed Also due to the intervention of Kitchener, the mobilisation of the Yeomanry, as part of the Territorial Force, was held back. Shown first in the Army List was the Supplementary Reserve Cavalry comprising the North Irish Horse and the South Irish Horse, to which was added the King Edward's Horse (The King's Overseas Dominions Regiment) on its formation and the 2nd Regiment King Edward's Horse, by December 1914. These four are listed here because of their similarity in background, although technically not Yeomanry. The Yeomanry were shown as 54 Regiments in the Army

List for August 1914 including the 1st and 2nd Lovat's Scouts as separate Regiments and The Scottish Horse even though it was two regiments, only shown as one. It was not until the Welsh Horse was formed, that the list showed 55 and the 2nd and 3rd Scottish Horse made up the number to 57 and this led to their beginning a truly Heinz Varieties situation. Of these 57 First Line Units, only The Queen's Own Oxfordshire Hussars served throughout the war as conventional cavalry regiment and it also had the distinction of becoming the first Yeomanry to exchange shots with the enemy. The analysis and employment of these regiments has been summarised by Brigadier James[3] in masterly fashion:

- 18 Regiments went dismounted to Gallipolli in 1915 (12) and Egypt in 1916 (6). They formed twelve infantry battalions in 1917 for the 74th (Yeomanry) Division which went to France in 1918: Ayr, Cheshire, Denbigh, 1st Devon, N Devon, Fife & Forfar, Glamorgan, E Kent, W Kent, Lanark, Montgomery, Norfolk, Pembroke, Shropshire W Somerset, Suffolk, Sussex and Welsh Horse.
- 9 Regiments went to Egypt, mounted, in 1915 and seven of them served in Gallipolli (Dismounted). Three went to Salonika for 1916-17. They were all dismounted in Egypt in 1918 and formed five machine gun battalions which went to France: Bucks, Berks, Lincoln, City of London, 2nd Co of London, 3rd Co of London, South Notts Hussars, Warwick and E Riding.
- 7 Regiments went to Egypt, mounted, in 1915 and six of them served in Gallipolli (dismounted). Two went to Salonika for 1916-17 and back to Egypt. They all remained, mounted, in Palestine until the end of the war: Dorset, Gloucester, Herts, 1st Co of London, Sherwood Rangers, Stafford and Worcester.
- 7 Regiments went to France in 1915-16 as squadrons of divisional cavalry and became corps cavalry regiments in 1916. They were absorbed in infantry battalions in 1917: Hampshire, Lancashire Hussars, Duke of Lancaster's, Glasgow, Westmorland & Cumberland, Wiltshire and Yorkshire Hussars.
- 4 Regiments went to France in 1914-15 and joined cavalry brigades. In 1918 they were absorbed in cavalry regiments: Bedford, Essex, Leicester and N Somerset.
- 4 Regiments went to Gallipolli, dismounted, in 1915 and then to Egypt. Converted to infantry in

1916 and went to Salonika and France in 1918: 1st and 2nd Lovat's Scouts and 1st and 2nd Scottish Horse.

- 3 Regiments went to France in 1914-15 as divisional cavalry and became corps cavalry regiments in 1916. They remained as corps troops until the end of the war, two in France (one as cyclists) and one in Italy: Northampton, Northumberland and Yorkshire Dragoons.
- 2 Regiments went to France in 1915 as squadrons of divisional cavalry and then to Salonika. Here, in 1916, they became corps cavalry regiments and remained in Salonika: Lothian's & Border Horse and Surrey.
- 1 Regiment went to France, mounted, in 1914 and served throughout the war: Oxfordshire.
- 1 Regiment went to Egypt, mounted, in 1915 and to Gallipolli dismounted. Then back to Egypt and remounted to Salonika in 1916 until the end of the war: Derbyshire.
- 1 Regiment went to Gallipolli, dismounted, in 1915. Then to Egypt and in 1916 converted to a machine gun squadron: 3rd Scottish Horse.

If any proof is needed to demonstrate the adaptability and flexibility of the Yeomanry Corps as a whole, the reader should consider that period between the 1st Line leaving the home shores and the end of the war: twenty-nine regiments served as infantry; ten regiments served as part of the Machine Gun Corps; four regiments were absorbed into other cavalry regiments; five served divisionally as squadrons before reforming as corps cavalry regiments; eight regiments served as mounted troops following dismounted service in Gallipolli; A solitary regiment from Oxford gained the prize of uninterrupted regimental service. The contribution rendered by these regiments is next considered under the campaign headings. Initially a large number of mainly infantry divisions gobbled up Yeomanry squadrons, before these were concentrated at Corps level. The translation of the horsed brigades, dismountings and remountings is traced in the various theatres.[3][4][5][6]

Brigadier James listed how the stresses of change worked through the brigade and divisional structure and also repeated the exercise for the Second Line Regiments. Two of these are of specific interest; The 2/2nd County of London Yeomanry being absorbed into both the Tank Corps and infantry during 1916 and the 2/1st Northumberland Hussars going to France in 1917 as Corps Cavalry Regiment and being absorbed

into the infantry, whilst the 2nd King Edward's Horse were eventually absorbed into the Tank Corps in August 1917.

The 2nd-Line served almost exclusively within the United Kingdom and mainly as Cyclists although all were originally formed as mounted units. The Third Line were in a similar though even less favoured position and generally they became affiliated to the reserve cavalry regiments, where they provided a variable source of manpower. Toward the end of the war all those passed as fit were fed to the Infantry.

The 1st Cavalry Division was named on 16th September 1914 from what in August had been styled 'The Cavalry Division'. The 2nd Cavalry Division was formed when its elements arrived on the Aisne on 13th September 1914. The 3rd Cavalry Division began formation near Salisbury from 19th September 1914. These three divisions served throughout the war on the Western Front in France and Belgium. The Reserves formed into the 1st and 2nd Mounted divisions, of which the 1st Mounted Division changed brigade nomenclature, from April 1916 and again in July 1916 when it became 1st Cyclist Division, only to be broken up in November 1916. The 2nd Mounted Division was a wartime creation and adopted numbered brigades (with sub-titles) from inception at Churn on 2nd September 1914, was reorganised as the result of Gallipoli on 4th September 1915, again from 1st December 1915 and then broken up on 21st January 1916. Apart from Home service it was in Egypt, Gallipoli and Egypt again. The 2nd/2nd Mounted Division formed on 6th March 1915, became 3rd Mounted on 20th March 1916, became 1st Mounted in July 1916, the Cyclist Division on 4th September 1917 and survived the war, only with significant changes in personnel. The 4th Mounted Division was formed on 20th March 1916, became the 2nd Cyclist Division in July 1916 and was broken up by 16th November 1916. The Yeomanry Mounted Division was a Palestine creation, being formed at Khan Yunis between 20th June and 22nd July 1917. It was reorganised, Indianised and designated 1st Mounted division on 24th April 1918 and redesignated 4th Cavalry Division on 22nd July 1918. It had total war service. Given these dates it is possible to fix the disposition of the numerous Yeomanry brigade formations and their constituents.

The initial 1st, 3rd and 4th Mounted divisions and 57th, 59th-62nd and 64th-69th divisions had wholly

Chapter 7

United Kingdom service, whilst the 70th Division was never formed. The 43rd-45th, 71st-73rd and 75th divisions had no Yeomanry element.

Cycling to War

A few of the 1st Line Yeomanry were converted to Cyclists: The North Irish Horse in March 1918 as part of V Corps Cycle Battalion and the Yorkshire Dragoons during February 1918. In the case of the 2nd line, 12 Cyclist Regiments were formed from 24 Yeomanry regiments. This enabled horses to be freed up for other duties. Some were first formed individually. All were amalgamated during November 1916 and resumed a separate status from March 1917. The 2nd Line Cyclists Regiments are shown listed in Table 12.

Infantry

By the middle of the war most of the infantry regiments were forming battalions numbered in double figures. Any of the 1st and 2nd Line Yeomanry could through the play of events find themselves dismounted. Sometimes they were 'converted' or 'formed' into infantry battalions creating a new title. In other instances large drafts were absorbed into existing battalions, presumably to make good battlefield losses and the titles were adjusted to reflect the Yeomanry addition. These specific battalion creations are shown under the theatre of origin.

Third Line Formations

The 3rd line was more problematical. It was last formed and got last pick of everything. The formations were more theoretical than real. There were 14 Reserve Regiments of Cavalry, which were affiliated to 'the Yeomanry' or the other way about. As a draft finding resource, it played a useful part in feeding both the 2nd line and the infantry.

Table 12 2nd Line Yeomanry Cyclist Regiments

Cyclist Regiments	Comprising 2nd Line Yeomanry
1st (Lovat's Scouts) Cyclist Regt	2/1st & 2/2nd Lovat's Scouts
2nd (Pembroke and Glamorgan) Y Cyclist Regt	2/1st Pembroke & Glamorgan
3rd (Montgomery and Denbigh) Y Cyclist Regt	2/1st Montgomery & Denbigh
4th (R 1st Devon and N Devon) Y Cyclist Regt	2/1st R N Devon & R 1st Devon
5th (W Somerset and Cy of London) Y Cyclist Regt	2/1st W Som, COLY & 1st NIH
6th (1st and 3rd Co of London) Y Cyclist Regt	2/1st & 2/3rd County of London
7th (Suffolk and Norfolk) Y Cyclist Regt	2/1st Suffolk & Norfolk
8th (Surrey and Sussex) Y Cyclist Regt	2/1st Surrey & Sussex
9th (East Kent & West Kent) Y Cyclist Regt	2/1 E Kent Y & W Kent
10th (Wiltshire and North Somerset) Y Cyclist Regt	2/1 N Somerset & R Wiltshire
11th (Hampshire and Berkshire) Y Cyclist Regt	2/1st Berks, Hants & Oxford
12th (Gloucester & Worcester) Y Cyclist Regt	2/1 Gloucester & QO Worcs H

Virtually all the remaining 2nd Line were also formed into cyclist units, starting from July 1916 and lasting with few exceptions until the end of the war. Three

Table 13 Other 2nd Line Yeomanry converted to Cyclists Regiments

Ayrshire	Lancashire Hussars	Sherwood Rangers
Buckingham	Leicester	Shropshire
Cheshire	Lincoln	Stafford
Derby	Lothian & Border Horse	Surrey
Dorset	2/2nd Lovat's Scouts	Warwick
Essex	S Nottinghamshire Hussars	W'morland & C'berland
Fife & Forfar	Queen's Own Oxford	York Dragoons
Hertford	Pembroke	E Riding of Yorkshire
Lanark	2/1st Scottish Horse	Yorkshire Hussars
Duke of Lancaster's	2/3rd Scottish Horse	

The Machine Gun Corps [7][8]

An interested party in the 1st line Yeomanry was the Machine Gun Corps. At the start of the war the Maxim-Vickers machine gun was the sort of weapon the War Office wasn't sure about. Trench warfare changed all that. Properly manned and tactically deployed it had an immense potential for slaughter. Its killing power could seal-off whole areas of front. If artillery was King of the battlefield this gun was Queen. The other side of the coin was the need for and availability of trainable crews of muscular proportions able to handle the weighty weapon. Added to this came the need for an immense ammunition train to satisfy its insatiable appetite. It is open to debate whether the Machine Gun Corps in any of its parts could be properly described as 'dismounted' because

managed brief periods of being remounted: Dorset from March to September 1917, Lincoln from November 1916 to August 1917 and Stafford the same. The regiments identified with this phase are shown in Table 13.

of the nature of its equipment and the urgency with which it needed to move.

The formation was by Royal Warrant dated 11th October 1915 and Army Order of 22nd October 1915. Initially it comprised three branches covering Cavalry, Infantry and the Motor Machine Gun Service. It will be remembered that the RNAS had earlier deployed armoured cars and these were armed with this weapon. Later the Heavy Branch was formed on 18th November 1916 and withdrawn on 27th July 1917 to form the Tank Corps, into which the Motor Machine Gun Service was then gradually absorbed. In this the 2nd King Edward's Horse supplied a significant manpower.

Initial deployments were as companies or squadrons, placed at Brigade disposal, so that individual sections moved into the regimental areas to provide cross-lacings of fire support. Later the weapon was raised to Divisional status during March 1918 and a fourth, the ex Divisional one, added to what then became MG battalions. These moves had almost certainly been ghosted beforehand. Now the Lieutenant-Colonel in charge doubled as the divisional Machine Gun Officer. This took in all the guns previously in the hands of regiments, including the Royal Field Artillery. A pool of high quality and available manpower was an opportunity not to be passed-up by *Johnny come lately* and a number of Yeomanry were recruited to the cause.

One is entitled to ask what relevance the Yeomanry had to the Machine Gun Corps and it was this: They were horse trained soldiers, accustomed to dismounted action and generally born and bred countrymen used to heavy manual labour. Such a unit required the transport of a normal brigade, infantry protection when in the line and an army of belt fillers when business was brisk. Stragglers up and down the axis of the front were rounded up for this duty. There were other considerations for this new weapon, new to the extent it was going to be used in a different way. Chief amongst these was the need for mobility, in either moving up or retiring, during the course of a battle and for the provision of concrete emplacements to provide a firm foundation for sustained fire.

There were 64 guns, each pair requiring a four horse drawn double limber. The gun detachment each of six men, plus the command structure each called for transport to respond to the tactical need. Thus a section of four guns had 32 Other Ranks and from

eight to sixteen to help with the loads This totalled some 750 to 900 men for the battalion and about the same number of horses with attendants and other necessaries, working between the front and rear echelon areas. his was a further example of the rush to technology overwhelming the divisional structure. If such a battalion was set out properly, it was possible to substantially thin-out the line, but at a price. German infiltration tactics, of the *stalking method*, often led to guns being bombed, whilst a large squad of belt loaders was necessary to sustain the rate of fire. Lastly moving required a degree of co-ordination. Instances arose where they were excluded from the movement plan or even stripped of their transport, left to make shrift for themselves and having to move back onto unprepared positions. During the Palestine Campaign the Yeomanry provided personnel to the Machine Gun Corps and earlier during October 1916 the 1/3rd Scottish Horse less a company, for service with The Imperial Camel Corps! Five Yeomanry battalions were formed from April 1918.

Beasts of Burden

In an earlier chapter the duties of Cavalry were enumerated, but nothing given on husbandry. The Egyptian Theatre, leading as in did into the Sinai and the sands of Arabia, had to consider how to get the best mileage from its beasts. The horse was good on all but loose sand, of which there was lots. Its best range was two and a half to three days without water: It sweated a lot and after such a period did not respond well and human beings got to be much the same after a single day. The camel could go without for five days, even six at a stretch. It hardly sweats because it has only small glands, one behind each ear and another two under the tail. It coped well with soft sand, in contrast to rocky going, because of large, soft foot pads. It carried nearly twice as much as a horse, yet existed on a more Spartan diet. Unfortunately it was less well understood by the European and could be unpredictable, whilst the horse was apt to panic and stampede in its presence. The shortage of good mounts or mounts of any kind, was a frequent handicap in campaigning and as Tylden relates the horsed Yeomanry frequently had a band of stragglers following behind, mounted on mules, donkeys and even asses! The shortage of shoeing materials, up front, was such that shot horses had their shoes and even the nails taken. A necessary precursor to campaigns was a careful logistic study, whilst troops in the field had to make a dash to secure well sites, which were as important to survival as defeating the enemy.

Chapter 7

Horse Power This is the imperial unit of power equal to 550 foot-pounds of work per second or about three-quarters of a kilo-watt and comes to us from the mining industry in which James Watt worked. It came about with a horse pulling a small loaded cart up an inclined shaft. The cavalry horse is open to more rule of thumb considerations, but it seems likely it has an output above this figure, besides which it brings a line of skills to bear on military problems. The characteristics, qualities and performance of the horse were considered by Tylden[9].

"The horse's versatility in performing many and various tasks has been well known since time immemorial. He could be packed for one thing and to this day he has no equal for riding. His back seem to have been made for man's saddle. He was strong and could cover great distances. He could walk, trot, gallop, turn, halt and plunge at the slightest beckon of his master. He could jump, swim rivers and pick his way down a mountain side with more skill and courage than any animal known. In battle he proved supreme, for warriors found in him unmatchable speed of movement. When packed he bore his load well. He was sure-footed and could easily carry up to 250 lb. He performed hazardous marches across fields and valleys and hills that other animals could not have endured. Above all he was a loyal companion."

"He also stood fire well, much better than the mule, though like his master he had his limitations....Like most of his kind when introduced to drill, to which he was unaccustomed, he picked it up quickly. The horse also stands cold, which would too much for camels and mules and would kill a dog. Even when half starved and short of water he will carry on until he can not go another yard".

"A modern estimate of the work a horse in condition should do in a day, when forming part of a large body of cavalry, is from 20-25 miles. Most of this would be done at a walk, at an average pace of four miles an hour. A march of 40-45 miles a day would constitute a forced marched and might have to be done at five to six miles an hour, necessitating the occasional use of a trot, a pace averaging eight miles an hour. The smaller the body of cavalry involved the quicker the rate of marching might be and at the strength of a regiment a 30 mile march might be done at the rate of six miles an hour, thus giving the horse time to rest. Whatever the distance to be covered cavalry had to be prepared to go into action at once and to deliver a charge at the rate of

12 miles an hour, perhaps followed by a fast pursuit of a broken enemy." Whether these values pertain to the heat of Sinai and Palestine is not stated, but one presumes these values needed trimming for extremes of climate.

"Two basic problems are firstly to shoe the horny feet which otherwise wear down on rough stony ground until the horse has to be rested and secondly the growth of the winter coat which may clash with the climate when transported across the Equator ", as occurred in the Boer War.

"One of the horse's most useful characteristics is his ability to see at night; only a few seem unable to do so. ...Horses vary like human beings. ...Someone must break and accustom him to his new profession and someone must ride him and keep him in the ranks. The professional creed of the Cavalryman, from as early as 1800 was *The Rider must live only for his horse, which is his legs, his safety and his reward.*" Obviously such deeply held feelings go the longest way to explain the extreme reluctance with which horses were given up for mere machines.

Next, there was the vexed question of husbandry during the Palestine Campaign, to which Croft [10] provides an insight. "The prime difficulty facing the advance of mounted troops against the Turks centred on the lack of water. At times horses and mules were without for 60-80 hours and not infrequently columns were going in practically the opposite direction to operational requirements. The charge at Huj by the Worcestershire and Warwickshire Yeomanry was deprived of covering fire from their RHA Battery and MG Squadron due to distant watering."

"Good regular grooming was essential, as it was like massage for a human being. At each hourly halt the horses' mouths, nostrils and eyes were wiped with a wet cloth and this always seemed to refresh the horses greatly and to relieve the symptoms of distress due to thirst. A little water was also mixed with the feeds, when grains were crushed or bran available. It was found that horses which were off their feed, owing to exhaustion, would often eat well if fed by hand with small balls of grain slightly moistened with water."
Grooming was particularly important along the back where the saddle rested. If this was neglected, sore backs would result, making the horse unfit for purpose. It appears that the British generally had a better record than the French in this respect and as a consequence

got a better mileage from their four legged friends. The problem of watering has to be understood as a personal matter between horse and trooper. The watering took place, often after a hard days march interspersed with fighting. The arrangements were often primitive in the extreme, involving a canvas bucket, a long rope and a deep well. Watering could stretch into the early hours of the morning, whilst the man himself had to attend personal needs. Such forces required men of superlative leadership and the Troopers a selfless devotion, forged by the relationship with the horse. The Yeomanry did so very well under these exacting conditions and without sounding pompous exemplified the highest traditions of the service.

Camel Capabilities and Peculiarities [11][12] As with the earlier paragraph on horses, something should be said, if only to explain some of the comical situations open to the intending handler. In essence the camel is a long range horse. Taken with the rider, as a weapons system it was analogous to the Mustang escort fighter aircraft of The Second World War. It carried a load of 450 lb for up to five days without re-supply at an average of six miles per hour for about as long as the rider could stay in the saddle: Possibly a distance of 300 miles. This relied on specific breeds of animal. Using selected beasts and careful loading much greater performance was possible, as instanced in work with Lawrence at the end of the Palestine Campaign. By further reducing loads and choosing only the best animals Lawrence found it possible to treble the daily rate of march, to the eternal irritation of the Turks!

Often GHQ Planners became mesmerised by camel performance to the extent that their riders were taken to have equal properties, with dire results on a number of occasions. This inadequate grasp of staff essentials and the attendant logistics was often to mar the efficiency of British efforts and extended to the slow removal of the wounded and injured.

The camel is easily broken for riding but responds poorly to urging and so requires careful handling and for these reasons it is usual to employ skilled attendants. For lack of these considerations an erstwhile docile beast is transformed into something moody, independent minded and downright vicious. It will pursue or spit in the eye of one to whom it has taken a dislike, drawing a gobbet from the first portion of its stomach. It can bite and pin a body down whilst it pummels with its knees before squeezing the life

from one, by bearing down with its chest. The unwary rider may have his legs nibbled if inattentive, besides which it has the disconcerting habit of kicking sideways. It seems immune to pain and senseless to discomfort, for which reason it needs careful and regular inspection when packed.

It makes a fearful noise during grooming or mounting-up. Few things upset it, though when something does it is not always apparent what. This said it seems generally agreed that the Scottish bagpipes succeed in setting off a stampede, for which reason an order was issued restricting their play within a half-mile radius. It can subsist on a meagre diet of thorny scrub and quench its thirst on brackish waters, drinking 16-26 gallons and a little more after a short rest. Large flat feet with twin pads enable it to spread its load and not sink into soft sand. The use of such a beast in the deserts of Egypt and Sinai provided the Military with a logistic miracle. Loading them into cattle trucks required an element of guile, in which they were blind folded and pushed from behind, in the opposite from the intended direction. When released they shot backwards into the open truck. The first time this was tried the offside door had been left open allowing the camel to land on the far side of the track.

In discussing the breed we are talking of a group known as the Dromedary or Arabian Runner, not to be confused with the Bactrian or Asiatic camel with two humps which latter animal is the equivalent of the Scammell lorry and best in the cold thin air of the Pamirs. This said the pure Arabian camel is far too light. The Mehari breed is about right, matching the Egyptian and Sinai need. A Bactrian bull crossed with an Algerian female Dromedary throws a good tempered animal of medium weight, able to undertake hard work and withstand a good measure of cold.

For obvious reasons loads need to be distributed evenly and a saddle is used, not that the rider is provided with stirrups. In place of the bridle, a single rope is attached to the right nostril, though the rider suggests a direction by leg pressure. In mounting from the left or nearside, the rider pulls the head round, gripping the nose, steps onto the neck and thence into the saddle. As the camel rises rear legs first it is important to 'lean over backwards' to maintain balance and maybe this is where the phrase originates.

Loads, apart from the rider are distributed around the saddle. A 50 lb. dhurra bag of native maize was

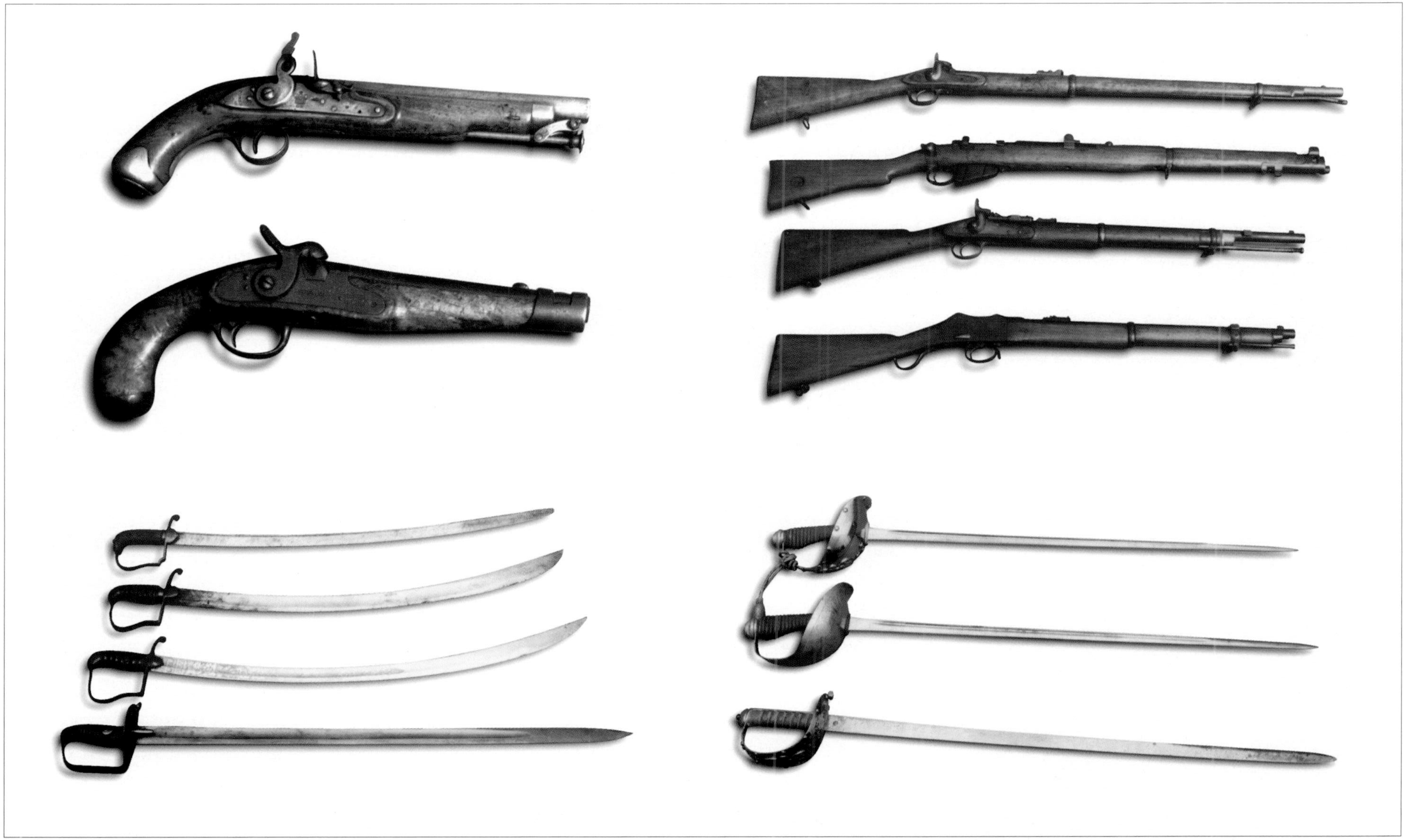

Patrick Mileham

Plate 5   Yeomanry Weaponry. Only the Short Lee Enfield rifle (2nd right) and the Cavalry Sabre (2nd right) were truly effective and are of post Boer War vintage.

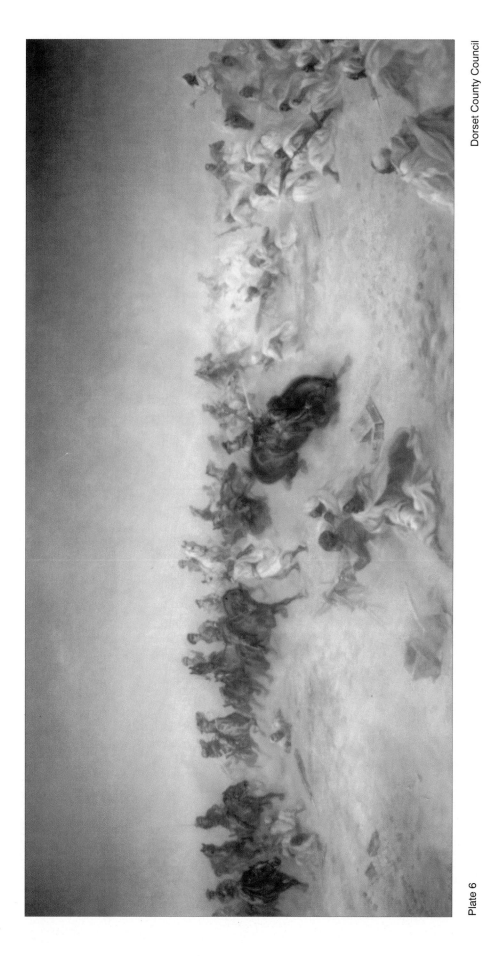

Plate 6

Dorset County Council

Charge of the Queen's Own Dorset Yeomanry - Agagia, 26th February 1916. The Senussi tribesmen were a thorn in the side of the British in Egypt and were ably assisted by Turkish and German agents landed by submarine. Until the British adopted camels this enemy proved elusive.

commonly hung on the neck. It was important to ensure a good padded fit for the saddle. Seemingly the camel will not complain over a cutting load, rubs and sores and only at grooming time are these discovered. Grooming was most important, as with horses, if only to remove the loathsome huge ticks which generally gathered under the poor animals tail, gorging themselves on its blood.

The camel can walk and trot, the latter producing a not unpleasant backward and forward rocking motion, which provides for a speed of from four to ten miles an hour, for as long as the rider can keep in the saddle. At the canter or gallop more skill was necessary than the ordinary trooper was likely to possess and in the case of runaways it invariably resulted in the rider being thrown from a great height with consequent injury. Only hard tugging on the headrope was likely to avert disaster, but even then the nostril could be torn before the camel answered. Camels with a bad nature, usually amongst those supplied as remounts, arrived with a muzzle and after some experience of the havoc these could wreak, they were 'found dead' the following morning and no effort was made to trace the culprits. Most will be familiar with the ornamental cord around Arab headress which served as a hobble, so that unattended animals could not wander off. Virtually all camels are branded with characteristic marks showing unambiguously their point of origin and it seems there is no record of falsified markings.

The Campaign Theatres

The Home Front A brief study reveals Britain's inability to arm, field or accommodate armies commensurate with the scale of the conflict even during the initial two years of the war. This constituted an industrial defect and chiefly a lack of strategic planning. Despite a supposed leadership in the Industrial Revolution, she was never able to support her armies properly, even down to the building of barracks on Salisbury Plain. That this should most seriously curtail the efforts of the Territorial Force had little to do with them as such, except to say a force without equipment was impossible to train and had limited military value. In the allocation of scarce resources Kitchener elected to put his New Armies first.

The 1st Mounted Division brought together 12 Yeomanry regiments and supporting arms and a single paragraph from Becke [4] illustrates the reality of the dilemma. "As the 1st-line mounted brigades departed overseas they were replaced by 2nd-line formations; but as late as July 1915, there were 2nd-line RHA Batteries without harness, guns or wagons. (Some batteries only obtained two 12-pounder guns, wagons and harness in September, 1915.) In July, many 2nd-line signal troops were without the necessary equipment, even for training; machine guns were still lacking; entrenching tools, swords, and rifles were required for instructional purposes; and very few men in 2nd-line units had fired a recruits' course of musketry. Not until October, 1915 were rifles available for every man." This was acknowledged by breaking up a number of divisions and only forming new ones as our expanded productive capacities caught up. It can be remarked somewhat cynically that if the British had difficulty in making sufficient rifles it did not apply to bicycles. Two of the Home divisions were devoted to cycles alone whilst virtually every division in the field had its cycle company. The Home Army was made a laughing stock, because it was something more on paper than based in fact. As the casualties mounted overseas it became something of a political embarrassment. The leading contenders were 'brought to the ring to dance according to their skill'. These are next described under theatre headings.

The British Expeditionary Force and Later Forces to the Western Front. This front was always to be the largest as it was where both sides had agreed a decision should be made. When the line gelled it stretched from Nieuport on the Channel coast to the Swiss frontier in the region of Basle. As the various phases of the campaigns played through the size and complexity of the forces increased. The initial phase was the encounter battles of Mons, which surprised the Germans to the extent that their initial thrusts were deflected and the strategic intent became dislocated. However pressure was still brought to bear on Antwerp, as had been foreseen and the Admiralty felt obliged to provide a fronting operation, as they were responsible for the vital ports of re supply. In an act of rare generosity the War Office loaned them the Queen's Own Oxfordshire Hussars as screening cavalry, but were unable to provide artillery, hence the Royal Naval Brigade and the later Division were always in a vulnerable position. The Yeomanry in this action earned the distinction of being the first Territorial Cavalry on the British side to exchange fire with the enemy.

Many Yeomanry regiments were split into squadrons

to provide divisional cavalry and later concentrated into regiments at Corps level during 1916. Some additional mobility was afforded divisions by the provision of cyclist companies and even regiments. The wide scale use of a cavalry force however was an impossibility here, though the use of horses was common enough hauling artillery and supplies and so was their vulnerability, with upwards of 500,000 killed. Regimental movements for the Western Front are listed in Table 14.

Table 14 Regimental Movements To and From the Western Front Theatre

Regt	Date	To Theatre or Formation	Date	To Theatre or Formation
NIH A Sqn	19 08 14	Le Havre, GHQ Tps	04 01 16	55 Div Cav
	10 05 16	VII Corps Cav Regt		
F(B) Sqn	18 11 15	Le Havre as 33rd Div Cav	19 04 16	49th Div Cav & 32nd Div Cav
	25 05 16	Became B Sqn	21 06 16	joined X Corps Cav Regt
C Sqn	22 08 14	GHQ Tps	14 04 15	3rd Div Cav
	11 05 16	X Corps Cav Regt		
D Sqn	02 05 15	51st Div Cav	10 05 16	VII Corps Cav Regt
E Sqn	01 01 16	34th Div Cav	10 05 16	VII Corps Cav Regt
1st NIH	10 05 16	fr A, D, and E Sqns	16 07 17	XIX Corps Cav Regt
	07 09 17	V Corps Cav Regt	14 03 18	V Corps Cyclist Bn
2nd NIH	21 06 16	fr B, C + 6th(I) Dgns service sqn	Aug 17	Broken up
	25 09 17	B&C abs by 9RIF	11 11 18	(North Irish Horse) added
SIH A Sqn	12 09 15	21st Div Cav	11 05 16	XV Corps Cav Regt
	Nov 16	IX Corps Cav Regt	16 01 17	XVIII Corps Cav Regt
B(S) Sqn	17 08 14	GHQ Tps	04 05 15	2nd Div Cav
	15 05 16	to I Corps Cav Regt as S Sqn		
C Sqn	16 12 15	16th Div Cav	17 05 16	I Corps Cav Regt
E Sqn	17 03 16	39th Div Cav	17 05 16	I Corps Cav Regt
F Sqn	18 05 17	Arrived France	27 05 17	XVIII Corps Cav Regt
S(B) Sqn	25 11 15	32nd Div Cav	14 05 16	XV Corps Regt as B Sqn
	21 11 16	IX Corps Cav Regt	Jan 17	XVIII Corps Cav Regt
1st SIH	17 05 16	C E S sqns form I Corps Cav	Aug 17	dismtd and amal 2nd SIH
2nd SIH	May 17	A B F Sqns f XVIII C Cav	Aug 17	and trained at Etaples as Inf.
			01 09 17	f 7RIR
KEH RHQ &	22 04 15	47th Div Cav	01 06 16	IV Corps Cav Regt
C	02 06 15	12 Div Cav	01 06 16	IV Corps Cav Regt
A Sqn	22 04 15	48th Div Cav	01 06 16	IV Corps Cav Regt
B Sqn	17 07 17	XVIII Corps Cav Regt	Nov 17	IV Corps Cav Regt
KEH	21 12 17	KEH to Italy XI Corps	16 03 18	to France with XI Corps
Regt divided	May 18	A Sqn, XI. B Sqn, I. C Sqn, XIII	Oct 18	C Sqn=III Corps
2KEH	04 05 15	Canadian Cav Bde		Dismtd as Seely's Detacht
	Sep 15	Canadian Cav Bde	27 01 16	mounted again as GHQ Tps
B Sqn	23 03 16	56th Div Cav till 30 05 16	Jun 16	Regt as XIV Corps Cav
	06 08 17	to UK, Regt broken up		Abs by Tank Corps, **Wareham**
AY	May 18	arr as 12RSF, 229th Bde, 74th div	21 06 18	to 94th Bde, 31st Div
BedsY	10 06 15	9th Cav Bde, 1st Cav Div	10 03 18	withdrawn, dismtd, mounted
	Apr 18	Returned to 9th Cav Bde		Abs 8th/15th/19th Hussars
BY	26 06 18	fr Taranto as C Bn MGC	19 08 18	redes 101st Bn MGC
RBH	as BY			
CY	07 05 18	arr 10KSLI, 231st Bde, 74th Div		
DenY	May 18	arr 24RWF, 231st Bde, 74th Div	21 06 18	to 94th Bde, 31st div
R1DY	07 05 18	arr 16DR, 229th Bde, 74th Div		
RNDY	as R1DY			
EY	01 12 14	Le Havre	12 12 14	8th Cav Bde, 3rd Cav Div
	Mar 18	withdrawn, dismounted	28 03 18	Mounted to 1st Cav Div
	04 04 18	Regt split up to 1st Cav Div		Sqns to 2 DG, 5 DG, 11th Hus
FFY	07 05 18	arr 14BW, 229th Bde, 74th Div		
GY	07 05 18	arr 24WR, 231st Bde, 74th Div		
QORGY A	01 09 15	Le Havre	30 04 16	attchd 2nd Cav Div till 14 05 16
Sqn	21 05 16	joined V Corps Cav Regt		
	13 05 15	Le Havre to join 9th Div	10 05 16	V Corps Cav Regt formed with RHQ & B
B Sqn	13 05 17	Dismounted		Sqn LBH
	23 08 17	Infantry training	23 09 17	abs by 18HLI

Regt	Date	To Theatre or Formation	Date	To Theatre or Formation
HCY A Sqn	20 01 17	Le Havre with 58th Div	25 01 17	rejoined Regt in IX Corps
B Sqn	25 06 16	Le Havre with 60th Div	28 08 16	RHQ joined IX Corps
& RHQ	08 07 16	B Sqn attchd XVII C till 04 09 16	05 09 16	to Cav Corps Tps
	19 01 17	rejoined IX Corps Cav Regt		
C Sqn	26 06 16	Le Havre with 61st Div	31 05 16	attchd 1st Cav Div till 16 06 16
	17 06 16	joined IX Corps Cav Regt	Jan 17	Regt concentrated
	25 07 17	Regt left IX Corps	25 08 17	Dismtd to infantry trg
	25 09 17	abs 15HR		
	12 11 17	to Italy with 41st Div	04 03 18	to France with 41st Div
HY B Sqn	04 07 16	with 11th Div	12 07 16	Attchd VI Corps
	e 1917	joined XVIII Corps Cav Regt	27 05 17	To GHQ Trps
	06 07 17	returned to Egypt		
REKY	07 05 18	as 10TB, 230th Bde, 74th Div		
RWKY		as REKY		
LHY B Sqn	Mar 16	to France	27 04 16	Attchd 2nd Indian Cav Div
& RHQ	11 05 16	VIII Corps Cav Regt		
C Sqn	01 02 16	Le Havre	10 05 16	VIII Corps Cav Regt
D Sqn	10 11 15	Le Havre	13 04 16	Attd 2 Indian Div till 26 04 16
	11 05 16	VIII Corps Cav Regt formed	Jul 17	dismtd to infantry trg
	24 09 17	abs by 18KR	11 02 18	(Lancashire Hussars Yeo) added
LanY	as AY			
DLOY	28 08 15	Le Havre with 23rd Div	20 04 16	Attd 1st Cav div till 04 05 16
RHQ&CSqn	14 05 16	III Corps Cav Regt		
D Sqn	23 05 15	Le Havre with 14th Div	14 05 16	III Corps Cav Regt
	May 16	Corps Cav Regt formed	24 07 17	RHQ & 2 sqns to GHQ Tps
	28 08 17	Dismtd to infantry trg	24 09 17	Abs by 12MR
LY	03 11 14	France to 7th Cav Bde 12 11 14	Nov 17	8th Cav Bde
	14 03 18	withdrawn and returned	04 04 18	split, sqn to 4 Hus, 5 and 16 L
LncY	01 06 18	fr Egypt as D Bn MGC	19 08 18	redes 102nd Bn MGC
1WDY	01 06 18	fr Egypt as F Bn MGC	19 08 18	redes 104th Bn MGC, 2nd Army
2WDY		Went to France, dismtd end 1915	Sum 16	Retd to Wool, abs Tank Corps
LBH RHQ &	27 09 15	Le Havre, with 25th Div	11 05 16	V Corps Cav Regt
B Sqn	23 07 17	Dismtd to inf trg	Sep 17	Abs by 17RS
A Sqn	28 09 15	To France with 26th Div	17 12 15	To Salonika
D Sqn	06 09 15	To France with 22nd Div	05 11 15	To Salonika
LncY	01 06 18	fr Egypt as D Bn MGC	19 08 18	redes 102nd Bn MGC, 1st Army
RR	01 06 18	fr Egypt as E Bn MGC	19 08 18	redes 103rd Bn MGC, 1st Army
SS	as RR			
1LS	06 07 18	fr Salonika as 10CH	06 07 18	to L of C
?other LS	1916-18	13 Detchmts, Corps Tps as OP's	Aug 17	became Groups 1-4
			end 17	No4 Group to Italy
MY	as DenY			
NorY	07 05 18	as 12NR, 230th Bde, 74th Div	21 06 18	to 94th Bde, 31st Div
NY	04 11 14	To France with 8th Div		
RHQ & B A	14 04 15	To 6th Div	09 05 16	VI Corps Cav Regt
Sqn	13 04 15	To 4th div	11 05 16	VI Corps Cav Regt
C Sqn	12 04 15	To 5th Div	11 05 16	VI Corps Cav Regt
	Sum 17	? 4th Army Tps attd ? XV Corps	11 11 17	To Italy
2/1 NY ?Sqn	Nov 16	in France	Aug 17	abs by Tank Corps
NH	06 10 14	Landed Zeebrugge with 7th Div	Apr 15	Regt split up
RHQ&ASqn	13 05 16	XIII Corps Cav Regt		
B Sqn	13 04 15	To 1st Div	18 04 16	XIII Corps Cav Regt
C SQn	12 04 15	To 8th Div	13 05 16	XIII Corps Cav Regt
	Aug 17	Regt left for VIII (or XIV) Corps	Nov 17	III Corps
	08 10 18	XII Corps Cav Regt		
2/1NHY	19 03 17	Le Havre	26 03 17	joined as XIX Corps Cav Regt
	28 08 17	To inf trg	25 09 17	Abs by 9NF
SNH	29 06 18	f Egypt as B Bn MGC	19 08 18	redes 100th Bn MGC, 4th Army
QOOH	22 09 14	Dunkirk with 2nd Mtd Div	22 09 14	to GHQ Tps
	31 10 14	2nd Cav Bde, 1st Cav Div	11 11 14	4th Cav Bde, 2nd Cav Div
PY	as GY			
SH	24 06 18	as 13BW, to 149th Bde, 50th Div		
SY	as CY			
NSY	03 11 14	France	13 11 14	6th Cav Bde, 3rd Cav Div
	10 03 18	Dismounted	Apr 18	Sqns to above, 1D, 3DG, 10Hus
WSY	07 05 18	as 12SLI, 229th Bde, 74th Div		
SufY	07 05 18	as 15SR, 230th Bde, 74th Div		

Regt	Date	To Theatre or Formation	Date	To Theatre or Formation
SurYA Sqn	21 10 14	to France		
C Sqn	11 03 16	29th Div, 11-19 May XV CCR	19 05 16	III CCR with 2 Sqns DLOY
	24 07 17	dismtd to inf trg	26 09 17	abs 10RWS, 124th Bde, 41st Div
SusY	07 05 18	as 16RSR, 230th Bde, 74th Div		
WCY RHQ &	27 04 15	Le Havre with 20th Div	30 04 16	Attd 2nd Cav Div till 14 05 16
D Sqn	15 05 16	XI Corps Cav Regt		
B Sqn	Jul 15	To France with 15th Div	02 04 16	Attd 1st Cav Div till 16 04 16
	15 05 16	XI Corps Cav Regt		
C Sqn	Jul 15	To France with 18th Div	15 05 16	XI Corps Cav Regt
	30 05 16	Attd 1st Cav Div till 20 06 16	21 07 17	Dismtd to inf trg
	22 09 17	Abs 7BR		
WY	as SNH			
WH	as MY			
RWY RHQ &	04 12 15	Le havre with 38th div	02 04 16	Attd 1st Cav Div till 17 04 16
D Sqn	01 05 16	Attd III CCR till 20 05 16	21 05 16	XV Corps Cav Regt
A Sqn	04 06 16	Le Havre with 40th Div	21 06 16	IX Corps Cav Regt
	19 11 16	XV Corps Cav Regt		
B Sqn	06 05 16	Le Havre with 41st DivXV Corps Cav Regt	01 06 16	Attd 2nd Cav Div till 20 06 16
	22 06 16	Abs by 6WR	03 09 17	Dismtd to inf trg
	26 09 17			
YD RHQ &B	01 08 15	Le Havre with 37th Div	May 16	II Corps Cav Regt
A SQn	16 07 15	Le Havre with 17th Div	May 16	II Corps Cav Regt
C Sqn	20 07 15	Le Havre with 19th Div	21 04 16	Attd 3rd Cav Div till 09 05 16
	May 16	II Corps Cav Regt	12 05 16	Regt concentrated
	Oct 17	Cav Corps Tps	06 12 17	Lucknow Cav Bde, 4th Cav Div
	27 02 18	Regt dismtd	16 03 18	II Corps Cyclist Bn
YHY	18 04 15	Le Havre with 50th Div	10 05 16	XVII Corps Cav Regt
RHQA Sqn	28 02 15	Le Havre with 46th Div	05 05 16	XVII Corps Cav Regt
B Sqn	16 04 15	Le Havre with 49th div	08 05 16	XVII Corps Cav Regt
C Sqn	26 08 17	Regt dismtd to inf trg	13 11 17	Abs by 9WYR
ERY	as LncY			

The Egyptian Theatre of Operations The fact of hostilities with Turkey effectively produced a second war, with GHQ Cairo at its hub. The campaigns in Gallipolli, the Balkans, Egypt itself and the Sinai, Palestine, Syria and even Mesopotamia each worked on or within the perimeter of the Ottoman Empire. Viewed from the west it was a most unwelcome development, though it could hardly have come as much of a surprise considering the political ineptitude with which affairs with Turkey had been handled. For Egypt the war meant it became a vast transit house and initially not a very secure one, besides which it greatly interfered with its normal peacetime occupations at the cross-roads of international trade and commerce.

Egypt occupied a political no-man's land as it recognised Turkey as its suzerain power, whilst sitting astride the Suez Canal, so much a British strategic interest. Immediately this latter was threatened the British moved in troops and when Turkey opted to side with Germany, Britain declared war on 5th November 1914. A passive British front opened along the canal facing Sinai and elsewhere, whilst a Turkish scheme for stirring up the Senussi in the west of Egypt was engineered with German help. It was this that brought the Yeomanry into the frame. Prior to the arrival of the 2nd Mounted Division, which completed its arrival on 29th April 1915, the Yeomanry were represented by Biscoe's Brigade, consisting of 1/1 Hertford, 1/2 County of London and a single Squadron of the Duke of Lancaster's Yeomanry. The idea to dismount the 2nd Mounted Division to assist in the Gallipolli Campaign was not a matter decided without serious misgivings by the Egyptian authorities. With the minor inconvenience of the Senussi and German submarines, Egypt became the chief baggage handlers for Gallipolli.

The post Gallipolli situation. Following the withdrawal of the 2nd Mounted Division from Gallipolli, some elements were used to strengthen the Western Frontier Force. A twin-pronged column was sent in from Mutrah on 25th December 1915, to surprise the enemy at Wadi Majid in which the Yeomanry comprised, the Royal Bucks Hussars, two Troops of Duke of Lancaster's, one Troop of Derbyshire, two Troops of City of London and a Squadron of Hertford Yeomanry. The odd composition of the Force is most probably explained by the facts of re-equipping, retraining and recovering from sickness.

The white man lost much face as the result of the Gallipolli outcome and the Egyptian Authorities had to tackle the Senussi all over again. They inhabited the Western Oases and the area where the Libyan Plateau ascends hundreds of feet above the waters of the Nile. The romantic notion of rolling sand dunes is a misnomer, though the soft going played hell with conventional cavalry operations, mounted as they were on horses. There was also the scarcity of water. Eventually the area was mapped and brought under scrutiny by a combination of air and motor patrols, yet in the meantime something more immediate was required. The initial response was to have a Camel Transport Corps bring life-giving water to the cavalry and there was already in being a fighting unit in the Indian Bikanir Camel Corps. It used larger than average beasts and mounted two men, the rear one acting as a tail gunner! Previously there had been raised a Sudan Camel Corps and although British officered it was a native unit. Before that Napoleon had something similar to the Bikanir Corps.

All these Corps had rendered good service though when it was suggested a wholly White or European Corps be formed the idea met an official frown. It was an anathema to Regular Cavalry Colonels to have camels mentioned in the same context as horses. Moving camels in the mass always succeeded in stampeding cavalry. They said they had an unfavourable impression formed from their encounters with the Transport Corps and, beside this, they could foresee the situation where they were used as a draft supplying source with themselves relegated to Staff duties. Nevertheless the idea went ahead because of the urgent need to have an effective remedy over internal security and the restive presence of saddle trained Australians and New Zealanders.

The Imperial Camel Corps: Nomina Desertis Inscripsimus *Our name is written in the desert.* This motto was adopted by The Australian 15th Light Horse, subsequent to their service with the Corps. It seems at least probable it served unofficially as a general motto before that. This Egyptian initiative bucked the trend to dismounting. Any general account of the Yeomanry would be incomplete without quoting the contribution made by this predominantly Australian and New Zealand force, which nevertheless contrived to include a battalion of Yeomen and a machine gun section. The initial force was Authorised during November 1915. Thus the troops returning from Gallipoli were canvassed for volunteers and the Yeomanry was asked to provide a Battalion and an MG Squadron. When fully fitted-out it comprised a

1st Battalion from the Australian Light Horse of four companies and a 3rd and 4th Battalion each with three companies of Australians and a fourth of New Zealanders. The 2nd Battalion consisted of six companies in which the first was made up from Infantry and its composition is listed in Table 15. 'As a subsidiary to the Battle of Bersheba (Oct 1917) a portion of No.5 Company blocked the Hebron Road at Yuta drawing upon themselves the Turkish reserve divisions and after a very heroic stand, suffering a third casualties, had to surrender.' [13] The remainder of the Battalion was made up as shown below, though it rarely acted together. Some 30 Pembroke Yeomen were later seconded from the 24th (Pembroke and Glamorgan Yeomanry) Battalion, The Welsh Regiment and it seems likely there were others periodically, as the necessity arose to maintain numbers.

Table 15 Composition of 2nd Bn ICC

Coy	Yeomanry as sections from the 17 Regts)
6	Cheshire, Shropshire, Montgomery, Denbigh
7	Scottish Horse, Lanark, Fife and Forfar, Ayrshire
8	Buckingham, 2CoLY, Berkshire, Dorset
9	3rd County of London (SS), City of London (RR)
10	ER of Yorkshire, Staffordshire, Lincolnshire

The scheme of manning was reminiscent of the Boer War. Each company was divided into four sections of 35 men under a subaltern. This was further divided into four man messing groups. On this manning and taking into account Headquarters staff, Lewis gun sections, Medical, Quartermaster, Veterinary and other personnel, the complement of five companies amounted to approximately 30 officers and 800 NCO's and men, with the best part of 1000 camels. The Imperial Camel Corps included its own Field Ambulance and as a whole numbered approximately 2,800 all ranks and when at full establishment it could put 1,800 rifles into the firing line. It came with 36 Lewis guns or three per Company, eight Vickers Maxim's and the Singapore and Hong Kong Mountain Battery with its six nine-pounder guns. Everything was carried packed on camels.

The Corps was never large as the above digest shows, but ultimately it provided a vital hinge upon which Allenby could turn Lawrence's desert force of Arab Irregulars to best advantage. It also provided a necessary buffer between the strait lace of the military reality on the one hand and the more cavalier attitude of the Arab irregulars. The manner in which it was built up meant it rarely if ever acted as a Brigade, which it most nearly resembled. For these reasons there are no precise formation or disbandment dates.

When particular components ran out of soft sand areas with little likelihood of their coming back to them, they were re-converted to the original Light Horse. Nevertheless it comprised a most determined band of fellows who actually succeeded in operating in the cold, damp and rocky tracts of the Trans-Jordan for a period, against all the rules. At the time of its break-up the British Companies survived until 1919 and in August 1918 Companies 7 and 10 served on the Hejaz with Lawrence and are mentioned by him in his *Seven Pillars of Wisdom.* The Machine Gun Squadron was re-deployed against the Senussi and were mounted on machine gun cars in the Western Desert.

The camel carried an infinite variety of loads apart from riders. Large fantassies or water containers were common enough, but they were packed with guns of various sizes, cacolot panniers for carrying the wounded either sitting up or stretchered, apart from general supplies, boxes of explosives and ammunition and general stores. Lawrence reputedly won a bargaining match with Allenby's Quartermaster at dinner by insisting a riding camel was of no use for pack work, but then he wanted 2000 camels 'to win Damascus' and gambled rightly that the latter didn't know any better!

The Egyptian Theatre as a base for offensive operations From the withdrawal to Egypt the 2nd Mounted Division returned to their horses, as will be recounted later. Those other Yeomanry, who had come to Gallipolli later, remained dismounted and formed the basis for the 74th Yeomanry Division. There were others who, even at this late stage, came to Egypt with their horses.

Work had to be performed within Egypt to maintain the status quo and although it had troubles enough of its own the men coming from Gallipolli had to be brought back to health to serve a larger design. This was more a matter of time though it also called for a combination of rest, feeding and medical treatment. The initial steps were taken to dislodge the Turks facing the Suez Canal. However the large loss of materiel had to be replaced by fresh imports and until this process was substantially completed the creation

of fully complemented divisions was impractical, indeed the decision was taken to break up the 2nd Mounted Division before the associated troops were ready to resume their duties.

The year 1916 had a big element of planning and directly these forces were recovered and reorganised they were sped off on a variety of errands. The Egyptian Expeditionary Force was created by the amalgamation of the Mediterranean Expeditionary Force and the Egyptian Force on 20th March 1916. This was in effect a first shake-out for the Yeomanry. It provided the first clear distinction between the mounted and dismounted elements in the Yeomanry. These forces are listed in Table 16.

Table 16 Egypt, Spring 1916

Force	Brigades etc	Regiments of Yeomanry etc
Canal	8th Mtd Bde	City of London, 1st Co of London, 3rd Co of London
Defences	3rd Dismtd Bde	E Kent, W Kent, Sussex, Welsh H, Norfolk, Suffolk
	42nd Div Mtd	A Sqn DLOY
	52nd Div Mtd	HQ and C Sqn, R Glasgow
	1st Dismtd Bde(attd)	1st, 2nd, 3rd Scottish Horse, Ayrshire, Lanark
	54th Div Mtd	A Sqn, HQ and MG Section, Hertford
WFF	5th Mtd Bde (Indpt)	Warwick, Gloucester, Worcester
Troops	6th Mtd Bde (Indpt)	Buckingham, Berkshire, Dorset
	22nd Mtd Bde	Lincoln, Stafford, E Riding of Yorkshire
	4th Dismtd Bde	Shrops, Denbigh, Cheshire, Glam, Montgomery, Pembroke

Thus the aftermath of Gallipolli made 1916 a year of retrenchment for the Egyptian Theatre. The many pillared frontier twixt the continents of Africa and Asia traces its way through rock and sand from Rafa to Akaba, both occupied by the Turkish. The latter held an embarrassingly strong flanking position, until Lawrence took it out later on 6th July 1917, something that GHQ Cairo could not accept until independently verified. Rafa felt an earlier impact delivered by the Anzac Division, the Imperial Camel Corps and the 5th Mounted Yeomanry Brigade on 9th January 1917. This signalled the end of an embattled Egypt. Something had been done to secure the Egyptian Base in the creation of the Camel Corps. The 2nd Mounted Division had been remounted. Now something was needed to create a worthwhile force from the large number of Yeomanry without horses.

To enter Palestine at first required the dislodgement of the Turks occupying a number of prepared positions within Sinai and a long approach march. The 5th Mounted Brigade took a lead in this at Katia and Oghratina, before the Anzac contingents were deployed across the Suez Canal. Then followed the attack on Rafa. Shimmering in the mind's distance lay

Damascus, the oldest continuously occupied city in the World. It held the key to unlock the Ottoman Empire. Only a dreamer would have looked in that direction at the time the British shook off their recent defeat. This dreamer was lost in the sandy wastes of Arabia. All the British could provide at this stage was sound administration and if Britain had a ragbag army in the Canal Zone, at least General Murray was a superb organiser. Whilst holding the Sinai Front the most active preparations went forward to extend road, rail and pipeline links against the then vague prospect that an army could be cobbled together to wrest the Levant from Anatolia.

The forces in Egypt at this time are shown listed in Table 17 at the end of this chapter.

The Gallipolli Theatre of operations The difference between strategy and tactics is never more startlingly demonstrated than by the affairs connected with that barren peninsula. The strategic concept was brilliant: Take the Dardanelles and the nearby sole munitions arsenal and Turkey was effectively out of the war, whilst the gateway to our Russian ally was opened. Unfortunately our intentions were so laboriously telegraphed to the enemy, to make them fully awakened to our designs. In addition there was no agreement between the Royal Navy and the Army over how this should be done and the latter was split between London and Cairo, besides which the Western Front did not want to know of other's problems, having enough of their own. The British with an unerring grasp of military imperatives appointed a general who, amongst other things, was good at poetry. Some forces were cobbled together, whilst our ideas of beach landings hadn't much advanced since the days of the Crimea. Thus the campaign opened on 18th March 1915.

The 2nd Mounted Division was dismounted and sent forward on 6th August, because events were not proceeding according to plan. Before this a considerable argument had arisen in posting it at all and whatever the niceties this caused further delays. Two Regiments were added to the force and the Artillery and horses withdrawn. The Brigades however more nearly approximated to battalions since five officers and 100 men from each Regiment had to stay behind to look after the horses, thus the division could field no more than 5000 rifles when it arrived at Suvla Bay on 17th August 1915. They were followed in

September by two further Brigades direct from the United Kingdom without horses, but with their gear packed according to the upside-down philosophy. This was followed in October by a further four Brigades. In total the campaign took in 31 regiments of Yeomanry, of which all the regiments of the initial contingent were withdrawn during the first days of November and the remainder at the retiral on 8/9th January 1916. This account is not over heroics or casualties, great and grievous as they were, yet the campaign transformed the Yeomen who survived into battle hardened veterans. TheForce make-up is shown in Table 18.

Table 18 Dismounted Yeomanry to Gallipolli

Dismounted Brigades	All 1st Yeomanry Regiments
August	
1st (S Midlands) Regt of Y	Warwick, Gloucester,Worcester
2nd (S Midlands) Regt of Y	Buckingham Hus, Dorset Berkshire
3rd Notts & Derby Regt of Y	Sherwood Rangers, S Notts, Derby
4th London Regt of Yeo	1st County of London, 1st City of London
5th Yeomanry Regt	Hertford, 2nd County of London
September	
Scottish Horse Bde	1st, 2nd, 3rd Scottish Horse
1st Highland	1st & 2nd Lovat's Scouts, Fife & Forfar
October	
2nd SW	1st Devon, R N Devon Hus, W Somerset
1st Eastern	Norfolk, Suffolk Hus, Welsh H
1st S Eastern	E Kent, W Kent, Sussex

The British had and still have a pronounced reticence against parading success or failure, as it is considered bad form. The consequence of this national foible is for no matter to be properly thought through or managed on a team basis. The leadership erects a wall of face-saving oriental fatalism when a plan fails to work and even subsequent commissions of enquiry find it impossible to penetrate the fog of self delusion. The expedition was certainly a fatal blunder; ill-conceived, badly planned and impossible to execute. They fought a redoubtable foe. The weather varied from extremely hot, leading to all forms of contagion, to very cold and damp, such that some were drowned, frost-bitten and even frozen to death. The campaign achieved nothing for the employment of 480,000 soldiers, of which 252,000 were killed, wounded, missing, prisoners, dead of disease or evacuated sick. The Turks suffered 218,000 casualties of whom 66,000 perished. The booty left behind was immense. It took two years to clean up the ground. [1] The Yeomanry associated with this campaign are listed in Table 19.

The Palestine Theatre of Operations and *the Road to Damascus* The invasion of Palestine was signalled on the 26th March 1917, by the 1st Battle of Gaza.

Chapter 7

Table 19 Regimental movements to and from the Gallipolli Theatre

Regt	Date	To Theatre or Formation	Date	To Theatre or Formation
AY	11 10 15	Fr UK to Helles	Jan 16	To Mudros for Egypt
BY	Aug 15	Fr Egypt to Gallipolli	Dec 15	To Egypt
RBH	as BY			
DY	as BY			
R1DY	09 10 15	Fr UK to Gallipolli	30 12 15	Landed Egypt
RNDY		as R1DY		
DorY	as BY			
FFY	26 09 15	Fr Egypt to Gallipolli	Dec 15	To Egypt
RGH	as BY			
HY	as BY			
REKY	08 10 15	Fr UK to Gallipolli	Jan16	To Mudros for Egypt
WKY		as REKY		
LY	11 10 15	Fr UK to Helles	Jan 16	To Mudros for Egypt
RR	as BY			
1CoLY	as BY			
WD	as BY			
SS	as BY			
1LS	26 09 15	Fr Egypt to Gallipolli	Dec 15	To Egypt
2LS	as 1LS			
NorY	10 10 15	Landed Anzac	Dec 15	To Egypt
SR	18 08 15	Landed Suvla	Dec 15	To Egypt
SNH	as SR			
1SH	02 09 15	Landed Suvla	28 12 15	Landed Egypt
2SH	as 1SH			
3SH	as 1SH			
WSY	09 10 15	Landed Suvla, attchd 11th Div	Dec 15	To Egypt
SufY	10 10 15	Landed Anzac, attchd 54th Div	Dec 15	To Egypt
SusY	08 10 15	Landed Helles, attchd 42nd Div	Dec 15	To Mudros for Egypt
WarY	18 08 15	Landed Gallipoli,	Dec 15	To Egypt
WH	10 10 15	Landed Anzac, attchd 54th Div	Dec 15	To Egypt
WorY	18 08 15	Landed Suvla	Nov 15	To Egypt

Most of the troops hoofed it into Palestine from Egypt, as opposed to landing and the same applied to Syria. As the consequence the campaign dates tend to blur. Notwithstanding mere dates, this country was set to become the scene of the largest mounted operations of the war. Eventually the formations evolved into three Corps. Yeomanry operations employed a mounted division, a dismounted infantry division each with attendant machine gun formations, attachments to divisional and corps cavalry, a battalion of the Imperial Camel Corps with a machine gun squadron.

The mounted portion took longer to stabilise so that a number of the remounted brigades had first served either independently or as parts of the Imperial Mounted Division, the Australian Mounted Division and the Anzac Mounted Division before forming the Yeomanry Mounted Division. The last building block fell into place when the 8th Mounted Brigade joined the Yeomanry Mounted Division from Salonica on 21st July.

The major battles fought during 1917 broke the back of enemy resistance. Each was presaged by careful preparation and the addition of reserves as these became available. The First Battle of Gaza used the Desert Column made up from the Anzac and Imperial Mounted divisions each with a brigade of Yeomanry and the Imperial Camel Corps with its Yeomanry battalion and machine gun section. The Second Battle of Gaza over 17th-19th April involved the same forces plus the use of four additional infantry divisions. The 74th Division was brought in reserve to the 2nd Battle of Gaza, although then deficient in artillery. The next stage was to re-arrange formations and to bring into being an essential flanking forces aptly named the Desert Mounted Corps. As from April 1917 Table 20 lists the disposition of forces.

Chapter 7

General Allenby assumed command of the EEF on 28th June 1917 and one of his first positive steps was to stiffen the army by purging Cairo of ineffectual Staff. He was a big, born in the saddle, cavalryman and much needed in view of the troops composing his command. The Australians had earlier shown their

talented amateur, since the forces were predominantly wartime recruits put into war-formed units. Also it was the only British theatre to make a wholesale use of mounted troops, whether on horse or camel and even cavalry sabres were re-issued later in the campaign.

Table 20 Palestine, Spring 1917

Force.	Brigades etc.	Regiments etc.
52nd Div	Div Mtd	C Sqn R Glasgow Y
53rd Div	Div Mtd	A Sqn DLOY
54th Div	Div Mtd	A Sqn Hertford Y
74th Div	Div Mtd	A Sqn WD
	229th Infantry Bde	16th(R 1st Devon and R N Devon Yeomanry) Bn Devonshire Regt
	(2nd Dismtd Bde)	12th(W Somerset Yeomanry) Bn Somerset L I
		12th (Ayr and Lanark Yeomanry) Bn Royal Scots Fusiliers
		14th (Fife and Forfar Yeomanry) Bn Black Watch
	230th Infantry Bde	10th (R E Kent and W Kent Yeomanry) Bn E Kent Regt
	(3rd Dismtd Bde)	16th (Sussex Yeomanry) Bn Sussex Regiment
		15th (Suffolk Yeomanry) Bn Suffolk Regiment
		12th (Norfolk Yeomanry) Bn Norfolk Regiment
	231st Infantry Bde	10th (Shropshire & Chester Yeomanry) Bn Shropshire L I
	(4th Dismtd Bde)	24th (Denbigh Yeomanry) Bn R Welch Fusiliers
		24th (Pembroke & Glamorgan Yeomanry) Bn Welch Regt
		25th (Montgomery & Welsh H Yeo) Bn R Welch Fusiliers
Desert Column		
ANZAC Mtd D	22nd Mtd Bde	Lincoln, Stafford and E Riding of Yorkshire Yeomanry
IMD	5th Mtd Bde	Warwick, Gloucester, and Worcester Yeomanry
IMD	6th Mtd Bde	Buckingham, Berkshire, and Dorset
ICC	2nd Bn + MG Sec	

From the beginning General Allenby had the problem of keeping together, for his use, those forces of his own creation. The scheme of campaign was for a strong infantry arm on the left flank, near enough the coast to receive logistic support from the sea, thus relieving pressure on his tenuous land lines. The centre was for the Cavalry, using the desert and on its right flank the Camel Corps to maintain the best possible liaison with Lawrence and his Arab Irregulars. By a series of feints he hoped to unbalance the Turks. He could hardly believe his luck when vital rail links were severed and otherwise impregnable enemy defences were rendered useless by Lawrence. At critical periods supplies and reinforcements were denied to Turkish positions and luck favoured those ready to exploit such an opportunity. During August 1917 there was a further reorganisation, leading to what was known as The Egyptian Expeditionary Force, listed in Table 21.

characteristic respect for authority in burning down the Happy Quarter of Cairo, when they encountered a sellers market on their return from Gallipolli. They would have eaten a lesser man and nevertheless made a good attempt on him. The basis of his plan was the creation of three forces, which whilst independent within themselves would be able to co-operate in joint ventures, the more so as they got their desert feet and acknowledged their respective strengths and weaknesses. It seems that Allenby got to all the places a general shouldn't be, winning great respect from the common soldiery and thereby succeeded in igniting the critical mass; Something where the whole was greater than the sum of the parts and tempered dreams became a reality!

What faith Allenby initially placed in Lawrence working the desert right flank we shall never know, but then the latter started to deliver undreamed of results. This was to be the war of the

Table 21 Palestine, August 1917

Force	Brigades etc	Regiments etc
Desert Mtd Corps	Corps Mtd Tps	2nd County of London Yeomanry
	7th Mtd Bde	SRY, SNH
	Yeomanry Mtd Div	
	6th Mtd Bde	RBH, QODY, BYH and 17th MG Sqn
	8th Mtd Bde	MxY, RR, SS and 21st MG Sqn
	22nd Mtd Bde	QOSY, LncY, ERY and 18th MG Sqn
XX Corps	74th Infantry Div	229th, 230th and 231st Bdes
Force	Brigades etc	Regiments etc
XXI Corps	Corps Mtd Tps	Regt of 3 Sqns from of RGOY, DLOY and HertsY

The Third Battle of Gaza took longer to organise and

commenced from 27th October till 6th November. By this time the XXth, XXIst and Desert Mounted Corps had been created which included the Yeomanry Mounted Division. Immediately following, on 8th November the Yeomanry were engaged once more at Huj. All of the fighting in Palestine was distinguished by the scale of its movement and against that of the Western Front by an absence of attrition. It can be said the GOC-in-C recaptured the initiative at a difficult time in military history, quite apart from winning the campaign and did so on the most meagre of resources.

By the Spring of 1918 the cause was not in doubt, besides which the Western Front was making impassioned pleas for help in the face of a determined German offensive. This led to a succession of changes affecting the Yeomanry. The 74th (Yeomanry) Division was dispatched complete to France in May. The Yeomanry Mounted Division was indianised at the same time and successively renamed the 1st Mounted Division and the 4th Cavalry Division. Five machine gun battalions were formed, dismounting nine regiments from the brigades, and these went to France between June and August. The Imperial Camel Corps Brigade was broken up in June, which allowed the Australians and New Zealanders to return to their divisions as light horse. The 2nd Battalion was retained on a variety of duties, part of it to assist Lawrence on the Hejaz railway, whilst the 26th (Scottish Horse) Sqn, Machine Gun Corps ended the war in machine gun cars on the Egyptian Western Frontier. The combination of moves allowed the remaining five mounted regiments to join the newly formed 4th and 5th Cavalry divisions, whilst the corps cavalry regiments remained in place as before: The Worcester Yeomanry with XX Corps and the Hertford Yeomanry with XXI Corps. The effect of these moves is summarised in Table 22 at the end of this chapter.

Macedonia. No attempt will be made here to describe the tangled web of history which has developed around Salonika since before the days of Alexander the Great. The campaign, as such it was to become had been forced on unwilling Statesmen and their Military. The landing of forces came at a time when things were going particularly badly at Gallipolli, the Grand Senussi had decided to attack us from Western Egypt, our hold on the Suez Canal was likely to be threatened

directly pressure was relaxed elsewhere and a disastrous siege was in progress at Kut in Mesopotamia. These problems were additional to affairs on the Western Front, with its own insatiable appetites. To satisfy the Macedonian requirement troops were wrenched from the Gallipolli battlefield and thrown down onto the quayside to await re-equipping with such basics as blankets, greatcoats and serge uniforms. Added to the misery was the wet weather which persisted for days following disembarkation.

On 7th October 1915 a Composite Yeomanry Regiment arrived from Egypt made up of Squadrons from the Nottinghamshire (Sherwood Rangers) Yeomanry, the Derbyshire Yeomanry and the South Nottinghamshire Hussars, hastily transferred from the 7th Mounted Brigade. This latter Brigade next arrived on 7th February 1916 and again took command of them. The incidence of malaria was such the South Nottinghamshire Hussars had to be formed into a Composite Regiment with two Squadrons of the Derbyshire Yeomanry. A further Composite Regiment was formed at the end of August from the HQ, MG and a single squadron of Derbyshire Yeomanry and two squadrons of Lothian's and Border Horse, taken from the 22nd and 26th Divisions.

Headquarters 8th Mounted Brigade arrived on 16th November, followed by their City of London, 1st County of London and 3rd County of London Yeomanry. At this time two of the dismounted Yeomanry Battalions which had been promised duly arrived in the form of the 10th (Lovat's Scouts) Bn Cameron Highlanders and the 13th (Scottish Horse) Bn Black Watch (The Royal Highlanders).

As at December 1916 XII Corps had mounted troops in the Lothian's and Border Horse less a squadron and XVI Corps the Surrey Yeomanry less the squadron with 27th Division. By 14th September 1918 the Yeomanry was reduced to the Lothian's and Border Horse with XII Corps, less a squadron, the XVI Corps with the Surrey Yeomanry, less a squadron and the Derbyshire Yeomanry as GHQ Troops. Between the crumbling Ottoman and Austro-Hungarian Empires, the lost Russian influence and dubious Greek intentions the British were pleased to disentangle themselves. Movements in this theatre are listed in Table 23.

Chapter 7

Table 23 Regimental Movements to and from the Macedonian Theatre of operations

Regt	Date	To Theatre or Formation	Date	To Theatre or Formation
DerY	06 02 16	Fr Egypt with 7th Mtd Bde		Remained mostly as GHQ Tps
RR	16 11 16	Fr Egypt as 8th Mtd Bde	04 06 17	To Egypt
SS	as RR			
LBHA Sqn	17 12 15	Fr France, with 26th Div	29 11 16	Attd 8th Bde until 11 01 17
	11 05 17	To XII Corps Cav Regt	28 09 18	To Bulgaria
D Sqn	05 11 15	Fr France	25 09 18	To Bulgaria
A&D Sqns	Jan 19	S Russia(Batum, Tiflis, Kars)	Apr 19	This period with 27th Div
1LS/2LS	20 06 16	Fr Egypt , landed Salonika	01 11 16	Joined 27th Div
	06 07 18	Left Div for France		
SRY	07 02 16	Fr Egypt with what became	04 07 17	To Egypt (torpedoed)
SNH	07 02 16	Fr Egypt with 7th Mtd Bde	29 06 17	To Egypt
1SH/2SH	21 10 16	Fr Egypt, landed Salonika	01 11 16	Joined 27th Div
	24 06 18	Left Div for France, via Italy		
SurYASqn	11 02 16	Fr France, landed Salonika	27 12 16	Two sqn Corps Cav Regt
B Sqn	02 12 16	Fr France, landed Salonika	27 12 16	formed till end of war

Italy The Italian Front faced on Austria. Hostilities opened on 23rd May 1915, although war with Germany was not declared until 27th August and the British involvement didn't begin until 28th October 1917 when XIV Corps arrived, followed by XI Corps in December. The primary military need in a country devoid of natural resources was Artillery. There followed some juggling with the forces until XI Corps returned to France. It brought with it and took away 1st King Edward's Horse. XIV Corps brought the Northamptonshire Yeomanry. Included in the Army Troops was No. 4 Group Lovat's Scouts acting as Anti-Aircraft Artillery and front spotters! These forces remained in place until after the Armistice came into effect on 4th November 1918. Regimental Formations in the Italian Theatre are shown in Table 24 at the end of this chapter.

Mesopotamia. As mentioned earlier this was primarily an Indian show although hardly excusing the disastrous siege at Kut. The Western component of the forces was the 13th Division which left Egypt handing over its defences along the Suez Canal to the Ayrshire and Lanarkshire Yeomanry on the 12th February 1916. They sailed for Basra and moved to the front on 2nd April in time for the third attempt to relieve Kut al Amara, which was unsuccessful. They remained in Mesopotamia until the end of the conflict, receiving orders on 1st November 1918 to cease hostilities at once.

The Divisional Cavalry, D Squadron Hertford Yeomanry, although already in Egypt actually joined the Division on 8th July 1916 and remained until 20th November, was then attached to the Remount Depot at Amara until 31st December, when it joined a Squadron of 10th Lancers and two Squadrons of 32nd Lancers to form III (Tigris) Corps Cavalry Regiment. As with the Cavalry in the Egyptian Theatre, it was actively engaged in horse borne fighting against the Turks. The forces involved are listed in Table 25 at the end of this chapter.

Chapter 7

Table 17 Regimental movements to and from the Egyptian Theatre (including Gallipolli)

Regt	Date	To Theatre or Formation	Date	To Theatre or Formation
AY	07 02 16	Fr Mudros, to 1st Dismtd Bde f with LanY,	16 10 16	2nd Dismtd Bde
	04 01 17	12RSF	07 05 18	To France
BY	09 04 15	Fr UK, 2nd S Midlands Mtd Bde	14 08 15	To Gallipolli dismtd
	30 11 15	Fr Gallipolli	Jan 16	To 6th Mtd Bde, Imp Mtd Div
	Jun 17	Bde to Yeo Mtd Div	04 04 18	f with RBH, C Bn MGC
			21 06 18	To France
RBH	as BY			
CY	20 03 16	Fr UK dismtd	20 03 16	formed part 4th Dismtd Bde
	02 03 17	f 10KSLI	07 05 18	To France
DenY	20 03 16	Fr UK dismtd	20 03 16	formed part 4th Dismtd Bde
	23 12 16	f 24RWF, 231st Bde, 74th Div	07 05 18	to France
DerY	09 04 15	Fr UK, Notts&Derby Mtd Bde	14 08 15	To Gallipolli, dismtd
	28 11 15	Fr Gallipolli	Jan 16	Left 2nd Mtd Div
	06 02 16	To Salonika, with 7th Mtd Bde		
R1DY	30 12 15	Fr Gallipolli	Feb 16	abs by 2nd Dismtd Bde
	04 01 17	f 16DR, 229th Bde, 74th Div	07 05 18	To France
RNDY		as R1DY		
DorY	20 04 15	Fr UK, with 2nd Mtd Div	14 08 15	To Gallipolli, dismounted
	30 11 15	Fr Gallipolli	21 01 16	Div broken up, to 6th Mtd Bde
	Feb 17	To Imp Mtd Div	Jun 17	To Yeo Mtd Div
	Jul 18	Now 10th Cav Bde, 4th Cav Div		
FFY	28 12 15	Fr Gallipolli	Feb 16	To 2nd Dismtd Bde
	21 12 16	f 14BW	07 05 18	To France
GY	15 03 16	Fr UK, dismtd	20 03 16	Abs 4th Dismtd Bde
	02 02 17	F 24WR	07 03 18	To France
RGH	24 04 15	Fr UK, with 2nd Mtd Div	17 08 15	To Gallipolli
	24 11 15	Fr Gallipolli	21 01 16	Div broken up, to 5th Mtd Bde
	Feb 17	Bde to Imp Mtd Div	Jun 17	Became Australian Mtd Div
	Aug 18	then 13th Cav Bde, 5th Cav Div		
HY	20 09 14	fr UK, to form Yeo Mtd Bde with 2CoLY	17 08 15	To Gallipolli, joined 2nd Mtd Div, as 5th Mtd Bde
		Fr Gallipolli, left 2nd Mtd Div for WFF		
	30 11 15	To 54th Div	Mar 16	Regt as Div Cav
		To Palestine		
RHQ&ASqn	20 03 16	XXI Corps Cav Regt	Sep 16	RHQ broken up
ASqn	1917-8	To 11th Div	1919	To Tripoli
B Sqn	26 08 17	Fr France, to Depot Sqn, Zeitoun	04 07 16	To France
	11 03 16	To Mesopotamia	09 05 18	Joined A Sqn, XXI Corps Cav Regt, Palestine
	06 07 17			
D Sqn				
	29 03 16			
REKY	05 02 16	Fr Mudros, abs by 3rd Dismtd Bde	01 02 17	f with WKY 10TB
			07 05 18	To France
WKY		as REKY		
LanY	07 02 16	Fr Mudros, to 1st Dismtd Bde	16 10 16	To 2nd Dismtd Bde
	04 01 17	As AY		
LH HQ &B Sqn	12 01 16	Fr UK	06 03 16	to France
C Sqn ?	01 02 16	to France		
D Sqn?	10 11 15	to France		
DLOY ASqn	30 09 14	Fr UK		
LncY	27 11 15	Fr UK	07 04 18	f with ERY D Bn MGC
	01 06 18	to France		
Regt	Date	To Theatre or Formation	Date	To Theatre or Formation
RR	06 05 15	Fr UK, as part of 2nd Mtd Div	18 08 15	Dismounted to Gallipolli
	29 11 15	Fr Gallipolli and mtd again	21 01 16	2nd Mtd Div broken up, to Suez Canal as part of 8th Mtd Bde
	16 11 16	To Salonika	04 06 17	Fr Salonika
	07 04 18	f with SS E Bn MGC	01 06 18	Arrd France
1CoLY	28 04 15	Fr UK, with London Mtd Bde	18 08 15	To Gallipolli, dismounted
	27 11 15	Fr Gallipolli and mtd again	Jan 16	2nd Mtd Div broken up, to Suez Canal as part of 8th Mtd Bde
	Nov 16	To Salonika	21 07 17	to Yeo Mtd Div
	04 0617	Fr Salonika	22 07 18	Then 11th Cav Bde, 4th Cav Div
	24 04 18	Div became 1st Mtd Div		

Chapter 7

2CoLY	25 09 14	Fr UK	19 01 15	Part of Yeo Mtd Bde with HY
	18 08 15	To Gallipolli, dismtd & attd to 2nd Mtd Div, in 5th Mtd Bde	29 11 15	Fr Gallipolli, left div, mounted
	Apr 16	Attd 6th Mtd Bde, WFF	Jan 17	Regt split up
RHQ&C Sqn		Northern Canal Defences		
A Sqn	14 01 17	53rd Div till 14 02 17	05 04 17	74th Div till 23 08 17
B Sqn	17 01 17	Depot Sqn Zeitoun till Aug		
	Aug 17	Regt now XX Cav Corps Regt	Jul 17	C Sqn at Zeitoun till Sep 17
	Apr 18	Fr XX Corps, f F Bn MGC	01 06 18	Landed in France
SS	as RR			
1LS	28 12 15	Fr Gallipolli	27 09 16	f with 1/2nd LS and coy from 1/3rd SH, 10CH
	20 10 16	To Salonika		
2LS	as 1LS			
MY	20 03 16	Fr UK and WFF	04 03 17	f with WHY 25RWF
	07 05 18	to France		
NorY	25 12 15	Fr Gallipolli	22 02 16	f 3rd Dismtd Bde. Suez Canal Formed 12NR
	Jul 16	Western Frontier Force	07 02 17	
	07 05 18	To France		
SRY	24 04 15	Fr UK, 2nd Mtd Div	18 08 15	To Suvla, dismtd
	28 11 15	Fr Suvla	21 01 16	2nd Mtd Div broken up
	07 02 16	To Salonika (soon 7th Mtd Bde)	Jun 17	Fr Salonika (torpedoed)
	04 07 17	Fr Mudros, attd Desert Mtd C	May 18	to new 2nd Mtd Div
	Jul 18	as 14th Cav Bde, 5th Cav Div		
SNY	24 04 15	Fr UK	18 08 15	To Suvla, dismtd
	28 11 15	Fr Suvla	21 01 16	2nd Mtd div broken up
	07 02 16	To Salonika (soon 7th Mtd Bde)	29 06 17	Fr Salonika, attd Desert Mtd C
	08 04 18	f with WksY B Bn MGC	26 05 18	Fr Alexandria (torpedoed)
	27 05 18	To Egypt	18 06 18	To France (via Taranto)
PY	Mar 16	Fr UK, dismtd	20 03 16	Abs by 4th Dismtd Bde
	02 02 17	f with GY 24WR		231st Bde, 74th Div
			07 05 18	To France
1SH	28 12 15	Fr Suvla	Feb 16	Abs in 1st Dismtd Bde, attd 52nd Suez Canal
	01 10 16	f with 2SH 13BW		Defences.
	21 10 16	To Salonika		with 1/2nd Scottish Horse
2SH	as 1SH			
3SH	as 1SH		01 10 16	to 26MG less Coy to 10CH
ShropY	14 03 16	Fr UK, dismtd	20 03 16	Abs 4th Dismtd Bde with WFF
	02 03 17	f with CY 10KSLI	07 05 18	To France
WSY	31 12 15	Fr Suvla	Feb 16	Abs by 2nd Dismtd Bde, WFF
	04 01 17	f 12SLI	07 05 18	To France
SY	09 11 15	Fr UK	c Apr 16	to 22nd Mtd Bde, WFF
	Feb 17	Bde to ANZAC Mtd Div	Jun 17	to Yeo Mtd Div
	Apr 18	Div became 1st Mtd Div	Jul 18	12th Cav Bde, 4th Cav Div
SufY	23 12 15	Fr Anzac	22 02 16	3rd Dismtd Bde, Suez Canal
	Jul 16	to WFF		
	05 01 17	f 15SR	07 05 18	To France
SurY CSqn	02 04 16	Fr UK	11 03 16	To France
SusY	07 02 16	Fr Mudros, abs in 3rd Dismtd Bde, on Suez Canal Defences	Jul 16	To WFF
	03 01 17	f 16RSR	07 05 18	To France
WkY	24 04 15	Fr UK	18 08 15	To Gallipolli, dismtd
	27 11 15	Fr Gallipolli	Jan 16	2nd Mtd Dive broken up, Bde became 5th Mtd
	Feb 17	to Imp Mtd Div		Bde and Indpt
	Jun 17	became Australian Mtd Div	08 04 18	f with SNH B Bn MGC
	26 05 18	sailed Alexandria, torpedoed	29 06 18	Arrd France via Taranto
WH	26 12 15	Fr Anzac	22 02 16	3rd Dismtd Bde formed, on Suez Canal
	Jul 16	To WFF		Defences
	04 03 17	f with MY 25RSF	07 05 18	To France
WorY	22 04 15	Fr UK	18 08 15	To Suvla
	30 11 15	Fr Suvla	Jan 16	Bde became 5th Mtd Bde, Indpt
	Feb 17	To Imp Mtd Div	Jun 17	Div became Australian Mtd Div
	05 05 18	Became XX Cav Corps Regt		
ERY	28 11 15	Fr UK	Apr 16	Changed to 22nd Mtd Bde, WFF
	Feb 17	To Anzac Mtd Div	Jun 17	To Yeomanry Mtd Div
	07 04 18	f with LncY D Bn MGC	01 06 18	Arrd France

Chapter 7

Table 22 Regimental Movements to and from the Palestine Theatre

Regt	Date	To Theatre or Formation	Date	To Theatre or Formation
AY	Jan 17	+LanY = 12RSF, 229 Bde, 74 Div	May 18	to France
BYH	Feb 17	with 6th Mtd Bde to IMD	Jun 17	to YMD
	04 04 18	with RBH formed C Bn MGC	21 06 18	to France via Taranto
RBH	as BYH			
CY	02 03 17	+SY=10KSLI, 231Bde, 74Div	May 18	to France
DenY	Feb 17	formed 24RWF, 231Bde, 74Div	May 18	to France
R1DY	04 01 17	+RNDY= 16DR, 229Bde, 74Div	07 05 18	to France
RNDY		as R1DY		
DorY	Feb 17	with 6th Mtd Bde to IMD	Jun 17	to YMD
	Jul 18	then 10th Cav Bde, 4th M Div	28 11 18	To Syria till Jul 19
FFY	21 12 16	formed 14BW, 229Bde, 74 Div	07 05 18	to France
GY	02 02 17	+PY= 24TWR, 231Bde, 74Div	May 18	to France
RGH	Feb 17	with 5th Mtd Bde to IMD	Jun 17	Div became Aus Mtd Div
	Aug 18	now 13th Cav Bde, 5th C Div	Oct 18	To Syria till Jun 19
HYASq	26 08 17	fr 54Div to XXI CCR	09 05 18	B Sqn joined A Sqn
2ICC		part ICCB in DMC		
REKY	01 02 17	+WKY= 10TB,230Bde, 74Div	07 05 18	to France
WKY		as REKY		
LanY	as AY			
LncY	Feb 17	to Anzac M Div with 22mtd Bde	Jul 17	Bde to YMD
	07 04 18	+ERY formed D Bn MGC	17 08 18	to France
RR	Jun 17	fr Salonika as 8MtdBde to YMD	07 04 18	with SS formed E Bn MGC
			01 06 18	to France
1CoLY	Jun 17 22	fr Salonika as 8MtdBde to YMD	24 04 18	Div became 1st Mtd Div
	07 18	then 11th Cav Bde, 4th C Div		
WD A	05 04 17	with 74th Div till 23rd Aug	Aug 17	XX Corps Cav Regt
Sqn	Apr 18	formed F Bn MGC	19 08 18	to France
SS	as RR			
MY	04 03 17	+WHY= 25RWF, 231Bde, 74Div	May 18	to France
NorY	07 02 17	formed 12NR, 230 Bde, 74th div	07 05 18	to France
Regt	Date	To Theatre or Formation	Date	To Theatre or Formation
SRY	04 07 17	fr Salonika as 7th Mtd Bde, attchd	May 18	to new 2nd Mtd Div
	c1918-9	DMC	Jul 18	became 14th Cav Bde, 5th
		To Syria till 07 10 19		C Div
SNH	Jun 17	fr Salonika as 7th Mtd Bde, atchd	Apr 18	with WY formed B Bn MGC
	27 05 18	DMC	18 06 18	survivors for France
		left Egypt, torpedoed		
Regt	Date	To Theatre or Formation	Date	To Theatre or Formation
PY	as GY			
SY	as CY			
WSY	04 01 17	formed 12SLI, 229Bde, 74Div	May 18	to France
StfY	Feb 17	22nd Mtd Bde to Anzac M Div	Jun 17	to YMD
	Apr 18	became 1st Mtd Div	Jul 18	as 12th Cav Bde, 4th Cav
	c1918-9	To Syria till Jun 19		Div
SufY	05 01 17	formed 15SR, 230Bde, 74Div	May 18	to France
SusY	03 01 17	formed 16RSR, 230Bde, 74Div	07 05 18	to France
WY	Feb 17	with 5th Mtd Bde to IMD	Jun 17	became Aus Mtd Div
	Apr 18	with SNH formed B Bn MGC	26 05 18	left Egypt, torpedoed
	21 06 18	survivors left again for France		
WHY	as MY			
WorY	Feb 17	with 5th Mtd Bde to IMD	Jun 17	Div became Aus Mtd Div
	05 05 18	left to become XX CCR	c1918-9	To Syria till Jun 19
ERY	as LY			

Table 24 Regimental Movements to and from the Italian Theatre of Operations

Regt	Date	To Theatre or Formation	Date	Disposals
KEH	15 12 17	Fr France to XI Corps	16 03 18	To France
HCY	12 11 17	Fr France with 41st Div	04 03 18	To France
1LS/2LS	end 17	Fr France 4th Group to GHQ Tps		As AA or front observers
NorY	10 11 17	Fr France as XIV C Cav Regt	18 04 18	Became GHQ Tps
	09 10 18	XIV Corps reformed		Reverted to Corps Cav Regt

Chapter 7

Table 25 Regimental Movements to and from the Mesopotamian Theatre of operations

Regt	Date	Disposals	Date	To Theatre or Formation
HY D Sqn	29 03 16	Fr Egypt, to L of C	08 07 16	To 13th Div
	Dec 16	III(Tigris) Corps Cav Regt	06 08 17	15th Indian Div
	Apr 18	NW Persia L of C	Oct 18	retd, then to India Jan-Aug 19

References

1 Terraine. J. The Smoke and the Fire - Myths and Anti-Myths of War 1861-1945. (Leo Cooper, London, 1992)
2 Winter. D. Haig's Command - A Reassessment. (Viking, London, 1991)
3 James Brig. EA. Historical Records of British Cavalry and Yeomanry Regts in the Great War - 1914-18. (1969)
4 Becke. Maj AF. Order of Battle - History of the Great War, Parts 1, 2a, 2b, 3a, 3b, 4 and 5a. (HMSO, 1935-45)
5 Gould RW. Locations of British Cavalry, Infantry and Machine Gun Units 1914-1924
6 Frederick JBM. Lineage Book of British Land Forces - Vol 1. (Microform Academic Publishers. Wakefield, 1984)
7 Chappell. M. The Vickers Machine Gun - No.8 (Wessex Military Publishing, Okehampton, 1989)
8 Hutchison. Lt-Col GS. Machine Guns,Their History & Tactical Deployment. 1916-22) (MacMillan, London, 1938)
9 Tylden. Maj G. Horses and Saddlery. (Army Museums and Ogilby Trust,JAA Allen, London, 1965)
10 Croft. Maj, The Rev J. Palestine September 1918. (SAHR, Vol LXX, Spring 1992)
11 Langley. E and G. Sand, Sweat and Camels. (Australia)
12 Inchbald. G. The Imperial Camel Corps. (Johnson, London 1970)
13 Haigh Bryant J. The Imperial Camel Corps 1916-1918. (Military Historical Soc. Vol XXIV, 93 Aug 1973, pp15-18)

Plate 7/1 The Tank Museum, Bovington

Scottish Horse or Lovat Scouts Armoured Car? Many private enterprise attempts were made tp create these vehicles during The Great War. This example utilised a Rolls Royce chassis, held at a premium during 1914-15.

Plate 7/2 The Tank Museum, Bovington

Westmorland & Cumberland Yeomanry Armoured Car.

Plate 7

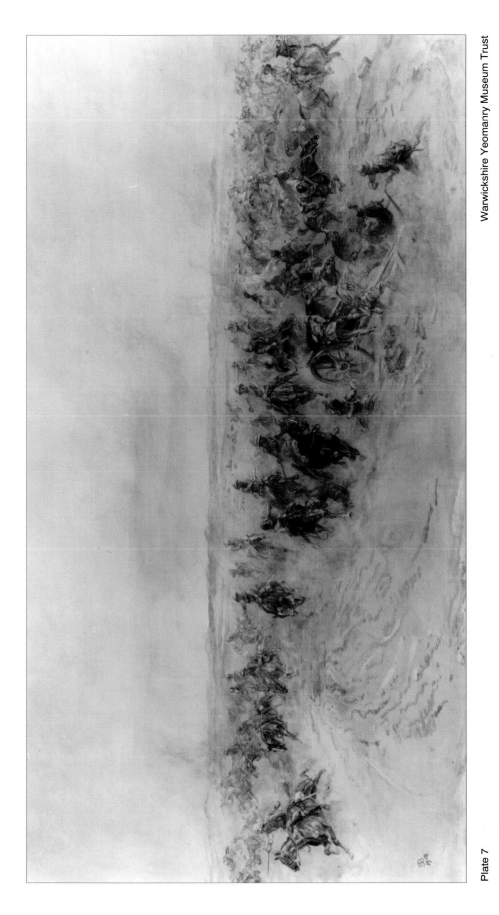

Storming the Turkish guns at Huj. Not an operation to be undertaken lightheartedly or without careful reconnoitre.

Warwickshire Yeomanry Museum Trust

Plate 8

by the late JP Beadle Esq. Hung in The
Army Staff College, Camberley

The charge of the 6th Mounted Brigade at El Mughar - 13th November 1917. The Royal Bucks Hussars are in the lead with the Queen's Own Dorset Yeomanry to the left and the Berkshire Yeomanry in support.

Plate 7/3   Pembroke Yeomanry Historical Trust

The Face of War. Lt. GA Sherian-Shedden MC.
Pembroke Yeomanry, attached to Machine-Gun
Corps.

Plate 7/4   Pembroke Yeomanry Historical Trust

Camel Patrol. A Squadron, Pembroke Yeomanry attatched to Imperial Camel
Corps, 1917.

The Royal Gloucestershire Hussars

'Aftermath' - The capture of the Turkish guns at Huj. The not so glamorous task of sorting out and tidying up after the victory.

Anonymous

'To take our horses and give us bicycles' - R.I.P. (Return if Possible)

Plate 7/7 Imperial War Museum

Imperial Camel Corps Beer Wagon. Two camels in harness.

Plate 7/8 The Imperial War Museum

The Imperial nature of the Imperial Camel Corps - Australians, United Kingdom, New Zealanders and Sikhs.

Plate 7/9   The Westminster Dragoons

Arrival in Jerusalem. The Westminster Dragoons were amongst the first Yeomanry to enter Jerusalem, 9th December 1917. Note the additional bandolier around the horse's neck

Plate 7/10   Imperial War Museum

Bogged Camel - Solving such a predicament calls for courage. Camels kick sideways.

Plate 7/11   Imperial War Museum

Members of Imperial Camel Corps at the Mitla Pass - Some British members of the Imperial Camel Corps joined Lawrence at the end of their service in Palestine.

 Imperial War Museum

'Sudani' - Portrait of a camel. Note the branding marks on the neck, there is no record of these marks being forged.

 Imperial War Museum

Infantry Battalion Machine Gun Limber - Such a unit included 32 such limbers and a total of over 800 horses. Two of the horse or mules were commonly fitted with pack-harness hangers to walk-up the Vickers guns and equipment to the firing emplacements.

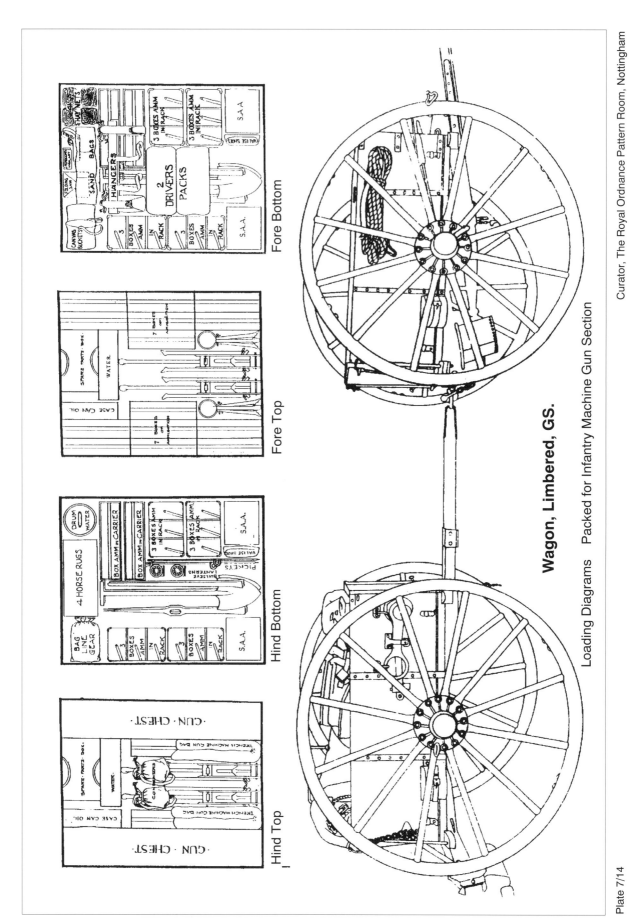

Fore Bottom

Fore Top

Hind Bottom

Hind Top

Wagon, Limbered, GS.

Loading Diagrams   Packed for Infantry Machine Gun Section

Curator, The Royal Ordnance Pattern Room, Nottingham

Wagon, Limbered, GS.   The illustration indicates the extensive nature of the stores carried by the Infantry Machine Gun Section.

8. Aftermath

Clearing the Decks

The effect of a long war was for all manner of formations to be created. In the post-war run-down virtually all war-formed units vanished. The 2nd and 3rd line regiments of the Yeomanry were either re-united with their 1st or kindred regiment, or disbanded. The 1st regiments were then either disembodied or disbanded. The fact was the Territorial Force ceased to exist from the time of embodiment and the commencement of hostilities and at the end of this period required to be reformed. An important distinction is made here, since disbandment constitutes a break in service, whilst disembodiment does not. Soundings taken, by those charged with the responsibility for reforming the Reserve Army decided who went where and ascertained if they were willing. Those found a slot were subsequently *Reconstituted* and those unable or unwilling were *Disbanded* and not reformed. The large number of Yeomanry serving with the Infantry and the Machine Gun Corps, as named units, it appears were both disbanded and disembodied indiscriminately, only to be reconstituted. From the point of reconstitution, it was possible for a regiment to resume its former status and in selected cases, for it to be transferred to another Arm of the service.

Yeomanry Formations

The fourteen most senior regiments of Yeomanry, taken from the deficient War Office list of precedence and were allowed to keep their horse and these are listed in Table 26.

Table 26 Yeomanry to Keep Horses

Ayrshire	Staffordshire
Cheshire	Warwickshire
Lanarkshire	R Wiltshire
Duke of Lancaster's Own	Yorkshire Dragoons
Leicestershire	Yorkshire Hussars
Northumberland	1st Lovat Scouts
Sherwood Rangers	2nd Lovat Scouts
Shropshire	Scottish Horse
N Somerset	The Inns of Court

To these were added the Scouts in the form of the Lovat Scouts and the Scottish Horse and these were followed in the 1930's by The Inns of Court Regiment.

Transfer or Disband

Royal Tank Regiment The Yeomanry owes a debt of gratitude to this Regiment for a timely intervention, during the post war reformation. The other side of the coin was the sound investment they made in building a significant Reserve Armour capability. As we shall see the Yeomanry was responsible for doubling a significant number of tank regiments, during a time of crisis. By way of history the Tank Detachment was formed secretly on 16th February 1916, mainly under Royal Navy auspices. It was re-designated in March as the Armoured Car Section, Motor Machine Gun Service. The Tank Corps and latterly the Royal Tank Regiment achieved a remarkable feat of survival. At last the Cavalry was confronted by the uncomfortable facts of life. The 'Tanks' as part of the Machine Gun Corps was then formed into the Heavy Branch of the Motor Machine Service on 18th November 1916. This was withdrawn on 27th July 1917 to form the Tank Corps. Next, the remainder of the Motor Machine Gun Service was gradually disbanded with the personnel going to the Tank Corps. Later it was further re-designated on the 18th October 1923 as the Royal Tank Corps. Then, just after the outbreak of the Second World War, actually 4th September 1939, it became a wing of the Royal Armoured Corps as the Royal Tank Regiment. By such peregrinations, the founder of the armoured movement in Britain was thus classified as the most junior of the Cavalry and so amply demonstrates the specious arguments over precedence! Whatever, out of the post-war reformation of the Territorial Army, the Tank Corps was able to sponsor eight Armoured Car Companies, to which the following Yeomanry were transferred and these are shown in Table 27.

Table 27 Armoured Car Companies

19th (1st) (TA)	21 05 20	The Lothian and Border Horse
20th (2nd) (TA)	06 01 21	The Fife and Forfar Yeomanry
21st (TA)	14 07 21	The R Gloucestershire Hussars
22nd (4th) (TA)	26 03 20	The Westminster Dragoons
23rd (5th) (TA)	25 09 20	3rd/4th Co of London Yeo (SS)
24th (TA)	14 07 21	The Derbyshire Yeomanry
25th (7th) (TA)	01 03 22	The Northamptonshire Yeo
26th (TA)	23 08 20	E Riding of Yorkshire Yeomanry

The Royal Regiment of Artillery No amount of tank talk can disguise the fact that The Great War was largely fought if not won by sheer weight of artillery: That is the nature of siege warfare. Given time, tanks and a manual of tactical doctrine, would have provided a convincing though not necessarily bloodless victory. As it was, they severely dented the front and succeeded in disrupting the military balance. But such a dent needed an accompanying exploitation and a strategic understanding. This was primarily a Cavalry responsibility and they muffed it. As with so many brilliant military notions, it takes at least half a generation to inculcate the philosophy at the level necessary to give it an opportunity to germinate.

In the meantime the Artillery had a vast field park of guns, available for the Reserve Army, designed and built for horse traction. With varying degrees of enthusiasm 27 Yeomanry were transferred to the Royal Regiment. As the consequence of these transfers, a number of those named have subsequently made a return to the Yeomanry proper. Others, by dint of association became anti-tank gunners, as listed in Table 28, very often manning self-propelled tracked vehicles.

Table 28 Conversions to Artillery

Bedford	Lancashire Hussars
Berkshire	City of London (RR)
Buckinghamshire	Montgomeryshire
Denbighshire	Norfolk
R 1st Devon	S Nottingham Hussars
R N Devon	Oxfordshire
Dorset	Pembroke
Essex	W Somerset
Glamorganshire	Suffolk
R Glasgow	Surrey
Hampshire	Sussex
Hertfordshire	W'moreland & Cum'land
R E Kent	Worcestershire
R W Kent	

Royal Signals The 1st County of London Yeomanry was transferred to the Royal Signals, which had just recently been separated from the Royal Engineers. They were to form the Divisional Signal Regiment for the 2nd Cavalry Division.

Scouts Two regiments of Lovat Scouts and the Scottish Horse were reconstituted as Scouts.

Disbandments The Lincolnshire Yeomanry was disbanded on the 17th December 1920, apparently due to an unwillingness to join the Artillery. The following units, not properly Yeomanry, are mentioned to complete the picture: Both the North Irish Horse and the South Irish Horse were disbanded on 31st July 1922, with the latter never reformed. The King Edward's Horse was disbanded on 31st March 1924 and not reformed, whilst the 2nd King Edward's Horse had already been absorbed into the Tank Corps during May 1917, with a reserve squadron disbanded in Kilkenny at the end of 1918 and never reformed.

Engineer Commander Benson Freeman RN
This man had more to do with chronicling the Yeomanry than anyone alive or dead. It was a tragedy he passed off the scene, as the result of a motoring accident in 1928, before completing his self-appointed task. His work with Fellows on precedence speaks for itself and is reproduced here, in its entirety, as Appendix D. To be provocative, it is possible to argue the case from the re-acceptance dates of 1802-03 and like his list of what might have been, develop a new wrangle. He would have loved this.

Thoughts on Armour
From Versailles the British had a Tank Corps the Germans none, but by 1926, British developments were down to a snails pace, being starved of trained manpower, design resources and equipment budgets. The lack of competent designers, available to the Cavalry Arm was to become farcical, as Correlli Barnett relates in excruciating detail in his Audit of War.[4] The extent of British developments was piecemeal and blinkered and precisely the thinking Fuller[2] had warned against. As was to be expected, there were differing opinions on how to progress. Few had an overall concept and those that had found it difficult to sell, because it cost a lot of money and they were too far down the pecking order for scarce funds. Tanks found little favour with the 'Establishment', nor were exercises conducted in an even-handed manner.[3] Worst of all, no effort was made at the top to revise battle doctrine, not at least until the sweep of events in Poland, and all this was to show through in the early days of The Second World War as our armour was committed in 'penny packets'.

Chapter 8

The dangers of a poor or non existent Staff had been foreseen before, both by Cardwell and Haldane and here again there was this absence of quality thinking at a crucial level. Critics of this view may say it was hardly the concern of the Reserve Army. However, the whole is the sum of the parts, in which the Regular Army is the no more than caretaker of the Country's defence during times of peace, though not the predominant part of the muscle during war. It is the Nation in arms which bears the brunt of a bankrupt military mentality. The Achilles Heel of the Reserve Army is the preponderance of staff positions held by non-reservists, who are unprepared to fight their corner for the best reason: They don't belong. Viewing the other side, there was hardly any secret what the Germans were planning and how it was to be achieved, because our Military Attachés attended many of their manoeuvres: Somehow nobody believed it could be done.

The Rest
A considerable post-war controversy arose within the tank owning nations as to which Arm should be responsible for tactical doctrine and the development of the weapon to achieve its ends. Certainly most Cavalry Arms did not embrace it, because it meant abandoning horses. Equally, with a somewhat *dog in the manger* attitude, they were unwilling to have anyone usurp their function. In the United States lobbying reached the Congress, who were prevailed upon to enact legislation, defining tank development as the prerogative of the Infantry! And this possibly explains some of those quaint castles on tracks gifted us at the start of the war. Elsewhere, strong arguments were put forward for the tank as a purely Infantry support weapon. The main sense in finding it this billet was the potentially large funds available to an established Arm: Hardly the soundest of arguments, but at least pragmatic. The essence of the 1920's however, was not so much the lack of money as the poverty of thought, except in Germany and latterly Russia.

Germany, debarred by the Peace Treaty from having tanks, spent nearly ten years with its best military brains, coming to terms with the implications of armoured warfare. Also, if they couldn't play at home they would '*play away*'; Russia and Sweden were the selected venues. But first, let us understand the grand design. What was the gospel according to Fuller and others, was it complete, could the mechanical answers be found to fit the theories and did it all hang together?

Kenneth Macksey[3], quotes a paragraph, written by Guderian, the inventor of the Panzer Division, in his memoirs dealing with 1929[4]. This stated with startling clarity what he considered armoured warfare was about, after he had wrestled with the problem for many years:

"My historical studies, the exercises carried out in England and our own mock-ups had persuaded me that tanks would never be able to produce their full effect until other weapons on whose support they must inevitably rely were brought to their standard of speed and of cross-country performance. In such a formation of all arms, the tanks must play the primary role, the other weapons being subordinated to the requirements of the armour. It would be wrong to include tanks in infantry divisions: what was needed were armoured divisions which would include all the supporting arms needed to allow tanks to fight with full effect."

The Germans held no monopoly over armoured philosophy, but kept themselves well informed on developments, particularly doctrine. Thus they were perceptive enough to engineer the removal of their opposite numbers during the Stalin purges of the 1930's. Presumably they gathered this intelligence during the period of joint ventures, but not unfortunately for them, the very separate development of the T34!

When it came to the Second World War, it was the gulf in thinking between the Germans and the rest that produced the former's dominance in armoured affairs. Piece by piece, British equipment, was as good and sometimes better than the German, but it was reduced to tatters by the absence of a cohesive philosophy. The British did not lack clear sighted military thinkers. Unfortunately their thoughts and published papers, were ignored or belittled by their seniors, yet avidly studied by others.

It is against this philosophical background that Germany set about remodelling its Cavalry: Not that all their Military were convinced. The blueprint called for an integrated divisional formation with a combination of sufficient power for the assault and mobility for the pursuit, a capable logistic tail and above all, superb radio communications. This was an expensive option for a country in straightened economic circumstances, but harking back to Nolan, it would produce a force above comparison with the competition. And so it was to prove, so long as the essential balance within the force was preserved.

References

1 Barnett. C. The Audit of War. (Macmillan, London 1986)
2 Fuller. JFC. Armoured Warfare. (Eyre and Spottiswood, London 1943 (1932 Lectures)
3 Macksey. K. The Tank Pioneers. (Jane's, London 1981)
4 Guderian. H. Panzer Leader. (Michael Joseph, London 1952)

"YOU OUGHT TO HAVE PULLED UP—THE POLICEMAN WAVED HIS HAND." "I NEVER TAKE ANY NOTICE OF THEIR FAMILIARITY."

Plate 7/15

Punch

First aid Nursing Yeomanry, November 20, 1918

Plate 8/1   The Tank Museum, Bovington, Dorset.

Armoured Car Camp - Very likely Salisbury Plain where eight squadrons of the Royal Tank Corps, formed in the Yeomanry were annually exercised.

Plate 8/2   The Imperial War Museum

Horse Power - Whilst a small portion of the Yeomanry was mechanised there remained the 2nd Cavalry Division in Palestine as a fully horsed formation.

Plate 8/3

9th/12th Royal Lancers

Visions Past. Gilbert Holiday was the artist. Although depicting an imaginary scene from the 9th Lancers in the 1920s, it is representative of the strong bond existing between horse and man in any cavalry unit.

A

H I S T O R Y

O F   T H E

Y E O M A N R Y   C A V A L R Y   F O R C E

O F

G R E A T   B R I T A I N

FROM THE INCEPTION OF THE YEOMANRY FORCE IN 1794
TO PRESENT TIMES

By

Benson Freeman.   O.B.E.,   F.R.His.S.
(late Engineer Commander Royal Navy)

ILLUSTRATED.

Army Museums Ogilby Trust

The Ghost of Benson Freeman - The author was killed in a motorcycling accident during 1928. A considerable coverage had been made up to the time of his untimely death and there has been an obvious intention to bring everything together as a single work.

9. The Second World War

Political Muscle

The seeds of war were first sown by terms planted in the Peace Treaty at Versailles and more particularly the appendices hanging thereto. If Hitler was a gambler he was onto a winning streak. The shake-out from the earlier war divided power groups differently: Notably Italy and then Japan felt like Germany that a share of the profits of empire was their due, but the latter was more intent on gathering together lost ethnic minorities scattered around her borders. However, whilst this made good politics, the real quest was for *living room* which caught the ear of countries further East. The horrendous conflict in the Russia's effectively sidelined the remainder of the war, large in the popular imagination as it appeared. It also had a schizophrenic effect on democracy. In a Parthian shot, Fuller exposed the core of the conflict as an unedifying choice between fascism from the North Sea to Vladivostok or communism from Vladivostok to the North Sea, whilst damning the doctrine of *unconditional surrender*, but then soldiers are obliged to pursue more pedestrian objectives.

War Preparedness

By dint of hard professional endeavour the Germans solved the problems wrapped within the Panzer philosophy. (One might add, with not a little help from the peace loving Swedes and their erstwhile Russian enemies.) Thus it was 'Son of Schleiffen' when unleashed, cleared Europe and took France out of the war. Such forces had taken ten patient years of improvisation, argument, development and manoeuvre to reach something still short of perfection. It is unclear what philosophy ruled in Britain though up to the time of El Alamein it was closely identified with 'penny packets' which was a prescription for disaster against those of the 'gathering flood'. Where the Germans fielded fully integrated armoured divisions the Allies were still working up to improvised brigades. Losses at Dunkirk are often cited as the reason for a poor showing, yet Germany replaced hugely greater losses of materiel under far more difficult conditions later in the war. Further, important as the hardware was, the soft thinking of the inter-war years had allowed an intellectual and cultural gap to open, so difficult to bridge in the cauldron of war. Accordingly, the humiliation of the Germans and the economics of Bedlam in the Twenties ran on into the Thirties, whilst military inaction at home departed from that place to Cloud Nine! In tracing the build-up of British armour the phasing is complicated by the frequent movement of regiments between brigades and brigades between divisions. Indeed, with the benefit of hindsight, perhaps the largest number were ineffectual and more in the mind than actuality. The real problem was not so much the absence of battle-worthy vehicles, as properly trained and tested armoured field commanders'.

It will be remembered that the planning of the 1920's period allowed the Territorial Army fourteen regiments of Cavalry, eight Armoured Car companies and two regiments of Scouts. From the Munich crisis onwards this was re-thought, though it did not call for immediate mechanisation. The Armoured Car companies became regiments and threw off seven more, whilst the Inns of Court adopted the armoured rôle, was joined by the reformed North Irish Horse and The Lovat Scouts was embodied without change of rôle as Scouts, bringing the total to 33 regiments. During 1940-45 period seven regiments converted to Royal Artillery, two to Infantry, (the Yorkshire Dragoons without formally leaving the Yeomanry, were converted after embodiment to 'Motorised Infantry'), two to Signals, one was later absorbed into its armoured companion and three were placed into suspended animation. Thus the war served Yeomanry varied downwards from 22 to 18 regiments and are listed in Table 29.[1][3]

Chapter 9

Table 29 Wartime Served Yeomanry

From	Date	Regiment	Disposal	Date
Yeo	15 02 40	The Ayrshire Yeomanry	RA. S/A 4/2/46 recon to RAC	01 01 47
Yeo	00 00 42	Cheshire Yeomanry	R Sigs, S/A & recon to RAC	01 01 47
RTC	30 04 39	The Derbyshire Yeo	Redes & recon to RAC	01 01 47
1st	24 08 39	2nd Derbyshire Yeo	Disbanded 14/6/47	******
RTC	30 04 39	Fife and Forfar Yeo	Redes, S/A 9/45 & recon to RAC	01 01 47
1st	24 08 39	2nd Fife and Forfar Yeo	S/A 9/45 & disbanded 1/1/47	******
RTC	30 04 39	R Gloucestershire Hus	Redes, S/A 1946 & recon to RAC	01 01 47
1st	24 08 39	2nd R Gloucestershire Hus	S/A 15/1/43 & disbanded 1/1/47	******
Joins	00 11 40	The Inns of Court Regt	S/A 3/47 and recon to RAC	00 03 47
Yeo	15 02 40	Lanarkshire Yeo Regt	RA.S/A 15/2/42 recon to RAC	01 01 47
Yeo	15 01 40	The D of Lancaster's O Yeo	RA S/A 4/2/46 recon to RAC	01 01 47
Yeo	15 02 40	Leicestershire Yeo Regt	RA. S/A 31 12 46 recon to RAC	01 01 47
RTC	30 11 40	2nd Co of Lon Yeo (W D)	Redes, S/A 1946 & recon to RAC	01 01 47
RTC	30 04 39	3/4th Co of Lon Yeo (SS)	Redes, S/A 1945 & recon to RAC	01 01 47
3rd	27 09 39	4th Co of London Yeo (SS)	Absorbed by 3rd 1/8/44	******
RTC	30 04 39	1st Lothian and Border H	Redes, S/A 1945 & recon to RAC	01 01 47
1st	24 08 39	2nd Lothian and Border H	S/A later, amal with 1st 1/1/47	******
Scouts	01 09 39	The Lovat Scouts	S/A 20/1/47 & recon to RAC*	01 01 47
RTC	00 04 39	The Northamptonshire Yeo	Redes, S/A 18/08/45, recon to RAC	01 01 47
1st	27 09 39	2nd Northamptonshire Yeo	S/A 18/8/44 & amal with 1st 1/1/47	******
New	26 09 39	North Irish Horse	S/A 30/4/45 & recon to RAC	01 01 47
Yeo	01 09 40	The N Somerset Yeomanry	RSigs 21 03 42 recon RAC	01 01 47
Yeo	15 02 40	Northumberland Hussars	RA, S/A 1/12/46 & recon RAC	01 01 47
Scouts	15 02 40	The Scottish Horse Regt	RA. S/A 1/3/46 recon to RAC	01 01 47
Yeo	12 04 41	The Sherwood Rangers Y	S/A 01 03 46 & recon to RAC	01 01 47
Yeo	15 02 40	Shropshire Yeomanry Regt	RA. S/A15/03/46 & recon to RAC	01 01 47
Yeo	12 04 41	The Staffordshire Yeo	S/A 01 03 46 & recon to RAC	01 01 47
Yeo	12 04 41	The Warwickshire Yeo	S/A later & recon to RAC	01 01 47
Yeo	12 04 41	The R Wiltshire Yeomanry	S/A 1945 & recon to RAC	01 01 47
Yeo	00 12 40	The Q's O Yorkshire Dgns	Inf, S/A 9/44 & recon to RAC	01 01 47
RTC	30 04 39	The East Riding Yeomanry	Redes, S/A later & recon to RAC	01 01 47
1st	25 06 40	2nd East Riding Yeomanry	Inf. S/A 12/46 & recon to Infantry	******
Yeo	19 12 44	The Yorkshire Hussars	Inf Recce. S/A & recon to RAC	01 01 47

At the divisional level there were twelve formations during the war, though ten if we accept that 1st Cavalry became 10th Armoured and the 79th was formed to develop, supply and fight specialised equipment for others and not to serve as a divisional formation. Of the remaining ten; The 8th Armoured was formed on 5th July 1942 till the end of that year, but was never up to strength nor operated as a formation, the 42nd Armoured from 1st November 1941 for just under two years serving in the United Kingdom only and the 9th Armoured from 1st December 1940 till 31st July 1944, disbanding after wholly United Kingdom service. This left seven actual fighting formations which served as follows; The Guards Armoured Division forming on 17th June 1941, but with a fighting life of just under a year, between 28th June 1944 and 11th June 1945 when it reverted to Infantry, though at no time having Yeomanry; The 1st Armoured, without any Yeomanry component, spending an uncomfortable month and two days in France during 1940 where it was never up to establishment but later in Africa from 13th November 1941, taking a fulsome part in the fighting for eighteen months and in Italy until October 1944, at which point it was stripped of its brigades; The 2nd starting life in

the United Kingdom on 15th December 1939, serving in Egypt and Libya between 1st January and 9th May 1941 whence it was disbanded on the 10th because its Headquarters was captured, but again without Yeomanry; The 6th forming in the United Kingdom on 12th September 1940, serving in North Africa, Italy and Austria between 22nd November 1942 till 31st August 1945; The 7th forming on 3rd September 1939 in Egypt, as The Armoured Division where it was formerly the Mobile Division. Then serving from there into Libya, Italy and NW Europe until 31st August 1945, with a short spell from 4th January to 7th June 1944 in the United Kingdom; The 10th forming in Palestine on 1st August 1941 and disbanding in Egypt on 18th June 1944 after some service in Syria. It was badly under-equipped; And lastly the 11th forming in the United Kingdom on 9th March 1941, serving in NW Europe from 13th June 1944 to 31st August 1945.

It follows from this that any Yeomanry must have fought either in these four divisions or otherwise independent brigades. In a conflict lasting 70 months the British armoured active overseas service amounted to 225 divisional months, with an average of slightly over three months per division in operational theatres, which even then includes a number of backwaters. As the general rule an armoured division included a single tank brigade of three regiments, so that the number of regimental months in a theatre of fighting operations was 675 in which the Yeomanry gave 416, making a contribution of just over 60%. This somewhat fragile statistic is supported by Joslen and also underwrites the Shavian quip that 'those that can, do and those that can't, teach!' And all this was achieved substantially on the back of borrowed equipment and the vital supply of spare parts, courtesy of the United States of America. It should make us less than sanguine over our military capabilities then as now, which is no cheap jibe at those in uniform, though perhaps the Military could have given more credit to their civilian helpers in uniform.

Feeling for a Cavalry Solution

Mercifully, German armour was not all Panther and Tiger tanks, due to the rush with which Hitler brought Germany to war. Nevertheless the British had their problems replenishing weapon stocks following Dunkirk. This was not entirely centred on producing tanks in sufficient quantity, but with designing them to take account of battlefield experience timeously. Here the most favoured element continued to be reliability, whilst the chief constraint over hitting power was the provision of a large turret ring to house anti-tank guns we seemed gifted at making. The dearth of both design and productive capacity, led to a mass of imports. The Sherman became the common building block; it was cheap, reliable and packed like a shoe box into a ship's hold. It did the sort of things a tank was supposed to, but in the face of first class opposition it had to give ground. Very often additional fittings in the form of welded-on spare tracks links and sand bags, were provided to make up for thin armour but this overloaded the suspension, causing breakdowns. Whatever the Allied shortcomings, the failure or inability on the part of the enemy, to maintain an essential element of air power within the Panzer formations, enabled us to manage the problem of German armoured superiority with tank busting aircraft.

Anti-Tank Artillery

The Royal Artillery got into the act when a number of the Yeomanry regiments, previously transferred during the early twenties, were re-equipped and trained as anti-tank gunners. These are summarised in Table 30.

Table 30 Anti-Tank Regiments formed from Yeomanry

Date	Regimental details
28 11 38	53rd (Worcestershire & Oxfordshire Yeomanry) Anti-Tank Regiment, RA (TA)
28 11 38	54th (Queen's Own Royal Glasgow Yeo) Anti-Tank Regiment, RA (TA)
28 11 38	55th (Suffolk & Norfolk Yeomanry) Anti-Tank Regiment, RA (TA)
1939	63rd Anti-Tank Regiment RA (TA) duplicate of 53rd
1939	64th Anti-Tank Regiment RA (TA) duplicate of 54th
01 06 39	65th Anti-Tank Regiment RA (TA) duplicate of 55th
12 09 41	102nd (Northumberland Hussars) Anti-Tank Regiment RA (TA) after assumed subtitle
04 07 42	149th (The Lancashire Yeomanry) Anti-Tank Regiment, RA (TA)

There were and possibly still are peculiarities of organisation between combatant nations. Whether an eminently suitable gun was an infantry, cavalry or artillery piece became a matter for debate during the war on both the British and German sides. British guns underwent a variety of deployments. To get the right mix of forces in an armoured engagement it was possible to have (even at platoon level) members of the three Arms working together, but each using similar equipment! Following a different shaft of logic, the German gun was under Armoured, Artillery, Heavy Artillery or even Air Force control, dependent upon prime function and calibre. To a General in the field, this could lead to strained relations. To get the equipment, one was obliged to take a unit with training that was often woefully inappropriate to a new role. Since high calibre and muzzle velocity were the main features for armoured use, the situation produced an unfair demand on scarce anti-aircraft guns then under airforce control; All the more humiliating because of a failed air power. The problem was never properly resolved and caused a number of 'own goals': So never let it be said the British held a monopoly of the problems! There were reported instances of the British using anti-aircraft guns in the anti-tank role, but only *in extremis*. This was short-sighted, but perhaps correct, having regard to their scarcity. The famous 88mm gun on the other side was primarily an anti-aircraft weapon of World War One vintage, yet it enjoyed a far greater utility knocking out tanks, whether it was mounted in a tank or trailed behind a Half-track. Unfortunately the AA gun is designed for use with the barrel in the vertical position, meaning it is confined to a sit-up-and-beg attitude to accommodate a substantial recoil and thus it was not the neatest piece to disguise on the battlefield. By the end of the war the Germans had redesigned the cradle and running gear to bring this height down to under five feet, making it comparatively invisible.

The Funnies [2][3]

Strangely the 79th Armoured Division became the largest armoured formation within the Allied Army, although it was to have no direct tactical employment as such. It was designed to develop and apply battlefield solutions to problems likely to be encountered from the Normandy Landings until the conclusion of hostilities in Europe. At one stage it had five armoured brigades comprising 17 regiments. There were 21,430 all ranks and 1,566 tracked vehicles. There was a whole brigade of Assault Royal Engineers. Working in between them were six Yeomanry regiments.

To support maintenance and repair there was a staff of 3,300 REME personnel, whilst radio communications employed 2,450 radios operating as far apart as 400 miles. Obviously, something had convinced Montgomery of the utility of such a formation. The concept, when carefully thought through, amounted to no flight of fantasy and if it gobbled up a large share of logistic support it obtained the economies of scale and specialisation.

Prior to November 1943 it had been recognised that the invasion of Europe would present the assaulting armies with some novel problems and that to wait until the troops were stranded on a beach was not the time to begin reaching for a solution. Also it was decided, against the conventional wisdom, that armour up front was the only sure way of shooting infantry onto their objectives without incurring unacceptable casualties. Special measures were necessary in any case to land armour on beaches as opposed to a harbour quayside. The problems in order were, floating tanks ashore under their own power, clearing mines, removing obstructions, taking out strong points such as pillboxes and gun emplacements, bridging and filling anti-tank ditches, whilst contending with a maelstrom of opposition.

Montgomery felt it worthwhile to reverse the normal deployment of infantry and armour. The getting of armour ashore dry shod at the same time as a few commandos could not be relied upon, so that the tanks themselves were made to float using inverted collapsible canvas skirts and each was driven by twin propellers. These were called DD tanks, after the duplex mechanism for track and propeller drive. Mines were a delaying tactic to which the British applied flailing chains to provide a safe lane for the following traffic and these were known as 'crabs'. Clearing obstructions was the preserve of the Royal Engineers. The armoured bulldozer was one of the equipments used, however concrete emplacements such as pillboxes and sea walls were treated by a Petard mortar firing something christened the 'flying dustbin' which was most effective provided the target was within 70 yards range. Other Royal Engineer equipment included bridge and matting layers and fascine droppers, each designed to cover gaps or boggy portions of ground. At the stage that rivers had to be crossed it was found necessary to apply hard matting on the further bank to enable DD tanks and Buffaloes to exit satisfactorily. Lastly came the 'crocodiles' or flame throwers. Although not properly a member of this family of unconventional equipment, it fitted well into the management structure. At the front it could help infantry smoke out obstinate pockets of resistance. Later in the campaign came the Buffalo tracked amphibian needed to ferry men and supplies across flooded terrain and river obstacles.

It was inevitable that the Yeomanry should be drawn into these developments and their later battlefield use. Due to the rough weather at the time of the Normandy Landings the British DD tanks landed dry shod. The Westminster Dragoons made the assault with their Crab flail tanks and were joined afterwards by the Lothian and Border Horse for the remainder of the campaign in North-Western Europe. The Staffordshire Yeomanry were withdrawn from the battlefield to undergo DD training in time for the crossing of the Maas at Xanten and were joined by the 44th Royal Tank Regiment. At this time there was a very watery situation so the Northamptonshire Yeomanry and The East Riding Yeomanry each manned Buffaloes to transport of troops and supplies.

The divisional structure was extremely flexible so as to enable visiting units to receive essential training in the minimum of time, either within the theatre or in the United Kingdom. This was particularly appropriate as fresh obstacles presented themselves such as the Rhine crossing.

Other Adaptations and Ruses

Although no part of The Funnies story, in a further epic of determined ingenuity, it was found possible to squeeze our best anti-tank gun, the 17 pounder, into a Sherman which was aptly re-named the *Firefly*. With a modified turret and turret ring, it provided an answer to all save the most feared German 88mm gun. Unfortunately this breakthrough came too late for all of the leading waves of the D-Day forces.

In a similar way to the Germans using the sturmgeshutz or fixed turret principle, the British fitted a variety of tank chassis' with larger calibre guns, both anti-tank and field. The lack of a proper turret made their use open to some restriction, as the Germans experienced, but it was both a quick and economical way of overcoming a shortfall in production and provided a useful capability: This paved the way to track borne artillery. Lastly in a comic deception, phoney units were created in the form of the 3rd Royal Gloucestershire Hussars and the 4th Northampton Yeomanry, equipped with inflatable

dummy tanks in service during May, June and July 1944, at the time of the Normandy landings. Also included was a Jeep-borne track printer to fool those making a fleeting air reconnaissance. This continued a deception at the time of El Alamein and an even earlier one of dummy horses by the Australians in Egypt and Palestine during the Great War.

Summary of the Yeomanry Force[1][3]

Dunkirk (May-June 1940) , El Alamein (23rd October 1942) and D-Day (6th June 1944) were the principal signposts of the war. The protagonists were considerably more sophisticated than in The Great War and the Brigade or Brigade Group played a more significant rôle than previously. Despite the terror inspired by the Panzer divisions and the widespread use of aircraft, like its earlier counterpart, it employed a vast artillery Arm. Again, in Table 31, the formations which served purely in the UK are ignored.

Table 31 Disposition of Yeomanry During The Second World War

Division	From	To	Yeomanry	Theatres
6th Armd (Div Tps)	10 11 40	31 08 45	1 Derby Yeo	N Africa 43, Italy 44, Austria 45.
10th Armd (Div Tps)	21 08 42	10 09 42	2 Derby Yeo	Palestine and Egypt (Alam el Halfa)
11th Armd (Div Tps)	25 03 43	17 08 44	2 N Yeo	NW Europe (see 33rd Bde)
79th Armoured			see	27th, 30th, 31st & 33rd Armd Bdes
48th Infantry	03 09 39	27 04 40	Lothians	France & Belgium from Jan-Apr 40
50th Infantry	D-Day	assault	W Dgns	D-Day, NW Europe. (see 30th Bde)
51st Infantry	03 09 39	29 03 40	1 FF Yeo	France
	20 01 44	31 08 45	2 Derby Yeo	NW Europe
1st Armd Recce Bde	30 03 40	25 11 40	1ER Yeo	France & UK
	07 04 40	17 06 40	1FF Yeo	France & UK
2nd Armd Bde	07 07 42	13 07 42	3 CLY(SS)	Defence of El Alamein
	24 08 42	18 12 42	Yorks Dgns	Battle of El Alamein
4th Armd Bde	04 10 42	15 11 42	2 Derby Yeo	El Alamein
	13 07 43	28 07 44	3 CLY(SS)	Sicily, Italy, D-Day
	29 07 44	31 08 45	3/4 CLY(SS)	France and Germany
	14 06 45	31 08 45	1 ER Yeo	Germany (see 33rd Armd Bde)
8th Armd Bde	01 08 41	30 08 45	Notts Yeo	El Alamein, UK, D-Day, Germany
	01 08 41	13 02 44	Staffs Yeo	El Alamein, N Africa and UK
9th Armd Bde	03 08 41	27 05 43	R Wilts Y	Palestine, El Alamein, Syria
	13 08 43	08 10 44	ditto	Palestine, Egypt, Italy
	03 08 41	27 05 43	Warwick Y	Palestine, El Alamein, Syria
	23 08 43	08 10 44	ditto	Palestine, Egypt, Italy
	10 10 41	13 03 42	Yorks H	Iraq, Palestine
21st Armoured Bde	11 06 45	11 08 45	NIH	Italy
22nd Armd Bde	03 09 39	16 09 43	3 CLY(SS)	UK, El Alamein, Libya
	03 09 39	16 09 42	R Glos H	UK, El Alamein, Libya
	03 09 39	29 07 44	4 CLY(SS)	UK, El Alamein, Libya, UK, NW Eu
24th Armd Bde	09 12 42	15 01 43	2 R Glos H	Egypt,
26th Armoured Bde	12 10 40	31 08 45	2 Lothians	UK, N Africa, Italy, Austria
27th Armd Bde (79th Divn)	14 02 44	29 07 44	ER Yeo	UK, D-Day, Caen. Early DD tanks and Buffaloes
	14 02 44	29 07 44	Staffs Yeo	UK, D-Day, Caen. DD tanks
	D-Day	Training	Notts Yeo	DD tanks (see 8th Armd Bde)
29th Armd Bde	07 06 41	31 08 45	2 FF Yeo	UK, NW Europe
30th Armd Bde (79th Armd Divn)	09 03 41	31 08 45	1 Lothians	UK, NW Europe. Crabs = Flails UK, NW Europe.
	08 03 41	31 08 45	W Dgns	Crabs = Flails
31st Armd Bde (79th Armd Divn)	02 02 45	06 06 45	1 FF Yeo	NW Europe. Crocodile F Throwers
	18 04 45	26 04 45	Staffs Yeo	NW Europe. DD tanks
33rd Armd Bde	17 03 44	18 08 45	1 N Yeo	Caen, NW Europe. Buffaloes
	16 08 44	23 04 45	1 ER Yeo	NW Europe. DD and Buffaloes
(79th Armd Divn)	26 04 45	26 06 45	Staffs Yeo	NW Europe. DD tanks

Chapter 9

Division	From	To	Yeomanry	Theatres
34th Armd Bde	06 06 45	31 08 45	1 FF Yeo	Germany
87th Dummy Tanks	26 05 44	11 07 44	4 N Yeo	Dummy tanks. Egypt, UK
	26 05 44	11 04 44	3 R Glos H	Dummy tanks. Egypt, UK
4th Cav Bde	03 12 39	02 10 40	R Wilts Yeo	UK, Palestine
	08 01 41	31 07 41	ditto	Palestine, Iraq, Syria
	15 11 39	21 03 41	N Som Y	UK, Palestine
	22 03 41	31 07 41	Warwick Y	Palestine, Iraq, Syria
5th Cav Bde	03 09 39	18 03 42	Yorks Dgns	UK, Palestine, Syria, Palestine
	03 09 39	22 03 41	Yorks H	UK, Palestine
	03 09 39	02 02 41	Notts Yeo	UK, Palestine
	21 03 41	07 06 41	Cheshire Y	UK, Palestine
	15 07 41	21 03 42	ditto	Syria, Palestine
	20 03 41	20 03 42	N Som Yeo	Palestine, Syria, Palestine
	30 04 41	04 06 41	Staffs Yeo	Palestine
6th Cav Bde	03 09 39	20 03 41	Cheshire Y	UK, Palestine
	03 09 39	28 04 41	Staffs Yeo	UK, Palestine
	05 06 41	31 07 41	ditto	Palestine
	03 09 39	21 03 41	Warwick Y	UK, Palestine
	03 10 40	07 01 41	R Wilts Yeo	Palestine,
	23 03 41	31 07 41	Yorks H	Palestine
21st Army Tank Bde	04 12 44	10 06 45	NIH	Italy
25th Army Tank Bde	03 09 42	03 12 44	NIH	UK, N Africa, Italy
31st Army Tank Bde	02 11 44	01 02 45	1 FF Yeo	NW Europe
1st Support Group	29 01 42	11 02 42	NH	Libya. 102(NH) Atk Regt RA
2nd Support Group	01 03 40	06 02 41 23	NH	UK, Egypt 102(NH) LAA/Atk Regt
	07 02 41	02 41	ditto	Egypt. 102(NH) Atk Regt RA
7th Motor Bde	24 10 44	18 12 44	Lovat Scouts	Italy. Redes 18th Inf Bde
GHQ BEF	May	1940	1 Lothians	United Kingdom
21st Army Group	23 05 44	15 05 45	Inns of Crt	UK and NW Europe
	15 05 45		1 ER Yeo	NW Europe
Italy & Balkans	27 12 44	13 05 45	Lovat Scouts	Italy & Balkans. Under Infantry
HQ 8th Army		15 1 43	2 R Glos H	In quarantine (S A)

Special Forces

Curiously, of all the Yeomanry related forces only one formation was embodied without a formally stated change of role. Reconstituted on 7th February 1920 as the 1st and 2nd Lovat's Scouts Yeomanry, they were transferred to the Scouts on 1st July 1920 as the 1st and 2nd Lovat Scouts (TA). Amalgamated to form The Lovat Scouts (TA) during August 1922, they were subsequently embodied on 1st September 1939, ultimately to achieve mobility on skis and to work as hill fighters, in Italy. Regimental disposals to various Theatres are listed in Tables 32-37.

Table 32 Regimental disposals to France and Belgium Theatre [5]

Regiment	Command	Dates	Command	Dates
1LBH	48 Inf Div	Jan 40 - Apr 40	51 Inf Div	Apr 40 - Jun 40
1FFY	50 Inf Div	Jan 40 - Apr 40	1 Armd Recce Bde	Apr 40 - Jun 40
	2 Armd Recce Bde	Jun 40		
ERY	GHQ BEF	Jan 40 - Mar 40	1 Armd Recce Bde	Mar 40 - Jun 40

Table 33 Regimental disposals to North Africa Theatre

Regiment	Command	Dates	Command	Dates
WksY	9 Armd Bde	May 42 - Dec 42	9 Armd Bde	Mar 44 - Apr 44
YH	GHQ MEF	Nov 43 - Dec 43		
SRY	8 Armd Bde	Feb 42 - Nov 43		
StfY	8 Armd Bde	Feb 42 - Nov 43		
RWY	9 Armd Bde	May 42 - Dec 42	9 Armd bde	Mar 44 - Apr 44
YD	GHQ BTE	May 42 - Aug 42	2 Armd Bde	Aug 42 - Dec 42
1DY	6 Armd Div	Nov 42 - Mar 44		
2DY	8 Armd Div	Jul 42 - Dec 42	4 Armd Bde	Oct 42 - Nov 42
	GHQ MEF	May 43 - Jun 43		
2RGH	22 Armd Bde	Oct 41 - Sep 42	24 Armd Bde	Dec 42 - Jan 43
2LBH	26 Armd Bde	Nov 42 - Mar 44		
SS	22 Armd Bde	Oct 41 - Sep 42	GHQ BTE	Sep 42 - Jul 43
4CoLY	22 Armd Bde	Oct 41 - Sep 43		
NIH	25 Tank Bde	Feb 43 - Apr 44		

Chapter 9

Table 34 Disposal to Sicily Theatre

Regiment	Command	Dates
SS	4 Armd Bde	Jul 43 - Sep 43

Table 35 Disposals to the Italian Theatre

Regiment	Command	Dates
WksY	9 Armd Bde	May 44 - Oct 44
RWY	9 Armd Bde	May 44 - Oct 44
1DY	6 Armd Bde	Mar 44 - May 45
2LBH	26 Armd Bde	Mar 44 - May 45
SS	4 Armd Bde	Sep 43 - Jan 44
4CoLY	22 Armd Bde	Sep 43 - Dec 43
NIH	21 Tank Bde	Dec 44 - Jun 45

Table 36 Regimental disposals to N W European Theatre

Regiment	Command	Dates	Command	Dates
SRY	8 armd Bde	Jun 44 - Aug 45		
StfY	27 Arme Bde 33 Armd Bde	Jun 44 - Jul 44 Apr 45 - Jun 45	(79 Armd Div)	Sep44 - Apr 45
2DY	51 Inf Bde	Jun 44 - Aug 45		
1LBH	Jun 44 - Aug 45			
1FFY	(79 Armd Div) 31 Armd Bde	Oct 44 - Nov 44 Feb 45 - Jun 45	31 Tank Bde 34 Armd Bde	Nov 44 - Feb 45 Jun 45 - Aug 45
2FFY	Jun 44 - Aug 45			
WD	30 Armd Bde	Jun 44 - Aug 45		
SS	4 Armd Bde	Jun 44 - Aug 45		
4CoLy	22 armd Bde	Jun 44 - Aug 44		
1NY	33 Armd bde	Jun 44 - Aug 44		
2NY	11 Armd div	Jun 44 - Aug 45		
ERY	27 armd Bde 21st Army Grp	Jun 44 - Aug 44 May 45	33 Armd Bde 4 Armd Bde	Sep 44 - Apr 45 Jun 45 - Aug 45
Inns Crt	I Corps	Jun 44 - Aug 45		

Table 37 Regimental disposals to Austrian Theatre

Regiment	Command	Dates
1DY	6 Armd Div	May 45 - Jul 45
2LBH	26 Armd Bde	May 45 - Jul 45

References

1 Joslen, Lt-Col HF. Orders of Battle - Second World War, 1939-1945. Vols 1&2. (W.O. &. HMSO 1960)

2 Fletcher. David. The Vanguard of Victory - The 79th Armoured Division. (HMSO, 1984)

3 Divisional authors. The Story of the 79th Armoured Division - No imprint, Germany, July 1945

4 Bellis, Malcolm. Data File 5 - British Armoured and Infantry Regiments 1939-45

5 Frederick Dr JBM, Lineage Book of British Land Forces. (Microform Academic Publishers. Wakefield, 1984)

6   Regimental and Honour Titles with Battle Honours for The Second World War. (Consolidation of RUSI J).

Plate 9/1   The Tank Museum, Bovington, Dorset.

Davis Escape Apparatus - some confidence building initiative was
necessary when asking the tank driver to stay at his controls, ten
foot beneath the water.

Plate 9/2   The Tank Museum, Bovington, Dorset.

Launching a DD Tank - Special ramps were needed to avoid shearing the propellers during
the launching operation from the LCT. Once in the water the tank was far less visible and in
danger of being run down by oncoming craft.

Plate 9

Wiltshire Yeomanry Matilda Tanks at El Alamein. At the start of the war this regiment was part of the 2nd Cavalry Division but was able to re-equip in time for this vital battle.

Plate 10

Crossing the Rhine at Zanten. The Staffordshire Yeomanry was equipped with DD tanks. Assualt Engineers have pegged out matting to enable them to mount the bank. The artist has used a little guile to incorporate his logo as the 27th Armoured Brigade sign was a Seahorse. The present location of the original is unknown.

Copyright Terence Cuneo

Plate 11

Author's Collection

Scottish Yeomanry Badging

Plate 9/3   The Tank Museum, Bovington, Dorset.

'What a Tangle' - Flail mine clearance was a great concept, however chains could be blown off and the debris collected meant that the odd mine was left in place.

Plate 9/4   The Tank Museum, Bovington, Dorset.

Flailing in Action - The driver of the vehicle was more or less blind to what was going on. A delicate touch was needed to beat the ground clear and to reverse out avoiding exploding untouched mines.

Plate 9/5   The Tank Museum, Bovington, Dorset.

Flame Thrower in action. An incidious weapon using jellied petroleum and a high pressure delivery system which made the operators quite as vulnerable as the enemy.

Plate 9/6   The Tank Museum, Bovington, Dorset.

The Flame Thrower equipment.

Buffoloes mounting a river bank. Both the Northamptonshire Yeomanry and the East Riding Yeomanry were equipped with this useful vehicle.

Buffoloes closing the logistic gap.

Epilogue

Retreads

As with the case of The Great War, the initial steps were taken to secure an actual peace following the battlefield surrender. However, this post war scene differed greatly from the earlier one. The quid pro quo of United States material help during and following the war was an almost unrestricted entry into the British sphere of (pre-war) influence and more importantly her trading markets. The spectre of vanishing Empire must have appeared to the statesmen of the period if not to the public at large. This was to have a profound influence over the continued existence of the reserve army and its Yeomanry constituents, as events proved. Perhaps the effects were muted because, at this time, huge forces were required to stabilise a crumbling Europe and Germany in particular, which in collapsing threatened to bring down all around. Also it was not long before soldiers 'up front' started to question the motives of their erstwhile allies, the Russians. In this they joined Fuller's appreciation of dictatorships which posed the question whether it was best to have Fascism from the North Sea to the Pacific or Communism from the Pacific to the North Sea. [1] Always the mother of compromise, Britain and her allies elected for something in between.

Demobilisation followed and the Territorial Army awaited recall. It took some time to establish a requirement. Most field forces were demobilised during 1946, but by no means all. Whereas the former war was one fought principally by artillery, hence the large surplus of it at its conclusion, the second was more 'balanced', if war can be described that way. Granted, artillery remained a highly significant portion of the effort, but mechanised cavalry, infantry and air power were very important factors in achieving the military solution. Henceforth, artillery, if it wished to be counted in, had to be capable of high mobility, both in keeping up with the fight and in rapid re deployment in the face of counter-bombardment.

It is an unfortunate feature of a prolonged conflict to end up with huge quantities of part used materiel, mainly fit for fighting yesterday's war. In this instance it enabled the Yeomanry to re-establish itself with a large number of armoured regiments. These in turn could rely upon the support of other Arms better suited to the needs of mobility. However, until the effects of the 'Cold War' began to penetrate, there was no need to develop fresh lines of weaponry: It was a case of wearing out the old. It is from this point that we take up the Yeomanry tale.

On the 14th March 1946, Mr Lawson stated in the House of Commons that he was determined in view of the great services of the old Territorial Army to retain most if not all first-line units. He followed this on 27th June with a further statement that the force was to be reconstituted. This was followed on 19th November by Mr Bellinger defining the rôles as: Anti-aircraft defence, the provision of units to the Regular Army and the provision of second-line defence. The force was to be reconstituted with effect from 1st January 1947, with the following timetable:

1st January
Official date of reconstitution of the Territorial Army with all formation commanders to be appointed
1st February
Appointment of unit commanding officers to be completed
1st March
The completion of regular permanent staff cadres
1st April
The commencement of general recruiting

The War Office next announced on 5th December that the new Territorial Army was to consist of six infantry divisions; the 42nd, 43rd, 44th, 50th, 51st/52nd, 53rd; the 16th Airborne Division; two armoured divisions, the 49th and 56th; plus a number of independent

Epilogue

Armoured and Infantry Brigades, Army Groups RA and RE and AA Command organised into five Groups, plus Coast Artillery Brigades, 101st and 105th consisting of 31 regiments, eventually reduced to 18 by 1956 and then converted to other branches or other arms. This compared with a pre-war Territorial Army of 150,000 soldiers disposed over 12 infantry divisions, two cavalry brigades, two anti-aircraft divisions, some coastal defence artillery and lines-of-communication units.

An interim measure was the continuation of conscription, with an individual twelve month commitment. This gave way to the scheme for the 18 month 'National Serviceman' (later increased to two years) and soon these recruits started to arrive in theTerritorial Army to fulfil a part-time obligation. Thus for the first time the TA was not all volunteer. New initiatives were taken to integrate the Yeomanry reserve units with the army by linking them to Regular Regiments of the Royal Armoured Corps who became responsible for providing Permanent Staff, Instructors, Training Officers and for filling key appointments when suitable persons were unavailable from local sources. In the past there had been no direct link between these Regiments because, with a few exceptions, the Regular Regiments of the Corps had no County or Territorial background and continued to be recruited from the whole of the United Kingdom. The regiments selected to serve at that time are shown in Table 38

Table 38 Regiments, Rôle, Allocation to Formations & Affiliations from 1947

Regiments	Rôle	Allocation to Formations	Affiliations
The Ayrshire Yeomanry	Armd Regt	30th Indep Armd Bde	The Royal Scots Greys
52nd (Lowland) Div refmd	wef 01 01 51	taking above under command	
The Cheshire Yeomanry	Armd Regt	23rd Indep Armd Bde.	5th R Inniskilling Dragoon Gds.
1st Derbyshire Yeomanry	Armd Car Regt	49th (WR & Midlands) Armd Div	12th Royal Lancers
1st Fife & Forfar Yeo	Armd Car Regt	Corps Troops	1st Royal Dragoons.
The Q's O R Glasgow Y	Armd Reg	30th Indep Armd Bde	The Royal Scots Greys
52nd (Lowland) Div refmd	wef 01 01 51	taking above under command	
1st R Glous'shire Hussars	Armd Car Regt	Corps Troops	11th Hussars.
Inns of Court Regiment	Armd Car Regt	56th (London) Armd Div	The L Guards & R Hse Guards
North Irish Horse,	Armd Car Regt	107th (Ulster) Indep Inf Bde Gp.	1st King's Dragoon Guards.
The Lanarkshire Yeo	Armd Regt	30th Indep Armd Bde	9th Queen's R Lancers
52nd (Lowland) Div refmd	wef 01 01 51	taking above under command	
The D of Lancaster's O Y	Div Regt RAC	42nd (Lancashire) Inf Div	14th/20th King's Hussars
The Leicestershire Yeo	Armd Regt	9th Indep Armd Bde Gp	7th Queen's Own Hussars
The C of Lon Y (RR)	Armd Regt	56th (London) Armd Div	The Queen's Bays.
2nd CoLY (W Dgns)	Armd Regt	56th (London) Armd Div	2nd RTR.
3rd CoLY (SS)	Armd Regt	56th (London) Armd Div	2nd RTR.
1st Lothians & Border H	Armd Regt	30th Indep Armd Bde	4th RTR.
52nd (Lowland) Div refmd	wef 01 01 51	taking above under command	
C (Lovat Scouts) Sqn, ScH	01 01 49	conv to RA	fr The Scottish Horse
1st Northamptonshire Y	Div Regt RAC	44th (Home Counties) Inf Div	8th King's R Irish Hussars
The N'thumberland H	Div Regt RAC	50th (Northumbrian) Inf Div	15th/19th The King's R H
The Notts (S Rangers) Y	Armd Regt	9th Indep Armd Bde	17th/21st Lancers
The Scottish Horse	Div Regt RAC	51st/52nd (Scottish) Inf Div	4th/7th R Dragoon Guards
HQ 51/52 (Sc) Inf Div	wef 01 09 48	redes HQ 51(Hd) Inf Div	
The Shropshire Yeo	Div Regt RAC	53rd (Welsh) Inf Div	4th Queen's O Hussars
The N Somerset Y	Div Regt RAC	16th Airborne Division	3rd The King's O Hussars.
The Staffordshire Yeo	Armd Regt	23rd Indep Armd Bde	16th/5th Lancers
The Warwickshire Yeo	Armd Regt	9th Indep Armd Bde	13th/18th Royal Hussars
The R Wiltshire Yeo	Div Regt RAC	43rd (Wessex) Inf Div	10th Royal Hussars.
Q's O Worcs H fr 01 09 50	Armd Regt	Corps Troops	7QOH & 13/18RH
The Yorkshire Dragoons	Armd Regt	49th (WR & Midlands) Armd Div	9th Queen's R Lancers
1st E Riding Y	Armd Regt	49th (WR & Midlands) Armd Div	3rd Carabiniers
The Yorkshire Hussars	Armd Regt	49th (WR & Midlands) Armd Div	8th King's R Irish Hussars
40th RTR	Armd Regt	23rd Indep Armd Bde	1st RTR.
41st RTR	Armd Regt	23rd Indep Armd Bde	3rd RTR.
42nd RTR	Armd Regt	56th (London) Armd Div	8th RTR.
43rd RTR	Armd Regt	9th Indep Armd Bde	7th RTR.
44th/50th RTR	Armd Rept Gp	Army Troops	5th RTR.
45th/51st RTR	Armd Regt	49th (WR & Midlands) Armd Div	6th RTR.

Continuity of Service and a Will to Survive Some regiments were not well placed at the time the Territorial Army was reformed. From April 1939 duplicate units had been formed, from the parent regiments. At the conclusion of hostilities these were the first to go, on the assumption that the parent would soon follow, leaving the latter to become available for reconstitution on 1st January 1947. This worked well for the Yeomanry as such, but the large Corps of Yeomanry Artillery dating from the 1920s has to be remembered. The Worcestershire Yeomanry was amongst these, having been converted within the Royal Artillery on 3rd November 1943 to 53rd Airlanding Light Regt RA (Worcestershire Yeomanry) (TA). To secure the continuity the regiment went into suspended animation on 1st January 1947, with the personnel posted to a new 'war-formed' 53rd A/L Lt Regt, RA with the same 210-212 Bty numbers. The way was then clear to reconstitute a TA unit on that date as 300th (Queen's Own Worcestershire Yeomanry) Anti-Tank Regt RA (TA). Of importance was its Subsequent conversion on 1st September 1950 to The Queen's Own Worcestershire Hussars, RAC (TA) and amalgamation on 1st October 1956 with The Warwickshire Yeomanry RAC (TA).

The Lovat Scouts made a brief appearance as C (Lovat Scouts) Sqn, The Scottish Horse until transfer to the Royal Artillery. As from 1st January 1949, 677 Mountain Regt RA (Lovat Scouts) (TA) was formed with the Uist and Inverness Batteries using Pack Horse and Jeepborne 4.2 inch mortars. On 22nd May 1950 this was reorganised to form 850 Mountain Battery RA (Lovat Scouts) (TA) which was then amalgamated with 532 Regt on 30th September 1950, followed by the Battery disbanding on 5th April 1954. That Regiment was redesignated as 540 LAA Regt RA (TA) (Lovat Scouts) on 4th November 1954. Two further amalgamations took place wef 31st October 1956 and 1st May 1961, but without change of title. This was not the end of the matter as the disbandment of the TA and formation of the T&AVR set the fight for survival off once again.

The above history traces the tortuous road to survival. There must be other examples of the need to reconstitute a Territorial Army unit, where the vesting date clashed with military need, leading to the forming of 'empty shells' to take the personnel from a unit which now needed to be disbanded to enable the Territorial Army to reform. At first sight it appears as an 'Alice in Wonderland' situation, though any other treatment would have either created a break in service or had a serving regiment transferred to the Territorial Army, which was not the intention.

As far as possible the Regular and the affiliated TA Regiments were employed in the same rôle and previous close associations between Regular and TA Regiments were maintained. Because there were more Territorial Army than Regular Regiments in the RAC, a number of instances arose where two Territorial Army Regiments were affiliated to the same regiment. The prospect of Regular COs having to source the Permanent Staff on such a scale must have been daunting. On the addition of the Queen's Own Worcestershire Yeomanry, with effect from 1st September 1950, there were twenty-eight Yeomanry and six RTR(TA) regiments serving in the armoured rôle, this being the post-war peak.

West of Suez
The disbandment of AA Command, with effect from 10th March 1955, brought extensive amalgamations and a few disbandments of RA(TA) regiments and supporting units, but this did not greatly affect the Yeomanry. Nine AA Regiments were placed in suspended animation, including 295th (Hampshire Carabiners Yeomanry) HAA Regiment RA (TA) and fifteen regiments were disbanded.

The forty-two AA Regiments which survived by amalgamation (thirty-two LAA, two LAA/SL and eight HAA) were, except for the ten Divisional LAA Regiments, grouped into 30th, 31st, 33rd and later 34th, AA Brigades RA(TA), 2nd and 7th AGRA (TA) [which at first had both Regular and TA units] and 41st and 42nd AGRA (AA) (TA), with 40th AGRA (AA) (TA) taking over the TA units of 2 AGRA (AA), with effect from 1st July 1959.

Trials in Germany had indicated how the Armoured Division was too cumbersome to exploit the opportunities created by the use of tactical nuclear weapons. As constituted, such a division had too few infantry for sustained fighting. However, the infantry required special equipment if they were to be enabled to integrate with other more mobile Arms and much of this development was still in its infancy! It was recognised how essential it was to have formations able to move quickly and which depended principally upon the fighting abilities of skilfully-used armoured regiments. Each formation would have to be compact and not 'cluttered up' with the all the units necessary to give it this sustained fighting capacity. Therefore it had to be a specialised formation comprising only armour and the minimum of supporting units. For those occasions when it had to perform tasks outwith such a remit, there was a need to group under it additional infantry, armoured or engineer units, according to the task. This indeed was an echo from the past. The reader might like to turn back some pages to refresh their memory on Guderian's thinking during 1929 and to ask themselves whether this consideration arose wholly as the result of battlefield nuclear weapons? The writer thinks not, nor should the politicians of the period have dressed-up an economic argument in pseudo-military jargon! Indeed, despite those prognostications, the effect was not to rectify the supposed short-comings of the Armoured Division, but to curtail it. And again, it was the case of, too little too late, when making-up glaring deficiencies in the equipment range, so necessary for battlefield mobility.

Thus, a Nation-wide, reorganisation took place after Annual Camps in 1956 and was completed for 'teeth arms' with effect from 31st October 1956. 'Drastic reductions' were announced on 20th December 1955 by The Secretary of State for War, Mr Head, to The House of Commons. Only two Territorial Army Divisions [43rd (Wessex) and the 53rd (Welsh)] were to be kept at full strength to meet Britain's NATO requirement, together with six armoured regiments, in 22nd and 23rd Armoured Brigades until 1961, for NATO reinforcement.

This resulted in HQ 52nd (Lowland) Division being reorganised as HQ 52 (Lowland) Infantry Division, the three Brigades becoming 155th, 156th and 157th [the latter two by redesignation and reorganisation of HQs 30th (Lowland) Armoured and 264th (Scottish) Beach Brigades]. Thus, The Scottish Horse amalgamated with The Fife and Forfar Yeomanry, as F&FY/ScH and became Recce Regiment of 51st (Highland) Infantry Division and the Lanarkshire, Lothians and Border, and Queen's Own Royal Glasgow Yeomanry amalgamated as The Queen's Own Lowland Yeomanry, to become Recce Regiment for 52 (Lowland) Infantry Division, whilst the Ayrshire Yeomanry reorganised as a Corps Armoured Delivery Regiment.

The 49th (West Riding and North Midland) and 56th (London) Armoured divisions also reorganised as Infantry Divisions. The three Yorkshire Yeomanry

Regiments amalgamated to form the Queen's Own Yorkshire Yeomanry, the Recce Regiment for 49th Infantry Division. The City of London Yeomanry reorganised as an infantry battalion, whilst The Inns of Court Regiment took under command The Northamptonshire Yeomanry as a fourth, 'D', Squadron.

In East Anglia and the East Midlands, The Leicestershire Yeomanry and the Derbyshire Yeomanry amalgamated to form the Recce Regiment of the reconstituted 54th (East Anglian) Infantry Division. HQ 89th AGRA(Fd) (TA) reorganised as HQ RA 54 (EA) Infantry Division, its four Medium Regiments [from the Hertfordshire, Essex, Suffolk and Bedfordshire Yeomanry] becoming three Field and one Light Regiments in the Divisional Artillery.

HQs 86th, 88th and 90th AGRAs (Fd) were disbanded, only the 87th continuing until the next major reorganisation in 1961. Again, several ex-Yeomanry artillery regiments were involved in moves and/or reorganisation.

The 16th Airborne Division was reduced to 44th Independent Parachute Brigade Group, thus The North Somerset Yeomanry amalgamated with 44th/50th RTR as an Armoured Regiment in support of 43rd (Wessex) Infantry Division and 16th Airborne Divisional Signal Regiment (Middlesex Yeomanry) reduced to 44th Independent Parachute Signal Squadron, later redesignated 305 Signal Squadron (Parachute Brigade) (TA).

Finally the Headquarters of 101st, 102nd and 105th Coast Brigades, the remaining three of the initial five Brigades formed in 1947, were disbanded, with the eighteen Coast Regiments disposed by reduction to extra sub-units or by conversion to other branches of The Royal Artillery or to other arms.

After the reductions by amalgamation, reorganisation etc, there remained nineteen Yeomanry Regiments and the 40th/41st RTR (TA).

By 1961 the reduced commitments made further economies possible, and in a further major reorganisation, completed by 1st May 1961, the traditional Divisional Organisation was swept away and the Headquarters of TA Divisions were amalgamated with District Headquarters as Headquarters Division/Districts. 56th (London)

Infantry Division was reduced to a Brigade, 56th (London) Infantry Brigade, under command of 54th (East Anglian) Division/District and HQ 48th Infantry Division (TA) was reformed and concurrently amalgamated with HQ West Midland District as HQ 48 Division (TA)/ West Midland District. Two further Districts were formed in HQ Yorkshire District from HQ Catterick Area and HQ Aldershot District taking under command certain TA units not under command of Division/Districts.

The total number of RAC(TA) units at this point was twenty Yeomanry (incluxsive of the Pembroke Yeomanry Sqn) and 40th/41st RTR. The practical effects of these measures are listed in Tables 39 and 40.

Table 39 Yeomanry Amalgamations, Rôle, Allocation, Dates and Affiliations c. 1956-7

Regiment	Rôle	Allocation	Date	Affiliation
The Ayrshire Yeomanry	Armd Del Regt	Corps Troops	No change	The R Scots Greys
Westminster Dragoons	Armd Regt	3 Inf Div	No change	2nd RTR
The Cheshire Y	Armd Regt	23 Armd Bde	No change	3Carabiniers / 5RInkilling Dgn Gds
The FF Yeo / Sc Hse	Recce Regt	51 Inf Div	31 10 56	4th/7th RDG & 1st R Dragoons
R Gloucestershire Huss	Recce Regt	43 Inf Div	No change	11th Hussars
Inns of Court Regt	Recce Regt	56 Inf Div	31 10 56	The Life Guards and RHG
N Irish Horse	Recce Regt	107 Indep Bde Gp	No change	1st King's Dragoon Guards
The City of London (RR) *	conv Inf	See later	01 10 56	
3rd/4th CoLY (SS)	Recce Regt	44 Inf Div	No change	6th RTR & 8th RTR.
The DLOY	Recce Regt	42 Inf Div	No change	3KOH & 14/20 RH
The Leics & Derby Y	Recce Regt	54 Inf Div	09 02 57	12th Royal Lancers
The Q'sOLY	Recce Regt	52 Inf Div	20 10 56	4th RTR & 7th RTR
The N'land Hussars	Recce Regt	50 Inf Div	No change	15th/19th King's Royal Hussars
The Sherwood Rgers Y	Armd Regt	3 Div	No change	17th/21st Lancers
The Shropshire Yeo	Recce Regt	53 Inf Div	No change	The Queen's Bays & 4QOH
The NSY/44RTR	Armd Regt	22 Armd Bde	31 10 56	3rd & 5th RTR
The Staffs Yeo	Armd Regt	23 Armd Bde	No change	16th/5th The QR Lancers
QO Warks & Worcs Y	Armd Regt	22 Armd Bde	01 10 56	7QOH & 13/18RH
The R Wilts Yeo	Armd Regt	22 Armd Bde	No change	10th Royal Hussars
The QO Yorkshire Yeo	Recce Regt	49 Inf Div	01 11 56	8th K R Irish H &9th Q R Lancers
40th/41st RTR	Armd Regt	23 Armd Bde	02 11 56	1st RTR
42nd RTR *	conv Inf		01 09 56	
43rd RTR *	conv Inf		01 11 56	
45th/51st RTR *	conv Inf		30 10 56	

Table 40 1961-67 Changes in Yeomanry Rôle

Regiment	Rôle	Date	Affiliations till 31 03 67
The Ayrshire Y	Armd Del Recce Regt	01 02 61	The R Scots Greys
Berks and W'minster D	Armd Car Regt	01 05 61	2nd RTR
The Cheshire Y	Recce Regt	01 02 61	3rd Carabiniers
Fife and Forfar Y/ Scottish Horse	No change		4th/7th R Dragoon Gds
The R Gloucestershire Hussars	No change		11th Hussars
Inns of Court and City Y (new orgnisation) Northants Y reorg as 250 Indep Fd Sqn RE	Recce Regt	01 05 61	The Life Gds & R Hse Gds
North Irish Horse	No change		5 R Irish DG & QRIH
Kent and CoLY (SS)	Recce Regt	01 05 61	The Royal Dragoons
The Duke of Lancaster's Own Y	No change		14/20 Hussars
The Leics and Derby (PAO) Y	No change		9th/12th Lancers
The Q's O Lowland Yeomanry	No change		4 RTR
The Northumberland Hussars	No change		15th/19th K R Hussars
The Sherwood Rangers Y	Recce Regt	01 02 61	17th/21st Lancers
The Shropshire Y (Pembroke Y thirdSabre Sqn)	Recce Regt	01 05 61	1QDG
NSY/44RTR redes NS&BY	No change	Apr 1965	3rd & 5th RTR
The Staffordshire Y	Recce Regt	01 02 61	16th/5th The Q R Lancers
Q's O Warks & Worcs Y	Recce Regt	01 02 61	Queen's Own Hussars
The R Wilts Yeomanry (PWO),	No change		10th Royal Hussars
The Q's O Yorkshire Yeomanry	No change		13/18 H
40/41 RTR (TA)	No change		1 RTR

Epilogue

Territorial Army Disbandment and the T&AVR

The Territorial Army was disbanded and replaced on 1st April 1967 by a group of reserve formations called The Territorial and Army Volunteer Reserve (T&AVR). At first it had been proposed as The Army Volunteer Reserve (AVR), but under much pressure the title was changed ahead of inception. It may be observed the Government was out of sympathy with the military, but it also coincided with a time for economic restraint and when the forces were urgently in need of an expensive refurbishment: effectually the stock of worthwhile re-treads had run out. In the absence of these, there was little purpose for the manpower, so the majority had to go. The problem called for an entirely new canvas. It was impossible to align the moneys with the perceived military need, so virtually the whole of the Yeomanry was disbanded. Details of the disbandment of the Territorial Army and formation of the Territorial and Army Volunteer Reserve were promulgated in Special Army Orders 1-5 of 1967. In essence the legislation created a four-part Army reserve with the following functions:

T&AVR I

About 1,700 men drawn from the 'Ever Readies' and liable to serve for up to six months of any year in a U.N. peace keeping force. It was to be joined by a further 3,500 men from the Regular Army Reserve. These people also topped up a number of specialised vacancies not generally carried in a peace time army.

T&AVR II

About 49,000 men organised in Independent or Sponsored units. This was very similar to the former Territorial Army and AER with slightly enhanced training requirements. Such a force was to be called to arms when warlike operations were in preparation or in progress.

T&AVR III

A Home Defence Force of 22,500, including 1,300 women, comprising 87 infantry type units, with an average of three units to each of the 27 civil defence sub-regions. (Its annual expenditure was limited to £3m!)

T&AVR IV

A miscellany of units, mainly University OTC's and Bands.

The T&AVR I and II were known collectively as 'The Volunteers', whilst T&AVR III were called 'The Territorials'. In a cynical gesture the Government stated how *it was anxious to foster close links between the Independent units of T&AVR II and III*, but the great differences in their rôles, liabilities, equipment and training meant the T&AVR III had to constitute separate units and have their own independent command structure.

SAO 2 was the Succession Warrant establishing the link between the former TA unit and the successor T&AVR unit, whilst SAO 14 of 1967 authorised T&AVR Unit and Sub-unit Titles.

With effect from 1st April 1967, a Category IIA unit was formed called The Royal Yeomanry Regiment (V) with personnel drawn from five Yeomanry regiments. Fifteen Category III, Home Service units were formed and one Band survived as a Category IV unit, whose title was confirmed by Army Order 39/1968. These formations are listed in Table 41.

Table 41 T&AVR Formations

Category IIA
The Royal Yeomanry Regiment (V)
Category III
The Ayrshire (Earl of Carrick's Own) Y (T)
The Cheshire Y (Earl of Chester's Territorials)
The Devonshire Territorials (R Devon Y & The 1st Rifle Vols)
The Duke of Lancaster's Own Yeo (RTR)(T)
The Fife and Forfar Yeomanry/Scottish Horse (T)
The Leicestershire and Derbyshire (PAO) Y (T)
North Irish Horse (T)
The Northumberland Hussars (T)
The Queen's Own Lowland Yeomanry (T)
The QO Warwickshire and Worcestershire Y (T)
The Queen's Own Yorkshire Yeomanry (T)
The Royal Gloucestershire Hussars (T)
The Sherwood Rangers Yeomanry (T)
The Shropshire Yeomanry (T)
The Staffordshire Yeomanry (QOR Regiment)(T)
Category IV
The R Yeomanry Band (Inns of Court and City Yeo)

In addition to the above which all formed part of the Royal Armoured Corps, there were other affiliations and these details and the later developments may be traced in Appendix E. By SAO 26/1969 Units in T&AVR I, IIA and IIB, III and IV were redesignated as either Group A or B. Units recruited locally and established in T&AVR Centres became 'Independent' units, whilst those recruited nationally and administered by the Central Volunteer Headquarters of each Arm or Service became known as 'Sponsored' units, which later around 1980 were redesignated 'Specialist'.

The T&AVR III units soldiered on until 1968, but were run down and ceased to function by 31st December. Disbandment commenced on 1st January 1969, along with the Civil Defence and the Auxiliary

Fire Service and was to have been completed by the 31st, under SAOs 25 and 26 of 1969. Many of their personnel, however, transferred to other units, either as individuals or to sub-units formed within the existing establishments of former T&AVR II units of the Royal Artillery, Royal Engineers, Royal Signals, Infantry, Royal Corps of Transport, the Royal Army Medical Corps and Royal Electrical and Mechanical Engineers. (see again Appendix G)

Under the terms of SAO 26/1969 ninety Cadres were formed to carry on the tradition of the former T&AVR III units. Each was permitted to form a Cadre retaining a similar title, or form part of a unit or sub-unit of similar title, or both. Each Cadre had a Major commanding, a Captain, a Subaltern (who might be replaced by a Captain if fully qualified or was a Q.M.), a Warrant Officer II, a Company Quartermaster Sergeant or Staff Sergeant, a Sergeant, a Corporal and a single Private Soldier. Those of the Yeomanry Arm, the titles of which were confirmed by AO 13/1971, are listed in Table 42.

Table 42 Formation of Cadres

The Royal Wiltshire Yeomanry (Prince of Wale's Own)
The Queen's Own Warwickshire and Worcestershire Y
The Queen's Own Yorkshire Yeomanry
The Sherwood Rangers Yeomanry
The Staffordshire Yeomanry (Queen's Own Royal Regt)
The Shropshire Yeomanry
The Ayrshire (Earl of Carrick's Own) Yeomanry
The Cheshire Yeomanry (Earl of Chester's)
The Leicestershire and Derbyshire (PAO) Yeomanry
The Duke of Lancaster's Own Yeomanry (RTR)
The Queen's Own Lowland Yeomanry
The Northumberland Hussars
The Royal Gloucestershire Hussars
The Royal Devon Yeomanry/1st Rifle Volunteers
The Highland Yeomanry
Inns of Court and City Yeomanry
North Irish Horse

For a further demonstration of the will to survive, we must turn to the Pembroke Yeomanry. When 4th Welch (T) was disbanded on 31st March 1969, most of the personnel of the Battalion elected to go to a newly formed 'shadow' sub-unit of 157 (W&M) Regiment RCT (V), 224 (West Wales) Sqn RCT (V), which formed in Carmarthen, Haverfordwest and Llanelli. A Shadow unit was one which was not officially recognised nor established and no extra strength or equipment was authorised. It was formed strictly within the existing establishment therefore, presumably to save money. A Troop, 224 (WW) Sqn was at Haverfordwest and Cadre 4 Welch was also formed at Llanelli, with effect from 1st April and later expanded on 1st April 1971 to form 4th RRW. A parade was

held on 15th March 1982 to bestow the title A (Pembroke Yeomanry) Troop and later on 21st February 1987 to confer the designation on 224 (Pembroke Yeomanry) Sqn, still within 157 (W&M) Transport Regt RCT (V). Thus the line of succession continues through 224 Sqn and not 4 Welch.

It will be noticed how The Royal Wiltshire Yeomanry formed a Cadre from part of The Royal Wiltshire Territorials, that of The Highland Yeomanry was from the Fife and Forfar Yeomanry/Scottish Horse and Inns of Court and City Yeomanry came from part of The London Yeomanry and Territorials. With effect from 1st April 1971 all but 15 of the Cadres were disbanded to form 21 additional units. Those of the Yeomanry were disposed to form an Armoured Car Regiment and three further Regiments in an infantry rôle as listed in Table 43.

Table 43 Formation of T&AVR Yeomanry Regiments

The Queen's Own Yeomanry (with the temporary designation 2nd Armoured Car Regiment), consisting of:
RHQ
HQ (Northumberland Hussars) Sqn
Y (Queen's Own Yorkshire Yeomanry) Sqn
A (Ayrshire Yeomanry) Sqn
C (Cheshire Yeomanry) Sqn
The Wessex Yeomanry (redesignated The Royal Wessex Yeomanry in 1979), consisting of squadrons from:
RHQ
HQ Sqn
A (Royal Gloucestershire Hussars) Sqn
B (Royal Wiltshire Yeomanry)
C (Royal Gloucestershire Hussars) Sqn
D (Royal Devon Yeomanry/1st Rifle Volunteers) Sqn
The Queen's Own Mercian Yeomanry, consisting of:
RHQ
HQ Sqn
A (Queen's Own Warwickshire and Worcestershire Yeomanry) Sqn
also X Troop (The Warwickshire Regiment, Royal Artillery) A Sqn
B (Staffordshire Yeomanry) Sqn
C (Shropshire Yeomanry) Sqn
The Duke of Lancaster's Own Yeomanry comprising
A,B and D Squadrons.

There were two further sub-units formed in other units:

A (Sherwood Rangers) Sqn, 3rd Bn The
Worcestershire and Sherwood Foresters Regt
(29th/45th Foot)
The Leicestershire & Derbyshire (PAO) Yeomanry
Sqn, 7th (Volunteer) Bn The Royal Anglian Regiment

There then remained four Cadres; The Queen's Own Lowland Yeomanry, The Highland Yeomanry, Inns of Court and City Yeomanry, North Irish Horse. All had in 1969 provided a number of volunteers for other sub-units, which perpetuated their sub-titles and these were now disbanded with effect from 1st April 1975. Also at this time the two squadrons mentioned above were redesignated as Companies.

The name 'Territorial Army' was restored with effect from 7th August 1979, although not reflected in unit titles.

In the 'Phase II Expansion' which took place over the period 1986-1990 a fourth Armoured Car Squadron was added from 1st April 1986 to The Queen's Own Yeomanry as D (Northumberland Hussars) Sqn.

The Defence Committee's 4th Report on 'Options for Change' in The Reserve Forces, dated 26th February 1992, made a further 'in depth' assessment of their place in the scheme of defence. On the one hand it wished to review the present freedom for improving the quality of the Reserves and on the other to form a more strategic assessment of needs and to achieve this it issued a Defence Open Government Document as the basis for discussion. The first objective worked on a Reserve Army model for 60-65,000 personnel. It concluded there was the need for:

- A credible rôle for the Territorial Army
- A requirement for a higher standard of training
- The need for better conditions of service
- A need to reduce the load on the individual by reducing the span of command
- A need for realistic funding

The report called for the Home Service Force to be absorbed by the Territorial Army (henceforth to be known as National Defence (ND)), for modern equipment to be brought in and for a realistic figure to be arrived at by MOD for Man Training Days, to have the Territorial Army attain standards closely comparable with Regular Army performance. It went on to propose the reduction in infantry battalions from 41 to 36, but of three company strength, meaning these came down from 164 to 109. The Royal Artillery was recommended to lose six out of 28 Batteries. The 200 (Sussex Yeomanry) Fd Battery RA was converted to 127 (Sussex Yeomanry) Field Squadron, Royal Engineers to enable the whole of an RA regiment to concentrate in a single Military District further North. Nevertheless, the Royal Engineers suffered a net loss

of one squadron from a previous 39 but increased its strength by 16% because full manning was introduced. The Royal Signals was to be retained at 11 regiments. The Army Air Corps was recommended to double to two squadrons, whilst REME was destined to increase 40% and the RCT was to lose 13% because the 3rd and 4th Lines had ceased to exist. It was acknowledged that the Parachute Regiment was no longer to remain in the parachute rôle. The ARMCO was recommended to adopt smaller units and to await the development of some unspecified voluntary proposals. Turning to the RAC, an Armoured Reconnaissance Regiment was proposed for the ARRC, against two withdrawn from the NATO commitment. Two existing regiments were to be amalgamated, whilst a new one was to be formed in Scotland. The upshot of these proposals was for the number of 'sabre' squadrons to reduce from 18 to 17. The 'Options for Change' initiative of 1992 resulted in the distribution of Squadrons as shown in Table 44.

Table 44 Redistribution of Yeomanry Squadrons

The Royal Yeomanry
HQ (Westminster Dragoons) Sqn
A (Royal Wiltshire Yeomanry) Sqn
B (Leicestershire and Derbyshire Yeomanry) Sqn
C (Kent and Sharpshooters Yeomanry) Sqn
Band - Inns of Court and City Yeomanry
The Royal Wessex Yeomanry
HQ (Royal Gloucestershire Hussars) Sqn
A (Royal Gloucestershire Hussars) Sqn
B (Royal Wiltshire Yeomanry) Sqn
D (Royal Devon Yeomanry) Sqn
Band - The Royal Gloucestershire Hussars
The Royal Mercian and Lancastrian Yeomanry
HQ (Shropshire Yeomanry) Sqn
A (QO Warwickshire and Worcestershire Yeomanry) Sqn
B (Staffordshire Yeomanry) Sqn
D (Duke of Lancaster's Yeomanry) Sqn
The Queen's Own Yeomanry
HQ (Northumberland Hussars) Sqn
Y (Yorkshire Yeomanry) Sqn
B (Sherwood Rangers Yeomanry) Sqn
C (Cheshire Yeomanry) Sqn
D (Northumberland Hussars) Sqn
The Scottish Yeomanry
HQ (Lothians and Border Horse) Sqn
A (Ayrshire (Earl of Carrick's Own) Yeomanry Sqn
B (Lanarkshire and QOR Glasgow Yeomanry) Sqn
C (Fife and Forfar/Scottish Horse) Sqn
North Irish Horse (Independent Squadron)

In addition to the Yeomanry which survives as part of The Royal Armoured Corps in the traditional 'mounted' rôle, there are sub-units in The Royal Regiment of Artillery, The Corps of Royal Engineers, The Royal Corps of Signals, The Infantry and The

Royal Logistic Corps. These units are listed with an outline of their succession in Appendix E

Conclusion and Rôle of the Present Day Territorial Army

Two hundred years is a significant time in the history of any military force. Even the Regular Army, through the quirks of history, cannot pre-date 1660. However the auxiliary forces can smile, for they number at least two units going back to the 1500s in The Honourable Artillery Company and Inns of Court Regiment from November 1584, which later opted for a cavalry rôle. Somehow the Reserve Forces survive. There is the composite nature of the Regiments, though in modern times a clear distinction has to be drawn between different traditions and common aims, whilst its Regular counterpart has had to accommodate this awkward principle for much longer.

The purpose of the Territorial Army has been sharpened by the addition of modern equipment, comparable to its Regular counterparts. Enhanced training under the 'Options for Change' philosophy is on-going and a further announcement is due in the not too distant future. Reference to Table 45 shows how the Yeomanry has permeated the Territorial Army with its unit and sub-unit appellations. It seems obvious to suppose that the scale of equipment and the units under command will continue to shadow national requirements.

A year ago the Territorial Army consisted of about 60,000 men and 10,000 women. Some small portion may be mobilised at any time that warlike preparations are in process and of course the whole of it directly a defence need arises. Each member has to undergo a minimum of 44 days training a year, of which 15 is spent at an annual camp, though many undertake to do more. Pay and conditions are in line with those of their Regular counterparts. Selected Territorial Army personnel now staff positions normally filled by the Regular Army. It may be to cover ad hoc events, such as 'The Year of the Yeomanry', when an enhanced Public Relations effort is required, but it had already extended to The Gulf War, Northern Ireland and selected Staff positions enabling hand picked personnel to serve, train and acquire special skills. Thus, the T&AVR is designed to function by supplying:

- Units necessary to bring the Regular Army up to field strength
- Specialists not generally required by the Army

during peacetime
- Units to defend vital Home installations and maintain internal security

The present wisdom dictates that on mobilisation the undernoted units would be added to the Order of Battle. Given this fabric, it now possible to trace those with Yeomanry appellations across the Territorial Army as a whole.

1	Armoured Reconnaissance Regiment - RAC
4	Wheeled Reconnaissance Regiments -RAC (plus an Independent Squadron in Ireland)
2	Field Regiments - RA
3	Air Defence Regiments - RA
9	Engineer Regiments - RE
9	Signal Regiments
36	Infantry Battalions
2	Special Air Service Regiments
12	Transport Regiment - RLC

An Outsiders Perception of the Yeomanry

The current armoured era is gripped in a turmoil of change, with most of the options costing a lot of money. Nor is the land battle any longer seen as won entirely by land forces, but it is an old nostrum that one cannot hold land without men on the ground. There is no sure way forward except that the basic building block is, as ever, configured around *man* and despite the varieties of equipment, there is little enough which can be done to change him fundamentally. Besides this the Volunteer Reserve Forces (VRFs) operate under obvious training time constraints in which two rôles have been identified as offering an optimum solution for the funds available. Firstly there is armoured reconnaissance in support of a NATO commitment and secondly home based reconnaissance using Landrovers as part of the national defence (ND) effort. All this requires sound, basic military training using principles which have hardly altered since Napoleonic times (eyes and ears) and are as totally relevant today as for the Yeomanry formed during that early period. Looking back to those early days and what Nolan later had to say about Light Cavalry, let us now put the story together for today, with all of its internal combustion engines, transistors, yet notionally the same yeomen!

The Armoured Reconnaissance Regiment The Queen's Own Yeomanry of four medium tracked reconnaissance sabre squadrons of Scimitars, with an RHQ and HQ Squadron has been tasked to join the Allied Command Europe Rapid Reaction Corps

Epilogue

(ARRC) Force in Germany, should a requirement arise. The capability and tactical doctrine for the reconnaissance force has changed very little over the years, although the equipment and speed of reaction is vastly enhanced. Its may be described in the following terms. It is fast, lightly armoured and equipped with powerful communications. It has an excellent cross-country mobility and range. It is not designed to fight its way forward against an anti-tank screen, though it must be prepared to fight to carry out its mission. Its duties include:

1. Conducting reconnaisance in advance of the forward troops when contact with the enemy has yet to be made or has been lost. *This is the primary and by far the most important task.*
2. Liaising with Armoured Battlegroup Recce Troops and assisting during operational moves.
3. Watching exposed flanks and covering withdrawals. *The wide front the regiment is able to cover enables it to give early warning of enemy threats, whilst due to its mobility, it can impose considerable delay upon enemy movement.*
4. Taking up a line of observation. *This will generally be behind an obstacle, such as a river or defile, saving the use of infantry.*
5. Pursuit and capture of 'spent' or retreating enemy

forces. *The bold use of force can create confusion in a disorganised enemy by destroying his communications and supply services*
6. Participation in Depth air/land battle - *attrition by air, depth Fire Artillery etc (as in Gulf).*

Elements of the Reconnaisance Regiment are appointed to a task to answer specific questions. When required to report on the enemy they must retain contact once they have made it, until they are released from their task. They must use their speed and silence to obtain information, only fighting for it when forced to do so. Having obtained information, they have excellent communications on which to pass it back. Their task is not accomplished until their report has been acknowledged. They are frequently assisted by and co-operate with air reconnaissance in the execution of their task. In the performance of these many and varied duties they have to ensure they open the way and do not impede the progress of their own columns.

The more usual task in a defensive scenario is to identify the scale and direction of enemy thrusts and to impose maximum delay. *The basic requirement laid on all recce forces is to obtain accurate information on the enemy and to ensure this reaches those in command quickly.* An organisation chart for this type of regiment appears here.

Armoured Reconnaissance Regiment - Tracked [2]

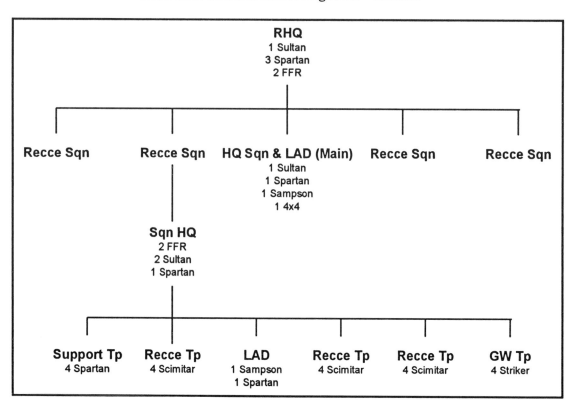

ND Soft Skin Vehicle Reconnaissance The Landrover may be described as softskinned, however equipped, though it has a well earned reputation for rugged reliability. A further attraction is that it may be serviced in the local civilian garage. The remaining four (ND) regiments comprise three long range radio equipped Landrover (FFR) Squadrons, with RHQ and HQ Squadron support. It will be apparent that these vehicles are unable to engage an enemy to any degree, although the SAS contrived a number of long range missions into Iraq to destroy Scud missile sites, using essentially the same equipment, during the Gulf War.

The ND rôle commenced with the task of duplicating a UK communications network against the possibility that Warsaw Pact special forces might deliver a pre-emptive strike to take-out existing ones. When those forces crumbled that capability was retained as a basic building block of good training and as a precaution in an uncertain world. The availability of trained crews enables a wide range of reconnaissance drills to be practised, whatever the scenario. At the same time personnel may be turret trained or in servicing a range of equipment. The definitive rôle can be summarised as follows:

- Reinforcement of tracked recce units with trained crews
- Duplication of nationwide RAC TA units
- Performance of light and medium range recce duties in support of hard topped formations.

An organisation chart for the ND Reconnaissance Regiment is shown here.

Radio Communications Guderian at an early stage in his career was advised to take a communications course in preference to virtually anything else offered. It seems that this advice remains as good today as it was then. Since that time technology has taken giant strides. Without rapid communications a commander is deprived of information, upon which to base vital decisions or even to react responsibly to an ongoing situation. This has nothing to do with cunning cyphers and code words; just simple information. Many older yeomen will recall the roar of static, the painstaking netting-in procedure for the '19 Set' and the inexplicable 'dead areas' with the numerous exhortations 'to search boldly' across the frequency band, and no end of naughty little tricks to lock-on again after a rough ride. No doubt there remain problems, though most of them seem to be a thing of the past. Since these recce regiments live by stealth, anything noisy, all lit up or emitting high electronic radiation is out! Also taking a leaf from the Second World War U-Boats, transmission times can be minimised using the 'blip' technique, making direction finding a virtual impossiblity. A further advance is scored by micro-miniaturisation, such that long range and dependable messages can transmitted from lightweight manpacked sets. In all cases frequencies may be set as for hi-fi stacks at home, though there remains the requirement for aerial tuning. These facilities open a new vista in reconnaissance philosophy. The problem today is the likelihood of too much, rather too little information, which takes time to absorb and therefore clutters the mind.

Currently used is the Clansman range of equipment,

Reconnaissance Regiment (ND) - (Wheeled)

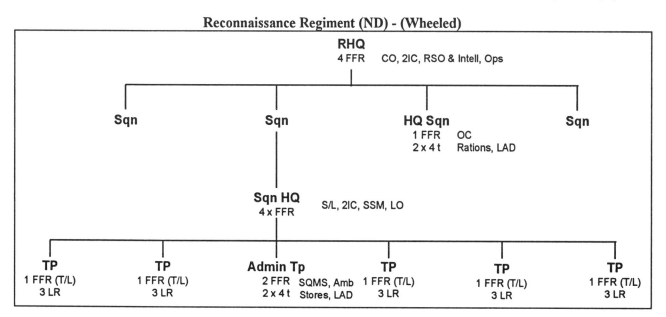

though it seems due for replacement at the turn of the century by Bowman. That Racal-BCC project is likely to make use of packet radio technology. The production phase is likely to involve all the major players in this field, under such project titles as Arrowhead, Yeoman and Crossbow. It remains a truism that the best equipment can be brought to naught by sloppy and indeciplined operation. The proper use of radio is best demonstrated by an economy of traffic, the optimum use to which information may be put and the minimum value it offers to an eavesdropper. The business of electronic counter measures (ECM) is a further area for the radioman.

Clansman Range of Radio Equipment

Type	Frequency	Range	Kg.
Mold telephone	UHF		
PRC 320 mp	2 - 29.999	50 km	11.0
PRC 352 mp	30 - 75.975	16 km	9.2
VRC 353 vm	30 - 75.975	30 km	22.0

The latest technology for combat radio is thought to be embodied in Scimitar (Plessey) and Jaguar (Racal Tacticom) ranges, designed to provide a secure combat net communications system to include a frequency agile ability for use in areas where the electronic counter measures (ECM) threat is high. These equipments are man portable or vehicle mounted - Stay Tuned!

Electronic Counter Measures Equipment

Type	Frequency	Chan	Kg.
H (HF radio) mp	1.6 - 30MHZ	284000	4.0
V (VHF) v or mp	30 - 88MHZ	2320	4.8
M (pocket VHF)	68 - 88MHZ	800	0.5

Sourcing Equipment

It will be apparent to the reader how important equipment is to attain the performance standards of a modern army. Less visible have been economy measures aimed at clarifying and simplifying their design and procurement. This has been more one of *not re-inventing the wheel.* Where good quality civilian items are available, they are now taken, such as the power train of Scimitar (Ford owned Jaguar Cars) and Landrover (BMW/Honda?), still slogging it out after numerous competitors such as the Champ have been proven expensive failures. Naturally there are exceptions, though it is refreshing to note mistakes in buying poor equipment are now admitted, such as under the *Combat Vehicle Reconnaissance(Tracked) or* CVR(T) programme. The replacement of the

vehicle fleet for Armoured Reconnaissance is now under the study programme *Future Family of Light Armoured Vehicles* (FFLAV) and *Light Armoured Vehicle Strategy* (LAVS) / *Tactical Reconnaissance Armoured Combat Equipment* (TRACER). Strangely, these are the updated versions of the Guderian programme for Half-Track vehicles pioneered in neutral Sweden during the 1920s. And surprise, surprise, it seems likely that an international consortium will be employed to produce them, such: Alvis, GKN and Vickers / Krauss Maffei, Thyssen Henschel and surely Porsche / Renault, Panhard and even Citrôen (of early self-centering track fame) / and Oto Melara. The present reduction in World tension makes it unlikely that these fleets will be deployed until after the year 2000, though there must be some fascinating types under-going trials!

It has been recognised that as the equipment enables more daunting tasks to be undertaken so the pressure on the individual increases to move onto more complex projects. Thus it becomes a matter of concern to reduce the burden of command on *all individuals* and to make it a matter of personnel selection, with matching pay and conditions to induce the right type of volunteer to come forward. The yeoman of 200 years ago was determined, resourceful and a proud man able to make his mark in society: it must be presumed he is still to be found.

The Royal Artillery includes 100th (Yeomanry) Field Regiment with three Batteries plus the Glamorgan Yeomanry Troop as part of a Battery in 104th Light Aid Defence Regiment. The Royal Engineers have two squadrons representing the Yeomanry. The Royal Signals number the 71st (Yeomanry) Signal Regiment and no less than an additional seven representative Squadrons, so important is the consideration which must be given to radio traffic. At the time of writing the Infantry Arm has 36 Battalions though the Yeomanry is represented in only three and in the Special Air Service Regiments not at all. Lastly, the Royal Logistic Corps, the successor to the Royal Corps of Transport, which has served as a friendly haven in the past, (indeed some of the last Yeomanry to be reformed came from that source), now it is down to the Pembrokeshire (Castlemartin) Squadron.

From the original Corps of Yeomanry, there are now the following, either serving as Recce, or with the other Arms and Services. The listing shown in Table 45, relies upon each carrying an appropriate appellation in unit titles or sub-title. There may be others, although the claim at the time of writing cannot be made with

Epilogue

certainty, though any omissions are regretted.

Table 45 Yeomanry Presence within the TA

County or Name Unit	RAC Sqn	RA Bty	RE Sqn	R Sig Sqn	Inf Coy	RLC Sqn
Ayr Yeo	1					
BYH				1		
CY	1			1		
DLOY	1					
EY				OCA1		
FFY/SH	1					
GY		Tp				
HBY		1				
HCY			1			
IC&CY	+			1		
KSY	1			2		
LDY	1					
L&RGY	1					
L&BH	1					
LS				Parts	of 2	
MxY				OCA1		
NH	2					
NIH	1			1		
Pemb(CM)Y						1
QOOH				1		
QOWWY	1			1		
RDY	1					
RGH	+2					
RWY	2					
SNH		+1				
SNY		1				
SRY	1					
StaffsY	1					
SyY					1	
SxY			1			
SY	1			1		
WDGN	1					
YorksY	1					
Totals	**22**	**4**	**2**	**11**	**3**	**1**

+ = Band in addition   OCA = Band under Old Comrades Assn

Finis

References

1 Fuller Maj-Gen JFC. Decisive Battles of the World. Vol III (Eyre & Spottiswood London 1956)
2 Heyman Charles editor. The British Army - A Pocket Guide. (R&F Military Publishing Barnsley 1993)

Plate 10/1   RAC, Bovington.

Fox Armoured Car. The lightweight armoured tracked vehicle did not exist when this first
came into service. The turret, with 30mm Rarden cannon has gone on to serve the Scimitar
and a range of other vehicles.

Plate 10/2   Racal Tacticom

Fitted for Radio (FFR) Landrover. Here a dual Jaguar 50w VHF station is combined with
100w VRQ 319 HF station. Such equipment is specifically designed to operate where
electronic counter measures (ECM) are in play. The picture is representative of modern
field radio, most of which may be man-packed. The Yeomanry uses the Clansman series
though much lighter 'packet techniques' are due to be introduced by 1999.

Plate 10/3   RAC, Bovington.

Scimitar at Speed. Not able to mix it with the big boys, but able to take care of itself and to do a useful reconnaissance job.

Plate 10/4   RAC, Bovington.

Scimitar showing its items of field equipment. The power train is from Ford owned Jaguar Cars.

Plate 10/7

Plate 10/6

Plate 10/7

Major J.S. Selby-Bennett TD,
The Royal Wiltshire Yeomanry

Yeomanry Montage showing exercises in the ND Role using FFR Landrover.

Racal Tacticom

Plate 10/9

Racal Tacticom

Plate 10/8

Radioman. Manpacked radio equipment.

.

Appendix A

Legislation

The Volunteer Act : 17th April 1794
"Act for encouraging and disciplining such Corps or Companies of Men, as shall voluntarily inrol themselves for the Defence of their Counties, Towns, or Coasts, or for the General Defence of the Kingdom, during the present War.

Whereas the utmost exersions are now requisite for increasing the Military Force in this Kingdom:

Be it therefore enacted by the King's most excellent Majesty, by and with the Advice and consent of the Lords Spiritual and Temporal, and Commons, in this present Parliament assembled, and by the Authority of the same, That any Corps or Company of Volunteers who are now, or shall be hereafter formed, in any Counties or Towns in GREAT BRITAIN, during the Continuance of the present War, under Officers having Commission from his Majesty, or from the Lieutenants of Counties, or others who may be specially authorised by his Majesty for that Purpose, and who shall at any Time, on being called upon, by special direction of his Majesty, in case of actual Invasion, or Appearance of Invasion, voluntarily march out of their respective Counties or Towns, or shall voluntarily assemble within same, to repel such invasion, or shall voluntarily march on being called upon, in pursuance of an Order from his Majesty, or from the Lord Lieutenant or Sheriff of the County, to act within the County or the adjacent Counties, for the Suppression of Riots or Tumults, shall in such Cases be entitled to receive Pay , in such Manner , and at such Rates, as the Officer and Soldiers of his Majesty's Regular Forces do now receive; and shall, during the Time of their being continued in such Service, and to receiving pay as above, be subject to Military Discipline as the rest of his Majesty's Militia and Regular Troops: Provided always, That no Officer or Soldier of any Volunteer Corps shall be liable to be tried or punished by any Court Martial at any Time, unless such Court Martial be composed entirely of Officers serving in Volunteer Corps, formed as aforesaid, such Court Martial to be assembled by Warrant under his Majesty's Sign Manual, or by Warrant from some General or other Officer duly authorized to hold Courts Martial.

II.   And be it further enacted, That it shall be lawful for all Mayors, Bailiffs, Constables, Tithingmen, Headboroughs, and other Chief Magistrates and Officers of the Cities, Towns, Parishes, Tithings, and Places and (in their Default or Absence) for any one Justice of the Peace inhabiting within or near any such City, Town, Parish, Tithing, or Place (but for no others); and they or he are or is hereby required to quarter and billet the Serjeants, Corporals, and Drummers of such Corps or Companies as aforesaid, and their Horses, in Inns, Livery Stables, Alehouses, Victualling Houses, and all Houses of Persons selling Brandy, Strong Waters, Cyder, Wine, or Metheglin, by Retail, upon Application made to any such Mayors, Bailiffs, Constables, Tithingmen, Headboroughs, or other Chief Magistrates or Officers, by his Majesty's Lieutenant, or by the Officer commanding the said Corps or Companies.

III.   And be it further enacted by the Authority aforesaid, That if the Officer commanding any such Corps or Company as aforesaid shall discharge from such Corps or Company any Person who shall have been inlisted or inrolled as aforesaid; and if such Person shall refuse or neglect, on being required by such Commanding Officer, to deliver up any Arms, Accoutrements, or Clothing, which shall have been entrusted to his Custody, every Person so refusing or neglecting shall, on being convicted thereof before any Justice of the Peace of the County within which such Corps or Company shall have been formed, forfeit and pay the Sum of ten Pounds, to be levied by the Distress and Sale of the Offender's Goods and Chattels by Warrant under the Hand and Seal of such Justice, rendering the Overplus (if any) on Demand, after deducting the Charges of such Distress and Sale, to the Person whose Goods and Chattels shall have been so distrained and fold; and for Want of sufficient Distress, such Justice is hereby required to commit such Offender to the Common Gaol of the County, Riding, or Place, where such Offence shall have been committed, for any Time not exceeding one Month; and the Monies arising by such Penalty shall be paid to the Treasurer of the County, Riding, or Place, where such Offence shall have been committed, to be applied as Part of the Stock of such County, Riding, or Place.

IV. And be it further enacted by the Authority aforesaid, That all Commissioned Officers of the said Corps, who shall be disabled in actual Service, shall be entitled to Half Pay; and all Non-commissioned Officers and Soldiers so disabled, to the Benefit of the Chelsea Hospital; and the Widows of the Commissioned Officers killed in Service, to a Pension for Life.

V. And be it further enacted by the Authority aforesaid, That no Person who shall be inlisted or inrolled in any Corps or Company of Volunteers as aforesaid shall, during the Time that he is serving in the said Corps or Company, be liable to serve personally, or to provide a Substitute to serve in the Militia, provided he shall produce to the Deputy Lieutenants, assembled at the Subdivision Meetings, holden in the several Counties, for the Purpose of hearing Appeals against the Militia List returned from each Parish, an Affidavit of his having been inrolled as aforesaid, and a Certificate signed by the Commanding Officer of the said Corps or Company, that he has, for the Space of Six Weeks immediately preceding such Subdivision Meeting, punctually attended at all such Times and Places as may have been agreed upon for the Exercise of such Corps or Company.

VI. Provided always, and be it enacted, That this Act shall have Continuance during the present War, and no longer."

Appenxix A

Legislation: Appendix A2

The Continuation Act : 22nd June 1802
Anno Quadragesimo Secundo Georgii III. Regis. C A P. LXVI An Act to enable His Majesty to avail himself of the Offers of certain Yeomanry and Volunteer Corps to continue their Services.

His Majesty may accept the Service of any Corps of Yeomanry or Volunteers on such Conditions as He may think proper.
Whereas it is expedient to enable His Majesty to avail himself of the Offers of certain Yeomanry and Volunteer Corps to continue their Services: And whereas it would tend to encourage the Continuance of such Corps of Yeomanry and Volunteers, if Persons enrolled and serving therein were to be exempted from serving personally, or providing Substitutes, for the Militia, under certain Regulations; be it therefore enacted by the King's most Excellent Majesty, by and with the Advice and Consent of the Lors Spiritual and Temporal, and Commons, in the present Perliament assembled, and by the Authority of the same., That it shall be lawful for his His Majesty to accept the Offers of service of any Corps of Yeomanry or volunteers already formed, or have served during the late War, and that may be willing to continue to serve, and also to accept the Offers of service of any Corps of Yeomanry or Volunteers that may at any Time hereafter be formed, upon such Terms and conditions respectively, as may to His Majesty seem fit and proper.

Persons inrolled in such Corps, and returned in the Master Roll required by this act., ans certified to have attended the Exercise of their Corps shall be exempted to serve in the militia.
II. And be it further enacted, That every Person inrolled or to be inrolled and serving in any Corps of Yeomanry or Volunteers in *Great Britain,* which shall hereafter be continued or formed in *Great Britain,* with the Approbation of His Majesty, under Officers having Commissions from His Majesty, or Lieutenants of counties, or others who may be specially authorized by His Majesty for that Purpose, who shall have attended the Exercise of his Corps on a certain Number of Days of Muster and Exercise, and shall be returned in the Muster Rolls required by this Act, and certified to have attended the respective Number of days therein mentioned, unless prevented in Manner therein mentioned, shall be exempt from being liable to serve personally or to provide a substitute in the Militia of *Great Britain.*
Exemption not to be allowed unless Muster Rolls in the Form annexed marked (A) that shall be transferred to the Lieutenant of the County, etc. and the Commanding Officer that annex a Certificate in the Form annexed, marked (B) that he has not inserted the name of any Person who has nmot attended Exercise Five Days, etc.
III. Provided always, and be it further enacted, That no such Exemption shall be claimed or allowed in the present or any future Year respectively, unless Muster Rolls in the Form in the Schedule to this Act annexed, marked (A.), shall, within Three Months after passing of this Act, for the present Year, and on or before the Twenty-first Day of *September* for any future Year, in which such Exemption may be claimed, be transmitted to the Lieutenant of the County, Riding, or Place within which such Corps of Yeomanry or Volunteers shall be continued or formed, or to some Person duly authorized by him to receive the same, which Muster Rolls shall be by him sent to the Clerk of the General Meetings of the said County, Riding, or Place, on or before the First Day of *October* next following, who shall thereupon transmit Extracts therefrom, containing the Names of the said Persons in each Subdivision, to the Clerks of Subdivision Meetings, who are hereby required forthwith to enter such Exemption on the Rolls of such Militia; and the Commanding Officer so transmitting the same shall annex thereto a Certificate, in the Form in the Schedulke to this Act annexed, marked (B.), signed by himself, certifying that he has not, to the best of his knowledge and, Belief, inserted in the said Muster Rolls the Name of any Person who has not attended, properly armed and equipped, at the Muster and Exercise of the Corps to which he shall belong, Five Days at the least in the course of the Year preceeding such Certificate, unless prevented by actual Sickness, such Sickness to be certified by some Medical Practitioner to such Commanding Officer as aforesaid, unless his Name shall be found on the last Muster Rolls which shall have been transmitted and certified pursuant to this Act.

Appendix A

Persons resigning or discharged from such Corps shall lose the Benefit of Exemption from serving in the Militia.

IV. And be it further enacted, That in the said Muster Rolls there shall be inserted the Name of every Person inrolled in any such Corps as aforesaid, who shall, since the Date of the last Muster Roll, have notified to the Commanding Officer thereof his Intention of discontinuing his Service therein, or have been discharged from such Corps, on Account of Non-attendance, or otherwise; and that if any such Person, during the Period of his having been enrolled in such Corps, shall have been drawn for the Militia, and shall have been exempted from Service therein, on Account of his Enrolment and Service in such Yeomanry and Volunteer Corps, he shall, on such Resignation or discharge as aforesaid, be liable to serve for the District in which he was drawn, in the same Manner as if he had not been exempted; and if there shall be at that Time no Vacancy for the District for which he was drawn, he or his Substitute shall be accounted a Supernumery for the same, until a Vacancy shall arise.

Exemption not to be alloed, unless the Commanding Officer certify on the Muster Roll that the Corps has been inspected Once at least in the preceding Year.

V. And be it further enacted, That no Person shall be entitled to claim such Exemption as aforesaid, by reason of his Enrolment and Service in any Corps of Yeomanry or Volunteers, or by reason of being returned in any such Muster Rolls as aforesaid, unless the Commanding Officer thereof shall, at the Time of transmitting the Muster Rolls of such Corps in the manner directed by this Act, certify at the Foot thereof, that such Corps has been inspected at least Once in the Space of the preceding Year, by some General or Field Officer of His Majesty's Regular Forces, or if such Inspection shall not have taken place, that such Corps is ready and willing to be inspected, at its usual Place or Places and Times of Meeting; Copies of which Certificates shall be certified by such Lieutenant to the Clerk of the General Meeting, and by him to the Subdivision Meetings, together with the Muster Rolls.

Clerks of the County General Meetings shall transmit to the Secretary of state Abstracts of the Muster Rolls in the Form annexed, marked (C.)

VI. And be it further enacted, That the Clerks of the General Meetings of the several Countiews and Places in *Great Britain*, shall Once in every Year transmit to One of His Majesty's Principal Secretaries of state, Abstracts, in the Form in the Schedule to this Act annexed, marked (C.), of the several Muster Rolls so sent to them respectively within the Year; which Abstracts shall express the Names of the several Corps, the Number of Persons enrolled and serving therein, and the Number in every such Corps exempted from serving in the Militia respectively.

Persons returned in any such Mustyer Roll as having used any Horse for the Service shall be exempted from the Duty granted by 42 Geo. 3. c. 37, in respect of such Horse, and also from duties granted by 41 Geo. 3. c. 69. Claim of such Exemption shall be proved by the Certificate of the Commanding Officer.

VII. And be it further enacted, That every Person enrolled and serving in any Corps of Yeomanry or Volunteer Cavalry, after passing of this Act, who shall be returned in any such Muster Roll as aforesaid, as having used any Horse, Mare, or Gelding for such Service during such Days of Muster and Exercise as aforesaid, shall be exempt from Payment of the Duties granted by and consolidated in an Act, passed in the forty-second Year of the Reign of His present Majesty, intitled, *An Act for granting to His Majesty certain additional Duties on Servants, Carriages, Horses, Mules and Dogs, and for consolidating the same with the present Duties thereon,* in respect of such Horse, Mare, or Gelding; and also from the Duties granted by an Act, passed in the Forty-first Year of the Reign of His present Majesty, intitled, *An Act transferring the receipt and Management of certain Duties on Certificates for wearing Hair powder, or using Armorial Bearings, from the commissioners of Stamps to the commissioners for the Affairs of Taxes; and also for making further Provisions in the respect to the said duties so transferred in respect of such Persons using Hair Powder:*and every Person enrolled and serving in any Corps of Volunteer Infantry after passing of this Act, who shall be returned in any such Muster Roll as aforesaid, shall be exempt from the Payment of the said last mentioned Duties, in respect of such Person; such Exemption to be returned and claimed in the

Manner in which Exemptions are directed to be returned and claimed by the said last mentioned Acts respectively: Provided always, that every Claim of either of such last mentioned Exemptions, shall be proved by the Certificates under the Hand of the Officer Commanding the Corps in which such Person shall be enrolled, in the Form in the schedule to this act annexed, marked (D.); which Certificate shall, between the fifth Day of *April* and the Firsdt Day of *May* in every Year, be delivered to the Surveyor or Insperctor of the Districtwhere such Corps shall be enrolled; and every Person claiming to be exemp from the said Duties, or either of them, shall be charged and chargeable thereto, unless such Certificates as aforesiad shall have been delivered pursuant to the provisions of this act; any Thing in any Act to the contrary thereof notwithstanding.

Persons who have served in any disbanded Corps entitled to be exempted from the Duties on Horses or for using Har Powder before the passing of this Act, may claim such Exemption for the Year commencing from April 5, 1802. Persons providing Horses between April 5, 1801 and April 5, 1802, for others serving in any Corps shall be exempted from the Duty thereon.

VIII. Provided always, and be it enacted, That every Person who shall have been enrolled, and shall have served in any such Yeomanry or volunteer Corps which shall have been or shall be disbanded, so as to entitle such Person to be exempted from the said last mentioned duties on Horses, or for using Hair Powder, by the Laws in force, at and immediately before the passing of this Act, for the Year commencing from the Fifth Day of **April** One thousand eight hundred and two, shall, in respect of such Service have and claim the like Exemption from the said last mentioned Duties for the said Year, as if this Act had not passed, to be claimed and proved in like Manner as is directed by the said Laws now force: Provided always, that every Person who shall have provided between the fifth Day od B AprilB One thousand eight hundred and one and the Fifth Day of BAprilB One thousand eight hundred and two, any Horse, Mare, or Gelding, for any Person serving in any Corps of Yeomanry or Volunteer Cavalry, or who shall have at his or her Expence furnished an horse, Mare, or Gelding, shall be exempted of every Horse, Mare, or Gelding so by him provided and furnished as aforesaid.

Horses going to or returning from the Place of Exercise of any Corps exempted from Toll, etc.

IX. And be it further enacted, That no Toll shall be demanded or taken at any Turnpike Gate or Bar, for any Horse, Mare, or Gelding, furnished by or for any Persons belonging to any Corps of Yeomanry or Volunteer Cavalry, and rode by them in going to or returning from the Place appointed for and on the Days of Exercise; any Thing contained in any Act or Acts to the contrary notwithstanding: Provided always, that such Persons shall be dressed in the Uniform of their respective Corps, and have their Arms, Furniture, and Accoutrements, according to the Regulations provided for such Corps respectively, at the Time of claiming such Exemption as aforesiad.

Corps who shall, on being called on, voluntaritl march out of the Counties etc. or assembled therein to repel Invasion, or to suppress Riots, shall be entitled to receive Pay as the Regulars, and shall then be subject to Military Discipline: But Courts Martial shall be composed of Officers serving in Yeomanry or Volunteer Corps.

X. And be it further enacted, That every Corps of Yeomanry or Volunteers which shall hereafter be continued or formed in any Counties or Towns in *Great Britain* with the Approbation of His Majesty, under Officers having Commission from His Majesty, or from the Lieutenant of Counties, or others who may be specially authorized by His Majesty for that Purpose, and who shall at any Time, on being called upon by special Direction of His Majesty, in case of actual Invasion, or Appearance of Invasion, voluntarily march out of their respective Counties or Towns, or shall voluntarily march, on being called upon in pursuance of any order from His Majesty, or from the Lieutenant or sheriff of the County, to act within the County, or the adjacent Counties, for the suppression of Riots or Tumults, shall in such Cases, be entitled to receive Pay, in such Manner and at such Rates as the Officers and Soldiers of His Majesty's Regular Forces, and shall, during the Time of their being continued in such Service, and so receiving Pay as above, be subject to Military discipline, and be entitled to be quartered and billetted, as the Rest of His Majesty's Regular and Militia Troops: Provided always, that no Officer or soldier of any Yeomanry or Volunteer Corps shall be liable to be tried or punished by any Court Martial at any Time, unless such Court Martialbe composed entirely of Officers serving in the Yeomanry or Volunteer Corps formed as aforesaid, such Court Martial to be assembled by Warrant under His Majesty's Sign Manual, or by Warrant from some General or other Officer duly authorized to hold courts Martial.

Magistrates etc. shall quarter Serjeants, etc. of such Corps and their Horses in Inns, etc. on Application for that Purpose.
XI. *And be it further enacted, That it shall be lawful for all Mayors, Bailiffs, constables, Tythingmen, Headboroughs, and other Chief Magistrates and Officers of Cities, Towns, Parishes, Tythings, and Places in* **England,** *and (in their Default or Absence), for any One Justice of the Peace inhabiting within or near any such City, Town, Parish, Tything, or Place (but for no others), and they or he are or is hereby required to quarter and billet the Serjeants, Corporals, and Drummers of such Corps as aforesaid, and their Horses, in Inns, Livery StablesAlehouses, Victualling Houses, and all Houses of Person's selling Brandy, Strong Waters, Cyder, Wine, or Metheglin, by Retail, upon Applicationmade by any such Mayors, Bailiffs, constables, Tythingmen, Headboroughs, or other Chief Magistrates or Officvers, by His Majesty's Lieutenant, or by Officers commanding said Corps; and that it shall be lawful in* **Scotland** *for allJustices of the Peace and Magistrates of Cities, Towns, and Places, and they and each of them are and is herteby required to quarter and billet such Serjeants, Corporals, and Drummers of His Majesty's Regular Forces are at present quartered and billetted in* **Scotland.**

Persons refusing to deliver up Arms etc. provided at the Public Expence, shall forfeit 10 l.
 XII. And be it further enacted, That every Person who shall have received or shall hereafter receive Arms or accoutrements, or Cloathing, from the publick Stores or at the publick Expence, or at the expence or Charge of any Subscription for providing such Articles, and who upon quitting any such Corps, or being discharged therefrom,or upon the disbanding of any such Corps, shall refuse or neglect, on being lawfully required, to deliver up any such Arms, Accoutrements, or Cloathing, shall, on being convicted thereof before any Justice of the peace of the County within which such Corps or company shall have been formed, forfeit and pay the Sum of Ten Pounds, to be levied by Distress and Sale of the Offender's Goods and Chattels, by Warrant under the Hand and Seal of such Justice, rendering the Overplus (if any), on Demand, after deducting the Charges of such Distress and Sale, to the Person whose Goods and Chattelsshall have been so distrained and sol; and for Want of such sufficient Distress, such Justice is hereby required to commit such Offender to the common Gaol of the County, Riding, or Place, where the Offence shall have been committed, for nay Time not exceeding Two Months, and the Monies arising by such Penalty shall bevpaid to thew Treasurerr of the County, Riding, or Place, where such Offence shall have been committed, to be applied as Part of the Stock of such County, Riding, or Place.

Officers disabled in actual Service entitled to Half Pay, and non-commissioned Officers and Soldiers to **Chelsea** *Hospital, etc.*
XIII. And be it further enacted, That all Commissioned Officers of the said Corps, who shall be disabled in actual Service, shall be entitled to Half Pay, and all Non-commissioned Officers and Soldiers disabled, to the benefit of *Chelsea* Hospital, and the Widows of Commissioned Officers killed in the Service, to a Pension for Life.

The Forms of Muster Rolls, etc. hereto annexed, or of a similar Import deemed valid.
XIV. And be it further enacted, That the Muster Rolls, Returns, and Certificates respectively, made up , returned, and certified according to the several Forms thereoff, (A.), (B.), (C.), and (D.) annexed to this Act, shall be deemed to be sufficient and valid for the Purposes of the same; but that if, from any Variation of Circumstances, or other Reason, these Forms should not be strictly adhered to, Instruments of a similar Import shall, nevertheless, be deemed sufficient for the purposes aforesaid.

Legislation: Appendix A3

Appenxix A

The Riot Act of 1715
Anno primo GeorgII Regis. Stat. 2. A.D.1714. C A P. V.
An Act for preventing Tumults and riotous Assemblies and for the more speedy and effectual punishing the Rioters *13 H. 4. c. 7. 2 H. 5. c. 8. st. 2. c. 9. 8 H. 6. c. 14. 9 H. 7. c. 13. H. H. P. C. Vol. 2. 197.*

Twelve Persons or more, unlawfully assembled, after the last of July 1715, and not dispersing after commanded by one Justice, etc. by Proclamation, shall be adjudged Felons without Benefit of Clergy.
'I. Whereas of late many rebellious Riots and Tumults have been in divers Parts of this Kingdom, to the Disturbance of the publick peace, and the endangering of his Majesty's Person and Government, and the same are yet continued and fomented by Persons disaffected to his Majesty, presuming so to do, for that the Punishments provided by the Laws now in being are not adequate to such heinous Offences; and by such Rioters his Majesty and his Administration have been most maliciously and fasely traduced, with an Intent to raise Divisions, and to alientate the Affections of the People from his Majesty. Therefore for the preventing and suppressing of such Riots and Tumults, and for the more speedy and effectual punishing the Offenders therein; Be it enacted by the King s most Excellent Majesty, by and with the Advice and Consent of the Lords Spiritual and Temporal, and of the Commons, in this present Parliament assembled, and by the Authority of the same, That if any Persons to the Number of twelve or more, being unlawfully, riotously, and tumultously assembled together, to the Disturbance of the Publick Peace, at any Time after the last Day of July in the year of our Lord one thousand seven hundred and fifteen, and being required or commanded by any one or more Justice or Justices of the Peace, or by the Sheriff of the County, or his Under-sheriff, or by the Mayor, Bailiff or Bailiffs, or other Head-officer, or Justice of the Peace of any City or Town-corporate, where such Assembly shall be, by Proclamation to be made in the King s name, in the Form herein after directed, to disperse themselves, and peaceably to depart to their Habitations, or to their lawful Business, shall, to the Number of twelve or more (notwithstanding such Proclamation made) unlawfully, riotously, and tumultously remain or continue together by the Space of one Hour after such Command or Request made by Proclamation, that then such continuing together to the Number of twelve or more, after such Command or Request made by Proclamation, shall be adjudged Felony without Benefit of Clergy, and the Offenders therein shall be adjudged Felons, and shall suffer Death as in case of Felony without Benefit of Clergy.

How the Proclamation shall be made.
II. And be it further enacted by the Authority foresaid, That the Order and Form of the Proclamations that shall be made by the Authority of this Act, shall be as hereafter followeth (that is to say) the Justice of the Peace, or other Person authorized by this Act to make the said Proclamation shall, among the said Rioters, or as near to them as he can safely come, with a loud Voice command, or cause to be commanded Silence to be, while Proclamation is making, and after that, shall openly and with loud Voice make or cause to be made Proclamation in these Words, or like in Effect:
The Proclamation.
Our Sovereign Lord the King chargeth and commandeth all Persons, being assembled, immediately to disperse themselves, and peaceably to depart to their Habitations, or to their lawful Business, upon the Pains contained in the Act made in the first Year of King George, for preventing Tumults and riotous Assemblies.
                                                                                    God save the King

Justices, etc. to report to the Place. And every such Justice and Justices of the Peace, Sheriff, Under-sheriff, Mayor, Bailiff, and other Head-officer, aforesaid, within the Limits of their respective Jurisdictions, are hereby authorized, impowered and required, on Notice or Knowledge of any such unlawful, riotous and tumultuous Assembly, to resort to the Place where such unlawful, riotous, and tumultuous Assemblies shall be, of Persons to the Number of twelve or more, and there to make or cause to be made Proclamation in Manner aforesaid.

Persons so assembled and not dispersing within an hour, to be seized. And if they make Resistance, the Persons killing them etc. to be indemnified.

Appendix A

III. And be it further enacted by the Authority aforesaid, That if such Person so unlawfully, riotously , and tumultously assembled, or twelve or more of them after Proclamation made in Manner aforesaid shall continue together and not disperse themselves within one Hour, That then it shall and may be lawful to and for every Justice of the Peace, Sheriff, or Under-sheriff of the County where such Assembly shall be, and also to and for every High or Petty-constable, and other Peace-officer within such Countyu, and also to and for every Mayor, Justice of the Peace, Sheriff, Bailiff, and other Head-officer, High or Petty-constable, and other Peace-officer of any City or Town-corporate where such Assembly shall be, and to and for such other Person and Persons as shall be commanded to the assisting unto any such Justice of the Peace, Sheriff, or Under-sheriff, Mayor, Bailiff, or other Head-officer aforesaid (who are hereby authorized and impowered to command all his Majesty s Subjects of Age and Ability to be assisting to them therein) to seize and apprehend, and they are hereby required to seize and apprehend such Persons so unlawfully, riotously and tumultously continuing together after Proclamation made, as aforesaid, and forthwith to carry the Persons so apprehended before one or more of his Majesty s Justices of the Peace of the County or Place where such Persons shall be so apprehended, in order to their being proceeded against for such their Offences according to Law; and that if the Persons so unlawfully, riotously and tumultously assembled, or any of them, shall happen to be killed, mained or hurt, in the dispersing, seizing or apprehending, or endeavouring to disperse, seize or apprehend them, by reason of their resisting the Persons so dispersing,, seizing or apprehending, or endeavouring to disperse, seize or apprehend them, that then every such Justice of the Peace, Sheriff, Under-sheriff, Mayor, Bailiff, Head-officer, High or Petty-constable or other Peace-officer, and all and singular Persons, being aiding and assiting to the, or any of them, shall be free, dishcarged and indemnified, as well against the King s Majesty, his Heirs and Successors, as against all and every other Person and Persons, of, for, or concerning the killing, maiming, or hurting of any such Person or Persons so unlawfully, riotously and tumultously assembled, that shall happen to be so killed, mained or hurt, as aforesaid.

Pulling down etc. any Church etc. Felony without Benefit of Clergy. 1 W.&M. Sess. 1. c. 18.

IV. And be it further enacted by the Authority aforesaid, That if any Persons unlawfully, riotously and tumultously assembled together, to the Disturbance of the publick Peace, shall unlawfully, and with Force demolish or pull down, or begin to demolish or pull down any Church or Chapel, or any Building for religious Worship certified and registered according to the Statute made in the first Year of the Reign of the late King William and Queen Mary, intituled, An Act for exempting their Majesties Protestant Subjects dissenting from the Church of England from the Penalties of certain Laws, or any Dwelling-house, Barn, Stable, or other Out-house, that then every such demolishing, or pulling down, or beginning to demolish, or pull down, shall be adjudged Felony without Benefit of Clery, and the Offenders therein shall be adjudged Felongs, and shall suffer Death as in case of Felony without Benefit of Clergy.

Opposing, etc. the making of such. Proclamation, Felony without Benefit of Clergy. And Persons to assembled, if the Proclamation be hindred, shall nevertheless suffer as Felons.

V. Provided always, and be it further enacted by the Authority aforesaid, That if any Person or Persons do, or shall, with Force and Arms, wilfully and knowingly oppose, obstruct, or in any manner wilfully and knowingly let, hinder or hurt any Person or Persons that shall begin to proclaim, or go to proclaim according to the Proclamation hereby directed to be made, whereby such Proclamation shall not be made, that then every such opposing, obstructing, letting, hindring or hurting such Person or Persons, so beginning or going to make such Proclamation , as aforesaid, shall be adjudged Felony without Benefit of Clergy, and the Offenders therein shall be adjudged Felons, and shall suffer Death as in case of Felony, without Benefit of Clergy; and that also every such Person or Person so being unlawfully, riotously and tumultously assembled, to the Number of twelve, as aforesaid, ore more, to whom proclamation should or ought to have been made if the same had not been hindred, as aforesaid, shall likewise, in case they or any of them to the Number of twelve or more, shall continue together, and not disperse themselves within our Hour after such Lett or Hindrance so made, having Knowledge of such Lett or Hindrance so made, shall be adjudged Felons, and shall suffer Death as in case of Felony, with Benefit of Clergy.

Appenxix A

How the damges shall be made good, if any Church, etc. be demolished, etc. 27 Eliz. c.13.
VI. And be it further enacted by the Authority aforesaid, That if after the said last Day of July one thousand seven hundred and fifteen, any such Church or Chapel, or any such Building for religious Worship or any such Dwelling-house, Barn, Stable, or other Out-house, shall be demolished or pulled down wholly, or in Part, by any Persons so unlawfully, riotously and tumultously assembled, that then, in case such Church, Chapel, Building for religious Worship, Dwelling-house, Barn Stable or Out-house, shall be out of any City or Town, that is either a County of inself, or is not within any Hundred, that then the Inhabitants of the Hundred in which such Damage shall be done, shall be liable toyhield Damaged to the Person or Persons injured and damnified by such demolishing or pulling down wholly or in Part; and such Damages shall and may be recovered by Action to be brought in any of his Majestys Courts of Record at Westminster, (wherein no Essoin, Protection, or Wager of Law, or any Imparlance shall be allowed) by the Person or Persons damnified thereby, against any two or more of the Inhabitants of such Hundred, such Action for Damages to any Church or Chapel to be brought in the Name of the Rector, Vicar or Curate of such Church or Chapel that shall be so damnified, in Trust for applying the Damages to be recovered in rebuilding or repairing such Church or Chapel; and that Judgement being given for the Plaintiff or Plaintiffs in such Action , the Damages so to be recovered shall, at the Request of such Plaintiff or Plaintiffs, his or their Executors or Administrators, be raised and levied on the Inhabitants of such Hundred, and paid to such Plaintiff or Plaintiffs, in such Manner and Form, and by such Ways and Means, as are provided by the Statute made in the seven and twentieth Year of the Reign of Queen Elizabeth, for reimbursing the Person or Persons on whom any Money recovered against any Hundred by any Party robbed , shall be levied: And in case of any such Church, Chapel, Building for religious Worship, Dwelling-house, Barn, Stable, or Out-house so damnified, shall be in any6 City or Town that is either a County of itself, or is not within any Hundred, than then such Damages shall and may be recovered by Action to be brought in Manner aforesaid (wherein no Essoin, Protection or Wager of Law, or any Imparlance shall be allowed) against two or more Inhabitants of such City or Town; and Judgement being given for the Plaintiff or Plaintiffs, his or their Executors or Administrators, made to theJustices of the Peace of such City or Town, at any Quarter-Sessions to be holden for the said City or Town, and paid to such Plaintiff or Plaintiffs, in such Manner and Form, and by such Ways and Means, as are provided by the said Statute made in the seven and twentieth Year of the Reign of Queen Elizabeth, for reimbursing the Person or Persons on whom any money recovered against any Hundred by any Party robbed, shall be levied.

This Act to be read at the Quarter-Sessions, etc.
VII. And be it further enacted by the Authority aforesaid, That this Act shall be openly read at every Quarter-Sessions, and at every Leet or Law-day.

Prosecution within twelve months.
VIII. Provided always, That no Person or Persons shall be prosecuted by virtue of this Act, for any Offence or Offences committed contgrary to the fame, unless such Prosecution be commenced within twelve Months after the Offence committed.

Sheriffs, etc. in Scotland to have the same Power as Justices, etc. have in England. Punishment of Persons offending in Scotland. Damages of any Church, etc. pulled down, etc. in Scotland, how to be recovered, and of whom.
IX. And be it further enacted by the Authority aforesaid, That the Sheriffs and their Deputies, Stewarts and their Deputies, Bailies of Regalities and their Deputies, Magistrates of Royal Boroughs, and all other inferior Judges and Magistrates, and also all High and Petty-constables, or ther Peace-officers of any County, Stewartry, City, or Town, within that Part of Great Britain called Scotland, shall have the same Powers and Authority for putting this present Act in Execution within Scotland, as the Justices of the Peace and other Magistrates aforesaid, respectively have by virtue of this Act, within and for the other Parts of this kingdom; and that all and every Person and Persons who shall at any Time be convicted of any the Offences aforementioned, within that Part of Great Britain called Scotland, shall for every such Offence incur and suffer the Pain of Death, and Confiscation of Moveables: And also that all Prosecutions for repairing the Damages of any Church or Chapel, or any

Appendix A

Building for Religious Worship, or any Dwelling-house, Barn, Stable, or Out-house, which shall be demolished or pulled down in whole or in part, within Scotland, by any Persons unlawfully, riotously or tumultuously assembled, shall and may be recoved by summar Action, at the Instance of the Party aggrieved, his or her Heirs, or Executors, against the County, Stweartry, City or Borough respectively, where such Disorders shall happen, the Magistrates being summoned in the ordinary Form, and the several Counties and Stewartries called by edictal Citation at the Market-cross of the Head-borough of such County or Stewartry respectively, and that in general, without mentioning their Names and Designations.

To what places in Scotland this Act shall extend.

X. Provided, and it is hereby declared, That this Act shall extend to all Places for religious Worship, in that Part of Great Britain called Scotland, which are tolerated by Law, and where his Majesty King George, the Prince and Princess of Wales, and their Issue are prayed for in express Words.

Appendix B

Precedence

Fellows & Freeman On The Precedence of the Yeomanry Regiments
From Appendix 'D' to South Nottinghamshire Hussars Yeomanry

As the question of its Regimental Precedence was of such burning importance to the South Notts. Hussars, this appendix was specially written at the instance of Colonel Sir Lancelot Rolleston. Each Regiment has been carefully checked from the formation of its original troop or troops, the dates in the original Establishment Book in every instance have been verified by the letter or letters offering the services of the corps. Disbandments and reductions and the re-raising of Corps have been verified by the Official Letter Books. In the case of the regiments raised after the Boer War, the dates of the Royal signature in the Submission Book at the War Office Library have been accepted, not the later dates of the *London Gazette*.

The introduction, giving a few brief notes of the origin of the Yeomanry Force, the author thought necessary, as so many absurd statements have been made regarding the Force having been originally raised in 1761 and other quite erroneous dates. The many volumes are not given in detail, as for a regimental history this appendix is already of abnormal length, but no date has been inserted of which there is the slightest doubt as to its absolute correctness.

THE PRECEDENCE OF THE YEOMANRY REGIMENTS

(1) Introductory Notes

The origin of the Militia is shrouded in antiquity, but to the Yeomanry Force a date of its first inception can be definitely assigned. Pitt, addressing the House of Commons on March 5th, 1794, on various measures for strengthening the internal means of resistance, made his speech remarkable as affording the first mention of the expression 'Yeoman Cavalry'. He said, after the enumeration of several propositions for defence of the kingdom: "As an augmentation of the cavalry for internal defence was a very natural object, they might under certain circumstances have a species of cavalry consisting of Gentlemen and Yeomanry, who would not be called upon to act out of their respective counties except on the pressure of emergency, or in cases of urgent necessity." Shortly after this, and during the same month of March, a plan was sent round to the Lords-Lieutenant of counties, included in which were the provisions that authorized the Lords-Lieutenant to embody troops of Yeoman Cavalry. (All the dates of formation, etc., have been taken from the War Office and Home Office letter books, etc., deposited in the Public Record Office. Reference has been made to official returns to verify the fact that the troops and regiments were not only authorized, but actually embodied. The London and provincial Press back files have also been referred to for a like purpose, together with old Army Lists and the records of those regiments who have published their history.)

The Militia Force originally included troops of horse as well as regiments of infantry, and although mustering in considerable numbers at the time of the Armada, the mounted portion of the old Constitutional Army had by the time of the Second George to all intents and purposes ceased to exist. To meet the threatened Jacobite rising, various Associations for Defence were formed in the counties during 1744. One of these associations - the Northamptonshire - is of peculiar interest, for amongst its proposals was the offer of a regiment of light horse to which 'five hundred and thirty substantial freeholders, yeomen and yeomen's sons, etc.,' had appended their signatures, who had agreed to mount and clothe themselves, and to 'serve within the Realm, where ever His Majesty's Service shall require, upon our being paid Trooper's Pay during the time we shall be employed and being paid for our horses if lost in the service.' Here is the germ of the idea of Yeoman Cavalry, for not only was

Appendix B

the composition of the proposed regiment that of a Yeomanry Corps, but the conditions of service very much those on which the Yeomanry Force half a century later were called into being.

The landowners of Yorkshire in September, 1745, raised a regiment of light cavalry which received the King's permission to be styled the Royal Regiment of Hunters, the unit being disbanded on the suppression of rebellion, and here again was another corps that foreshadowed the Yeomanry Force.

On the reorganization of the Militia in 1757, the Force was to consist of infantry regiments only, and no provision was made for any mounted troops.

In 1779 that famous and unique corps, the London and Westminster Light Horse Volunteers, sprang into being, and demonstrated the possibility of citizen cavalry, for the cavalry arms had become so technical as to be considered outside the scope of all but professional soldiers. This regiment was discontinued in 1783, and their standards - presented for their services in suppressing the Gordon Riots - lodged in the Tower, and it is interesting to note were again taken into use on the regiment being re-established as Yeomanry in 1794. Only one other corps of cavalry of this period has a direct connection with the Yeomanry, the Norfolk Rangers, organized by the Marquess Townshend, who was convinced of what he had seen in the American War of Independence of the utility of Volunteer Light Cavalry. This Corps was never officially disbanded and was in being, even if officially forgotten, and finally reorganized in 1794 into a Corps of Yeomanry.

Although to Pitt must be given the credit of the inception of the Yeomanry Force, there is little doubt that in the framing of the Government circular he was largely influenced by the various proposals that had been made to the Government. As early as February, 1793, a meeting was held at Dover to form a Regiment of Volunteer Light Horse for the Cinque Ports, followed by a meeting at Canterbury, convened the following month, to raise a Regiment of Volunteer Cavalry for East Kent. Over two thousand pounds was subscribed at the latter meeting, for the men of Kent acutely felt the insecurity of their narrow strip of sea frontier; but the King's Ministers, however, refused this offer of service, and the subscriptions, less expenses, were returned to the donors. Towards the close of the year 1793, the Lord-Lieutenant of Dorset proffered the services of a Corps of Guides to be raised by the Gentlemen and Yeomanry of Dorset; and in February, 1794, plans were submitted by the counties of Berks, Rutland, etc., for an armed Yeomanry based on the ideas that Arthur Young, the famous Suffolk agriculturist, had for the past two years been endeavouring to impress on the landed classes. Young's conception of a 'Militia of Property' expanded in his well-known pamphlet entitled 'The Example of France a Warning to England' went through four editions, and made a great sensation at this period. Young, who afterwards enrolled himself as a private in one of the Yeomanry troops - that of Bury St Edmunds - was regarded by many of his fellow-countrymen for some years afterwards as the originator of the Yeomanry movement.

Following the issue of the Government circular in March, 1794, meetings of the various counties were held both in London and in the counties themselves, and corps of Yeomanry were rapidly organized.

Had no disbandment taken place, the following list gives the precedence of the regiments as originally raised. As some counties organized more than one regiment, the table below gives the precedence not only of the country, but the regiments themselves. In all cases the precedence is based on the date of acceptance of the senior troop of the Regiment. (Corps were accepted for Bedfordshire, Glamorganshire, Roxburghshire during 1794, but these corps, however, did not materialize.)

The first corps to be raised was the Cinque Ports Yeomanry Cavalry, Pitt himself being the Lord Warden of the Ports; but it must be remembered that the Marquess Townshend's Norfolk Rangers were still a corporate body, and there is evidence that the Corps was in existence in the years 1792 and 1793, and was re-enrolled, with the addition of two extra troops, in June, 1794. Its members simply subscribed to the new (Yeomanry) conditions, and no letter can be found in the Home Office or War Office Letter Books in which there is an offer of service. The Rangers were disbanded in the reductions of 1828, but had they survived there is little doubt that they could

Appendix B

easily have made good their claim to a continuous existence from the year 1782, the only case of a corps originating from a date previous to 1794.

The table given below shows the original precedence of the various regiments of the Force, based on the date entered in the official establishment book of the senior troop. Only some twelve regiments were originally organized as regiments, the remainder of the corps being organized in troops or squadrons. As some counties had more than one regiment, the regimental and not the county precedence is consequently given. The dates given are those in the establishment book and have been verified by letters from the Home Secretary's letter books, the only exceptions being when a corps, owing to delays caused by its organization, has been by Royal Authority ordered to have its date of commissioning antedated.

The numbers enrolled in the Yeomanry corps not being considered sufficient, the Provisional Cavalry Act was passed in 1796; and almost immediately a clause was inserted to the effect that in counties where the Yeomanry Force was three-fourths of the number to be levied for the Provisional Cavalry, those counties should be exempted from the operation of the Act. This compulsory levy of men and horses met with intense and long-maintained opposition, and, as Windham said in the House of Commons, "it passed over the country like a blight." Pitt stated, when introducing this Bill, that the number of horses kept for pleasure in England and Wales amounted to no less than two hundred thousand; some gentlemen kept ten, and some twenty, and he proposed that those keeping ten should find one horse and rider; those keeping twenty, two; and so on.

1	Norfolk Rangers	00 09 82	27	Mid-Norfolk (Clackclose)	05 06 94
2	Cinque Ports	23 03 94	28	Hertforshire	08 06 94
3	Rutlandshire	25 03 94	29	N Cornwall (Launceston)	09 06 94
4	Dorsetshire	29 03 94	30	Sussex	23 06 94
5	E Kent	16 04 94	31	Lincs Lt Horse Rangers (Kesteven)	05 07 94
6	W Kent	16 04 94	32	Lincs (Holland)	09 07 94
7	Huntingdonshire	17 04 94	33	Warwickshire	16 07 94
8	1st (W) Berks (Abingdon)	20 04 94	34	North Riding	18 07 94
9	Pembrokeshire (Castlemartin)	22 04 94	35	Royal E Devon	21 07 94
10	Leicestershire	01 05 94	36	Herefordshire	08 08 94
11	Surrey	01 05 94	37	Notts (Sherwood Rangers)	09 08 94
12	Suffolk	01 05 94	38	Notts (Southern)	09 08 94
13	Northamptonshire	03 05 94	39	Yorkshire Dragoons	13 08 94
14	E Riding	03 05 94	40	Yorkshire Hussars	13 08 94
15	S Buckinghamshire	08 05 94	41	Staffordshire	21 08 94
16	Mid-Buckinghamshire	08 05 94	42	Derbyshire	25 08 94
17	N Buckinghamshire	08 05 94	43	Worcestershire	14 09 94
18	London and Westminster Lt Horse	09 05 94	44	Forfarshire	15 12 94
19	1st Devonshire	15 05 94	45	N Shropshire	11 01 95
20	E Somersetshire	28 05 94	46	S Shropshire	08 03 95
21	N Hampshire	31 05 94	47	E Hants (Portsdown)	28 04 95
22	Carmarthenshire	31 05 94	48	Denbigh (Wrexham)	23 05 95
23	E Norfolk (Hingham)	31 05 94	49	Durham	07 07 95
24	W Somersetshire	03 06 94	50	Gloucestershire	30 07 95
25	Wiltshire	04 06 94	51	Cambridgeshire	14 11 95
26	S Hants (New Forest)	05 06 94			

Appendix B

Those who had only one horse were to be balloted for, and those chosen to mount one man for the Force. This was a reversion to the old feudal system almost, and put the yeomen and farmers in a much closer and dangerous contact with the Militia ballot than was considered comfortable. In addition, the farmers and gentlemen had to ride in the ranks with their servants, and the result was not only a large augmentation of the existing troops and regiments of Yeomanry, but many fresh corps were formed in 1797 and 1798. Northumberland, Cheshire, Lancashire, Oxfordshire, Essex, Bedfordshire and Monmouthshire, who up to the passing of the Act had possessed no Yeomanry troops, now commenced to raise such corps. In Wales corps were raised in Flintshire and Glamorganshire, the latter county having offered a corps in 1794, which, though accepted, failed to materialize; and as regards the Kingdom of Scotland, the whole of the Lowland Counties, who had hitherto been without any Yeomanry, now commenced to raise Yeomanry troops. In addition to this large increase of the Yeomanry Force, its efficiency was largely increased by various troops of several counties, now uniting themselves into county regiments.

The preliminaries of peace between England and France were signed on October 1st, 1801, and on the 10th of that month a Government circular was issued requesting a renewal of services when peace was definitely established, which resulted in practically every corps assenting to continue. The Government had already found the Yeomanry not only quite as effective in quelling riots and tumults as the Regular and Fencible Cavalry, and had also realized the small cost of the whole Yeomanry Force, when compared to the upkeep of the thirty odd regiments of Fencible Cavalry that had been raised at the same time as the Yeomanry, who were now in the process of being disbanded.

On March 28th, 1802, a definite treaty was signed at Amiens, and although the Regular Army was immediately reduced, and the Militia disembodied, the Government, while retaining none of the Infantry Volunteers, were prepared to accept all Yeomanry Corps who might tender a renewal of their service. By far the greater part of the Force elected to continue, but the Regiments of Dorsetshire, Leicestershire, and the Southern Regiment of the West Riding (now Yorkshire Dragoons) were amongst the few corps who declined to serve on. The bulk of the cavalry troops of the various Volunteer Associations - a sort of Town Guards that had been raised in 1798 - were also disbanded, with the exception of a few troops who were transformed into Yeomanry troops.

On the renewal of the war on May 12th, 1803, the disbanded regiments were not only re-raised, but the Yeomanry Force was augmented to some thirty-six thousand officers and men, exclusive of the Irish Yeomanry. For the next two years the nation lived in daily fear of Napoleon's threatened invasion, and the Yeomanry, in addition to their weekly drills, were now embodied for spells of permanent duty. A circular was issued towards the close of 1803 directing the various unregimented troops to combine so as to form regiments, but although several counties regimented their old troops, the bulk of the independent troops managed to evade the order. The victory of Trafalgar in 1805 brought its much-needed relaxation to the Yeomanry. Drills were now less frequent, many corps dispensed with permanent duty and a few corps disbanded themselves. Napoleon's overthrow in 1814 resulted in several more corps withdrawing their services, amongst whom was the Dorset Regiment, who for a second time was disbanded. The escape of the Emperor from Elba, and the victory of Waterloo followed so quickly on each other that there was little opportunity for the Yeomanry to show their desire to again augment their numbers. Another circular, ordering the regimentation of those single troops and squadrons, had been issued in 1813, but only resulted in the bulk of the single troops ignoring the order, for which the Government were largely to blame, as there was no provision made in funds to assimilate the uniform of the various troops that might desire to adopt one uniform for the whole regiment.

The industrial outlook after the peace was now very serious, and from 1817 to 1819 it appeared at times as if the country was on the verge of open rebellion. Lord Sidmouth - himself an old Yeomanry Commandant (Woodley Squadron, Berkshire) decided to largely augment the Yeomanry, and many new regiments were raised - only, after performing 'yeoman service' in the suppression of these riots, to be ruthlessly disbanded in the wholesale reductions of 1828. These reductions had actually commended in 1824, when the Government ordered a

Appendix B

searching inspection to be made into the Force, especially the single-troop units and independent squadrons, with the natural result that a good many of these small corps disbanded themselves.

The Force, which had reached an establishment of over thirty-three thousand and had been already reduced to thirty-one thousand, now was to consist of but some seven thousand seven hundred and twenty-five officers and men, the following corps, some twenty-two in number (containing one hundred and forty-four troops) alone being retained. To their credit, the following sixteen corps, containing sixty-six troops and a total strength of three thousand one hundred and fifty-two men, offered to continue their services *and were accepted* without either pay or allowances. These patriotic corps were:

Retained	At no pay or allowances
Ayrshire	Second (or Mid) Buckinghamshire
Cheshire (King's)	1st Cornwall
Glamorganshire (Gower or Swansea)	2nd Cornwall
Eastern Glamorganshire	Denbighshire
Central Glamorganshire	Derbyshire
Lanarkshire	Royal 1st Devon
Lancashire (Duke of Lancaster's Own)	North Devon
Leicestershire	South Devon
Midlothian	Glasgow
Northumberland	East Lothian
South Nottinghamshire	Oxfordshire
Sherwood Rangers	Bloxham and Banbury (Oxon)
Renfrewshire	Pembrokeshire (Castlemartin)
North Shropshire	West Somerset
South Shropshire	East Somerset (Taunton)
North Somersetshire	Westmoreland
Stirlingshire	
Staffordshire	
Warwickshire	
Wiltshire	
Yorkshire Hussars	
SW Yorkshire (now Yorks Dragoons)	

The remainder of the Yeomanry corps, many of whom were compact regiments, some one hundred and two in number, and containing some three hundred and fifty-four troops, were selected for disbandment. The total number of corps thus serving being raised to 38, containing 210 troops and an establishment of 10,877 privates.

The outbreak of the agricultural riots in the south of England - now without Yeomanry, except the two Regiments of Wilts and North Somerset, on pay and allowances, and the three Devon and one Bucks Corps, not on pay - resulted in a panic-stricken Government once again turning to the Force, which was within a few months brought up to a strength of some twenty thousand men. The Reform Riots followed, with the terrible orgies at Bristol, which scenes of bloodshed would have been equalled by the dangerous mobs at Derby and Nottingham, (At Nottinghamshire the historic castle was burnt by the mob.) and several other cities, had it not been for the firm hand kept on the mobs by the local Yeomanries. But the King's ministers had learnt no lesson for the future, and in 1838 the Force was again reduced from 92 corps, with 337 troops and some eighteen thousand men, to 46 corps containing 251 troops and some thirteen thousand five hundred men. Even then there were to be found nine corps willing to serve without pay and allowances - namely, the South Bucks or Taplow Corps, the West Essex, the Andover and Lymington Troops in Hampshire, the Taunton and Ilminster Troops in Somerset, the Long Melford and Suffolk Borderers in Suffolk, and in Sussex the Petworth Troop; these corps being again placed on pay in 1843, when fresh disorder again called for more Yeomanry, and two regiments, the 2nd West York and the Midlothian were also revived.

In 1846 the East Lothian (later the Lothian and Border Horse) were re-raised; and as a result of the Chartist movement, the Glasgow and Lancashire Hussars were organized in 1848. Industrial troubles in Scotland caused the Forfarshire Yeomanry to be revived in 1856, this Regiment being disbanded, however, in 1862, and was the last regiment to be raised under the old order of things as Yeomanry Cavalry.

The Force, owing to an efficient police force being at last established, were gradually relieved of their duties in aid of the Civil Power, and the trend of events on the Continent caused them to be gradually brought back to their original status as the cavalry of the Home Defence Army. In 1860 the corps numbered forty-nine, but by 1871 were reduced to forty-five, of which three were but single-troop corps. These three latter units were disbanded, and the Force was now organized in forty-two regiments.

The South and North Shropshire were amalgamated in 1872, the Midlothian were disbanded in 1873, and the West Essex in 1877, and the Force remained at thirty-nine regiments until the 2nd West York Yeomanry were broken up for want of officers in 1894. On the experience of the Boer War (including the double regiments of the Lovat's Scouts and Scottish Horse, but not including the two Irish regiments), eighteen new regiments were raised, bringing the total to fifty-six regiments, of which one, the King Edward's Oversea Horse, was in 1908 transferred to the Special Reserve (Militia).

(2) The Proposed Precedence Table

Tradition related that a dispute between the Light Troop of the Honourable Artillery Company and the Brighton Troop of the Middlesex Hussars, as to which was the senior unit and so entitled to lead the march past, at a Volunteer Review held at Brighton on Easter Monday, 1884, was the immediate cause of the question of the precedence to the Yeomanry regiments being brought under official consideration.

The question of the Honourable Artillery Company's position in the Citizen Forces of the Crown was quickly settled. That ancient body was in future to rank after the Militia, and to take precedence before the Yeomanry and Volunteer Forces. The Yeomanry were to rank after the Honourable Artillery Company and before the Volunteer Force, and now came the question of the individual precedence of the regiments of the Force.

During the autumn of 1884 a project was started for the authorization by Her Majesty the Queen of a 'Table of Precedence' for the several regiments of Yeomanry Cavalry in Great Britain. A considerable amount of correspondence took place between the War Office and the Colonels of the Regiments and on December 5th, 1884, the 'Proposed Precedence Table for Yeomanry Cavalry Regiments' was issued. As will be seen from the Table - of which an exact copy is given - in many cases only the dates of the year are given. The proposed table was as follows:-

1	Derbyshire	00 10 31	21	North Devon	1804
2	Ayrshire	1792	22	Lanarkshire	1819
3	Yorkshire Hussars	1792	23	Northumberland	00 12 19
4	1st Devon	1793	24	Westmoreland and Cumberland	1819
5	Hampshire	1793	25	Notts. (Southern Notts.)	1826
6	Pembroke	1793	26	Duke of Lancaster's Own	1827
7	Denbigh	1794	27	Dorset	16 12 30
8	West Somerset	1794	28	Herts	22 12 30
9	Stafford	1794	29	West Kent	00 12 30

10	Warwick	1794	30	Berkshire	12 02 31
11	Sherwood Rangers	1795	31	Middlesex	03 03 31
12	Oxford	1796	32	Suffolk	07 04 31
13	Bucks	1797	33	Worcester	29 04 31
14	North Somerset	09 03 97	34	Gloucester	00 04 34
15	Royal Wiltshire	13 06 98	35	2nd West York	14 07 43
16	Shropshire	27 06 98	36	East Lothian	00 06 46
17	Cheshire	1803	37	Lancashire Hussars	05 09
18	Leicester	1803	38	Lanarkshire (Glasgow)	21 04 49
19	Montgomery	1803	39	East Kent	20 11 53
20	1st West York	15 08 03			

The Derbyshire claim was based on a printer's error in a Parliamentary return issued in the 'fifties, giving amongst other information the date various Yeomanry corps were supposed to have been raised, the date 1831 having been shown in error as 1731. The Ayrshire, Yorkshire Hussars, 1st Devon, Hampshire and Pembroke Regiments, it will be noted, are, for no apparent reason, claiming a date before even the Yeomanry were called into being. The South Notts., Duke of Lancaster's Own, and the Gloucester Yeomanries are dating only the claims from the regimentation of their various troops. Other dates can be recognized as dates, when the establishment was fixed by an augmentation or reduction of strength; and, finally, the East Kent modestly volunteer to occupy the last place in the list, based on their change of designation to 'Mounted Rifles' which took place twenty-three years after their being re-raised to suppress the agricultural riots of 1830. Further comment on this haphazard table would be superfluous.

(3) The Official Table of Precedence

The Secretary of State for War now called upon the Commanding Officers for more detailed statements, and the various claims made by the regiments were again examined. To do the War Office justice, a straightforward attempt was made to give each regiment its proper order; the precedence was not to be balloted for as had been done in the case of the Militia regiments. Each regiment was to base its actual precedence from the *continuous service of its earliest troop*, and on January 27th, 1885, the following official table was issued. The dates on which the table was based were issued separately to the Regiments in a circular letter dated January 27th, 1885, and the full date is given when known; but they are of no real importance, as they are, with few exceptions, hopelessly incorrect. To be brief, the table is valueless. For one thing, the original dates were taken from the 1794-95 and succeeding Militia and Volunteer Lists, and the date of commissioning a corps was (with a few exceptions when a unit was antedated) always later than that of the date of official acceptance of a corps. Secondly, no account has been taken that the following nine regiments served without pay and allowances from 1828 until they were again placed on the paid lists in 1830-31, viz.: Denbighshire, Westmorland and Cumberland, Pembrokeshire, Buckinghamshire, Derbyshire, 1st Devon, North Devon, West Somerset and Oxfordshire. Also one date, that of the South Notts., is still the date of the amalgamation of the independent troops in Southern Nottinghamshire to form that corps; and, finally, in the later regiments in the table a large proportion are based on dates when merely their establishments were revised. An example is here given: the Montgomeryshire were accepted as a corps of four troops on January 13th, 1831. On February 25th, 1831, a fifth troop was approved, but on September 16th, 1831, the establishment was again fixed at four troops; and the establishment in officers and men was finally fixed on September 27th, 1831, which date was borne for a long time in the War Office entry books, and so was accepted as the date when the Montgomeryshire Yeomanry had been re-raised.

(1)	Royal Wiltshire	21 06 94	(21)	Bucks.	08 12 30
(2)	Warwickshire	16 07 94	(22)	Derbyshire	08 12 30
(3)	Yorkshire Hussars	13 08 94	(23)	Dorset	08 12 30
(4)	Sherwood Rangers	15 08 94	(24)	Gloucestershire	1830

Appendix B

(5)	Staffordshire	20 09 94	(25)	Herts.	1830
(6)	Shropshire	17 04 95	(26)	Berks.	04 03 31
(7)	Ayrshire	26 07 03	(27)	Middlesex	1831
(8)	Cheshire	13 08 03	(28)	Royal 1st Devon	1831
(9)	Yorkshire Dragoons	15 08 03	(29)	Suffolk	1831
(10)	Leicestershire	05 09 03	(30)	North Devon	1831
(11)	North Somerset	1803	(31)	Worcestershire	29 04 31
(12)	Duke of Lancaster's	22 08 19	(32)	West Kent	1831
(13)	Lanarkshire	02 11 19	(33)	West Somerset	1831
(14)	**Northumberland**	**20 11 19**	**(34)**	**Oxfordshire**	**1831**
(15)	South Notts.	1826	(35)	Montgomeryshire	27 09 31
(16)	Denbighshire	1830	(36)	2nd West York	1843 (disb 1894)
(17)	Westmorland and Cumberland	1830	(37)	Lothians and Berwick	1846
(18)	Pembrokeshire	23 07 30	(38)	Glasgow	1848
(19)	East Kent	30 11 30	(39)	Lancashire Hussars	1848
(20)	Hampshire	30 11 30			

How careless was the research made is seen from the fact that the letters raising the various corps and the disbanding of the same are all in Home Office letter books at the Public Record Office. As for the regiments that continued to serve, the letter books for 1828, contain the correspondence requesting that permission, and later the letter books of 1830 and 1831 make it clear that those corps were once more placed on pay and allowances. Also there are complete lists of these corps serving without pay in the correspondence between the Home Secretary when requesting exemption from the Horse Tax for these regiments from the Commissioners of Taxes. It may be stated that only some four or five dates are correct, and that not a single regiment has got its correct precedence number, with the exception of the last four regiments and that was almost by accident, as they have been shown with incorrect dates.

In 1894 the 2nd West York Regiment was disbanded and the 37th, 38th and 39th Regiments took the numbers 36, 37 and 38 respectively. On reorganization of the Yeomanry in 1901, the following regiments were raised and allocated the following numbers:-

39	Surrey	30 04 01	48	Bedfordshire	23 08 01
40	Fife and Forfar	18 05 01	49	Essex	08 11 01
41	Norfolk	24 05 01	50	King's Colonials	29 11 01
42	Sussex	11 06 01	51	North of Ireland	07 01 02
43	Glamorgan	21 06 01	52	South of Ireland	07 01 02
44	Lincolnshire	26 06 01	53	Northamptonshire	14 02 02
45	City of London (Rough Riders)	23 07 01	54	East Riding of Yorkshire	15 04 02
46	2nd Co of London (Westminster)	23 07 01	55	Lovat Scouts (two regiments)	20 02 03
47	3rd Co of London (Sharpshooters)	23 07 01	56	Scottish Horse (two regiments)	03 03 03

The above dates are *not* the dates the regiments received the approval of their Sovereign, but the somewhat later dates when notified in the *London Gazette*. The two Irish regiments and the King's Colonials were later transferred to the Special Reserve, and on Lovat's Scouts being definitely split into separate regiments, the following regiments were numbered as below:

In 1914, shortly after the outbreak of the war, a Welsh Yeomanry Regiment was raised in South Wales, and as it was administered by the Glamorganshire Territorial Force Association, the War Office bent on maintaining

50	Northamptonshire	52	1st Lovat Scouts
51	East Riding	53	2nd Lovat Scouts
		54	Scottish Hse (two regts)

the quite incorrect character of the Precedence Table, gave this new regiment the number 44, so as to follow the Glamorganshire Regiment. The correct number would have been the 57th, as the Scottish Horse had added a third regiment on mobilization. The Lincolnshire Yeomanry now became the 45th, and all units junior to the Lincoln Regiment were fleeted up one number.

(4) The Correct Precedence Table

This table is based on the official date of acceptance of the earliest troop forming the regiment, unless that unit has been by Royal Authority antedated in its commissioning, which was sometimes done in cases where troops had been already raised, but delay had ensued in the transmission of their offers of service. Such examples are found in the Royal First Devon, the late East Devon, Derbyshire, Staffordshire and Warwickshire Regiments.

From 1794 to the middle of 1798, as the Lords-Lieutenant of counties were empowered to accept corps, the date of acceptance as entered in the establishment book is always that of the *date of the letter in which Lord-Lieutenant offered the services of the corps, but in later years the Establishment Book enters as the date of acceptance the date of the letter in which the Home Secretary notified His Majesty's acceptance of the corps.*

In the case of the Regiments raised after the Boer War, the date of the Sovereign's approval of the submission, and not the date notified in the London Gazette, is taken as the date of official acceptance.

The following Table gives the Correct Precedence of the Yeomanry Regiments as they stood at the close of the Great War, 1919:- (The official numbers given are those at the conclusion of the Great War.)

No. 1. The Pembrokeshire (Castlemartin) Yeomanry Hussars Accepted April 22nd, 1794 (two Pembroke troops accepted, but only one, the Castlemartin, raised); commissioned August 31st, 1794. Took part in the capture of the French invading force at Fishguard, 1797. No letter re-accepting the Corps (one troop) can be found at the Record Office, but the monthly returns are rendered from 1795 to August, 1803, without a break. On August, 1803, augmented to two troops. Ordered to be disbanded in 1828 reductions, but offer accepted to serve without pay and allowances on January 11th, 1828. Placed on pay January 27th, 1831. Regiment has thus had a continuous existence since April 22nd, 1794. (Official No. 18.)

No. 2. The Royal Buckinghamshire Yeomanry Hussars Accepted May 8th, 1794 (five troops as Bucks Armed Yeomanry). Renewed service September 30th, 1802. The Aylesbury and Buckingham Squadrons formed into the 2nd or Mid Bucks Yeomanry Cavalry on August 16th, 1803. North and South Bucks Regiments disbanded in 1828, but Mid Bucks accepted without pay December 15th, 1827, and placed on pay December 8th, 1830. **Note:** Not commissioned until May 13th, 1795, as the officers were at first only commissioned by the Lord-Lieutenant. Regiment has never been disbanded, and dates from May 8th, 1794. (Official No. 21.)

No. 3. The Royal First Devonshire Yeomanry Hussars Raised and enrolled on May 15th, 1794. Letter of service delayed until August 3rd, 1794, which date was entered in the Establishment Book, but by the King's approval the Corps was commissioned to date from May 15th, 1794. This Corps, known as the First Devon Troop, was formed into the First Devon Regiment in 1801, which Regiment renewed their services November 5th, 1802. Offered to serve without pay January 5th, 1828, accepted, and placed on pay January 17th, 1831. The Regiment has never been disbanded, and dates from May 15th, 1794. (Official No. 28.)

Appendix B

No. 4. The West Somersetshire Yeomanry Hussars Accepted June 3rd, 1794 (Brymore or Bridgewater Troop), and commissioned July 24th, 1794. Formed with other troops into West Somerset Regiment Yeomanry Cavalry in 1798. Renewed offer of service December 21st, 1802; officially accepted February 2nd, 1803. Ordered to be disbanded 1828, but accepted without pay January 31st, 1828, and placed on pay and allowances May 28th, 1831. Never disbanded, and date from June 3rd, 1794. (Official No. 33.)

No. 5. The Prince of Wales' Own Royal Wiltshire Yeomanry Hussars Accepted June 4th, 1794 (nine troops) and commissioned June 21st, 1794. Regimented 1797. Renewed service August 31st, 1802. Never disbanded, but date from June 4th, 1794. (Official No. 1.)

No. 6. The Warwickshire Yeomanry Hussars Accepted July 17th, 1794, but commissioned by King to date from July 16th, 1794 (four troops). Regimented 1797. Renewed service October 13th, 1802. Never disbanded, but date from July 16th, 1794. (Official No. 2.)

No. 7. The Sherwood Rangers Yeomanry (Hussars) Accepted August 9th, 1794 (three troops), and commissioned August 15yh, 1794. Disbanded except Newark Troop, who were re-accepted June 22nd, 1802. Regimented May 27th, 1828, as the Sherwood Rangers Yeomanry Cavalry. Never disbanded. Through the continued service of the Newark Troop, date from August 9th, 1794. (Official No. 4.)

No. 8. The Alexandra Princess of Wales' Own Yorkshire Yeomanry Hussars Accepted August 13th, 1794, as 2nd or Northern Regiment of West Riding Yeomanry Cavalry and commissioned same date. Renewed service July 25th, 1802, and on October 9th, 1802, styled 1st Regiment West Riding Yeomanry Cavalry. Never disbanded, but date from August 13th, 1794. (Official No. 3.)

No. 9. The Queen's Own Royal Staffordshire Yeomanry Hussars Accepted September 20th, 1794, but actually raised July 4th, 1794 - i.e. enrolled - and in consequence dated back by King's approval and commissioned to August 21st, 1794. Renewed service September 16th, 1802. Originally formed as a regiment, and have never been disbanded, but date from August 21st, 1794. (Official No. 5.)

No. 10. The Derbyshire Yeomanry Dragoons Accepted September 16th, 1794 (raised in July, 1794), and commissioned by the King August 25th, 1794. Renewed service accepted April 7th, 1803. Ordered to be disbanded 1828, but three troops on April 2nd, 1828, offered to serve without pay; but in May, 1829, two of these troops withdrew their offer, leaving only one troop (the Radbourne Troop), which was placed on pay December 14th, 1830. Note: The Radbourne Troop absorbed portions of the other two troops. Radbourne Troop and other troops regimented into Derbyshire Yeomanry Cavalry, 1864. Regiment never entirely disbanded, and date from August 25th, 1794. (Official No. 22.)

No. 11. The Shropshire Yeomanry Dragoons Accepted January 11th, 1795 (Market Drayton Troop), and commissioned same date. This Troop united to 3rd or North Shropshire Corps. In 1872 amalgamated to South Shropshire Regiment as the Shropshire Yeomanry Cavalry. Never disbanded, but date from January 11th, 1795. (Official No. 6.)

No.12.   The Denbighshire Yeomanry Hussars Accepted May 23rd, 1795 (Wrexham Troop), and commissioned June 3rd, 1795. Renewed service 1802, and increased to a corps of three troops 1803, and in 1820 to five troops designated Denbighshire Yeomanry Cavalry. Ordered to be disbanded in 1828, but accepted without pay February 21st, 1828. Placed on pay January 5th, 1831. Never disbanded, but date from May 23rd, 1795. (Official No. 16.)

No. 13. The Earl of Chester's Cheshire Yeomanry Hussars Accepted June 5th, 1797 (Macclesfield Troop), and commissioned June 21st, 1797. Renewed service accepted October 6th, 1802, and on July 26th, 1803, formed into Earl of Chester's Regiment of Yeomanry Cavalry. Never disbanded, and date from June 5th, 1797. (Official No. 8.)

No. 14. The South Nottinghamshire Yeomanry Hussars Accepted May 23rd, 1798 (enrolled March and April), Holme Pierrepont Troop. Commissioned June 20th, 1798. Holme Troop re-accepted renewal of services June 22rd, 1802, and regimented July 21st, 1826, to form Southern Nottinghamshire Regiment of Yeomanry Cavalry. Note the Nottingham (Town) Troop raised August 9th, 1794, disbanded in 1802. Regiment has thus continued service through the Holme Troop from May 23rd, 1798. (Official No. 15.)

No. 15. The Royal North Devonshire Yeomanry Hussars Accepted May 23rd, 1798 (as Jame, later Bideford, Troop), and commissioned June 27th, 1798; renewed services accepted November 5th, 1802, and on March 20th, 1803, formed with other troops into North Devon Regiment of Yeomanry Cavalry. (Note: Barnstaple Troop, accepted April 29th, 1798, was disbanded March 20th, 1805.) North Devon ordered to be disbanded, but services without pay accepted January 5th, 1828, and placed on pay January 17th, 1831. Never disbanded, and date from May 23rd, 1798. (Official No. 30.) (The Royal North Devon Hussars bear the same date - May 23rd,1798 - as the South Notts. Hussars - but the South Notts. Hussars were not only commissioned some seven days earlier, but had been actually enrolled in March, 1798.)

No. 16. The Earl of Carrick's Own Ayrshire Yeomanry Hussars Accepted May 29th, 1798 (Carrick Troop); commissioned July 19th, 1798. Renewed services accepted October 22nd, 1802, and augmented to three troops 1803. Never disbanded, and date from May 29th, 1798. (Official No. 7.)

No. 17. The Queen's Own Oxfordshire Yeomanry Hussars Accepted July 26th, 1798 (North Wootton Troop), and commissioned September 6th, 1798. Renewed services accepted September 27th, 1802 In 1818 regimented to form North-West (later 1st) Regiment of Oxfordshire Yeomanry Cavalry. Ordered to be disbanded 1828, but accepted without pay March 22nd, 1828, and placed on pay December 8th, 1830. Never disbanded, and date from July 26th, 1798. (First Yeomanry Regiment to go on active service in Great War.) (Official No. 34.)

No. 18. The North Somersetshire Yeomanry Dragoons Accepted June 20th, 1798 (Frome Troop), but disbanded in 1802, as were all other North Somerset troops at Bath, Road and Wolverton, Mells, and Beckingham. Re-raised as Frome Troop August 13th, 1803, and united in 1804 with East Mendip Corps to form the Frome and East Mendip Regiment of Yeomanry Cavalry, which in 1814 was designated North Somerset Yeomanry Cavalry. Having been disbanded in 1802, the Regiment dates from August 13th, 1803. (Official No. 11.)

No. 19. The Queen's Own Yorkshire Yeomanry Dragoons Accepted as 1st or Southern Regiment of West Riding Yeomanry Cavalry August 13th, 1794, but disbanded in 1802. Re-raised on August 15th, 1803, as the 2nd or Southern Regiment of West Riding Yeomanry Cavalry. Later became South-West Yorkshire Yeomanry Cavalry, and then 1st West York, and finally Yorkshire Dragoons. Date from August 15th, 1803. (Official No. 9.)

No. 20. The Prince Albert's Own Leicestershire Yeomanry Hussars Accepted May 1st, 1794 (commissioned May 9th, 1794), as a regiment, but disbanded 1802. Re-raised September 5th, 1803 (commissioned September 5th, 1803) as a regiment. Dates from September 5th, 1803. (Official No. 10.)

No. 21. The Duke of Lancaster's Own Yeomanry Dragoons Accepted April 5th, 1798 (Bolton Troop), which after renewing services in 1802 (August 3rd) was disbanded in 1814. The Furness Troop accepted August 23rd, 1819 (commissioned September 22nd, 1819), was on August 18th, 1828, regimented with Bolton and Wigan Troop as Lancashire Regiment of Yeomanry Cavalry. Dates from August 23rd, 1819. (Official No. 12.)

Appendix B

No. 22. The Westmorland and Cumberland Yeomanry Hussars Accepted October 7th, 1819 (commissioned October 22nd, 1819). Ordered to be disbanded 1828, but services accepted without pay April 24th, 1828, and again placed on pay May 28th, 1831. Note: Originally raised as Westmorland Yeomanry Cavalry; title changed to Westmorland and Cumberland Cavalry in 1843. Dates from October 7th, 1819. (Official No. 17.)

No. 23. The Lanarkshire Yeomanry Lancers Accepted November 2nd, 1819 (commissioned November 17th, 1819). Dates from November 2nd, 1819. (Official No. 13.)

No. 24. The Northumberland Yeomanry Hussars Accepted as Newcastle Troop, February 23rd, 1797 (commissioned March 9th, 1797) but disbanded in 1802. Re-raised (accepted) November 20th, 1819 (commissioned December 7th, 1819) as Northumberland and Newcastle Regiment of Yeomanry Cavalry. Dates from November 20th, 1819. (Official No. 14.)
Note: The junior Regiment retained as cavalry.

No. 25. The Duke of Connaught's Own Royal East Kent Yeomanry Mounted Rifles Accepted April 16th, 1794 (commissioned April 19th, 1794) as Independent Troops; renewed services August 13th, 1802. Partially regimented 1803, actually regimented in 1813; disbanded 1828. Re-raised (accepted) November 30th, 1830. (Kent was the first county to make offer of Yeomanry in 1830.) Dates from November 30th, 1830. (Official No. 19.)

No. 26. The Hampshire Yeomanry Carabiniers Accepted as North Hants Yeomanry Cavalry (one troop, later three troops) May 31st, 1794 (commissioned May 31st, 1794) but disbanded 1828. Re-raised (accepted) November 30th, 1830. Date from November 30th, 1830. Note: Re-raised as North Hampshire Yeomanry Cavalry, became Hampshire Yeomanry Cavalry 1848. (Official No. 20.)

No. 27. The Hertfordshire Yeomanry Dragoons Accepted June 8th, 1794 (commissioned June 21st, 1794), as independent troops. Renewed services accepted August 31st, 1802; disbanded as South Herts. 1824. Re-raised (as South Herts.) and accepted December 4th, 1830. Designated Hertfordshire Yeomanry Cavalry 1872. Date from December 4th, 1830. (Official No. 25.)

No. 28. The Queen's Own Dorsetshire Yeomanry Hussars Accepted March 29th, 1794 (commissioned May 9th, 1794) but disbanded in 1802. Re-raised (accepted) May 27th, 1803, but disbanded June 14th, 1814. Again re-raised (accepted) December 8th, 1830. Raised each time as a county regiment. Date from December 8th, 1830. (Official No. 23.)

No. 29. The Duke of Cambridge's Middlesex Yeomanry Hussars Accepted (Uxbridge Troop) April 7th, 1797 (commissioned May 12th, 1797); disbanded 1802. Re-raised (accepted) December 10th, 1830, as Uxbridge Troop. Date from December 15th, 1830. (Official No. 27.)

No. 30. The Royal Gloucestershire Yeomanry Hussars Accepted (Cheltenham Troop) July 30th, 1795 (commissioned August 15th, 1795). Renewed service August 1st, 1802; disbanded 1814. Note: All Gloucester troops disbanded by 1828. Re-raised (accepted) as independent troops December 15th, 1830 (Marshfield Troop). Regimented in 1834. Date from December 15th, 1830. (Official No. 24.)

No. 31. The Queen's Own West Kent Yeomanry Hussars Accepted April 16th, 1794 (commissioned April 19th, 1794) as independent troops. Regimented 1797; disbanded 1825. Re-raised as independent troops, Chislehurst Troop being accepted December 18th, 1830. Regimented 1831. Date from December 18th, 1830. (Official No. 32.)

No. 32. The Montgomeryshire Yeomanry Dragoons Accepted September 9th, 1803, but disbanded 1828. Re-raised (accepted) January 13th, 1831. Date from January 13th, 1831. (Official No. 35.)

Appendix B

No. 33. The Royal Berkshire (Hungerford) Yeomanry Dragoons Accepted April 20th, 1794 (Abingdon Troop); commissioned May 16th, 1794. Renewed services accepted August 31st, 1802. Regimented 1803, but disbanded 1828. Re-raised (accepted) March 4th, 1831, as Hungerford Troop. Increased to a corps of three troops, designated Berkshire (Hungerford) Yeomanry Cavalry, 1853. Date from March 4th, 1831. (Official No. 26.)

No. 34. The Duke of York's Own Loyal Suffolk Yeomanry Hussars Accepted May 4th, 1794 (commissioned May 9th, 1794). Renewed service October 8th, 1802, but disbanded in 1828. Re-raised April 7th, 1831, 1st Loyal Suffolk Troop. Ordered to be disbanded, but accepted to serve without pay, June, 1838; placed on pay list 1843. Regimented 1868. Date from April 7th, 1831. (Official No. 29.)

No. 35. The Queen's Own Worcestershire Yeomanry Hussars Accepted September 14th, 1794, and commissioned same date; renewed service August 31st, 1802, but disbanded 1828. Re-raised (accepted) as a regiment April 29th, 1831. Dates from April 29th, 1831. (Official No. 31.)

No. 36. The Lothian and Border Yeomanry Horse Accepted May 7th, 1797 (commissioned June 1st, 1797). Renewed services July 13th, 1802. Ordered to be disbanded, but one troop (4th) accepted to serve without pay, March 27th, 1828; replaced on pay 1831, and augmented, but disbanded 1838. Re-raised (accepted) May 16th, 1846. Date from May 16th, 1846. (Originally the East Lothian Yeomanry Cavalry.) (Official No. 36.)

(The Prince of Wales' Own 2nd West Yorkshire Yeomanry Cavalry would have preceded the Lothian and Border Horse. Accepted at Halifax May 7th, 1798, and Huddersfield May 15th, 1798, but both units disbanded 1802. Re-raised as West Yorkshire Yeomanry Cavalry August 15th, 1803, but disbanded July 20th, 1810. Re-raised (accepted) as Huddersfield Squadron March 12th, 1817, but disbanded April 10th, 1826. Re-raised (accepted) June 2nd, 1843, but disbanded 1894. (Official No. 36.))

No. 37. The Queen's Own Royal Glasgow Yeomanry Dragoons Accepted March 20th, 1797 (commissioned July 5th, 1797), but disbanded in 1802. Re-raised (accepted October 21st, 1819), ordered to be disbanded 1828, but retained without pay, December, 1828. The Glasgow Troop was never formally disbanded, but by the Home Secretary of State's correspondence appears to have gradually dwindled away. Re-raised (accepted) July 22nd, 1848, as Glasgow Yeomanry Cavalry (commissioned December 22nd, 1848). Date from July 22nd, 1848. (Official No. 37.)

No. 38. The Lancashire Yeomanry Hussars Accepted as Ashton Yeomanry Cavalry May 2nd, 1798 (commissioned June 2nd, 1798); renewed services August 3rd, 1802, but disbanded May 28th, 1823. Re-raised (accepted) at Ashton as Lancashire Hussars August 31st, 1848 (commissioned September 5th, 1848). In both cases the Corps were raised by the Gerard family. Date from August 31st, 1848. (Official No. 38.)

No. 39. The Fifeshire and Forfarshire Yeomanry Dragoons Accepted June 17th, 1797 (Kirkcaldy Troop); renewed service December 21st, 1802. Kirkcaldy Troop amalgamated to Fife Yeomanry Cavalry Regiment, 1803, but disbanded 1828. Re-raised as Fife Regiment of Yeomanry Cavalry April 12th, 1831, but disbanded 1838. Re-raised as Fife Volunteer Mounted Rifles (later Light Horse), June 7th, 1860, and on May 7th, 1901, the King approved the amalgamation with Forfar Light Horse as the Fife and Forfar Imperial Yeomanry. Date from June 7th, 1860. **Note:** The Yeomanry were originally all volunteer cavalry. (Official No. 49.)

No. 40. The Queen Mary's Surrey Yeomanry Lancers Accepted as Surrey Regiment of Yeomanry Cavalry, May 1st, 1794 (commissioned May 9th, 1794). Renewed service October 31st, 1802, but disbanded 1828. Re-raised (accepted) Southwark Troop January 17th, 1831, which was amalgamated to Surrey Regiment of Yeomanry Cavalry; accepted March 31st, 1831, but the Regiment was disbanded June 26th, 1848. Re-raised (accepted by King Edward) April 12th, 1901, but not gazetted until April 30th, 1901. Date from April 12th, 1901. (Official No. 39.)

Appendix B

No. 41. The King's Own Royal Norfolk Yeomanry Dragoons Accepted September, 1782 (commissioned Octoer, 1782), as the Norfolk Rangers, and were actually serving at the time of the inception of the Yeomanry Force in 1794. Augmented in 1794, and renewed service December 8th, 1802, but disbanded in 1828, as were the 2nd or Mid and 3rd or East Regiments of Norfolk Yeomanry Cavalry. Re-raised (accepted) as Norfolk (actually a revival of the Mid Regiment) January 17th, 1831, but were disbanded April 26th, 1849. On May 14th, 1901, the King approved of the King's Own Norfolk Regiment of Imperial Yeomanry being raised, and the Regiment was gazetted May 24th, 1901. Date from May 14th, 1901. (Official No. 41.)

No. 42. The Lincolnshire Yeomanry Lancers Accepted as independent troops June 5th, 1794 (commissioned July 5th, 1794). Renewed service February 22nd, 1802, but disbanded 1828. Re-raised as North Lincoln Regiment of Yeomanry Cavalry, April 6th, 1831, but were disbanded December 13th, 1846. Approved by the King May 18th, 1901, but were for some reason not notified in the *London Gazette* until June 26th, 1901, and so were given the precedence No. 44 instead of 42, and on the raising of the Welch Horse in 1914 were incorrectly given the No. 45. Date from May 18th, 1901. (Official No. 45.) (Regiment disbanded A.O. 512, November, 1920.)

No. 43. The Sussex Yeomanry Dragoons Accepted June 23rd, 1794 (commissioned June 23rd, 1794), as independent troops. Renewed services July 26th, 1802, but disbanded 1828. Re-raised as Petworth Troop March 28th, 1831, and Arundel and Bramber Corps May 18th, 1831; latter Corps disbanded August 26th, 1848. Approved by the King to revive Sussex Regiment, June 4th, 1901, and gazetted June 11th, 1901. Date from June 4th, 1901. (Official No. 42.)

No. 44. The Glamorganshire Yeomanry Dragoons Accepted June 26th, 1794, but were not raised until April, 1797. Renewed services August 20th, 1802. All three Glamorgan corps were retained, but were all disbanded July 11th, 1831, by order of the Home Secretary on account of their supposed conduct at the Merthyr Tydvil riots, when several rioters were killed. Accepted by the King June 14th, 1901, and gazetted on June 21st, 1901. Date from June 14th, 1901. (Official No. 43.)

No. 45. The City of London Yeomanry Lancers (The Roughriders) Accepted as Loyal Islington Troop April 26th, 1798, but disbanded 1802. Re-raised as Loyal Islington (accepted) on July 9th, 1803; became Loyal London V.C. August 21st, 1803, but disbanded 1814. Accepted by the King July 18th, 1901, and gazetted July 23rd, 1901. Date from July 18th, 1901. (Official No. 46.)

(The Roughriders and the Sharpshooters were both raised from the ex-members of the Roughriders and Sharpshooters Battalions of Imperial Yeomanry who had returned and also were at the time on service in South Africa, and were allowed the war honour "South Africa, 1900-1902". These Battalions were first formed in December, 1899, and the date of these Regiments might have been antedated to these dates. The same remarks apply to the Lovat's Scouts and Scottish Horse, who were also allowed the South African honours. The Bedfordshire, Glamorganshire and Sussex Imperial Yeomanry honours were, however, not allowed to the newly raised home regiments.)

No. 46. The Westminster Yeomanry Dragoons Accepted March 16th, 1797, as Westminster Volunteer Cavalry; renewed service September 27th, 1802, but gradually dwindled and by 1826 consisted of a weak troop which dissolved itself. Accepted by the King July 18th, 1901, and gazetted July 23rd, 1901. Date from July 18th, 1901. (Official No. 47.)

(The famous London and Westminster Light Horse Volunteers are a distinct Corps from the City of London and the Westminster Yeomanry Regiments. The London and Westminster Light Horse were raised August 21st, 1779, and were accepted by the King on December 7th, 1779, and were disbanded on May 14th, 1783, when the standards of the Corps were lodged in the Tower of London. On May 8th, 1794, re-enrolled and were accepted by the King, May 12th, 1794; renewed services 1802, but were finally disbanded June 26th, 1829, and their standards for a second time lodged in the Tower. It is a matter for regret that the standards were not again unfurled on the Yeomanry reorganization after the Boer War. The claim of the Queen's Westminster Volunteers to be the representatives of the London and Westminster Light Horse, also the Westminster Volunteer (actually Yeomanry) Cavalry is, of course, quite absurd, and no person with but the weakest knowledge of military history would consider such an assumption. The London and Westminster Light Horse were far more a City of London Regiment than anything else, and their connection with Westminster was purely nominal; in fact, by far the greater number of its opulent privates lived in the Kentish suburbs towards the east or the northern parts of Middlesex. The Westminster Cavalry were on the same allowances as a Yeomanry corps, the term "Volunteer Cavalry" being the more popular in the case of urban corps than the designation 'Yeomanry Cavalry'.)

No. 47. The 3rd County of London Yeomanry Hussars (The Sharpshooters) Accepted by the King July 18th, 1901, and gazetted July 23rd, 1901. Date from July 18th, 1901. (Official No. 48.)

No. 48. The Bedfordshire Yeomanry Lancers Accepted October, 1794, but not raised until May 3rd, 1797. Renewed service October 26th, 1802, but disbanded in 1809. Re-raised August 4th, 1817, but disbanded 1828. Accepted by the King August 10th, 1901, and gazetted August 23rd, 1901. Date from August 10th, 1901. (Official No. 49.)

No. 49. The Essex Yeomanry Dragoons Accepted April 8th, 1797; renewed service October 26th, 1802, but all Essex Yeomanry troops disbanded 1828. Re-raised as West Essex February 10th, 1831. From May 12th, 1838, to 1843 served without pay, but finally disbanded in 1877. Accepted by the King October 28th, 1901, and gazetted November 8th, 1901. Date from October 28th, 1901. (Official No. 50.)

No. 50. The Northamptonshire Yeomanry Dragoons Accepted May 3rd,1794, as a regiment (commissioned May 9th, 1794); renewed services September 27th, 1802, but disbanded 1828. Re-raised as independent troops December 27th, 1830, but the last troop (the Royal Kettering) disbanded in 1873. Accepted by the King February 7th, 1902, and gazetted February 14th, 1902. Date from February 7th, 1902. (Official No. 51.)

No. 51. The East Riding Yeomanry Lancers Accepted May 3rd, 1794 (commisioned May 23rd, 1794); renewed service August 31st, 1802, but disbanded 1814. Accepted by the King April 2nd, 1902, and gazetted April 15th, 1902. Date from April 2nd, 1902. (Official No. 52.)

No. 52. The First Lovat Yeomanry Scouts Accepted by the King February 11th, 1903, as a double regiment, and gazetted February 20th, 1903. Date from February 11th, 1903. (Official No. 53.)

No. 53. The Second Lovat Yeomanry Scouts Accepted by the King February 11th, 1903 as a double regiment, and gazetted February 20th, 1903. Definitely separated from 1st Regiment April 1st, 1908. Date from February 11th, 1903. (Official No. 54.)

No. 54. The First Scottish Yeomanry Horse Accepted as Perthshrie Yeomanry Cavalry June 20th, 1798, and renewed service 1802, but were disbanded 1808. Re-raised May 13th, 1817, but disbanded 1828. Accepted by the King February 16th, 1903, and gazetted March 3rd, 1903. Date from February 16th, 1903. (Official No. 55.)

No. 55. The Second Scottish Yeomanry Horse Accepted by the King as a double regiment February 16th, 1903, and gazetted March 3rd, 1903. Date from February 16th, 1903. (Official No. 55.)

No. 56. The Third Scottish Yeomanry Horse Raised from the existing two regiments on reorganization on mobilization (peace organization of eight squadrons being reduced to two regiments of three squadrons each,

Appendix B

leaving two surplus squadrons, from which on August 26th, 1914, the Third Regiment was formed.) Date from February 16th, 1903. (**Official No. 55.**)

NOTE: The three Scottish Horse Regiments were treated as a brigade, and, being under their original Commanding Officer - Colonel the Duke of Atholl - were thus, unlike the Lovat's Scouts, not definitely separated.

No. 57. The Welch Yeomanry Horse Accepted August 15th, 1914. Raised in Southern Welsh counties, and was, on being administered by Glamorgan Territorial Force Association, given a precedence number following that of the Glamorgan Regiment of Yeomanry - i.e. No. 45 - a quite incorrect procedure.   Disbanded on demobilization in 1919. (**Official No. 44.**)

Conclusion

The following fourteen regiments were retained as cavalry. Had a correct Precedence Table been issued they would have borne the numbers given in the brackets: (and) Thus the fourteen regiments would have stood as follows:-

No	Actually Retained	No	Would have stood	Date
(5)	Royal Wiltshire	1	Pembrokeshire (Castlemartin)	22 04 94
(6)	Warwickshire	2	Royal Bucks Hussars	08 05 94
(8)	Yorkshire Hussars	3	Royal First Devon	15 05 94
(7)	Sherwood Rangers	4	West Somersetshire	03 06 94
(9)	Staffordshire	5	Royal Wiltshire	04 06 94
(11)	Shropshire	6	Warwickshire	16 07 94
(16)	Ayrshire	7	Sherwood Rangers	09 08 94
(13)	Cheshire	8	Yorkshire Hussars	13 08 94
(18)	North Somersetshire	9	Staffordshire	21 08 94
(19)	Yorkshire Dragoons	10	Derbyshire	25 08 94
(20)	Leicestershire	11	Shropshire	11 01 95
(21)	Duke of Lancaster's Own	12	Denbighshire Hussars	23 05 95
(23)	Lanarkshire	13	Cheshire	05 06 97
(24)	Northumberland Hussars	14	South Notts. Hussars	23 05 98

The following regiments would *not* have been retained (seven in number):

(16)	Ayrshire	29 05 98	(21)	D of Lancas ter's Own	23 08 19
(18)	North Somersetshire	13 08 03	(23)	Lanarkshire	02 11 19
(19)	Yorkshire Dragoons	15 08 03	(24)	Northumberland Huss	20 11 19
(20)	Leicestershire	05 09 03			

The injustice of converting the Pembrokeshire, Bucks, Royal 1st Devon, West Somerset, Derbyshire, Denbighshire, and South Notts. Regiments into units of other arms is obvious.

Appendix C

The Yeomanry, Volunteer and Volunteer Association Cavalry -
Bibliography & Spreadsheets for: 1794-1802 and 1802-1828.

UK Yeomanry Formations (1794-1967)

The French Revolution may have commenced during 1789, but it was the execution of the French King on 21 January 1793 which prompted England to sever diplomatic relations with France two days later, who in turn declared war directly their ambassador had returned home during the following eight days. These events unleashed a fervent of popular patriotism in Britain. Eventually these focused on Parliament who were prompted by Peel to pass the Volunteers Act (34 GIII c.31) on 17 April 1794. The advent of this Act led to the widespread creation of volunteer companies amongst them Troops of Yeomanry. These were created particularly to defend our coasts and the maritime counties were in the forefront these developments.

Most of the early Troops were independent although formed under the Lords Lieutenant of the various counties, who were also responsible for commissioning the officers. This commissioning of officers was no mere formality, since the issue of arms and ammunition to formations could not be authorised until it had occurred. These units also had no standard size and during the period of risk, lasting until the Battle of Trafalgar in 1805, very little consolidation took place. Where more than one Toop came together, the formation generally became known as a Corps of Yeomanry Cavalry, although this term was applied indiscriminately to single troops. Single Troops tended to lapse during any periods of inactivity, whilst others became better standardised. Regimenting generally took place where five or more troops came together.

With the French Wars concluded the need for Yeomanry was decided at the county level depending upon the internal security needs, prompted by a Government with a perennial need for economy. Leading up to both 1828 and 1838, the Government pressing for further economies, led to a range of disbandments, re-raisings and further disbandments and to less numerous but better consolidated formations.

The War Office took over the Yeomanry from the Home Office during 1856. By 1885 the various regiments were based upon establishments using three basic building blocks, with matching permanent staffs. This situation prevailed until the outbreak of the Boer War in 1899. Under the Cardwell reforms those with less than four troops were not trained at Government expense and their retention was based on the likely need for local ceremonial.

For the Boer War, the Regular Army adopted a four company battalion plan when employing the Yeomanry, that is to say the Yeomanry as such were not embodied. The Yeomanry on the Home Establishment was debarred by Statute from serving overseas, nevertheless enabling legislation was rushed through Parliament for its members to serve overseas in these specially created battalions. Thereafter a stream of volunteers very often as complete companies and regiments were released to serve. Any shortfall in professional staff was made good by the Regular Army, who ensured a proper integration in the command structure. A large number of new yeomanry regiments were raised and added their members to the Imperial field force. This latter component was not entered onto the Home Establishment until after the war was concluded.

Until The Great War the Yeomanry had fought one actual war as mounted infantry. The impasse following the failure of the German offensive largely destroyed the cavalry role. Except for the Middle East there was no largescale use for cavalry. That they could adapt to other things there was no doubt.

The aftermath saw the military becoming more artillery oriented. Since most was horse drawn, it was natural to convert the Yeomanry to this role. A more interesting development was the creation of eight Armoured Car

Appendix C

Companies under the auspices of the newly created Royal Tank Corps. Just 14 regiments remained as horse mounted soldiers.

The advent of World War II saw the Yeomanry doubling their formations by splitting existing regiments and retraining. Some were armoured and a few became especially innovative, as specialised armour employed at the D-Day landings. Others, erstwhile artillery, became expert in the anti-tank role, at a time when German armour was virtually unassailable in conventional combat. Sadly, little was done to employ their talent in the reconnaissance role!

The reformation of the Territorial Army after the World War Two enabled a small number to return to armour: The horses were now gone. The general trend however was to wear out the old equipment and the lack of modern replacements reflected Britain's reduced role east of Suez. These changes showed in the amalgamations of 1957. A further enactment of this scenario came in 1967 with the disbandment of the Territorial Army in toto. A smaller but better equipped reserve took its place, in which a small Yeomanry element was retained. The foregoing account reviews the history of the Yeomanry in a general way. Problems are encountered when getting down to the details and nowhere is this more apparent than during the early days.

It may be thought that the creation or disbandment of a Corps were clearcut historical events, unfortunately things never run so smoothly. The cycle of events usually started with a meeting, which was convened to sound local opinion and to list suitable recruits. The proposal was submitted to the Lord Lieutenant of the county, to gain acceptance. Given an acceptance it was possible for the leaders of that movement to agree amongst themselves who should become officers and if these were accepted the names went forward for Gazetting. Only at this stage was it possible for arms to be issued by the Board of Ordnance. Now until arms were issued there was no ability to train, hence mustering was impractical. Commonly the date of acceptance, either by the Lord Lieutenant or later the Sovereign is taken as the seniority date yet, as the foregoing explains, that was rather meaningless, as was the date of first commission, or even muster, since the body remained largely untrained. Similarly, disbandments were often preceeded by periods of uncertainty and a falling off in attendance, down to the point where there was no effective Corps was in being and only rarely were the necessary preliminaries followed leading to a formal disbandment.

At this range, the absence of a date of one sort and the other cannot stop the creation of a record, so in reading contemporary papers the most appropriate date is selected. During periods of National economy, stratagems of serving for no pay, standing down or continuing service 'on foot' were added nuances which blurr distinction and unless such dates can be found in official records they are disregarded although noted. Notwithstanding these considerations there are still a number of records which are incomplete and readers having useful information are asked to put this on the record.

The following list of counties indicates whether a Yeomanry Unit is known to exist and there follows a two part scheme of spreadsheeting, covering the date spans: 1794 - 1802 and 1802 - 1828. Two further appendices trace the story to the disbandment of the Territorial Army and the development of the Territorial and Army Volunteer Reserve.

England   **County**
Bedfordshire
Berkshire
Buckinghamshire
Cambridgeshire & Isle of Ely
Cheshire
Cornwall
Cumberland

Appendix C

Derbyshire
Devonshire
Dorsetshire
Durham County
Essex
Gloucestershire
Hampshire & Isle of Wight
Herefordshire
Hertfordshire
Huntingdonshire & Peterborough
Kent
Lancashire
Leicestershire
Lincolnshire
London
Norfolkshire
Northamptonshire
Northumberland
Nottinghamshire
Oxfordshire
Rutland
Shropshire
Somerset
Staffordshire
Suffolk, East & West
Surrey
Sussex, East & West
Warwickshire
Westmorland
Wiltshire
Worcestershire
Yorkshire Ridings
    East
    North
    West

Ireland

(Irish Horse)
(North Irish Horse)
(South Irish Horse)

Isle of Man

Wales

Angelsey	See Denbigh
Brecknockshire	No records
Caernarvonshire	See Denbigh
Cardiganshire	See Pembroke
Carmarthenshire	
Denbighshire	
Flintshire	
Glamorganshire	
Merionethshire	No records

	Monmouthshire	
	Montgomeryshire	
	Pembrokeshire	
	Radnorshire	No records
	Wales	See Montgomery
Scotland	Aberdeenshire	
	Angus	
	Argyllshire	See Perth
	Ayrshire	
	Banffshire	No records
	Berwickshire	
	Buteshire	No records
	Caithness	See Inverness
	Clackmannanshire	
	Dumbartonshire	
	Dumfriesshire	
	East Lothian	
	Fifeshire	
	Glasgow	See Lanark
	Invernessshire	
	Kincardineshire	No records
	Kinrossshire	
	Lanarkshire	
	Midlothian	
	Moray	See Inverness & Perth
	Nairnshire	See Perth
	Orkney	See Inverness
	Peeblesshire	
	Perthshire	
	Renfrewshire	
	Ross & Cromarty	See Inverness
	Roxburghshire	
	Selkirkshire	
	Stirlingshire	
	Sutherlandshire	See Inverness
	West Lothian	
	Wigtownshire	
	Zetland	See Inverness

To illustrate the creation, development and later curtailment of the numerous Corps of Volunteer and Yeomanry Cavalry two "Spreadsheets" have been created where each independent Corps is shown, line by line, starting where possible with an 'Acceptance' date or other date co-incident with its formation, such as the date of the first officer commissioned. Using the scheme of coding marks shown below, these data have been concentrated onto a minimum number of sheets. Chart layout follows a simple alphabetical listing by counties, with the surviving Corps heading those from which they derive. The Lothians are shown as such and divided into Mid, East and West respectively, similarly Yorkshire is divided into Ridings. Man and Wight are shown as 'Isles of'. The position in the chart provides no indication of precedence. Also, to accommodate the data, the names of Corps are necessarily trancated. The supporting bibliography appears as part of Appendix C, with two spreadsheets for 1794-1802 and 1802-1828.

Appendix C

Line Entries To illustrate the creation, development and later curtailment of the numerous Corps of Volunteer and Yeomanry Cavalry two 'Spreadsheets' have been used, starting where possible with an 'Acceptance' date. A spreadsheet is effectively a infinitely large graph paper, able to accommodate the variety of data mentioned below. Using the scheme of coding marks, these have been concentrated onto the following sheets. Layout follows a simple alphabetical listing of counties, with surviving Corps heading those from which they derive.

Date Panel Where an Acceptance date by the Lord Lieutenant or the Sovereign is available this is first shown. In its absence, the date of first officer commissioned is noted, failing which dates are taken from history books, Newspapers and other comtemporary records. Aside from getting a confident lead on the year of formation, no great importance is attached to the dates as such.

Spreadsheet Coding Marks

A	a	Amalgamation
C	c	Cadre/converted
D	d	Disbandment/one inferred
F	f	Formed
L	l	Lapsed or lapsing inferred
M	-	Maintained
N	-	Service at No Pay
R	r	Regimented or semi-regtd
S	s	Secession
No		Troops
Date	(date)	Definitive date or surmise
*	?	See manuscript/ uncertain

Year Cells Simple numbers are used to indicate the number of Troops in a Corps. Regimentation and amalgamations are shown by a new entry with as 'R' and 'A' set immediately above a group of Corps, shown 'a', forming the amalgamation. The reforming of Corps, a common occurrence following the 1828 economies is shown by 'r'. Disbandments and Lapsing appear as 'D' and 'L' and 'd' or 'l' when inferred. An 's' is used for any portion of a Corps seceding.   It is necessary to scan a column to establish relationships. During 1828 and 1838 Corps were differentiated as paid, maintained or serving for no pay or allowances, indicated as 'P', 'M' and 'N'. Over the period 1801-1803 there are few records of disbandment yet a long line of acceptances!

Generalities The period 1794-1802 is the most confused because 70 boxes of the Official records possibly remain unsorted, although archived in the Public Records Office at Kew. The 'Associations' figure in the Yeomanry and Volunteer Lists for 1799 and 1800. The watershed for the Yeomanry was the Peace of Amiens, commencing 27th March 1802 which required the Continuation Act of 22nd June 1802 to set the clock going again. Theoretically from 1802 all the information is in the Public domain.

Bibliography The authority for these entries has been obtained from the following sources. These are arranged by Counties, following the pattern established by AS White in Bibliography of Regimental Histories of the British Army, (SAHR and Army Museums, Ogilby Trust. 1965) with suitable additions.

Ayr Benson Freeman, Engineer Commander RN. No. 6 The Cummingham and Cumnock Yeomanry Cavalry, 1817-1828. (War Office Library, London)
Steel Brownlie, Maj.W. Proud Trooper, The Ayrshire Yeomanry.   (Collins, 1964, London)

Bedford Benson Freeman, Engineer Commander RN. Some Notes on the Bedfordshire Lancers. (Bedford Times 12th Feb-20th Aug, 1926)

Berkshire Tylden, Maj. G. The Yeomanry in Berkshire. (SASHR Vol 28 pp96-101. 1950)
Benson Freeman edited A French. the Eastern Berkshire Yeomanry Cavalry. Extracts from Reading Mercury.
Pearsblake Maj JB. The Berkshire Yeomanry, An interesting resume of its history, status and work. The Whitehall Review

Appendix C

Berwick Benson Freeman, Engineer Commander RN. No. 1 The Berwickshire Yeomanry, 1797-1828. (Kelso Mail, 1906). See also 19th Armoured Car Company

Buckingham Swann, Maj-Gen. JC. The Citizen soldiers of Buckinghamshire, 1795-1926. pp16-30. (Hazell, Watson and Viney, London)
Beckett, IFW. The Local Community and the Amatuer Military Tradition: A Case Study of Victorian Buckinghamshire. (SAHR, Summer and Autumn, 1981)

Carnarvon North Wales Yeomanry Cavalry. Peter Longworth, private communication.

Cheshire Leary, F. The Earl of Chester's Regt of Yeomanry Cavalry. (Ballantyne, Edinburgh, 1898)
Benson Freeman, Engineer Commander RN. Forgotten Cheshire Regiments. (The Cheshire sheaf, 3rd Series, Vol 6. Dec, 1906)
Benson Freeman, Engineer Commander RN. No. 19 The Prince Regent's South Cheshire Yeomanry Cavalry. (W O Library, London (see C Sheaf)
Benson Freeman, Engineer Commander RN. No. 20 The Western Cheshire Yeomanry Cavalry. (War Office Library, London (see C Sheaf)
Yeomanry Corps of Cheshire. Peter Longworth, private communication.

Cornwall The Yeomanry of Cornwall. See Devon.
Cornish Yeomanry Corps. Peter Longworth, private communication.

Cumberland May, RK. The Cumberland Rangers. (SAHR Com 1328, Vol 69, 280, Autumn 1991)

Denbigh Benson Freeman, Engineer Commander RN. Historical Records of the Denbighshire Imperial Yeomanry, from their formation in 1795 till 1906, with a note on the Flintshire, Royal Maylor and Carnarvonshire Yeomanry Corps. (Woodall, Minshall and Thomas, Wrexham 1909)
North Wales Yeomanry Cavalry. Peter Longworth, private communication.

Derby Colville, Lt-Col CR. A Record of the Volunteer Cavalry of Derbyshire, 1794-1864. (Bemrose, London. 1868,)

Devon Benson Freeman, Engineer Commander RN. Edited Earl Fortescue. The Yeomanry of Devon, 1794-1927. (St Catherine Press, London 1927)
The Yeomanry Corps of Devon. Peter Longworth, private communication.

Dorset Glyn, Maj RH. A Short Account of the Q's O Dorset Yeo. (Q'sODY Old Comrades Association. H Ling, Dorchester 1948)
Thompson, CW. Records of the Dorset Yeo (Q's O). (Dorset County Chronicle, Dorchester. 1894)

East Lothian see Midlothian

Essex Burrows, JW. (In association with) The Essex Yeomanry. (TA Assn, Southend-on-Sea, 1925)
Lennard, TB. Barstable & Chafford Tp of Vol Cav (1798). (Essex Review, pp64-75, Vol XXII, 1913)
Cranmer-Byng, JL. Essex Prepares for Invasion, 1796-1805. (Essex Review, pp127-134, Vol LX, 1951 and pp43-47, 57-74 Vol LXI, 1952)
The Yeomanry of Essex. WY Carman. Draft data sheet.
Private communication Lt-Commdr Keith Hook.

Fife Burgoyne, Capt G. The Fife and Forfar Imperial Yeomanry and its Predecessors. (JG Innes, Fife Herald and Journal, Cupar, Fife. 1904)
Sellar, RJB. By F & Ff Y Assn. The Fife and Forfar Yeomanry, 1919-1956. (W Blackwood, Edinburgh and London 1960)
Ogilvie, Maj. DD. The Fife and Forfar Yeomanry, 1914-1919. (J Murray, London 1921)

Flint North Wales Yeomanry and Cavalry Corps. Peter Longworth, private communication.

Forfar see Fife

Glasgow see Lanark

Gloucester Morgan, ET. A Brief History of the Bristol Vols. (Bristol Times and Mirror, Bristol 1908)
Austin, R. Early Years of the Royal Gloucester Yeomanry Cavalry (Titus Wilson, Kendal, no date)
Quin, WHW. The Yeo Cav of Gloucestershire and Monmouth. (Westlery's Library, Cheltenham, 1898)

Hampshire Benson Freeman, Engineer Commander RN. Historical Records of the Hampshire Yeomanry Regiments. (Published serially in the the Hampshire Chronicle from July, 1923)

Hertford Griffith, Maj ALP. A Brief Record of the Hertford Yeomanry Cavalry and Hertford Artillery. (G Reasy, Hertford, 1927)

Invernessshire Melville, Maj ML Story of the Lovat Scouts, 1900-1980. (The St Andrew Press, Edinburgh, 1981)
Barlow, L and Smith, RJ. The Uniforms of the British Yeomanry force, 1794-1914: No.8 Lovat Scouts. (Robert Ogilby Trust. Spelmount, Tunbridge Wells, 1985)

Ireland see Appendix H

Kent Harris, Col Lord. A Century of Yeoman Service. (The Kentish Express, Ashford, 1899)
Edmeades, Lt-Col. JF. His. Records of the W Kent (Q's O) Yeo, 1794-1909. (A Melrose, London 1909)

Lanark The Queen's Own Royal Glasgow Yeomanry, 1848-1948. R Maclehose, privately 1949
Wood, RE. The Lanarkshire Yeomanry, 1819-1910. (No imprint, Edinburgh, 1910)

Lancashire Lancashire's Part-Time Soldiers, 1690-1890. Borough of Blackburn. No date
Barlow, L and Smith, RJ. The Uniforms of the British Yeomanry force, 1794-1914: No.6 The Duke of Lancaster's Own Yeomanry. (Robert Ogilby Trust. Spelmount, Tnbridge Wells, 1983)
Fell, A. A Furness Chronicle. (Kitchin, Ulverston, 1937)
Hargreaves, Col. P and Benson Freeman, Engr Comdr RN. Old Time Yeomanry: The Manchester Corps. (Published serially in the Chester courant from Mar 2nd, 1910. Last article in series missing.)

Leicester Codrington, Col Sir G. (printed privately) An Outline of the History of the Leicestershire (Prince Albert's Own) Yeomanry. (Eyre and Spottiswood, Chiswick Press, 1955.)
Codrington, Col. GR. Yeomanry Cavalry. (SAHR Vol IX, pp 134-142, 1930)

London Barlow, L and Smith, RJ. The Unifroms of the British Yeomanry Force, 1794-1914: No.5 3rd County of London (Sharpshooters). (Robert Ogilby Trust. Spelmount, Tunbridge Wells, 1983)

Isle of Man Benson Freeman, Engr Comdr RN. No.12 Manx Yeo. Cav. (Manx Sun and WO Library, London)

Sargent, BE. A Military History of the Isle of Man. (T Buncle, Arbroath, 1947)

Middlesex Stonham, CS and Benson Freeman, Engineer Commander RN. Edited by JS Judd. Historical Records of the Middlesex Yeomanry, 1797-1927. (published by Regimental Committee, Chelsea, 1930)
Stonham, CS and Benson Freeman, Engineer Commander RN. No.34 The Loyal Middlesex Light Horse Yeomanry Cavalry. (War Office. Library, London.)

Midlothian Marshall, Maj JR. Outline of the Regimental History of the 19th (Lothians and Border Horse Armoured Car Company). (T Allan, Edinburgh, 1928)

Monmouth (See also Gloucester) Benson Freeman, Engineer Commander RN. No.18 The loyal Monmouthshire Yeomanry Cavalry. (War Office Library, London 1927)

Montgomery Williams, Lt-Col RW Wynn and Benson Freeman, Engr Comdr RN. His. Records of the Yeo. and Vols of Montgomeryshire, 1803-1908. (Woodall, Minsell, Thomas, Oswestry, 1909)

Norfolk Harvey, Lt-Col JR . The Records of the Yeomanry Cavalry of Norfolk. (Jarrold, London , 1908)
Bastin J. The Norfolk Yeomanry in Peace and War - 1782-1961. The Iceni Press, Fakenham, 1986.

Northumberland Pease, H. His. of the N'berland (Huss) Yeo, 1819-1919. (Constable, London 1924)

Nottingham Fellows, Maj. G and Benson Freeman, Engineer Commander RN. Historical Records of the South Nottinghamshire Hussars, 1794-1924. (Gale and Polden Aldershot, 1928)
Barbour, Lt-Col DC. A Short History of the Sherwood Rangers, 1794-1953. (Sissons, Worksop, 1953)

Oxford Keith-Falconer, A. Oxfordshire Hussars in the Great War, 1914-1918. (J Murray, London, 1927)

Peebles Benson Freeman, Engr Comdr RN. No.2 The Peebleshire Yeomanry Cavalry. (Kelso Mail, 1906)

Pembroke Meyrick, Sir TF and Howell, RL. History of the Pembroke Yeomanry. (Also earlier work by Col FC Meyrick) published by the Regiment, Haverfordwest, 1959)

Perth Edited by the Marchioness of Tullibardine. A Military History of Perthshire 1660-1902. The Perthshire Yeomanry 1794-1902. (R and J Hay, Perth, 1908)
Edited by Marchioness of Tullibardine. Mil. history of Perthshire, 1899-1902. (R and J Hay, Perth, 1908)
Barlow, L and Smith, RJ. Uniforms of the British Yeomanry Force, 1794-1914: No.8 The Scottish Horse. (Robert Ogilby Trust, Spelmount, Tunbridge Wells, 1985)

Ross and Cromarty see Inverness

Roxburgh Benson Freeman, Engineer Commander RN. No.3 The Roxburghshire Light Dragoons Yeomanry Cavalry, 1797-1828. (Kelso Mail, 1906)

Rutland see Leicestershire

Selkirk Benson Freeman, Engineer Commander RN. No.4 Selkirkshire Light Dragoons Yeomanry Cavalry, 1797-1828. (Kelso Mail 1906)

Shropshire (Salop) Gladstone, EW. The Shrops Yeo, 1795-1945. (The Whitethorn Press, Bristol, 1953)
Shropshire Yeomanry Cavalry Corps. Peter Longworth, private communication.

Somerset Morgan, ET. A Brief History of the Bristol Volunteer. (Bristol Times and Mirror, Bristol, 1908)
Fisher, WG . A History of the Someset Yeomanry, Volunteer and Territorial Units. (Goodman, Taunton, 1924)
Barlow, L and Smith, RJ The Uniforms of the British Yeomanry force 1794-1914: No.2 North Somerset Yeomanry. (Robert Ogilby Trust. Spelmount, Tunbridge Wells)

Stafford Webster, PCG. Records of Q's O R Regt of Staffs Yeo. (Longmans Green, London 1870)

Stirling Mileham, Maj PJR. The Stirlingshire Yeomanry Cavalry and the Scottish Radical Disturbances of April 1820. (SAHR, Vol LXIII, p 21-30, Spring 1985 and pp 104-112, Summer.)

Suffolk See Norfolk, Chapter IX, pp325-332 Harvey.

Surrey Harrison-Ainsworth, ED. His. & Records of the Surrey (QMR) Yeo. (CF Layton, London 1928)

Sussex Madden, Capt CH .The Volunteer Forces of Sussex. (Sussex Co Magazine, pp 539-543, Vol 13)
Hudson, A. Volunteer Soldiers in Sussex During the Revolutionary and Napoleonic Wars, 1793-1815. (Sussex Archeological Collections, pp 161-181, 122, 1984)
Barlow, L and Smith, RJ. The Uniforms of the British Yeomanry force, 1794-1914: No.1 The Sussex Yeomanry. (The Robert Ogilby Trust, Spelmount, Tunbridge Wells.)

Warwick Barlow, L and Smith, RJ. The Uniforms of the British Yeomanry force, 1794-1914: No.9 Warwickshire and Worcestershire Yeomanry. (Spelmount, Tunbridge Wells)

Westmorland Barlow, L and Smith, RJ. The Uniforms of the British Yeomanry Force, 1794-1914: No.4 Westmorland and Cumberland Yeomanry. (Robert Ogilby Trust. Spelmount, Tunbridge Wells)

Wiltshire Graham, H . Annuls of the Yeo. Cavalry of Wiltshire, 1794-1884. (Marples, Liverpool, 1886)
Wiltshire Yeomanry and Cavalry Corps. Peter Longworth, private communication.

Worcester QL, Privately printed. The Yeo. Cavalry of Worcs, 1794-1913. (G Simpson, Devizes, 1914)
The Uniforms of the British Yeomanry force, 1794-1914: No.9 The Warwickshire and Worcestershire Yeomanry. (The Robert Ogilby Trust. Spelmount, Tunbridge Wells)
Worcestershire Yeomanry and Cavalry Corps. Peter Longworth, private communication.

Yorkshire: North Riding An alphabetical List of the Officers of the Yorkshire Hussars from the formation of the Regiment to the Present time. HS Smith. Simpkin, Marshall, London, 1853
Barlow, L and Smith, RJ. The Uniforms of the British Yeomanry force, 1794-1914: No.3 The Yorkshire Hussars. Robert Ogilby Trust. Spelmount, Tunbridge Wells,

Yorkshire: West Riding Barlow, L and Smith, RJ. The Uniforms of the British Yeomanry Force, 1794-1914: No.7 The Yorkshire Dragoons. (Robert Ogilby Trust. Spelmount, Yunbridge Wells)

General Works with Yeomanry etc references
Frederick, Dr JBM . Lineage Book of British Land Forces, 1660-1978. (Microform Academic Publishers, Wakefield, 1984)
Mileham, Maj PJR . The Yeomanry Regiments: A Pictorial History. (Spelmount, Tunbridge Wells, 1985)
Marquess of Cambridge. The Volunteer Army of Great Britain in the Year 1806: The James Willson Chart. (SAHR, Vol XXXI, pp 113-126 and 163-174.)

Appendix C

White, AS. A Bibliography of Regimental Histories of the British Army. Section IV, Auxilliary Forces, Yeomanry pp 161-178. (SAHR and Robert Ogilby Trust, London, 1965)

Yeomanry and Volunteer Cavalry Returns - Parliamentary Session Papers

The sessional papers are bound together in successive volumes, in which each page is given a handwritten folio number. These numbers are in distinction to those which are usually printed on the individual papers circulated for Member's use, which only afterwards are brought together to form the volumes concerned.

Volunteer and Yeomanry Lists

28 07 94	23 04 99	01 10 04	30 09 20
14 05 95	21 04 00	14 10 05	20 09 25
10 07 96	01 06 01	31 03 07	00 01 37
22 06 97	15 07 03	31 07 17	00 04 50

Year	Vol	Pages	Subject
	XLV	910	Return of Yeomanry Cavalry and Volunteer Cavalry
	XI	1-65	Abstract of Volunteer and Yeomanry Corps Accepted by H M
		209-249	Accounts of Corps on Permanent Pay and Duty
1806	X	1-101	Returns of Volunteer Corps of Cavalry, Infantry and Artillery
1810	XIII	351	1797
1812	IX	209-218	1803-4
1817	XIII	225-228	Return of the Yeomanry and Volunteer Cavalry in Great Britain
1821	XV	131	Establishment and Effective Strengths of Corps of Yeo and Vols
1822	XIX	277	Sums Which Have Been Issued On Account of Corps of Yeo Cav
1828	XVII	251	Manner of How £153,148 was Expended for Volunteer Corps (1827), Corps to be Maintained for £66,212
		283-287	Dates of Call-outs for Actual Service During Last 10 Years
1829	XVI	178-183	Expense of Vol and Yeo Corps Aaiding Civil Power (1816-1829)
1831-2	XXVII	123	Return of Volunteers of All Ranks
		451-3	Return Stating Date when Corps of Yeomanry First Embodied
1834	XLII	89-91	Return of Number of Tps, Officers and Men and Expense in 1833
		97	Sums Voted and Expended by Yeo and Vol Corps (1816-1834)
1835	XXXVIII	153-4	1834, Corps, Troops, Numbers and Expense of the Yeomanry
1836	XXXVIII	131-3	1835, ditto
1837-8	XXXVII	163-5	1836, ditto
		167-9	1837, ditto
		171-4	Reduction and Retention of Yeom,anry Corps, 1827 versus 1838
1839	XXXI	309	1838, Corps, Troops, Numbers and Expense of Yeomanry
1842	XXVII	264-5	1840 and 1841, ditto
1843	XXXI	171	Abstract of Expense of Yeomanry 1816-1842
		175-7	1842, Corps, Tps, Numbers, Expense New Tps and Return to Pay
1844	XXXIII	217	Costs for Yeo Corps Noted in Aid to the Civil Power 1840-1-2
1847	XXXVI	81-6	1842-6, Corps, Troops, Numbers and Expense of Yeomanry
1847-8	XLi	87	1829, 1835, 1840 1847, Numbers of Officers and Men in Yeo
1850	XXXV	128-139	1843-4 till 1848-9, Corps, Numbers Assembled, Duty Days Including Aid to Civil Power

County	Formed	Volunteer or Yeomanry Corps	1794	1795	1796	1797	1798	1799	1800	1801	1802
Ayr	19 07 97	Carrick & 1st Regiment				1					
Bedford	03 05 97	Bedfordshire/Odell				2		1			
	15 05 98	Loyal Warden Troop					1				
	15 05 98	Ampthill					1		d		
	12 05 98	Bedford Association					1				
	15 06 98	Luton & Dunstable Association					1				
Berkshire	20 04 94	Abingdon	1								
	28 07 98	Wickham									
	23 04 98	Newbury Assn (Donnington)					1				
	01 06 98	Hungerford Assn.	1								
	30 09 00	Windsor					1				
	21 03 00	Loyal Wargrave Rangers					1				
	11 05 98	Woodley with Reading					2	1			
	24 05 98	Thatcham Assn					1				
	00 06 98	Maidenhead United Cav Assn					1				
	03 07 94	Reading	1								
Berwick	23 05 94	Berwickshire YC				2				3	
Bucks	08 05 94	Buckinghamshire Armed Y	5			6					
	20 05 98	Aylesford					1				
	28 08 98	Winslow					1				
	13 05 95	Fenny Stratford		1							
	29 08 98	Eton (Dismounted)							1		
Cambridge	14 11 96	Uxbridge (07 04 97)			1						
	20 08 98	Loyal Whittlesey Assn.	2								
Carmarthen	31 05 94	Carmarthen	2								
Carnarvon	21 01 95	Carnarvon		1						D	
Cheshire	05 06 97	Macclesfield				1					
	07 07 98	Nether Knutsford Assn.				1					
	17 01 97	Chester				3					
	24 05 98	Stockport					1				
Cinque Ports	23 03 94	Cinque Ports	1								
	04 06 94	Lydd	1								
Cornwall	09 06 94	Launceston G & Y	1								
	16 04 97	Falmouth G & Y				1					
	04 10 97	Cornwall G & Y (Eliot & Carew)					2				
	30 05 98	Helston G & Y					1				
	07 09 97	Penryn Cavalry Assn				1	(05 07 98?)				
	01 10 01	Penwith Y Lt Dgns. (Cam. & Illogan)								1	
	07 09 97	Trelawney Coldrennick				1					
Cumberland	16 10 98	Eskdale Five Kirks					1				
	25 10 98	Cumberland					1				
	15 10 01	Penrith								1	
Denbigh	23 05 95	Wrexham		1							
	04 07 99	Denbigh Assn.						1	a		
	11 11 00	Denbigh Legion/Foresters							R		
Derby	25 08 94	Derby Regiment	3	5							
Devon	28 02 01	First Devon								R	R
	15 05 94	First Devon Pynes	1		2					a	
	20 06 98	Devonshire									
	06 04 97	Portsdown									
	18 10 98	Bere Forest Rangers									
	1797	Crediton Volunteer Cavalry					1			a	
	11 04 97	Tiverton Volunteer Cavalry					1			a	
	23 05 98	Exmouth/Woodbury					1		2	a	
	08 06 98	Cullumpton Assn. (VC 18 06 00)					1			a	
	07 07 98	Exeter Assn. (YC 04 02 01)					1				a
	27 11 00	Bicton								1	a
	23 05 98	Jame later Bideford Assn						1			
	29 04 98	Barnstable Association						1			

County	Formed	Volunteer or Yeomanry Corps	1794	1795	1796	1797	1798	1799	1800	1801	1802
	28 08 01	Hemyock 2nd								a	
	14 12 96	R E Devon			R					5	6
	13 07 01	Hemyock								a	
	21 07 94	Axminster	1		2a						
	20 06 98	Plympton					1				
	20 06 98	Teignmouth					1				
	18 06 98	Chudleigh Assn					1				
	18 06 98	Plymouth Dock Assn. (D'port)					1				
	30 07 98	Plymouth Assn.					1				
	11 08 01	Ippleden (S D YC)					?			1	
Dorset	29 03 94	Volunteer Dorset Rangers	6			7	9				
Dunbarton	21 07 98	Dumbarton					2				
Dumfries	14 10 98	Dumfriesshire Y C					1				
Durham	07 07 95	Mr Methokl of Durham		1							
	05 06 98	Ryton					1				
	29 05 98	Staindrop					1				
	28 05 98	North Durham					1				
	28 05 98	Usworth Legion					1				
	14 06 98	Axwell Assn.					1				
	22 01 99	Darlington						1			
	16 03 99	Durham Assn. (YC 11 09 01)						1		1	
	28 07 98	Gibside Assn					1				
	05 07 98	Bishopwearmouth Assn					1				
	17 03 97	Easington Ward Assn.				1					
E Lothian	07 05 97	E Lothian (Haddington)				3					
Essex	24 05 98	2nd E Essex or Kelvedon					1				
	08 04 97	1st Essex Tp later Sqn				1					
	21 02 98	2nd Essex Chelmesford					1				
	05 04 98	3rd Essex Tp					1				
	14 02 98	4th Essex Tp					1				
	00 05 98	5th L Essex Harlow					1				
	07 06 98	Aveley Assn (later pt of Barstable)									
	25 04 97	West Essex				1					
	20 06 98	Harlow					1				
	20 05 98	Stebbing					1			D	
	29 05 98	Halstead Assn.					1				
	26 06 98	Hatfield Peverill					1				
	03 04 00	Epping Forest							1		
	31 05 98	Tendring					1			D	
	29 05 98	C Hedingham/Hinckford Assn.								D	
	06 09 98	Waltham					1				
	20 05 98	Haverhill					1			D	
	20 06 98	Havering /Bar & Chafford					1				
	18 05 98	Barstable & Chafford					1				
	20 06 98	Chelmesford 2nd E Tp?					1	1			
	31 05 98	Uttlesford & Clavering					1			D	
	25 04 97	W Essex									
	1798	Saling					1				
Fife	17 06 97	Kirkaldy				1	a				
	29 07 97	Fifeshire YC				1	R				
	06 03 98	Fifeshire (R Northern) YC				1	a				
	16 05 98	F'shire E District					a				
	20 03 97	F'shire W District				1	a				
	14 04 98	Strath Eden					a				
Flint	26 07 97	Mold				1					
Forfar	15 12 94	Forfar	2	3a							
	1794	Meigle YC	1	a							
Glamorgan		Glamorgan East					2				
	08 04 97	Swansea VC (Legion 13 08 00)					1				

County	Formed	Volunteer or Yeomanry Corps	1794	1795	1796	1797	1798	1799	1800	1801	1802
	27 06 98	Cardiff						1			
	26 04 97	Neath				1					
	07 06 98	Fairwood				1		1			
Gloucester	30 07 95	Cheltenham		1	r		a				
	26 10 96	R Gloucester Hussars			R		a				
	01 10 95	Minchin Hampton		1	a						
	10 03 97	Gloucester				1	R				
	1795	Wootton under Edge		1	a						
	01 02 97	Cotswold				1	a				
	01 11 97	Bristol 1st				1	d				
	01 11 97	Bristol 2nd				1					
	01 04 97	Henbury				1					
	24 05 98	Longtree Bisley Whitstone					1				
	11 07 98	Northwick					1				
	11 07 98	Dursley					1				
Hampshire	31 05 94	N Hants (Basingstoke)	1	3				1			
	25 07 98	Bramdean Assn.									
	00 03 97	Fawley Light Dragoons				1					
	31 05 98	Fordingbridge						1			
	12 05 98	Ringwood						1			
	05 06 94	S Hants (Christchurch)	1				2				
	10 05 96	Alton & Petersfield				1					
	28 04 95	SE Hants (Portsdown)		1			2				
	02 03 97	Southampton				1					
	05 06 94	New Forest VC (Rangers 1797)	2								
	18 10 98	Bere Forest						1			
	31 05 94	Basingstoke Mr Lefevre					2				
Hereford	08 08 94	Hereford	2								
	15 03 98	Leominster Assn.						1			
Hertford	08 06 94	Hartford	5				6				
	10 05 98	Hertford VC					1				
	17 05 98	Beechwood					1				
	00 12 97	Horse Artillery				1					
	21 06 94	Hertfordshire Eastern	1								
	21 06 01	Hertfordshire Southern								1	
	21 06 94	Hertfordshire Western	1								
	21 06 94	Hertfordshire Northern	1								
	21 06 94	Hertfordshire Midland or Centre	1								
	19 07 98	Caistor or Castor					1				
	28 05 98	Sawbridgeworth Assn					1				
	17 05 98	Hertfordshire					1				
	24 05 98	St Albans					1				
Huntingdon	17 04 94	Huntingdon	1				2				
	16 03 97	Erpington & Eynsford					1				
Kent	23 03 97	East Kent				r					
	19 04 94	Nonington	1			2					
	23 03 94	Walmer & Deal (Cinque Ports)	1								
	19 04 94	Wingham East & West	1								
	24 05 98	Denton					1				
	17 08 94	Rolvenden				1					
	19 04 94	Provender	1			2	3	1			
	13 07 94	Thanet Isle of	1								
	00 06 94	Blenhooth	1								
	13 06 98	Woolwich Assn. (VC 24 09 01)					1			a	
	19 06 00	Blackheath							1	R	
	23 02 97	2nd Nonington (Bridgehill)				1					
	17 06 94	Coxheath	1		2	a					
	12 04 96	Evington later Elham	1								
	23 02 97	Barham Downs					1				

County	Formed	Volunteer or Yeomanry Corps	1794	1795	1796	1797	1798	1799	1800	1801	1802
	07 04 97	West Kent				R					
	16 04 94	Sevenoaks	1			a					
	16 04 94	Tonbridge	1			a					
	16 04 94	Farningham	1			a					
	16 04 94	Cobham E	1			a					
	10 02 97	Cobham W				a					
	05 06 98	Sheppey I of Assn. (Mr Shove)						1	2		
	16 04 94	Chislehurst	1			a					
	07 06 94	Tunbridge Wells & Deptford	1								
	26 05 98	Deptford Assn.						1			
	16 04 94	Evington	1			a					
	29 08 98	Peckham							1		
	1798	Kent Guides						1			
Lanark	20 03 97	Glasgow Lt H (Lower Ward)				1					D
	1799	R Glasgow YC						1			
Lancashire	23 03 97	Liverpool Light Horse				1					
	06 06 98	Loyal Blackburn Assn.						1			
	12 07 98	Atherton Assn.						1			
	05 04 98	Bolton						2			
	11 05 97	Manchester & Salford					3	6			
	02 06 98	Ashton in Makerfield Assn.						1			
	00 05 98	Manchester Light Horse						1			
	27 06 98	Oldham Assn.						1			
Leicester	01 05 94	Leicestershire Lt Horse	R								
	25 07 98	Ashby-de-la-Zouch Assn.						1			
	11 07 98	Lutterworth						1			
Lincoln	05 06 94	Lincoln Lt Horse Rangers	2								
	09 07 94	Holland	1								
	06 06 98	Gainsborough						1	1		
	11 07 98	Market Raisen							1		
	09 07 94	Spalding & Long Sutton (Scrope)	2								
	23 07 94	Sir J Trollope	1								
	29 07 94	Lovedon & Grantham					1				
	03 06 95	S Holland tp							1		
	30 05 99	Louth or Ardee Cavalry					1				
	00 01 97	Boston									
Linlithgow	08 03 97	Linlithgow Kirtlesdown					1				
London	16 03 97	Westminster VC					1				
	26 04 98	Islington (L London) Assn. (Y 14 05 01)						1			
	12 05 94	London & Westminster Lt Horse	6								
Man Isle of	1793 !!	Constitutional Dragoons	1		D		a				
	1796	Manx Yeomanry Cavalry N			1			a			
	late 1798	Manx Yeomanry Cavalry S					r	a			
	17 01 99	Manx G & Yeomanry C						R			
Middlesex	29 05 98	Middx Lt H (Hackney)					1				
	14 08 98	Clerkenwell Assn. (to London later)					1				*
	17 05 98	Twickenham					1				
	12 05 97	Uxbridge					1	2			
Midlothian	15 06 97	R Midlothian					1		3		
	10 12 97	Edinburgh					2		a		
	10 12 97	Midlothian VC					1				
Monmouth	13 07 98	Loyal Monmouth						1			
	29 05 98	Chepstow						1			
Norfolk	29 09 94	Norfolk Rangers (Sep 1783)	1								
	19 07 98	Freebridge & Smithdon						1			
	22 06 98	Swaffham Assn.						1			
	22 06 98	E Dereham Assn.						1			
	05 06 94	2nd or Mid (Clackclose)	1								
	31 05 94	3rd or E (Higham)									

County	Formed	Volunteer or Yeomanry Corps	1794	1795	1796	1797	1798	1799	1800	1801	1802
	19 07 98	Freebridge Lynn						1			
	19 07 98	Attleburgh						1			
	18 03 95	Blofield & Walsingham		1							
	09 12 94	Loddon & Clavering	1								
	19 07 98	Holkham					2				
	23 03 97	Norwich Lt Horse				1					
	17 04 95	Tunsted & Happing		1							
	20 06 98	Yarmouth					1				
	30 10 94	1st E Dereham	1								
	19 07 98	Shropham & Guiltcross					1				
	04 03 97	S Erpingham & Eynsford				1					
Northampton	03 05 94	Northampton	R								
	25 08 98	Wallington						1			
	19 04 98	Northampton County					1				
	13 06 98	Wellingborough Assn.					1				
	20 07 98	Thrapston Assn.					1				
Nothumberland	04 07 98	Northumberland					1				
	25 07 98	Percy Tenantry					1				
	23 02 97	Newcastle-upon-Tyne Assn.					1				
	19 03 99	Cheviot Legion						1			
	22 08 98	Hexham Assn.									
	20 08 98	Bywell Assn.									
	11 09 98	Glendale Mr carr					1				
	00 05 98	N Shields						1			
Nottingham	15 08 94	Sherwood Rangers	R				7				
	09 08 94	Retford, Rufford, Clumber	a								
	09 08 94	Mansfield	a								
	09 08 94	Newark	a								
	09 08 94	Nottingham	a								
	23 05 98	1st Holme Pierrepoint					a				
	23 05 98	Bingham					a				
	22 04 98	Bunny Park					a				
Oxford	24 06 98	Worksop Assn.					1				
	09 06 98	Watlington					1				
	20 06 98	Buckland & Shrivenham									
	21 07 98	Bullington, Dor'r & Thame					1				
	26 07 98	Oxford (Wootton)					1				
	27 09 98	Bloxham & Banbury					1				
	20 06 98	Buckland & Shrivenham					1				
Pembroke	22 04 94	Castlemartin	1								
	00 05 98	Narberth					1				
	17 04 01	Haverfordwest								2	
	17 07 94	Pembroke	R				5				4
Perth	20 06 98	Perthshire					1				
	28 08 98	Carse of Gowrie					1	a			
Roxburgh	(10 08 94)	Roxburghshire	?			3					
Rutland	25 03 94	Rutland Legion	3			4					
Selkirk	15 02 97	Selkirk				1					
Shropshire	17 04 95	1st Corps Wrekin		2			4R				
	08 03 95	Wellington		1			2				
	05 06 98	Haleowen					1				
	27 06 98	Shropshire C					1				
	17 05 98	Shropshire 1st Corps					1				
	20 06 98	Shropshire C 2nd					1				
	05 06 98	Hales Owen					1				
	16 08 98	Ludlow & B Castle					1				
	20 06 98	Brimstree Loyal Legion Assn.					R				
	20 06 98	Shifnal					a				
	22 08 98	Apley					a				

County	Formed	Volunteer or Yeomanry Corps	1794	1795	1796	1797	1798	1799	1800	1801	1802
	20 06 98	2nd Shrewsbury Corps					3				
	11 01 95	Market Drayton		1							
	06 04 97	Oswestry Rangers				1		2			
	27 06 98	3rd Prees Corps					2				
	11 06 98	4th Pimhill Lt Horse Corps					1				
Somerset	19 07 98	E Somerset Regt of Y					R	R			
	28 05 94	Castle Cary	1				a				
	07 05 94	Taunton (Hanning)	1				a	?			
	30 07 94	North Perrott	1				a				
	30 07 94	Yoevil	1				a	?			
	01 09 94	Martock	1				a				
	07 09 99	Wincanton				1	a				
	1798	Crewkerne					1				
	21 06 94	Taunton	1				a				
	27 11 99	Taunton (3rd)						2			
	18 07 98	West Somerset					R	R		7	
	03 06 94	Brymore (Bridgwater)	1				a				
	22 08 98	Langport					1	a			
	1797?8	Dulverton				?	1	a			
	24 08 94	Milverton	2				a				
	18 01 97	Wellington			1		a				
	1794	Wiveliscombe						a			
	28 07 98	Road & Woolverton Assn.					1				
	11 03 96	Dunster half Troop			½						
	24 12 00	Monksilver Half Tp/ D & M						½	1		
	20 06 98	Frome Assn.					1				
	23 10 98	Mells Assn.					1				
	1798	Doulting Half Troop/ C&D					½				
	1798	Cranmore Half Troop					½				
	23 05 98	Bath V Lt Horse					1				
	07 07 98	Doddington Assn.					1				
	1798?	Wells					?				
	29 06 98	Beckington Assn.					1				
	1798	Wrington					1				
Stafford	04 07 94	Staffordshire	R				R				
	21 08 94	Stafford	a								
	21 05 98	R Staffs Pottery Assn.									
	1794	Newcastle u Lyme	a								
	23 05 98	Loyal Walsall Lt horse					a				
	31 05 98	Hanley					a				
	29 05 98	Stone & Eccleshall					a				
	18 06 98	Bilston Assn.					a				
	00 05 98	Wolverhampton Assn.					a				
	06 07 98	Tamworth Assn.	a								
	24 06 98	Handsworth Assn.					1				
	29 05 98	Needwood					1				
Stirling	25 07 98	Stirling YC					1				
	04 08 98	Strath Enrick							1		
	31 05 98	Baldernock became S Lennox							1		
Suffolk	04 05 94	Suffolk	1								
	1794	Bury St Edmunds Assn.	1								
	1794	Eye (Suffolk Borderers)	1								
	07 08 00	Ipswich	1								
	1794	Botesdale	1								
	24 05 98	Ickworth	1								
	1798	Farnham					1				
	1794	Lowestoft	1								
	1794	Saxmunden	1								
	1794	Stowmarket	1								

County	Formed	Volunteer or Yeomanry Corps	1794	1795	1796	1797	1798	1799	1800	1801	1802
	1798	1st or Blithing Troop					1				
	13 01 95	5th Troop		1							
Surrey	01 05 94	Surrey	R								
	30 09 98	Southwark						1			
	30 05 98	Croydon Assn.					1				
	1799	Guildford & Blackheath						1			
	00 05 98	Mitcham					1				
	30 05 98	Clapham Assn.					1				
	18 07 98	Wimbledon Assn.					1				
	15 06 98	Woking Assn.					1				
	19 07 98	Wandsworth Assn.					1				
	26 07 98	Loyal Lambeth Assn.					1				
	30 05 98	Battersea, S'ham & Tooting Assn.					1				
	30 05 98	Beddington & Carshalton Assn.					1				
	16 10 01	Surrey Volunteer Guides								1	
	10 07 98	Reigate, Mersham & Galton					1				
Sussex	23 06 94	Sussex	R8								
	12 08 95	Parham		1							
	24 05 98	Minsteed					1				
	26 06 94	Hastings	1								
	07 06 97	Sussex Artillery				1					
	18 07 98	Sussex guides					1				
	31 07 94	Rye	1								
	23 06 94	W Hoathley	1								
	23 06 94	Petworth	1								
	00 02 95	North Pevensey		1							
	11 08 95	Arundel & Bramber		1							
	24 11 94	Midhurst	1								
	03 06 95	Lewes		1							
	15 04 95	Chichester & Arundel		1							
Warwick	27 01 97	Warwick				R					
	02 10 97	Earl of home				2					
	05 06 98	Ryton Assn.						1			
	04 07 98	Eglington						2			
	08 07 98	Knightlow						1			
	05 08 94	Earl of Aylesford	5								
	01 10 95	Hampton		1							
	16 07 94	Packington	1			a					
	16 07 94	Birmingham	1			a					
	04 10 97	Loyal Birmingham				1		D			
	16 07 94	Rugby	1			a					
	16 07 94	Kineton	1			a					
	08 07 95	Nuneaton		1							
	22 04 97	Coventry				2					
	01 01 95	Forest of Arden		1							
	04 09 97	Warwick Borough				2					
	08 07 98	Edgehill						1			
Wigtown	04 09 97	Wigtown				1					
Wight	27 03 00	Isle of Wight						1			
	19 04 98	East Medina						1		1	
	17 05 98	West Medina						1		1	
Wiltshire	04 04 97	Wiltshire				R					
	09 08 98	Westbury Assn (VC 24 09 01)						1		d	
	04 06 94	Devizes	1			a					
	04 06 94	Bradford,Trowbridge,Melksham	1			a					
	04 06 94	Chippenham & Calne	1			a					
	04 06 94	Malmesbury	1			a					
	04 06 94	Swindon	1			a					
	04 06 94	Everley	1			a					

County	Formed	Volunteer or Yeomanry Corps	1794	1795	1796	1797	1798	1799	1800	1801	1802
	30 06 94	Hindon	1			a					
	07 07 94	Warminster	1		.	a					
	07 07 94	Sarum or Salisbury	1			a					
	03 08 98	Melksham					1				
	05 01 96	Marlborough		1		a					
	14 06 98	Deptford						1			
		Dinton								d	
	04 06 94	Draycott (Hon Windsor)	1								
Worcester	14 09 94	Worcester	1		2						
	1798	City of Worcester					1				
	1798	Kidderminster VC					1				
	23 05 98	Bromsgrove Assn.					1				
	17 07 98	Dudley					1				
	00 04 98	Stourbridge					1				
	00 04 98	Stourbridge 2nd					1				
	1798	Kings Norton					1				
York ER	03 05 94	ER Yeomanry	3								
	08 07 98	Yorkshire Wolds						1			
	24 07 98	Scarborough						1			
	04 07 94	Hull	1								
York NR	18 07 94	Newburgh Rangers	1								
	18 07 94	Kiplin & Langton	1								
	18 07 94	Helmsley	1								
	18 07 94	Barton le Street	1								
York WR	13 08 94	1st or S Corps then Regt	9								
	05 07 98	Rotherham & Sheffield					1				
	13 08 94	2nd or N then 1st Regt	5						D		R
	11 05 97	Leeds				1					
	21 06 98	Wakefield Assn.	a				1				
	09 06 98	York City & Staincross					1				
	22 05 98	Halifax Assn.					1				
	22 05 98	Huddersfield Assn.					1		D		

Yeomanry History 1802-1828

Date Accepted	Yeomanry Corps	1802	1803	1804	1805	1806	1807	1808	1809	1810	1811	1812	1813	1814	1815	1816	1817	1818	1819	1820	1821	1822	1823	1824	1825	1826	1827	1828
1806	Angus				1									1														
1806	Western Troop				1																							
22 10 02	Carrick & 1st Regiment	1	3														4		5								6	M
27 06 17	Cumnock & 2nd Regt																5										D	
30 10 03	Bedfordshire Corps		R			r	r	r																				
16 09 02	Bedfordshire/Odell	2	a		D																							
20 08 03	Woburn Squadron		2a				D																					
26 10 02	Warden Troop		a			s		D									1	(04 08 17)										
04 08 17	Leighton later B'shire YC																1	3	5								D	
04 08 17	Harrold																1								d			
21 03 04	1st Berkshire			R										R					5									
31 08 02	Abingdon	1	a																									
30 09 03	Hungerford		1	a																								
22 08 03	Donnington/Newbury		1	a	(05 05 04)																							
05 09 03	White Horse Sqn		2	a																								
14 01 20	Eastern Berkshire Regt																		R				D					
30 09 02	Loyal Windsor Cavalry	1				D																						
22 03 03	Wargrave		1											a					D									
08 10 02	Woodley	1												a														
24 02 03	Thatcham		1																									
13 08 03	Aldermaston		1																									
13 07 03	Maidenhead		1																									
23 12 02	Berwickshire Y C	3	4																									
16 07 03	1st or S Buckingham		9																									
30 09 02	Taplow Tp of 1st Regt																										s	
16 07 03	2nd or Mid Buckingham		6																								R	N
16 07 03	3rd or N Buckingham		6																									
02 11 03	Aylesford Legion C		1																									
00 12 04	Bute VC			1																								
17 10 03	Arrington		1																									
04 08 03	Doddington		1																									
30 08 03	Whittlesey		1																									
13 10 02	Carmarthen	1	2											r														
13 10 02	2nd Western Carmarthen	1																										
12 11 19	Carnarvon																		1									
16 09 02	1st Cheshire	2	6			a								8					10							R		M
26 07 03	Cheshire Y C		R																									
1806	Cheshire Legion					R								d														
22 08 03	Norton		1																									
12 08 03	Stockport		1											D														
	Knutsford																											
06 10 02	Macclesfield	1																										
	Adlington																				1							
13 08 03	Western Cheshire		6					D											1					L				
20 11 19	Wirral																		1					L				
16 11 19	2nd Cheshire																		6									
13 08 02	Lydd	1																										
13 08 02	Walmer	1																										
05 09 03	Clackmannan & Kinross		1														2											
05 07 03	E Cornwall or Antony		1																								a	
13 04 03	L Meneage (1st DoC)		R		1									R			R										R	
13 04 03	Helston YC		a																								s	N
13 04 03	Trelowarren		a																									
24 09 03	Penryn		a																									
20 08 03	Killigrew or Bodrean Y		1											a			s	a										
16 07 03	St Germans Y, CC, ECY		1											a				a										
16 07 03	WPenwith G Mountsbay		G	Y										a														
23 05 03	Penwith, Camborne GYC		2			1								a			s	a										
1817	2nd D of C (Penwith)																R	R										N
30 11 19	3rd D of C (N C Hussars)																		R								R	
	Eskdale 5 Kirks					1																						
18 05 03	Cumberland Rangers		1			7	formerly Edenside Rangers																					
01 08 06	Cumberland C																											
17 03 03	Wrexham		3																5	R								N

181

Date	Yeomanry Corps	1802	1803	1804	1805	1806	1807	1808	1809	1810	1811	1812	1813	1814	1815	1816	1817	1818	1819	1820	1821	1822	1823	1824	1825	1826	1827	1828
17 03 03	Denbigh Lgn (V Tp 14 07 03)		1					D																				
07 04 03	Derbyshire YC		6																									N
16 06 03	Derbyshire VC	4	a																									
05 07 17	R E Derby (Shipley)																1										D	
26 01 20	N Derbyshire																			R							D	
02 06 17	Hopton																1			a								
1820	Wirksworth																			a								
1820	Bakewell																			a								
1828	Radbourne																									s		
16 09 17	Alfreton																1										D	
29 12 19	N High Peak																				1						D	
	Chaddesdon & Morley																											
26 02 28	Chesterfield																										1	
05 11 02	R 1st Devon YC		R8																Ten								8	N
16 06 03	Exeter A	a																										
25 06 03	Salcombe	1	a																									
20 03 03	N Devon		R8																									N
05 11 02	Stevenstone	1	a																									
00 12 04	Torrington	1	a																									
05 11 02	Bideford A to Y	1	a																									
00 12 04	Holsworthy		1																									
29 10 02	Hemiock	1						s																				
17 02 03	Hemyock 2nd		1																									
29 10 02	Culmstoke	1						s																				
12 10 03	Upottery		1					s																				
12 10 03	Churchstanton		1					s																				
12 10 03	Barnstable		1	D (20 03 05)																								
05 11 02	R E Devon	6																										
1802	R E Devon Squadron	2						1																				
13 10 03	E Devon Legion		4					D											4								
22 08 03	S Devon Legion		9		8									6						D								
05 11 02	South Devon	1	a																								2	N
12 10 03	Teignmouth		a																	a								
1803	Stokeleigh		a																	a								
20 03 03	Plymouth Dock		a																	1							D	
1820	Chudleigh																			a								
1802	Ippleden	1												D					2	2a								
1820	South Hams Yeo																			R	9						D	
03 04 17	Bridport Lt Horse																1							D	(26 05 24)			
1803	Ermington S Regt		a																	s				D				
22 08 03	Kingsbridge S Regt		a																	s				D				
1803	Devonport		a																	s							D	
12 10 03	Teignbridge Sqn		2a																	2s							D	
12 10 03	Torbay		a																									
31 11 03	Corps of Guides		G					3					4									a						
30 11 13	Coleridge 100 Troop												a															
	Dart & Erme																			s		R					D	
08 11 03	Swimbridge																											
27 05 03	Dorset Yeomanry Cavalry		7											D (14 06 14)														
01 11 03	Dorset C Sadborough		1																				(24 12 27)				D	
03 04 17	Bridport Light Horse																1							(26 05 24)	D			
09 05 03	Dumbarton		2																	3								
22 02 03	R Dumfries		2		3												5											
16 09 02	Durham	3																										
24 11 02	Darlington Legion	1	2																									
16 09 02	Staindrop	1																										
1817	S Tyne Hussars																1											
13 10 02	North Durham	1																										
13 08 02	Usworth Legion	2	4																									
00 12 04	Ravensworth																			1								
00 12 04	1st Stockton																			1								
00 12 04	2nd Stockton																			1								
1815	Gibside													1														
05 11 02	Loyal Axwell	1																										
1806	Bywell					1								1														

Date	Yeomanry Corps	1802	1803	1804	1805	1806	1807	1808	1809	1810	1811	1812	1813	1814	1815	1816	1817	1818	1819	1820	1821	1822	1823	1824	1825	1826	1827	1828
1806	Coquet Dale Rangers					1																						
18 08 03	Glendale		1																									
30 07 03	Percy Tenantry		R			6																						
13 07 02	E Lothian (Haddington)	2	4																					1				N
31 01 14	1st Essex Yeomanry Cav													R	(see sub-units)													
10 08 03	1st E Essex Colchester		2										D															
06 09 03	2nd E Essex or Kelvedon		1											a	D													
06 09 03	1st Essex Legion		1			3																						
26 10 02	1st Essex Tp later Sqn	1							2																			
26 10 02	2nd Essex Chelmesford	1												a														
26 10 02	3rd Essex Tp	1												a	D													
26 10 02	4th Essex Tp (Harlaw)	1		D																								
10 08 03	Essex Union Legion		R			6																						
26 10 02	5th Essx Tp	1	4	a																								
26 10 02	Threshwell 100	1		D										a														
26 10 02	Halstead	1												a														
26 10 02	Hatfield Peverill	1			D																							
17 12 03	East Essex Legion																											
1806	West Essx Legion					3																						
26 10 02	Epping Forest	1			D																							
26 10 02	Haverhill	1												a														
26 12 02	Havering /Bar & Chafford	2	3	A		4													D									
26 10 02	Chafford& Barstable	1	2	a																								
	Aveley																											
09 05 03	Wakering		1											a		D												
26 10 02	Uttlesford & Clavering	1		D																								
06 10 03	Barford & Clufford		1																									
03 03 03	R Regiment Fifeshire		7			R																						
21 12 02	Kirkaldy YC		1			a																						
1803	F'shire E District		?																									
1822	F'shire Tp of Lancers																											
03 08 02	Mold Corps G & YC	1	2																									
12 06 03	Maylor Legion		4																6									
18 11 02	Forfar	1																										
00 07 03	Forfar W or Meigle		1																									
31 08 02	Cardiff Yeomanry	1																										M
31 08 02	Fairwood	1																										M
31 08 02	Swansea	1	2																									M
01 08 02	Cheltenham	1												D														
22 08 03	Gloucester																											
22 09 03	Gloucester		1																									
13 08 03	Bristol		3												d													
01 09 03	Longtree Bisley		1												d													
12 07 03	Stow		1												d													
22 08 03	2nd GA or Dodington		1												d													
12 08 03	Cirencester		1												d													
08 11 03	Tewkesbury		1												d													
13 09 03	Dursley		1												d													
22 08 03	Grumbold's Ash		1												d													
08 11 03	Winterbourne		1												d													
05 09 03	Tortworth		1												d													
06 09 02	N Hants (Basingstoke)	2	4			2																						
01 09 03	Ringwood		2																									
06 09 02	S Hants (Christchurch)	8																										
09 05 03	SE Hants (Portsdown)		4																									
06 09 02	NE or Alton	2	3																									
08 08 03	Dogmersfield		1																									
06 09 02	Fawley	1																										
16 07 03	Bere Forest		1																									
	New Forest																											
08 08 03	Whitchurch		1																									
01 09 03	Fordingbridge		1																									
	Southampton																											
27 09 02	Hereford	1	3																									
04 07 03	Leominster		1																									

Date	Yeomanry Corps	1802	1803	1804	1805	1806	1807	1808	1809	1810	1811	1812	1813	1814	1815	1816	1817	1818	1819	1820	1821	1822	1823	1824	1825	1826	1827	1828
16 09 02	Hertfordshire	1																						D				
16 09 02	Beechwood	1																										
20 08 03	Flying Artil		1																									
	Hertfordshire 2nd																											
31 08 02	Northern Tp	1																										
31 08 02	Eastern Tp	1																										
13 08 02	Southern Legion	1																										
13 08 02	Midland or Center Tp	1																										
07 05 03	Western Tp		1																									
13 09 03	Ashridge		1																									
22 12 02	Sawbridgeworth																											
05 11 02	Huntingdon	2	3																									
13 08 02	East Kent		r										R															
13 08 02	Nonington	1	a										a															
13 08 02	Denton	1											a															
13 08 02	Provender	2											2a															
13 08 02	Thanet Isle of	1											a															
27 08 03	Coxheath																											
	Cobham																											
05 05 04	Tunbridge																											
	Tunbridge Wells																											
02 11 03	Aylesford Legion C																											
13 08 02	Barham Downs	1																										
13 08 02	Elham	1																										
14 06 03	Bridge Hill 2nd Non		1																									
30 07 03	Corps of Guides		1																									
13 08 02	West Kent	8																						D				
14 12 03	Sheppey I of Mr Shove		1																									
13 08 02	Chislehurst	1																										
16 09 02	Deptford	1																										
06 08 03	Ifield Court		1																									
22 08 03	Maidstone (Hunton)		1																									
06 09 03	Penshurst		1																									
06 09 03	Squirries		1																									
	Sevenoaks																											
Dec-04	Farningham																											
13 08 02	Blackheath	2																										
22 08 03	Hunton		1																									
1818	Kinross YC																1											
05 07 03	Kirkcudbright		4																									
26 07 03	Royal Glasgow		1										D							1	(21 10 20)							N
1820	Kilbride																			1								
02 11 19	Lanark (Upper Ward)																		1									M
1821	Airdrie																				1							
1819	Cambuslang																		1									
03 08 02	Liverpool Light Horse	1	2																									
18 08 28	Lancashire																										R	M
03 08 02	Bolton-le-Moor	1											D							1	2						1	a
03 08 02	Loyal Ashton	1																						D	(28 05 25)			
23 08 19	Furness																		1								a	
17 08 03	Manchester Light Horse		3			2																						
20 10 19	Wigan																		1								a	
09 08 03	Preston		1																									
05 09 03	Leicestershire Lt Horse		9																									M
05 09 03	Lutterworth		1																									
05 09 03	Ashby-de-la-Zouch		1																									
22 02 03	Spalding		1																									
17 11 03	Holland S																											
22 02 03	Market Raisin		1																									
12 08 03	Louth		1																									
12 08 03	Lovedon		1																									
1817	North Lincoln																1											
28 07 03	Lincoln Lt H Rgrs (F & B)		3																									
20 01 03	Bourne East		1																									
15 08 03	Boston		1																									

Date	Yeomanry Corps	1802	1803	1804	1805	1806	1807	1808	1809	1810	1811	1812	1813	1814	1815	1816	1817	1818	1819	1820	1821	1822	1823	1824	1825	1826	1827	1828
03 09 03	Ness		1																									
03 09 03	Lincoln City		1																									
30 07 05	North Wold					1																						
15 08 03	Grantham		1																									
31 08 02	Linlithgow Kirtlesdown	2																										
01 07 02	London&Westminster	6																										
27 09 02	Westminster VC	1																								D		
19 05 00	Flying Artillery																											
09 07 03	L London (Islington)		3			4							D															
25 06 03	Manx G & Yeomanry C																								D			
05 09 03	R Spelthorne Hus (Legion)		1							D																		
12 10 03	Edmonton		1							D																		
31 01 03	R Midlothian Cav		6											5														M
1819	R Edinburgh VC													d					1									
06 11 02	Chepstow	1																				1						
22 08 03	Monmouthshire		1																									
14 06 22	2nd Monmouth																					1						
09 09 03	Montgomery Legion		3											4						6								
08 12 02	Norfolk Rangers	2	a																									
16 09 03	Holkham		a																									
22 10 02	Lynn & Freebridge	1	a																									
13 08 03	Smithdon & BrotherX		a																									
23 09 03	Marshland		a																									
10 12 03	1st W Regt of N Y		R																							D		
02 09 03	Clackclose		a																									
22 10 02	Erpingham & Eynesford		a																									
22 10 02	1st Dereham	1	a																									
22 10 02	2nd or E Dereham	1	a																									
22 10 02	Swaffham	1	a																									
09 07 03	S Greenoe		a																									
05 09 03	Wymondham		a																									
07 01 04	2nd Mid Regt of N Y		R																							D		
22 10 02	Blofield&SWalsham	1	a																									
22 10 02	Tunstead & Happing	1	a																									
22 10 02	Loddon	1	a																									
22 10 02	Norwich Lt Horse	1	a																									
22 10 02	Yarmouth	1	a																									
01 01 04	3rd E Regt N Y		R																							D		
22 10 02	Hingham	1																										
16 09 03	Downham																				1							
1806	Rainham					2																						
08 11 03	Capt Savorey		1																									
13 08 02	Northampton	1																										
12 07 03	Peterborough		3																									
16 09 02	Wellinborough	1																										
27 09 02	Northamptonshire	ll																										
02 09 03	Northampton Y Inf		1																									
30 06 03	Thrapston to N'ts Y		1																									
30 07 03	Percy Tenantry		6																									
12 02 05	Flying Artillery			1																								
12 02 03	Cheviot Legion		4																a									
13 08 02	Bywell	1																										
18 08 03	Glendale		1																a									
1805	Coquetdale Rangers			1																								
20 11 19	N'land & Newcastle																		R									M
22 06 02	Newark	1																										
27 05 28	Sherwood Rangers YC																										R	M
08 08 03	Retford		1											D						1							a	
08 08 03	Mansfield		1																								a	
08 08 03	Notts (Chaplin)		1					D												1						a		
08 08 03	Notts (Wright)		1																									
05 09 03	Rufford		1																									
22 06 02	Holmepierrepoint		1																							a		
22 03 03	Bunny		1																D							a		
1803	Worksop (VA)		1																					1				

Date	Yeomanry Corps	1802	1803	1804	1805	1806	1807	1808	1809	1810	1811	1812	1813	1814	1815	1816	1817	1818	1819	1820	1821	1822	1823	1824	1825	1826	1827	1828
21 07 26	S Nottingham																									R		M
25 08 17	Watnall																1									a		
25 08 17	Wollaton																1									a		
13 07 03	L Oxfordshire		1											3	a													
12 12 18	NW Oxfordshire																	R				a						
13 08 02	Watlington	1																					D					
13 08 02	Bullingdon, Dorchester & T	1																					D					
12 05 17	1st Oxfordshire YC																1					R						N
27 09 02	Wootton North	1																a										
10 11 02	Bloxham & Banbury	2																										N
20 08 03	Oxford C (Morrell)		1																				D					
13 07 03	Oxford C (Francis)																											
03 09 03	Ploughley (Bicester)		1			D																						
23 05 03	Peeblesshire YC		1																		2							
28 07 03	Castlemartin		2						1																			N
10 12 03	Haverfordwest																											
1802	Dungleddy	1																	2a									
09 11 03	N Pembroke		2a																									
07 11 03	Orielton Sir H Owen		2a																									
	Kinnaird																											
1803	Jordanston		1a																									
02 05 03	1st Tp Y (Rotch)																											
1803	Indpt Pem YC		R															a										
1819	Dungleddy YC																	R										
01 08 03	Perth (Kinnaird)		4				D									r												
1821	Renfrewshire Y Infantry																			1							
1820	Renfrew YC																		1								M
19 08 02	Roxburghshire	2															3		4		5							
03 08 02	Rutland	4																										
17 09 03	Wellington Lgn C												2	a														
05 06 98	Haleowen													a														
31 08 02	Selkirkshire	1																										
09 06 03	Hales Owen		1											a														
01 08 02	Ludlow & Bishop's Castle	1	3											2a														
04 06 02	Market Drayton	1	a	(to 3rd Corps 03 12 03)																								
16 04 14	S Shropshire VC													R														M
00 03 03	1st Shrewsbury Corps		2																									
26 10 02	Shrewsbury (Hon W Hill)																											
07 05 27	S Salopian YC																										R	
	Shropshire 2nd																											
05 11 02	Oswestry Rangers	2												2a	(05 05 14)													
04 06 03	3rd Prees Corps		4	5		5a																						
28 02 06	Shropshire 1st Regiment				R	a																						
	Shropshire Y C					R								5a														
01 08 03	Pimhill	1												a	(05 05 14)													
07 07 03	Bradford N/Acton Reynold		1	a																								
03 08 02	N Shropshire Y C	2	4											R														M
07 09 03	Acton Reynold		1																									
06 08 02	E Somerset Regt of Y	6	8				R																					N
15 09 03	East Coker		1				a																					
02 02 03	West Somerset		8																									N
21 06 15	North Somerset														R		R											M
13 08 03	Frome & East Mendip Regt			R	(10 06 04)									a														
1803	East Mendip Regiment		R	a																								
05 09 03	Mendip Corps		4																									
19 05 15	Stone Easton													a														
20 08 03	East Mendip Legion Cavalry		1			C																						
22 08 03	Bath		2										1	a														
24 02 17	East Harptree																2a											
14 04 17	Keynsham																a											
18 10 17	Bedminster																1	a										
22 08 03	Blagdon		1												D													
13 08 03	Wells		1																									
13 08 03	Selwood Forest Legion		2	d																								
05 09 03	Midsomer Norton		2																									

Date	Yeomanry Corps	1802	1803	1804	1805	1806	1807	1808	1809	1810	1811	1812	1813	1814	1815	1816	1817	1818	1819	1820	1821	1822	1823	1824	1825	1826	1827	1828
1820?	Bitton																											
16 09 02	Staffordshire	6	8																									M
16 09 02	Loyal Bilston	1																										
07 10 03	Stone & Eccleshall		1																									
07 10 03	Handsworth		1																									
07 10 03	Tamworth		1																									
12 08 03	Uttoxeter		1																									
1803	Batchacre																											
13 08 02	St Ninian's & Stirg	1	2																									M
27 09 02	Strath Enrick	1	a																									
19 03 03	Stirling East District		1																									
30 09 02	Stirling S Lennox	3		3																								
25 12 04	W Stirling V Legion																											
22 08 03	Suffolk		1											R														
08 08 03	Bury St Edmunds					3																						
20 07 03	Baberg		1																									n
1806	Woodbridge					4																						
28 07 03	Hadleigh		1																									n
08 10 02	1st Suffolk (Rous)	1																										
08 10 02	2nd Suffolk (Edgar)	1	3																									
08 10 02	3rd Suffolk (Maynard	1																										
08 10 02	4th Suffolk (Fowke)	1	3																									
08 10 02	5th Suffolk (Sparrow	1																										
20 07 03	6th Suffolk																											
28 07 03	7th Suffolk																											
22 08 03	8th Suffolk																											
05 09 03	9th (Southelmham		1																									
31 10 02	Surrey	6																										
21 08 03	Woking		1																									
21 08 03	Southwark		2																									
21 08 03	Guildford & Blackheath		2																									
21 08 03	Egham & Godley 100		1																									
21 08 03	Richmond & Kew Legion		1																									
22 08 03	Wimbledon Lt Horse		1																									
22 09 03	Lambeth		1																									
22 08 03	Wandsworth		2																									
22 08 03	Clapham		1																									
22 09 03	Croydon		1																									
13 08 02	Chichester Artillery	1																										
31 12 02	Petworth	1																										
21 11 02	Western Coast	1																										
23 11 02	Midhurst	1																										
23 11 02	Parham	1																										
	Hoathley W																											
23 11 02	Lewes	1																										
23 11 02	East Grinstead	1																										
26 05 03	Corps of Guides		1																									
13 06 03	Ashburnham		1																									
30 07 03	N Pevensey Legion		2																									
02 09 03	Ringmere		1																									
01 10 03	Rye		1																									
06 12 03	Henfield		1																									
20 10 03	Sussex C (Mr Curteis)		3																									
13 10 02	Warwick	?	5																									
13 10 02	Nuneaton	1																										M
09 09 03	Atherstone		1										D															
17 04 04	Coleshill			1									D															
13 10 02	Warwick Borough	1																										
27 09 02	Westminster	4																										
07 10 19	Westmoreland																	6									2	N
13 08 02	East Medene	1			a																							
13 08 02	West Medene	1			a																							
25 03 05	Isle of Wight Y C				2	2																						
13 08 02	Wigtown	1		a	s																						D	
15 09 03	Stranraer		1	a																								

Date	Yeomanry Corps	1802	1803	1804	1805	1806	1807	1808	1809	1810	1811	1812	1813	1814	1815	1816	1817	1818	1819	1820	1821	1822	1823	1824	1825	1826	1827	1828
15 09 03	Galloway Rangers			R	r												D											
31 08 02	Wiltshire	Ten																										M
01 12 03	Draycott (Hon Windsor)		1																									
	Corsham																											
	Ramsbury																											
	Potterne																											
	Westbury																											
	Dinton																											
	Pewsey																											
31 08 02	Worcester	2	3																									
15 11 02	Kidderminster	1																										
27 09 03	Wolverley		1																									
06 11 02	Stourbridge 1st	1																										
12 02 03	Broomsgrove		1																									
12 09 03	Stourbridge 2nd		1																									
27 09 03	Kingsnorton		1																									
22 11 03	Dudley		1																									
?	ER Yeomanry																											
31 08 02	Yorkshire Wolds	?	5											D														
19 08 03	Everingham		1																									
05 09 03	Grimston		2																									
30 09 02	Scarborough	1																										
21 08 03	Richmond Foresters		2																									
05 09 03	Newburgh Rangers		1																									
15 08 03	Kiplin & Langton		1																									
05 09 03	Helmsley		1																									
20 09 03	Black Hambleton		1																									
15 08 03	S Regt of WR		Twelve																									M
25 07 02	N Regt of WR	7	8	(15 08 03)													a											M
14 11 03	Cav attached		1																									
20 08 03	Harewood		1																									
20 08 03	Knaresborough		1																									
13 08 02	Leeds	1																										
15 08 03	West York		3																									
22 08 03	West Riding C (Stockeld)		1																									
07 09 03	Craven Legion		5																									
21 10 03	Barton-le-Street																											
20 12 17	Yorkshire Hussars																R											
13 09 20	SW Yorkshire																			R								
12 03 17	Huddersfeild																1											

Appendix D

Yeomanry Succession 1829 - 1967

Aberdeenshire

16 02 03	gazetted 30 03 03 as 2nd Regt Scottish Horse, from Aberdeen, Elgin, Kintore and Connel
01 04 08	2nd Scottish Horse (TF)
04 08 14	embodied as 1/2nd and brigaded with 1/1st and 1/3rd
17 10 16	amal with 1/1st and 1/3rd to form 13th Bn, The Black Watch. Now see Perthshire

Ayrshire

1829	Maintained as Ayrshire Yeomanry Cavalry
1850	Lapsed
1897	redes Ayrshire Yeomanry Cavalry (Earl of Carrick's Own)
1900-02	co-sponsored 17th Coy IY 6 (Sc) Bn with Lanarkshire Yeomanry
1901	redes Ayrshire IY
01 04 08	redes as Ayrshire Yeomanry (Earl of Carrick's Own)
04 08 14	embodied as 1/1st
04 01 17	amalgamated with 1/1st Lanark to form 12th Bn, The Royal Scots Fusiliers
28 05 19	disbanded
07 02 20	reconstituted as cavalry
03 09 39	embodied
15 02 40	*transferred to **Royal Artillery** as The Ayrshire Yeomanry Regt. RA (TA). Reorg 15 04 40 as 151st (Ayrshire Yeomanry) Field Regt. RA (TA). with P, Q, R and then 123-5 Btys. S/A 04 02 46, completed 28 02 46.*
14 01 41	*Duplicate 152nd (AY) Fd Regt RA. with P, Q, R, then 126-8 Btys S/A 10 11 45, disb 01 01 47*
01 01 47	reconstituted as an armoured regt.
31 03 67	disbanded.
	Successors - The Ayrshire (Earl of Carrick's) Own Yeomanry (T)

Bedfordshire

1900	28th(Bedfordshire) Company, IY, Compton's Horse
19 09 01	Bedfordshire Imperial Yeomanry raised
01 04 08	Bedfordshire Yeomanry
04 08 14	embodied as 1/1st
10 03 18	dismounted but soon remounted
1919 ca	disembodied
07 02 20	reconstituted
05 08 20	*transferred to **Royal Artillery** to form 10th (Bedford) Army Bde, RFA (TF). Redes 01 11 38 as 105th (Bedfordshire Yeomanry) Army Field Regt, RA (TA).with 417-8 Btys. Conv 01 11 39 to 52nd (Bedfordshire Yeomanry) Heavy Regt, RA (TA).with A, B, C, D Btys. Disb 20 06 40. RHQ reformed 10 03 43 as RHQ 52nd Heavy Regt, RA (Bedfordshire Yeomanry) (TA) from personnel of RHQ 174th Fd Regt, RA.. 52nd Regt in S/A 10 04 46. Reconst 01 0147 as 305th Bedfordshire Yeomanry) Medium Regt RA, (TA). Conv 31 10 56 as 305th (Bedfordshire Yeomanry) Light Regt, RA, (TA). Amal 01 05 61 with 286th (Hertfordshire Yeomanry Field Regt. See Hertfordshire.*
	***Duplicate** unit formed 1939 as 148th Field Regt, RA (TA). S/A 15 02 42 after loss at Singapore. Disb 01 01 47.*

Appendix D

Berkshire

1831	Troops raised, 12 Feb Woolley, 25 Feb Welford & Newbury, 4 Apr Hungerford, 12 Apr White Horse
1838	All except Hungerford disb
1846	First mention of Royal Berkshire Yeomanry Cavalry in the Reading Mercury
1900-01	sponsored 39th and 58th Companies IY
1901	The Berkshire Imperial Yeomanry (Hungerford)
01 04 08	Berkshire Yeomanry (Hungerford)
04 08 14	embodied as 1/1st
00 04 15	amal with 1/1st Dorset Y & 1/1st RBH to form 2nd South Midland Regt of Yeomanry
00 08 15	dismounted
00 12 15	reformed
04 04 18	converted as part of C Bn, MG Corps
00 08 18	redesignated as part of 101st Bn, MG Corps
1919	disbanded
07 02 20	reconstituted
22 06 21	*transferred to **Royal Artillery** and reorg as part of 99th (Buckinghamshire and Berkshire) Bde, RFA (TA). 395-6 Btys. Berkshire Yeomanry elements withdrawn 17 06 39 to form 145th Field Regt, RA (TA). New title authorised 17 02 42 and amended to "(Berkshire Yeomanry)" 12 05 42. S/A 01 06 46 less 395 Bty to 178th Fd Regt to be disb 14 09 46.*
01 05 61	*Regt reconst 01 01 47 as 345th (Berkshire Yeomanry) Medium Regt, RA, (TA). Amal 16 08 50 with 346th Med Regt without change of title. Amal 31 10 56 with 299th Field Regt RA (TA) to form 299th (Royal Buckinghamshire Yeomanry, Berkshire Yeomanry and The Queen's Own Oxfordshire Hussars) Field Regt, RA (TA)*
	Reorg: R (Berkshire Yeomanry) Bty amal with Westminster Dragoons to form The Berkshire and Westminster Dragoons, RAC (TA). *(Remainder of 299th amal with 431st Light Anti-Aircraft Regt and 143 Control and Reporting Section to form 299th (Royal Buckinghamshire Yeomanry, Queen's Own Oxfordshire Hussars, and Berkshire) Field Regt, RA (TA)*
	Successor - The Royal Yeomanry Regt (V). Also - A Coy (Berkshhire Y) The R Berkshire Territorials

Buckinghamshire

1829	At no pay as 2nd Bucks. Also indpt Taplow Tp
1829	Also indpt Taplow Troop at no pay, paid 27 12 30, no pay 1838, returned to pay 1843
1850	Both lapsed
1857	Buckinghamshire Yeomanry Cavalry (Royal Bucks Hussars)
1871	Taplow Troop disbanded
1900-02	sponsored 37th(Buckingham), 38th(High Wycombe), 56 & 57 Coys (IY)
1901	redes Buckinghamshire IY(Royal Bucks Hussars)
01 04 08	redes Buckinghamshire Yeomanry (Royal Bucks Hussars)
04 08 14	embodied as 1/1st
04 09 15	separate status
00 12 15	amal with 1/1st Dorset Y & 1/1st Berkshire Y to form 2nd S Midland Regt of Yeomanry
04 04 18	converted with Berks Y to form C Bn MG Corps
19 08 18	renamed 101st Bn MG Corps
1919	disbanded
07 02 20	reconstituted

Appendix D

29 04 21   *transferred to **Royal Artillery** and reorg as 99th (Buckinghamshire Yeomanry) Bde, RFA (TA) with HQ, 393-4 Btys.. Reorg 22 06 21 to include elements of Berkshire Yeomanry with title addition. Bde reorg 01 11 38 as Field Regt. Berkshire elements withdrawn 17 06 39. Title authorised 12 05 42 as 99th Field Regt, RA (Buckinhamshire Yeomanry) (TA). S/A 30 09 46. Reconst 01 01 47 as 299th (Buckinghamshire Yeomanry) Field Regt, RA (TA). Amal 15 09 50 to form 387th/299th (Royal Buckinghamshire Yeomanry and Queen's Own Oxfordshire Hussars) Field Regt, RA (TA). Renum 01 07 51 as 299th. Amal 31 10 56 with 345th (Berkshire Yeomanry) Medium Regt to form 299th (Royal Buckinghamshire Yeomanry, Berkshire Yeomanry and The Queen's Own Oxfordshire Hussars) Field Regt, RA (TA). Regt less R Bty amal with 431st Light Anti-Aircraft Regt and 143 Control and Reporting Section 01 05 61, to form 299th (Royal Buckinghamshire Yeomanry, Queen's Own Oxfordshire Hussars and Berkshire) Field Regt, RA (TA)*
            Successor: P Bty (Royal Bucks Yeomanry), The Buckinghamshire Regiment, RA (T)

Cambridge.
1829	Royston & Arrington enters at no pay, placed on pay 02 05 31
11 04 31	Whittlesea Tp raised, lapsed 1850

Cheshire
1829	Maintained as King's Cheshire
1900-02	sponsored 21st & 22nd Coys IY
1901	redes Cheshire IY(Earl of Chester's)
01 04 08	redes Cheshire Yeomanry(Earl of Chester's)
04 08 14	Embodied as 1/1st
02 03 17	amalgamated with 1/1st Shropshire Y to form 10th Bn KSLI
1918	reduced to a cadre
23 06 19	disembodied
07 02 20	reconstituted as Cheshire Yeomanry (Earl of Chester's)
01 09 39	embodied
09 09 41	transferred to RAC
1942	*transferred to **Royal Signals** as 5 Line of Communication Signals. Redes 00 02 45 17 L of C Signals. S/A 1945 ca.*
01 01 47	Reconst as an armd regt of the RAC (TA), The Cheshire Yeomanry (Earl of Chrester's Successor: The Cheshire Yeomanry (E of Chester's Territorials) & The Queen's Own Yeomanry.

Cornwall
1829	D of Cornwall's and 2nd Cornwall or Penwith accepted at no pay
14 03 31	D of Cornwall's paid and disb 1838
31 01 33	Penwith disb

Denbighshire
1829	Denbighshire at no pay
1831	Restored to pay
1850	Lapsed
1900-02	sponsored 29th Coy IY
01 04 08	designated Denbighshire Yeomanry
04 08 14	embodied as 1/1st
00 02 17	converted to 24th Bn. Royal Welsh Fusiliers
1919	disembodied
07 02 20	reconstituted

01 03 22   *transferred to **Royal Artillery** to form 61st Medium Bde, RGA (TA).   Redes 00 01 24 61st Carnarvon and Denbigh (Yeomanry) Medium Bde, RGA (TA).   Redes 01 11 38 61st Carnarvon and Denbigh (Yeomanry) Medium Regt, RA (TA) and subsequently reorg to provide for duplicate regt.   Both regts began S/A 01 03 46 and completed 13 03 46 and 17 03 46 respectively.   61st Regt reconst 01 01 47 as 361st (Carnarvon and Denbigh Yeomanry) MediumRegt, RA (TA). Amal 31 10 56 with 384th Light Regt RA (Royal Welch Fusiliers) (TA) to form 372nd (Flintshire and Denbighshire Yeomanry) Field Regt, RA (TA)*
*   **Duplicate** formed 1939 as 69th (Carnarvon and Denbigh Yeomanry) Med Regt, RA (TA) with 241-2 Bbtys from 61st Regt. Subtitle of regt authorised 17 02 42, disb 01 01 47.*
*   Successor: The Flintshire and Denbighshire Yeomanry, RA (T)*

Derbyshire
1829	Radbourne Tp accepted at no pay and returned to pay 14 12 30
15 12 31	Derby & Chaddeston Tp raised
1832	Tps raised, Worksworth 17 Jan and Repton & Gresley 9 Apr
1838	Worksworth, Repton & Gresley Tps disb
1864	Troops regimented as Derbyshire Yeomanry Cavalry
1900-02	sponsored 8th and 104th coys IY
1901	designated Derbyshire IY
01 04 08	designated Derbyshire Yeomanry
04 08 14	embodied as 1/1st
03 09 15	amal. with 1/1st Sherwood Rgrs and S Notts Y to form 3rd Notts & Derby Regt of Y
00 12 15	separate status
1919 ca	disembodied
07 02 20	reconstituted
14 07 21	*transferred to **Tank Corps** as 24th (Derbyshire Yeomanry) Armoured Car Company*
30 04 39	transferred to RAC
24 08 39	Redes 1st Derbyshire Yeomanry.
	Duplicate unit formed as 2nd Derbyshire Yeomanry RAC (TA). S/A c. 1946, disb 01 01 47.
01 09 39	1st regt embodied
01 01 47	pers of 1st regt redes 2/1st and disb 14 06 47.
01 01 47	reconstituted as The Derbyshire Yeomanry
09 02 57	Amalgamated with The Leicestershire Yeomanry. See Leicestershire

Devonshire
a.	**R 1st Devon and others**
1829	R 1st Devon, S Devon, E Devon all retained at no pay
1830-31	Returned to pay, 19 03 31, 23 02 31 & 27 12 30
17 01 31	NE Devon raised
1838	S Devon, E Devon & NE Devon disb
1871	redesignated Royal 1st Devonshire Yeomanry Cavalry
1900-02	co-sponsored 27 Coy IY with RNDH
1901	redesignated Royal 1st Devon IY
01 04 08	redesignated Royal 1st Devon Yeomanry
04 08 14	embodied as 1/1st
04 01 17	amal. (wef 21 12 16) with 1/1st RNDY to form 16th Bn The Devonshire Regiment.
28 06 19	disbanded
07 02 20	reconstituted as Royal 1st Devon Yeomanry

07 06 20   *Tsfd to **Royal Artillery** and organised as two btys of 11th (Devon) Army Bde, RFA (TA) and later part of 96th (Devon Yeomanry) Bde, RFA (TA) and later as a Field Bde. with HQ, 381-2 and 469 (newly) formed Btys. Reorg 01 11 38 as 96th (Royal Devon Yeomanry) Field Regt, RA (TA) with R N Devon Yeomanry. S/A 01 01 47 and concurrently reconst as 296th (Royal Devon Yeomanry), RA (TA); pers of former 96th Fd Regt continued in new war-formed 96th Fd Regt, RA until 11 01 47 when disb in SEALF. Amal 01 07 50 with 342nd (Royal Devon Yeomanry) Medium Regt, RA (TA) without change of title. Amal 01 05 61 with 256th (Wessex) Light Anti-Aircraft Regt, RA (TA) less P Bty, without change of title.*
*   Successor: The Devonshire Territorials(Royal Devon Yeomanry/ The 1st Rifle Volunteers).*

b.   North Devon
1829   N Devon accepted at no pay, returned to pay 29 04 31
1868   redesignated Royal North Devonshire Hussars
1900-01   co-sponsored 27 Coy, 7 Bn IY with above
1901   redesignated Royal North Devonshire IY
01 04 08   redesignated Royal North Devon Yeomanry
04 08 14   embodied as 1/1st
04 01 17   amalgamated with 1/1st R 1st Devon Y to form 16th Bn The Devonshire Regiment
28 06 19   disbanded
07 02 20   reconstituted
*07 06 20   transferred to **Royal Artillery** and reorg as two btys of 11th (Devon) Army Bde RFA (TA) and later as part of 96th (Devon Yeomanry) Bde, RFA (TA). **Duplicate** formed 08 07 39 by142nd Field Regt, RA (TA) taking 383-4 Btys from 96th Regt, plus 506 Bty formed. Title auth 17 01 42 as 142nd Field Regt, RA (Royal Devon Yeomanry) (TA). S/A 07 11 45. Reconst 01 01 47 as 342nd (Royal Devon Yeomanry) Medium Regt, RA (TA). Amal 01 07 50 with 296th (Royal Devon Yeomanry) Fd Regt, RA (TA).   See Royal 1st Devon Yeomanry*

Dorsetshire
08 12 30   Dorset YC raised
1830-31   Independent Tps raised, Charborough 16 12 30, Wimborne 21 02 31, Blandford 24 02 31, Isle of Purbeck & W'ham 25 02 31
12 08 35   Charborough disb and remaining indpt Tps 31 03 38
1857   Enters as Dorsetshire Yeomanry (Queen's Own)
1900-01   sponsored 26 Coy, 7 Bn IY
1901   designated Dorsetshire IY (Queen's Own)
01 04 08   designated Dorset Yeomanry (Queen's Own)
04 08 14   embodied as 1/1st
04 09 15   till 12/15 amal. with 1/1st RBH and 1/1st Berks Y to form 2nd S Midlands Regt of Y
13 07 19   reduced to cadre and later disembodied
07 02 20   reconstituted
*25 01 22   Transferred to **Royal Artillery** as 375-6 Btys of 94th (Somerset and Dorset Yeomanry) Bde, RFA (TA). Redes 01 11 38 94th (Queen's Own Dorset Yeomanry) Field Regt, RA (TA) with 218, 224 and 468 Bty formed later. 94th Regt to S/A 13 06 46. On 01 01 47, 94th reconst as 294th (Queen's Own Dorset Yeomanry) Field Regt, RA (TA) and 141st reconst as 341st (Queen's Own Dorset Yeomanry) Medium Regt, RA (TA). 341st Regt amal 01 07 50 with 294th Regt without change of latter title. Amal with 255th (West Somerset Yeomanry and Dorset Garrison) Med Regt, RA (TA) to form 250th (Queen's Own Dorset and West Somerset Yeomanry), RA (TA).*
*   **Duplicate** formed 1939 as 141st Field Regt, RA (Queen's Own Dorset Yeomanry) (TA) with 375-6 and later 505 Btys from 94th Fd Regt with title authorised 17 02 42. To S/A 11 12 45. Successor: A Coy (Queen's Own Dorset Yeomanry), The Dorset Territorials*

Essex
10 02 31   W Essex raised
1838   Accepted at no pay, returned to pay 1843
31 03 77   disbanded
13 02 02   raised as Essex IY
01 04 08   designated Essex Yeomanry
04 08 14   embodied as 1/1st and later disembodied
07 02 20   reconstituted

194

Appendix D

14 07 21   *Transferred to **Royal Artillery** as part of 104th (Essex Yeomanry) Bde, RFA (TA). Conv 01 11 38 to 104th (Essex Yeomanry) Regt, RHA (TA). ultimately with RHQ, 339, 463, 519 Btys. 104th Regt S/A 21 03 46. Reconst 01 01 47 as 304th (Essex Yeomanry) Medium Regt, RA (TA). Conv 31 10 56 to 304th (Essex Yeomanry - RHA) Field Regt, RA (TA). Amal 01 05 61 with other btys without change in title.*
*   **Duplicate** formed 1939 as 147th Regt. Conv 01 06 40 to Field Regt, RA (TA) with title authorised 17 02 42 as 147th Field Regt, RA (Essex Yeomanry) TA, ultimately with 413, 431, 511 Btys. S/A 04 02 46, complete 28 02 46 and disb 01 01 47.*
*   Successor: The Essex Yeomanry (RHA) RA (T)*
*   Note: A 191st Fd Regt, RA was formed in Dec 1942 and disb 31 01 45 using cadres from 147th and 86th Fd Regts.*

Fifeshire

12 04 31	Raised as a Regt
1838	Disb
07 06 60	raised as 1st Ad Bn, Fifeshire **MRV** with 4 coys 19 disembodied
00 09 60	consolidated to form 1st Fifeshire **MRVC**
1870	redes. 1st Fifeshire LHV Corps
1900-02	co-sponsored 20th Coy, 6 (Sc) Bn IY with Forfar Light Horse
00 05 01	amal with 1st Forfarshire Light Horse Volunteers to form Fifeshire and Forfarshire I Y
01 04 08	redes Fifeshire and Forfarshire Yeomanry
04 08 14	embodied as 1/1st
04 01 17	wef 21 12 16 as 14th Bn The Black Watch (R Highlanders)
24 07 19	disembodied
07 02 20	reconstituted
06 01 21	transferred to Tank Corps as 2nd Temp later 20th Armoured Car Coy.
30 04 39	trans to RAC (TA) as Fife & Forfar Y (TA)
24 08 39	Duplicate unit formed, 2nd fife and Forfar Yeomanry RAC (TA), S/A Sep45, disb 01 01 47
9/ 45+	suspended animation
01 01 47	recon. as The Fife and Forfar Yeomanry RAC(TA)
31 10 56	amal with The Scottish Horse to form The Fife and Forfar Y/Scottish Horse RAC(TA)
31 03 67	disbanded.
	Successors: The Fife and Forfar Yeomanry / Scottish Horse (T)

Flint

21 12 30	Maylor Tp raised and disb 1837
16 02 31	Flintshire raised and disb 1838

Forfarshire

1846	Forfarshire Yeomanry re-raised **NB Sometimes listed under Angus**
1862	disbanded
05 07 76	*1st Forfarshire **Light Horse Vol Corps** raised at Perth attchd 1st Fifeshire LHVC*
00 12 91	*redes 1st Forfarshire Light Horse Volunteers*
1900-02	co-sponsored 20th Coy IY
00 05 01	amal with 1st Fifeshire LHV. Now see Fife

Glamorganshire

1829	Glamorgan E, Fairwood & Swansea, Central Glamorgan each maintained
11 07 31	All Glamorgan Corps disb
00 08 01	raised as Glamorgan IY
01 04 08	designated Glamorganshire Yeomanry
04 08 14	embodied as 1/1st
02 02 17	till 1/3/17 amalgamated with 1/1st Pembroke Y to form 24th Bn. The Welsh Regt
05 07 19	disembodied
07 02 20	reconstituted

01 01 20   *transferred to **Royal Artillery** as part of 81st (Welsh) Bde, RFA (TA). Reorg 1939 as 81st (Welsh) Field Regt, RA (TA).(324 Bty Glamorgan). S/A 20 06 46. Reconst 01 01 47 as part of 281st (Welsh) Field Regt, RA (TA) and expanded so as to make whole regt Yeomanry. Redes 30 09 53 as 281st (Glamorgan Yeomanry) Field Regt, RA (TA). Amal 31 10 56 with other btys to form 282nd (Glamorgan and Monmouthshire) Field Regt, RA (TA).*
Successors: E(Glamorgan Yeomanry) Troop,211 (South Wales) Lt AD Bty, 104th Lt AD Regt, RA (Vols)
Surplus pers of P Bty 281 amal with 282 HAA W/S & 533 RASC as 509 Coy (MT) RASC to provide 223 (Welsh) Sqn RCT (V)

Gloucestershire
1830-31	Tps raised at Marchfield & Doddington 15 12 30, Fairford & Cirencester 10 02 31, Stroudwater 16 03 31, Tetbury 31 03 31, Gloucestershire 16 07 31, Wimbourne & Stapleton 12 12 31, Alveston 28 12 31
1834	Regimented
1900-02	sponsored 3rd Coy, 1 Bn IY
1901	designated Gloucestershire IY (Royal Gloucestershire Hussars)
01 04 08	designated Gloucestershire Yeomanry(Royal Gloucestershire Hussars)
04 08 14	embodied as 1/1st
04 09 15	till 12 15 amal. 1/1st Warwickshire and 1/1st Worcestershire Y to form 1st S Midland Bde
07 02 20	reconstituted
14 07 21	transferred to Tank Corps to form 21st Armoured Car Coy
30 04 39	transferred to RAC
24 08 39	redesignated 1st Royal Gloucestershire Hussars, with formation of **duplicate** unit.
01 09 39	embodied
15 1 43+	2nd RGH to S/A and disb 01 01 47
26 05 44	*3rd RGH formed as **dummy tank unit** for deception purposes till 11 07 44*
1946 ca	suspended animation
01 01 47	reconstituted as The Royal Gloucestershire Hussars
	Successors: B (The Royal Gloucestershire Hussars) Sqn, The Royal Gloucestershire Hussars (T)

Hampshire & Isle of Wight
1830-31	Tps raised, N Hants 30 11 30, Valley of Avon/ N Avon 07 12 30, (S Avon ?? ?? ??), Lymington 09 12 30, Fordingbridge 00 12 30, Romsey 27 01 31, New Forest East 22 01 31, New Forest West 08 02 31, Andover 27 12 31
1834	N Hants regimented
1838	Andover, Lymington serve at no pay and remaining six Tps disb
1843	Andover, Lymington returned to pay
1884/7	adopted title Carabiniers
1887	reorganised as Hampshire Yeomanry Cavalry (Carabiniers)
1900-02	sponsored 41st and 50th Coys IY
1901	redesignated Hampshire IY (Carabiniers)
01 04 08	redesignated Hampshire Yeomanry (Carabiniers)
04 08 14	embodied as 1/1st
27 09 17	absorbed into 15th Bn The Hampshire Regiment
07 11 19	disbanded
07 02 20	reconstituted
01 06 20	*Transferred **Royal Artillery** to form part of 7th (Hampshire) Army Bde, RFA (TF). Bde redes 00 07 37 95th(Hampshire Field Bde, RA (TA). Conv 01 10 37 to 72nd Hampshire) Anti-Aircraft Bde, RA (TA). Bde redes 01 11 38 as Regt and AA became HAA 01 06 40. S/A 30 01 45. Reconst 01 01 47 as 295th (Hampshire Carabiniers Yeomanry) Heavy Anti-Aircraft Regt, RA (TA). S/A 10 03 55. Resus 01 09 63 and amal with 457th Regt to form 457th (Wessex) Regt, RA (Hampshire Carabiniers Yeomanry) (TA). Desig 18 03 64 as 457th (Wessex) Hy AD Regt, RA (Hampshire Carabiniers Yeomanry) (TA).*
	Successor: HQ & C Coy (Wessex RA Princess Beatrice's), The Hampshire and Isle of Wight Territorials

Appendix D

Hertfordshire

1830-31	Tps raised, S Herts 04 12 30, Cashio 23 12 30, Dacorum 16 02 31, N Herts 16 02 31, Gilston 05 03 31
1843	Gilston disb
00 08 70	amalgamated to form Hertfordshire Yeomanry Cavalry
1874	redesignated Hertfordshire Yeomanry (Dragoons)
1900-01	sponsored 42nd Coy IY
1901	designated as Hertfordshire IY
01 04 08	redesignated Hertfordshire Yeomanry
04 08 14	embodied as 1/1st
00 09 15	amal. 1st/2nd Co of London Yeo (Westminster Dragoons) to form 5th Yeomanry Regt
00 12 15	resumed separate status
1919 ca	disembodied
07 02 20	reconstituted
00 03 20	*transferred **Royal Artillery** as part of 3rd East Anglian Bde, RFA (TF). Redes 01 06 24 as 86th(East Anglian) (Hertfordshire Yeomanry) Field Bde, RA (TA). Redes 01 11 38 as regt. with 341, 342 Btys and 462 formed in Regt. 14 01 41. S/A 14 04 46. Regt reconst 01 01 47 as 286th (Hertfordshire Yeomanry) Field Regt, RA (TA) and conv to Med Regt 01 10 54. Amal 10 03 55 with 479th Regt without change of title. Conv 31 10 56 to 286th (Hertfordshire Yeomanry) Field Regt, RA (TA). Amal 01 05 61 with 305th Regt to form 286th (Hertforshire and Bedfordshire Yeomanry) Field Regt, RA (TA)*
	*135th Regt formed 22 07 39 based on Bty from 86th Regt, to serve as **duplicate** unit.with 336, 334 Btys and 499 formed in Regt 22 07 39. S/A 15 01 42 as regt lost at Singapore. Disb 01 01 47.*
	79th Anti-Aircraft Regt, RA (TA) created 01 01 39 with Bty from 86th Regt and redes 01 06 40 with name as 79th (Hertfordshire Yeomanry) HAA. Regt, RA (TA). S/A 09 03 45. Reconst 01 01 47 as 479th Regt. Amal 10 03 55 as 286th Regt. 1956 Fd Regt, 1961 amal with 305 as 286 (Herts Beds Y) Fd Regt RA
	Successors: 201 (Hertfordshire and Bedfordshire Yeomanry) Med Bty, 100th (Eastern) Med Regt, RA (Vols); and No 2 (Hertfordshire Yeomanry) Coy and No 3 (Bedfordshire Yeomanry) Coy, The Bedfordshire and Hertfordshire Regt (T).

Inverness

1900-02	sponsored? 113th & 114th Coys IY
00 02 00	raised as 1st Mounted & 2nd Foot Companies, Lovat's Scouts
1901	2nd Contingent designated 99th & 100th Coys IY
1902	disbanded
01 03 03	authorised as two regts and later expanded into 1st and 2nd Lovat's Scouts Yeomanry
01 04 08?	
04 08 14	Both regiments embodied as 1/1st and 1/2nd
00 08 15	both dismounted
27 09 16	both amal with coy from 1/3rd Scottish Horse formed, 10th Bn, The Q's O Cameron Hldrs
1917	sharpshooter detachments formed and later 14 groups
17 04 19	disembodied
07 02 20	reconstituted as 1st & 2nd Lovat's Scouts Yeomanry
01 0 20	transferred to Scouts
00 08 22	2nd aml. with 1st to form The Lovat Scouts (TA)
01 09 39	embodied
20 01 47	suspended animation
01 01 47	reconstituted as a Sqn of the Scottish Horse RAC (TA)

01 01 49   *converted to **Royal Artillery** as 677th Mountain Regt, RA (Lovat Scouts) (TA). One bty reorg 22 05 50 as 850 Mtn Bty, RA (Lovat Scouts) (TA) and disb 05 04 54, personnel joining 532nd LAA.. Remainder of 677th Regt amal 30 09 50 with 532nd Regt and 540th Regt to form 532rd Light Anti-Aircraft Regt, RA (Lovat Scouts) (TA) which was renumbered 540th on 04 11 54. Amal 31 10 56 with 412th Regt without change of title*

Parts of regt to infantry 01 05 61. Remainder amal with 861 Indep LAA Bty to form 540th Light Anti-Aircraft Regt, RA (Lovat Scouts) (TA). Redes 18 03 64 540th Light Air Defence Regt, RA (The Lovat Scouts) (TA).

Successors: Orkney and Zetland (Lovat Scouts) Bty, The Highland Regiment, RA (TA); and A (Lovat Scouts) Coy, 3rd (T) Bn, Queen's Own Highlanders (Seaforth and Camerons)

Irish Horse   Yeomanry was formed before the Act of Union (1801) but under separate legislation. Many troops were formed both before and after this Act and as quickly disbanded, mainly as the result of the sectarian divide and difficulties in regulating affairs.

North Irish Horse (TA)
07 03 00	raised for South African War, posted to 60th Coy, 16th Bn. IY
07 01 02	reorganised as North of Ireland Imperial Yeomanry
07 07 08	placed on Special Reserve as North Irish Horse, approved 20 10 08
04 08 14	embodied and split into 6 independent squadrons
10 05 16	three Sqns to form 1st North Irish Horse
21 06 16	2nd NIH formed See WW1 table
1918	Disembodied
31 07 22	Disbanded
26 09 39	reformed in the Supplementary Reserve as North Irish Horse RAC.
30 04 45	S/A
01 01 47	reconstituted as North Irish Horse, RAC (TA)

Successors: D (North Irish Horse) Sqn, the Royal Yeomanry Regt (Vols); and North Irish Horse (T)

South Irish Horse
07 03 00	raised for South African War, posted to 61st Coy, 17th Bn IY
07 01 02	reorganised as South of Ireland Imperial Yeomanry
07 07 08	placed on Special Reserve as South Irish Horse, approved 20 10 08
04 08 14	embodied and split into 6 independent squadrons
17 05 16	three Sqns to form 1st South Irish Horse
00 05 17	2nd SIH formed
01 09 17	1st and 2nd SIH converted to 7th Bn, Royal Irish Regiment
18 04 18	reduced to cadre
00 06 18	reformed as a Bn
1919	disembodied
31 07 22	South Irish Horse disbanded

Kent
30 11 30	E Kent raised as a Regt
?? ?? ??	Tps raised, Faversham, Lydd(CP), Sellinge, Wye possibly as part of E Kent
1830	Tps raised Cobham East, Chislehurst (18 12 30), Sevenoaks, Tunbridge Wells/Deptford, Dartford, 1st Oxenhoath, Maidstone(Hunton), for later incorp with West Kent Regt
24 05 31	W Kent raised as a Regt
1838	Cobham East, Dartford, Sevenoaks, Tunbridge Wells/Deptford disb and possibly Chislehurst , Maidstone
00 06 56	designated Royal East Kent Regiment of Mounted Rifles
07 04 64	redesignated West Kent Yeomanry Cavalry(Queen's Own)
1888	redes Royal East Kent Mounted Rifles (The D of Connaught's Own)
1900-02	East Kent sponsored 33rd and 53rd Coys, 11th Bn. IY, and 43rd Coy, 14th Bn. IY. West Kent sponsored 36th Coy, 11th Bn IY
1901	Designated Royal East Kent Imperial Yeomanry Designated West Kent IY (Queen's Own)

Appendix D

01 04 08	redes R East Kent Yeomanry (D of Connaught's Own) (Mounted Rifles) redes West Kent Yeomanry (Queen's Own)
04 08 14	both Regts embodied as 1/1st
01 02 17	amalgamated with 1/1st W K Y to form 10th Bn E Kent Regt.
18 07 19	disembodied
07 02 20	reconstituted
20 08 20	*E & W Kent amal and trans to **Royal Artillery** to form part of 6th (Kent) Army Bde, RFA (TF). Redes 01 11 38 as 97th (Kent Yeomanry) Army Field Regt, RA (TA) and subsequently reorg into original and duplicate units. S/A 15 12 45. Reconst 01 01 47 as 297th (Kent Yeomanry) Light Anti-Aircraft Regt, RA (TA).*
01 05 61	amalgamated as Kent Yeomanry with 3rd/4th COLY to form Kent and Co of London Y See 3rd/4th County of London (Sharpshooters), RAC (TA) Successors - C(K&CLY)Sqn The Royal Yeomanry Regiment (V) Also - R(K&CLY)Bty, The London and Kent Reg RA (T) Also - A Kent & Co of London (Sharpshooters), 8th (T) Bn, The Queen's Regt (West Kent)

Kirkcudbright

1834	Troop raised and disb 1838

Lanarkshire

a.	**Upper Ward**
1829	Maintained
1900-02	co-sponsored 17th Coy, 6th (sc) Bn. IY with Ayrshire Yeomanry
1901	redes. Lanarkshire IY
01 04 08	redes. Lanarkshire Yeomanry
04 08 14	embodied as 1/1st
04 01 17	amal with 1/1st Ayrshire to form 12th Bn, The Royal Scots Fusiliers
1919	disembodied
07 02 20	reconstituted
01 09 39	embodied
15 02 40	*transferred to **Royal Artillery** as Lanarkshire Yeomanry Regt, RA (TA). Reorg 15 04 40 as 155th(Lanarkshire Yeomanry) Field Regt, RA (TA). S/A 15 02 42 after loss at Singapore.*
1941	*Duplicate formed as 156th (Lanark Y) Fd Rgt RA, with 591-3 Btys 01 01 43, S/A 27 12 45, disb 01 01 47.*
01 01 47	Reconst as the Lanark Yeomanry RAC(TA)
20 10 56	amal. with QORGY and 1st/2nd Lothians and Border Horse to form The Queen's Own Lowland Yeomanry RAC(TA), an armoured reconnaissance regt. Successor: The Queen's Own Lowland Yeomanry (T)
b.	**Lower Ward**
00 12 28	Accepted at no pay
1848	Regimented
1900-02	sponsored 18th and 108th Coys, 6th (Sc) Bn IY
1901	redes Lanarkshire I Y (Queen's Own Royal Glasgow and Lower Ward of Lanarkshire)
01 04 08	IY deleted
04 08 14	embodied as 1/1st
by02 16	redes Queen's Own Royal Glasgow Yeomanry
23 09 17	absorbed into 18th Bn, The Highland Light Infantry
1918	reduced to cadre
27 04 19	disembodied
07 02 20	reconstituted
21 02 22	*transferred to **Royal Artillery** to form 101st (Glasgow Yeomanry) Bde, RFA (TA). Redes 01 11 38 as 101st (Queen's Own Royal Glasgow Yeomanry) Army Field Regt, RA (TA). Conv 28 11 38 to part of 54th (Queen's Own Royal Glasgow Yeomanry) Anti-Tank Regt, RA (TA). S/A 25 02 42 after loss in Malaya. Reconst 25 06 43. S/A 07 03 46.* *Duplicate formed 1939 as 64th A Tk Regt, RA (Queen's Own Royal Glasgow Yeomanry) (TA). Title authorised 17 02 42. S/A 22 01 46. Disb 01 01 47.*
01 01 47	Reconst as the Queen's Own Royal Glasgow Yeomanry, RAC (TA)
20 10 56	Amal with Lanarkshire Yeomanry

Lancashire

1829	Duke of Lancaster's Own Yeomanry Cavalry maintained
31 08 48	Lancashire Hussars raised as a regiment
1858-9	L Huss, Liverpool troop replaced by one raised at Newton
1859	L Huss, Latham and Ormskirk troop raised and joins regiment
1900-2	DLOY co-sponsored ??
	L Huss co-sponsored 23rd & 32nd Coys IY also 77 Coy, 8th Bn IY(Manchester)
1901	Regts designated Duke of Lancaster's Own IY and Lancashire Hussars IY
01 04 08	redes as Duke of Lancaster's Own Yeomanry and Lancashire Hussars Yeomanry
04 08 14	both regts embodied as 1/1st
24 07 17	DLOY partially dismd and abs 24 09 17 by 12th Bn The Manchester Regt and reduced to a cadre 1918
24 09 17	L Huss absorbed into 18th Bn King's(Liverpool Regt)
14 05 18	reduced to cadre, 13 08 18 reconstituted as 13th Bn, 20 05 19 disembodied, 07 02 20 reconstituted
20 05 19	disembodied also A Sqn as independent during 1919
07 02 20	reconstituted as Duke of Lancaster's Own Yeomanry
14 06 20	*L Huss transferred to **Royal Artillery** to form 2nd (Lancashire) Army Bde, RFA (TF). Redes on 01 11 38 as 106th (Lancashire Yeomanry) Regt, RHA (TA). Conv 14 03 41 to 106thLight Anti-Aircraft Regt, RA (Lancashire Hussars) (TA). Disb 01 07 41, later considered S/A. Reconst 01 01 47 as 306th (Lancashire Hussars) Heavy Anti-Aircraft Regt, RA (TA). Amal 15 07 50 with 390th Regt to form 306th Heavy Anti-Aircraft Regt, RA (Lancashire Hussars) (TA). Conv 01 01 54 to Medium Regt. Amal 31 10 56 with 287th Regt to form 287th (1st West Lancashire) Field Regt, RA (TA).*
	Conv, 147th Anti-Tank Regt, RA (TA)
	***Duplicate** unit formed 1939 as 149th (Lancashire Yeomanry) Regt, RHA (TA). Conv 01 06 40 to Field Regt. Conv 01 07 41 to 149th Anti-Tank Regt, RA (Lancashire Yeomanry) (TA). Conv 30 05 42 to Field Regt. Conv 11 11 42 to Anti-Tank Regt. S/A 15 06 45. Reconst 01 01 47 without ref to Yeomanry.*
	Successor: A Troop (The Lancashire Hussars), P Bty (1st West Lancashire), The West Lancashire Regt, RA (T)
01 09 39	embodied
15 01 40	*transferred to **Royal Artillery** as Duke of Lancaster's Own Yeomanry Regt, RA (TA). Conv 15 04 40to form 77th (Duke of Lancaster's Own Yeomanry) Medium Regt, RA (TA). **Duplicate** formed as 78th Regt, RA (Auxiliary Police) (Duke of Lancaster's Own Yeomanry) (TA). S/A 15 04 46 and disb 01 01 47. 77th Regt began S/A 04 02 46, completed 25 02 46.*
01 01 47	Reconstituted as The Duke of Lancaster's Own Yeomanry RAC (TA)
	Successor: The Duke of Lancaster's Own Yeomanry RTR (T)

Leicestershire

1829	Maintained as Leicestershire YC
1900-2	sponsored 7th Coy, 4th Bn & 65th Coy 17th Bn IY
1901	designated as Leicestershire Imperial Yeomanry
01 04 08	designated Leicestershire Yeomanry (Prince Albert's Own)
04 08 14	embodied as 1/1st
1918	early part dismounted with North Somerset Y as an MG Bn
04 04 18	absorbed by units of 3rd Cavalry Bde
07 02 20	reconstituted as Leicestershire Yeo (Prince Albert's Own)
00 09 39	embodied
15 02 40	*transferred to **Royal Artillery** as Liecestershire Yeomanry Regt, RA (TA). Conv 15 04 40 to 153rd (Liecestershire Yeomanry) Field Regt, RA (TA). Ordered to disb 31 12 46 but amended to S/A. **Duplicate** formed 15 04 40 as154th (Leicestershire Yeomanry) Field Regt, RA (TA). S/A 07 11 45 and disb 01 01 47.*
01 01 47	reconstituted as The Leicestershire Yeomanry (Prince Albert 's Own)
09 02 57	amal. with Derbyshire Y to form The Leics and Derbyshire (P Albert's O) Y, RAC (TA)
	Successor: The Leicestershire and Derbyshire (Prince Albert's Own) Yeomanry (T)

Appendix D

Lincolnshire

1831	Lincoln Heath raised 21 Feb and N Lincoln 6 Apr
1838	Lincoln Heath disb
1846	N Lincoln disb
25 06 01	Lincolnshire Imperial Yeomanry raised
01 04 08	designated as Lincolnshire Yeomanry
04 08 14	embodied as 1/1st
07 04 18	converted as part of D (19 8 18 = 102nd) Bn MG Corps
20/11 or	17 12 20. disbanded (possibly unwilling to convert to RA)

London

a.   Inns of Court

00 04 32	reorganised as mixed cavalry and infantry formation from earlier units dating from November 1584 with title Inns of Court Regiment
00 11 40	transferred to RAC
00 03 47	S/A and reconstituted
31 10 56	amalgamated with Northamptonshire Yeomanry as 4th Sqn
01 05 61	(Prince Consort's Own) to form The Inns of Court and City Yeo RAC (TA) withdrawn to amalgamate with The City of London Yeomanry (Rough Riders), The Rifle Brigade Successor: HQ & A Coy (Inns of Court and City Yeomanry), The London Yeomanry and Territorials . Also as Band of The R Yeomanry Regt (V)

b.   1st CoLY/ City oLY- Rough Riders

17 03 00	Formed 20th Bn IY (Rough Riders) for the SA War comprising 72nd, 76th, 78th and 79th Coys IY
27 03 01	76th and 78th joined 85th, 86th and 87th Coys in 22nd Bn (Rough Riders)
23 07 01	reorganised as 1st County of London Imperial Yeomanry (Rough Riders)
24 08 01	renamed 1st City of London Imperial Yeomanry (Rough Riders)
01 04 08	redes City of London Yeomanry (Rough Riders)
04 08 14	embodied as 1/1st
04 09 15	amal. with 1/1st Co of London Yeo (Sharp Shooters) to form 4th London Regt of Yeo
00 12 15	resumed separate status
07 04 18	converted as part of E (19 8 18 = 103rd) Bn MG Corps
1919	disbanded
07 02 20	reconstituted
16 02 20	*transferred to **Royal Artillery** to form C Bty 11th (Honourable Artillery Company and City of London Yeomanry) Bde, RHA (TA). Bty expanded 29 09 38 to form 11th (City of London Yeomanry) Light Anti-Aircraft Bde, RA (TA). Redes 01 01 39 as Regt. 43 Bty formed in Regt 17 01 39, joining 101st LAA/Anti-Tank Regt on 15 02 40 and 61st LAA Regt 01 11 40. Disb 01 08 44. 283 Bty formed 09 06 41, to 17th LAA Regt 12 09 41 and to 1st Airborne Divn 02 07 42, reorg 04 12 42 as 1 A/L LAA Bty, began S/A 04 02 46, complete 13 02 46. Because of reconst of regt in TA 01 01 47, pers tsfd to new war-formed 11th LAA Regt, RA*
01 01 47	reconstituted as The City of London Yeomanry (Rough Riders) RAC (TA)
0110 56	*conv to **Infantry** bn of The Rifle Brigade (Prince Consort's Own) (TA) retaining title.*
01 05 61	amal with The Inns of Court Regt RAC (TA).

c.   Middlesex

10 12 30	Uxbridge Tp raised
1871	redesignated as Middlesex Yeomanry Cavalry (Uxbridge)
1884	redes as Middlesex (D of Cambridge's Hussars) Yeo Cavalry
1900-1	sponsored 34th, 35th Coys, 11 Bn and 62nd Coy, 14th Bn, 112th & 3 other Coys IY
1901	desig Middlesex IY (D of Cambridge's Hussars)
04 08 14	embodied as 1/1st
04 09 15	amal. with 1/1st C of London & 1/3rd Co of London Y to form 4th London Regt of Yeo.
00 12 15	resumed separate status
1919 ca	disembodied

07 02 20   *reconstituted & transferred to **Royal Signals** as 2nd Cavalry Divisional Signals, Royal Signals (Middlesex Yeomanry) (TA). Redes 1938 Mobile Divisional Signals, Royal Signals (Middlesex Yeomanry) (TA). Redes 1941 as 9th Armd Bde Sig Sqn, R Sigs (Middlesex Yeomanry) (TA) with S/A later. Reconst 01 01 47 as 16th Airborne Divisional Sigs, R Sigs (Middlesex Yeomanry) (TA). Redes 01 10 56 as Middlesex Yeomanry Signal Regt, R Sigs (TA). Redes 1959 as 40th Signl Regt, R Sigs (Middlesex Yeomanry) (TA). Amal 1961 with 47th (London) Signal Regt, R Sigs (TA).*

*   **Duplicate** unit formed in 1939 as 2nd Armoured Divisional Signals, R Sigs (Middlesex Yeomanry) (TA). Redes 08 11 41 as 22nd Armoured Bde Sig Sqn, R Sigs (Middlesex Yeomanry) (TA). S/A 1945 or later. Disb 01 01 47.*

*   Successors: 305 Sqn: 55 (Mersey and Thames) Signal Sqn, R Sigs (Vols) and 47th Regt: 31 (Grester London) Signal Regt, R Sigs (Vols)*

d.   **2nd CoLY - Westminster**

30 03 01   raised as 2nd County of London IY, sent out 24th Bn (Metropolitan Rifles) to SA (94th-97th Coys IY)

24 08 01   reorganised

01 04 08   additional sub-title '(Westminster Dragoons)' to perpetuate title of London and Westminster Light Horse raised 1779 and disbanded 1829 (no actual link)

04 08 14   embodied as 1/2nd

04 09 15   amal. till Dec with 1/1st Herts Y to form 5th Yeo Regt resuming separate status later

18 07 18   converted to F (19 08 18 = 104th) Bn MG Corps

1919   disbanded

07 02 20   reconstituted

26 03 20   *trans. to **Tank Corps** as 22nd (temp 4th) Armoured Car Coy (Westminster Dragoons)*

00 01 38   *expanded to 22nd Bn (Westminster Dragoons), Royal Tank Corps as officer producing unit. RTC redes 00 04 39 as Royal Tank Regt. Conv 00 09 39 as 102 OCTU*

30 11 40   converted as 2nd City of London Yeomanry (Westminster Dragoons) RAC

1943   allocated to Flail tanks

1946   suspended animation

01 01 47   reconstituted as armoured regt

01 09 51   redesignated The Westminster Dragoons (2nd C o L Y)

01 05 61   *amal. with R (Berkshire Yemanry) Bty of 299th Fd Regt RA (TA). See Berkshire.*

e.   **3rd CoLY - Sharpshooters**

07 03 00   raised 18th Bn IY comprising 67th, 70th, 71st, and 75th Coys IY.

05 03 01   23rd Bn of 90th-93rd coys raised

09 03 01   21st Bn of 80th-83rd coys raised

19 10 01   25th Bn of 115th-118th coys raised

23 07 01   reorganisation in UK and title 3rd County of London Imperial Yeomanry (Sharpshooters)

01 04 08   3rd County of London Yeomanry (Sharpshooters)

04 08 14   embodied as 1/3rd

04 09 15   till Dec 15 amalgamated with 1/1st City & 1/1st County of London Yeomanry to form 4th London Regt of Yeomanry but resumed separate status later

07 04 18   converted as part of E (19 08 18 = 103rd) Bn MG Corps

1919   disembodied

07 02 20   reconstituted

25 09 20   *transferred to **Tank Corps** as 5th, later 23rd (London) Armoured Car Company*

1938   *expanded into 23rd Cavalry Armoured Car Regiment*

30 04 39   transferred to RAC

24 08 39   redesignated 3rd County of London (Sharpshooters) RAC (TA)

01 08 44   amal. with 4th C o L Y (SS) to form 3rd/4th Co of London Yeomanry (Sharpshooters)

1945   suspended animation

01 01 47   reconstituted as an armoured regt

01 05 61   amal. with Kent Y to form Kent and County of London Yeomanry (Sharpshooters) RAC (TA). Successors: C (Kent and County of London Yeomanry) Sqn, The Royal Yeomanry Regt (Vols); R (Kent and County of London) Bty, Then London and Kent Regt, RA (T) and A (Kent and County of London Yeomanry(Sharpshooters)), 8th (T) Bn, The Queen's Regt (West Kent).

Appendix D

f.   **4th CoLY - King's Colonials/ King Edward's Horse**
29 11 01   4th County of London Imperial Yeomanry (King's Colonials) raised
07 04 05   re-designated King's Colonials, Imperial Yeomanry
12 07 10   re-designated King Edward's Horse (The King's Overseas Dominions Regiment)
1913   transferred to Special Reserve
04 08 14   embodied as 1st
00 08 19   disembodied
31 03 24   disbanded

g.   **2nd King Edward's Horse**
10 08 14   2nd King Edward's Horse raised
00 05 15   dismounted
27 01 16   mounted
00 05 17   absorbed into Tank Corps
00 08 14   reserve Sqn formed
00 02 17   expanded into Regt
1918   disbanded

h.   **4th CoLY (Sharpshooters)**
27 09 39   4th County of London Yeomanry (Sharpshooters) RAC formed
01 08 44   amalgamated with 3rd Regiment

Lothians & Borders

Berwickshire
1857   Troop reformed and amalgamated with E Lothian

East Lothian(Haddington)
1829   Served at no pay, placed on pay 1831 and disb 1838
1846   Re-raised
1857   Berwickshire Troop amalgamated
1888   augmented by Midlothian Troop
1892   aug. by W Lothian Troop to form Lothians and Berwickshire Yeomanry Cavalry Regt.
1900-02   sponsored 19th Coy IY
1901   designated Lothians and Berwickshire IY
01 04 08   redes Lothians and Border Horse Yeomanry
04 08 14   embodied as 1/1st
00 07 17   the Regiment less A & D sqns absorbed into 17th Bn, The Royal Scots
1919 ca   the A & D Sqns disembodied
07 02 20   reconstituted
21 05 20   *trans. to **Tank Corps** to form 1st, later 19th (Lothians and Border) Armoured Car Coy*
30 04 39   transferred to RAC(TA)
24 08 39   redes 1st Lothians and Border Horse Yeomanry. Suspended animation later
?? ?? ??   2nd Lothians and Border Horse Yeomanry formed as duplicate unit. S/A later
01 01 47   formed an armoured regt, 1st/2nd Lothians and Border Horse Yeomanry RAC(TA)
20 10 56   amal with Lanarkshire Yeomanry and Queen's Own Glasgow Yeomanry. See Lanarkshire

Midlothian
1829   Maintained and disb 1838
1843   Re-raised and lapsed 1850
1877   troop raised to augment East Lothian
1888   above troop amalgamated with East Lothian

West Lothian
1870   re-raised
1892   amal to join Lothians and Berwickshire Yeomanry Cavalry

Appendix D

Montgomeryshire

13 01 31	Raised and lapsed 1850
1900-02	sponsored 31st (2), 49th (2), 88th and 89th Coys I Y
1901	designated Montgomeryshire IY
01 04 08	redesignated Montgomeryshire Yeomanry
04 08 14	embodied as 1/1st
04 03 17	amal. with 1/1st Welsh Horse Yeomanry to form 25th Bn The Royal Welsh Fusiliers
1919 ca	disembodied
07 02 20	reconstituted
03 03 20	*Transferred to **Infantry** as two coys of 7th (Montgomeryshire) Bn, The Royal Welch Fusiliers (TA) which was embodied 01 09 39 and S/A 28 02 46. Bn reconst 01 01 47 and conv as 636th Light Anti-Aircraft Regt, RA (Royal Welch) (TA). Redes 1950/51 as 636th (Royal Welch) LAA Regt, RA (TA). Amal 10 03 55 with 635th Regt to form 446th (Royal Welch) Airborne Light Anti-Aircraft Regt, RA (TA). Conv and tsfd 01 07 56 as 6th/7th Bn, The Royal Welch Fusiliers (TA). 10th (Merionethshire and Montgomeryshire) Bn FOC 29 04 39 as duplicate to 7th Bn. Conv 01 08 42 as 6th Bn (Royal Welch), The Parachute Regt. Conv to Inf 00 07 46 as 10th (Merionethshire and Montgomeryshire) Bn of regt and S/A concurrently. Amal 01 01 47 with 7th Bn.*
	Successors: 6th/7th (T) Bn, The Royal Welch Fusiliers

b.	Welsh Horse Yeomanry (TF)
18 08 14	raised
00 09 15	dismounted
04 03 17	amal. as above and not reformed. Accorded seniority after Glamorgan Yeomanry because its connection with the Glamorgan TA Assn at time of formation in 1914.

Norfolkshire

17 01 31	Raised
1849	Disb
24 05 01	Norfolk IY raised by expansion of Norfolk Sqn of Suffolk Y
00 12 05	redesignated Norfolk IY (The King's Own Royal Regiment)
01 04 08	redesignated Norfolk Yeomanry (The King's Own Royal Regt)
04 08 14	embodied as 1/1st
00 09 15	dismounted
07 02 17	converted 12th Bn The Norfolk Regiment
03 06 19	disembodied
07 02 20	reconstituted as Norfolk Yeomanry (The King's Own Royal Regt)
00 05 22	*transferred to **Royal Artillery** to form 108th (Norfolk Yeomanry) Bde, RFA (TA). Redes 00 11 23 (Suffolk and Norfolk). Redes 01 11 38 108th (Suffolk and NorfolkYeomanry) Army Field Regt, RA (TA). Conv 28 11 38 to 55th (Suffolk and Norfolk Yeomanry)Anti-Tank Regt, RA (TA).*
	*Norfolk personnel subs organised as **duplicate** unit 65th Anti-Tank Regt, RA (Suffolk and Norfolk Yeomanry) (TA). Broken up 09 04 42 and btys to other regts and RHQ dispersed. Re-assembled 14 07 42 and redes 27 11 42 as 65th Anti-Tank Regt, RA (Norfolk Yeomanry) (TA). Began S/A 04 02 46, complete 28 02 46. Reconst 01 01 47 as 389th (The King's Own Royal Regiment, Norfolk Yeomanry) Light Anti-AircraftRegt, RA (TA). Amal 10 03 55 with 284th Regt, to form 284th (King's Own Royal Regiment, Norfolk Yeomanry) Light Anti-Aircraft Regt, RA (TA). Amal 01 05 61 with 358th Regt to form 308th (Suffolk and Norfolk Yeomanry) Fd Regt. See Suffolk*

Northamptonshire

27 12 30	Tps raised at B'ley & Churchwarden, Kettering, Oundle, Thrapston, Towcester, Wellingborough and paid from 1831
1838	All except Kettering and Towcester disb and these lapsed 1850
1857	Apparently various independent Troops
1873	Royal Kettering last troop disbanded
07 02 02	reformed as Northamptonshire Imperial Yeomanry
01 04 08	renamed Northamptonshire Yeomanry

Appendix D

04 08 14	embodied as 1/1st
1919 ca	disembodied
07 02 20	reconstituted
01 03 22	*transferred to Tank Corps as 7th, later 25th Armoured Car Company*
00 04 39	transferred to RAC as Northamptonshire Yeomanry
24 08 39	numbered as 1st
18 08 45	suspended animation
01 04 47?	reconstituted and amalgamated with 2nd Regt
31 10 56	amalgamated with Inns of Court as D Sqn
01 05 61	*Withdrawn, transferred, reorg and conv to form 250 (Northamptonshire Yeomanry) Field Sqn, RE (TA)*
	Successors: A Coy (northamptonshire Y), The Northamptonshire Regt (T)
27 09 39	2nd Regt formed
15 01 43	converted to light armd recce regt
18 08 44	disbanded or suspended animation
01 04 47?	amalgamated with 1st regt

Northumberland

1829	Maintained and lpsed 1850
1900-2	sponsored 14th, 15th, 55th and 105th Coys, 5th Bn IY
1901	designated Northumberland IY
01 04 08	redesignated Northumberland Yeomanry (Hussars)
04 08 14	embodied as 1/1st
1919 ca	disembodied
07 02 20	reconstituted
01 09 39	embodied
15 02 40	*transferred to Royal Artillery and conv to form 102nd Light Anti-Aircraft and Anti-Tank Regt Regt, RA (The Northumberland Hussars) (TA). Conv 14 03 41 as 102nd Anti-Tank Regt etc. Various changes with S/A 01 12 46.*
01 01 47	transferred and reconstituted as The Northumberland Hussars RAC (TA)
31 03 67	disbanded. Successors - The Northumberland Hussars (T) and The Q's Own Yeomanry
	Successor: The Northumberland Hussars (T)

Nottinghamshire

a.   **Sherwood Rangers**

1829	Maintained and lapsed 1850
1857	Enters as Nottinghamshire Yeomanry Cavalry (Sherwood Rangers) Regt
1900-2	sponsored 10th Coy, 3rd Bn IY
1901	designated Nottinghamshire IY (Sherwood Rangers)
01 04 08	redesignated Nottinghamshire Yeomanry (Sherwood Rangers)
04 08 14	embodied as 1/1st
18 08 15	dismounted
04 09 15	amal. with 1/1st NY (S Notts H) and Derby Y to form 3rd Notts & Derby Regt. of Y
00 12 15	separate status
07 10 19	reduced to cadre and subsequently disembodied
07 02 20	reconstituted
01 09 39	embodied
1940	served as Coast Artillery
12 04 41	transferred as Nottinghamshire Yeomanry (Sherwood Rangers)
01 03 46	suspended animation
01 01 47	reconstituted as The Nottinghamshire Yeomanry Sherwood Rangers) RAC (TA)
01 09 51	redesignated The Sherwood Rangers Yeomanry RAC (TA)
	Successors - B (Sherwood Rangers Yeomanry) Sqn, The Royal Yeomanry Regt (Vols) and The Sherwood Rangers Yeomanry (T)

b.   **Southern Nottinghamshire**

19 02 31?	Maintained
1900-02	sponsored 12th Coy, 3rd Bn. IY

1901	designated Nottinghamshire Imperial Yeomanry (S Notts Hus)
01 04 08	redesignated Nottinghamshire Yeomanry (Southern Notts Hus)
04 08 14	embodied as 1/1st
18 8 15	dismounted
04 09 15	amal. 1/1st Notts Y & 1/1st Derby Y to form 3rd Notts & Derbyshire Regt of Yeomanry
00 12 15	separate status
03 04 18	amalgamated with 1/1st Warwick Y to form B(19 8 18 = 100th) Bn MG Corps
1919 ca	disembodied
07 02 20	reconstituted
21 02 22	*transferred to **Royal Artillery** to form the 107th (The South Nottinghamshire Hussars Yeomanry) Bde, RFA (TF). Conv 01 11 38 to Regt RHA. Conv 18 04 42 to Field Regt. Reduced 06 06 42 to Medium Bty after heavy casualties. Regt reformed 21 03 44 as 107th Medium Regt, RA (The South Nottinghamshire Hussars Yeomanry) (TA). S/A 01 03 46. Reconst 01 01 47 as 307th (South Nottinghamshire Hussars Yeomanry) Field Regt, RA (TA). Redes 08 02 55 as 307th (RHA) (South Nottinghamshire Hussars Yeomanry) Field Regt, RA (TA)*
	***Duplicate** unit formed by 06 06 39 as 150th (South Nottinghamshire Hussars Yeomanry) Regt, RHA (TA). Conv 01 06 40 to Field Regt. Title auth 17 02 42 as 150th Field Regt, RA (The South Nottinghamshire Hussars Yeomanry) (TA). S/A 31 01 45. Reconst 01 01 47 as 350th (South Nottinghamshire Hussars Yeomanry) Heavy Regt, RA (TA) Amal 15 07 50 with 315th Regt without change of title. Amal 10 03 55 with 528th Regt to form bty of 350th (The Robin Hood Foresters) Hy Regt, RA (TA). 1956 reorg as 350(Robin Hood Foresters) Lt Regt RA. Regt broken up 01 05 61 and ceased to have any Yeomanry connections.(less R Bty reorg as 350(The Robin Hood Foresters) Fd Sqn RE in 49(West Riding) Div/Dist RE)*
	Successor: The South Nottinghamshire Hussars Yeomanry (RHA) RA (TA)
	Also - The Robin Hood (T) Bn, The Sherwood Forestoers (Notts & Derby Regt)

Oxfordshire

1829	Q's R Oxford and Watlington Tp at no pay and placed on pay 1830 and 1831 respectively
1838	Watlington Tp disb
1888	redesignated Queen's Own Oxfordshire Hussars
1900-01	sponsored 40th Cy, 10th Bn & 59th Coy, 15th Bn. IY
1901	reorganised & redesignated Oxfordshire IY(Q'sOOH)
01 04 08	redesignated Oxfordshire Y (Q'sOOH)
04 08 14	embodied as 1/1st
31 03 22	disembodied
18 04 22	*transferred to **Royal Artillery** to form part of 100th (Worcestershire and Oxfordshire Yeomanry) Bde RFA (TA). Conv 28 11 38 as 53rd (Worcesterdhire and Oxfordshire Yeomanry) Anti-Tank Regt, RA (TA). In 1939 Oxfordshire pers formed **duplicate** unit as 63rd Anti-Tank Regt, RA (TA). S/A after loss at Singapore 15 02 42. Title authorised 17 02 42 as 63rd Anti-Tank Regt, RA (Worcestershire and Oxfordshire Yeomanry) (TA)? Exchanges of pers and revised title as 63rd Anti-Tank Regt, RA (TA). S/A 18 05 46. Reconst 01 01 47 as 387th (Oxfordshire Yeomanry) Field Regt, RA (TA). Amal 15 09 50 with 299th Regt to form 387th/299th (Royal Buckinghamshire Yeomanry and Queen's Own Oxfordshire Hussars) Field Regt, RA (TA), renum 01 07 51 as 299th. Amal 31 10 56 with 345th Regt to form 299th (Royal Buckinghamshire Yeomanry, Berkshire Yeomanry and The Queen's Own Oxfordshire Hussars) Field Regt, RA (TA). Regt less R Bty amal with 431st Regt, and 143 Reporting Section to form 299th (Royal Buckinghamshire Yeomanry, #~Queen's Own Oxfordshire Hussarsand Berkshire) Field Regt, RA (TA)*
	Successor: A (Queen's Own Oxfordshire Hussars) Coy, The Oxfordshire Territorials

Pembrokeshire

1829	Castlemartin Tp at no pay, placed on pay 1831
1900-02	sponsored 30th Coy, 9th Bn. IY
1901	further sqn added
1901	designated Pembroke IY(Castlemartin)
01 04 08	redesignated Pembroke Yeomanry(Castlemartin)
04 08 14	embodied as 1/1st

00 01 15	dismounted
02 09 17	amalgamated with 1/1st Glamorgan Yeomanry to form 24th Bn, The Welsh Regt
05 07 19	disembodied
07 02 20	reconstituted
03 09 20	*transferred to **Royal Artillery** to form 102nd (Pembroke and Cardigan) Bde, RFA (TF). Redes 01 11 38 as 102nd (Pembroke and Cardigan) Army /field Regt, RA (TA). Conv 23 09 43 as 102nd Medium Regt, RA (Pembroke Yeomanry) (TA). S/A 15 01 46. Reconst 01 01 47 as 302nd (Pembroke Yeomanry)Field Regt, RA (TA). Amal 31 10 56 with 408th Regt without change of title.*
	***Duplicate** formed as 146th Field Regt, RA (Pembroke and Cardiganshire) (TA) 08 07 39. Conv 16 12 43 to Medium Regt. S/A 09 0146 and disb 01 01 47.*
01 05 61	converted as The Pembroke Y RAC(TA), an independent sqn affiliated to The Shropshire Yeomanry RAC(TA)
	Successor - A Coy (Pembroke Y), The 4th (T) Bn, The Welch Regt.

Perthshire

00 12 00	Raised by Caledonian Society of Johannesburg
15 12 00	gazetted
00 02 01	four sqns raised
1901	redes. 1st Scottish Horse
00 04 01	2nd Scottish Horse formed with Scots from UK and Australia, at first treated as Colonial Irregular Horse
00 05 01	a 5th sqn added from UK
1902	both units disbanded
30 03 03	1st and 2nd Regts accpted on 16 02 03 and gazetted as Scottish Horse Imperial Yeomanry
01 04 08	Imperial deleted
04 08 14	embodied as 1/1st and 1/2nd
00 08 14	1/3rd raised
00 10 16	1/3rd conv, less 1 sqn, to 26th Sqn Mg Corps
17 10 16	1/1st, 1/2nd and 1/3rd of 1 sqn each amal to form 13th Bn, The Black Watch
18 07 19	13th Bn, The Black Watch disembodied
15 09 19	26th Sqn MG Corps disbanded
07 02 20	recon as Scottish Horse Yeomanry
23 04 20	converted to Scottish Horse Scouts
15 02 40	*taken over as Scottish Horse Regt, **RA** (TA) and conv 15 04 40 to 79th (The Scottish Horse) Medium Regt, RA (TA). S/A 01 03 46.*
	***Duplicate** unit formed 15 04 40 as 80th (Scottish Horse) Medium Regt, RA (TA). S/A 24 11 45 and disb 01 01 47.*
01 01 47	recon as The Scottish Horse RAC(TA)
31 10 56	amal with The Fife and Forfar Yeomanry

Renfrewshire

1834	Four Tps raised and disb 1838

Shropshire

1829	North and South Salopian Regts maintained
27 04 72	the Shropshire Yeomanry Cavalry formed by amalgamation of 8 troops
1900-02	sponsored 13 Coy, 5th Bn. IY
1901	designated Shropshire IY
01 04 08	redesignated Shropshire Yeomanry
04 08 14	embodied as 1/1st
00 11 15	dismounted
02 03 17	amalgamated with 1/1st Cheshire Y to form 10th Bn, KSLI
1918	reduced to cadre
23 06 19	disembodied
07 02 20	reconstituted
01 09 39	embodied

15 02 40	*transferred to **Royal Artillery** as Shropshire Yeomanry Regt, RA (TA). Conv 15 04 40 as 75th (Shropsahire Yeomanry) Medium Regt, RA (TA). S/A 15 03 46.*
	***Duplicate** unit formed 15 04 40 as 76th (Shropshire Yeomanry) Medium Regt, RA (TA). S/A 10 11 45 and disb 01 01 47.*
01 01 47	reconstituted and transferred as The Shropshire Yeomanry RAC (TA)
01 05 61	Reorg as Regt with RHQ and two Sqns with Pembroke Y providing 3rd.
	Successors - The Shropshire Yeomanry (T) and The Mercian Yeomanry

Somerset

a.	**North Somerset**
1829	Maintained and regimented 1830
1841	Keynsham Tp disb
1844	Regimented and Wells Tp added
1900-02	sponsored 48th Coy, 7th Bn. IY
1901	designated as North Somerset IY
01 04 08	redesignated as North Somerset Yeomanry
04 08 14	embodied as 1/1st
1919 ca	disembodied
07 02 20	reconstituted
01 09 39	embodied
00 09 41	transferred to RAC (TA)
21 03 42	*transferred to **Royal Signals** to form 4th Air Formation Signals (North Somerset Yeomanry) absg existing unit. Renum 14th Air Formation Signals. S/A later.*
01 01 47	trans. and reconstituted as an airborne divisional regt, The N Somerset Y RAC (TA)
31 10 56	amal. with 44th/50th RTR to form The N Somerset Y/ 44th R Tank Regt, RAC (TA)
00 04 65	redes The North Somerset and Bristol Yeomanry RAC(TA)
	Successor: A Coy (N Somerset and Bristol Yeomanry), The Somerset Yeomanry and Light Infantry (T).

b.	**44th Bn RTC**
01 11 38	transferred and converted as 44 Bn RTC (TA)
00 04 39	trans. to RAC (TA) as 44th Bn R Tank Regt later 44th RTR, later suspended animation
01 01 47	reconstituted and amal to form 44th/50th RTR RAC (TA)
31 10 56	amalgamated with a.

c.	**50th Bn RTC**
31 03 39	formed as duplicate of b.
00 04 39	redes. 50th Bn RTR RAC (TA), later 50th RTR RAC (TA), later suspended animation
01 01 47	reconstituted and concurrently amalgamated with b.

d.	**West Somerset**
1829	At no pay, paid 1831
1900-01	sponsored 25th Coy, 2nd Bn. IY
1901	designated as West Somerset IY
01 04 08	redesignated West Somerset Yeomanry
04 08 14	embodied as 1/1st
00 09 15	dismounted
04 01 17	converted as 12th Bn Somerset Light Infantry
20 06 19	disembodied
07 02 20	reconstituted

Appendix D

01 06 20   *transferred to **Royal Artillery** to form 1st (Somerset) Army Bde, RFA (TF). Redes 25 01 22 as 94th (Dorset and Somerset Yeomanry) Bde, RFA (TA). Redes 01 11 38 55th (Wessex) Field Regt, RA (TA). S/A 31 12 46. Reconst 01 01 47 as 255th (Wessex) Medium Regt, RA (TA) and amal 01 07 50 with 421st Regt without change of title. Amal 31 10 56 with 421st Regt to form 255th (West Somerset Yeomanry and Dorset Garrison) Medium Regt, RA (TA). Amal 01 05 61 with 294th Regt to form 250th (Queen's Own Dorset and West Somerset Yeomanry) Medium Regt, RA (TA).*
*   **Duplicate** unit formed had no West Somerset Yeomanry connections (112th Field Regt, RA (TA).*
*   Successor: B Coy (West Somerset Yeomanry), The Somerset Yeomanry and Light Infantry (T)*

e.   **East Somerset Needs a resort**
1829   Taunton at no pay and placed on pay 1831
1830   Wincanton Tp raised
05 01 31   Mudford Tp raised
28 02 31   Ilminster Tp raised
03 03 31   Martock Tp raised
1832   Taunton Corps formed by amalg of Taunton, Kingston and Puriton Tps
1834   North Marsh Tp raised
1838   Martock and Mudford Tps disb
1838   Ilminster Tp at no pay, placed on pay 1843 and disb 1848
1842   Mells Tp disb
1843   Taunton Corps disb

Staffordshire
1829   Maintained as The Queen's Own Royal Regiment of Staffordshire Yeomanry Cavalry.
1900-02   sponsored 6th and 106th Coys, 4th Bn. IY
1901   designated Staffordshire IY (Queen's Own Royal Regt)
01 04 08   designated Staffordshire Y (Q'sORR)
04 08 14   embodied as 1/1st
19 12 19   reduced to cadre and later disembodied
07 02 20   reconstituted
01 09 39   embodied
12 4 41   converted to an armoured regt RAC (TA)
01 03 46   suspended animation
01 01 47   reconstituted as an armoured regt
00 04 58   converted to armoured car regt
00 10 60   converted to a reconnaisance regt
    Successor: The Staffordshire Yeomanry (Queen's Own Royal Regiment) (T).

Stirling
1829   Stirlingshire maintained and disb 1838

Suffolk
1829   Long Melford and Suffolk Borderers at no pay, placed on pay 25 04 31 and 20 07 31 respectively
07 04 31   1st L Suffolk raised
1838   These three Tps serving at no pay, paid from 1843
28 09 68   West Suffolk Yeomanry formed by amalgamation with Suffolk (Long Melford) Troop
1872   redes as Hussars
28 05 75   redesignated Suffolk Yeomanry Cavalry
01 06 83   (Loyal Suffolk Hussars) added
01 08 94   (Duke of York's Own) added
1900   Sponsored 43rd & 44th Coys, 12th Bn IY
1901   designated Imperial
01 04 08   Imperial deleted
04 08 14   embodied as 1/1st
00 12 15   dismounted
05 01 17   converted to form 15th Bn Suffolk Regt
29 06 19   disembodied

07 02 20	reconstituted
23 07 21	*transferred to **Royal Artillery** to form 103rd (Suffolk) Bde, RFA (TF). Conv 28 11 38 to 55th (Suffolk and Norfolk Yeomanry) Anti-Tank Regt, RA (TA). 220 Bt indpt 18 03 41 and disb 01 11 43. Many bty moves. Redes27 11 42 as 55th Anti-Tank Regt, RA (Suffolk Yeomanry) (TA). S/A 31 12 46. Reconst 01 01 47 308th (Suffolk Yeomanry) Anti-Tank Regt, RA (TA). Amal 01 09 50 358th Regt to form 358th (Suffolk Yeomanry) Medium Regt, RA (TA). Amal 31 10 56 with 419th Regt to form 358th (Suffolk Yeomanry) Field Regt, RA (TA). Amal 01 05 61 284th Regt to form 308th (Suffolk and Norfolk Yeomanry) Field Regt, RA (TA)*
	Successors: 202nd (Suffolk and Norfolk Yeomanry) Medium Bty, 100th (Eastern) Medium Regt, RA (Vols); and A and D (Suffolk and Norfolk Yeomanry) Coys, The Suffolk and Cambridgeshire Regt (T).

Surrey

17 01 31	Southwark Tp raised
31 03 31	Surrey Regt of YC raised and disb 1848
30 04 01	reformed as Surrey IY, a regiment of 4 troops
00 07 02	redesignated Surrey IY (The Princess of Wales's)
01 04 08	Imperial deleted
04 08 14	embodied as 1/1st
00 09 17	the Regt less C Sqn absorbed into 10th Bn, The Queen's (RWSR)
1919 ca	disembodied
07 02 20	reconstituted as Surrey Yeomanry (Queen Mary's Regt)(TA)
27 03 22	*transferred to **Royal Artillery** to form part of 98th (Surrey and Sussex Yeomanry) Bde, RFA (TA). Redes 01 11 38 as 98th (Surrey and Sussex Yeomanry, Queenary's) Army Field Regt, RA (TA). S/A 18 05 46. Reconst 01 01 47 as 298th (Surrey Yeomanry, Queen Mary's) Field Regt, RA (TA). Amal 01 05 61 with 263rd (less two btys),, 291st and 381st Regts to form 263rd (Surrey Yeomanry, Queen Mary's) Field Regt, RA (TA)*
	Successor: The Surrey Yeomanry (Queen Mary's Regiment) (T), comprising P and Q (Surrey Yeomanry, Queen Mary's) Btys.

Sussex

28 03 31	Petworth Tp raised, at no pay from 1838 , paid from 1843
18 05 31	Arundel & Bramber Tp raised and disb 1848
1880's	Brighton Troop of Middlesex Hussars serving!
00 09 01	the Sussex Imperial Yeomanry formed from nucleus of personnel who served in South Africa as 69th Coy IY and 3rd Tp 20th Coy (Fifeshire Lt Horse volunteers)
01 04 08	redesignated as Sussex Yeomanry
04 08 14	embodied as 1/1st
00 09 15	dismounted
03 01 17	converted to 16th Bn, Royal Sussex Regt
1919 ca	disembodied
07 02 20	reconstituted
09 10 20	*transferred to **Royal Artillery** to form 13th Army Bde, RFA (TA). 27 03 22 conv to include Surrey btys - see Surrey.*
	*Reorg 05 06 39 as **duplicate** unit of 98th Fd Regt and desig 144th Field Regt, RA (Surrey and Sussex Yeomanry, Queen Mary's)(TA) with title authorised 17 02 42. Began S/A 21 09 45, completed 11 10 45. Reconst 01 01 47 as 344th (Sussex Yeomanry) Light Anti-Aircraft and Searchlight Regt, RA (TA). Amal 30 06 50 with 605th Regt without change of title. Amal 10 03 55 with 258th, 313th and 641st Regts to form 258th (Sussex Yeomanry) Light Anti-AircraftRegt, RA (TA). Amal 01 05 61 with 257th Regt to form 257th (SussexYeomanry) Field Regt, RA (TA)*
	Successor: 200th (Sussex Yeomanry) Medium Bty, 100th (Eastern) Medium ?REgt, RA (Vols)

Warwickshire

1829	Maintained as as Warwickshire Regiment of Yeomanry Cavalry and lapsed 1850
1900-02	sponsored 5th and 103rd Coys, 5th Bn. IY
1901	designated Warwickshire IY
01 04 08	Imperial deleted
04 08 14	embodied as 1/1st

00 08 15	dismounted
04 09 15	amal. with 1/1st Worcs and 1/1st R Glos Hus to form 1st S Midlands Regt of Y
00 12 15	separate status
03 04 18	amalgamated with 1/1st S Notts Hussars to form B Bn (19 8 18 = 100th) MG Corps
1919 ca	disembodied
07 02 20	reconstituted
?	embodied
?	converted to Lorried Infantry
12 04 41	transferred to RAC (TA)
?	suspended animation
01 01 47	reconstituted as an armoured regt
01 10 56	amal. to form The Queen's Own Warwickshire and Worcestershire Yeomanry RAC (TA)
	Successor: The Queen's Own Warwickshire and Worcestershire Yeomanry (T)

Westmorland

1829	At no pay as Westmoreland & Cumberland Yeomanry Cavalry, placed on pay from 1831 and lapsed 1850
1900-02	sponsored 24th Coy, 8th Bn. IY
1901	Imperial added to title
01 04 08	Imperial deleted from title
04 08 14	embodied as 1/1st
22 09 17	absorbed into 7th Bn, The Border Regiment
00 12 18	reduced to cadre
24 04 19	disembodied
??	
07 02 20	disembodied
00 03 20	*transferred to **Royal Artillery**. Redes 1921 as 93rd (Westmorland and Cumberland Yeomanry) Bde, RFA (TA). Redes 01 11 38 as 51st(Westmorland and Cumberland) Field Regt, RA (TA) with 203 & 370 Btys. Amal 18 10 43 with 69th Regt to form 51st/69th Regt, RA (TA) serving in 16th Inf Bde, as Infantry with long range Penetration role in India and Burma 1943-44. S/A 14 10 44. Reconst 01 01 47 as 251st (Westmorland and ?Cumberland Yeomanry) Field Regt, RA (TA).*
???	*309(Westmorland and Cumberland) Coast Regt RA in 1948 had S Bty disb and remainder reorg as Fd Regt RA. The 251 amal 30 06 50 with 309th Regt without change of title. Redes 30 09 53 as 251st (Westmorland and Cumberland Yeomanry) Field Regt, RA (TA). Regt broken up 01 05 61, with Q Bty reorg as 851 (Westmorland and Cumberland Yeomanry) Indep Fd Bty, RA (TA). Duplicate formed 1939 as 109th (W&C) Fd Regt. with 204 & 369 Btys, plus 436 Bty formed 16 10 41 and 14 HAA Bty from 6th Coast Regt.. Amal with 69th Regt 18 10 43.*
	Successor: B (Westmorland and Cumberland Yeomanry) Co, 4th (T) Bn, The Border Regiment.

Wigtownshire

1834	Wigtown and Stanraer Tps raised and disb 1838

Wiltshire

1829	R Wiltshire maintained
11 12 30	Corsham Tp raised. ??Westbury and Dinton
1831	Pewsey Tp added to R Wilts, Potterne and Ramsbury Tps raised 15 and 20 Feb
1836	Potterne Tp disb
1838	Ramsbury Tp disb
1959-76	contained attached dismounted riflemen
23 4 63	redes The Prince of Wales's Own Regt of Wiltshire Yeomanry Cavalry
1900-01	sponsored 1st and 2nd Coys, 1st Bn. IY
1901	designated Royal Wiltshire Imperial Yeomanry (P of W's O R Regt)
01 04 08	Imperial deleted
04 08 14	embodied as 1/1st
26 09 17	absorbed into 6th Bn, The Duke of Edinburgh's (Wiltshire Regt)
13 05 18	reduced to Cadre
20 6 18	reconstituted and again reduced to Cadre

11 6 19	disembodied
07 02 20	reconstituted
01 09 39	embodied
00 01 41	B Sqn served as AA and Searchlight Bty
12 04 41	transferred to RAC (TA)
1945+	suspended animation
01 01 47	reconstituted as divisional regt RAC (TA)
	Successors: A (Royal Wiltshire Yeomanry) Sqn, The Royal Yeomanry Regiment (Vols) and B Coy (Royal Wiltshire Yeomanry), The Royal Wiltshire Territorials.

Worcestershire

29 04 31	raised and became The Queen's Own Worcestershire Hussars. Lapsed 1850
1900-02	sponsored 16th and 102nd Coys,5th Bn. IY
1901	designated as Worcestershire IY (The Q'sOWH)
01 04 08	Imperial deleted
04 08 14	embodied as 1/1st
04 09 15	amal. 1/1st Warwick and 1/1st R Glou Hus to form 1st S Midlands Regt of Yeomanry
0012 15	separate status
02 07 19	reduced to cadre and later disembodied
07 02 20	reconstituted
18 04 22	*transferred to **Royal Artillery** to form part of 100th (Worcestershire and Oxfordshire Yeomanry) Bde, RFA (TA). Redes 01 11 38 as Field Regtb and conv 28 11 38 as 53rd (Worcestershire and Oxfordshire Yeomanry) Anti-Tank Regt, RA (TA). Conv 03 11 43 to 53rd Airlanding Light Regt, RA (Worcestershire Yeomanry) (TA). S/A 01 01 47 with pers to new war-formed 53rd A/L Lt Regt, RA. TA unit reconst as 300th (Queen's Own Worcestershire Yeomanry) Anti-Tank Regt, RA (TA)*
01 09 50	converted to a regiment, The Queen's Own Worcestershire Hussars RAC (TA)
01 10 56	amalgamated with The Warwickshire Yeomanry

Yorkshire - East Riding

1902	Lord Wenlock's Horse raised following South African war
15 05 03	accepted as East Riding of Yorkshire Imperial Yeomanry
01 04 08	Imperial deleted
04 08 14	embodied as 1/1st
07 04 18	converted as part of D Bn (19 8 18 = 102nd) MG Corps
1919	disembodied
07 02 20	reconstituted
23 08 20	*trans. to Tank Corps as ER of Yorkshire, later 26th (ER of Yorkshire) Armed Car Coy.*
*30 0 39	transferred to RAC (TA) and mechanised as div cav
24 08 39	designated 1st East Riding Yeomanry, RAC (TA)
	2nd East Riding Yeomanry, RAC (TA) formed as a **duplicate** unit. *Conv 25 06 40 to **Infantry** as 10th (East Riding Yeomanry) Bn, The Green Howards (Alexandra, Princess of Wales's Own Yorkshire Regt). Conv to **parachutes** 01 01 43. S/A 00 12 46. Reconst 01 03 47 as 12th (Yorkshire) Bn of that regt. Amal 01 10 56 with 13th (Lancashire) Bn Parachute Regiment (TA).*
00 09 39	embodied
?	suspended animation
01 01 47	reconstituted as armoured regt, The East Riding of Yorkshire Yeomanry RAC (TA)
01 09 51	The East Riding Yeomanry RAC (TA)
01 11 56	amal to form The Queen's Own Yorkshire Yeomanry RAC (TA)

Yorkshire - West Riding
a.   1st W Yorkshire

1829	Maintained as SW Yorkshire (later 1st West York Yeomanry Cavalry. Lapsed 1850
1894	4th Sqn added from elements of disbanded 2nd WYYC
1888	redesignated as Yorkshire Dragoons
1897	redesignated as The Queen's Own Yorkshire Dragoons
1900-02	sponsored 11th, 111th Coys, 3rd Bn and part of 66th Coy, 16th Bn IY

Appendix D

1901	designated as Yorkshire Dragoons IY (Queen's Own)
01 04 08	Imperial deleted
04 08 14	embodied as 1/1st
00 02 18	converted to cyclists
1919 ca	disembodied
07 02 20	reconstituted
01 09 39	embodied
00 12 40	converted to a Motor Bn, 9th Bn KOYLI
00 09 44	suspended animation reverting to RAC (TA)
01 01 47	reconstituted as The Queen's Own Yorkshire Dragoons RAC (TA)
01 01 56	amalgamated to form QOYY. Successors - The Q O Yorkshire Y (T)

b.   **2nd W Yorkshire**

?? ?? ??	Morley and Agbrigg raised
1838	Disb
14 07 43	Redes 2nd West Yorkshire Yeomanry Cavalry (Prince of Wales's Own)
1894	Disbanded with elements transferred to form 4th Sqn Yorkshire Dragoons

c.   **Yorkshire Hussars**

1829	Maintained as Yorkshire Hussars. Lapsed 1850
25 12 63	redesignated with (Alexandra, Princess of Wales's Own) added
1900-02	sponsored 9th and 109th Coys, 3rd Bn. IY
1901	Imperial added to title
01 04 08	Imperial deleted from title
04 08 14	embodied as 1/1st
26 08 17	dismounted
13 11 17	absorbed into 9th Bn West Yorkshire Regt
05 07 19	disembodied
07 02 20	reconstituted as Yorkshire Hussars Yeomanry (Alexandra, Princess of Wales's Own)
01 09 39	embodied
12 04 41	transferred to RAC (TA)
19 12 44	converted as an infantry reconnaisance regt
?	suspended animation
01 01 47	reconstituted as armoured regt
01 11 56	amal. with The Q'sO Yorks Dgns and The ER Yeo to form The Q'sO Yorks Y RAC (TA) Successor: The Queen's Own Yorkshire Yeomanry (T).

d.   **N Yorkshire**

30 03 31	N York raised
1838	Disb

Appendix E

Territorial & Army Volunteer Reserve (T&AVR), 1967-1994

Notes:

1	The name Territorial Army was restored on 7th August 1979 although not reflected in titles.
2	Only units with Yeomanry connections are included and these are separated into groups in the order; Royal Armoured Corps - Royal Artillery - Royal Engineers - Royal Signals - Infantry - Royal Logistics Corps. Transfers are linked into the narrative.
3	No attempt has been made to ascribe precedence. The order of arrangement, so far as is possible, is alpha-numerical
4	Cadres constitute Units in their own right, hence they had first to be disbanded in 1971 when they were required to form sub-units of new units.

Appendix E1 Royal Armoured Corps

Ayrshire
01 04 67   The Ayrshire (Earl of Carrick's Own) Yeomanry (T)
01 04 69   reduced to Cadre, with some personnel to RCT
01 04 71   cadre disbanded to form Sqn in The Queen's Own Yeomanry, see also The Scottish Y

Berkshire and Westminster - See The Royal Yeomanry

Cheshire
01 04 67   The Cheshire Yeomanry (Earl of Chester's Territorials)
01 04 69   Cadre, The Cheshire Y (E of C'), also some personnel to 80 (Cheshire) Sigs (Y) Sqn, later redes (Cheshire Yeomanry)
01 04 71   Cadre disbanded to form Sqn in The Queen's Own Yeomanry

Devonshire
01 04 67   The Devonshire Territorials (Royal Devon Yeomanry/ The First Rifle Volunteers) was at first to be RA but later decided to affiliate with RAC and 5RTR
01 04 69   reduced to Cadre
01 04 71   Cadre disbanded to form Sqn in The Wessex Yeomanry

Fife and Forfar / Scottish Horse
01 04 67   The Fife and Forfar Yeomanry/Scottish Horse (T)
01 04 69   Cadre formed, The Highland Yeomanry with some personnel to newly formed RCT (Y) Sqn
01 04 75   Cadre disbanded
05 04 93   C Sqn formed in The Scottish Yeomanry

Gloucestershire
01 04 67   The Royal Gloucestershire Hussars (T)
01 04 69   reduced to Cadre
01 04 71   disbanded to form parts of The Wessex Yeomanry

Appendix E

Inns of Court and City of London
01 04 67   HQ and A Coys (Inns of Court and City of London) The London Yeomanry Territorials.
Note attachment of band to The Royal Yeomanry
01 04 69   reduced to Cadre with personnel to new formed R Sigs (Y) Sqn
01 07 75   Cadre disbanded

Kent and County of London - see The Royal Yeomanry

Lancaster
01 04 67   The Duke of Lancaster's Own Yeomanry (Royal Tank Regiment) (T) formed by
amalgamation of DLOY and 40/41 RTR (TA)
01 04 69   Cadre formed, with some personnel to new formed RE Sqn
01 04 71   Expanded to form the Duke of Lancaster's Own Yeomanry (Royal Tank Regiment)
29 02 72   redesignated The Duke of Lancaster's Own Yeomanry
01 04 92   RHQ, HQ, B and D Sqns merged with A Sqn reducing to one Sqn plus RHQ Cadre
01 07 92   B & D Sqn vols to A Sqn, to RE or Infantry
01 11 92   Regt reduced to Recce Sqn when both Regts disbanded and new Regt formed
The Royal Mercian and Lancastrian Yeomanry

Leicestershire and Derbyshire
01 04 67   The Leicestershire and Derbyshire (Prince Albert's Own) Yeomanry (T)
01 04 69   Cadre formed
01 04 71   Cadre disbanded to form Infantry (Y), see The Royal Anglian Regiment
01 05 92   New Sqn formed in The Royal Yeomanry from vols from Coy 7 (V) R Anglian at Liecester
01 04 75   Redes Coy

Lowland Yeomanry
01 04 67   The Queen's Own Lowland Yeomanry (T)
01 04 69   Cadre formed with vols to RCT (Y)
01 04 75   Cadre disbanded.
Successors - 225 (Queen's Own Lowland Yeomanry) Fuel Tanker Sqn, 154 Transport Regt

North Irish Horse
01 04 67   D (NIH) Sqn The Royal Yeomanry (V) formed, see also The North Irish Horse (T)
01 04 69   The North Irish Horse reduced to Cadre, also personnel to new formed R Sigs (Y) Sqn
01 04 75   Cadre disbanded
01 04 93   **Independent Recce Sqn, North Irish Horse RAC**   taken from The Royal Yeomanry

The Queen's Own Mercian Yeomanry
01 04 71   The regiment formed consisting:
A (Warwickshire and Worcestershire Y) Sqn
B (Staffordshire Y) Sqn
C (Shropshire Y) Sqn
X Troop from RA as part of A Sqn from Worcestershire RA
21 10 71   The title, The Mercian Yeomanry retroactive to 01 04 71
25 05 73   redesignated The Queen's Own Mercian Yeomanry
01 10 92   RHQ & HQ formed from pers of C Sqn which closed
See The Royal Mercian and Lancastrian Yeomanry

Appendix E

Royal Mercian and Lancastrian Yeomanry
01 10 92   The Royal Mercian and Lancastrian Yeomanry raised consisting
            RHQ & HQ Sqn formed from pers of C (Q'sOMY) Sqn
            A (QOW & WY) Sqn
            B (Staffordshire Y) Sqn
            D(DLOY) Sqn

Northumberland
01 04 67   The Northumberland Hussars (T)
01 04 69   Cadre formed
01 04 71   Cadre disbanded to form RHQ & NH (Northumberland Hussars) Sqn (at first HQ Sqn)
            The Queen's Own Yeomanry

Queen's Own Yeomanry
01 04 67   formed with provisional title 2nd Armoured Car Regiment with
            RHQ and LAD at Tynemouth and Hebburn
            A (Q's O Yorkshire Y) Sqn
            B (Ayrshire Y) Sqn
            C (Cheshire Y) Sqn
            HQ (Northumberland Hussars) Sqn
30 04 71   Redesignation approved: The Queen's Own Yeomanry
ca 11 72   HQ Sqn redes NH (Northumberland Hussars) Sqn
            Y (Queen's Own Yorkshire Yeomanry) Sqn, was A Sqn
            A (Ayrshire Yeomanry) Sqn, was B Sqn
            C (Cheshire Yeomanry) Sqn, renamed
01 04 86   D (Northumberland Hussars) Sqn formed
00 04 92   B (Sherwood Rangers Yeomanry) Sqn joined as new B Sqn from the R Yeomanry
01 11 92   A (Ayrshire Yeomanry) Sqn trans to Scottish Yeomanry

Royal Yeomanry
01 04 67   The Royal Yeomanry Regiment (V) formed with
            RHQ in London, HQ (Berkshire and Westminster Dragoons) Sqn
            A (Royal Wiltshire Yeomanry) Sqn
            B (Sherwood Rangers Yeomanry) Sqn
            C (Kent and County of London Yeomanry) Sqn
            D (North Irish Horse) Sqn
            Band (Inns of Court and City Yeomanry)
01 04 69   reorganised as four Armoured Car Sqns
09 05 67   redesignated The Royal Yeomanry
08 10 73   redes C Sqn subtitle (Kent and Sharpshooters Yeomanry) and 'and'
            replaces '&' in B & C Sqns subtitles
00 04 92   B Sqn to QOY as B Sqn
01 05 92   new formed B (L&DY) Sqn from R Anglian Regt
            redes C (K & SY) Sqn
01 11 92   D(NIH) Sqn reorg from Armoured Recce to ND Recce Sqn
01 04 93   D(NIH) Sqn leaves as Independent Sqn, see North Irish Horse

The Scottish Yeomanry
01 08 92   New Regiment. RHQ formed as Cadre

Appendix E

01 11 92   A (Ayrshire Yeomanry) Sqn trans from QOY
            B (Lanarkshire and QORGY) Sqn formed from vols 222 Sqn, 154 Regt RCT
            C (Fife and Forfar/ Scottish Horse) Sqn formed from vols 239 Sqn, 153 Regt RCT
            RHQ & HQ (Lothians and Border Horse) Sqn formed from vols 239 Sqn Regt RCT and
            225 Sqn 154 Regt RCT

Sherwood Rangers Yeomanry
01 04 67   B Sqn formed in The Royal Yeomanry Regiment and The Sherwood Rangers Yeomanry
01 04 69   Cadre formed
01 04 71   Cadre disbanded to form A (Sherwood Rangers) Sqn, 3rd (V) Bn The Worcestershire
            and Sherwood Foresters Regiment
01 04 75   Redes Coy

Shropshire
01 04 67   The Shropshire Yeomanry (T) formed
01 04 69   Cadre formed with some pers to (Shropshire Yeomanry) Sig Sqn
01 04 71   Cadre disbanded to form RHQ and C (Shropshire Yeomanry) Sqn, see Mercian Yeomanry

Staffordshire
01 04 67   The Staffordshire Yeomanry (QORR) (T)
01 04 69   Cadre formed
01 04 71   Cadre disbanded to form B Sqn in Mercian Yeomanry

Warwickshire and Worcestershire
01 04 67   The Queen's Own Warwickshire and Worcestershire Yeomanry (T)
01 04 69   Cadre formed, with some pers to 67 (QOWWY) Sig Sqn
01 04 71   Cadre disbanded to form A (Queen's Own Warwickshire and Worcestershire Yeomanry)
            Sqn, The Queen's Own Mercian Yeomanry

Wessex Yeomanry
01 04 71   The Wessex Yeomanry formed in an infantry rôle with the following sqns from Cadre:
            RHQ and A (Royal Gloucestershire Hussars) Sqn
            B (Royal Wiltshire Yeomanry) Sqn
            C (Royal Gloucestershire Hussars) Sqn
            D (Royal Devon Yeomanry/ 1st Rifle Volunteers) Sqn
16 09 74   Sub-title of D Squadron altered to Royal Devon Yeomanry. See later The Devonshire
            Territorials
01 04 92   C Sqn vols to HQ Sqn

Wiltshire
01 04 67   A (RWY) Sqn formed in The Royal Yeomanry Regt, also B Coy (RWY) The Royal Wiltshire
            Territorials
01 04 69   Cadre formed
01 04 71   Cadre disbanded to form B (Royal Wiltshire Yeomanry) Sqn The Wessex Yeomanry

Yorkshire
01 04 67   The Queen's Own Yorkshire Yeomanry (T)
01 04 69   Cadre formed
01 04 71   Cadre disbanded to form Y (Queen's Own Yorkshire Yeomanry) Sqn The Queen's
            Own Yeomanry (at first A Sqn)

Appendix E

Appendix E2 Royal Artillery

Buckinghamshire
01 04 67   P (RBY) Bty The Buckinghamshire Regt RA (T)
01 04 69   Cadre formed with some personnel to Infantry
01 04 71   Transferred to Infantry (Y), see Wessex Regt

Essex
01 04 67   The Essex Yeomanry RHA (T)
01 04 69   Cadre formed with some personnel to R Sigs (Y)
01 04 75   Cadre disbanded

Flintshire and Denbighshire
01 04 67   The Flintshire and Denbyshire Yeomanry RA (T)
01 04 69   Cadre formed
01 04 71   Cadre disb to form Infantry (Y)

Glamorgan - see 104th Regt RA (V)

Hertfordshire and Bedfordshire - see 100th Regt RA (V)

The Highland Regiment RA (T)
01 04 67   Orkney & Zetland (Lovat Scouts) Bty formed in The Highland Regiment RA (T) from
            540 Lt AD Regt RA (The Lovat Scouts) (TA)
01 04 69   Regiment reduced to Cadre. No 1 (LS) Coy, H'land Vols also formed from personnel
01 04 75   Cadre disbanded

Kent and London
01 04 67   R (K & CLY) Bty The London and Kent Regt RA (T)
01 04 69   Cadre formed with some personnel to R Sigs (Y)
01 04 71   Cadre disbanded to form Infantry

Lancashire
01 04 67   A Tp (The Lancashire Hussars), P Bty (1st West Lancashire) The West Lancashire
            Regt (RA) (T)
01 04 69   Cadre formed
01 04 75   Cadre disbanded

Nottinghamshire
01 04 67   South Notts Hussars Yeomanry (RHA) RA (T)
01 04 69   Cadre formed
01 01 70   307 (SNHY RHA)Bty RA (V)_raised
01 04 71   Cadre disbanded and personnel transferred to Infantry (Y)
00 00 92   307 Bty transferred to 100 (Yeomanry) Regt RA

Suffolk and Norfolk - see 100th Regt RA (V)

Surrey
01 04 67   The Surrey Yeomanry (QMR) RA (T)
01 04 69   Cadre formed
01 04 71   Cadre disbanded to Infantry (Y)

Appendix E

Sussex - see 100th Regt RA (V)

100th (Yeomanry) Field Regt
01 04 67   100 (E) Med Regt RA (V) formed with RHQ and HQ Bty and the following:
                200 (Sussex Yeomanry) Med Bty
                201 (Hertfordshire and Bedfordshire Yeomanry) Med Bty
                202 (Suffolk and Norfolk Yeomanry) Med Bty
31 10 70   100th Med Bty
00 09 76   100th (Y) Med Bty
01 04 78   Btys and Regt redes as Field
00 00 92   200 Bty transferred and converted to 127 (Sx Y) Fd Sqn, 78th (Fortress) Engr Regt RE (V)

104th Light Air Defence Regt RA (V)
01 04 67   211 (South Wales) AD Bty, E (Glamorgan Yeomanry) Troop forms part
31 01 70   100th Med Regt
01 04 71   Redes C (Glamorgan Yeomanry) Troop
01 04 78   aug to AD Bty

Appendix E3 Royal Engineers

Sussex
00 00 92   200 Field Bty RA reorg as 127 (Sussex Yeomanry) Field Sqn, 78th (Fortress)Engineer Regt RE (V)

Appendix E4 Royal Signals

31st (Greater London) Signal Regt (V)
01 04 67   47 (Middlesex Yeomanry) Sig Sqn

32nd (Scottish) Signal Regt (V)
01 04 69   69 (North Irish Horse) Sig Sqn

33rd (Lancashire and Cheshire) Signal Regt (V)
01 04 69   80 (Cheshire Yeomanry) Sig Sqn. Pers from T&AVR III joined and was then redes (Cheshire Yeomanry)

35th (South Midland) Signal Regt (V)
01 04 69   95 (Shropshire Yeomanry) Sig Sqn

37th (Wessex and Welsh) Signal Regt (V)
01 04 69   67 (Queen's Own Warwickshire and Worcestershire Yeomanry) Sig Sqn

38th Signal Regt (V)
01 04 93   70 (Essex Yeomanry) Sig Sqn trans from 71st Sig Regt

39th (City of London) Signal Regt
01 04 69   5 (The Queen's Own Oxfordshire Hussars) Sig Sqn

Appendix E

71 (Yeomanry) Signal Regt
01 04 69   RHQ and HQ Sqn
        68 (Inns of Court and City Yeomanry) Sig Sqn
        70 (Essex Yeomanry) Sig Sqn
        94 (Berkshire Yeomanry) Sig Sqn
        HQ (265 Kent and Sharpshooters Yeomanry) Sig Sqn
01 04 93   70 (Essex Yeomanry) Sig Sqn transferred to 38th Signal Regt (V)

Appendix E5 Infantry

7th (V) Battalion The Royal Anglian Regiment
01 04 71   Formed with HQ and sub-units from The Leicestershire and Derbyshire (Prince Albert's Own) Yeomanry Sqn from Cadre, The Leicestershire and Derbyshire (PAO) Yeomanry
01 04 75   Sqn redes a coy
31 10 75   Rebadged
00 00 92   redes and transferred as B Sqn to The Royal Yeomanry

The Bedfordshire and Hertfordshire Regiment (T)
01 04 67   Nos 2 (Hertfordshire Yeomanry) and 3 (Bedfordshire Yeomanry) Coys from RA (TA)
01 04 69   Cadre formed
01 04 71   Cadre disb to form B (Bedfordshire) Coy, 6th (V) Bn The Royal Anglian Regiment

The Royal Berkshire Territorials
01 04 67   A Coy (Berkshire Yeomanry) from the Berks & WD, RAC (TA) and B Coy (Berks Artillery) from 299th Field Regt RA (TA) and C Coy (R Berks) fr 4/6 R Berks
01 04 69   Cadre formed and personnel to R Sigs (Y)
01 04 71   Cadre disb to form C (Royal Berkshire) Coy, 2nd Bn The Wessex Volunteers

4th (T) Battalion The Border Regiment
01 04 67   B (Westmorland and Cumberland Yeomanry) Coy from RA (TA)
01 04 69   Cadre formed
01 04 71   Cadre disb to form B (4th Border Regiment) Coy, The Northumbrian Volunteers
01 04 75   C Coy 4 (V) KOR Border Regt on reorg

The Buckinghamshire Regiment
01 04 69   The Buckinghamshire Regiment RA (T) reduced to a cadre
01 04 71   Disb to form A Coy (Later B (Royal Buckinghamshire Yeomanry) Coy), 2nd Bn The Wessex Volunteers
01 04 75   Disb with pers to other Coys and trans to RGJ

The Devonshire Territorials (Royal Devon Yeomanry/ The 1st Rifle Volunteers)
01 04 69   Cadre formed
01 04 71   Cadre disb to form D (Royal Devon Yeomanry/1st Rifle Volunteers) Sqn, The Wessex Yeomanry
1973/4   Redes D (RDY) Sqn

Appendix E

The Dorset Territorials
01 04 67	HQ and A Coy (Queen's Own Dorset Yeomanry) from RA (TA)
01 04 69	Cadre formed
01 04 71	Cadre disb to form D (Queen's Own Dorset Yeomanry) Coy, 2nd Bn The Wessex Regiment (Volunteers)
00 00 78	trans as D (QODY) Coy 1st Wessex Regt (Rifle Vols)
00 00 92	trans as D Coy 4th (V) Devon and Dorset Regt

Hampshire and Isle of Wight Territorials
01 04 67	HQ and C Coy (Wessex Royal Artillery, Princess Beatrice's) from 457 (Wx) Hy AD Regt (Hampshire Carabiniers Y) RA (TA)
01 04 69	Cadre formed
01 04 71	Cadre disb

51st Highland Volunteers
01 04 67	B Coy (Seaforth) formed from 11th Bn Seaforth Highlanders and parts of 540th Lt AD Regt, (TA)
01 04 69	No 1 (Lovat Scouts) Coy formed
01 04 71	2nd Bn formed including A (Lovat Scouts) Coy by redes of No 1 Coy and B Coy from 1st Bn..
01 04 74	3rd Bn formed including B (Queen's Own Highlanders) Coy from 2nd Bn

5th (T) Battalion The Royal Irish Fusiliers
01 04 67	B Coy formed from elements of the North Irish Horse, RAC (TA)
01 04 69	Cadre formed
01 04 71	Cadre disb

The London Yeomanry and Territorials
01 04 67	HQ and A Coy (IC&CY) from Inns of Court and City Yeomanry, RAC (TA)
01 04 69	Cadre formed
01 04 75	Cadre disb

The Northamptonshire Regiment (T)
01 04 67	A Coy (Northamptonshire Yeomanry) from 250 Field Sqn, (NY) RE (TA)
01 04 69	Cadre formed
01 04 71	Cadre disb

The 7th (T) Battalion The Royal Northumberland Fusiliers
01 04 67	units formed partly with elements of the Northumberland Hussars, RAC (TA)
01 04 69	Cadre formed
01 04 71	Cadre disb

The Oxfordshire Territorials
01 04 67	HQ and A (QOOH) Coy from Q Bty of 299 (RBY, QOOH and Berks) Fd Regt RA (TA)
01 04 69	Cadre formed and some personnel to R Sigs (Y)
01 04 75	Cadre disb

3rd (T) Battalion Queen's Own Highlanders (Seaforth and Camerons)
01 04 67	A (Lovat Scouts) Coy from 540 Lt AD Regt, RA (Lovat Scouts) (TA)
01 04 69	Cadre formed, also No 1 (LS) Coy under 51st Highland Volunteers
01 04 71	Cadre disb to form HQ, 2nd Bn 51st Highland Vols. No 1 (LS) Coy trans as A (LS) Coy
00 00 91	After further reorg formed part of A (QOH & LS) Coy and D (Gordon Hldrs & LS) Coy
0 00 92	Made parts of C & D Coys in 2/51 Highland Volunteers

Appendix E

6th (T) Battalion The Queen's Regiment (Queen's Surreys)
01 04 67	Parts of HQ and A from parts of Kent and County of London Y (SS), RAC (TA)
01 04 69	Cadre formed
01 04 71	Bn reformed as 6th (V) Bn The Queen's Regt from Cadre and other Cadres with D Bty (Surrey Yeomanry) (Queen Mary's) Cadre, The Surrey Y (Queen Mary's Regiment)
01 04 75	Amal with 7th (V) Bn of same Regt to form 6th/7th (V) Bn with loss of Y tradition

8th (T) Battalion The Queen's Regiment (West Kent)
01 04 67	A (Kent and County of London Yeomanry Sharpshooters) Coy from part of that Regt
01 04 69	Cadre formed
01 04 71	Cadre disb

The Robin Hood (Territorial) Bn, The Sherwood Foresters (Notts & Derbys Regt)
01 04 67	Formed
01 04 69	Cadre formed,with some personnel to new formed RE unit
01 04 71	Cadre disb

The Somerset Yeomanry and Light Infantry (T)
01 04 67	A Coy (NS & Bristol Y) from the NS & Bristol Y and B Coy (WSY) from 250th (QOD & WSY) Medium Regt, RA (TA)
01 04 69	Cadre formed
01 04 71	Cadre disb to form A (Somerset Yeomanry Light Infantry) and B (Somerset Yeomanry Light Infantry) Coys, 6th Battalion The Light Infantry (V)
00 00 92	Amalg with A Coy without Yeomanry link

The Suffolk and Cambridgeshire Regiment (T)
01 04 67	A (S&Norfolk Y) Coy and D (Suffolk and Norfolk Yeomanry) from RA (TA)
01 04 69	Cadre formed
01 04 71	Cadre disb

3rd (V) Battalion The Royal Welch Fusiliers
01 04 71	Cadre tfd from RA (TA) and disb to form B (Flintshire and Denbighshire Y) Coy
00 00 90	Sub-titles dropped and Yeomanry link lost

The 4th (T) Battalion The Welch Regiment
01 04 67	A (Pembroke Yeomanry) Coy formed from Pembroke Yeomanry RAC (TA)
01 04 69	Cadre formed, with some personnel to RCT (Y)
00 03 71	By now des The 4th (Carmarthenshire and Pembrokeshire) Bn The Royal Regiment of Wales (24th/41st Foot)

Welsh Volunteers
01 04 67	A Coy formed from RA (TA)
01 04 71	Reorg with A Coy became A (4th Bn Royal Welch Fusiliers) Coy, 3rd (V) Bn The Royal Regiment of Wales (24th/41st Foot)

2nd Battalion The Wessex Volunteers
01 04 71	A Coy (later B) (Royal Buckinghamshire Yeomanry) Coy and D (Queen's Own Dorset Yeomanry) Coy from Cadres
30 03 72	Redes 2nd Battalion The Wessex Regiment (V)
01 04 75	B (RBY) Coy disb

Appendix E

The Royal Wiltshire Territorials
01 04 67   B Coy (Royal Wiltshire Yeomanry) from part of The Royal Wiltshire Y, RAC (TA)
01 04 69   Regt less B Coy transferred to RAC, Cadre formed
01 04 75   Cadre disb, but B Coy tfd to Wessex Yeomanry

The Worcestershire and Sherwood Foresters Regiment
01 04 71   Formed with A (Sherwood Rangers) Sqn from Cadre, The Sherwood Rangers Y and B
            (SNH) Bty from Cadre, The SNHY (RHA) RA and trans to infantry as 3rd (V) Battalion
            The Worcestershire and Sherwood Foresters Regiment
01 04 75   Disb. Personnel formed detached D Coy
00 00 78   B (LDY) Coy 3 (V) Bn The Worcestershire and Sherwood Foresters Regt formed
00 00 92   Yeomanry tradition lost in reorg

Appendix E6 Royal Corps of Transport and Royal Logistic Corps from 05 04 93
(All Regt RCT (V) redes Transport Regiments RCT (V) at end of 1977)

153 (Highland) Artillery Support Regt
01 04 67   Regt RCT (V)
01 04 69   239(Highland Yeomanry) Artillery Support Sqn, 153 (Highland) Regt RCT (V)
00 12 77   Redes 153 (H'land) Transport Regt RCT (V)
01 04 83   153 (H'land) Arty Support Regt, 239 (H'land Y) Arty Support Sqn
01 11 92   Vols from 239 Sqn tfd to C and HQ Sqn The Scottish Yeomanry
01 04 93   153 Rgt disb to form new Scottish Transport Regt without Yeomanry appellation

154(Lowland) Transport Regt
01 04 69   225 (Queen's Own Lowland Yeomanry) Sqn
01 11 92   Vols from 222 and 225 Sqns tfd to B Sqn or C Sqn and HQ The Scottish Yeomanry,
            respectively
01 04 93   154 Regt disb to form new Scottish Transport Regt without Yeomanry appellation

157 (Wales and Midlands) Transport Regt
01 04 69   224 (West Wales) Sqn formed but un-established
01 04 77   Sqn established with A (Pembroke Yeomanry) Troop
00 02 87   title transferred to 224 (West Wales) Sqn 157 (Wales and Midlands) Tpt Rgt (V)
05 04 93   became 224 (Pembroke Y) Engr Support Sqn 157 (W&M) Tpt Rgt Royal Logistics Corps

Appendix F

The Irish Yeomanry

Introduction

As part of the British Isles, Ireland has tended to be regarded, in the English imagination, as *one of us*. In reality it was something very different as its history has showed. It never attracted the Continental odium of 'perfidious Albion', since it had sought few external dealings.

The English were in some doubts, during 1793-96, whether to rule Ireland as a subordinate Kingdom or as an unruly Colony. The lack of decision ended up somewhere in between, so the Irish were relegated to a no-man's land and in this they were happy enough, if only to be left alone. Even the Act of Union little changed the practicalities, whilst it is at least questionable whether it didn't succeed in putting back their cause of democratic government a hundred years. The stumbling block for the colonial administrator, for Ireland became a colony by default, was the existence of a highly developed parliamentary system of government, with an excellent command of English.

Whatever the problems of government, the advent of the French Revolution, touched on a sensitive English nerve. Here was this relatively large and populated island likely to offer an open backdoor to an intending aggressor. As we shall see, it never turned out very well for the French, nor did they see any long term good in making a lodgement.

History

Continental peoples first populated Ireland around 6000 BC. From about 400 BC the Celtic tribes invaded from Britain and the Continent and took control. Saint Patrick brought Christianity in 432 AD. Viking raiders started arriving from 800 AD, established settlements and generally took over. They were eventually defeated in 1014 by Brian Boru and those that remained became absorbed into the Irish Race.

Normans from England were invited by one of their Kings during the 1160's to stabilise the warring factions, which they did until 1171. At this point a Baron Strongbow seized Leinster, making himself king and others followed suit by taking other land. This led to a visit by Henry II of England, to ensure the Barons remained loyal, by forcing them to recognize him as Lord of Ireland. Norman loyalty had weakened by 1300, as they intermingled with the Irish and adopted the latters language and customs.

In 1534, Henry VIII set about regaining England's influence and forced the Irish Parliament to declare him King of Ireland in 1541. This led to the establishment of English laws, whilst he tried without success to introduce Protestantism. Edward VI and his daughters, notably Elizabeth, continued these policies leading to the persecution of Catholics and the introduction of English settlers. As a consequence, a number of revolts occurred.

Oliver Cromwell took ruthless action, in the last of a series, by not only crushing the revolt but depriving Catholics of many political rights. By 1704, the Catholics held no more than a seventh of the land and were forbidden even to purchase, rent or inherit it. Also they were excluded from Parliament, the Army and restricted even in their rights to practice their religion.

During the 1700's the British maintained a tight control and even limited the powers of its Parliament. To this the Irish Protestants objected and demanded legislative freedom, which Great Britain met in 1782. The Irish Parliament then restored the right of Catholics to hold land and gave them back religious freedom, whilst still refusing political rights. Some Protestants in Parliament tried unsuccessfully to gain political rights for the Catholics. This failure led to the formation of the United Irishmen. Their first demand was for equal rights and then complete independence from British rule. Of course this threat to Protestant supremacy triggered the formation of the Orange Movement. Henceforth the scene was set for a three cornered fight, with the flames of dissent and misunderstanding fanned by secret minorities.

Appendix F

Ireland has had and has retained an essentially agricultural economy. There was no Industrial Revolution in the English sense. All the troubles were basically of other peoples making. A lot more could have been made of the Irish opportunity. Religion has been made the scapegoat for bungled politics.

The inability of the Irish Parliament to grant a balanced measure of Catholic emancipation allowed William Pitt, the then English Prime Minister, to engineer Ireland into becoming united with Great Britain. He therefore persauded both Parliaments to pass the Act of Union and on 1st January 1801 Ireland became part of the United Kingdom of Great Britain and Ireland. With this Act the Irish Parliament and colonial status was ended.

Although granted a 100 seats in the enlarged House of Commons, the operation of the British Test Act meant non-conformist representation, both Catholic and Protestant, was barred until its repeal in 1829. As with England, the denial of political self expression bottled-up all manner of emotions, leading to periodic riots. When these crimes could be explained in no meaningful fashion, they were reported as 'Outrages'.

This later repeal and the formation of properly organised Police led to more settled times, when the Yeomanry was discontinued in 1834. Secret Societies were abolished or at least outlawed in 1835, as the result of a petition to the King, so that theoretically the Orange Order lapsed at this time.

Constitution
The initial affect of the French war was to hasten the cause of Catholic emancipation. In retrospect, there now seems no reason to suppose that a Catholic plot existed for Ireland to offer the French a 'springboard' into England. What *was* required was a measure of automony and a heartfelt desire to be left in peace.

Only as a result of frustrating the development of constitutional measures at home was the United Irish Movement formed, bringing together such disparate bedfellows as Presbyterians and Catholics, because both espoused the radical cause. This grew out of the Defender Movement, designed to protect Catholics against Protestant assailants. Unfortunately it provoked the Battle of the Diamond, on 21st September 1795 and the killing of 45 Protestants, leading to the formation of the Orange Order, as we know it today.

The decision facing a devious and unrepresentative Irish Government, as opposed to Parliament, was whether to allow the latter to reform or to govern by force. They opted for force. In the process they suspended Habeas Corpus in November 1796 and imposed martial law in Ulster during 1797. It should be remarked that such a suspension was hardly a special Irish measure as the same instrument was at work within England.

Lord Camden, the Lord Lieutenant of Ireland, writing to The Duke of Portland in London on 9th March 1797, stated how he had ordered General Lake to disarm districts where outrages had been committed, to establish patrols for the arrest of all persons assembling by night and for the prevention of meetings. "If," he added, significantly - although armed with the powers of the Convention Act, the Insurrection Act and the Habeus Corpus Suspension Act - "the urgency of the case demands a conduct beyond what can be sanctioned by law, the General had orders from him not to suffer the cause of justice to be frustrated by their delicacy which might have possibly actuated the magistracy." If such malignancy was injected at the highest levels of the civil and military administration and Parliament made impotent, it was hardly strange to encounter deficient standards lower down the system. It is this consideration more than any other which must be borne in mind when judging the performance of the Irish Yeomanry.

Military Administration
At the time of the French war the Dublin based Parliament was unable to provide constitutional safeguards for the populace. Magistrates and the Military answered only to the Lord Lieutenant. In the case of the Yeomanry, legal and proper judicial measures, were frequently negatived by local magistrates and these people often doubled as their Commandants. Senior Generals, pressured into accepting Irish office, found troops corrupted by their

surroundings. That is to say acts of rape, pillage, house burning, murder, and illegal transportation to Australia or to service in the Fleet, against the civil population went uninvestigated and rarely punished.

One is tempted to say such stories were rumours put about by detractors of the Military, but this is not so. Sir Ralph Abercromby taking office as chief soldier in November 1797 was shocked by the lack of discipline shown by troops. He expressed his determination to stop military outrages, which in some cases had been perpetrated at the instigation of Government officials, by issuing an order reminding officers that though they might sometimes be called on to support the magistrates, they must not forget they were only called on to to support the laws of the land. Later, on 26th February 1798, the same man felt compelled to sanction an order which ran "The very disgraceful frequency of Courts Martial and the many complaints of irregularities in the conduct of troops in this Kingdom having too unfortunately proved the Army to be in a state of licentiousness, which must render it formidable to everyone but the enemy, it had become necessary to enjoin commanding officers to compel from all officers under their command the strictest and most unremitting attention to the discipline, good order and conduct of their men.... Standing Orders of the Kingdom positively forbid the troops to act (but in case of attack) without the presence and authority of a magistrate, should military assistance be requisitioned and precise orders are to be given to the officer commanding the party for the purpose." A shocked disbelief reverberated up and into the English House of Commons, where he was an elected member. The clash, when he heard of it, brought his resignation, since he felt unable to preside over the ruination of his troops.

Formation

It is not proposed by the writer to account for the Irish Yeomanry in the same manner as their United Kingdom counterparts, for the following reasons. Firstly it was established under separate legislation; An Act of the Irish Parliament for 1796-97. Secondly the Country was riven by legal impediments favouring a religeous and sectarian divide, yet the Yeomanry was commissioned to uphold the law. Lastly, there never was any long term intention of regimenting the numerous Cavalry Troops, nor the even more numerous Yeomanry Infantry. Directly the suppression of riot and rebellion was achieved, the Force was stood-down. All this said it holds *the unique distinction amongst the Yeomanry of engaging a foreign enemy on the field of battle and of suffering, at his hands, dead and wounded.*

Bridging the gap between the forces required to secure Ireland and the Regular Army units available were the Militia and the Fencibles. By 1796 it was apparent that something along the same lines as the English Yeomanry was necessary. However this strategem could not work on the same model. Also it was seen that a substantial Infantry element was required. The nature of Irish society meant that any Yeomanry required a centrallised control. Thus in the Autumn of 1796 the Armed Volunteer Yeomanry of Ireland was formed, consisting of District Cavalry and Infantry Corps. These units were administered from a Yeomanry Office established in Dublin Castle. The units absorbed the volunteers of half a generation before and many members saw service in both. The names of nearly 300 District Cavalry Corps of the Armed Volunteers were published in the Dublin Gazette for the period leading up to the 20th December 1796. The Force then amounted to about 10,000 Cavalry and as many Infantry.

The speed of formation was remarkable and far outstripped the developments in England. Each Troop served under a Captain assisted by two Lieutenants and numbered between 45 and 50 Troopers. Their members were exempt from the Militia ballot, which was a great inducement to enlist. The Corps were made up both of Catholics and Protestants with some of the Non-Conformist persuasion and wrung from a reluctant witness the admission that during the subsequent rebellion of 1798 they distinguished themselves 'by steadiness, bravery and perseverence'. Found of use then, they were continued as a permanent military force, to aid the Civil Power.

After the French expedition of 1797 to Bantry Bay both the Cavalry and Infantry elements were augmented to 14,000 and just prior to the rebellion of 1798 the establishment amounted to 15,000 Cavalry and 21,000 Infantry. As in England, the Yeomanry were employed in occasional duties, such as escorts and picquet guards at night, until April 1798, when permanent duty began. In May and June, the rebellion then raging, the whole

Appendix F

establishment was on duty. Following this the Cavalry element was reduced to 10,000 but the Infantry was further augmented to 40,000.

Subsequent employment varied with the circumstances. They were once more placed on permanent duty at the time of the Battle of Castlebar. In March 1799, Martial Law was withdrawn and this effectively drew a line between the Yeomanry in support of the Military and support of the civilian authorities; granted both powers remained vested in one man at Dublin. Almost immediately, in May 1799, an alarm was sounded of a French fleet sailing from Brest, but this never materialised.

Thenceforth the Yeomanry acted in a civil capacity. They undertook criminal investigative work now carried out by the Police and provided occasional escorts and picquets. "It may be conjectured that the Government, harassed as it was by lack of men to sustain the campaigns against Napoleon, had cast its eye on the Yeomanry as a possible fighting force for active service. They had shown their spirit in encounters with the rebels of 1798, a collection of men whose desparate valour and skilful tactics rendered them no mean antagonists even for regular troops."

During the war, particularly the period 1801-05 there was an attempt at welding together the Troops and Companies. "The small local units were brigaded together, so that they could in time of need be formed into battalions, and they were instructed in case of invasion to harass the enemy and endeavour to draw him into ambuscades. In 1804 circulars were issued asking the Yeomanry Corps if they would be willing, in the event of invasion, to march outside the districts in which they had originally volunteered to act, and in fact to extend their service to Ireland generally. The responses were equally divided --- In later years, however, some of the best Corps were put on *permanent pay*, or embodied for an indefinite term like the Militia ... In 1808 at least one Corps volunteered for the Peninsula, and in 1813 all were ready to serve anywhere in the United Kingdom, and some were willing to go to the Continent." However, directly the need for mobility was removed more of the horsed units became infantry and numbers fell away towards the end of the war.

There is no record of disbandment during the Peace of Amiens and with its expiry, a somewhat similar return to that of England, showing establishment was made to Parliament in London. This recorded acceptances of 125 mounted, 188 mixed mounted and dismounted Corps, besides which there were a further 728 Infantry only, making a total of 1041 Corps. The total for all ranks is given as 82,941 as at 13th December 1803. These figures derive from the 32 Counties, plus the cities of Cork and Dublin. The United Kingdom could have hardly been better defended.

The outcome of Trafalgar in 1805 saw a similar run-down in the reserve forces, to that in England. A return made on 21st May 1817 fails to differentiate between Infantry and Mounted Corps, but the 32 Counties and Dublin City are shown as providing 424 Corps, totalling 40,458 All Ranks. This halving in numbers reflects the end of the war with France.

In theory the Act of Union granted equal rights for access to markets. As in the United Kingdom, the end of the war gave rise to a recession and increased hardship for the population with consequent disturbances. When exposed to the full blast of England's Industrial Revolution, the effect was devastating. There was no further need for the Yeomanry, since large portions of the population opted to emigrate, rather than starve at home.

In the circumstances, the Yeomanry dwindled away, but also because the Authorities were disinclined to use them for security duties. However, by the 1830-1 period definite steps were taken to re-activate the Yeomanry: The costs were enormous because uniforms had gone to bits and a large number of the weapons were no longer operable.

Difficulties arose over the recovery of arms, or did they? A similar measure existed, to the English one, to charge £10 for those not returned, but this seems to have been looked upon more as a levy. When the Yeomanry came to be disbanded in 1834, somehow the return of arms was 'forgotten'. It also transpires from correspondence as late as 1843 that although the permanent staff were discharged and therefore no longer paid, the Yeomanry volunteers as such were never disbanded! The Irish wry sense of humour must have infected the Government of the day.

Invasion Scares

The French mounted four expeditions against Ireland: One was defeated en route and three made the shore line; Two of the latter got there anchors down, only one of which achieved a landing. The Dutch mounted a single expedition which was intercepted and badly beaten. Many other landings were planned, some resulting in mutiny and all without achieving practical results.

The one to Bantry Bay first arrived on the 21st December 1796, in scattered form. This action had been initiated, against a certain French reluctance, by Tone representing the United Irishmen. It started as a fleet of 34 ships, but only 28 made the rendezvous. Amongst the missing ships was the one carrying expedition's commander. On the morning of the 23rd it blew a gale. Sixteen vessels remained anchored in the bay, in a haphazrd manner, with the remainder blown out to sea.   Communication between vessels was difficult and when the gale strengthened, the Admiral in command ordered the fleet to cut their cables and run for home. Tone had a variety of alternative targets, such as Limerick by the Shannon and Belfast; but nothing came of these.

It is unclear what military force awaited on land. The force embarked for the venture numbered 15,000 troops, 40,000 stands of additional arms, a field park of 29 artillery pieces, 60,000 barrels of powder and 7,000,000 cartridges. The chance storm was truly a godsend to the British. It would appear that inklings of this invasion gave rise to the initial formation of the Yeomanry.

Next, the Dutch under prompting by Tone assembled a Fleet with 15,000 men, a field park of artillery, adequate stores and plenty of money on which to subsist once landed. This effort coincided with the mutinies at the Nore and Spithead. Once again the weather intervened and the British bluffed and blockaded the Texel with a scratch force of two ships, the Admiral pleading with the mutineers for the second ship. This led on to the Battle of Camperdown on 11th October 1797 and a straight 16:16 fight in which the Dutch lost 6,000 soldiers and eight ships.

The second assault by the French came on 22nd August 1798, when three frigates under English colours entered Killala Bay, County Mayo. No alarm was sounded until after a considerable force was landed, including an advance guard of 300 men, who marched on the town. This was poorly garrisoned by a party of the Prince of Wales' Fencibles and a few local Yeomanry, the whole not exceeding 60 men. These proceeded to offer a stout resistence until driven back into the castle and with a few killed and wounded, felt obliged to surrender. The landing force consisted of 1,060 men, 70 officers with two four pounder cannon and arms for 5,500. After the completion of landing stores, a reconnaisance was made on Ballina, which was repelled by a party of Carabineers and some Yeomanry. News of the landing reached the Dublin authorities that evening, who set about planning an attacking force.

Between the landing and the lead-up to the battle of Castlebar, a period of two weeks elapsed. From four and five thousand Irishmen joined the French. At the time of the battle, the Kilkenny and Longford Militias deserted to the French. On the British side, the plan was an unco-ordinated muddle and individual heroism was not enough to prevent the French carrying the day. The French occupation of Castlebar was conducted with restraint. They protected Protestants from abuse by the rebels. Whilst they ate and drank of the best and slept on fine beds, they fed their newly found rebel allies on potatoes and whiskey, leaving them to sleep on straw.

As a generality the French behaviour, both on and off the battlefield was of the most chivalrous kind. General Hubert aware that Lord Cornwallis was approaching with a force of 30,000, commenced a march on Sligo accompanied by a large group of rebels. In order to save a useless slaughter he surrendered on 8th September. Their opinion of the rebels was very poor. These souls were put to the sabre when found on the march by the British, or hung when at the halt. Of some 500 managing to be taken prisoner 17 drew lots to be hung. The French lesson from this campaign was that chance rebels were a doubtful advantage and that Ireland was not such an open backdoor on England as they had at first supposed. The British in seeking to press tightly behind a retreating enemy, mounted Light infantrymen behind Dragoons.

On the 27th October the same frigates which had landed Humbert re-appeared in Killala bay with a reputed force of 2,000 to reinforce his effort. They were intended to add to the diversion of the Brest inspired landing, destined for the NE coast of Ireland. When they sailed, the intelligence of the latter's surrender had not reached France. Before their anchors had touched bottom they were pursued by British cruisers, only managing to elude capture by superior sailing. Later, the Brest fleet numbering eight major vessels, was hounded by the British from the time they left port until three of the smallest ships returned home in a shattered state. This finally convinced the French Directory that attempts on Ireland were futile.

Rebellion

Rebellion or insurrection are one and the same thing; It's a matter of scale and also if successful they are not given that name. The Great Rebellion of 1798 opened on 23rd May in and around Dublin. By this time a well drilled and considerable force of Yeomanry existed. This was as well since the city was drained of Regular Army forces, called to more pressing duties elsewhere. Steps were taken to *purify* the Corps of unreliable Catholics and those who had taken or were suspected of taking the oath of the United Irishmen. Many such had joined the Yeomanry, not only to avoid service in the Militia but also to benefit from a military education for later use when instructing rebels.

The night preceeding, the Rathfarnham Yeomanry was raised from a picquet to full Troop strength. Directly rebels were confirmed as on the move, an express yeoman was dispatched to the Lord Lieutenant.

The Yeomanry at Dunlavin soon found themselves sandwiched between approaching rebels outwith the township and those inside. To complicate matters the gaol held 19 Saunders-Grove and nine Narrowmore Yeomen, adjudged traitors and unreliable. This group outnumbered the garrison, so after due consideration this group was led out and shot, whilst the remaining prisoners were released. This was summary in the extreme, but many yeomen, even officers had enrolled themselves, only to desert to the rebel cause. On the other side, rebels encountering members of the military, put them to death if they would not swear to their cause, whilst this was freely meted out to any Protestants, women and children included, unfortunate enough to be discovered by Catholic rebels in the South.

On the 24th of May, a Company of Infantry and a Troop of Cavalry, both Yeomanry were assailed at Monastereven. After repulsing an attack, the Cavalry charged putting the rebels to flight with more than 50 dead. This loyal band of defenders included 14 Catholics.

By the 29th May the loyalties within the Yeomanry could be properly judged. Almost the whole of Kildare was tainted. The Sleamarigue laid down their arms, the Castledermot had only five loyal men and the Athy Cavalry were publicly disarmed with their Captain imprisoned. The Rathangan, North Naas and Furnace Yeomanry were all extensivley disaffected. That of Clane, nominally 65 strong, could only muster 25 yeomen. Units within the metropolis were generally loyal. More insidious were the individual and secret members of the United Irish, who served as Yeomen and were liable to *sell the pass* at critical moments.

When the character of the rebellion turned from politics to religeous intolerance many of the Protestant rebels fell away. The St Sepulchre's Corps taking its turn of duty at Dolphin's barn provided such an instance. Being mainly Catholic and disaffected, their leader was hung on the information of a Republican Protestant Yeoman returning to the loyalist cause and the unit was disarmed on 3rd June and disbanded.

At Navan three Cavalry and an Infantry Corps, each Yeomanry, joined with the Reay Fencibles to storm the very steep, nearby Tara Hill, held by a force of 4000 rebels. This success had the excellent result of opening North and South communications with Dublin.

In Wexford, events took on a sullen tone before the rebellion. The initial defence of Enniscorthy by Royalists, followed by its abandonment, led to its burning and the massacre of Protestants, mostly out of irritation. Later

Appendix F

the rebels decamped to Vinegar Hill, where they numbered an estimated 10,000. The camp was a disorganised rabble and   soon divided into three groups.

One of these made for Gorey, where a Captain White of Yeomanry, decided to take the offensive with the parts of three Corps of Yeomanry, 25 Antrim and 25 North Cork Militias and 20 volunteer infantry; a total of 130 men, whilst the rebels numbered an estimated 2000. Fortune favoured the brave and with reinforcements expected from Dublin, the dust raised by this little force unsettled the rebels. The steady fire led by the Antrim band steadied the force, which routed the opposition. Only a late charge by the Cavalry avoided an immense slaughter.

The second party of rebels made along the river Slaney for Newton Barry. The defending commander decided to abandon the town in favour of high ground. This left it open to be plundered and the inhabitants massacred. A Captain Kerr of the Yeomanry, both mounted and dismounted and numbering 250, asked to permission to "conquer or die", which was granted. 'Nothing could surpass the desparate gallantry of these daring horsemen - while a heavy fire of grape from the guns and musketry drove the rebels from the town and enabled the cavalry to act'. The pursuit continued for three miles, leading to the disintegration of that rebel force.

The third portion of the Vinagar Hill rebels were in some trepidation, yet due to the mishandling of Royalist forces, half of the latter were defeated at Tubberneering. Random fights broke out all over Wexford with the most dreadful atrocities commited by both sides, including the Yeomanry. In subsequent operations the Yeomen were employed as guides and events stabilised. Gallant leadership helped to win a battle at Ross, where the Royal Irish Artillery made a signal contribution.

Yeomanry in the metropolis, now purged of unreliables, numbered 4000 and these were well armed and disciplined. With perfect confidence the city was entrusted to their protection.

The Military were planning for a battle at Arklow and proceded there to prepare the ground. It was a curious little army. The Cavalry, under a Colonel, numbered 154, drawn from the 4th Dragoon Guards, 5th Dragoons and the Ancient British. The Infantry, made up as three Brigades, comprised the Armagh, North Cork, Cavan and Antrim Militias, the Tyrone and Suffolk Light Companies, the Londonderry Grenadier Company and the Durham and Dunbarton Fencibles; these forces totalled 1323. Added to this were the Yeomanry Corps numbering 337, from North and South Arklow, Camolin, Coolgreney and Castletown of which 260 were mounted. Also included were a few guns. It was against this force, with time to prepare that a rebel army numbering between 25,000 to 31,000 approached. Luckily no more than 5000 of the latter had firearms and in their looting along the way, they had consumed much whiskey, making them poorly disciplined and incautious. The battle raged from the forenoon till darkness fell, making it impossible to pursue the retreating rebels. It was estimated that 1000 rebels perished, whilst the Royalists lost less than 70.

The Arklow battle, by 9th June, decided the fate of the rebellion. It also curtailed the fearful extent of atrocities on both sides. If the town had been lost there was the distinct likelihood that all Protestants in Wexford were to be massecred, even those Protestant leaders fighting on the rebel side; Feelings were bitter and extreme.

The concluding battle to take Vinegar Hill, included the Dunlavin Yeomanry in which a single man was wounded.

The dispersal of rebels led one party to attack Hacketstown. It was garrisoned by Yeomanry and 40 of the Antrim Militia and later reinforced with more Infantry and Cavalry till it numbered 200. These proceeded to thwart the rebel attack commenced at 6am on 25th June. Some 350 rebels were killed, before they withdrew during the early afternoon.

In the further pursuit of rebels, the Tinehaly Cavalry made a reconnaissance to Ballyellis. An impetuous attack led to the loss of two officers and 60 men. Carnew, with 50 Yeomen, was saved by a timely warning from retreating Cavalry. This attack was repulsed, but later the pursuing Yeomanry committed a blunder in attacking the rebels holding high ground. Some 60 Yeomanry infantry were able to contain the fight by occupying a house at the bottom of the hill and repelling attacks for 14 hours.

The rebels made a further stand at Ballygullen. The Artillery with four six-pounders and Yeomanry Cavalry under Captain White and the Fox Hunters under Lord Roden pressed them vigorously. Although the rebels continued as robbers, this was the end of the Wexford rebellion.

The attacks now transfer to the centre and North of Ireland, with Clonard as the first target, defended by a weak (under 30) Yeomanry garrison. Tyrrell, the commander was a self taught soldier and hearing of the approaching horde, made the best dispositions available. The rebel force of 300 Cavalry were repulsed and his force greatly discomforted the following Infantry. Later, with 27 reinforcements from the Northumberland Fencibles and the Kinnegrad Infantry, they wrought havoc amongst an estimated 400 rebel infantry, by killing over 200.

The seat of rebellion then changed to Ulster, where the first battle was at Antrim, in which The Belfast Yeomanry participated with the Antrim Yeomanry. The fighting commenced on 7th July. The result was decisive with the rebels losing 150 killed and a further 200 cut down in the subsequent rout.

The battles of Saintfield and Ballynahinch followed in which the Yeomanry played their part. Obviously the schism was deep, but nowhere as deep, as in the South. The fight when it came was political and did not cross the religeous divide.

Support of the Civil Power

The move from Martial Law to the Union was brief, but it provided time for tempers to cool. The summary methods of justice, were replaced by attempts to make the law work. Nevertheless, an Act of Indemnity was passed to protect those guilty of past wrong doing. It does well, however, to catalogue atrocities, such as are known, since these reveal the savagery of the times. In setting cases against the Yeomanry, it behoves one to remember how the members and their families suffered at the hands of rebels.

The standard gambits of the time included flogging, half-hanging and pitch capping (a paper hat lined with hot pitch applied to the head and subsequently raised with a consequent loss of hair and sometimes scalp) to extract information. Summary hangings were not unusual. Family homes were burnt, if it was suspected they harboured *criminal elements* or arms were found

The Yeomanry were not the architects of these clearly unconstitutional practices, but they were local and became caught up in them when attempting pacification. With few exceptions the Yeomanry in Ireland were led by Protestants, of the orthodox persuasion. This meant the leadership of a Troop was generally secure. Not all the troopers however were selected with similar beliefs, quite the contrary, meaning that some units embraced a *Trojan Horse*. In times of trouble it was possible for Yeomen to resign or desert and some did at the time of the rebellion to act as military instructors to the insurgents. Against this background of divided loyalties, early intelligence of proposed defaults in or by a Troop were eagerly sought so that units could be dis-armed. In the case of an officer, an informant could obtain £250 for a successful prosecution, with a further £250 going to the local infirmary.

The Militia and the Fencible Regiments were guilty of worse excesses. Those showing excessive zeal were rarely censured or brought to book.

As the result of religious intolerance, the political strands, within the country, were knitted differently. Presbyterians in Ulster and Catholics generally were discriminated against in favour of *Episcopaleans*, thus sapping social cohesion.

The repeal of the Test Act and the formation of properly organised police led to more settled times, when the Yeomanry was disbanded, in 1834. Secret Societies were abolished in 1835, as the result of a petition from the House of Commons to the King, so that in theory the Orange Order at least lapsed at about the same time!

Act Governing the Formation of the Irish Yeomanry

An Act for encouraging and disciplining Such Corps of Men as shall voluntarily enroll themselves under Officers to be commissioned by His Majesty, for the Defence of this Kingdom during the present War.

Whereas further exertions are now become necessary for the defence of this kingdom, and for the preservation and security of the lives and properties of his Majesty's subjects there-in: be it enacted by the King's most excellent Majesty, by and with the advice and consent of the lords spitual and temporal, and commons in this present parliament assembled, and by the authority of the same, That if any of his Majesty's loyal subjects in this kingdom, shall have voluntarily associated and enrolled themselves, or shall hereafter voluntarily associate and enroll themselves in troops or companies during the continuance of the present war, under officers having commissions from his Majesty, or from the chief governor or governors of this Kingdom, duly authorized thereto by his Majesty, for the protection of property, and preservation of the peace within the barony, city, or town wherein the place of first assembling shall be appointed in such commission, and within every barony, city, or town immediately adjoining thereto, every serjeant, trumpeter, drummer, and private therein, shall be entitled to receive such clothing, arms, and accoutrements, or allowances in lieu thereof, and also such pay, in such manner and at such rate, as his Majesty, or the chief governor or governors of this kingdom shall appoint, for every day, not exceeding two days in each week and he shall actually assemble and attend by order of his commanding officer for the purpose of being disciplined and exercised.

II.   And be it further enacted, That one serjeant, and one trumpeter or drummer in every such troop or company, shall be entitled to receive permanent or daily pay, to be appointed in like manner, during the continuance of such troop or company.

III.   And be it further enacted, That such enrolment nor the receiving of pay, or allowances as aforesaid, shall subject any person so enrolled, or receiving pay, to military discipline or duty, or to the provisions of any act for punishing mutiny and desertion.

IV.   And be it further enacted, that if the officer commanding any such troop or company as aforesaid, shall discharge from such troop or company any person; or if any person shall withdraw from such troop or company, who shall have been enrolled as aforesaid, and if such person shall refuse or neglect, on being required by such commanding officer to deliver up any arms, accoutrements, or clothing, which shall have been entrusted to his custody, every person so refusing or neglecting, shall, on bing convicted thereof before any justice of the peace of the county within which such troop or company shall have been formed, forfeit and pay the sum of ten pounds, to be levied by distress and sale of the offender's goods and chattels, by warrant under the hand and seal of such justice, rendering the overplus (if any) on demand, after deducting the charges of such distress and sale, to the person whose goods and chattels shall have been distrained and sold; and for want of such sufficient distress, such justice is hereby required to commit such offender to the common gaol of the county, city, or place where the offence shall have been committed, for any time not exceeding six months; the monies arising by such penalty, to be applied by the commanding officer to replace such arms, accoutrements, or clothing, and the overplus (if any) to form a stock-purse for the use of such troop or company.

V.   And be it further enacted, That if any such troop or company shall, in case of invasion, rebellion, or insurrection, or the paprehension thereof, voluntarily offer to act as a military corps, and to do duty as such, or to march wherever it shall be ordered, within this Kingdom, during the continuance of such invasion, rebellion, insurrection, or apprehension thereof, every person therein, who shall testify such his offer, by putting his name thereto, shall, upon such offer being accepted by his Majesty, or the chief governor or governors of this kingdom, be entitled, if a commissioned officer, to receive the same pay as officers of like rank receive in his Majesty's regular forces, and if a serjeant, trumpeter, drummer or private, the same pay daily as on the days of exercise, and each be subject, while he shall be so entitled, and at no other time, nor on any other ground or pretence to the like

Appendix F

military discipline as his Majesty's regular and militia forces during the time he shall have so offered for, and no longer.

VI. Provided always, That no officer or soldier of any such corps, shall be liable to be tried by any court-martial, unless such court-martial shall be composed entirely of officers serving in the corps formed as aforesaid, such courts-martial to be assembled by warrant from the chief governor or governors of this kingdom, or by warrant from some general or other officer duly authorized to order courts-martial to be holden.

VII. And be it enacted by the authority aforesaid, That all commissioned officers of such troops and companies, who shall be disabled in actual service, shall be entitled to half-pay, and all non-commissioned officers, privates, trumpeters, and drummers, to the benefit of the Royal Hospital at Kilmainham, and the widows of commissioned officers killed in service, to such pension for life, as is usually given to the widows of officers of like rank in his Majesty's regular forces.

VIII. And be it enacted, That no person who shall be enrolled in any such troop or company, as aforesaid, shall during the time he is serving in such corps, be liable to serve personally, or to provide a substitute to serve in the militia, provided he shall produce to the deputy governors assembled at a sub-division meeting, an affidavit of his being enrolled as aforesaid, and a certificate signed by his commanding officer, that he has for the space of six weeks immediately preceding such divisional meeting, punctually attended at all such times and places as may have been appointed for the exercise thereof, unless prevented therefrom by sickness, which sickness shall be stated in such certificate, and verified by oath.

IX. And be it further enacted, That every person who shall have entered into any such troop or company before the passing of this act, shall within ten days after the passing thereof, or at such other near and convenient time as shall be appointed by his commanding officer, and every other person who shall hereafter enroll himself in any such troop or company, shall at the time he shall enroll himself, take and subscribe the following oath or affirmation of allegiance.

I   do sincerely promise and swear, or affirm, that I will be faithful, and bear true allegiance to his Majesty king George the third, and that I will faithfully support and maintain the laws and constitution of this kingdom, and the succession to the throne in his Majesty's illustrious house.
So help me God.

Every which oath any magistrate is hereby empowered to administer, and the commanding officer shall transmit same to his Majesty's war-office without delay, to be enrolled from thence in his Majesty's court of chancery.

X. And be it further enacted, That if any officer shall admit or retain in his troop or company, any person who shall neglect to take and subscribe the same, or who upon being required thereto by him, shall refuse to take and subscribe it, he shall upon due conviction thereof in any court of record, be fined for every such offence in the sum of five hundred pounds, one-half thereof to be paid to the informer, and the other half to the treasurer of the infirmary of the county, town, or city, in which his troop or company shall be appointed to assemble, for the use of such infirmary.

XI. And be it enacted, That no constable or peace-officer appointed, or paid in pursuance of an act passed in the twenty-seventh year of his present Majesty's reign, entitled, *An act for the better execution of the law, and preservation of the peace within counties at large,* shall be admissible into any such troop or compony.

XII. And be it further enacted, That this act shall continue to the end of the present war, and no longer.

Author's Note

The foregoing account is written without malice or side. It attempts to provide a balance, yet it is perforce short and therefore selective. The account draws only from the sources given below, though there is so much more

Appendix F

easily available, generally from Public Libraries. Also, their is an extensive academic literature by researchers following a variety of persuasions. These serve to highlight the arbitrary nature of the cruelties perpetrated. Generally there is a start of the matter with bad law, which when enforced is flouted, whereby whole communities were criminalised. There follows the work of good men and rogues working both sides of a church divide which had neither connection with religion nor any God.

Reading List

1. The Constitutional and Parliamentary History of Ireland Till the Union. JG Swift MacNeill MP. Fisher Unwin, London 1917
2. History of the Irish Rebellion in 1798 etc. WH Maxwell. Bailey Brothers, London 1845
3. The War in Wexford: An Account of the rebellion in the South of Ireland in 1798. HFB Wheeler & AM Broadley. John Lane, The Bodley Head, London 1910
4. Ireland from the Union to Catholic Emancipation. DA Chart. JM Dent & Son, London 1910
5. Rural Disorder and Police Reform in Ireland. G Broeker. Routledge & Keegan Paul, London 1970
6. Parliamentary Papers, 1843 LI p401-2

Appendix F

Appendix G

Guidons, Battle Honours and Honourary Distinctions [1][2]

For many centuries Banners were found to be necessary to show the position of the commander and to form rallying points. The Standards and Guidons of cavalry and the Colours of infantry are all direct descendents of the Banners of Knights and Barons, whose followers made up the armies which fought at Crecy and Agincourt. Originally the distinguishing marks of the leaders, gradually the emblems became the means of identifying the units themselves. Heraldic schemes of the medieval period saw suprior knights riding under a square banner, whilst the knight of lesser degree carried a pennon or guidon on his lance which narrowed to a fork at the free end, sometimes referred to as a swallow tail. The word 'guidon' originates from the Old French 'guyd-homme' or leader of the horse. Particularly valorous conduct was often denoted by cutting off the forkends and the person thus distinguished became known as a knight banneret, later corrupted to baronet. Gradually these coloured emblems became the means of identifying groups of men rather than an individual leader. As the consequence they symbolised the fighting spirit of the group, so the practice arose of consecrating them.

The term 'colours' is now used to cover this group of banner flags carried by both Infantry and Cavalry. During the 17th Century Colours used to be carried by each infantry company and cavalry troop, the cavalry squadron being not formed till later. The number was reduced to three in each infantry regiment, in 1707 and thenceforth they were carried into battle by the musketeers on the flanks and the pikemen in the centre. This continued until the pike was abolished in 1747, when their number was reduced to two, comprising the Queen's Colour and the Regimental Colour and this is the position today. The last time these were carried into action was during the 1st Boer War, at the Battle of Majuba Hill in 1881. Nowadays, when a regiment goes to war it is usual for it to lodge its Colours in the Regimental Chapel or in a church with which it has a close association.

Cavalry Colours were regulated at the same time as the infantry by the Royal Warrants of 1747, 1751 and 1768, however, they were never regarded with the same veneration paid to those carried by the infantry. Household Cavalry and Dragoon Guards retained the rectangular Standard. The Guidon became the regulation Colour for Dragoons. Hussars and Lancers had neither Standards nor Guidons because their mode of operation called for concealment, accordingly they carried any Honours on their drum cloths. In 1834 Guidons were abolished for all Light Cavalry, thus until that date only Yeomanry designated as Dragoons had carried a Guidon. The Yeomanry designated as Dragoons carried Guidons from 1908, the majority being presented by King Edward VII in Windsor Great Park. Nineteen in all were presented in the early years, including those to both the 1st and 2nd Scottish Horse.

In 1956 Her Majesty Queen Elizabeth II authorised all cavalry and yeomanry regiments to carry Standards or Guidons, as many of the regiments no longer had mounted bands. The Royal Tank Regiments now carry Standards denoting the number of the regiment, whilst the Yeomanry, whether Dragoons, Hussars or Lancers each carry the Guidon. By tradition the Guidons of Light Cavalry and the Standards of Heavy Cavalry are at all times carried on parade by senior Warrant Officers and not by commissioned ranks. In a converse manner the two infantry Colours are carried by Officers but with a similar escort of Non-Commissioned Officers.

The Guidon is now of crimson silk damask, 2 feet 3 inches deep and 3 feet 5 inches to the points of the swallow tails, embroidered and fringed in gold. It is carried on a lance with cords and tassels of mixed crimson and gold. Since 1858 the lance has been surmounted with the lion and crown - the crest of England. All Standards, Guidons and Colours are supervised by the Garter-King-of Arms, who is Inspector of Regimental Colours. Also in 1858 the infantry Colours were reduced in size from 6 feet 6 inches flying by 6 feet deep on the Pike to 3 feet 9 inches long by 3 feet deep with a similar crest.

Their purpose now is to form a suitable centre for parades and ceremonial occasions. When uncased the Colours are saluted by all ranks in uniform: men in civilian clothes take off their hats. Only one Guidon is presented to a cavalry or yeomanry regiment.

Appendix G

Guidons display selected Battle Honours and any Honorary Distinction, with campaign scrolls with year dates. These are arranged around a centrally placed badge and circlet giving the name of the regiment. These appear on both or either the obverse and reverse sides. Battle Honours are most usually divided between both sides of the Guidon, by reason of the space limitation. The position of Honorary Distinctions is complicated in the instance of regiments which have resulted from amalgamation. Where this is awarded to one regiment and not the other (or others), it usually appears on the single side. When one appears it is usual for the badge to face the pike, although as with the Inns of Court and City Yeomanry, it appears on the reverse side of the Guidon facing *away* from the pike. This supports the principle for the junior regiment in an amalgamation to occupy the reverse side of the Guidon.

Collectively, the Yeomanry has been awarded Honorary Distinctions by The Royal Regiment of Artillery and the Royal Corps of Signals and these details are listed in the following tabulation. It is pertinent to add that the Royal Regiment classes its Guns as Colours and carries no Banner as such. Further afield the Infantry have been awarded Honorary Distinctions by the Royal Armoured Corps (5th Bn The King's Own Royal Regiment (Lancaster), the Royal Tank Regiment (23rd London Regiment, The Leeds Rifles and The West Yorkshire Regiment) and the Reconnaissance Corps (5th Bn The Gloucestershire Regiment and 5th Bn The Loyal Regiment (North Lancashire)). Conversely the infantry has honoured its own by granting an Honorary distinction to 17th Bn, The Parachute Regiment, formerly 9th Bn, The Durham Light Infantry.

The Inns of Court Regiment was authorised infantry Colours by King George V in 1935, but due to The Second World War, these were not presented until 26th May 1954, the Regiment then being unique as the only cavalry regiment to carry infantry Colours. Furthermore, as it was then classed as Hussars, it was the only Hussar regiment authorised to carry Colours of any description at that time. These Colours are layed up in Lincoln's Inn. Over the period 1956 to 1961, D (Northamptonshire Yeomanry) Sqn brought with it its Guidon and during this time both Guidon and Colours were carried at once, the Guidon being 'on the right of the line', if of course 'D' Sqn was on parade with The Regiment. The Inns of Court and City Yeomanry was presented with a Guidon on 14th June 1963.

Unique in the annals of British military history stands the Battle Honour 'Fishguard' awarded to the Pembroke Yeomanry for an action at Fishguard in Wales, representing the sole United Kingdom award to a British Army unit. This appeared on the 1854 Guidon and differed markedly from those in use today. In that instance the centre-piece was a large Prince of Wales feathers motif with three scrolls around, entitled - Castlemartin - Fishguard - Yeomanry in gold embroidery on a light blue ground and a gold bullion fringe. An account of this event is given below.

At the time of the South African War many of the regiments later to receive an award were not entered on the Home Establishment, indeed many had not then been formed. The initiative to send these troops to South Africa was entrusted to an Imperial Yeomanry Committee who accepted the assistance of various county committees, who in turn enlisted help from the various county Yeomanry.

The Pembroke (Castlemartin) Yeomanry during the French Revolutionary War[3]
"Early in the morning of 23rd April 1797 the Castlemartin Troop were called from Haverfordwest, crossing the Haven by ferry and that evening were at Fishguard with the 750 men commanded by Lord Cawdor who had been mustered to oppose 1,400 Frenchmen under William Tate, safely landed at Carreg Point the night before. This expedition, originally intended as a minor diversion in an ambitious invasion plan that came to nothing when the 15,000 men Louis Lazare Hoche had failed to land at Bantry Bay and 5,000 more under Quantin had abandoned their voyage to Newcastle off Dunkirk, ended ingloriously.

Tate, disillusioned as to the quality of his troops and the temper of the Welsh, misled by Lord Cawdor's firmness and a belief that the scarlet whittles of distant Welsh women were the red coats of the regulars into assuming a British superiourity that did not exist, surrendered upon Goodwick Sands on the morning of 24th February."

In consequence of this action a Royal Warrant of Queen Victoria dated 18th May 1853 was later granted to the Castlemartin Yeomanry Cavalry the Battle Honour **Fishguard**. The Regimental Cap Badge subsequently incorporated a scroll with the name **Fishguard**.

Tabulation of Battle Honours Awarded to Yeomanry Regiments [4][5][6]
(Those in bold type appear on the Guidon)

North Irish Horse (Hussars)

1914-24 **Retreat from Mons - Marne 1914 - Aisne 1914 - Armentières 1914 -** Somme 1914, 1918 - **Albert 1916 - Messines 1917- Ypres 1917 -** Pilckem - St Quentin - **Bapaume 1918 -** Hindenburg Line - Épéhy - St Quentin Canal - **Cambrai 1918 -** Selle - Sambre - France and Flanders, 1914-1918.

1939-45 **Hunt's Gap -** Sedjenane I - Tamara - Mergueb Chaouach - **Djebel Rmel - Longstop Hill, 1943 - Tunis -** North Africa, 1943 - Liri Valley - **Hitler Line - Advance to Florence - Gothic Line -** Monte Farneto - Monte Cavallo - **Casa Fortis -** Casa Bettini Lamone Crossing - Valli di Commacchio - **Senio - Italy 1944-45**

South Irish Horse

1914-24 **Loos - Somme, 1916, 1918 - Albert, 1916 - St Quentin - Rosières - Avre - Ypres, 1918 - Courtrai - France and Flanders, 1915-18.**

King Edward's Horse (The King's Oversea Dominions Regiment)

1914-24 **Loos - Ypres, 1917 - Pilckem - Cambrai, 1917 - Lye - Estaires - Hazebrouck - Pursuit to Mons - France and Flanders, 1915-17, 1918 - Italy, 1917-18.**

The Ayrshire Yeomanry (Earl od Carrick's Own) (Hussars)

1899-02 **South Africa, 1900-02**

1914-24 **Ypres, 1918 - France and Flanders, 1918 - Gallipolli, 1915 - Rumani - Egypt, 1916-17 - Gaza - Jerusalem - Tell 'Asur - Palestine, 1917-18.**

1939-45 **Honorary Distinction:** A Badge of the Royal Regiment of Artillery with year dates 1942-45 and three scrolls, North-West Europe, North Africa, Italy.

Bedfordshire Yeomanry (Lancers)

1914-24 **Somme, 1916, 1918 - Flers-Courcelette - Cambrai, 1917 - France and Flanders, 1915-18.**

Berks Yeomanry (Hungerford) (Dragoons)

1899-02 **South Africa, 1900-01**

1914-24 **Arras, 1918 - Scarpe, 1918 - Ypres, 1918 - Courtrai - France and Flanders, 1918 - Suvla - Scimitar Hill - Gallipolli, 1915 - Egypt, 1915-17 - Gaza - El Mughar -** Nebi Samwil - **Palestine, 1917-18.**

Buckinghamshire Yeomanry (Royal Bucks Hussars)

1899-02 **South Africa, 1900-01**

1914-24 **Arras, 1918 - Scarpe, 1918 - Ypres, 1918 - Courtrai - France and Flanders, 1918 - Suvla - Scimitar Hill - Gallipolli, 1915 - Egypt, 1915-17 - Gaza - El Mughar -** Nebi Samwell - **Palestine, 1917-18.**

Appendix G

The Cheshire Yeomanry (Earl of Chester's) (Hussars)
1899-02 **South Africa, 1900-01**
1914-24 **Somme, 1918 - Bapaume, 1918 - Hindenburg Line - Épéchy - Pursuit to Mons - France and Flanders, 1918 - Egypt, 1916-17 - Gaza. Jerusalem, Jericho, Tell'Asur** - Palestine, 1917-18
1939-45 **Syria, 1941.** Honorary Distinction: A Royal Corps of Signals Badge with year date **1945** and scroll **North -West Europe**

Denbighshire Yeomanry (Dragoons)
1899-02 **South Africa, 1900-01**
1914-24 **Ypres, 1918 - France and Flanders, 1918 - Egypt, 1916-17 - Gaza - Jerusalem - Jericho - Tell 'Asur - Palestine, 1917-18.**

Derbyshire Yeomanry (Dragoons)
1899-02 **South Africa, 1900-01**
1914-24 **Struma - Macedonia, 1916-18 - Suvla - Scimitar Hill - Gallipolli, 1915 - Egypt, 1915-16.**
1939-45 **Dives Crossing** - La Vie Crossing - Lisieux - **Lower Maas** - Ourthe - **Rhineland** - Reichwald - North-West Europe, 1944-45 - **Alam el Halfa** - **El Alamein** - **Medjez el Bab** - Tabourba Gap - Bou Arada - Kasserine - Steamroller Farm - Maknassy - Fondouk - **Kairouan** - El Kourzia - Tunis - North Africa, 1942-43 - **Cassino II** - Liri Valley - Aquino - Arezzo - Advance to Florence - **Argenta Gap** - Fossa Cembalina - Italy 1944-45.

Royal 1st Devon Yeomanry (Hussars)
1899-02 **South Africa, 1900-01**
1914-24 **Somme, 1918 - Bapaume, 1918 - Hindenburg Line -   Épéhy** - Pursuit to Mons - **France and Flanders, 1918 - Gallipolli, 1915 - Egypt, 1916-17 - Gaza - Jerusalem -** Tell 'Asur - **Palestine, 1917-18**

Royal North Devon Yeomanry (Hussars)
1899-02 **South Africa, 1900-01**
1914-24 **Somme 1918, Bapaume 1918, Hindenburg Line -** Épéhy - Pursuit to Mons - **France and Flanders 1918, Gallipolli 1915, Egypt 1916-17, Gaza, Jerusalem,** Tell 'Asur, **Palestine, 1917-18.**

Dorset Yeomanry (Queen's Own)
1899-02 **South Africa, 1900-01**
1914-24 **Suvla - Scimitar Hill - Gallipolli, 1915 - Agagiya - Egypt, 1915-17 - Gaza - El Mughar - Nebi Samwil -** Megiddo - Sharon - **Damascus - Palestine, 1917-18.**

Essex Yeomanry (Dragoons)
1914-24 **Ypres, 1915 - St Julien - Fresenberg - Loos - Arras, 1917 - Scarpe, 1917 - Some, 1918 - France and flanders, 1914-18.**

Fife and Forfar Yeomanry
1899-02 **South Africa, 1900-01**
1914-24 **Somme, 1918 - Bapaume, 1918 - Hindenburg Line -** Épéhy - Pursuit to Mons - **France and flanders, 1918 - Egypt, 1916-17 - Gaza - Jerusalem - Jericho -** Tell 'Asur - Palestine, 1917-18
1939-45 **Dunkirk, 1940 - Cheux - Bourguebus Ridge - Le Perier Ridge - Scheldt - Ourthe - Rhineland - Rhine - North-West Europe, 1944-45.**

Appendix G

Glamorgan Yeomanry (Dragoons)

1914-24 Somme, 1918 - Bapaume, 1918 - Hindenburg Line - Épéhy - Pursuit to Mons - **France and flanders, 1918 - Egypt, 1916-17 - Gaza - Jerusalem - Jericho - Tell 'Asur - Palestine, 1917-18.**

The Queen's Own Royal Glasgow Yeomanry

1914-24 **Loos - Ypres, 1917-18 - Paachendaele - Somme, 1918 - Bapaume, 1918 - Ancre, 1918 - Courtrai - France and Flanders, 1915-18**

1939-45 **Honorary Distinction:** A Badge of the Royal Regiment of Artillery with year-dates 1940, 42-45 and scrolls North-West Europe, North Africa, Sicily, Italy

Gloucestershire Yeomanry (Royal Gloucestershire Hussars)

1899-02 **South Africa, 1900-01**

1914-24 **Suvla - Scimitar Hill - Gallipolli,1915 - Rumani - Rafah - Egypt, 1915-17 - Gaza - El Mughar - Nebi Samwil - Jerusalem - Magiddo - Sharon - Damascus - Palestine, 1917-18.**

1939-45 **Tobruk, 1941 - Gubi I - Sidi Rezegh, 1941 - Chor es Sufan - Gazala - Bir el Aslagh - Cauldron - Alam el Halfa - West Point 23 - North Africa, 1941-42**

Hampshire (Carabiniers) Dragoons

1899-02 **South Africa, 1900-01**

1914-24 **Messines, 1917 - Somme, 1918 - St Quentin - Bapaume, 1918 - Arras, 1918 - Ypres, 1918 - Courtrai - France and Flanders, 1916-17, 1918 - Italy, 1917-18.**

Herts Yeomanry (Dragoons)

1899-02 **South Africa, 1900-01**

1914-24 **Suvla - Scimitar Hill - Gallipolli, 1915 - Suez Canal - Egypt, 1915-16 - Megiddo - Sharon - Damascus - Palestine, 1918.**

The Inns of Court Regiment, RAC, TA.

1899-02 **South Africa, 1900-01**

1939-45 **Normandy Landing - Caen - Bourguebas Ridge - Cagny - Catheolles - Amiens, 1944 - Antwerp - Hechtel - Rhine - Leese - Aller - North-West Europer, 1944-45.**

Royal East Kent (The Duke of connaught's Own) (Mounted Rifles) (Hussars)

1914-24 **Somme 1918, Bapaume 1918, Hindenburg Line, Épéhy, Pursuit to Mons, France and Flanders1918, Gallipolli 1915, Egypt 1916-17, Gaza,** Jerusalem, Tel 'Asur, **Palestine 1917-18**

West Kent Yeomanry (Queen's Own) (Hussars)

1914-24 **Somme, 1918 - Bapaume, 1918 - Hindenburg Line - Épéhy - Pursuit to Mons - France and Flanders, 1918 - Gallipolli, 1915 - Egypt, 1916-17 - Gaza -** Jerusalem - Tell 'Asur **- Palestine, 1917-18**

The Lanarkshire Yeomanry

1899-02 **South Africa, 1900-02**

1914-24 **Ypres, 1918 - France and Flanders, 1918 - Gallipolli, 1915 - Egypt, 1916-17 - Gaza - Jerusalem - Tell 'Asur - Palestine, 1917-18**

1939-45 **Honorary distinction:** A Badge of the Royal Regiment of Artillery, with year-dates 1941-45 and four scrolls: North-West Europe, Sicily, Italy, Malaya

Appendix G

The Lancashire Hussars Yeomanry
1899-02 **South Africa, 1900-02**
1914-24 **Somme, 1916, 1918 - Albert, 1916 - Ypres, 1917 - Pilckem - St Quentin -
St Rosieres - Lys - Kemmel** - Scherpenberg - **Hindenburg Line - Cambrai, 1918** - Selle -
France and flanders, 1916-18

The Duke of Lancaster's Own Yeomanry (Dragoons)
1899-02 **South Africa, 1900-02**
1914-24 **Somme, 1916, 1918 - Albert, 1916, 1918 - Ypres, 1917 - Passchendaele - St Quentin -
Bapaume, 1918 - Amiens - Hindenburg Line - Épéhy - Cambrai, 1918 - Selle - Sambre -
France and Flanders, 1915-18.**
1939-45 Honorary Distinction: A Badge of the Royal Regiment of Artillery, with year dates
1944-45 and two scrolls North-West Europe, Italy

The Leicestershire Yeomanry (Prince Albert's Own) (Hussars)
1899-02 **South Africa, 1900-02**
1914-24 **Ypres, 1914, 1915 - St Julien - Frezenberg - Arras, 1917 - Scarpe, 1917 - France and
Flanders, 1914-18.**
1939-45 Honorary Distinction: A Badge of the Royal Regiment of Artillery, with year dates 1942, 44-45
and scrolls North-West Europe, North Africa, Italy

Lincolnshire Yeomanry (Lancers)
1914-24 **Selle - Valenciennes - Sambre - France and flanders, 1918 - Egypt, 1915-17 - Gaza - El
Mughar - Nebi Samwil - Palestine, 1917-18**

City of London Yeomanry (Rough Riders) (Lancers)
1899-02 **South Africa, 1900-02**
1914-24 **Pursuit to Mons - France and Flanders, 1918 - Macedonia, 1916-17 - Suvla -
Scimitar Hill - Gallipolli, 1915 - Rumani** - Egypt, 1915-16 - **Gaza** - El Mughar -
Nebi Samwil - Palestine, 1917-18.
1939-45 Honorary distinction. A Badge of the Royal Regiment of Artillery, with year dates
1942-45 and two scrolls: North Africa, Italy.

1st County of London Yeomanry (Middlesex, Duke of Cambridge's Hussars)
1899-02 **South Africa, 1900-01**
1914-24 **Macedonia, 1916-17 - Suvla - Scimitar Hill - Gallipolli, 1915** - Egypt, 1915-16 - **Gaza** - El
Mughar - **Nebi Samwil - Megiddo - Sharon - Damascus - Palestine, 1917-18.**

2nd County of London Yeomanry (Westminster Dragoons)
1899-02 **South Africa, 1900-02**
1914-24 **Courtrai - France and Flanders, 1918 - Suvla - Scimitar Hill - Gallipolli,1915 -
Suez Canal - Egypt, 1915-17 - Gaza** - El Mughar - **Jerusalem - Palestine, 1917-18.**
1939-45 **Normandy Landing - Villers Bocage - Venraij - Meijel - Venlo Pocket - Roer -**
North-West Europe, 1944-45.

3rd County of London Yeomanry (Sharpshooters) (Hussars)
1899-02 **South Africa, 1900-02**
1914-24 **Pursit to Mons - France and flanders, 1918 - Suvla - Scimitar Hill - Gallipolli, 1915 - Egypt,
1915-16 - Gaza - El Mughar - Nebi Samwil - Palestine, 1917-18.**

Appendix G

1939-45   Villers Bocage - Odon - Defence of Rauray - **Caen** - Bourguebus Ridge - Falaise - Lower Maas - Rhineland - Hochwald - **Rhine** - Aller - **North-West Europe, 1944-45** - Tobruk, 1941 - Gubi I - Gabr Saleh - **Sidi Rezegh, 1941** - Chor es Sufan - Gazala - Cauldron - Hegiag el Raml - Mers Matruh - Minqar Qaim - Defence of Alamein Line - Deir el Shein - Ruweisat - Point 39 - Ruweisat Ridge - **Alam el Halfa** - **El Alamein** - Akerit - Djebel Roumana - Tunis - North Africa, 1941-43 - Termoli - **Sangro** - Fossacesia - Volturno Crossing - **Italy, 1943**

Lothians and Border Horse (Dragoons)
1899-02   **South Africa; 1900-01**
1914-24   **France and Flanders, 1915 - Doiran, 1918 - Macedonia, 1915-18**
1939-45   Somme, 1940 - Withdrawal to Seine - St Valery-en-Caux - **Falaise** - Faslaise Road - Laison - Le Havre - **Boulogne, 1944** - Calais, 1944 - Scheldt - **Westkapelle** - Geilenkirchen - Roer - Reichwald - North-West Europe, 1940, 1944-45 - Bou Arada - **Kasserine** - Thala - Fondouk - Sidi Ali - Bordj - Djebel - **Cassino II** - Liri Valley - Monte Picollo - Monte Retondo - Capture of Perugia - Advance to Florence - **Argenta Gap** - **Italy 1944-45**

The Lovat Scouts
1899-02   **South Africa, 1900-02**
1914-24   **France and Flanders, 1916-18 - Macedonia, 1916-18 - Gallipolli, 1915 - Egypt, 1915-16.**

Montgomeryshire Yeomanry (Dragoons)
1899-02   **South Africa, 1901**
1914-24   **Somme, 1918 - Bapaume, 1918 - Hindenburg Line - Épéhy - Pursit to Mons - France and Flanders, 1918 - Egypt, 1916-18 - Gaza - Jerusalem - Jericho - Tell 'Asur - Palestine, 1917-18.**

1914-24   Norfolk Yeomanry (The King's Own Royal Regiment) (Dragoons)
Ypres, 1918 - France and Flanders, 1918 - Gallipolli, 1915 - Egypt, 1915-17 - Gaza - Jerusalem - Tell 'Asur - Palestine, 1917-18

Northamptonshire Yeomanry (Dragoons)
1914-24   **Neuve Chapelle - Ypres, 1915 - Arras, 1917 - Scarpe, 1917 - France and flanders, 1914-17 - Vittorio Veneto - Italy, 1917-18.**
1939-45   **Odon - Cheux** - Defence of Rauray - **Caen** - Noyers - **Bourguebus Ridge** - **Mount Pincon** - Falaise - Falaise Road - Dives Crossing - Lisieux - **Le Havre** - **Lower Maas** - Venlo Pocket - Ourthe - **Rhine** - North-West Europe, 1944-45.

The Northumberland Hussars (Yeomanry)
1899-02   **South Africa, 1900-02**
1914-24   **Ypres, 1914 - Langemarck, 1914 - Gheluvelt - Neuve Chapelle - Loos - Cambrai, 1917 - Somme, 1918 - St Quentin - Albert, 1918 - Selle - Sambre - France and Flanders, 1914-18.**
1939-45   **Honorary Distinction:** A Badge of the Royal Regiment of Artillery, with year dates 1940-45 and five scrolls: North Africa, Greece, Middle East, Sicily, North-West Europe

The Nottinghamshire Yeomanry (Sherwood Rangers) (Hussars)
1899-02   **South Africa, 1900-02**
1914-24   **Struma - Macedonia, 1916-17 - Suvla - Scimitar Hill - Gallipolli, 1915 - Egypt, 1915-16 - Gaza - Damascus - Palestine, 1917-18.**

Appendix G

1939-45 **Normandy Landing** - Villers Bocage - Odon - Fontenay le Pesnil - Defence of Rauray - Mont pincon - Jurques - Noireau Crossing - Seine, 1944 - **Gheel** - Nederirijn - **Geilenkirchen** - Roer - Rhineland - Cleve - Goch - Weeze - **Rhine** - **North-West Europe, 1944-45** - **Alam el Halfa** - **El Alamein** - El Agheila - **Advance to Tripoli** - **Tebaga Gap** - Point 201 (Roman Wall) - El Hamma - Chebkjet en Nouiges - Enfidaville - Takrouna - **North Africa, 1940-43.**

Nottinghamshire Yeomanry (South Nottinghamshire Hussars)
1899-02 **South Africa, 1900-02**
1914-24 **Hindenburg Line** - **Épéhy** - St Quentin Canal - Beaurevoir - **Selle** - **Sambre** - France and Flanders, 1918 - **Struma** - Macedonia, 1916-17 - **suvla** - **Gaza** - **Scimitar Hill** - Gallipolli, 1915 - Egypt, 1915-16 - **Gaza** - **El Mughar** - **Nebi Samwil** - Palestine, 1917-18

Oxfordshire Yeomanry (Queen's Own Oxfordshire Hussars)
1899-02 **South Africa, 1900-01**
1914-24 **Messines, 1914** - **Armentières, 1914** - **Ypres, 1915** - St Julien - Bellewaarde - **Arras, 1917** - Scarpe, 1917 - **Cambrai, 1917, 1918** - **Somme, 1918** - St Quentin - **Lys** - Hazebrouck - Amiens - Bapaume, 1918 - **Hindenburg Line** - Canal du Nord - Selle - Sambre - **France and flanders, 1914-18.**

Pembroke Yeomanry (Castlemartin) (Hussars)
1794-01 **Fishguard**
1899-02 **South Africa, 1901**
1914-24 Somme, 1918 - Bapaume, 1918 - **Hindenburg Line** - **Épéhy** - Pursuit to Mons - **France and Flanders, 1918** - Egypt, 1916-17 - **Gaza** - **Jerusalem** - Jericho - **Tell 'Asur** - Palestine, 1917-18.

The Scottish Horse (Scouts)
1899-02 **South Africa, 1900-02**
1914-24 **The Hindenburg Line** - St Quentin Canal - Cambrai, 1918 - **Beaurevoir** - **Selle** - **Sambre** - **France and Flanders, 1918** - **Macedonia, 1916-18** - **Gallipolli, 1915** - Rumani - Egypt, 1915-16.
1939-45 Honorary Distinction: A Badge of the Royal Regiment of Artillery, with year dates 1943-45 and three scrolls, North-West Europe, Sicily, Italy.

Shropshire Yeomanry (Dragoons)
1899-02 **South Africa, 1900-02**
1914-24 **Somme, 1918** - **Bapaume, 1918** - **Hindenburg Line** - **Épéhy** - Pursuit to Mons - **France and Flanders, 1918** - Egypt, 1916-17 - **Gaza** - **Jerusalem** - Jericho - **Tell 'Asur** - Palestine, 1917-18.
1939-45 Honorary Distinction: A Badge of the Royal Regiment of Artillery with year dates 1943-45 and scrolls Sicily, Italy.

The North Somerset Yeomanry (Dragoons)
1899-02 **South Africa, 1900-01**
1914-24 **Ypres, 1914, 1915** - **Frezenberg** - Loos - **Arras, 1917** - Scarpe, 1917 - **France and flanders, 1914-18.**
1939-45 **Jebel Mazar, Syria, 1941. Honorary distinction:** A Badge of the Royal Corps of signals with year dates 1942-45 and four scrolls: North Africa, Sicily, Italy, North-West Europe

The Norfolk Yeomanry Trust

The Cheshire Yeomanry

The Wiltshire Yeomanry

Guidons. The Royal Wiltshire Yeomanry Guidon as presented 11th June 1961 showing obverse and reverse views.
The Cheshire Yeomanry Guidon, showing Honorary Distinction 'The Royal Coprs of Signals'.
Norfolk Yeomanry, King's Own Royal Regiment Guidon.

Plate 12

Plate 13

The Queen's Colour and The Regimental Colour of The Inns of Court. The Regiment was unique in carrying Infantry Colours and a Yeomanry Guidon. The Inns of Court and City Yeomanry now carries a Guidon the Reverse side of which displays the Honorary Distinction of The Royal Regiment of Artillery.

The North Somerset Yeomanry / 44th Royal
Tank Regimental Association.

Guidon of The North Somerset Yeomanry / 44th Royal Tank
Regiment, with Honorary Distinction The Royal Corps of
Signals.

Guidon of The Westminster Dragoons.

The Royal Tank Regiment

The Standard of the Royal Tank Regiment, carried by virtue of
their being 'Heavy Cavalry'.

'All Regiments, Regular and Territorial, carry the same Standard
with their individual Regimental Number above the letters R.T.R. at
the top right and bottom left hand corners of the Standard.

The reverse side of the Standard is identical except that it only
bears the single battle honour KOREA 1951-53.

Plate 14.

The Fife and Forfar Yeomanry / Scottish Horse

Guidon of The Fife and Forfar Yeomanry / Scottish Horse.
This carries this Honorary Distinction on the obverse,
whilst the Battle Honours are divided between the
obverse and reverse.

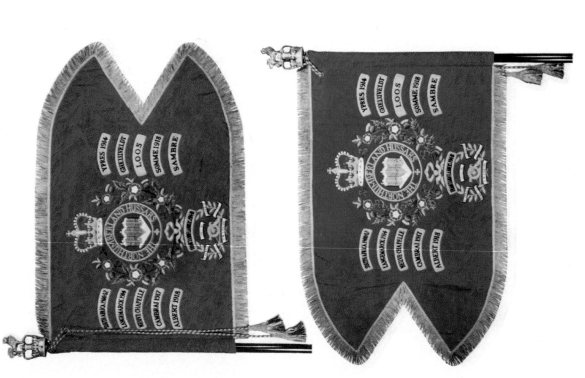

The Northumberland Hussars

Guidon of The Northumberland Hussars. It is noteworthy
that they carry the Honour Distinction of The Royal
Regiment of Artillery on both the obverse and reverse
sides and similarly their Battle Honours.

Plate 15

Appendix G

West Somerset Yeomanry (Hussars)
1899-02 **South Africa, 1900-01**
1914-24 **Somme, 1918 - Bapaume, 1918 - Hindenburg Line - Épéhy - Pursuit to Mons - France and flanders, 1918 - Gallipolli, 1915 - Egypt, 1916-17 - Gaza - Jerusalem -** Tell 'Asur - **Palestine, 1917-18.**

The Staffordshire Yeomanry (Queen's Own Royal Regiment) (Hussars)
1899-02 **South Africa, 1900-01**
1914-24 **Egypt, 1915-17 - Gaza - El Mughar - Nebi Samwil - Megiddo - Sharon - Damascus - Palestine, 1917-18.**
1939-45 **Normandy Landing - Caen - Troarn - Rhine - Lingen - North-Western Europe, 1944-45 - Syria, 1941 - Alam El Halfa - El Alamein - El Agheila - Advance on Tripoli - Tebaga Gap -** Point 201 (Roman Wall) - El Hamma - **Akerit -** Sebkret en Noual - Djebel el Telil - **Enfidaville -** Takrouna - North Africa, 1942-43.

Suffolk Yeomanry (The Duke of York's Own Loyal Suffolk Hussars)
1899-02 **South Africa, 1900-01**
1914-24 **Somme, 1918 - Bapaume, 1918 - Hindenburg Line - Épéhy - Pursuit to Mons - France and flanders, 1918 - Gallipolli, 1915 - Egypt, 1915-17 - Gaza - Jerusalem -** Tell 'Asur - Palestine, 1917-18.

Surrey Yeomanry (Queen Mary's Regiment) (Lancers)
1914-24 **Ypres, 1915 - France and Flanders, 1915 - Struma - Macedonia, 1916-18 - Egypt, 1915**

Sussex Yeomanry (Dragoons)
1914-24 **Somme, 1918 - Bapaume, 1918 - Hindenburg Line - Épéhy - Pursuit to Mons -** France and Flanders, 1918 - **Gallipolli, 1915 - Egypt, 1916-17 - Gaza - Jerusalem -** Tell 'Asur - Palestine, 1917-18.

The Warwickshire Yeomanry (Hussars)
1899-02 **South Africa, 1900-01**
1914-24 **Hindenburg Line - Épéhy - St Quentin Canal - Beaurevoir - Sambre - France and Flanders, 1918 - Suvla - Scimitar Hill - Gallipolli, 1915 -** Rumani - **Rafah - Egypt, 1915-17 - Gaza -** El Mughar - Nebi Samwil - Jerusalem - **Palestine, 1917-18.**
1939-45 **Iraq, 1941 - Syria, 1941 - El Alamein - North Africa, 1942 - Ficulle - Trasimene Line - Sanfatucchio - Advance to Florence - Campriano - Italy, 1944.**

Welsh Horse (Lancers)
1914-24 **Somme, 1918 - Bapaume, 1918 - Hindenburg Line - Épéhy - Pursuit to Mons - France and Flanders, 1918 - Gallipolli, 1915 - Egypt, 1915-17 - Gaza - Jerusalem - Jericho -** Tell 'Asur - **Palestine 1917-18.**

Westmorland and Cumberland Yeomanry (Hussars)
1899-02 **South Africa, 1900-01**
1914-24 **Ypres, 1917 - Poelcappelle - Passchendaele - Somme, 1918 -** St Quentin **- Bapaume, 1918 -** Amiens **- Albert, 1918 - Hindenburg Line - Épéhy -** Cambrai, 1918 - Selle - **Sambre - France and Flanders, 1915-18**

Appendix G

The Royal Wiltshire Yeomanry (Prince of Wales's Own) (Hussars)

1899-02	**South Africa, 1900-01**
1914-24	**Ypres, 1917** - Polygon Wood - **Broodseinde** - Poel-cappelle - Passchendaele - **Somme, 1918 - St Quentin - Bapaume, 1918 - Lys - Messines, 1918 - Bailleul - Kemmel - France and flanders, 1916-18.**
1939-45	Iraq, 1941 - **Palmyra** - Syria, 1941 - **El Alamein** - North Africa, 1942 - **Liri Valley - Advance to Tiber - Citta delia Pieve - Transimene Line - Advance to Florence - Monte Cedrone - Citta di Castello - Italy, 1944.**

Worcestershire Yeomanry (The Queen's Own Worcestershire Hussars)

1899-1902	**South Africa, 1900-02**
1914-1924	**Suvla - Scimitar Hill - Gallipolli, 1915 - Rumani - Rafah - Egypt, 1915-17 - Gaza** - El Mughar - Nebi Samwil - **Jerusalem - Megiddo** - Nablus - **Damascus - Palestine, 1917-18.**
1939-1945	**Honorary Distinction:** A Badge of the Royal Regiment of Artillery with year dates 1940, 44-45 and one scroll North-West Europe

The Yorkshire Dragoons Yeomanry (Queen's Own)

1899-02	**South Africa, 1900-02**
1914-24	**Cambrai, 1917 - Courtrai - France and Flanders, 1915-18.**
1939-45	**Syria, 1941 - El Alamein - Tebaga Gap - El Hamma - El Kourzia - Tunis - North Africa, 1942-43** -Anzio - **Rome** - Coriano - **Rimini Line - Ceriano Ridge - Italy, 1944.**

The Yorkshire Hussars Yeomanry (Alexandra, Princess of Wales's Own)

1899-02	**South Africa, 1900-02**
1914-24	**Arras, 1918 - Scarpe, 1918 Droocourt-Quéant - Hindenburg Line - Canal du Nord - Cambrai, 1918 - Selle - Valenciennes - Sambre - France and flanders, 1915-18.**

East Riding of Yorkshire Yeomanry (Lancers)

1914-24	**Sele - Valenciennes - Sambre - France and flanders, 1918 - Egypt, 1915-17 - Gaza - El Mughar - Nebi Samwil - Palestine, 1917-18**
1939-45	Withdrawal to Escaut - **St Omer la Bassee - Cassel - Normandy Landing - Cambes - Caen - Bourguebus Ridge** - La Vie Crossing - **Lisieux** - Foret de Bretonne - **Lower Maas - Venlo Pocket** - Ourthe - **Rhine** - North-West Europe, 1940, 1944-45.

References

1 'The Devil's Own'
   (Additional material has been included, taken from programmes issued at the time new Guidons have been presented to regiments.)
2 TJ Edwards MBE FRHistS Standards, Guidons and Colours of the Commonwealth Forces p9
3 Howell RL Lt-Col (Edited Glover DG Capt) The Pembroke Yeomanry Dyfed County Council Haverfordwest, 1987
4 Battle Honours Awarded for the Boer War - Individual regimental histories
5 Battle Honours Awarded for the Great War - Complete List Issued with Army Orders, War Office 27th February, 1925 HMSO
6 The Second World War Battle Honours. Consolidated from RUSI journals

Appendix H

First Aid Nursing Yeomanry

Introduction

The foundation and early growing pains of this gallant and determined little Corps have been detailed in chapter six. This covered events until after the 1914 Summer Camp. The Declaration of War which followed very soon revealed that 'kind words butter no parsnips', insofar as War Office then advised them to 'go home and sit still - No petticoats here!' when they put in an application for active duties. It will avoid a grating repitition by stating now that a string of vague assurances foundered upon the rock hard Victorian premise that women were not combatants and most of the decision takers hailed from that era. This continued into The Second World War, with the recreation of the women's services and the then belated acknowledgement that some were going into combat. It was a narrow drawn line and a face saving formula suiting official convenience. But the story hardly stops there, since later and to confound it all, the three Women's Services were scrapped to have them re-badged with their male counterparts! As the Queen said in Alice in Wonderland, "words mean what I want them to mean". The account which follows makes no attempt at history: it portrays acts of devotion and the often annoying capacity for intervention where officialdom bumbled.

Le bon Dieu protége ses petites Fannies

The Great War

After a few false starts the first substantial duty came with the Belgians, in manning a 100-Bed hospital at Lamarck, Calais. Some 8000 casualties were treated and transhipped to Cherbourg during five days of the Battle of Ypres. Besides this they helped establish and ran a convelescent home at St Inglevert, opened a soup kitchen and purchased and operated a much needed mobile baths unit providing 250 baths a day, with clothes disinfection. These operations ran for two years with 4000 Belgian soldiers treated for typhoid or minor wounds. In addition they founded a mobile canteen in a desolate area and ran a mobile cinema, self supported by a generator. They went on to help establish the Belgian concentration area at Tours. All these measures were designed to save and enhance the quality of life and were financed mainly from their own resources and fund raising efforts. Despite such obvious success it still remained a priority to obtain British service.

A British hospital was next established at Calais in June 1915 and on January 1916 their male drivers were released for more forward duties and replaced by FANY: at last they were officially driving for the British Army! The duties involved unloading wounded from trains, evacuating cases from hospitals into hospital ships and collecting the wounded brought down the St Omer Canal in barges. Calais harbour was a congested area, including the quays, making driving extremely difficult. On one occasion the Corps received congratulations for the feat of loading 300 stretcher cases into a ship in under two hours. This convoy was not relieved by the RAMC until May 1919! But before this, a further convoy was raised at St Omer, presumably to handle the same sort of disruptions which affected the Belgians mentioned below.

The Belgians also raised a convoy unit at Calais, but in the Autumn of 1916, based on the earlier prototype. The British Red Cross Committee which already shared an uneasy relationship with the St Johns Ambulance counterpart, got to hear of this and decided to take out any FANY involvement not in direct support of the British Army. This was the continuation of an old joust and MacDougall, the leading light of the period duly lifted the gauntlet. In a brilliant stroke, these FANYs were paraded for the Belgians to weigh, measure, photograph, finger-print and swear-in as Soldats de la Corps de Transport de Calais (Belge). The Belgians were not much amused by these party tricks, during a grim war, in which they had gone to great lengths to equip and support a useful. service. The upshot, when the self-advertised assassins arrived was to find the Belgians waiting with the FANYs resplendent in blue gorgets and silver badges of rank and the question "how can we help you, now that you venture upon Belgian soil?". This at last established the not unreasonable requirement for each army to make its own arrangements with FANY, directly. The Corps grew in stature and managed its own affairs, both administratively and technically. During October 1918 it advanced with the Belgians into Bruges. Here it encountered the mass of displaced civilians and released prisoners arriving by road and rail and managed the business of succouring the many ill, before re-routing the various parties.

Attempts to nurse the French encountered resistance, who wished to be seen as looking after their own. Thus, a new hospital established by them at Port à Binson, but commissioned by FANY from the end of 1916, saw them terminated on 19th January 1918. The French were lavish in their praise, treated the Corps better than most and came back many times for convoy services, but felt too proud to entrust their badly wounded to others. Having regard to the charades played by Britain, who can begrudge them their national pride? The VIth convoy was established, based on Amiens and was well treated. The VIIth was created, based on Epernay and had a very cold time. It carried 1817 cases by January 1918 and 1566 cases during the March 1918 offensive.

Nine other Ambulance Convoy units were established after the Calais prototype and 197 air raids were endured on that place alone. Four new convoys were created at the time of the Armistice and operated until April 1919, to be disembodied as opposed to disbanded.

It does well to reflect upon the bravery and self sacrifice of the Corps. Those empowered to sanction them made 95 French, Belgian as well as British awards with 15 Mentions in Despatches. This included 16 Military Medals, the majority gained at the time of the Ludendorf Offensive when it was entirely uncertain whether the front would hold. With the local ambulance service out of action, it was a matter of relief to have three units brought in to load up and carry away many wounded, despite exploding shells and gas. The flood of properly documented recommendations for decorations at this time led to an enquiry and later, perhaps a little shame facedly , to the awards mentioned.

The Peace

The Corps was allowed to continue after the war by the War Office, though under what authority is unclear. With the war over came the necessity to update Corps objectives and this was done. The Army, now without a female Service and recognising the contribution the Corps could make, provided support in the run-up to the General Strike. The proposed involvement had been foreseen as a requirement for a revised constitution. When the strike came they were able to serve and it set the stage for formal recognition. The plaudits when they came, were disproportionately large in relation to the service rendered, nevertheless Franklin, then in charge, recognised a good opportunity and pressed for recognition, enclosing a copy of the new constitution. She offered the Corps services to the War Office and suggested that it should be made official. In due course Army Order No 94, appeared in the Army List for 14th April 1927 stating: 'The First Aid Nursing Yeomanry (Ambulance Car Corps) has been officially recognised by the Army Council as a voluntary reserve transport unit. The Corps has placed its services at the disposal of the War Office for service in any national emergency .'

Work continued to increase expertise on the subjects of advanced driving, vehicle maintenance and what today is called orienteering. The Guards also assisted with quarter-master training and camp practice. Inreasingly through the 1930s the Corps title began to hamper rather than help its advancement and to strengthen its position this was changed to the Women's Transport Service (FANY). Although the War Office agreed to the entity and the continued recognition of its Headquarters, it became something impossible of fulfilment. Matters progressed well enough until the Munich crisis loomed, when plans were made to reform the various Women's Services, disbanded at the end of the last war. Here we are talking of what became a 200,000 strong Auxiliary Territorial Service (ATS) and immediately the War Office were on the horns of a dilemma. Instead of admitting the difficulties of administering two female organisations with entirely different 'codes of practice', it hoped the problem would go away, why we shall never know.

The initial strategem was to offer the headship of the new larger body to that of the smaller, and F.A.N.Y. the Corps being an obvious cadre for the large number of officers required by the infant ATS, but such blandishments were spurned by FANY. Later, a shot-gun wedding was reluctantly agreed and signed on 21st September 1938 bringing WTS(FANY) under ATS tutelage, against a further line of worthless assurances. From that point the majority of the Corps became members of Motor Driver Companies (Army), Auxiliary Territorial Service. They

Appendix H

wore a distinguishing shoulder flash (if recruited prior to 1st September 1941), shared the discomfort of a divided loyalty and ultimately served under the Army Act.

The Corps had now been in existence for 31 years and had trained consistently, in the memorable words of Captain Baker ALONG THE RIGHT LINES and thus it was off to a flying start in vehicle management and the formation of ten 150 strong companies. Very soon they had 1000 driver mechanics, had a recruiting drive underway for a further 500 and had initiated officer and NCO training courses. By comparison, the ATS were without uniforms, had few trained officers and very little in the way of military expertise. Nevertheless, the Corps natural free thinking and their easy self-confidence born out of experience and hard training continued to rub on their uncertain host's mind, who became preoccupied with dismantling the Corps Headquarters and everything it stood for. When they contrived its relocation to a Camberley Training Centre, in December 1939, they felt that at last they had administered the *coup de grâce*, but that was not to be.

It is not proposed to continue this dismal recital over a criminal abuse of splended resources, except to say the diversion of management effort by ATS to delay the WTS(FANY) work redounded on them when the moral probity of the General Duties Companies (ATS) was brought into question and an unfortunate reputation dogged them into 1942, finally requiring the Markham committee to scotch further rumours. The excuse behind War Office intentions towards the FANY was best explained in the minute from the Adjutant General of 7th February 1940, which later ran: 'The War Office has every desire to FANY continuing in existence but as a body separate from the ATS and outside War Office control; it desires to help the FANYs when possible and will gratefully accept its help so far as the War machine permits. It was agreed that the FANY might perform invaluable work as an entity with the French, Finns or other foreign Armies as time goes on, or under the Home Office.' This doesn't entirely square with the arm-twisting and protracted bargaining of the earlier period and perhaps a more straightforward statement could have been introduced *before* many of the half-baked negotiations were entered into. Since the Army had in a clumsy and messy way already achieved the best cut on FANY resources, the above statement has a patronising, if not downright dishonest ring to it.

The Second World War

The wartime account has to do mainly with Transport, for this was the primary area of expertise, but by no means the whole story. Free FANYs operated within and beyond the UK shores. There were the Secret FANYs, using their radio skills and also as Field Agents in the Occupied Countries.

The Transport operation was quickly made a success. Problems, such as arose, generally stemmed from the inexperience of ATS Staff Officers in transport matters or interference engineered from a high level over the flow of recruits and of those trained, into the system, much to the annoyance of Army Commands. When the Training Centre opened in February 1940 it came under the Director of Army Training and SE Command. Until July 1941 the cost of recruitment was taken by FANY and handled by volunteers working at their HQ. Hugh Popham writes of this period as an unhappy one for the Corps, where the majority of its members found themselves involuntarily entangled with a brand-new service tersely described by one Shelford Bidwell as 'a shambles' and the creation of which was 'one of the most outstanding feats of military organisation in the history of the British Army'! In turn the ATS charged the Corps with an over-relaxed standard of discipline and a misplaced sense of humour; indeed they adopted Guards standards of discipline when on duty and complete informality when off, whilst to the second charge they asked 'where might they be without a sense of humour?'

The first action for the Corps came with driving ambulances in France from April 1940, followed by evacuation through St Malo, after the Dunkirk débâcle. The number of Motor Companies reached 41 in 1942, at which time there was a rationalisation, when they were integrated as Command Mixed MT Companies.

The further history can be followed elsewhere as it would be difficult to separate specifically FANY activities. The appointment of Jean Knox as DATS, in July 1941, marked an immediate improvement in relations with Corps members. Later, Mary Baxter Ellis became DDATS and five Controllers and many Chief and Senior Commanders were FANY. It is noteworthy that as the war progressed there were numerous other 'non-combatant' jobs to be tackled and duties moved out from transport into AA Command and the RASC, to

Appendix H

designing camouflage, making maps with the RE, running the Army blood donor service, tracking ship movements, sorting letters in the Army Post Office, operating telephone switchboards and teleprinters with the Royal Signals, reconditioning salvaged ammunition and helping with instruction and film making for the training service. They also provided a small Military Police and a select handful of high-powered assistants to Commanders and Chiefs of Staff. Contingents started to go overseas again from 1941 onwards, where they moved-up close behind the victorious armies.

For the rôle of the Free FANYs we must return to the old London FANY HQ. The departure of Mary Baxter Ellis to Camberley was preceded by an urgent call to Northern Rhodesia to have Marian Gamwell return to hold the fort. The general support of these calls for personnel was met by the FANY Headquarters Attachment Unit, run voluntarily and without official funding. It was a general principle that *all* recruits should undergo a basic training to incalcate the Corps ethos, such as FANY history, tradition and discipline. It included teaching the basic skills in drill, map-reading, First Aid and Gas. Added to this came comprehensive mechanical and vehicle training for drivers, whilst others took courses appropriate to specialism. This form of solid background, given to carefully selected individuals, ensured both competence and confidence when called to act on their own initiative and helped protect the reputation of the Corps.

Finland presented the first challenge, so that on 1st February 1940 a 40-strong detachment took ambulances via Sweden to assist in the movement of the recently wounded resulting from the war with Russia. That operation was wound up by mid-Summer. A Canteen unit left for France, in the Spring of 1940 and operated with the Poles in Brittany, before being evacuated through St Nazaire. Thereafter a number of Canteens were attached to the Poles in the South of Scotland and operated alongside 10 ambulances presented by the British/American Red Cross Society. There were 250 Corps members serving with the Poles. And later they were to support the Poles again in Bari as Force 139, set up at the end of 1943. A single ambulance unit, at a later stage joined the French Maquis. Further afield, the Kenya Branch, the only one outside the UK, got their membership up to 600 and became the Women's Territorial Service (East Africa), serving on the same terms as the men. Although the UK link was severed, they were still known as FANYs. Their main duties comprised the guarding of civilian alien families for five months, whilst six high fliers joined the administration for the invasion of Abysinnia. Elsewhere at home, more bizarre employment came as wirelss operators for the auxilliary units of a clandestine army under a Major Colin Gubbins. Little talked about, their object was to provide communications between units in the event of Germany securing a foothold in the United Kingdom.

Secret FANYs were employed, both as wireless operators and in listening watches over covert actions on the Continent. This was a further Gubbins responsibility, acting as Director of Operations and Training for the Special Operations Executive (SOE), which went under the vague name of the Inter-Services Research Bureau. Starting work in July 1940 with a couple of FANY, it evolved into a sophisticated operation employing 2000 girls. As many were under 21, it required parental permission before they could proceed overseas and the advantage of a FANY membership eased the way, whilst their careful selection and training ensured few got into difficulties. A number of FANY entered Europe as agents or as wireless operators, running all the dangers implicit in such employment. A number were arrested but survived, though twelve were executed, generally after interrogation and torture. (Some 51 FANYs died on active service during the war, amongst them seven by shooting, three by lethal injection, one by gassing, one by extermination in Belsen, one in a shoot-out in France and one of meningitis in the field.)

SOE also had responsibilities toward the Far East, including Force 136. Some 500 FANYs were despatched at the rate of 30 every three weeks to fill jobs as secretaries, ciphers clerks and similar administrative posts, starting work in India.. Wth the end of hostilities on 14th August 1945 the War Office had no further requirement for them, though many of the senior people destined for senior administrative posts were quick to make ad hoc arrangements to retain their services as confidential secreataries and assistants. Then the flood of starved and brutalised prisoners of war had to be nursed and cared for, leading to further delays in the repatriation of FANY. The strangest episode concerned the rescue of 2000 men, women and children in up-country Sumatra, 500 miles from Padang. The few British were confined to camp, because of the uncertain political situation. The only available transport was arranged through the Japanese Headquarters and the Transport Company allocated to help, remained armed for their own protection. Thus a FANY Lieutenant, Canadian Joan Bamford-Fletcher found herself in sole command a convoy varying between 15-25 vehicles for thirty journeys over a two hour ferry, terrible tracks involving a climb to 5000 feet through mountains. Towards the end the Indonesians became bolder and started to barracade the way necessitating the use of a crash waggon to push these aside. The Japanese Captain was so impressed by the determination and courtesy with which she treated his men that he presented her with his 300 year old sword as a token of respect. The SOE is the subject of many publications that the reader requiring more information should refer elsewhere for more detailed information. The chaos in South-East Asia saw the Corps performing all manner of duties from Bangkok, Borneo, India, Murotai, Saigon, Singapore and Tokyo.

The FANY Corps reached a strength of 6000 at its peak, with 2000 serving with SOE which serves in itself as a high commendation when its existence had been no more than grudgingly recognised by the military heirarchy. Awards came in the form of three George Cross, two George Medal, one CBE, 12 OBE, 36 MBE, a King's Medal, a King's Commendation, ten BEM and 36 Mention in Despatches, besides 12 Croix de Guerre and a number of other foreign decorations. But now there was peace!

1946, *Arduis Invicta* - 'I Cope'

The end of a second war gave time to reflect upon the *raison d'etre*. The War Office at the end of 1947 made it known they had decided to retain the ATS and was unable to allot a role for the WTS(FANY). This coincided with Corps thinking that the cultivation of special skills, which the regular services tended to ignore, was more appropriate and that driving as an individual skill, no longer needed their management expertise.

Translating nascent philosophy into practicalities takes time and it was unwise to rush. The elements of Radio-Telecommunications, a knowledge of foreign countries and their language, secretarial and staff duties and welfare work fitted into the new thinking. It therefore needed the acceptance and approval by some department of officialdom saying it would call upon them to do certain specific jobs. So far as this applied to the peace-time, it meant an event of crisis proportions. They established a formal if tenuous link with the Communications Department of the Foreign Office. The end of hostilities had released a vast range of FANY personnel and expertise , more or less for their exclusive use and past experience had made them wise to their becoming entangled in a fight every time a larger group took it into its head to boss them about. Other groups of specialists had found their way into the system, to cite only the Special Air Service and the Commando as examples. None of these was particularly welcomed by their more conventional brethren within respective services, but they enjoyed powerful support at a higher level, for the reason they could achieve things that others could not. The fundamental need was one for establishing a compact group having the right qualities and the willingness to train appropriately during peacetime. FANY had few doubts that it could satisfy such an objective, very often and attractively at nil cost.

To put the organisation upon a broad footing county groups were established and a site selected for an annual camp and these were begun to flesh out the new thrust. The objectives were sharpened through the 1970s in a liaison with Metropolitan and City of London Police in manning a communications incident facility at the time of a major incident. A number of regional police forces also indicated an interest. The Corps Mobile Unit was created and practices commenced by attending Horse Trials and Tattoo events where the speedy transmission of data figured. By 1973 documentation sessions were conducted in the Central Casualty and Inquiry Bureau (CCB). This was of particular benefit at the time of the Moorgate Tube disaster, on 28th February 1975, because trained personnel were quickly available, to release police and others to more direct duties. Over 800 calls were handled on that Friday night and reliefs were sent in on Saturday morning. A similar contingency plan existed between Tower Hamlets and the Isle of Dogs in the event the Thames overflowed its banks and it came within 10 inches of that before the barrier at Woolwich was put into place.

History is difficult to tell in contemporary terms, though the response to bomb explosions are further examples where the Corps was able to provide a worthwhile service to ameliorate horrific circumstances. A further feather

Appendix H

in the cap came in 1983 when the Royal Signals approached the Corps and asked if they would be prepared to provide support in the small Army Communications Centres in the United Kingdom during times of tension or National Emergency when it became necessary to go over to 24-hour operation. Members of FANY sign the Official Secrets Act and undertake training sessions at 'Com-Cens' and other government communications centres. This reflects the new philosophy of complete integration between the sexes within the services and provides a more objctive basis in the allocation to task.

Meantime the language groups were getting into their stride, by offering a range of languages by practising with incoming country groups attending conferences and exhibitions. Even by the Spring of 1973 they could offer French, Italian, German, Spanish, Norwegian, Russian, Polish, Japanese, Swahili and Arabic. FANY have laid down they will not to compete with professional interpreters and that their services are provided free.

The currently active membership is about 140, counting the linguists, whilst the total Corps strength numbers 700-800 scattered across the British Isles. Recruitment provides about 30 new members per year. The Headquarters is based on the Duke of York's Barracks in Chelsea and is manned by an extremely small and hard working staff consisting of a CO, a Deputy, an Adjutant and a handful of part-time volunteers covering Quartermastering, Training, Finance and general administration. The Princess Royal, Princess Anne is the present Commandant-in-Chief so one might say the Corps is progressing ALONG THE RIGHT LINES!

Plate H1   Commandmant, First Aid
Nursing Yeomanry.

Early days of First Aid Nursing Yeomanry.

Plate H2   Commandmant, First Aid
Nursing Yeomanry.

FANY Sadie Bonnett receiving the Military Medal, France 1917.

Plate H3

Commandmant, First Aid
Nursing Yeomanry.

Calais Convoy.

Plate H4

Commandmant, First Aid
Nursing Yeomanry.

With the Belgians.

Plate H5

Commandmant, First Aid
Nursing Yeomanry.

Princess Elizabeth joins for training 1945.

Plate H6

Commandmant, First Aid
Nursing Yeomanry.

First Aid Nursing Yeomanry, Bangkok 1945.

Plate H7   Commandmant, First Aid
                                            Nursing Yeomanry.

Plate H8   Commandmant, First Aid
                                            Nursing Yeomanry.

Plate H9   Commandmant, First Aid
                                            Nursing Yeomanry.

Montage - The First Aid Nursing Yeomanry manning the City of London
Incident Communications Centre and other exercises including visitation
from their Colonel Commandant, HRH Ann, the Princess Royal.

Yeomanry Capbadges from the Boer War Onwards

Introduction

There seems to be no book or account on Yeomanry badging which might be described as definitive. Those given to collecting are not always into publishing, whilst those that publish are into borrowing and make numerous errors in writing the subject up, due to haste and ignorance. A further pitfall opens, particularly when attempting to provide worthwhile illustrations. The variety of metals and other materials employed in badge manufacture make it extremely difficult to do the subject justice, either photographically or by scanning, whilst the cost of individual colour printing is astronomical, though it may be necessary upon occasion. Over and above this there are numerous metal variants struck from the same dies and latterly to these have been added many bogus strikes using the original dies.

Most badge collectors take up the hobby from the time that Service Dress was introduced, which from the Yeomanry standpoint coincides with the Boer War. There were badges before that, available in small numbers and most often integral with the headgear and dress of the period. Despite the dating of the service periods, there was and is no such precision in the issue of the related badges. Granted, *what was worn had to be approved* but that did little to have an old badge set aside. Many regiments failed to mark specific periods, such as Imperial, whilst others are positively misleading. Some regiments have as few as two basic badges, covering a period of over ninety years, whilst others have contrived the issue of over ten.

The badging described here commences with those worn by the field forces formed in South Africa from 1899 onwards. At that time the troops had started to wear khaki 'service dress' and with it, most commonly, a slouch hat because of the climate. After the war it eventually gave way to a 'field service' cap, the service dress cap, the GS cap and the beret, but these forms were added to the existing modes of dress dating from the Victorian era. There were curious variants, for example the inverted flowerpot with brim, worn by The King's Colonials and the Bersaglier full dress hat of the North Irish Imperial Yeomanry, plus the earlier forms of head dress, some of which did not provide for the wearing of a badge of any kind, whilst others encouraged those of inordinate size. This latter class of badge is not further considered.

The conventional badging materials were yellow cartridge brass, reddish gilding metal, german silver or white metal and bronze, to which might be added silver. Metals were finished by gilding, plating in silver and sometimes chromium, whilst brass may be given a bronze finishing treatment and others were simply stained or painted. In addition any badge might be worn over patches of felt or tartan cloth, and combined with feathers, rosettes of corded silk, or both. Other methods of badge making included embroidery using both thread and sometimes gold, brass and silver wire. Following The Second World War the anodised aluminium badge arrived adding its garish gold and silver lacquered colours to the scheme. This is now in the process of being displaced by those of a metal composition material, which provides a better looking badge at a cheaper price.

The Boer War

The general method adopted for wearing the slouch hat was for the left side of the brim to be turned up against the crown. Later, at the time of The Great War, the United Kingdom adopted the Solar Topee and the New Zealanders wore the slouch hat without pinning back the brim, leaving the Australians alone to do so. Badging was to the fore. The large but dull nature of the slouch hat encouraged a degree of embellishment so that coloured patches of felt, cloth, feathers and corded silk ribbon rosettes were often added and placed immediately behind the badge itself. These elements of the badge design tended to be lost more easily and are rarely available to the collector today.

The Yeomanry was raised as a number of 'mounted rifle' companies, generally grouped in fours, forming battalions as an administrative device. Recruitment, most often, attracted the sponsorship of a Yeomanry regiment already on the Home Establishment and thus an approved capbadge was already in being or in the process of being approved. Some small number of whole new Yeomanry regiments were formed by notables during that period and they took the field as consolidated units, wearing a badge of their proprietors' choice. Some others, without sponsorship of any kind quickly developed a corporate identity and had badges of their own struck, for example the Irish at Kimberley. A consolidated summary of these Companies is shown in Table Ten which appears at the end of chapter five.

Imperial Yeomanry - April 1901 till 1908
By virtue of an Army Order, issued during April 1901, the entire Yeomanry was designated Imperial Yeomanry and most regiments already entered on the Home Establishment added the word *Imperial* to their regimental titles and this remained the case until the formation of the Territorial Force in 1908. Companies returning from South Africa dropped all unofficial badge designs, indeed they were disbanded. This applied equally to whole regiments, who had to await acceptance onto the Home Establishment, if that was their wish. Some twenty new regiments were admitted and each in course had a capbadge design approved. Often the badges, but not all, included the word 'Imperial' in the title.

Before the designation of the regiments was once again asserted as Dragoons, Hussars or Lancers under War office letter Y/Gen No./114. Q.M.G.7. (b) of 1st December, 1905, some bizarre dress patterns had been adopted. The North Irish Imperial Horse, for example, wore the Bersaglier bonnet; a Lancer tunic and trousers with a single broad stripe indicative of heavy cavalry. Lanarkshire although Lancers, wore an infantry spiked cloth helmet, whilst some regiments from earlier times had been 'awarded' the right to wear gold lace, as opposed to silver, the normal embellishment for reserve forces. This wide latitude allowed in dress led to the variety of capbadge types. The main thrust of the War Office letter was to standardise dress and its wearing., and whilst it asked for proposals, it clearly wanted these to fall in with one of the following: Dragoon pattern with helmet; Hussar pattern with busby; Lancer pattern with a Lancer cap; Special pattern with slouch hat. An order to remove gold lace from mess dress of Officers by 31st December 1909, went largely ignored. The minimum standard made Service dress obligatory and the remainder optional. Theoretically this promoted a matching standardisation in the badging, though it took years to work its way through, in fact so long as to make it unhelpful in the business of classification or date banding. It also made for a random hobby, in which experience rather than rules decided to which perid a badge should be apportioned. It is impossible to be dogmatic over metal colour worn with a particular uniform. Officers wore bronze badging with service dress, unless it was black denoting a Rifles connection, however the Dorset Yeomanry Other Ranks also used bronze, but Other Ranks more generally wore brass with service dress. Silver coloured badging and buttons commonly applied to full dress, when badges of rank were to be gold, though there were so many exceptions as to make any generalised statement unwise.

Yeomanry Territorial Force - 1908 till 1922
The Yeomanry regiments comprised in the Territorial Force dropped the title 'Imperial' and in appropriate cases badges were altered. A Special Reserve Cavalry was formed comprising the recently renamed King's Colonials, now King Edward's Horse, from 12th July 1910 and the North and South Irish Horse. This group was later renamed the Cavalry Militia. The first was disbanded on 31st March 1924, the second not re-recruited but reactivated in 1939 and the third disbanded on 31st July 1922 with the formation of The Irish Free State. These are treated as Yeomanry during their entire service period, out of equity.

Reconstitution of The Territorial Army - 1920 till 1939 and 1947 till the 1967 Disbandment
The Great War had shown there was no longer a requirement for a large number of mounted cavalry. This affected the Yeomanry in that only 14 were retained with horses to which were later added two regiments of Scouts. Additionally, eight became Armoured Car companies formed under the (Royal) Tank Corps and 26 converted to artillery. The Middlesex Yeomanry was converted to the newly formed Signal Corps, whilst the Montgomeryshire Yeomanry formed two coys in the 7th (Montgomeryshire) Bn, of the Royal Welch Fusiliers (TA). The war formed Welsh Horse was not re-raised, nor the Lincolnshire Yeomanry who declined to be converted. Those regiments converted commonly kept their badging in whole or in part, when serving in a new Arm or Corps.

The Second World War saw the disappearance of horsed units, although they served on as late as 1941 in Syria. A number of Yeomanry were re-rôled as artillery and earlier conversions went on to adapt as anti-tank gunners. Two further regiments, The Cheshire Yeomanry and North Somerset Yeomanry, converted to Royal Corps of Signals, a fact displayed on their Guidons. Lastly, the Yorkshire Dragoons, without formal change of rôle, converted to armoured motorised infantry.

Once again the Territorial Army was reconstituted in 1947, mostly under the Royal Armoured Corps and Royal Artillery titles, with the Middlesex Yeomanry remaining under the Royal Corps of Signals. A series of amalgamations followed, first with the disbandment of Anti-Aircraft artillery units and later some armour on the disappearance of the divisional organisations. This culminated in the disbandment of the Territorial Army as such and its replacement by a much smaller reserve on 1st April 1967.

The Territorial Army and Volunteer Reserve (TA&VR) - 1967 till the present day.

The reserve comprised four classes: Ever Readies, Volunteers, Territorials, and Miscellaneous (OTCs, bands etc). The main thrust was to reduce the 'Territorials' to Home Guard proportions, because it was impossible to align their scale of equipment and training with those termed 'Volunteers'. The ultimate fate here was the formation of eight man Cadres and the transfer of many Yeomen to 'other units'. This period produced some intriguing badges, in which Yeomanry and infantry composite formations strove to maintain an identiy. A new positive emphasis developed up to 1st April 1971 when the Cadres disbanded to form, or after forming numerous Volunteer units in the various Arms and Corps. Further regimental re-alignments re-surfaced, in the form of conversions to other Arms and Corps. The Yeomanry were now to be found in the Royal Engineers, Royal Signals, the infantry and the Royal Corps of Transport soon to be the Royal Logistic Corps. Over and above simple amalgamations came the *Composite Regiment*, embodying *regimental squadrons* and The Scottish Yeomanry was formed in 1993 following this principle.

Badge Illustrations

A representative selection of Yeomanry badge illustrations is shown later. An endeavour has been made to reveal the details and markings on each of the specimens, though for the reasons already stated, there are limitations. Further work is needed to perfect a number of the badge pictures. The arrangement follows the list below, which is approximately alphabetical, by county, whilst the badges are grouped against the regiments, in historical order when known. Latterly, a number of Yeomanry sub-titles have been interposed into those of the composite regiments, both within the Yeomanry proper and elswhere. These are not included within the lists so far discussed. Those Batteries and Squadrons carrying such appellations often wear their own badges or the capbadge of a parent along with their own collar dogs or shoulder titles, denoting Yeomanry origin. No attention has been paid to catalogue numbers, metal types, nor the mode of fixing to caps, as this lays outwith the scope of a work of this nature and such information is available elsewhere.

The photographic and associated techniques employed to produce these illustrations are diverse. It will be observed there is a considerable range in light and shade and some of the surfaces are excessively reflective. Since few of the badges are flat, side lighting introduces a degree of imbalance and a light tent was used to help diffusion. Where possible, groups of badges with similarly reflective surfaces have been taken together, enabling a narrower range of exposure to be employed. This was especially important for anodised aluminium, needing very subdued lighting. Nevertheless, it remains problemmatical to pick up all the details which are of vital concern to the collector; lettering and regalia being two of the most important. In the instance of colourful items a limited number of colour photographs were taken, but mainly for future use. There is nothing new about this except that with the over 350 badges here, it makes the project labour intensive and some decision had to be taken to contain costs. The individual badge prints were regrouped and captioned in a philatelic manner and then scanned, from which the printer prepared his plates.

As a matter of record the photographic details were as follows:

Ilford XP2 film was used, which is fast and fine grained, yielding exceptional sharpness and a full range of tones, including excellent highlight and shadow detail. A Sinar 5 x 4 inch camera with a 240mm lens, stopped to 22.66 *f* was used for black and white work. This value was adjusted to 11.66 *f* when checking out possible results by Polaroid and to 16.33 *f* for the small number of colour shots.

An exposure of 1/60th second daylight flash, employed a 'light tent' in which the subjects to be shot were lit without directional light, in a totally diffused lighting environment. The of brilliance of anodised aluminium specimens was dulled using a spray agent, also reflections into the camera lens were deflected by tilting the specimen, which is responsible for a low degree of image distortion in a few cases.

To attain the highest quality from the negatives, the printing employed Ilford multigrade 111 RC De Luxe paper, which has a variable contrast range comprising six grades, from which to select the particular level desired.

The resultant prints were guillotined into individual specimen and remounted on card in regimental and historical order and scanned for printing. A 600 dpi desktop scanner was used along with Adobe Photoshop for retouching and Quark Xpress software with an Apple MacIntosh Quadra 700. The images were scanned for black and white and colour separations. In the instance of the Field forces used in the Boer War, a single page was prepared in colour and appears as Plate Eleven

About half of the badges appearing here are from the author's collection, whilst the remainder and by far the more difficult portion have been very kindly made available by Lieutenant Commander Keith Hook, RD, RN (Retd). Particular credit is given to Jim MacDonald of BPC acting a private capacity, to Richard Thomson of Borowski Image Communications and John Black of Training Management Systems Limited in helping the author to 'crack' a difficult nut.

Badge Listing Order

1 The Ayrshire (Earl of Carrick's Own) Y
2 Bedfordshire Yeomanry
3 The Berkshire Yeomanry
4 The Berkshire and Westminster Dgns
5 The Royal Buckinghamshire Hussars
6 The Cheshire Yeomanry (Earl of Chester's)
7 Denbighshire Yeomanry, Caernarvon & Denbigh Yeomanry, Flint and Denbigh Y
8 The Derbyshire Yeomanry
9 Royal First Devon Yeomanry
10 Royal Devon Yeomanry
11 The Royal North Devonshire Yeomanry
12 The Queen's Own Dorset Yeomanry
13 Queen's Own Dorset & West Somerset Y
14 The Essex Yeomanry
15 The Fife and Forfar Yeomanry
16 The Fife & Forfar Yeomanry/Scottish Hse
17 The Glamorgan Yeomanry
18 The Queen's Own Royal Glasgow Yeomanry
19 The Royal Gloucestershire Hussars
20 The Hampshire Carabiniers Yeomanry
21 Hertfordshire Yeomanry
22 The Hertfordshire and Bedfordshire Y
23 The Inns of Court Regiment
24 Inns of Court and City Yeomanry
25 North Irish Horse
26 South Irish Horse
27 The Royal East Kent Yeomanry (The Duke of Connaught's Own Mounted Rifles)
28 The Queen's Own West Kent Yeomanry
29 The Kent and CoLY (Sharp Shooters)

31 The Queen's Own Lowland Yeomanry
32 The Lancashire Hussars
33 The Duke of Lancaster's Own Yeomanry
34 The Prince Albert's Own Leicestershire Y
35 The Leicestershire and Derbyshire (Prince Albert's Own) Yeomanry
36 The Lincolnshire Yeomanry
37 The London Yeomanry & Territorials
38 The City of London Y (Roughriders)
39 1st County of London Yeomanry (Middlesex, Duke of Cambridge's Huss)
40 Westminster Dragoons (2nd CoLY)
41 3rd CoLY(Sharp Shooters)
42 4th County of London Imperial Yeomanry (King's Colonials) later King Edward's Horse (King's Overseas Dominions Regt)
43 Lothians & Berwickshire Imperial Yeomanry/ The Lothians and Border Horse
44 The Lovat Scouts
45 The Queen's Own Mercian Yeomanry
46 Queen's Own Mercian & Lancastrian Y
47 Montgomeryshire Yeomanry
48 The King's Own Royal Norfolk Yeomanry
49 The Northamptonshire Yeomanry
50 The Northumberland Hussars
51 Notts: The Sherwood Rangers Yeomanry
52 The South Nottinghamshire Hussars
53 The Queen's Own Oxfordshire Hussars
54 Pembroke Yeomanry (Castlemartin)
55 The Queen's Own Yeomanry
56 The Scottish Horse
57 The Scottish Yeomanry

1 The Ayrshire (Earl of Carrick's Own) Yeomanry

2 Bedfordshire Yeomanry

3 The Berkshire Yeomanry

4 The Berkshire and Westminster Dragoons

5 The Royal Buckinghamshire Hussars

6 The Cheshire Yeomanry (Earl of Chester's)

7 Denbighshire Yeomanry, Caernarvon & Denbigh Yeomanry, Flint and Denbigh Yeomanry

8 The Derbyshire Yeomanry

9 Royal First Devon Yeomanry

10 Royal Devon Yeomanry

11 The Royal North Devonshire Yeomanry

12 The Queen's Own Dorset Yeomanry

13 The Queen's Own Dorset and West Somerset Yeomanry

14 The Essex Yeomanry (continued)

14 The Essex Yeomanry

15 The Fife and Forfar Yeomanry

16 The Highland Yeomanry later The Fife & Forfar Yeomanry / Scottish Horse

17 The Glamorgan Yeomanry

18 The Queen's Own Royal Glasgow Yeomanry

19 The Royal Gloucestershire Hussars

20 The Hampshire Caraniniers Yeomanry

21 Hertfordshire Yeomanry

22 The Hertfordshire and
Bedfordshire Yeomanry

23 The Inns of Court Regiment

24 Inns of Court and City Yeomanry

25 North Irish Horse

26 South Irish Horse

27 The Royal East Kent Yeomanry
(The Duke of Connaught's Own Mounted Rifles)

28 The Queen's Own West Kent Yeomanry

29 The Kent and County of London Yeomanry (Sharp Shooters)

30 The Lanarkshire Yeomanry

31 The Queen's Own Lowland Yeomanry

32 The Lancashire Hussars

33 The Duke of Lancaster's Own Yeomanry

34 The Prince Albert's Own Leicestershire Yeomanry

35 The Leicestershire and Derbyshire (Prince Albert's Own) Yeomanry

36 The Lincolnshire Yeomanry

37 The London Yeomanry & Territorials

38 The City of London Yeomanry (The Roughriders)

39 1st County of London Yeomanry (Middlesex, Duke of Cambridge's Hussars)

40 Westminster Dragoons (2nd County of London Yeomanry)

41 3rd County of London Yeomanry (Sharp Shooters)

42 4th County of London Imperial Yeomanry (King's Colonials) later King Edward's House

(King's Overseas Dominions Regiment)

43 The Lothians and Berwickshire Imperial Yeomanry later The Lothians and Border Horse

44 The Lovat Scouts

45 The Queen's Own Mercian Yeomanry

46 The Queen's Own Mercian and Lancastrian Yeomanry

47 Montgomeryshire Yeomanry

48 The King's Own Royal Norfolk Yeomanry

49 The Northhamptonshire Yeomanry

50 The Northumberland Hussars

51 Notts: The Sherwood Rangers Yeomanry

52 The South Nottinghamshire Hussars

53 The Queen's Own Oxfordshire Hussars

54 Pembroke Yeomanry (Castlemartin)

55 The Queen's Own Yeomanry

56 The Scottish Horse

57 The Scottish Yeomanry

58 The Shropshire Yeomanry

59 The North Somerset Yeomanry

60 The North Somerset Yeomanry /
44th Royal Tank Regiment

61 The West Somerset Yeomanry

62 The Staffordshire Yeomanry (Queen's Own Royal Regiment)

63 The Duke of York's Own Loyal Suffolk Hussars

64 The Suffolk and Norfolk Yeomanry

65 The Surrey Yeomanry (Queen Mary's Regiment)

66 The Sussex Yeomanry

67 The Warwickshire Yeomanry

68 The Queen's Own Warwickshire and Worcestershire Yeomanry

69 Welsh Horse

70 Westmorland and Cumberland Yeomanry

71 The Royal Wiltshire Yeomanry (Prince of Wales's Own)

72 The Queen's Own Worcestershire Hussars

73 The Queen's Own Yorkshire Dragoons

74 The Yorkshire Hussars (Alexandra, Princess of Wales's Own)

75 Yorks: The East Riding Yeomanry

76 The Queen's Own Yorkshire Yeomanry

77 First Aid Nursing Yeomanry and Women's Transport Service F.A.N.Y.

78 Imperial Yeomanry and Yeomanry Cadets

79 Imperial Yeomanry Hospital

80 Trade Badges

INDEX